Knowledge and Value

SECOND EDITION

A Project of the

DEPARTMENT OF PHILOSOPHY, BROOKLYN COLLEGE OF THE CITY UNIVERSITY OF NEW YORK

with the advice and assistance of Howard W. Hintz *

William A. Gerhard †

John Hospers

Philip M. Kretschmann

Martin E. Lean

Julius Portnoy

Elmer Sprague

Paul W. Taylor

H. Van Rensselaer Wilson

---

* Professor Howard W. Hintz (1903–64) was Chairman of the Brooklyn College Department of Philosophy from 1953 to 1963, and Coordinating Adviser of the first edition of *Knowledge and Value.*

† Professor William A. Gerhard (1915–64) was a member of the Brooklyn College Department of Philosophy from 1949 until his death.

Knowledge and Value

SECOND EDITION

Edited by

ELMER SPRAGUE
PAUL W. TAYLOR

Brooklyn College
of
the City University of New York

HARCOURT, BRACE & WORLD, INC.

NEW YORK · CHICAGO · SAN FRANCISCO · ATLANTA

God offers to every mind its choice between truth and repose. Take which you please—you can never have both. Between these, as a pendulum, man oscillates. He in whom the love of repose predominates will accept the first creed, the first philosophy, the first political party he meets—most likely his father's. He gets rest, commodity and reputation; but he shuts the door of truth. He in whom the love of truth predominates will keep himself aloof from all moorings, and afloat. He will abstain from dogmatism, and recognize all the opposite negations between which, as walls, his being is swung. He submits to the inconvenience of suspense and imperfect opinion, but he is a candidate for truth, as the other is not, and respects the highest law of his being.

—RALPH WALDO EMERSON

Preface

In this second edition of *Knowledge and Value* we have made two principal changes: a reorganization of the contents and the inclusion of new selections. These changes are intended as improvements in the ordering and coverage of material for students in introductory philosophy. The book has three parts: Knowledge, Persons, and the World; Philosophy and the Knowledge of God; and Values and Their Justification. Each part contains several chapters, each consisting of a set of readings that focus attention upon one basic philosophical problem falling under the heading. The book is so arranged that the student can begin with any of the three parts. However, the ordering of the chapters in each part and the ordering of the readings in each chapter are based on the principle that the consideration of some problems is a necessary preliminary to the consideration of others.

We have continued to adhere to the twofold purpose of the first edition: to enable students to understand what philosophical problems are and how philosophers have carried on their thinking about them, and to stimulate students to think philosophically about these problems. Accordingly, we have retained the questions at the end of each reading not only as a review for the student but also as a guide to further reflection. The bibliographies at the end of each chapter, which have been brought up to date, are a guide for further study. We have also continued the practice of introducing each reading by a headnote, hoping by this means to overcome a sense of being lost which students sometimes suffer when they are first given a philosopher's work to read. Finally, as in the first edition, we have made the readings of substantial length in order to allow a philosopher to develop his argument in his own way. Thus we hope to have avoided, or at least to have minimized, distortion caused by the imposing of editorial judgment on original philosophical writing.

We offer this second edition of *Knowledge and Value* to old and new friends with the continued hope that it will provide the occasion for good reading and the opportunity for hard and satisfying thought.

ELMER SPRAGUE
PAUL W. TAYLOR

June, 1966
Brooklyn, New York

Acknowledgments

We thank all the authors, editors, and publishers who have kindly granted permission for the reprinting of their material in this book. The source of each reading selection is stated at the end of its headnote, and specific indebtedness to author, editor, or publisher is noted at the beginning of each selection. We gratefully acknowledge our debt to the staff of the Brooklyn College Library for their cooperation and assistance. This book owes much to the free use we have made of the philosophy collections of the Brooklyn College Library, the Brooklyn Public Library, and the New York Public Library.

This anthology had its origin in the syllabus and in the two earlier collections of readings prepared for an introductory course in philosophy prescribed for all undergraduate students in Brooklyn College. The first of these earlier collections of readings was edited by the late Professor William A. Gerhard and Professor Martin E. Lean, with the advice and assistance of the Brooklyn College Department of Philosophy. The second collection was edited by Professors Martin E. Lean and Paul W. Taylor, also with the advice and assistance of the Brooklyn College Department of Philosophy. In their preparation of the first edition of the present anthology the editors are indebted to the following colleagues for their advice and assistance: the late Professors Howard W. Hintz and William A. Gerhard, and Professors Walter Cerf, John Hospers, Philip M. Kretschmann, Martin E. Lean, Julius Portnoy, and H. Van Rensselaer Wilson. Special acknowledgment is due Professor Howard W. Hintz for his services as coordinating adviser of the first edition. During his chairmanship of the Brooklyn College Philosophy Department, he gave the editors unfailing support and encouragement in the making of this anthology; and his indefatigable efforts in no small measure made possible its publication. While his untimely death precluded our enjoying his aid in the preparation of the second edition, it is still a small reflection of the boundless vigor and enthusiasm which he brought to the discussion of philosophical problems. We also wish to acknowledge the large and friendly assistance of our fellow teachers on other campuses, Professors Raziel Abelson, Annette C. Baier, Douglas Browning, Albert W. Fenske, Robert Hoffman, and Kendall C. King, who commented on the usefulness of the first edition and the value of our proposed improvements in the second edition.

The preparation of this second edition has been the sole responsibility of the editors. It is in a very real sense a joint enterprise. We have worked closely together on all the chapters, and we, rather than our advisers, bear responsibility for whatever shortcomings the book may have.

E. S.
P. W. T.

Contents

Chapter 7. Proving God's Existence

Chapter 8. God and the Natural Order   395

Part Three
VALUES
AND THEIR JUSTIFICATION   431

Chapter 9. Freedom of the Will   435

Knowledge and Value

SECOND EDITION

Philosophy

The selections in this anthology introduce the reader to certain problems (the nature of knowledge, the nature of reality, the nature of science, the nature of the self, the existence of God, the possibility of miracles, the significance of evil, the nature of human freedom, the nature of morality, the nature of beauty) which are treated by philosophers, but which are not their exclusive property. For the problems of philosophy may be of interest to anyone; they may cut across other disciplines, such as the natural and social sciences, mathematics, and history, and involve other enterprises, such as religion, politics, and art. But if these problems are not the exclusive property of philosophers, what is it that makes them philosophical? Is their association only accidental? Or are they philosophical because they share some common characteristic or because they are amenable to some common method of investigation? In short, "What is philosophy?"

In considering answers to "What is philosophy?" the reader may be helped if he notices the similarity of this question to other questions he may already have considered, such as, "What is poetry?," "What is art?," or "What is music?" The answers to such questions may be given in at least two ways. In the case of poetry, for example, the answer may be a description of who the poets are and what they have done, or it may be a statement of what poets ought to do. The first answer might list, for example, both Robert Frost and Edith Sitwell as poets, whereas the second answer might exclude the writings of one or the other. It would seem that the best definition of poetry might mingle these descriptive and prescriptive elements; however, anyone who seeks such a definition must ascertain if, and how, these elements are to be combined.

Defining philosophy is perhaps even more difficult than defining poetry. That philosophers recognize these difficulties is apparent in the answer which is sometimes given to the question "What is philosophy?": *The definition of philosophy is one of the problems of philosophy.* In answering this question we have tried to avoid some of the difficulties by offering a descriptive answer. Yet we are apologetic about what we shall say, for our answer must characterize an enterprise which in the Western world has been carried on by many thousands of men in many different circumstances for some twenty-five hundred years. A short description of philosophy can only be an approximation of the truth, offered with respect-

1

ful nods to both the long history of the subject and the wide range of philosophical schools in existence today.

As a first approximation, we shall say that philosophy is the study of those subjects which may be understood only by considering the ways in which they are talked about. In this anthology, the consideration of such subjects as knowledge, reality, the self, God, human freedom, morality, and beauty illustrates this definition of philosophy. When we say that one understands these subjects by considering the ways in which they are talked about, we are not saying that philosophy is about nothing but words, but rather that philosophical subjects have their life in our language (in our speaking and writing to one another), and that finding out how these subjects are talked about (or are to be talked about) is the way to discover their natures. Writings that we count as philosophical will usually turn out to be either (1) the investigation of the meaning of some old term, or the proposal of some new term, in order to advance some area of philosophical enquiry, (2) the criticism of the use of some term, or (3) some combination of these activities. Philosophical understanding, then, turns not on making some discovery in the world, but on deciding how to talk.

Other subjects besides those noticed by philosophers share the characteristic of being understandable only through noticing how they are talked about. Here are two simple non-philosophical illustrations. Take our use of the word "meal" as a collective name for the food which is eaten at a given time. Suppose we say to someone who has eaten servings of roast beef, potatoes, oven-browned carrots, sliced tomatoes, and apple pie, "You have eaten a good meal," and he replies, "Well, I ate roast beef and potatoes (and so on through

the list), but I didn't eat a meal." Clearly we cannot show such a person some *thing* to set him straight about what a meal is. What we must do is teach him how to use the word "meal": eating a meal is eating food in just the way that he has been eating it. Meal is a subject which is to be understood only by learning how to talk about it.

The second example is drawn from our notions of "penny" and "cent." Suppose that someone asks you to explain what a penny is in the coinage of the United States of America. The easiest thing to do would be to show him one of the coins we call a penny, or failing that, to show him a picture. Suppose next that he asks you to explain what a cent is. You might say that a cent is a penny. Then is "cent" another name for a penny? Yes; but then, no. A penny is one cent, but "cent" means more than "penny." Using United States coins, you can certainly give someone one cent by giving him a penny; but you can also give him a cent by giving him a nickel and receiving four pennies in change. To understand "cent," then, one must understand the uses of pieces of United States money; but cent is not itself a piece of money. As a unit of money value, it has its life in our use of money, and we explain the meaning of "cent" to someone by explaining to him how to talk about the relative values of pieces of United States money, as he uses them.

"Meal" and "cent," then, are both examples of subjects which have this characteristic in common with philosophical subjects: we find out about them by learning how to talk about them. They also share another characteristic with philosophical subjects. They are useful in organizing our experience of the world. At the simplest level, consider our example of a meal.

A man might consume vast quantities of beef and potatoes and never know the word "meal," and neither his appetite nor his capacity need suffer. But once he has the notion of a meal, he may refer to what he has eaten without having to recite a menu. Or consider the notion of a cent. A person may have a pocketful of coins, but unless he knows their relative values based on the notion of cent, he is an innocent in the marketplace. Once he has grasped the uses of "cent," though, his thought about the coins is organized, and the possibilities of buying and selling open before him.

Now something must be said of the way philosophical subjects differ from subjects like "meal" and "cent." There are two large differences. The first is the fundamental importance of philosophical subjects to a reflective person: the matters about which he believes that it is possible to have knowledge, the things which he counts as real, and the acts which he regards as good are among the crucial and pervasive considerations that shape his life.

The second large difference between "meal" and "cent" and philosophical subjects is to be found in the general agreement about what a meal and a cent are and the lack of any such general agreement about how a given philosophical subject is to be defined. Knowledge, reality, and goodness, for example, can be and have been characterized in many different and sometimes incompatible ways. This elasticity of characterization, far exceeding that of "meal" and "cent," is a necessary property of philosophical subjects. Of course, ultimately, one characterization of a given philosophical subject might come to prevail—agreement among philosophers is conceivable. But in the history of philosophy it has certainly not been achieved.

It follows that in an anthology of this kind, the reader must not expect one answer to such questions as "What is knowledge?," "What is reality?," and "Is there a God?" Although a given philosopher may offer only one answer, philosophy, viewed as a collective though not necessarily cooperative enterprise, offers many answers. One man's having produced, say, an analysis of reality or of moral good, in no way precludes another man from developing his own thoughts on these topics, just as Jane Austen's novels did not render Dickens' unnecessary, and Mozart's symphonies did not foreclose the possibility of Tschaikowsky's writing his. Of course philosophers may share viewpoints and methods, and when there is agreement, a given philosopher may accept the work of others without feeling a need to redo it, even though he may still feel a need to put his own stamp on it. But we do not mean to say that all philosophy is beyond the reach of rational examination, and it is to this topic that we must now turn.

The first task in reading philosophy is to get clear what the author is saying—to follow his directions for talking about a subject which can only be known by learning how to talk of it.

The reader's second task is to evaluate what the philosopher has said. How is this evaluation to be carried out? An old rule states that we should ask of every piece of philosophy: is it consistent with the world? And, is it consistent with itself? The value of these rules can only be learned in practice, and readers who are studying philosophy with a teacher will have the advantage of his example to guide them. The following three incidents from the life of Plato's contemporary, Diogenes, illustrate how philosophy may be evaluated by questioning its *consistency with the world*. For example, Diogenes "replied to one who had been asserting that there was no such thing as motion, by getting up and walking away." [1]

In another situation, Diogenes criticized Plato:

> Plato defined man thus: "Man is a two-footed, featherless animal," and was much praised for the definition; so Diogenes plucked a cock and brought it into his school, and said "This is Plato's man." On which account this addition was made to the definition, "With broad flat nails." [2]

The last sentence shows that the charge of inconsistency with the world is not a fatal criticism, since the philosopher is able to amend his directions for talking about something.

In this final example, Diogenes charged that Plato talked of things which do not exist.

> When Plato was discoursing about his "ideas," and using the nouns "tableness" and "cupness"; "I, O Plato!" interrupted Diogenes, "see a table and a cup, but I see no tableness or cupness." Plato made answer, "That is natural enough, for you have eyes, by which a cup and a table are contemplated; but you have not intellect, by which tableness and cupness are seen." [3]

The issue between Diogenes and Plato might be put in the following way: Diogenes is saying that the world contains only what he can see, and he can see only cups. Plato is saying that if there are cups there must also be cupness. Diogenes and Plato espouse com-

peting worlds, and Plato's includes more items than Diogenes'.

The examination of a philosophy by considering its *consistency with itself* is a process capable of several variations, of which the following are some of the more important. At the very simplest one may consider whether what a philosopher says on one page is consistent with what he says on any other page. A slightly more sophisticated activity is to consider whether he uses any of his terms ambiguously, and if he does, whether the ambiguity permits him to draw conclusions which a straightforward use of the terms would rule out. Do his statements have implications which he does not follow out, but which, when they are brought into the open, contradict his previously stated views? An example of testing a philosophy for consistency with itself is Socrates' examination of Euthyphro's definitions of "piety," which appears as the first selection in this book under the heading "A Philosopher at Work."

While each philosopher, at least at first acquaintance, must be credited with trying to speak sensibly about philosophical subjects and trying to be consistent with both the world and himself, philosophy itself is a chorus of many voices saying many different things. We have tried to show why this is so; and thus we have tried to arm our readers against those first and fatal reactions to philosophy wherein it is regarded as a meaningless game, or an idle pastime, or at worst the manufacture of nonsense. No one who understands the place of organizing concepts in the life of a reflective person can fail to appreciate the importance of philosophy, the enterprise of proposing, analyzing, and criticizing those concepts.

Philosophical thinking is a lifetime activity. The problems it deals with are

[1] "Diogenes Laertius," *The Lives and Opinions of Eminent Philosophers*, trans., C. D. Yonge, George Bell & Sons, London, 1895, p. 231.
[2] *Ibid.*
[3] *Ibid.*, p. 236.

so complex and far-reaching that no final, universally acceptable solutions have yet been found. The only thing we can do is to carry on our philosophical thinking as clearly and as carefully as possible, hoping that we may advance a little toward more enlightened points of view. Meanwhile, we must live our practical lives. How can this be done in a rational way if we cannot arrive at final conclusions concerning a true world view and philosophy of life? We can only live according to tentative conclusions, re-examining them as our philosophical thinking develops. Such a life has been called "the life of reason." To live this kind of life is to live as a thinking being.

PLATO

(427?–347 B.C.)

Euthyphro

To illustrate the Introduction to this book we offer a word portrait by Plato of a philosopher at work. Plato, one of the triad of great Greek philosophers, stands between his teacher, Socrates (469–399 B.C.), and his pupil, Aristotle (384–322 B.C.). Socrates wrote nothing; and those of Aristotle's works which have survived are in a state that requires much editorial effort to make them intelligible. It is no wonder then that the twenty-four of Plato's dialogues which have come down to us comparatively intact, and splendid in their range and power of thought, are regarded as one of the great cultural treasures of the world.

The *Euthyphro* belongs to the set of early dialogues in which Plato both illustrates Socrates' method of doing philosophy and endeavors to vindicate the manner of his life to those Athenians who had sought and achieved Socrates' execution by the state. Indeed, the dramatic occasion of this dialogue is a conversation which Socrates is supposed to have had on his way to be tried for his life, one of the charges against him being that of impiety. Although Plato shows Socrates coming to no philosophical conclusion in the *Euthyphro,* he nonetheless has Socrates describe the kind of philosophical

knowledge which Plato thought was most valuable: "Remember that I did not ask you to give me two or three examples of piety, but to explain the general form which makes all pious things to be pious." This search for "general forms" was the philosophical mission of Plato's own life. But it is just because the dialogue is inconclusive that *Euthyphro* is an excellent illustration of the philosopher at work. Undistracted by the need to evaluate any conclusion, we may concentrate wholly on watching Socrates do philosophy.

As becomes a philosopher, Socrates' interest in piety is a second-order interest. He has no desire to propose his own theory of piety. He is interested in the notion simply because, as with every other notion, it is worthwhile being clear about what one has in mind when one talks of it. Euthyphro claims to be an expert on piety, and Socrates decides to test this claim. He prods Euthyphro through several different accounts of the meaning of "piety"; and in each instance Socrates succeeds in showing either that what Euthyphro says about piety makes no sense, i.e., is too muddled to be allowed to stand, or is self-contradictory. Thus Socrates' analysis exemplifies the philosopher's two basic tests of the clarity of first-order statements: Do they make sense? Are they self-contradictory? Notice that Socrates makes no suggestions about the nature of piety until Euthyphro feels that he can say no more without assistance. Then, as a philosopher, Socrates scrutinizes the definitions which he offers Euthyphro with the same care that he gave to Euthyphro's own.

In examining this dialogue the reader will do well first to make a note of each definition of "piety" as it is offered, and then to summarize briefly the points that Socrates makes against it. Thus he will be better able to judge the effectiveness of Socrates' criticism and determine whether Euthyphro, at some stage of the dialogue, might have made a stronger case for what he says than he is here given credit for. It must be noticed that at least some of Euthyphro's difficulties stem from the peculiarities of Greek religion. Would his task be easier if he were a monotheist? How? Finally, the reader should try to decide what definition of "piety" would satisfy himself; and then he should see whether he can defend it successfully against Socrates' kind of criticism. The way to learn philosophy is by doing it.

The entire dialogue is reprinted here. The translation from the Greek is by Benjamin Jowett, as revised in 1953 by order of the Jowett Copyright Trustees.

From *The Dialogues of Plato,* 4th ed., translated
by Benjamin Jowett, 1953.
Reprinted by permission of Oxford University Press.

PERSONS OF THE DIALOGUE: Socrates, Euthyphro
SCENE: The Porch of the King Archon

EUTHYPHRO. What can have happened, Socrates, to bring you away from the Lyceum? and what are you doing in the Porch of the King Archon? Surely you cannot be concerned in a suit before the King, like myself?

SOCRATES. Not in a suit, Euthyphro; prosecution is the word which the Athenians use.

EUTH. What! I suppose that someone has been prosecuting you, for I cannot believe that you are the prosecutor of another.

SOC. Certainly not.

EUTH. Then someone else has been prosecuting you?

SOC. Yes.

EUTH. And who is he?

SOC. A young man who is little known, Euthyphro; and I hardly know him: his name is Meletus, and he is of the deme of Pitthis. Perhaps you may remember his appearance; he has a beak, and straight hair, and a beard which is ill grown.

EUTH. No, I do not remember him, Socrates. But what is the charge which he brings against you?

soc. What is the charge? Well, rather a grand one, which implies a degree of discernment far from contemptible in a young man. He says he knows how the youth are corrupted and who are their corruptors. I fancy that he must be a wise man, and seeing that I am the reverse of a wise man, he has found me out, and is going to accuse me of corrupting his generation. And of this our mother the state is to be the judge. Of all our political men he is the only one who seems to me to begin in the right way, with the cultivation of virtue in youth; like a good husbandman, he makes the young shoots his first care, and clears away us whom he accuses of destroying them. This is only the first step; afterwards he will assuredly attend to the elder branches; and if he goes on as he has begun, he will be a very great public benefactor.

EUTH. I hope that he may; but I rather fear, Socrates, that the opposite will turn out to be the truth. My opinion is that in attacking you he is simply aiming a blow at the heart of the state. But in what way does he say that you corrupt the young?

soc. In a curious way, which at first hearing excites surprise: he says that I am a maker of gods, and that I invent new gods and deny the existence of the old ones; this is the ground of his indictment.

EUTH. I understand, Socrates; he means to attack you about the familiar sign which occasionally, as you say, comes to you. He thinks that you are a neologian, and he is going to have you up before the court for this. He knows that such a charge is readily received by the world, as I myself know too well; for when I speak in the assembly about divine things, and foretell the future to them, they laugh at me and think me a madman. Yet every word that I say is true. But they are jealous of us all; and we must be brave and go at them.

soc. Their laughter, friend Euthyphro, is not a matter of much consequence. For a man may be thought clever; but the Athenians, I suspect, do not much trouble themselves about him until he begins to impart his wisdom to others; and then for some reason or other, perhaps, as you say, from jealousy, they are angry.

EUTH. I have no great wish to try their temper towards me in this way.

soc. No doubt they think you are reserved in your behavior, and unwilling to impart your wisdom. But I have a benevolent habit of pouring out myself to everybody, and would even pay for a listener, and I am afraid that the Athenians may think me too talkative. Now if, as I was saying, they would only laugh at me, as you say that they laugh at you, the time might pass gaily enough with jokes and merriment in the court; but perhaps they may be in earnest, and then what the end will be you soothsayers only can predict.

EUTH. I dare say that the affair will end in nothing, Socrates, and that you will win your cause; and I think that I shall win my own.

SOC. And what is your suit, Euthyphro? are you the pursuer or the defendant?

EUTH. I am the pursuer.

SOC. Of whom?

EUTH. When I tell you, you will perceive another reason why I am thought mad.

SOC. Why, has the fugitive wings?

EUTH. Nay, he is not very volatile at his time of life.

SOC. Who is he?

EUTH. My father.

SOC. My dear Sir! Your own father?

EUTH. Yes.

SOC. And of what is he accused?

EUTH. Of murder, Socrates.

SOC. Good heavens! How little, Euthyphro, does the common herd know of the nature of right and truth! A man must be an extraordinary man, and have made great strides in wisdom, before he could have seen his way to bring such an action.

EUTH. Indeed, Socrates, he must.

SOC. I suppose that the man whom your father murdered was one of your family—clearly he was; for if he had been a stranger you would never have thought of prosecuting him.

EUTH. I am amused, Socrates, at your making a distinction between one who is a member of the family and one who is not; for surely the pollution is the same in either case, if you knowingly associate with the murderer when you ought to clear yourself and him by proceeding against him. The real question is whether the murdered man has been justly slain. If justly, then your duty is to let the matter alone; but if unjustly, then proceed against the murderer, if, that is to say, he lives under the same roof with you and eats at the same table. In fact, the man who is dead was a poor dependant of mine who worked for us as a field labourer on our farm in Naxos, and one day in a fit of drunken passion he got into a quarrel with one of our domestic servants and slew him. My father bound him hand and foot and threw him into a ditch, and then sent to Athens to ask an expositor of religious law what he should do with him. Meanwhile he never attended to him and took no care about him; for he regarded him as a murderer, and thought that no great harm would be done even if he did die. Now this was just what happened. For such was the effect of cold and hunger and chains upon him, that before the messenger returned from the expositor, he was dead. And my father and family are angry with me for taking the part of the murderer and prosecuting my father. They say that he did not kill him, and that if he did, the dead man was but a murderer, and I ought not to take any notice, for that a son is impious who prosecutes a father for murder. Which shows, Socrates, how little they know what the gods think about piety and impiety.

soc. Good heavens, Euthyphro! and is your knowledge of religion and of things pious and impious so very exact, that, supposing the circumstances to be as you state them, you are not afraid lest you too may be doing an impious thing in bringing an action against your father?

euth. The best of Euthyphro, that which distinguishes him, Socrates, from the common herd, is his exact knowledge of all such matters. What should I be good for without it?

soc. Rare friend! I think that I cannot do better than be your disciple. Then before the trial with Meletus comes on I shall challenge him, and say that I have always had a great interest in religious questions, and now, as he charges me with rash imaginations and innovations in religion, I have become your disciple. You, Meletus, as I shall say to him, acknowledge Euthyphro to be a great theologian, and so you ought to approve of me, and not have me into court; otherwise you should begin by indicting him who is my teacher, and who will be the ruin, not of the young, but of the old; that is to say, of myself whom he instructs, and of his old father whom he admonishes and chastises. And if Meletus refuses to listen to me, but will go on, and will not shift the indictment from me to you, I cannot do better than repeat this challenge in the court.

euth. Yes, indeed, Socrates; and if he attempts to indict me I am mistaken if I do not find a flaw in him; the court will be occupied with him long before it comes to me.

soc. And I, my dear friend, knowing this, am desirous of becoming your disciple. For I observe that no one appears to notice you—not even this Meletus; but his sharp eyes have found me out at once, and he has indicted me for impiety. And therefore, I adjure you to tell me the nature of piety and impiety, which you said that you knew so well, in their bearing on murder and generally on offences against the gods. Is not piety in every action always the same? and impiety, again—is it not always the opposite of piety, and also the same with itself, having, as impiety, one notion or form which includes whatever is impious?

euth. To be sure, Socrates.

soc. And what is piety, and what is impiety?

euth. Piety is doing as I am doing; that is to say, prosecuting anyone who is guilty of murder, sacrilege, or of any similar crime—whether he be your father or mother, or whoever he may be—that makes no difference; and not to prosecute them is impiety. And please to consider, Socrates, what a notable proof I will give you that this is the law, a proof which I have already given to others—of the principle, I mean, that the impious, whoever he may be, ought not to go unpunished. For do not men acknowledge Zeus as the best and most righteous of the gods? and yet they admit that he bound his father (Cronos) because he wickedly devoured his sons, and that he too had punished his own father (Uranus) for a similar reason, in a nameless manner. And yet when I proceed against my father, they are angry with me. So inconsistent are they in their way of talking when the gods are concerned, and when I am concerned.

soc. May not this be the reason, Euthyphro, why I am charged with impiety—that I cannot away with these stories about the gods? that, I suppose is where people think I go wrong. But as you who are well informed about them approve of them, I cannot do better than assent to your superior wisdom. What else can I say, confessing as I do, that I know nothing about them? Tell me, for the love of Zeus, whether you really believe that they are true.

euth. Yes, Socrates; and things more wonderful still, of which the world is in ignorance.

soc. And do you really believe that the gods fought with one another, and had dire quarrels, battles, and the like, as the poets say, and as you see represented in the works of great artists? The temples are full of them; and notably the robe of Athene, which is carried up to the Acropolis at the great Panathenaea, is embroidered with them throughout. Are all these tales of the gods true, Euthyphro?

euth. Yes, Socrates; and, as I was saying, I can tell you, if you would like to hear them, many other things about the gods which would quite amaze you.

soc. I dare say; and you shall tell me them at some other time when I have leisure. But just at present I would rather hear from you a more precise answer, which you have not as yet given, my friend, to the question, "What is 'piety'?" When asked, you only replied, "Doing as you do, charging your father with murder."

euth. And what I said was true, Socrates.

soc. No doubt, Euthyphro; but you would admit that there are many other pious acts?

euth. There are.

soc. Remember that I did not ask you to give me two or three examples of piety, but to explain the general form which makes all pious things to be pious. Do you not recollect saying that one and the same form made the impious impious, and the pious pious?

euth. I remember.

soc. Tell me what is the nature of this form, and then I shall have a standard to which I may look, and by which I may measure actions, whether yours or those of anyone else, and then I shall be able to say that such and such an action is pious, such another impious.

euth. I will tell you, if you like.

soc. I should very much like.

EUTH. Piety, then, is that which is dear to the gods, and impiety is that which is not dear to them.

SOC. Very good, Euthyphro; you have now given me the sort of answer which I wanted. But whether what you say is true or not I cannot as yet tell, although I make no doubt that you will go on to prove the truth of your words.

EUTH. Of course.

SOC. Come, then, and let us examine what we are saying. That thing or person which is dear to the gods is pious, and that thing or person which is hateful to the gods is impious, these two being the extreme opposites of one another. Was not that said?

EUTH. It was.

SOC. And well said?

EUTH. Yes, Socrates, I think so.

SOC. And further, Euthyphro, the gods were admitted to have enmities and hatreds and differences?

EUTH. Yes, that was also said.

SOC. And what sort of differences creates enmity and anger? Suppose for example that you and I, my good friend, differ on the question which of two groups of things is more numerous; do differences of this sort make us enemies and set us at variance with one another? Do we not proceed at once to counting, and put an end to them?

EUTH. True.

SOC. Or suppose that we differ about magnitudes, do we not quickly end the difference by measuring?

EUTH. Very true.

SOC. And we end a controversy about heavy and light by resorting to a weighing machine?

EUTH. To be sure.

SOC. But what are the matters about which differences arise that cannot be thus decided, and therefore make us angry and set us at enmity with one another? I dare say the answer does not occur to you at the moment, and therefore I will suggest that these enmities arise when the matters of differ-ence are the just and unjust, good and evil, honourable and dishonourable. Are not these the subjects about which men differ, and about which when we are unable satisfactorily to decide our differences, you and I and all of us quarrel, when we do quarrel? [1]

EUTH. Yes, Socrates, the nature of the differences about which we quarrel is such as you describe.

SOC. And the quarrels of the gods, noble Euthyphro, when they occur, are of a like nature?

EUTH. Certainly they are.

[1] Cf. 1 *Alcib*. III foll.

soc. They have differences of opinion, as you say, about good and evil, just and unjust, honourable and dishonourable: there would be no quarrels among them, if there were no such differences—would there now?

euth. You are quite right.

soc. Does not each party of them love that which they deem noble and just and good, and hate the opposite?

euth. Very true.

soc. But, as you say, one party regards as just the same things as the other thinks unjust—about these they dispute; and so there arise wars and fightings among them.

euth. Very true.

soc. Then the same things are hated by the gods and loved by the gods, and are both hateful and dear to them?

euth. It appears so.

soc. And upon this view the same things, Euthyphro, will be pious and also impious?

euth. So I should suppose.

soc. Then, my friend, I remark with surprise that you have not answered the question which I asked. For I certainly did not ask you to tell me what action is both pious and impious; but now it would seem that what is loved by the gods is also hated by them. And therefore, Euthyphro, in thus chastising your father you may very likely be doing what is agreeable to Zeus but disagreeable to Cronos and Uranus, and what is acceptable to Hephaestus but unacceptable to Hera, and there may be other gods who have similar differences of opinion.

euth. But I believe, Socrates, that all the gods would be agreed as to the propriety of punishing a murderer: there would be no difference of opinion about that.

soc. Well, but speaking of men, Euthyphro, did you ever hear anyone arguing that a murderer or any sort of evil-doer ought to be let off?

euth. I should rather say that these are the questions which they are always arguing, especially in courts of law: they commit all sorts of crimes, and there is nothing which they will not do or say in their own defence.

soc. But do they admit their guilt, Euthyphro, and yet say that they ought not to be punished?

euth. No; they do not.

soc. Then there are some things which they do not venture to say and do: for they do not venture to argue that if guilty they are to go unpunished, but they deny their guilt, do they not?

euth. Yes.

soc. Then they do not argue that the evil-doer should not be punished, but they argue about the fact of who the evil-doer is, and what he did and when?

euth. True.

soc. And the gods are in the same case, if as you assert they quarrel about just and unjust, and some of them say while others deny that injustice is done among them. For surely neither god nor man will ever venture to say that the doer of injustice is not to be punished?

EUTH. That is true, Socrates, in the main.

soc. But they join issue about the particulars—gods and men alike, if indeed the gods dispute at all; they differ about some act which is called in question, and which by some is affirmed to be just, by others to be unjust. Is not that true?

EUTH. Quite true.

soc. Well then, my dear friend Euthyphro, do tell me, for my better instruction and information, what proof have you that in the opinion of all the gods a servant who is guilty of murder, and is put in chains by the master of the dead man, and dies because he is put in chains before he who bound him can learn from the expositors of religious law what he ought to do with him, is killed unjustly; and that on behalf of such an one a son ought to proceed against his father and accuse him of murder. How would you show that all the gods absolutely agree in approving of his act? Prove to me that they do, and I will applaud your wisdom as long as I live.

EUTH. No doubt it will be a difficult task; though I could make the matter very clear indeed to you.

soc. I understand; you mean to say that I am not so quick of apprehension as the judges: for to them you will be sure to prove that the act is unjust, and hateful to all the gods.

EUTH. Yes indeed, Socrates; at least if they will listen to me.

soc. But they will be sure to listen if they find that you are a good speaker. There was a notion that came into my mind while you were speaking; I said to myself: "Well, and what if Euthyphro does prove to me that all the gods regarded the death of the serf as unjust, how do I know anything more of the nature of piety and impiety? For, granting that this action may be hateful to the gods, still piety and impiety are not adequately defined by these distinctions, for that which is hateful to the gods has been shown to be also dear to them." And therefore, Euthyphro, I do not ask you to prove this; I will suppose, if you like, that all the gods condemn and abominate such an action. But I will amend the definition so far as to say that what all the gods hate is impious, and what they love pious or holy; and what some of them love and others hate is both or neither. Shall this be our definition of piety and impiety?

EUTH. Why not, Socrates?

soc. Why not! certainly, as far as I am concerned, Euthyphro, there is no reason why not. But whether this premise will greatly assist you in the task of instructing me as you promised is a matter for you to consider.

EUTH. Yes, I should say that what all the gods love is pious and holy, and the opposite which they all hate, impious.

soc. Ought we to inquire into the truth of this, Euthyphro, or simply to accept it on our own authority and that of others—echoing mere assertions? What do you say?

EUTH. We should inquire; and I believe that the statement will stand the test of inquiry.

soc. We shall soon be better able to say, my good friend. The point which I should first wish to understand is whether the pious or holy is beloved by the gods because it is holy, or holy because it is beloved of the gods.

EUTH. I do not understand your meaning, Socrates.

soc. I will endeavour to explain: we speak of carrying and we speak of being carried, of leading and being led, seeing and being seen. You know that in all such cases there is a difference, and you know also in what the difference lies?

EUTH. I think that I understand.

soc. And is not that which is beloved distinct from that which loves?

EUTH. Certainly.

soc. Well; and now tell me, is that which is carried in this state of carrying because it is carried, or for some other reason?

EUTH. No; that is the reason.

soc. And the same is true of what is led and of what is seen?

EUTH. True.

soc. And a thing is not seen because it is visible, but conversely, visible because it is seen; nor is a thing led because it is in the state of being led, or carried because it is in the state of being carried, but the converse of this. And now I think, Euthyphro, that my meaning will be intelligible; and my meaning is that any state of action or passion implies previous action or passion. It does not become because it is becoming, but it is in a state of becoming because it becomes; neither does it suffer because it is in a state of suffering, but it is in a state of suffering because it suffers. Do you not agree?

EUTH. Yes.

soc. Is not that which is loved in some state either of becoming or suffering?

EUTH. Yes.

soc. And the same holds as in the previous instances; the state of being loved follows the act of being loved, and not the act the state.

EUTH. Certainly.

soc. And what do you say of piety, Euthyphro: is not piety, according to your definition, loved by all the gods?

EUTH. Yes.

soc. Because it is pious or holy, or for some other reason?

EUTH. No, that is the reason.

soc. It is loved because it is holy, not holy because it is loved?

EUTH. Apparently.

soc. And it is the object of the gods' love, and is dear to them, because it is loved of them?

EUTH. Certainly.

SOC. Then that which is dear to the gods, Euthyphro, is not holy, nor is that which is holy dear to the gods, as you affirm; but they are two different things.

EUTH. How do you mean, Socrates?

SOC. I mean to say that the holy has been acknowledged by us to be loved because it is holy, not to be holy because it is loved.

EUTH. Yes.

SOC. But that which is dear to the gods is dear to them because it is loved by them, not loved by them because it is dear to them.

EUTH. True.

SOC. But, friend Euthyphro, if that which is holy were the same with that which is dear to the gods, and were loved because it is holy, then that which is dear to the gods would be loved as being dear to them; but if that which is dear to them were dear to them because loved by them, then that which is holy would be holy because loved by them. But now you see that the reverse is the case, and that the two things are quite different from one another. For one (θεοφιλές) is of a kind to be loved because it is loved, and the other (ὅσιον) is loved because it is of a kind to be loved. Thus you appear to me, Euthyphro, when I ask you what is the nature of holiness, to offer an attribute only, and not the essence—the attribute of being loved by all the gods. But you still do not explain to me the nature of holiness. And therefore, if you please, I will ask you not to hide your treasure, but to start again, and tell me frankly what holiness or piety really is, whether dear to the gods or not (for that is a matter about which we will not quarrel); and what is impiety?

EUTH. I really do not know, Socrates, how to express what I mean. For somehow or other the definitions we propound, on whatever bases we rest them, seem always to turn round and walk away from us.

SOC. Your words, Euthyphro, are like the handiwork of my ancestor Daedalus; and if I were the sayer or propounder of them, you might scoffingly reply that the products of my reasoning walk away and will not remain fixed where they are placed because I am a descendant of his. But now, since these propositions are your own, you must find some other gibe, for they certainly, as you yourself allow, show an inclination to be on the move.

EUTH. Nay, Socrates, I think the gibe is much to the point, for you are the Daedalus who sets arguments in motion; not I, certainly, but you make them move or go round, for they would never have stirred, as far as I am concerned.

SOC. Then I must be a greater than Daedalus: for whereas he only made his own inventions to move, I move those of other people as well. And the beauty of it is, that I would rather not: for I would give the wisdom of Daedalus, and the wealth of Tantalus, to be able to detain them and keep them fixed. But enough of this. As I perceive that you are spoilt, I will myself endeavour to show you how you might instruct me in the nature of

piety; and I hope that you will not grudge your labour. Tell me, then—
Is not all that is pious necessarily just?

EUTH. Yes.

SOC. And is, then, all which is just pious? or, is that which is pious all
just, but that which is just is only in part, and not all, pious?

EUTH. I do not understand you, Socrates.

SOC. And yet I know that you are as much wiser than I am, as you are
younger. But, as I was saying, revered friend, you are spoilt owing to the
abundance of your wisdom. Please to exert yourself, for there is no real difficulty in understanding me. What I mean I may explain by an illustration of
what I do not mean. The poet (Stasinus) sings—

Of Zeus, the author and creator of all these things,
He will not speak reproach: for where there is fear there is also reverence.

Now I disagree with this poet. Shall I tell you in what respect?

EUTH. By all means.

SOC. I should not say that where there is fear there is also reverence; for
I am sure that many persons fear poverty and disease, and the like evils,
but I do not perceive that they reverence the objects of their fear.

EUTH. Very true.

SOC. But where reverence is, there is fear; for he, who has a feeling of
reverence and shame about the commission of any action, fears and is afraid
of an ill reputation.

EUTH. No doubt.

SOC. Then we are wrong in saying that where there is fear there is also
reverence; and we should say, where there is reverence there is also fear. But
there is not always reverence where there is fear; for fear is a more extended
notion, and reverence is a part of fear, just as the odd is a part of number,
and number is a more extended notion than the odd. I suppose that you
follow me now?

EUTH. Quite well.

SOC. That was the sort of question which I meant to raise when I asked
whether the just is always the pious, or whether it is not the case that where
there is piety there is always justice, but there may be justice where there is
not piety; for justice is the more extended notion of which piety is only a
part. Do you dissent?

EUTH. No, I think that you are quite right.

SOC. Then, if piety is a part of justice, I suppose that we should inquire
what part? If you had pursued the inquiry in the previous cases; for instance,
if you had asked me what is an even number, and what part of number the
even is, I should have had no difficulty in replying, a number which is not
lopsided, so to speak, but represents a figure having two equal sides. Do you
not agree?

EUTH. Yes, I quite agree.

soc. In like manner, I want you to tell me what part of justice is piety or holiness, that I may be able to tell Meletus not to do me injustice, or indict me for impiety, as I am now adequately instructed by you in the nature of piety or holiness, and their opposites.

euth. Piety or holiness, Socrates, appears to me to be that part of justice which attends to the gods, as there is the other part of justice which attends to men.

soc. That is good, Euthyphro; yet still there is a little point about which I should like to have further information, What is the meaning of "attention"? For attention can hardly be used in the same sense when applied to the gods as when applied to other things. We do so apply it, do we not? For instance, horses are said to require attention, and not every person is able to attend to them, but only a person skilled in horsemanship. Is it not so?

euth. Certainly.

soc. I should suppose that the art of horsemanship is the art of attending to horses?

euth. Yes.

soc. Nor is everyone qualified to attend to dogs, but only the huntsman?

euth. True.

soc. And I should also conceive that the art of the huntsman is the art of attending to dogs?

euth. Yes.

soc. As the art of the oxherd is the art of attending to oxen?

euth. Very true.

soc. In like manner holiness or piety is the art of attending to the gods? that would be your meaning, Euthyphro?

euth. Yes.

soc. And is not attention always designed for the good or benefit of that to which the attention is given? As in the case of horses, you may observe that when attended to by the horseman's art they are benefited and improved, are they not?

euth. True.

soc. As the dogs are benefited by the huntsman's art, and the oxen by the art of the oxherd, and all other things are tended or attended for their good and not for their hurt?

euth. Certainly, not for their hurt.

soc. But for their good?

euth. Of course.

soc. And does piety or holiness, which has been defined to be the art of attending to the gods, benefit or improve them? Would you say that when you do a holy act you make any of the gods better?

euth. No, no; that was certainly not what I meant.

soc. And I, Euthyphro, never supposed that you did. I asked you the question about the nature of the attention, because I thought that you did **not.**

EUTH. You do me justice, Socrates; that is not the sort of attention which I mean.

soc. Good: but I must still ask what is this attention to the gods which is called piety?

EUTH. It is such, Socrates, as servants show to their masters.

soc. I understand—a sort of ministration to the gods.

EUTH. Exactly.

soc. Medicine is also a sort of ministration or service, having in view the attainment of some object—would you not say of health?

EUTH. I should.

soc. Again, there is the art which ministers to the shipbuilder with a view to the attainment of some result?

EUTH. Yes, Socrates, with a view to the building of a ship.

soc. As there is an art which ministers to the housebuilder with a view to the building of a house?

EUTH. Yes.

soc. And now tell me, my good friend, about the art which ministers to the gods: what work does that help to accomplish? For you must surely know if, as you say, you are of all men living the one who is best instructed in religion.

EUTH. And I speak the truth, Socrates.

soc. Tell me then, oh tell me—what is that fair work which the gods do by the help of our ministrations?

EUTH. Many and fair, Socrates, are the works which they do.

soc. Why, my friend, and so are those of a general. But the sum of them is easily told. Would you not say that the sum of his works is victory in war?

EUTH. Certainly.

soc. Many and fair, too, are the works of the husbandman, if I am not mistaken; but their sum is the production of food from the earth?

EUTH. Exactly.

soc. And of the many and fair things done by the gods, what is the sum?

EUTH. I have told you already, Socrates, that to learn all these things accurately will be very tiresome. Let me simply say that piety or holiness is learning how to please the gods in word and deed, by prayers and sacrifices. Such piety is the salvation of families and states, just as impiety, which is unpleasing to the gods, is their ruin and destruction.

soc. I think that you could have answered in much fewer words the substance of my questions if you had chosen. But I see plainly that you are not disposed to instruct me—clearly not: else why, when we reached the point, did you turn aside? Had you only answered me I should have truly learned of you by this time the nature of piety. But I must follow you as a lover must follow the caprice of his beloved, and therefore can only ask again, what is the pious, and what is piety? Do you mean that they are a sort of science of praying and sacrificing?

EUTH. Yes, I do.

soc. And sacrificing is giving to the gods, and prayer is asking of the gods?

EUTH. Yes, Socrates.

soc. Upon this view, then, piety is a science of asking and giving?

EUTH. You understand me capitally, Socrates.

soc. Yes, my friend; the reason is that I am a votary of your science, and give my mind to it, and therefore nothing which you say will be thrown away upon me. Please then to tell me, what is the nature of this service to the gods? Do you mean that we prefer requests and give gifts to them?

EUTH. Yes, I do.

soc. Is not the right way of asking to ask of them what we want?

EUTH. Certainly.

soc. And the right way of giving is to give to them in return what they want of us. There would be no meaning in an art which gives to anyone that which he does not want.

EUTH. Very true, Socrates.

soc. Then piety, Euthyphro, is an art which gods and men have of trafficking with one another?

EUTH. That is an expression which you may use, if you like.

soc. But I have no particular liking for anything but the truth. I wish, however, that you would tell me what benefit accrues to the gods from our gifts. There is no doubt about what they give to us, for there is no good thing which they do not give; but how they get any benefit from our gifts to them is far from being equally clear. If they give everything and get from us nothing, that must be a traffic in which we have very greatly the advantage of them.

EUTH. And do you imagine, Socrates, that any benefit accrues to the gods from our gifts?

soc. But if not, Euthyphro, what is the meaning of the gifts we offer to the gods?

EUTH. What else but tributes of honour; and, as I was just now saying, what pleases them?

soc. Piety, then, is pleasing to the gods, but not beneficial or dear to them?

EUTH. I should say that nothing could be dearer.

soc. Then once more the assertion is repeated that piety is that which is dear to the gods?

EUTH. Certainly.

soc. And when you say this, can you wonder at your words not standing firm, but walking away? Will you accuse me of being the Daedalus who makes them walk away, not perceiving that there is another and far greater artist than Daedalus who makes things that go round in a circle, and he is yourself; for the argument, as you will perceive, comes round to the same point. Were we not saying that the holy or pious was not the same with that which is loved of the gods? Have you forgotten?

EUTH. I quite remember.

soc. And are you not now saying that what is dear to the gods is holy; and is not this the same as what is loved of them—do you see?

EUTH. True.

soc. Then either we were wrong in our former assertion; or, if we were right then, we are wrong now.

EUTH. It appears so.

soc. Then we must begin again and ask, What is piety? That is an inquiry which I shall never be weary of pursuing as far as in me lies; and I entreat you not to scorn me, but to apply your mind to the utmost, and tell me the truth. For, if any man knows, you are he; and therefore I must hold you fast, like Proteus, until you tell. If you had not certainly known the nature of piety and impiety, I am confident that you would never, on behalf of a serf, have charged your aged father with murder. You would not have run such a risk of doing wrong in the sight of the gods, and you would have had too much respect for the opinions of men. I am sure, therefore, that you know the nature of piety and impiety. Speak out then, my dear Euthyphro, and do not hide your knowledge.

EUTH. Another time, Socrates; for I am in a hurry, and must go now.

soc. Alas! my friend, and will you leave me in despair? I was hoping that you would instruct me in the nature of piety and impiety; and then I might have cleared myself of Meletus and his indictment. I would have told him that I had been enlightened by Euthyphro, and had given up rash innovations and speculations in which I indulged only through ignorance, and that now I am about to lead a better life.

QUESTIONS

1. Give the steps of the argument by which Socrates shows that the definition, "Piety is that which is dear to the gods," leads to a self-contradiction. What new definition is offered to escape this self-contradiction?
2. State in your own words what point Socrates is making by means of the discussion about whether piety is loved by the gods because it is holy, or is holy because it is loved by the gods.
3. Through his questioning, Socrates gets Euthyphro to define piety as one part of justice. What part of justice does Euthyphro say it is? Show how Socrates criticizes this definition, and state why you think his criticism is, or is not, valid.
4. Socrates is in quest of a definition of "piety." What kind of definition is he seeking when he says: "Remember that I did not ask you to give me two or three examples of piety, but to explain the general form which makes all pious things to be pious"? After reading the selection by Black in Chapter 4, what comments would you make about Socrates' view of what a definition is?
5. If we assume that Socrates is doing what Plato thinks a philosopher should do, while Euthyphro is not, what is Plato's conception of the aim of philosophizing? Of the proper method of philosophizing?

Part One

KNOWLEDGE, PERSONS, AND THE WORLD

Part One introduces the reader to a set of philosophical topics which are related to the notion of knowledge. The discussion of knowledge has always had a central place in philosophy. Philosophers have assumed, practically from the beginning of the subject, the task of distinguishing what can be known with certainty from that which is uncertain. The results of philosophers' work in this area should be of use to anyone in any sort of intellectual endeavor. But philosophers have also put their conclusions to their own special uses, for each philosopher may employ his criterion of certain knowledge to justify his own claims to knowledge and to judge the claims of his fellow philosophers. So the definition of knowledge is of interest not only because of the attention philosophers have given it, but also because of its usefulness in the construction and criticism of philosophies.

THE PROBLEM OF KNOWLEDGE

"Knowledge" is an ambiguous term; the first two chapters in this part treat two of its meanings. Some philosophers have thought of knowledge as something in the mind. Locke is a representative of this point of view, and Chapter 1, "Knowing and the Known," opens with his description of knowledge as ideas in the mind of the knower. This view is criticized by Professor Ryle; he and Waismann offer accounts of knowledge which refer not to the contents of the mind, but to the abilities of the knower.

Someone's knowledge may also be thought of as the true statements which he can make; Chapter 2, "Knowing and Stating One's Knowledge," contains readings about the classification of statements according to differences in the ways that their meaning and truth are to be ascertained. The classifi-

cation of statements serves in its turn, then, as a clue to the way our claims to know are to be justified.

METAPHYSICS

The metaphysician wants to give an account of what there is, an account that will both comprehend everything and explain why everything is as it is. In Chapter 3, "Metaphysics," the reader is introduced to metaphysics by way of its links to questions which are part of the problem of knowledge. In the first two readings, Berkeley and Lord Russell explore, from different points of view (Idealism and Materialism, respectively), the connection between claims about what we can know and what there is. In the last two readings, A. J. Ayer and W. H. Walsh consider the meaning and truth of metaphysicians' statements about what there is.

SCIENCE

The scientist, too, wishes to give an account of what there is. While his claims may ultimately be no less comprehensive than the metaphysician's, his methods appear to be more piecemeal. In Chapter 4, "The Scientist's Knowledge," the first reading is an examination of scientific method and the knowledge it yields. The second is a discussion of the problem of defining science and scientific method. The last is an examination of the relation of scientific knowledge to everyday knowledge.

PERSONS

In the first four chapters of Part One, the reader will repeatedly meet references to persons as knowing, perceiving, conceiving, having experiences, and encountering the world. But what sort of thing is a person? In the first two selections in Chapter 5, "Mind,

Body, Self and Immortality," the reader is introduced to two opposing claims about persons. Bishop Butler argues that a person is solely a mental (or spiritual) entity. Baron d'Holbach argues that a person is solely a material entity. In the third selection Hume advances the thesis that "the self" is a meaningless concept, and in the last selection Professor Ryle suggests some remedies for our paradoxical thoughts about the self.

At the head of Part One stands a reading drawn from Descartes' *Meditations*. In it the reader may encounter the several problems included in Part One, entwined in the thought of one man. In considering Descartes' philosophy, the reader may come to appreciate both the interconnectedness of the problems considered in this part and the pressing need for later philosophers to separate these problems for fuller and clearer discussion.

RENÉ DESCARTES

(1596–1650)

Meditations on the First Philosophy

René Descartes was born at La Haye, Touraine, France. He was educated at the Jesuit school in La Flèche and at the University of Poitiers, where he studied law. As a young man he spent several years in soldiering and travel, but his thoughts were never far from mathematics and the sciences, and he finally decided to devote himself to a life of study. He settled first in France, but in 1628 he moved to Holland, where he spent almost all the rest of his life. As a mathematician, Descartes is remembered for his discovery of analytic geometry. Although he wrote on theoretical physics and carried out investigations in physiology, he made no lasting contribution to these sciences. His great ambition was to work out an entire reconstruction of all knowledge (including religious knowledge) which would be as clear and as certain as mathematics. It was with this goal in mind that he wrote his

chief philosophical works: *Rules for the Direction of the Mind* (1628); *Discourse on the Method of Rightly Conducting the Reason and Seeking for Truth in the Sciences* (1637); and *Meditations on the First Philosophy* (1641).

In the history of philosophy Descartes' works mark the change from philosophy as the technical concern of theologians disputing among themselves to philosophy as the concern of anyone who is able and willing to think clearly. Doubtless we should claim too much if we said that Descartes was the first modern to think for himself. But by offering his intellectual biography to the general reader in both the *Discourse* and the *Meditations,* Descartes became the exemplar of modern man thinking for himself. Even though many of his successors did not accept Descartes' solutions to the problems of philosophy, all were impressed by the larger implications of his way of doing philosophy. For Descartes replaces the practice of citing an authority as the guarantee of truth with the more exacting program of discovering truth by the careful exercise of his own intellectual powers.

The large theme underlying all of Descartes' philosophical work is the nature and capacities of the human mind. This theme is the touchstone of the reading before us. As Descartes pursues it, he considers a wide range of philosophical problems: the limits of skepticism, the foundations of human knowledge, the nature and existence of the self, proofs for the existence of God, the extent of our knowledge of the world, and the relation between God, individual minds, and the world. Thanks to the brevity of Descartes' work, the interdependence of all these topics may be quickly appreciated. The topics themselves continue to engage philosophers today. While Descartes' views never enjoyed an unchallenged reign, they have often been assumed as a starting point by his critics as well as his followers; and they are not without their influence today. Therefore, both because of Descartes' comprehensiveness and his importance to later philosophy, we have drawn a reading from his *Meditations* to serve as an introduction to and general survey of Part One.

The reader should keep in mind the general plan of the *Meditations*. Des-cartes proceeds from the simplest matters to more complex topics which can only be understood if first the simplest matters are clearly understood. Each part of the *Meditations* is thought of as the work of a day; the opening and closing passages of each meditation are breaks in the rigorous progress of the argument, where Descartes reviews what he has accomplished and assesses what must be done next. Descartes begins the *Meditations* by surveying different kinds of knowledge to see whether any is indubitable. He does indeed discover one piece of knowledge that withstands all doubt, and this discovery leads him to a limited reliance on the powers of his own mind. From this starting point, he is able to offer a proof of the existence of God; with God to serve as a guarantor, he goes on to argue for order in the natural world and the reliability of his own senses and reason.

This reading is followed by a set of objections to certain points in Descartes' philosophy which were advanced by his contemporaries, and Descartes' replies to these objections. The reader should consider these objections and replies not only for their relevance to Descartes' philosophy, but as examples of the way any piece of philosophy may be criticized and defended.

This reading is selected from *Meditations on the First Philosophy,* translated from the Latin by E. S. Haldane and G. R. T. Ross.

From *The Philosophical Works of Descartes,* Vol. I, translated by E. S. Haldane and G. R. T. Ross, Cambridge University Press, London, 1931. Reprinted by permission of the publisher.

MEDITATION I.

Of the things which may be brought within the sphere of the doubtful.

It is now some years since I detected how many were the false beliefs that I had from my earliest youth admitted as true, and how doubtful was everything I had since constructed on this basis; and from that time I was convinced that I must once for all seriously undertake to rid myself of all the opinions which I had formerly accepted, and commence to build anew from the foundation, if I wanted to establish any firm and permanent structure in the sciences. But as this enterprise appeared to be a very great one, I waited until I had attained an age so mature that I could not hope that at any later date I should be better fitted to execute my design. This reason caused me to delay so long that I should feel that I was doing wrong were I to occupy in deliberation the time that yet remains to me for action. To-day, then, since very opportunely for the plan I have in view I have delivered my mind from every care [and am happily agitated by no passions] [1] and since I have procured for myself an assured leisure in a peaceable retirement, I shall at last seriously and freely address myself to the general upheaval of all my former opinions.

Now for this object it is not necessary that I should show that all of these are false—I shall perhaps never arrive at this end. But inasmuch as reason already persuades me that I ought no less carefully to withhold my assent from matters which are not entirely certain and indubitable than from those which appear to me manifestly to be false, if I am able to find in each one some reason to doubt, this will suffice to justify my rejecting the whole. And for that end it will not be requisite that I should examine each in particular, which would be an endless undertaking; for owing to the fact that the destruction of the foundations of necessity brings with it the downfall of the rest of the edifice, I shall only in the first place attack those principles upon which all my former opinions rested.

DOUBTS ABOUT KNOWLEDGE GAINED THROUGH THE SENSES

All that up to the present time I have accepted as most true and certain I have learned either from the senses or through the senses; but it is sometimes proved to me that these senses are deceptive, and it is wiser not to trust entirely to any thing by which we have once been deceived.

[1] This translation is from the Latin version of the *Meditations*. Additional readings from the French version are inserted within brackets.—Eds.

But it may be that although the senses sometimes deceive us concerning things which are hardly perceptible, or very far away, there are yet many others to be met with as to which we cannot reasonably have any doubt, although we recognise them by their means. For example, there is the fact that I am here, seated by the fire, attired in a dressing gown, having this paper in my hands and other similar matters. And how could I deny that these hands and this body are mine, were it not perhaps that I compare my-self to certain persons, devoid of sense, whose cerebella are so troubled and clouded by the violent vapours of black bile, that they constantly assure us that they think they are kings when they are really quite poor, or that they are clothed in purple when they are really without covering, or who imagine that they have an earthenware head or are nothing but pumpkins or are made of glass. But they are mad, and I should not be any the less insane were I to follow examples so extravagant.

At the same time I must remember that I am a man, and that conse-quently I am in the habit of sleeping, and in my dreams representing to my-self the same things or sometimes even less probable things, than do those who are insane in their waking moments. How often has it happened to me that in the night I dreamt that I found myself in this particular place, that I was dressed and seated near the fire, whilst in reality I was lying undressed in bed! At this moment it does indeed seem to me that it is with eyes awake that I am looking at this paper; that this head which I move is not asleep, that it is deliberately and of set purpose that I extend my hand and perceive it; what happens in sleep does not appear so clear nor so distinct as does all this. But in thinking over this I remind myself that on many occasions I have in sleep been deceived by similar illusions, and in dwelling carefully on this reflection I see so manifestly that there are no certain indications by which we may clearly distinguish wakefulness from sleep that I am lost in astonishment. And my astonishment is such that it is almost capable of persuading me that I now dream.

DOUBTS ABOUT MATHEMATICAL KNOWLEDGE

Now let us assume that we are asleep and that all these particulars, e.g. that we open our eyes, shake our head, extend our hands, and so on, are but false delusions; and let us reflect that possibly neither our hands nor our whole body are such as they appear to us to be. At the same time we must at least confess that the things which are represented to us in sleep are like painted representations which can only have been formed as the counter-parts of something real and true, and that in this way those general things at least, i.e. eyes, a head, hands, and a whole body, are not imaginary things, but things really existent. For, as a matter of fact, painters, even when they study with the greatest skill to represent sirens and satyrs by forms the most strange and extraordinary, cannot give them natures which are entirely new, but merely make a certain medley of the members of different animals; or if their imagination is extravagant enough to invent something so novel that nothing similar has ever before been seen, and that then their work represents a thing purely fictitious and absolutely false, it is certain all the same that the colours of which this is composed are necessarily real. And for the same reason, although these general things, to wit, [a body], eyes, a head, hands, and such like, may be imaginary, we are bound at the same time to confess that there are at least some other objects yet more simple and more universal, which are real and true; and of these just in the same way as with certain real colours, all these images of things which dwell in our thoughts, whether true and real or false and fantastic, are formed.

To such a class of things pertains corporeal nature in general, and its extension, the figure of extended things, their quantity or magnitude and number, as also the place in which they are, the time which measures their duration, and so on.

That is possibly why our reasoning is not unjust when we conclude from this that Physics, Astronomy, Medicine and all other sciences which have as their end the consideration of composite things, are very dubious and uncertain; but that Arithmetic, Geometry and other sciences of that kind which only treat of things that are very simple and very general, without taking great trouble to ascertain whether they are actually existent or not, contain some measure of certainty and an element of the indubitable. For whether I am awake or asleep, two and three together always form five, and the square can never have more than four sides, and it does not seem possible that truths so clear and apparent can be suspected of any falsity [or uncertainty].

Nevertheless I have long had fixed in my mind the belief that an all-powerful God existed by whom I have been created such as I am. But how do I know that He has not brought it to pass that there is no earth, no heaven, no extended body, no magnitude, no place, and that nevertheless [I possess the perceptions of all these things and that] they seem to me to exist just exactly as I now see them? And, besides, as I sometimes imagine that others deceive themselves in the things which they think they know best, how do I know that I am not deceived every time that I add two and three, or count the sides of a square, or judge of things yet simpler, if anything simpler can be imagined? But possibly God has not desired that I should be thus deceived, for He is said to be supremely good. If, however, it is contrary to His goodness to have made me such that I constantly deceive myself, it would also appear to be contrary to His goodness to permit me to be sometimes deceived, and nevertheless I cannot doubt that He does permit this.

There may indeed be those who would prefer to deny the existence of a

God so powerful, rather than believe that all other things are uncertain. But let us not oppose them for the present, and grant that all that is here said of a God is a fable; nevertheless in whatever way they suppose that I have arrived at the state of being that I have reached—whether they attribute it to fate or to accident, or make out that it is by a continual succession of antecedents, or by some other method—since to err and deceive oneself is a defect, it is clear that the greater will be the probability of my being so imperfect as to deceive myself ever, as is the Author to whom they assign my origin the less powerful. To these reasons I have certainly nothing to reply, but at the end I feel constrained to confess that there is nothing in all that I formerly believed to be true, of which I cannot in some measure doubt, and that not merely through want of thought or through levity, but for reasons which are very powerful and maturely considered; so that henceforth I ought not the less carefully to refrain from giving credence to these opinions than to that which is manifestly false, if I desire to arrive at any certainty [in the sciences].

But it is not sufficient to have made these remarks, we must also be careful to keep them in mind. For these ancient and commonly held opinions still revert frequently to my mind, long and familiar custom having given them the right to occupy my mind against my inclination and rendered them almost masters of my belief; nor will I ever lose the habit of deferring to them or of placing my confidence in them, so long as I consider them as they really are, i.e. opinions in some measure doubtful, as I have just shown, and at the same time highly probable, so that there is much more reason to believe in than to deny them. That is why I consider that I shall not be acting amiss, if, taking of set purpose a contrary belief, I allow myself to be deceived, and for a certain time pretend that all these opinions are entirely false and imaginary, until at last, having thus balanced my former prejudices with my latter [so that they cannot divert my opinions more to one side than to the other], my judgment will no longer be dominated by bad usage or turned away from the right knowledge of the truth. For I am assured that there can be neither peril nor error in this course, and that I cannot at present yield too much to distrust, since I am not considering the question of action, but only of knowledge.

I shall then suppose, not that God who is supremely good and the fountain of truth, but some evil genius not less powerful than deceitful, has employed his whole energies in deceiving me; I shall consider that the heavens, the earth, colours, figures, sound, and all other external things are nought but the illusions and dreams of which this genius has availed himself in order to lay traps for my credulity; I shall consider myself as having no hands, no eyes, no flesh, no blood, nor any senses, yet falsely believing myself to possess all these things; I shall remain obstinately attached to this idea, and if by this means it is not in my power to arrive at the knowledge of any truth, I may at least do what is in my power [i.e. suspend my judgment], and with firm purpose avoid giving credence to any false thing, or being imposed upon by this arch deceiver, however powerful and deceptive he may be. . . .

MEDITATION II.

Of the Nature of the Human Mind;
and that it is more easily known than the Body.

INDUBITABLE TRUTH

The Meditation of yesterday filled my mind with so many doubts that it is no longer in my power to forget them. And yet I do not see in what manner I can resolve them; and, just as if I had all of a sudden fallen into very deep water, I am so disconcerted that I can neither make certain of setting my feet on the bottom, nor can I swim and so support myself on the surface. I shall nevertheless make an effort and follow anew the same path as that on which I yesterday entered, i.e. I shall proceed by setting aside all that in which the least doubt could be supposed to exist, just as if I had discovered that it was absolutely false; and I shall ever follow in this road until I have met with something which is certain, or at least, if I can do nothing else, until I have learned for certain that there is nothing in the world that is certain. Archimedes, in order that he might draw the terrestrial globe out of its place, and transport it elsewhere, demanded only that one point should be fixed and immoveable; in the same way I shall have the right to conceive high hopes if I am happy enough to discover one thing only which is certain and indubitable.

I suppose, then, that all the things that I see are false; I persuade myself that nothing has ever existed of all that my fallacious memory represents to me. I consider that I possess no senses; I imagine that body, figure, extension, movement and place are but the fictions of my mind. What, then, can be esteemed as true? Perhaps nothing at all, unless that there is nothing in the world that is certain.

But how can I know there is not something different from those things that I have just considered, of which one cannot have the slightest doubt? Is there not some God, or some other being by whatever name we call it, who puts these reflections into my mind? That is not necessary, for is it not possible that I am capable of producing them myself? I myself, am I not at least something? But I have already denied that I had senses and body. Yet I hesitate, for what follows from that? Am I so dependent on body and senses that I cannot exist without these? But I was persuaded that there was nothing in all the world, that there was no heaven, no earth, that there were no minds, nor any bodies: was I not then likewise persuaded that I did not exist? Not at all; of a surety I myself did exist since I persuaded myself of something [or merely because I thought of something]. But there is some deceiver or other, very powerful and very cunning, who ever employs his ingenuity in deceiving me. Then without doubt I exist also if he deceives me, and let him deceive me as much as he will, he can never cause me to be nothing so long as I think that I am something. So that after having reflected well and carefully examined all things, we must come to the definite conclusion that this proposition: I am, I exist, is necessarily true each time that I pronounce it, or that I mentally conceive it.[2]

DESCARTES, A THING WHICH THINKS

But I do not yet know clearly enough what I am, I who am certain that I am; and hence I must be careful to see that I do not imprudently take some other object in place of myself, and thus that I do not go astray in respect of this knowledge that I hold to be the most certain and most evident of all that I have formerly learned. That is why I shall now consider anew what I believed myself to be before I embarked upon these last reflections; and of my former opinions I shall withdraw all that might even in a small degree be invalidated by the reasons which I have just brought forward, in order that there may be nothing at all left beyond what is absolutely certain and indubitable.

What then did I formerly believe myself to be? Undoubtedly I believed

---

[2] In his *Discourse on the Method of Rightly Conducting the Reason,* Descartes proves his existence in the following way:

. . . I noticed that whilst I thus wished to think all things false, it was absolutely essential that the 'I' who thought this should be somewhat, and remarking that this truth '*I think, therefore I am*' was so certain and so assured that all the most extravagant suppositions brought forward by the sceptics were incapable of shaking it, I came to the conclusion that I could receive it without scruple as the first principle of the Philosophy for which I was seeking.

And then, examining attentively that which I was, I saw that I could conceive that I had no body, and that there was no world nor place where I might be; but yet that I could not for all that conceive that I was not. On the contrary, I saw from the very fact that I thought of doubting the truth of other things, it very evidently and certainly followed that I was; on the other hand if I had only ceased from thinking, even if all the rest of what I had ever imagined had really existed, I shall have no reason for thinking that I had existed. From that I knew that I was a substance the whole essence or nature of which is to think, and that for its existence there is no need of any place, nor does it depend on any material thing; so that this 'me,' that is to say, the soul by which I am what I am, is entirely distinct from body, and is even more easy to know than is the latter; and even if body were not, the soul would not cease to be what it is.

Discourse, Part IV.—Eds.

myself to be a man. But what is a man? Shall I say a reasonable animal? Certainly not; for then I should have to inquire what an animal is, and what is reasonable; and thus from a single question I should insensibly fall into an infinitude of others more difficult; and I should not wish to waste the little time and leisure remaining to me in trying to unravel subtleties like these. But I shall rather stop here to consider the thoughts which of themselves spring up in my mind, and which were not inspired by anything beyond my own nature alone when I applied myself to the consideration of my being. In the first place, then, I considered myself as having a face, hands, arms, and all that system of members composed of bones and flesh as seen in a corpse which I designated by the name of body. In addition to this I considered that I was nourished, that I walked, that I felt, and that I thought, and I referred all these actions to the soul: but I did not stop to consider what the soul was, or if I did stop, I imagined that it was something extremely rare and subtle like a wind, a flame, or an ether, which was spread throughout my grosser parts. As to body I had no manner of doubt about its nature, but thought I had a very clear knowledge of it; and if I had desired to explain it according to the notions that I had then formed of it, I should have described it thus: By the body I understand all that which can be defined by a certain figure: something which can be confined in a certain place, and which can fill a given space in such a way that every other body will be excluded from it; which can be perceived either by touch, or by sight, or by hearing, or by taste, or by smell: which can be moved in many ways not, in truth, by itself, but by something which is foreign to it, by which it is touched [and from which it receives impressions]: for to have the power of self-movement, as also of feeling or of thinking, I did not consider to appertain to the nature of body: on the contrary, I was rather astonished to find that faculties similar to them existed in some bodies.

But what am I, now that I suppose that there is a certain genius which is extremely powerful, and, if I may say so, malicious, who employs all his powers in deceiving me? Can I affirm that I possess the least of all those things which I have just said pertain to the nature of body? I pause to consider, I revolve all these things in my mind, and I find none of which I can say that it pertains to me. It would be tedious to stop to enumerate them. Let us pass to the attributes of soul and see if there is any one which is in me? What of nutrition or walking [the first mentioned]? But if it is so that I have no body it is also true that I can neither walk nor take nourishment. Another attribute is sensation. But one cannot feel without body, and besides I have thought I perceived many things during sleep that I recognised in my waking moments as not having been experienced at all. What of thinking? I find here that thought is an attribute that belongs to me; it alone cannot be separated from me. I am, I exist, that is certain. But how often? Just when I think; for it might possibly be the case if I ceased entirely to think, that I should likewise cease altogether to exist. I do not now admit anything which is not necessarily true: to speak accurately I am not more than a thing which thinks, that is to say a mind or a soul, or an understanding, or a reason, which are terms whose significance was formerly unknown to me. I am, however, a real thing and really exist; but what thing? I have answered: a thing which thinks.

And what more? I shall exercise my imagination [in order to see if I am not something more]. I am not a collection of members which we call the human body: I am not a subtle air distributed through these members, I am not a wind, a fire, a vapour, a breath, nor anything at all which I can imagine or conceive; because I have assumed that all these were nothing. Without changing that supposition I find that I only leave myself certain of the fact that I am somewhat. But perhaps it is true that these same things which I supposed were non-existent because they are unknown to me, are really not different from the self which I know. I am not sure about this, I shall not dispute about it now; I can only give judgment on things that are known to me. I know that I exist, and I inquire what I am, I whom I know to exist. But it is very certain that the knowledge of my existence taken in its precise significance does not depend on things whose existence is not yet known to me; consequently it does not depend on those which I can feign in imagination. And indeed the very term *feign* in imagination [3] proves to me my error, for I really do this if I imagine myself a something, since to imagine is nothing else than to contemplate the figure or image of a corporeal thing. But I already know for certain that I am, and that it may be that all these images, and, speaking generally, all things that relate to the nature of body are nothing but dreams [and chimeras]. For this reason I see clearly that I have as little reason to say, 'I shall stimulate my imagination in order to know more distinctly what I am,' than if I were to say, 'I am now awake, and I perceive somewhat that is real and true: but because I do not yet perceive it distinctly enough, I shall go to sleep of express purpose, so that my dreams may represent the perception with greatest truth and evidence.' And, thus, I know for certain that nothing of all that I can understand by means of my imagination belongs to this knowledge which I have of myself, and that it is necessary to recall the mind from this mode of thought with the utmost diligence in order that it may be able to know its own nature with perfect distinctness.

But what then am I? A thing which thinks. What is a thing which thinks? It is a thing which doubts, understands, [conceives], affirms, denies, wills, refuses, which also imagines and feels.

Certainly it is no small matter if all these things pertain to my nature. But why should they not so pertain? Am I not that being who now doubts nearly everything, who nevertheless understands certain things, who affirms that one only is true, who denies all the others, who desires to know more,

[3] Or 'form an image' (effingo).

is averse from being deceived, who imagines many things, sometimes indeed despite his will, and who perceives many likewise, as by the intervention of the bodily organs? Is there nothing in all this which is as true as it is certain that I exist, even though I should always sleep and though he who has given me being employed all his ingenuity in deceiving me? Is there likewise any one of these attributes which can be distinguished from my thought, or which might be said to be separated from myself? For it is so evident of itself that it is I who doubts, who understands, and who desires, that there is no reason here to add anything to explain it. And I have certainly the power of imagining likewise; for although it may happen (as I formerly supposed) that none of the things which I imagine are true, nevertheless this power of imagining does not cease to be really in use, and it forms part of my thought. Finally, I am the same who feels, that is to say, who perceives certain things, as by the organs of sense, since in truth I see light, I hear noise, I feel heat. But it will be said that these phenomena are false and that I am dreaming. Let it be so; still it is at least quite certain that it seems to me that I see light, that I hear noise and that I feel heat. That cannot be false; properly speaking it is what is in me called feeling; [4] and used in this precise sense that is no other thing than thinking.

From this time I begin to know what I am with a little more clearness and distinction than before; but nevertheless it still seems to me, and I cannot prevent myself from thinking, that corporeal things, whose images are framed by thought, which are tested by the senses, are much more distinctly known than that obscure part of me which does not come under the imagination. Although really it is very strange to say that I know and understand more distinctly these things whose existence seems to me dubious, which are unknown to me, and which do not belong to me, than others of the truth of which I am convinced, which are known to me and which pertain to my real nature, in a word, than myself. But I see clearly how the case stands: my mind loves to wander, and cannot yet suffer itself to be retained within the just limits of truth. Very good, let us once more give it the freest rein, so that, when afterwards we seize the proper occasion for pulling up, it may the more easily be regulated and controlled.

KNOWING WAX AND KNOWING THE MIND

Let us begin by considering the commonest matters, those which we believe to be the most distinctly comprehended, to wit, the bodies which we touch and see; not indeed bodies in general, for these general ideas are usually a little more confused, but let us consider one body in particular. Let us take, for example, this piece of wax: it has been taken quite freshly from the hive, and it has not yet lost the sweetness of the honey which it

[4] Sentire.

contains; it still retains somewhat of the odour of the flowers from which
it has been culled; its colour, its figure, its size are apparent; it is hard, cold,
easily handled, and if you strike it with the finger, it will emit a sound.
Finally all the things which are requisite to cause us distinctly to recognise
a body, are met with in it. But notice that while I speak and approach the
fire what remained of the taste is exhaled, the smell evaporates, the colour
alters, the figure is destroyed, the size increases, it becomes liquid, it heats,
scarcely can one handle it, and when one strikes it, no sound is emitted.
Does the same wax remain after this change? We must confess that it
remains; none would judge otherwise. What then did I know so distinctly
in this piece of wax? It could certainly be nothing of all that the senses
brought to my notice, since all these things which fall under taste, smell,
sight, touch, and hearing, are found to be changed, and yet the same wax
remains.

Perhaps it was what I now think, viz. that this wax was not that sweetness of honey, nor that agreeable scent of flowers, nor that particular whiteness, nor that figure, nor that sound, but simply a body which a little while
before appeared to me as perceptible under these forms, and which is now
perceptible under others. But what, precisely, is it that I imagine when I form
such conceptions? Let us attentively consider this, and, abstracting from all
that does not belong to the wax, let us see what remains. Certainly nothing
remains excepting a certain extended thing which is flexible and movable.
But what is the meaning of flexible and movable? Is it not that I imagine
that this piece of wax being round is capable of becoming square and of
passing from a square to a triangular figure? No, certainly it is not that,
since I imagine it admits of an infinitude of similar changes, and I nevertheless do not know how to compass the infinitude by my imagination, and
consequently this conception which I have of the wax is not brought about
by the faculty of imagination. What now is this extension? Is it not also
unknown? For it becomes greater when the wax is melted, greater when it is
boiled, and greater still when the heat increases; and I should not conceive
[clearly] according to truth what wax is, if I did not think that even this
piece that we are considering is capable of receiving more variations in extension than I have ever imagined. We must then grant that I could not even
understand through the imagination what this piece of wax is, and that
it is my mind [5] alone which perceives it. I say this piece of wax in particular,
for as to wax in general it is yet clearer. But what is this piece of wax which
cannot be understood excepting by the [understanding or] mind? It is certainly the same that I see, touch, imagine, and finally it is the same which
I have always believed it to be from the beginning. But what must particularly be observed is that its perception is neither an act of vision, nor of
touch, nor of imagination, and has never been such although it may have

[5] entendement F., mens L.

appeared formerly to be so, but only an intuition [6] of the mind, which may be imperfect and confused as it was formerly, or clear and distinct as it is at present, according as my attention is more or less directed to the elements which are found in it, and of which it is composed.

Yet in the meantime I am greatly astonished when I consider [the great feebleness of mind] and its proneness to fall [insensibly] into error; for although without giving expression to my thoughts I consider all this in my own mind, words often impede me and I am almost deceived by the terms of ordinary language. For we say that we see the same wax, if it is present, and not that we simply judge that it is the same from its having the same colour and figure. From this I should conclude that I knew the wax by means of vision and not simply by the intuition of the mind; unless by chance I remember that, when looking from a window and saying I see men who pass in the street, I really do not see them, but infer that what I see is men, just as I say that I see wax. And yet what do I see from the window but hats and coats which may cover automatic machines? Yet I judge these to be men. And similarly solely by the faculty of judgment which rests in my mind, I comprehend that which I believed I saw with my eyes.

A man who makes it his aim to raise his knowledge above the common should be ashamed to derive the occasion for doubting from the forms of speech invented by the vulgar; I prefer to pass on and consider whether I had a more evident and perfect conception of what the wax was when I first perceived it, and when I believed I knew it by means of the external senses or at least by the common sense [7] as it is called, that is to say by the imaginative faculty, or whether my present conception is clearer now that I have most carefully examined what it is, and in what way it can be known. It would certainly be absurd to doubt as to this. For what was there in this first perception which was distinct? What was there which might not as well have been perceived by any of the animals? But when I distinguish the wax from its external forms, and when, just as if I had taken from it its vestments, I consider it quite naked, it is certain that although some error may still be found in my judgment, I can nevertheless not perceive it thus without a human mind.

But finally what shall I say of this mind, that is, of myself, for up to this point I do not admit in myself anything but mind? What then, I who seem to perceive this piece of wax so distinctly, do I not know myself, not only with much more truth and certainty, but also with much more distinctness and clearness? For if I judge that the wax is or exists from the fact that I see it, it certainly follows much more clearly that I am or that I exist myself from the fact that I see it. For it may be that what I see is not really wax, it may also be that I do not possess eyes with which to see anything; but it

[6] inspectio.
[7] sensus communis.

cannot be that when I see, or (for I no longer take account of the distinction) when I think I see, that I myself who think am nought. So if I judge that the wax exists from the fact that I touch it, the same thing will follow, to wit, that I am; and if I judge that my imagination, or some other cause, whatever it is, persuades me that the wax exists, I shall still conclude the same. And what I have here remarked of wax may be applied to all other things which are external to me [and which are met with outside of me]. And further, if the [notion or] perception of wax has seemed to me clearer and more distinct, not only after the sight or the touch, but also after many other causes have rendered it quite manifest to me, with how much more [evidence] and distinctness must it be said that I now know myself, since all the reasons which contribute to the knowledge of wax, or any other body whatever, are yet better proofs of the nature of my mind! And there are so many other things in the mind itself which may contribute to the elucidation of its nature, that those which depend on body such as these just mentioned, hardly merit being taken into account.

But finally here I am, having insensibly reverted to the point I desired, for, since it is now manifest to me that even bodies are not properly speaking known by the senses or by the faculty of imagination, but by the understanding only, and since they are not known from the fact that they are seen or touched, but only because they are understood, I see clearly that there is nothing which is easier for me to know than my mind. But because it is difficult to rid oneself so promptly of an opinion to which one was accustomed for so long, it will be well that I should halt a little at this point, so that by the length of my meditation I may more deeply imprint on my memory this new knowledge.

MEDITATION III.

Of God: that He exists.

I shall now close my eyes, I shall stop my ears, I shall call away all my senses, I shall efface even from my thoughts all the images of corporeal things, or at least (for that is hardly possible) I shall esteem them as vain and false; and thus holding converse only with myself and considering my own nature, I shall try little by little to reach a better knowledge of and a more familiar acquaintanceship with myself. I am a thing that thinks, that is to say, that doubts, affirms, denies, that knows a few things, that is ignorant of many [that loves, that hates], that wills, that desires, that also imagines and perceives; for as I remarked before, although the things which I perceive and imagine are perhaps nothing at all apart from me and in themselves, I am nevertheless assured that these modes of thought that I call perceptions and imaginations, inasmuch only as they are modes of thought, certainly reside [and are met with] in me.

And in the little that I have just said, I think I have summed up all that I really know, or at least all that hitherto I was aware that I knew. In order to try to extend my knowledge further, I shall now look around more carefully and see whether I cannot still discover in myself some other things which I have not hitherto perceived. I am certain that I am a thing which thinks; but do I not then likewise know what is requisite to render me certain of a truth? Certainly in this first knowledge there is nothing that assures me of its truth, excepting the clear and distinct perception of that which I state, which would not indeed suffice to assure me that what I say is true, if it could ever happen that a thing which I conceived so clearly and distinctly could be false; and accordingly it seems to me that already I can establish as a general rule that all things which I perceive [8] very clearly and very distinctly are true.

At the same time I have before received and admitted many things to be very certain and manifest, which yet I afterwards recognised as being dubious. What then were these things? They were the earth, sky, stars and all other objects which I apprehended by means of the senses. But what did I clearly [and distinctly] perceive in them? Nothing more than that the ideas or thoughts of these things were presented to my mind. And not even now do I deny that these ideas are met with in me. But there was yet another thing which I affirmed, and which, owing to the habit which I had formed of believing it, I thought I perceived very clearly, although in truth I did not perceive it at all, to wit, that there were objects outside of me from which these ideas proceeded, and to which they were entirely similar. And it was in this that I erred, or, if perchance my judgment was correct, this was not due to any knowledge arising from my perception.

But when I took anything very simple and easy in the sphere of arithmetic or geometry into consideration, e.g. that two and three together made five, and other things of the sort, were not these present to my mind so clearly as to enable me to affirm that they were true? Certainly if I judged that since such matters could be doubted, this would not have been so for any other reason than that it came into my mind that perhaps a God might have endowed me with such a nature that I may have been deceived even concerning things which seemed to me most manifest. But every time that this preconceived opinion of the sovereign power of a God presents itself to my thought, I am constrained to confess that it is easy to Him, if He wishes it, to cause me to err, even in matters in which I believe myself to have the best evidence. And, on the other hand, always when I direct my attention to things which I believe myself to perceive very clearly, I am so persuaded of their truth that I let myself break out into words such as these: Let who will deceive me, He can never cause me to be nothing while I think that I am, or some day cause it to be true to say that I have never been, it being true now to say that I am, or that two and three make more or less than five, or any

---

[8] Percipio, F. nous concevons.

such thing in which I see a manifest contradiction. And, certainly, since I have no reason to believe that there is a God who is a deceiver, and as I have not yet satisfied myself that there is a God at all, the reason for doubt which depends on this opinion alone is very slight, and so to speak metaphysical. But in order to be able altogether to remove it, I must inquire whether there is a God as soon as the occasion presents itself; and if I find that there is a God, I must also inquire whether He may be a deceiver; for without a knowledge of these two truths I do not see that I can ever be certain of anything.

THOUGHTS AND IDEAS

And in order that I may have an opportunity of inquiring into this in an orderly way [without interrupting the order of meditation which I have proposed to myself, and which is little by little to pass from the notions which I find first of all in my mind to those which I shall later on discover in it] it is requisite that I should here divide my thoughts into certain kinds, and that I should consider in which of these kinds there is, properly speaking, truth or error to be found. Of my thoughts some are, so to speak, images of the things, and to these alone is the title 'idea' properly applied; examples are my thought of a man or of a chimera, of heaven, of an angel, or [even] of God. But other thoughts possess other forms as well. For example in willing, fearing, approving, denying, though I always perceive something as the subject of the action of my mind,[9] yet by this action I always add something else to the idea[10] which I have of that thing; and of the thoughts of this kind some are called volitions or affections, and others judgments.

Now as to what concerns ideas, if we consider them only in themselves and do not relate them to anything else beyond themselves, they cannot properly speaking be false; for whether I imagine a goat or a chimera, it is not less true that I imagine the one than the other. We must not fear likewise that falsity can enter into will and into affections, for although I may desire evil things, or even things that never existed, it is not the less true that I desire them. Thus there remains no more than the judgments which we make, in which I must take the greatest care not to deceive myself. But the principal error and the commonest which we may meet with in them, consists in my judging that the ideas which are in me are similar or conformable to the things which are outside me; for without doubt if I considered the ideas only as certain modes of my thoughts, without trying to relate them to anything beyond, they could scarcely give me material for error.

But among these ideas, some appear to me to be innate, some adventi-

---

[9] The French version is followed here as being more explicit. In it 'action de mon esprit' replaces 'mea cogitatio.'
[10] In the Latin version 'similitudinem.'

tious, and others to be formed [or invented] by myself; for, as I have the power of understanding what is called a thing, or a truth, or a thought, it appears to me that I hold this power from no other source than my own nature. But if I now hear some sound, if I see the sun, or feel heat, I have hitherto judged that these sensations proceeded from certain things that exist outside of me; and finally it appears to me that sirens, hippogryphs, and the like, are formed out of my own mind. But again I may possibly persuade myself that all these ideas are of the nature of those which I term adventitious, or else that they are all innate, or all fictitious: for I have not yet clearly discovered their true origin.

ADVENTITIOUS IDEAS, THEIR IMPLICATIONS

And my principal task in this place is to consider, in respect to those ideas which appear to me to proceed from certain objects that are outside me, what are the reasons which cause me to think them similar to these objects. It seems indeed in the first place that I am taught this lesson by nature; and, secondly, I experience in myself that these ideas do not depend on my will nor therefore on myself—for they often present themselves to my mind in spite of my will. Just now, for instance, whether I will or whether I do not will, I feel heat, and thus I persuade myself that this feeling, or at least this idea of heat, is produced in me by something which is different from me, i.e. by the heat of the fire near which I sit. And nothing seems to me more obvious than to judge that this object imprints its likeness rather than anything else upon me.

Now I must discover whether these proofs are sufficiently strong and convincing. When I say that I am so instructed by nature, I merely mean a certain spontaneous inclination which impels me to believe in this connection, and not a natural light which makes me recognise that it is true. But these two things are very different; for I cannot doubt that which the natural light causes me to believe to be true, as, for example, it has shown me that I am from the fact that I doubt, or other facts of the same kind. And I possess no other faculty whereby to distinguish truth from falsehood, which can teach me that what this light shows me to be true is not really true, and no other faculty that is equally trustworthy. But as far as [apparently] natural impulses are concerned, I have frequently remarked, when I had to make active choice between virtue and vice, that they often enough led me to the part that was worse; and this is why I do not see any reason for following them in what regards truth and error.

And as to the other reason, which is that these ideas must proceed from objects outside me, since they do not depend on my will, I do not find it any the more convincing. For just as these impulses of which I have spoken are found in me, nothwithstanding that they do not always concur with my will, so perhaps there is in me some faculty fitted to produce these ideas without the assistance of any external things, even though it is not yet known by me; just as, apparently, they have hitherto always been found in me during sleep without the aid of any external objects.

And finally, though they did proceed from objects different from myself, it is not a necessary consequence that they should resemble these. On the contrary, I have noticed that in many cases there was a great difference between the object and its idea. I find, for example, two completely diverse ideas of the sun in my mind; the one derives its origin from the senses, and should be placed in the category of adventitious ideas; according to this idea the sun seems to be extremely small; but the other is derived from astronomical reasonings, i.e. is elicited from certain notions that are innate in me, or else it is formed by me in some other manner; in accordance with it the sun appears to be several times greater than the earth. These two ideas cannot, indeed, both resemble the same sun, and reason makes me believe that the one which seems to have originated directly from the sun itself, is the one which is most dissimilar to it.

All this causes me to believe that until the present time it has not been by a judgment that was certain [or premeditated], but only by a sort of blind impulse that I believed that things existed outside of, and different from me, which, by the organs of my senses, or by some other method whatever it might be, conveyed these ideas or images to me [and imprinted on me their similitudes].

IDEAS OF SUBSTANCES, THEIR OBJECTIVE REALITY

But there is yet another method of inquiring whether any of the objects of which I have ideas within me exist outside of me. If ideas are only taken as certain modes of thought, I recognise amongst them no difference or inequality, and all appear to proceed from me in the same manner; but when we consider them as images, one representing one thing and the other another, it is clear that they are very different one from the other. There is no doubt that those which represent to me substances are something more, and contain so to speak more objective reality within them [that is to say, by representation participate in a higher degree of being or perfection] than those that simply represent modes or accidents; and that idea again by which I understand a supreme God, eternal, infinite, [immutable], omniscient, omnipotent, and Creator of all things which are outside of Himself, has certainly more objective reality in itself than those ideas by which finite substances are represented.

Now it is manifest by the natural light that there must at least be as much reality in the efficient and total cause as in its effect. For, pray, whence can the effect derive its reality, if not from its cause? And in what way can this cause communicate this reality to it, unless it possessed it in itself? And from this it follows, not only that something cannot proceed from nothing, but likewise that what is more perfect—that is to say, which has more reality within itself—cannot proceed from the less perfect. And this is not only evidently true of those effects which possess actual or formal reality, but also of the ideas in which we consider merely what is termed objective reality. To take an example, the stone which has not yet existed not only cannot now commence to be unless it has been produced by something which possesses within itself, either formally or eminently, all that enters into the composition of the stone [i.e. it must possess the same things or other more excellent things than those which exist in the stone] and heat can only be produced in a subject in which it did not previously exist by a cause that is of an order [degree or kind] at least as perfect as heat, and so in all other cases. But further, the idea of heat, or of a stone, cannot exist in me unless it has been placed within me by some cause which possesses within it at least as much reality as that which I conceive to exist in the heat or the stone. For although this cause does not transmit anything of its actual or formal reality to my idea, we must not for that reason imagine that it is necessarily a less real cause; we must remember that [since every idea is a work of the mind] its nature is such that it demands of itself no other formal reality than that which it borrows from my thought, of which it is only a mode [i.e. a manner or way of thinking]. But in order that an idea should contain some one certain objective reality rather than another, it must without doubt derive it from some cause in which there is at least as much formal reality as this idea contains of objective reality. For if we imagine that something is found in an idea which is not found in the cause, it must then have been derived from nought; but however imperfect may be this mode of being by which a thing is objectively [or by representation] in the understanding by its idea, we cannot certainly say that this mode of being is nothing, nor, consequently, that the idea derives its origin from nothing.

Nor must I imagine that, since the reality that I consider in these ideas is only objective, it is not essential that this reality should be formally in the causes of my ideas, but that it is sufficient that it should be found objectively. For just as this mode of objective existence pertains to ideas by their proper nature, so does the mode of formal existence pertain to the causes of those ideas (this is at least true of the first and principal) by the nature peculiar to them. And although it may be the case that one idea gives birth to another idea, that cannot continue to be so indefinitely; for in the end we must reach an idea whose cause shall be so to speak an archetype, in which the whole reality [or perfection] which is so to speak objectively [or by representation] in these ideas is contained formally [and really]. Thus the light of nature causes me to know clearly that the ideas in me are like [pictures or] images which can, in truth, easily fall short of the perfection of the objects from which they have been derived, but which can never contain anything greater or more perfect.

And the longer and the more carefully that I investigate these matters, the more clearly and distinctly do I recognise their truth. But what am I to conclude from it all in the end? It is this, that if the objective reality of any one of my ideas is of such a nature as clearly to make me recognise that it is not in me either formally or eminently, and that consequently I cannot myself be the cause of it, it follows of necessity that I am not alone in the world, but that there is another being which exists, or which is the cause of this idea. On the other hand, had no such an idea existed in me, I should have had no sufficient argument to convince me of the existence of any being beyond myself; for I have made very careful investigation everywhere and up to the present time have been able to find no other ground.

THE IDEA OF GOD, AND A PROOF
OF GOD'S EXISTENCE

But of my ideas, beyond that which represents me to myself, as to which there can here be no difficulty, there is another which represents a God, and there are others representing corporeal and inanimate things, others angels, others animals, and others again which represent to me men similar to myself.

As regards the ideas which represent to me other men or animals, or angels, I can however easily conceive that they might be formed by an admixture of the other ideas which I have of myself, of corporeal things, and of God, even although there were apart from me neither men nor animals, nor angels, in all the world.

And in regard to the ideas of corporeal objects, I do not recognise in them anything so great or so excellent that they might not have possibly proceeded from myself; for if I consider them more closely, and examine them individually, as I yesterday examined the idea of wax, I find that there is very little in them which I perceive clearly and distinctly. Magnitude or extension in length, breadth, or depth, I do so perceive; also figure which results from a termination of this extension, the situation which bodies of different figure preserve in relation to one another, and movement or change of situation; to which we may also add substance, duration and number. As to other things such as light, colours, sounds, scents, tastes, heat, cold and the other tactile qualities, they are thought by me with so much obscurity and confusion that I do not even know if they are true or false, i.e. whether the ideas which I form of these qualities are actually the ideas of real objects or not [or whether they only represent chimeras which cannot exist in fact]. For although I have before remarked that it is only in judgments that falsity, properly speaking, or formal falsity, can be met with, a certain material falsity may nevertheless be found in ideas, i.e. when these ideas represent what is nothing as though it were something. For example, the ideas which I have of cold and heat are so far from clear and distinct that by their means I cannot tell whether cold is merely a privation of heat, or heat a privation of cold, or whether both are real qualities, or are not such. And inasmuch as [since ideas resemble images] there cannot be any ideas which do not appear to represent some things, if it is correct to say that cold is merely a privation of heat, the idea which represents it to me as something real and positive will not be improperly termed false, and the same holds good of other similar ideas.

To these it is certainly not necessary that I should attribute any author other than myself. For if they are false, i.e. if they represent things which do not exist, the light of nature shows me that they issue from nought, that is to say, that they are only in me in so far as something is lacking to the perfection of my nature. But if they are true, nevertheless because they exhibit so little reality to me that I cannot even clearly distinguish the thing represented from non-being, I do not see any reason why they should not be produced by myself.

As to the clear and distinct idea which I have of corporeal things, some of them seem as though I might have derived them from the idea which I possess of myself, as those which I have of substance, duration, number, and such like. For [even] when I think that a stone is a substance, or at least a thing capable of existing of itself, and that I am a substance also, although I conceive that I am a thing that thinks and not one that is extended, and that the stone on the other hand is an extended thing which does not think, and that thus there is a notable difference between the two conceptions— they seem, nevertheless, to agree in this, that both represent substances. In the same way, when I perceive that I now exist and further recollect that I have in former times existed, and when I remember that I have various thoughts of which I can recognise the number, I acquire ideas of duration and number which I can afterwards transfer to any object that I please. But as to all the other qualities of which the ideas of corporeal things are composed, to wit, extension, figure, situation and motion, it is true that they are not formally in me, since I am only a thing that thinks; but because they are merely certain modes of substance [and so to speak the vestments under which corporeal substance appears to us] and because I myself am also a substance, it would seem that they might be contained in me eminently.

Hence there remains only the idea of God, concerning which we must consider whether it is something which cannot have proceeded from me myself. By the name God I understand a substance that is infinite [eternal, immutable], independent, all-knowing, all-powerful, and by which I myself and everything else, if anything else does exist, have been created. Now all these characteristics are such that the more diligently I attend to them, the

less do they appear capable of proceeding from me alone; hence, from what
has been already said, we must conclude that God necessarily exists.

For although the idea of substance is within me owing to the fact that
I am substance, nevertheless I should not have the idea of an infinite substance—since I am finite—if it had not proceeded from some substance which
was veritably infinite.

THE IDEA OF THE INFINITE

Nor should I imagine that I do not perceive the infinite by a true idea,
but only by the negation of the finite, just as I perceive repose and darkness
by the negation of movement and of light; for, on the contrary, I see that
there is manifestly more reality in infinite substance than in finite, and therefore that in some way I have in me the notion of the infinite earlier than the
finite—to wit, the notion of God before that of myself. For how would it be
possible that I should know that I doubt and desire, that is to say, that something is lacking to me, and that I am not quite perfect, unless I had within
me some idea of a Being more perfect than myself, in comparison with
which I should recognise the deficiencies of my nature?

And we cannot say that this idea of God is perhaps materially false and
that consequently I can derive it from nought [i.e. that possibly it exists in
me because I am imperfect], as I have just said is the case with ideas of heat,
cold and other such things; for, on the contrary, as this idea is very clear
and distinct and contains within it more objective reality than any other,
there can be none which is of itself more true, nor any in which there can
be less suspicion of falsehood. The idea, I say, of this Being who is absolutely perfect and infinite, is entirely true; for although, perhaps, we can
imagine that such a Being does not exist, we cannot nevertheless imagine
that His idea represents nothing real to me, as I have said of the idea of cold.
This idea is also very clear and distinct; since all that I conceive clearly and
distinctly of the real and the true, and of what conveys some perfection, is
in its entirety contained in this idea. And this does not cease to be true
although I do not comprehend the infinite, or though in God there is an
infinitude of things which I cannot comprehend, nor possibly even reach in
any way by thought; for it is of the nature of the infinite that my nature,
which is finite and limited, should not comprehend it; and it is sufficient
that I should understand this, and that I should judge that all things which
I clearly perceive and in which I know that there is some perfection, and
possibly likewise an infinitude of properties of which I am ignorant, are in
God formally or eminently, so that the idea which I have of Him may become the most true, most clear, and most distinct of all the ideas that are
in my mind.

. . .

MEDITATION IV.

Of the True and the False.

I have been well accustomed these past days to detach my mind from my senses, and I have accurately observed that there are very few things that one knows with certainty respecting corporeal objects, that there are many more which are known to us respecting the human mind, and yet more still regarding God Himself; so that I shall now without any difficulty abstract my thoughts from the consideration of [sensible or] imaginable objects, and carry them to those which, being withdrawn from all contact with matter, are purely intelligible. And certainly the idea which I possess of the human mind inasmuch as it is a thinking thing, and not extending in length, width and depth, nor participating in anything pertaining to body, is incomparably more distinct than is the idea of any corporeal thing. And when I consider that I doubt, that is to say, that I am an incomplete and dependent being, the idea of a being that is complete and independent, that is of God, presents itself to my mind with so much distinctness and clearness—and from the fact alone that this idea is found in me, or that I who possess this idea exist, I conclude so certainly that God exists, and that my existence depends entirely on Him in every moment of my life—that I do not think that the human mind is capable of knowing anything with more evidence and certitude. And it seems to me that I now have before me a road which will lead us from the contemplation of the true God (in whom all the treasures of science and wisdom are contained) to the knowledge of the other objects of the universe.

For, first of all, I recognise it to be impossible that He should ever deceive me; for in all fraud and deception some imperfection is to be found, and although it may appear that the power of deception is a mark of subtilty or power, yet the desire to deceive without doubt testifies to malice or feebleness, and accordingly cannot be found in God.

In the next place I experienced in myself a certain capacity for judging which I have doubtless received from God, like all the other things that I possess; and as He could not desire to deceive me, it is clear that He has not given me a faculty that will lead me to err if I use it aright.

*   *   *

ORIGIN OF ERROR

Whereupon, regarding myself more closely, and considering what are my errors (for they alone testify to there being any imperfection in me), I answer that they depend on a combination of two causes, to wit, on the faculty of knowledge that rests in me, and on the power of choice or of free will—that is to say, of the understanding and at the same time of the will. For by the understanding alone I [neither assert nor deny anything, but] apprehend [11] the ideas of things as to which I can form a judgment. But no error is properly speaking found in it, provided the word error is taken in its proper signification; and though there is possibly an infinitude of things in the world of which I have no idea in my understanding, we cannot for all that say that it is deprived of these ideas [as we might say of something which is required by its nature], but simply it does not possess these; because in truth there is no reason to prove that God should have given me a greater faculty of knowledge than He has given me; and however skilful a workman I represent Him to be, I should not for all that consider that He was bound to have placed in each of His works all the perfections which He may have been able to place in some. I likewise cannot complain that God has not given me a free choice or a will which is sufficient, ample and perfect, since as a matter of fact I am conscious of a will so extended as to be subject to no limits. And what seems to me very remarkable in this regard is that of all the qualities which I possess there is no one so perfect and so comprehensive that I do not very clearly recognise that it might be yet greater and more perfect. For, to take an example, if I consider the faculty of comprehension which I possess, I find that it is of very small extent and extremely limited, and at the same time I find the idea of another faculty much more ample and even infinite, and seeing that I can form the idea of it, I recognise from this very fact that it pertains to the nature of God. If in the same way I examine the memory, the imagination, or some other faculty, I do not find any which is not small and circumscribed, while in God it is immense [or infinite]. It is free-will alone or liberty of choice which I find to be so great in me that I can conceive no other idea to be more great; it is indeed the case that it is for the most part this will that causes me to know that in some manner I bear the image and similitude of God. For although the power of will is incomparably greater in God than in me, both by reason of the knowledge and the power which, conjoined with it, render it stronger and more efficacious, and by reason of its object, inasmuch as in God it extends to a great many things; it nevertheless does not seem to me greater if I consider it formally and precisely in itself: for the faculty of will consists alone in our having the power of choosing to do a thing or choosing not to do it (that is, to affirm or deny, to pursue or to shun it), or rather it consists alone in the fact that in order to affirm or deny, pursue or shun those things placed before us by the understanding, we act so that we are unconscious that any outside force constrains us in doing so. For in order that I should be free it is not necessary that I should be indifferent as to the choice of one or the other of two contraries; but contrariwise the more I lean to the one—whether I recognise clearly that the reasons of the good and true are to be

[11] percipio.

found in it, or whether God so disposes my inward thought—the more freely do I choose and embrace it. And undoubtedly both divine grace and natural knowledge, far from diminishing my liberty, rather increase it and strengthen it. Hence this indifference which I feel, when I am not swayed to one side rather than to the other by lack of reason, is the lowest grade of liberty, and rather evinces a lack or negation in knowledge than a perfection of will: for if I always recognised clearly what was true and good, I should never have trouble in deliberating as to what judgment or choice I should make, and then I should be entirely free without ever being indifferent.

From all this I recognise that the power of will which I have received from God is not of itself the source of my errors—for it is very ample and very perfect of its kind—any more than is the power of understanding; for since I understand nothing but by the power which God has given me for understanding, there is no doubt that all that I understand, I understand as I ought, and it is not possible that I err in this. Whence then come my errors? They come from the sole fact that since the will is much wider in its range and compass than the understanding, I do not restrain it within the same bounds, but extend it also to things which I do not understand: and as the will is of itself indifferent to these, it easily falls into error and sin, and chooses the evil for the good, or the false for the true.

. . .

MEDITATION V.

Of the essence of material things, and, again, of God, that He exists.

. . . Now (after first noting what must be done or avoided, in order to arrive at a knowledge of the truth) my principal task is to endeavor to emerge from the state of doubt into which I have these last days fallen, and to see whether nothing certain can be known regarding material things.

But before examining whether any such objects as I conceive exist outside of me, I must consider the ideas of them in so far as they are in my thought, and see which of them are distinct and which confused.

In the first place, I am able distinctly to imagine that quantity which philosophers commonly call continuous, or the extension in length, breadth, or depth, that is in this quantity, or rather in the object to which it is attributed. Further, I can number in it many different parts, and attribute to each of its parts many sorts of size, figure, situation and local movement, and, finally, I can assign to each of these movements all degrees of duration.

And not only do I know these things with distinctness when I consider them in general, but, likewise [however little I apply my attention to the matter], I discover an infinitude of particulars respecting numbers, figures, movements, and other such things, whose truth is so manifest, and so well accords with my nature, that when I begin to discover them, it seems to me that I learn nothing new, or recollect what I formerly knew—that is to say, that I for the first time perceive things which were already present to my mind, although I had not as yet applied my mind to them.

And what I here find to be most important is that I discover in myself an infinitude of ideas of certain things which cannot be esteemed as pure negations, although they may possibly have no existence outside of my thought, and which are not framed by me, although it is within my power either to think or not to think them, but which possess natures which are true and immutable. For example, when I imagine a triangle, although there may nowhere in the world be such a figure outside my thought, or ever have been, there is nevertheless in this figure a certain determinate nature, form, or essence, which is immutable and eternal, which I have not invented, and which in no wise depends on my mind, as appears from the fact that diverse properties of that triangle can be demonstrated, viz. that its three angles are equal to two right angles, that the greatest side is subtended by the greatest angle, and the like, which now, whether I wish it or do not wish it, I recognise very clearly as pertaining to it, although I never thought of the matter at all when I imagined a triangle for the first time, and which therefore cannot be said to have been invented by me.

Nor does the objection hold good that possibly this idea of a triangle has reached my mind through the medium of my senses, since I have sometimes seen bodies triangular in shape; because I can form in my mind an infinitude of other figures regarding which we cannot have the least conception of their ever having been objects of sense, and I can nevertheless demonstrate various properties pertaining to their nature as well as to that of the triangle, and these must certainly all be true since I conceive them clearly. Hence they are something, and not pure negation; for it is perfectly clear that all that is true is something, and I have already fully demonstrated that all that I know clearly is true. And even although I had not demonstrated this, the nature of my mind is such that I could not prevent myself from holding them to be true so long as I conceive them clearly; and I recollect that even when I was still strongly attached to the objects of sense, I counted as the most certain those truths which I conceived clearly as regards figures, numbers, and the other matters which pertain to arithmetic and geometry, and, in general, to pure and abstract mathematics.

A NEW DEMONSTRATION OF GOD'S EXISTENCE

But now, if just because I can draw the idea of something from my thought, it follows that all which I know clearly and distinctly as pertaining to this object does really belong to it, may I not derive from this an argument demonstrating the existence of God? It is certain that I no less find the idea of God, that is to say, the idea of a supremely perfect Being, in me, than that of any figure or number whatever it is; and I do not know any less clearly and distinctly that an [actual and] eternal existence pertains to this nature than I know that all that which I am able to demonstrate of some figure or number truly pertains to the nature of this figure or number, and therefore, although all that I concluded in the preceding Meditations were found to be false, the existence of God would pass with me as at least as certain as I have ever held the truths of mathematics (which concern only numbers and figures) to be.

This indeed is not at first manifest, since it would seem to present some appearance of being a sophism. For being accustomed in all other things to make a distinction between existence and essence, I easily persuade myself that the existence can be separated from the essence of God, and that we can thus conceive God as not actually existing. But, nevertheless, when I think of it with more attention, I clearly see that existence can no more be separated from the essence of God than can its having its three angles equal to two right angles be separated from the essence of a [rectilinear] triangle, or the idea of a mountain from the idea of a valley; and so there is not any less repugnance to our conceiving a God (that is, a Being supremely perfect) to whom existence is lacking (that is to say, to whom a certain perfection is lacking), than to conceive of a mountain which has no valley.

But although I cannot really conceive of a God without existence any more than a mountain without a valley, still from the fact that I conceive of a mountain with a valley, it does not follow that there is such a mountain in the world; similarly although I conceive of God as possessing existence, it would seem that it does not follow that there is a God which exists; for my thought does not impose any necessity upon things, and just as I may imagine a winged horse, although no horse with wings exists, so I could perhaps attribute existence to God, although no God existed.

But a sophism is concealed in this objection; for from the fact that I cannot conceive a mountain without a valley, it does not follow that there is any mountain or any valley in existence, but only that the mountain and the valley, whether they exist or do not exist, cannot in any way be separated one from the other. While from the fact that I cannot conceive God without existence, it follows that existence is inseparable from Him, and hence that He really exists; not that my thought can bring this to pass, or impose any necessity on things, but, on the contrary, because the necessity which lies in the thing itself, i.e. the necessity of the existence of God determines me to think in this way. For it is not within my power to think of God without existence (that is of a supremely perfect Being devoid of a supreme perfection) though it is in my power to imagine a horse either with wings or without wings.

And we must not here object that it is in truth necessary for me to assert that God exists after having presupposed that He possesses every sort of perfection, since existence is one of these, but that as a matter of fact my original supposition was not necessary, just as it is not necessary to consider that all quadrilateral figures can be inscribed in the circle; for supposing I thought this, I should be constrained to admit that the rhombus might be inscribed in the circle since it is a quadrilateral figure, which, however, is manifestly false. [We must not, I say, make any such allegations because] although it is not necessary that I should at any time entertain the notion of God, nevertheless whenever it happens that I think of a first and a sovereign Being, and, so to speak, derive the idea of Him from the storehouse of my mind, it is necessary that I should attribute to Him every sort of perfection, although I do not get so far as to enumerate them all, or to apply my mind to each one in particular. And this necessity suffices to make me conclude (after having recognised that existence is a perfection) that this first and sovereign Being really exists; just as though it is not necessary for me ever to imagine any triangle, yet, whenever I wish to consider a rectilinear figure composed only of three angles, it is absolutely essential that I should attribute to it all those properties which serve to bring about the conclusion that its three angles are not greater than two right angles, even although I may not then be considering this point in particular. But when I consider which figures are capable of being inscribed in the circle, it is in no wise necessary that I should think that all quadrilateral figures are of this number; on the contrary, I cannot even pretend that this is the case, so long as I do not desire to accept anything which I cannot conceive clearly and distinctly. And in consequence there is a great difference between the false suppositions such as this, and the true ideas born within me, the first and principal of which is that of God. For really I discern in many ways that this idea is not something factitious, and depending solely on my thought, but that it is the image of a true and immutable nature; first of all, because I cannot conceive anything but God himself to whose essence existence [necessarily] pertains; in the second place because it is not possible for me to conceive two or more Gods in this same position; and, granted that there is one such God who now exists, I see clearly that it is necessary that He should have existed from all eternity, and that He must exist eternally; and finally, because I know an infinitude of other properties in God, none of which I can either diminish or change.

. . .

MEDITATION VI.

Of the Existence of Material Things, and of the real distinction between the Soul and Body of Man.

Nothing further now remains but to inquire whether material things exist. And certainly I at least know that these may exist in so far as they are considered as the objects of pure mathematics, since in this aspect I perceive them clearly and distinctly. For there is no doubt that God possesses the power to produce everything that I am capable of perceiving with distinctness, and I have never deemed that anything was impossible for Him, unless I found a contradiction in attempting to conceive it clearly.

. . .

RELIABILITY OF THE SENSES

But I am in the habit of imagining many other things besides this corporeal nature which is the object of pure mathematics, to wit, the colours, sounds, scents, pain, and other such things, although less distinctly. And inasmuch as I perceive these things much better through the senses, by the medium of which, and by the memory, they seem to have reached my imagination, I believe that, in order to examine them more conveniently, it is right that I should at the same time investigate the nature of sense perception, and that I should see if from the ideas which I apprehend by this mode of thought, which I call feeling, I cannot derive some certain proof of the existence of corporeal objects.

And first of all I shall recall to my memory those matters which I hitherto held to be true, as having perceived them through the senses, and the foundations on which my belief has rested; in the next place I shall examine the reasons which have since obliged me to place them in doubt; in the last place I shall consider which of them I must now believe.

First of all, then, I perceived that I had a head, hands, feet, and all other members of which this body—which I considered as a part, or possibly even as the whole, of myself—is composed. Further I was sensible that this body was placed amidst many others, from which it was capable of being affected in many different ways, beneficial and hurtful, and I remarked that a certain feeling of pleasure accompanied those that were beneficial, and pain those which were harmful. And in addition to this pleasure and pain, I also experienced hunger, thirst, and other similar appetites, as also certain corporeal inclinations towards joy, sadness, anger, and other similar passions. And outside myself, in addition to extension, figure, and motions of bodies, I remarked in them hardness, heat, and all other tactile qualities, and, further, light and colour, and scents and sounds, the variety of which gave me the means of distinguishing the sky, the earth, the sea, and generally all the other bodies, one from the other. And certainly, considering the ideas of all these qualities which presented themselves to my mind, and which alone I perceived properly or immediately, it was not without reason that I believed myself to perceive objects quite different from my thought, to wit, bodies from which those ideas proceeded; for I found by experience that these ideas presented themselves to me without my consent being requisite, so that I could not perceive any object, however desirous I might be, unless it were present to the organs of sense; and it was not in my power not to perceive it, when it was present. And because the ideas which I received through the senses were much more lively, more clear, and even, in their own way, more distinct than any of those which I could of myself frame in meditation, or than those I found impressed on my memory, it appeared as though they could not have proceeded from my mind, so that they must necessarily have been produced in me by some other things. And having no knowledge of those objects excepting the knowledge which the ideas themselves gave me, nothing was more likely to occur to my mind than that the objects were similar to the ideas which were caused. And because I likewise remembered that I had formerly made use of my senses rather than my reason, and recognised that the ideas which I formed of myself were not so distinct as those which I perceived through the senses, and that they were most frequently even composed of portions of these last, I persuaded myself easily that I had no idea in my mind which had not formerly come to me through the senses. Nor was it without some reason that I believed that this body (which by a certain special right I call my own) belonged to me more properly and more strictly than any other; for in fact I could never be separated from it as from other bodies; I experienced in it and on account of it all my appetites and affections, and finally I was touched by the feeling of pain and the titillation of pleasure in its parts, and not in the parts of other bodies which were separated from it. But when I inquired, why, from some, I know not what, painful sensation, there follows sadness of mind, and from the pleasurable sensation there arises joy, or why this mysterious pinching of the stomach which I call hunger causes me to desire to eat, and dryness of throat causes a desire to drink, and so on, I could give no reason excepting that nature taught me so; for there is certainly no affinity (that I at least can understand) between the craving of the stomach and the desire to eat, any more than between the perception of whatever causes pain and the thought of sadness which arises from this perception. And in the same way it appeared to me that I had learned from nature all the other judgments which I formed regarding the objects of my senses, since I remarked that these judgments were formed in me before I had the leisure to weigh and consider any reasons which might oblige me to make them.

But afterwards many experiences little by little destroyed all the faith which I had rested in my senses; for I from time to time observed that those towers which from afar appeared to me to be round, more closely observed seemed square, and that colossal statues raised on the summit of these towers, appeared as quite tiny statues when viewed from the bottom; and so in an infinitude of other cases I found error in judgments founded on the external senses. And not only in those founded on the external senses, but even in those founded on the internal as well; for is there anything more intimate or more internal than pain? And yet I have learned from some persons whose arms or legs have been cut off, that they sometimes seemed to feel pain in the part which had been amputated, which made me think that I could not be quite certain that it was a certain member which pained me, even although I felt pain in it. And to those grounds of doubt I have lately added two others, which are very general; the first is that I never have believed myself to feel anything in waking moments which I cannot also sometimes believe myself to feel when I sleep, and as I do not think that these things which I seem to feel in sleep, proceed from objects outside of me, I do not see any reason why I should have this belief regarding objects which I seem to perceive while awake. The other was that being still ignorant, or rather supposing myself to be ignorant, of the author of my being, I saw nothing to prevent me from having been so constituted by nature that I might be deceived even in matters which seemed to me to be most certain. And as to the grounds on which I was formerly persuaded of the truth of sensible objects, I had not much trouble in replying to them. For since nature seemed to cause me to lean towards many things from which reason repelled me, I did not believe that I should trust much to the teachings of nature. And although the ideas which I receive by the senses do not depend on my will, I did not think that one should for that reason conclude that they proceeded from things different from myself, since possibly some faculty might be discovered in me—though hitherto unknown to me—which produced them.

But now that I begin to know myself better, and to discover more clearly the author of my being, I do not in truth think that I should rashly admit all the matters which the senses seem to teach us, but, on the other hand, I do not think that I should doubt them all universally.

DISTINCTION BETWEEN MIND AND BODY

And first of all, because I know that all things which I apprehend clearly and distinctly can be created by God as I apprehend them, it suffices that I am able to apprehend one thing apart from another clearly and distinctly in order to be certain that the one is different from the other, since they may be made to exist in separation at least by the omnipotence of God; and it does not signify by what power this separation is made in order to compel me to judge them to be different: and, therefore, just because I know certainly that I exist, and that meanwhile I do not remark that any other thing necessarily pertains to my nature or essence, excepting that I am a thinking thing, I rightly conclude that my essence consists solely in the fact that I am a thinking thing [or a substance whose whole essence or nature is to think]. And although possibly (or rather certainly, as I shall say in a moment) I possess a body with which I am very intimately conjoined, yet because, on the one side, I have a clear and distinct idea of myself inasmuch as I am only a thinking and unextended thing, and as, on the other, I possess a distinct idea of body, inasmuch as it is only an extended and unthinking thing, it is certain that this I [that is to say, my soul by which I am what I am], is entirely and absolutely distinct from my body, and can exist without it.

I further find in myself faculties employing modes of thinking peculiar to themselves, to wit, the faculties of imagination and feeling, without which I can easily conceive myself clearly and distinctly as a complete being; while, on the other hand, they cannot be so conceived apart from me, that is without an intelligent substance in which they reside, for [in the notion we have of these faculties, or, to use the language of the Schools] in their formal concept, some kind of intellection is comprised, from which I infer that they are distinct from me as its modes are from a thing. I observe also in me some other faculties such as that of change of position, the assumption of different figures and such like, which cannot be conceived, any more than can the preceding, apart from some substance to which they are attached, and consequently cannot exist without it; but it is very clear that these faculties, if it be true that they exist, must be attached to some corporeal or extended substance, and not to an intelligent substance, since in the clear and distinct conception of these there is some sort of extension found to be present, but no intellection at all. There is certainly further in me a certain passive faculty of perception, that is, of receiving and recognising the ideas of sensible things, but this would be useless to me [and I could in no way avail myself of it], if there were not either in me or in some other thing another active faculty capable of forming and producing these ideas. But this active faculty cannot exist in me [inasmuch as I am a thing that thinks] seeing that it does not presuppose thought, and also that those ideas are often produced in me without my contributing in any way to the same, and often even against my will; it is thus necessarily the case that the faculty resides in some substance different from me in which all the reality which is objectively in the ideas that are produced by this faculty is formally or eminently contained, as I remarked before. And this substance is either a body, that is, a corporeal nature in which there is contained formally [and really] all that which is objectively [and by representation] in those ideas, or it is God Himself, or some other creature more noble than body in which that same is contained eminently. But, since God is no deceiver, it is very manifest that He does not communicate to me these ideas immediately and by Himself, nor yet by the intervention of some creature in which their reality is not formally, but only eminently, contained. For since He has given me no faculty to recognise that this is the case, but, on the other hand, a very great inclination to believe [that they are sent to me or] that they are conveyed to me by corporeal objects, I do not see how He could be defended from the accusation of deceit if these ideas were produced by causes other than corporeal objects. Hence we must allow that corporeal things exist. However, they are perhaps not exactly what we perceive by the senses, since this comprehension by the senses is in many instances very obscure and confused; but we must at least admit that all things which I conceive in them clearly and distinctly, that is to say, all things which, speaking generally, are comprehended in the object of pure mathematics, are truly to be recognised as external objects.

As to other things, however, which are either particular only, as, for example, that the sun is of such and such a figure, etc., or which are less clearly and distinctly conceived, such as light, sound, pain and the like, it is certain that although they are very dubious and uncertain, yet on the sole ground that God is not a deceiver, and that consequently He has not permitted any falsity to exist in my opinion which He has not likewise given me the faculty of correcting, I may assuredly hope to conclude that I have within me the means of arriving at the truth even here. And first of all there is no doubt that in all things which nature teaches me there is some truth contained; for by nature, considered in general, I now understand no other thing than either God Himself or else the order and disposition which God has established in created things; and by my nature in particular I understand no other thing than the complexus of all the things which God has given me.

But there is nothing which this nature teaches me more expressly [nor more sensibly] than that I have a body which is adversely affected when I feel pain, which has need of food or drink when I experience the feelings of hunger and thirst, and so on; nor can I doubt there being some truth in all this.

Nature also teaches me by these sensations of pain, hunger, thirst, etc., that I am not only lodged in my body as a pilot in a vessel, but that I am very closely united to it, and so to speak so intermingled with it that I seem to compose with it one whole. For if that were not the case, when my body is hurt, I, who am merely a thinking thing, should not feel pain, for I should perceive this wound by the understanding only, just as the sailor perceives by sight when something is damaged in his vessel; and when my body has need of drink or food, I should clearly understand the fact without being warned of it by confused feelings of hunger and thirst. For all these sensations of hunger, thirst, pain, etc. are in truth none other than certain confused modes of thought which are produced by the union and apparent intermingling of mind and body.

Moreover, nature teaches me that many other bodies exist around mine, of which some are to be avoided, and others sought after. And certainly from the fact that I am sensible of different sorts of colours, sounds, scents, tastes, heat, hardness, etc., I very easily conclude that there are in the bodies from which all these diverse sense-perceptions proceed certain variations which answer to them, although possibly these are not really at all similar to them. And also from the fact that amongst these different sense-perceptions some are very agreeable to me and others disagreeable, it is quite certain that my body (or rather myself in my entirety, inasmuch as I am formed of body and soul) may receive different impressions agreeable and disagreeable from the other bodies which surround it.

.   .   .

A FAREWELL TO DOUBT

From this it is quite clear that, notwithstanding the supreme goodness of God, the nature of man, inasmuch as it is composed of mind and body, cannot be otherwise than sometimes a source of deception. For if there is any cause which excites, not in the foot but in some part of the nerves which are extended between the foot and the brain, or even in the brain itself, the same movement which usually is produced when the foot is detrimentally affected, pain will be experienced as though it were in the foot, and the sense will thus naturally be deceived; for since the same movement in the brain is capable of causing but one sensation in the mind, and this sensation is much more frequently excited by a cause which hurts the foot than by another existing in some other quarter, it is reasonable that it should convey to the mind pain in the foot rather than in any other part of the body. And although the parchedness of the throat does not always proceed, as it usually does, from the fact that drinking is necessary for the health of the body, but sometimes comes from quite a different cause, as is the case with dropsical patients, it is yet much better that it should mislead on this occasion than if, on the other hand, it were always to deceive us when the body is in good health; and so on in similar cases.

And certainly this consideration is of great service to me, not only in enabling me to recognise all the errors to which my nature is subject, but also in enabling me to avoid them or to correct them more easily. For knowing that all my senses more frequently indicate to me truth than falsehood respecting the things which concern that which is beneficial to the body, and being able almost always to avail myself of many of them in order to examine one particular thing, and, besides that, being able to make use of my memory in order to connect the present with the past, and of my understanding which already has discovered all the causes of my errors, I ought no longer to fear that falsity may be found in matters every day presented to me by my senses. And I ought to set aside all the doubts of these past days as hyperbolical and ridiculous, particularly that very common uncertainty respecting sleep, which I could not distinguish from the waking state; for at present I find a very notable difference between the two, inasmuch as our memory can never connect our dreams one with the other, or with the whole course of our lives, as it unites events which happen to us while we are awake. And, as a matter of fact, if someone, while I was awake, quite suddenly appeared to me and disappeared as fast as do the images which I see in sleep, so that I could not know from whence the form came nor whither it went, it would not be without reason that I should deem it a spectre or a phantom formed by my brain [and similar to those which I form in sleep], rather than a real man. But when I perceive things as to which I know distinctly both the place from which they proceed, and that in which they are, and the time at which they appeared to me; and when, without any interruption, I can connect the perceptions which I have of them with the whole course of my life, I am perfectly assured that these perceptions occur while I am waking and not during sleep. And I ought in no wise to doubt the truth of such matters, if, after having called up all my senses, my memory, and my understanding, to examine them, nothing is brought to evidence by any one of them which is repugnant to what is set forth by the others. For because God is in no wise a deceiver, it follows that I am not deceived in this. But because the exigencies of action often oblige us to make up our minds before having leisure to examine matters carefully, we must confess that the life of man is very frequently subject to error in respect to individual objects, and we must in the end acknowledge the infirmity of our nature.

Objections and Replies

Before the *Meditations* were published, Descartes' friend, Mersenne, showed the work to a number of philosophers and theologians and asked for their comments. These comments along with Descartes' answers were then published as part of the first edition of the *Meditations* under the title "Objections and Replies." The selected excerpts here illustrate both the criticisms most often thought of when Descartes' philosophy is discussed and the defense which Descartes offered. The reader may serve as an umpire between Descartes and his critics, taking care to consider in each exchange just how decidable the issue is and on what grounds it is to be decided.

From *The Philosophical Works of Descartes,* Vol. II, translated by E. S. Haldane and G. R. T. Ross, Cambridge University Press, London, 1931. Reprinted by permission of the publisher.

1. THINKING IMPLIES EXISTENCE

Gassendi[1]

. . . you recognize at least that you exist; *which thus establishes the* conclusion that this proposition:—I am, I exist, is true each time that you pronounce it, or that you mentally conceive it. *But I don't see that you needed all this mechanism, when you had other grounds for being sure, and it was true, that you existed. You might have inferred that from any other activity, since our natural light informs us that whatever acts also exists.* (From the "Fifth Set of Objections.")

Descartes

. . . what grounds have you for saying *that there was no need of such an elaborate mechanism in order to prove that I exist?* Really these very words of yours give me the best grounds for believing that my labours have not yet been sufficiently great, since I have as yet failed to make you understand the matter rightly. When you say that *I could have inferred the same conclusion from any of my other actions,* you wander far from the truth, because there is none of my activities of which I am wholly certain (in the sense of having metaphysical certitude, which alone is here involved), save thinking alone. For example you have no right to make the inference: *I walk, hence I exist,* except in so far as our awareness of walking is a thought; it is of this alone that the inference holds good, not of the motion of the body, which sometimes does not exist, as in dreams, when nevertheless I appear to walk. Hence from the fact that I think that I walk I can very well infer the existence of the mind which so thinks, but not that of the body which walks. So it is also in all other cases.

2. DESCARTES IS THOUGHT ALONE

Gassendi

You add that it is thought alone which cannot be separated from you. *Truly it is impossible to deny this of you, if you are primarily Mind alone and refuse to allow that your substance can be distinguished from the substance of the soul except in thought; though here I pause and ask whether, when you say* that thought cannot be separated from you, *you mean that you, as long as you exist, think to an indefinite extent. This is indeed in conformity*

[1] Pierre Gassendi (1592–1655), French mathematician and Materialist philosopher.— Eds.

with the pronouncement of those celebrated philosophers who, in order to prove your immortality, assumed that you were in perpetual motion, or, as I interpret it, thought continuously. But this will not gain the adhesion of those who cannot comprehend how you can think during a lethargic sleep, or while in the womb. Besides, I have a difficulty here as to whether you think that you have been infused into the body or one of its parts during the uterine stage of existence or at birth. But I should be loth to be troublesome with my enquiries, or to reflect whether you remember what your thoughts were when in the womb, or in the days, months, and years succeeding your birth; or, if you replied that you had forgotten, to ask why this was so. Yet I suggest that you should remember how obscure, how meagre, how nearly non-existent your thought must have been during those periods of life. (From the "Fifth Set of Objections.")

Descartes

You have a difficulty, however, you say, *as to whether I think that the soul always thinks.* But why should it not always think, when it is a thinking substance? Why is it strange that we do not remember the thoughts it has had when in the womb or in a stupor, when we do not even remember the most of those we know we have had when grown up, in good health, and awake? For the recollection of the thoughts which the mind has had during the period of its union with the body, it is necessary for certain traces of them to be impressed on the brain; and turning and applying itself to these the mind remembers. Is it remarkable if the brain of an infant or of one in a stupor is unfit to receive these residual impressions?

3. THOUGHT, AN ATTRIBUTE OF BODY

Divers Theologians and Philosophers [2]

. . . pray remember that it was not as an actual fact and in reality, but merely by a mental fiction, that you so stoutly resisted the claim of all bodies to be more than phantasms, in order that you might draw the conclusion that you were merely a thinking being; for otherwise there is perhaps a risk you might believe that you could draw the conclusion that you were in truth nothing other than mind, or thought, or a thinking being. This we find worthy of mention only in connection with the first two Meditations, in which you show clearly that it is at least certain that you, who think, exist. But let us pause a little here. Up to this point you know that you are a being that thinks; but you do not know what this thinking thing is. What if that

[2] This group is not further identified by Mersenne, who collected their remarks for the "Second Set of Objections" to the *Meditations*.—Eds.

were a body which by its various motions and encounters produces that which we call thought? For, granted that you rejected the claim of every sort of body, you may have been deceived in this, because you did not rule out yourself, who are a body. For how will you prove that a body cannot think, or that its bodily motions are not thought itself? Possibly even, the whole bodily system, which you imagine you have rejected, or some of its parts, say the parts composing the brain, can unite to produce those motions which we call thoughts. 'I am a thinking thing,' you say; but who knows but you are a corporeal motion, or a body in motion? (From the "Second Set of Objections.")

Descartes

. . . if any people deny that they have distinct ideas of mind and body, I can do nothing further than ask them to give sufficient attention to what is said in the Second Meditation. I beg them to note that the opinion they perchance hold, namely, that the parts of the brain join their forces with the soul to form thoughts, has not arisen from any positive ground, but only from the fact that they have never had experience of separation from the body, and have not seldom been hindered by it in their operations, and that similarly if anyone had from infancy continually worn irons on his legs, he would think that those irons were part of his own body and that he needed them in order to walk.

4. APPREHENDING THE INFINITE

Caterus [3]

. . . *'I apprehend clearly and distinctly an infinite being; hence it is something true and real.' But will not someone ask, 'Do you apprehend clearly and distinctly an infinite being?' But what then is the meaning of that well-worn maxim known to all?—The infinite quâ infinite is unknown. For if, when I think of a chiliagon and have a confused representation of some figure, I do not have a distinct image of the chiliagon or know it, because I do not have its thousand sides evident and distinct before my mind, shall I not be asked,—how can the infinite be thought of distinctly and not confusedly, if the infinite perfections of which it is composed cannot be perceived clearly, and, as it were, with true distinctness of vision?* (From the "First Set of Objections.")

Descartes

. . . prudently he here enquires *whether I know the infinite distinctly and clearly*; and although I have tried to anticipate this objection, yet it

---

[3] Identified simply as "a priest of Alkmaar," in Holland.—Eds.

occurs so spontaneously to each one, that it is worth while to give it a detailed reply. Therefore here, to start with, I shall say that the infinite *quâ* infinite is in nowise comprehended, but that nevertheless it is understood, in so far as clearly and distinctly to understand a thing to be such that no limits can be found in it is to understand clearly that it is infinite.

Here indeed I distinguish between *the indefinite* and *the infinite*, and that alone do I properly speaking call infinite in which nowhere are limits to be found; in this sense God alone is infinite. That moreover in which only in a certain aspect do I recognize no limit, as e.g. the extension of imaginary space, the many in number, or the divisibility of the parts of quantity, and other similar things, I call indeed *indefinite* but not *infinite*, because such things are not limitless in every respect.

Besides that, I distinguish between the formal notion of the infinite or infinity and the thing which is infinite; for as for infinity, even though we understand it to have as much positive reality as may be, yet we understand it only in a certain negative fashion, from the fact, namely, that we perceive no limitation in the thing; but the thing itself which is infinite is indeed positively understood, though not adequately, i.e. we do not comprehend the whole of what is intelligible in it. But it is just as when gazing at the sea, we are said to behold it, though our sight does not cover it all nor measures its immensity; if indeed we view it from a distance in such a way as to take in the whole with a single glance, we see it only confusedly, as we have a confused image of a chiliagon, when taking in all its sides at the same time; but if from near at hand we fix our glance on one portion of the sea, this act of vision can be clear and distinct, just as the image of a chiliagon may be, if it takes in only one or two of the figure's sides. By similar reasoning I admit along with all theologians that God cannot be comprehended by the human mind, and also that he cannot be distinctly known by those who try mentally to grasp Him at once in His entirety, and view Him, as it were, from a distance. . . . But those who try to attend to His perfections singly, and intend not so much to comprehend them as to admire them and to employ all the power of their mind in contemplating them, will assuredly find in Him a much ampler and readier supply of the material for clear and distinct cognition than in any created things.

5. ORIGIN OF THE IDEA OF A PERFECT BEING

Divers Theologians and Philosophers

. . . from the idea of a supreme being, which, you contend, cannot be by you produced, you are bold enough to infer the necessary existence of the supreme being from which alone can come that idea that your mind perceives. Yet we find in our own selves a sufficient basis on which alone to

erect that said idea, even though that supreme being did not exist, or we were ignorant of its existence and did not even think of it though it did exist. Do I not see that I, in thinking, have some degree of perfection? And therefore I conclude that others besides me have a similar degree, and hence I have a basis on which to construct the thought of any number of degrees and so to add one degree of perfection to another to infinity, just as, given the existence of a single degree of light or heat, I can add and imagine fresh degrees up to infinity. Why, on similar reasoning, can I not add, to any degree of being that I perceive in myself any other degree I please, and out of the whole number capable of addition construct the idea of a perfect being? 'But,' you say, 'an effect can have no degree of perfection or reality which has not previously existed in its cause.' In reply we urge (passing by the fact that experience shows us that flies and other animals, or even plants are produced by the sun, rain and the earth, in which life, a nobler thing than any merely corporeal grade of being, does not exist, and that hence an effect can derive from its cause some reality which yet is not found in the cause) that that idea is nothing but an entity of reason, which has no more nobility than your mind that thinks it. Besides this, how do you know that that idea would have come before your mind if you had not been nurtured among men of culture, but had passed all your life in some desert spot? Have you not derived it from reflections previously entertained, from books, from interchange of converse with your friends, etc., not from your own mind alone or from a supreme being who exists? You must therefore prove more clearly that that idea could not present itself to you unless a supreme being did exist; though when you show this we shall all confess ourselves vanquished. But it seems to be shown clearly that that idea springs from previous notions by the fact that the natives of Canada, the Hurons, and other savages, have no idea in their minds such as this, which is one that you can form from a previous survey of corporeal things, in such a way that your idea refers only to this corporeal world, which embraces all the perfections that you can imagine; hence you would have up to this point no grounds as yet for inferring more than an entirely perfect corporeal Entity, unless you were to add something else conducting us to the [knowledge of the] incorporeal or spiritual. Let us add that you can construct the idea of an angel (just as you can form the notion of a supremely perfect being) without that idea being caused in you by a [really existing] angel; though the angel has more perfection than you have. (From the "Second Set of Objections.")

Descartes

. . . when you say that *in ourselves there is a sufficient foundation on which to construct the idea of God,* your assertion in no way conflicts with my opinion. I myself at the end of the Third Meditation have expressly said that *this idea is innate in me,* or alternatively that it comes to me from no other source than myself. I admit that *we could form this very idea, though we did not know that a supreme being existed,* but not that we could do so *if it were in fact non-existent,* for on the contrary I have notified that *the whole force of my argument lies in the fact that the capacity for constructing such an idea could not exist in me, unless I were created by God.*

6. NECESSITY OF GOD'S EXISTENCE

Gassendi

You next attempt the proof of God's existence and the vital part of your argument lies in these words: When I think attentively I clearly see that the existence can no more be separated from the essence of God than can there be separated from the essence of a triangle the equality in magnitude of its three angles to two right angles, or the idea of a mountain from the idea of a valley; so that there is no less incongruity in our conceiving a God (i.e. a Being who is supremely perfect) to Whom existence is lacking (i.e. in Whom a certain perfection is missing), than to think of a mountain which is not accompanied by a valley. *But we must note that a comparison of this kind is not sufficiently accurate.*

For though you properly enough compare essence with essence, in your next step it is neither existence with essence, nor property with property that you compare, but existence with property. Hence it seems that you either ought to have said that God's omnipotence can no more be separated from His essence than can that equality in magnitude of the angles of a triangle from its essence; or at least, that God's existence can no more be separated from His essence than the existence from the essence of a triangle. Thus taken, each comparison would have proceeded on correct lines, and the truth would have been conceded, not only of the former but of the latter, although this would not be evidence that you had established your conclusion that God necessarily exists, because neither does the triangle necessarily exist, although its essence and its existence cannot in reality be severed, howsoever much the mind separates them or thinks of them apart, in the same way as the Divine essence and existence may be thought of separately.

Next we must note that you place existence among the Divine perfections, without, however, putting it among the perfections of a triangle or of a mountain, though in exactly similar fashion, and in its own way, it may be said to be a perfection of each. But, sooth to say, existence is a perfection neither in God nor in anything else; it is rather that in the absence of which there is no perfection.

This must be so if, indeed, that which does not exist has neither perfection nor imperfection, and that which exists and has various perfections, does not have its existence as a particular perfection and as one of the number

*of its perfections, but as that by means of which the thing itself equally
with its perfections is in existence, and without which neither can it be said
to possess perfections, nor can perfections be said to be possessed by it. Hence
neither is existence held to exist in a thing in the way that perfections do,
nor if the thing lacks existence is it said to be imperfect (or deprived of a
perfection), so much as to be nothing.*

*Wherefore, as in enumerating the perfections of a triangle you do not
mention existence, nor hence conclude that the triangle exists, so, in enumerating the perfections of God, you ought not to have put existence among
them, in order to draw the conclusion that God exists, unless you wanted to
beg the question.* (From the "Fifth Set of Objections.")

Descartes

Here I do not see to what class of reality you wish to assign existence,
nor do I see why it may not be said to be a property as well as omnipotence,
taking the word property as equivalent to any attribute or anything which
can be predicated of a thing, as in the present case it should be by all means
regarded. Nay, necessary existence in the case of God is also a true property
in the strictest sense of the word, because it belongs to Him and forms part
of His essence alone. Hence the existence of a triangle cannot be compared
with the existence of God, because existence manifestly has a different relation
to essence in the case of God and in the case of a triangle.

Nor is it more a begging of the question, *to enumerate existence among
the things belonging to the essence of God,* than to reckon the equality of
the three angles of a triangle to two right angles among the properties of the
triangle.

Nor is it true *that essence and existence can be thought, the one apart
from the other in God,* as in a triangle, because God *is* His existence, while
a triangle is not its own existence. I do not, nevertheless, deny that existence
is a possible perfection in the idea of a triangle, as it is a necessary one in the
idea of God; for this fact makes the idea of the triangle one of higher rank
than the ideas of those chimerical things whose existence can never be
supposed. . . .

QUESTIONS

1. State the grounds on which Descartes attempts to doubt the senses as a basis
   for genuine knowledge. Give your reasons for thinking that he succeeded, or
   that he failed, in this attempt.
2. State the grounds on which Descartes attempts to doubt that "two and three
   together always form five." Give your reasons for thinking that he succeeded,
   or that he failed, in this attempt.
3. Why does Descartes find that the mind (or self) and God are more easily
   known than any other thing?
4. Descartes' famous conclusion, "I think; therefore, I am," has been criticized

as meaning no more than "There is a thought." How do you think that he might reply to such a criticism?

5. What is Descartes trying to show about our knowledge of the world by his discussion of knowing a piece of wax?

6. State all the premises Descartes must accept in each of his arguments to prove that God exists. Tested by his own method of doubt, are his proofs of God's existence acceptable? Why or why not?

7. According to Descartes, what part does God play in our knowledge of the world? Why are we sometimes mistaken in our knowledge?

8. How does Descartes prove that corporeal objects exist? What is his final justification of perceptual knowledge? Does it square with his rationalist theory of knowledge?

9. How do you know you are not dreaming right now? Does Descartes offer a satisfactory resolution of this dilemma?

10. For each set of extracts from the "Objections and Replies" state the issue and consider which side puts forth the better case. Can you think of any variations on these objections or of any additional philosophical objections to Descartes' *Meditations?* Try to think of the answers which Descartes might make to these new objections.

SUGGESTED FURTHER READING

Bouwsma, O. K., *Philosophical Essays,* University of Nebraska Press, Lincoln, 1965. "Descartes' Skepticism of the Senses"; "Descartes' Evil Genius"; "On Many Occasions I Have in Sleep Been Deceived."

Malcolm, Norman, *Dreaming,* Routledge and Kegan Paul, London, 1959.

Sesonske, Alexander, and Noel Fleming, eds., *Meta-Meditations: Studies in Descartes,* Wadsworth, Belmont, Calif., 1965. (Anthology.)

Chapter 1. Knowing and the Known

There is a cluster of questions which form the chief part of the problem of knowledge: What is knowledge? How am I able to have knowledge? What is the relation between my knowledge and the things which I know something about; and does my being able to know a thing have any implications for the nature of that thing? The answer to any one of these questions will have a bearing on the answers to the others, and many philosophers have worked out comprehensive theories of knowledge which would answer all of these questions. John Locke is one such philosopher; the selection covering the main parts of his theory of knowledge forms the mainstay of this chapter.

One of the notable features of Locke's theory of knowledge is the dichotomy between internal, mental objects (ideas) and external, physical objects. But assuming this dichotomy, one is soon faced with the question of how these two kinds of objects are related. If I can know only the ideas in my mind, how can I tell whether they represent anything outside the mind? As we shall see in Chapter 3, one of Locke's successors, Berkeley, evades this problem by arguing that there is really only one kind of object: a mental object or idea. But there is another line of attack to which the dichotomy between internal objects of knowledge and external reality is open, namely that the dichotomy rests on a mistaken attempt to reduce observing to having sensations. This line of attack is carried out in Professor Gilbert Ryle's "Sensation and Observation." He argues that we should abandon the search for a special, mental object of knowledge; as a replacement for these old theories, he offers a dispositional account of knowing.

The last selection in this chapter, Friedrich Waismann's consideration of "Facts and Language," carries the examination of the relation between the observer and what he observes a step further. Locke characterized the observer's mind as a white paper ready to take the impress of the outside world when mind and world meet. Waismann argues against this picture of the completely passive observer by pointing out the ways in which the observer's use of language to describe the world disposes him to pick out those features of the world which he can describe and to ignore those which he has not been taught to talk about. Thus, facts, those features of the world which we take notice of, are more closely tied to what we can say than might originally have been supposed.

1. JOHN LOCKE

(1632–1704)

An Essay Concerning Human Understanding

John Locke was born at Wrington, Somerset, in England, and was educated at Westminster School and Oxford. He was a friend of the chemist Robert Boyle, and was himself an amateur in chemistry; but he finally expressed his scientific bent in the study and practice of medicine. He was a close associate of

Thomas Sydenham, a famous physician, who was endeavoring to introduce into England a science of medicine based on observation and taught by demonstration. Through his writings Locke made important contributions to the cause of civil liberty and religious toleration in England, and his political ideas had a great influence on the Founding Fathers of the United States. As for philosophy, Locke said that Descartes' books were the first to give him a relish for philosophical studies. Locke's principal writings are: *Two Treatises of Government* (1690); *Letters on Toleration* (1689, 1690); and *An Essay Concerning Human Understanding* (1690).

In his theory of knowledge, Locke holds that knowing is having ideas in one's mind. This part of his theory is compatible with Descartes' views. But Descartes and Locke differ in their accounts of the origin of the ideas in the mind. Descartes, whose philosophy is an example of what is sometimes called "rationalism," holds that at least some of our ideas are innate; Locke holds that our minds are not furnished with ideas until experience supplies them. Locke's philosophy is, thus, an example of what is sometimes called "empiricism." Indeed, Locke is often regarded as the founder of the empirical school of philosophy, for his work points the way to the empirical criterion of knowledge: If we can support our assertions about the world by an appeal to direct experience, we have knowledge. Otherwise, we do not.

While Locke is an influential figure in the history of philosophy, his work has received substantial criticism. For example, to Locke, the mind is passive. Thus, instead of our being able to speak of a person as performing mental tasks (e.g., looking, tasting, wondering, considering, imagining, reasoning), we must understand a person as the mere spectator of an internal dance of ideas which just happens to be going on in his mind. Many philosophers have considered this description of our mental life to be inadequate, and the reader should give careful attention to the question of its accuracy.

The reading begins with Locke's attempt to show how all the ideas which make up our knowledge originate in sense experience and in the mind's "reflection" on its own operations. Locke imagines the mind at birth to be like a blank sheet of paper on which experience begins to write and leave its mark. First the mind has "simple ideas," among which are its ideas of the qualities of objects. Then it builds up "complex ideas," among which are its ideas of the objects ("substances") which have these qualities. Locke goes on to consider the nature of knowledge. Knowledge, he says, is the perception of the agreement or disagreement of our ideas. This raises the question of how we can know whether our knowledge, which is limited to our ideas, does in fact correspond to the real world outside our ideas. The reading concludes with Locke's attempt to answer this question.

The reading is from Books I, II, and IV of *An Essay Concerning Human Understanding*. Locke's original chapter titles are retained in this selection.

INTRODUCTION

An inquiry into the understanding, pleasant and useful. Since it is the *understanding* that sets man above the rest of sensible beings, and gives him all the advantage and dominion which he has over them, it is certainly a subject, even for its nobleness, worth our labor to inquire into. The understanding, like the eye, whilst it makes us see and perceive all other things, takes no notice of itself; and it requires art and pains to set it at a distance, and make it its own object. But whatever be the difficulties that lie in the way of this inquiry, whatever it be that keeps us so much in the dark to ourselves, sure I am that all the light we can let in upon our own minds, all the acquaintance we can make with our own understandings, will not only be very pleasant, but bring us great advantage in directing our thoughts in the search of other things.

Method. It is worth while to search out the bounds between opinion and knowledge, and examine by what measures, in things whereof we have no certain knowledge, we ought to regulate our assent, and moderate our persuasions. In order whereunto, I shall pursue this following method:

First, I shall inquire into the original of those *ideas,* notions, or whatever else you please to call them, which a man observes, and is conscious to himself he has in his mind; and the ways whereby the understanding comes to be furnished with them.

Secondly, I shall endeavor to show what *knowledge* the understanding hath by those ideas, and the certainty, evidence, and extent of it. . . .

Our capacity suited to our state and concerns. Though the comprehension of our understandings comes exceeding short of the vast extent of things, yet we shall have cause enough to magnify the bountiful Author of our being for that proportion and degree of knowledge He has bestowed on us, so far above all the rest of the inhabitants of this our mansion. Men have reason to be well satisfied with what God hath thought fit for them, since He has given them, as St. Peter says, whatsoever is necessary for the conveniences of life, and information of virtue; and has put, within the reach of their discovery, the comfortable provision for this life and the way that leads to a better. How short soever their knowledge may come of an universal or perfect comprehension of whatsoever is, it yet secures their great concernments that they have light enough to lead them to the knowledge of their Maker, and the sight of their own duties. . . .

. . . Our business here is not to know all things, but those which concern our conduct. If we can find out those measures whereby a rational creature, put in that state which man is in in this world, may and ought to govern his opinions and actions depending thereon, we need not be troubled that some other things escape our knowledge.

. . . Were the capacities of our understandings well considered, the extent of our knowledge once discovered, and the horizon found which sets the bounds between the enlightened and dark parts of things—between what is and what is not comprehensible by us—men would, perhaps with less scruple, acquiesce in the avowed ignorance of the one, and employ their thoughts and discourse with more advantage and satisfaction in the other.

What "idea" stands for. . . . Before I proceed on to what I have thought on this subject, I must here, in the entrance, beg pardon of my reader for the frequent use of the word "idea" which he will find in the following treatise. It being that term which, I think, serves best to stand for whatsoever is the *object* of the understanding when a man thinks, I have used it to express whatever is meant by phantasm, notion, species, or whatever it is which the mind can be employed about in thinking; and I could not avoid frequently using it.

I presume it will be easily granted me, that there are such *ideas* in men's minds. Everyone is conscious of them in himself; and men's words and actions will satisfy him that they are in others.

Our first inquiry, then, shall be, how they come into the mind.

OF IDEAS IN GENERAL, AND THEIR ORIGINAL

Idea is the object of thinking. Every man being conscious to himself that he thinks, and that which his mind is applied about whilst thinking being the ideas that are there, it is past doubt that men have in their minds several ideas, such as are those expressed by the words whiteness, hardness, sweetness, thinking, motion, man, elephant, army, drunkenness, and others: it is in the first place then to be inquired, How he comes by them? . . .

All ideas come from sensation or reflection. Let us then suppose the mind to be, as we say, white paper, void of all characters, without any ideas; how comes it to be furnished? Whence comes it by that vast store, which the busy and boundless fancy of man has painted on it with an almost endless variety? Whence has it all the materials of reason and knowledge? To this I answer, in one word, from experience. In that all our knowledge is founded, and from that it ultimately derives itself. Our observation, employed either about external sensible objects, or about the internal operations of our minds, perceived and reflected on by ourselves, is that which supplies our understandings with all the materials of thinking. These two are the fountains of knowledge, from whence all the ideas we have, or can naturally have, do spring.

The objects of sensation, one source of ideas. First, our senses, conversant about particular sensible objects, do convey into the mind several distinct perceptions of things, according to those various ways wherein those objects do affect them; and thus we come by those ideas we have of yellow, white, heat, cold, soft, hard, bitter, sweet, and all those which we call sensible qualities; which when I say the senses convey into the mind, I mean, they from external objects convey into the mind what produces there those perceptions. This great source of most of the ideas we have, depending wholly upon our senses, and derived by them to the understanding, I call *sensation.*

The operations of our minds, the other source of them. Secondly, the other fountain, from which experience furnisheth the understanding with ideas, is the perception of the operations of our own mind within us, as it is employed about the ideas it has got; which operations, when the soul comes to reflect on and consider, do furnish the understanding with another set of ideas which could not be had from things without; and such are perception, thinking, doubting, believing, reasoning, knowing, willing, and all the different actings of our own minds; which we, being conscious of, and observing in ourselves, do from these receive into our understandings as distinct ideas, as we do from bodies affecting our senses. This source of ideas every man has wholly in himself; and though it be not sense as having nothing to do with external objects, yet it is very like it, and might properly enough be called *internal sense.* But as I call the other sensation, so I call this *reflection,* the ideas it affords being such only as the mind gets by reflecting on its own operations within itself. By reflection, then, in the following part of this discourse, I would be understood to mean that notice which the mind takes of its own operations, and the manner of them, by reason whereof there come to be ideas of these operations in the understanding. These two, I say, viz., external material things as the object of sensation, and the operations of our own minds within as the objects of reflection, are, to me, the only originals from whence all our ideas take their beginnings. The term *operations* here, I use in a large sense, as comprehending not barely the actions of the mind about its ideas, but some sort of passions arising sometimes from them, such as is the satisfaction or uneasiness arising from any thought. . . .

OF SIMPLE IDEAS

~ *Uncompounded appearances.* The better to understand the nature, manner, and extent of our knowledge, one thing is carefully to be observed concerning the ideas we have; and that is, that some of them are *simple,* and some *complex.*

Though the qualities that affect our senses are, in the things themselves, so united and blended that there is no separation, no distance between them;

yet it is plain the ideas they produce in the mind enter by the senses simple and unmixed. For though the sight and touch often take in from the same object, at the same time, different ideas—as a man sees at once motion and color, the hand feels softness and warmth in the same piece of wax—yet the simple ideas thus united in the same subject are as perfectly distinct as those that come in by different senses; the coldness and hardness which a man feels in a piece of ice being as distinct ideas in the mind as the smell and whiteness of a lily, or as the taste of sugar and smell of a rose: and there is nothing can be plainer to a man than the clear and distinct perception he has of those simple ideas; which, being each in itself uncompounded, contains in it nothing but *one uniform appearance or conception in the mind,* and is not distinguishable into different ideas.

The mind can neither make nor destroy them. These simple ideas, the materials of all our knowledge, are suggested and furnished to the mind only by those two ways above mentioned, viz., sensation and reflection. When the understanding is once stored with these simple ideas, it has the power to repeat, compare, and unite them, even to an almost infinite variety, and so can make at pleasure new complex ideas. But it is not in the power of the most exalted wit or enlarged understanding, by any quickness or variety of thought, to *invent* or *frame* one new simple idea in the mind, not taken in by the ways before mentioned; nor can any force of the understanding *destroy* those that are there: the dominion of man, in this little world of his own understanding, being much-what the same as it is in the great world of visible things; wherein his power, however managed by art and skill, reaches no farther than to compound and divide the materials that are made to his hand but can do nothing towards the making the least particle of new matter, or destroying one atom of what is already in being. The same inability will everyone find in himself, who shall go about to fashion in his understanding any simple idea not received in by his senses from external objects, or by reflection from the operations of his own mind about them. I would have anyone try to fancy any taste which had never affected his palate, or frame the idea of a scent he had never smelt; and when he can do this, I will also conclude that a blind man hath *ideas* of colors, and a deaf man true, distinct notions of sounds. . . .

OF SIMPLE IDEAS OF REFLECTION

Simple ideas of reflection are the operations of the mind about its other ideas. The mind, receiving the ideas mentioned in the foregoing chapters from without, when it turns its view inward upon itself, and observes its own actions about those ideas it has, takes from thence other ideas, which are as capable to be the objects of its contemplation as any of those it received from foreign things.

The idea of perception, and idea of willing, we have from reflection.
The two great and principal actions of the mind, which are most frequently
considered, and which are so frequent that everyone that pleases may take
notice of them in himself, are these two: *perception* or *thinking,* and *volition*
or *willing.* . . .

OF SIMPLE IDEAS OF BOTH
SENSATION AND REFLECTION

Ideas of pleasure and pain.   There be other simple ideas which convey
themselves into the mind by all the ways of sensation and reflection: viz.,
pleasure or delight, and its opposite, pain or uneasiness; power, existence,
unity.

SOME FARTHER CONSIDERATIONS CONCERNING
OUR SIMPLE IDEAS OF SENSATION

Ideas in the mind, qualities in bodies.   To discover the nature of our
ideas the better, and to discourse of them intelligibly, it will be convenient
to distinguish them, as they are *ideas or perceptions in our minds,* and as
they are *modifications of matter in the bodies that cause such perception
in us:* that so we may not think (as perhaps usually is done) that they are
exactly the images and resemblances of something inherent in the subject;
most of those of sensation being in the mind no more the likeness of something existing without us than the names that stand for them are the likeness
of our ideas, which yet upon hearing they are apt to excite in us.

Whatsoever the mind perceives in itself, or is the immediate object of
perception, thought, or understanding, that I call *idea;* and the power to
produce any idea in our mind, I call *quality* of the subject wherein that
power is. Thus a snowball having the power to produce in us the ideas of
white, cold, and round, the powers to produce those ideas in us as they are
in the snowball, I call qualities; and as they are sensations or perceptions in
our understandings, I call them ideas; which ideas, if I speak of them sometimes as in the things themselves, I would be understood to mean those
qualities in the objects which produce them in us.

Primary qualities.   Qualities thus considered in bodies are: *First* such
as are utterly inseparable from the body, in what estate soever it be; and such
as, in all the alterations and changes it suffers, all the force can be used upon
it, it constantly keeps; and such as sense constantly finds in every particle of
matter which has bulk enough to be perceived, and the mind finds inseparable from every particle of matter, though less than to make itself singly be
perceived by our senses: v.g., take a grain of wheat, divide it into two parts,

each part has still solidity, extension, figure, and mobility; divide it again, and it retains still the same qualities: and so divide it on till the parts become insensible, they must retain still each of them all those qualities. For, division (which is all that a mill or pestle or any other body does upon another, in reducing it to insensible parts) can never take away either solidity, extension, figure, or mobility from any body, but only makes two or more distinct separate masses of matter of that which was but one before; all which distinct masses, reckoned as so many distinct bodies, after division, make a certain number. These I call *original* or *primary qualities* of body, which I think we may observe to produce simple ideas in us, viz., solidity, extension, figure, motion or rest, and number.

Secondary qualities. *Secondly,* such qualities, which in truth are nothing in the objects themselves, but powers to produce various sensations in us by their primary qualities, i.e., by the bulk, figure, texture, and motion of their insensible parts, as colors, sounds, tastes, etc., these I call *secondary* qualities. To these might be added a third sort, which are allowed to be barely powers, though they are as much real qualities in the subject as those which I, to comply with the common way of speaking, call qualities, but, for distinction, *secondary* qualities. For, the power in fire to produce a new color or consistency in wax or clay, by its primary qualities, is as much a quality in fire as the power it has to produce in me a new idea or sensation of warmth or burning, which I felt not before, by the same primary qualities, viz., the bulk, texture, and motion of its insensible parts.

How primary qualities produce ideas in us. The next thing to be considered is how bodies produce ideas in us; and that is manifestly by impulse, the only way we can conceive bodies to operate in.

If, then, external objects be not united to our minds when they produce ideas therein, and yet we perceive these original qualities in such of them as singly fall under our senses, it is evident that some motion must be thence continued by our nerves, or animal spirits, by some parts of our bodies, to the brain or the seat of sensation, there to produce in our minds the particular ideas we have of them. And since the extension, figure, number, and motion of bodies of an observable bigness, may be perceived at a distance by the sight, it is evident some singly imperceptible bodies must come from them to the eyes, and thereby convey to the brain some motion which produces these ideas which we have of them in us.

How secondary. After the same manner that the ideas of these original qualities are produced in us, we may conceive that the ideas of secondary qualities are also produced, viz., by the operation of insensible particles on our senses. For it being manifest that there are bodies, and good store of bodies, each whereof are so small that we cannot by any of our senses discover either their bulk, figure, or motion (as is evident in the particles of the air and water, and others extremely smaller than those, perhaps as much smaller than the particles of air or water as the particles of air or water are smaller than peas or hailstones) : let us suppose at present that the different motions and figures, bulk and number, of such particles, affecting the several organs of our senses, produce in us these different sensations which we have from the colors and smells of bodies, v.g., that a violet, by the impulse of such insensible particles of matter of peculiar figures and bulks, and in different degrees and modifications of their motions, causes the ideas of the blue color and sweet scent of that flower to be produced in our minds; it being no more impossible to conceive that God should annex such ideas to such motions, with which they have no similitude, than that He should annex the idea of pain to the motion of a piece of steel dividing our flesh, with which the idea hath no resemblance.

What I have said concerning colors and smells may be understood also of tastes and sounds, and other the like sensible qualities; which, whatever reality we by mistake attribute to them, are in truth nothing in the objects themselves, but powers to produce various sensations in us, and depend on those primary qualities, viz., bulk, figure, texture, and motion of parts as I have said.

Ideas of primary qualities are resemblances; of secondary, not. From whence I think it is easy to draw this observation, that the ideas of primary qualities of bodies are resemblances of them, and their patterns do really exist in the bodies themselves; but the ideas produced in us by these secondary qualities have no resemblance of them at all. There is nothing like our ideas existing in the bodies themselves. They are, in the bodies we denominate from them, only a power to produce those sensations in us; and what is sweet, blue, or warm in idea, is but the certain bulk, figure, and motion of the insensible parts in the bodies themselves, which we call so.

Flame is denominated hot and light; snow, white and cold; and manna, white and sweet, from the ideas they produce in us, which qualities are commonly thought to be the same in those bodies that those ideas are in us, the one the perfect resemblance of the other, as they are in a mirror; and it would by most men be judged very extravagant, if one should say otherwise. And yet he that will consider that the same fire that at one distance produces in us the sensation of warmth, does at a nearer approach produce in us the far different sensation of pain, ought to bethink himself what reason he has to say that this idea of warmth, which was produced in him by the fire, is actually in the fire, and his idea of pain which the same fire produced in him the same way is not in the fire. Why are whiteness and coldness in snow and pain not, when it produces the one and the other idea in us, and can do neither but by the bulk, figure, number, and motion of its solid parts?

The particular bulk, number, figure, and motion of the parts of fire or snow are really in them, whether anyone's senses perceive them or no; and therefore they may be called *real* qualities, because they really exist in those bodies. But light, heat, whiteness, or coldness, are no more really in them than sickness or pain is in manna. Take away the sensation of them; let not the eyes see light or colors, nor the ears hear sounds; let the palate not taste, nor the nose smell; and all colors, tastes, odors, and sounds, as they are such particular ideas, vanish and cease, and are reduced to their causes, i.e., bulk, figure, and motion of parts. . . .

Pound an almond, and the clear white color will be altered into a dirty one, and the sweet taste into an oily one. What real alteration can the beating of the pestle make in any body, but an alteration of the texture of it?

Ideas being thus distinguished and understood, we may be able to give an account how the same water, at the same time, may produce the idea of cold by one hand, and of heat by the other; whereas it is impossible that the same water, if those ideas were really in it, should at the same time be both hot and cold. For if we imagine warmth as it is in our hands, to be nothing but a certain sort and degree of motion in the minute particles of our nerves or animal spirits, we may understand how it is possible that the same water may at the same time produce the sensation of heat in one hand, and cold in the other; which yet figure never does, that never producing the idea of a square by one hand which has produced the idea of a globe by another. But if the sensation of heat and cold be nothing but the increase or diminution of the motion of the minute parts of our bodies, caused by the corpuscles of any other body, it is easy to be understood that if that motion be greater in one hand than in the other, if a body be applied to the two hands, which has in its minute particles a greater motion than in those of one of the hands, and a less than in those of the other, it will increase the motion of the one hand, and lessen it in the other, and so cause the different sensations of heat and cold that depend thereon. . . .

Three sorts of qualities in bodies. The qualities then that are in bodies, rightly considered, are of three sorts:

First, the bulk, figure, number, situation, and motion or rest of their solid parts; those are in them, whether we perceive them or not; and when they are of that size that we can discover them, we have by these ideas of the thing as it is in itself, as is plain in artificial things. These I call *primary qualities.*

Secondly, the power that is in any body, by reason of its insensible primary qualities, to operate after a peculiar manner on any of our senses, and thereby produce in us the different ideas of several colors, sounds, smells, tastes, etc. These are usually called *sensible qualities.*

Thirdly, the power that is in any body, by reason of the particular constitution of its primary qualities, to make such a change in the bulk, figure, texture, and motion of another body, as to make it operate on our senses differently from what it did before. Thus the sun has a power to make wax white, and fire, to make lead fluid. These are usually called *powers*.

The first of these, as has been said, I think may be properly called real, original, or primary qualities, because they are in the things themselves, whether they are perceived or no; and upon their different modifications it is that the secondary qualities depend.

The other two are only powers to act differently upon other things, which powers result from the different modifications of those primary qualities. . . .

OF OUR COMPLEX IDEAS OF SUBSTANCES

Ideas of particular substances, how made. The mind being, as I have declared, furnished with a great number of the simple ideas conveyed in by the senses, as they are found in exterior things, or by reflections on its own operations, takes notice, also, that a certain number of these simple ideas go constantly together; which being presumed to belong to one thing, and words being suited to common apprehensions, and made use of for quick despatch, are called, so united in one subject, by one name; which, by inadvertency, we are apt afterward to talk of and consider as one simple idea, which indeed is a complication of many ideas together: because, as I have said, not imagining how these simple ideas can subsist by themselves, we accustom ourselves to suppose some *substratum* wherein they do subsist, and from which they do result; which therefore we call *substance*.

Our obscure idea of substance in general. So that if anyone will examine himself concerning his notion of pure substance in general, he will find he has no other idea of it at all, but only a supposition of he knows not what support of such qualities which are capable of producing simple ideas in us; which qualities are commonly called accidents. If anyone should be asked, what is the subject wherein color or weight inheres, he would have nothing to say but, the solid extended parts. And if he were demanded, what is it that solidity and extension inhere in, he would not be in a much better case than the Indian who, saying that the world was supported by a great elephant, was asked what the elephant rested on; to which his answer was, a great tortoise; but being again pressed to know what gave support to the broad-backed tortoise, replied—something, he knew not what. And thus here, as in all other cases where we use words without having clear and distinct ideas, we talk like children: who, being questioned what such a thing is which they know not, readily give this satisfactory answer, that it is *something;* which in truth signifies no more, when so used, either by children or men, but that they know not what; and that the thing they pretend to know and talk of is what they have no distinct idea of at all, and so are perfectly ignorant of it, and in the dark. The idea, then, we have, to which we give the *general* name substance, being nothing but the supposed, but unknown, support of those qualities we find existing, which we imagine cannot subsist *sine re substante,* "without something to support them," we call that support *substantia;* which, according to the true import of the word, is, in plain English, standing under, or upholding.

Of the sorts of substances. An obscure and relative idea of substance in general being thus made, we come to have the idea of particular sorts of substances, by collecting such combinations of simple ideas as are by experience and observation of men's senses taken notice of to exist together, and are therefore supposed to flow from the particular internal constitution or unknown essence of that substance. Thus we come to have the ideas of a man, horse, gold, water, etc., of which substances, whether anyone has any other clear idea, farther than of certain simple ideas coexistent together, I appeal to everyone's own experience. It is the ordinary qualities observable in iron or a diamond, put together, that make the true complex idea of those substances, which a smith or a jeweler commonly knows better than a philosopher; who, whatever substantial forms he may talk of, has no other idea of those substances than what is framed by a collection of those simple ideas which are to be found in them. Only we must take notice that our complex ideas of substances, besides all these simple ideas they are made up of, have always the confused idea of something to which they belong, and in which they subsist: and therefore when we speak of any sort of substance, we say it is a thing having such or such qualities; as, body is a thing that is extended, figured, and capable of motion; spirit, a thing capable of thinking; and so hardness, friability, and power to draw iron, we say, are qualities to be found in a loadstone. These and the like fashions of speaking intimate that the substance is supposed always something, besides the extension, figure, solidity, motion, thinking, or other observable ideas, though we know not what it is.

No clear or distinct idea of substance in general. Hence, when we talk or think of any particular sort of corporeal substances, as horse, stone, etc., though the idea we have of either of them be but the complication or collection of those several simple ideas of sensible qualities which we used to find united in the thing called horse or stone; yet because we cannot conceive how they should subsist alone, nor one in another, we suppose them existing in, and supported by, some common subject; which support we denote by the name substance, though it be certain we have no clear or distinct idea of that thing we suppose a support.

As clear an idea of spirit as body. The same happens concerning the operations of the mind; viz., thinking, reasoning, fearing, etc., which we, concluding not to subsist of themselves, nor apprehending how they can belong to body, or be produced by it, we are apt to think these the actions of some other substance, which we call *spirit;* whereby yet it is evident, that having no other idea or notion of matter but something wherein those many sensible qualities which affect our senses do subsist; by supposing a substance wherein thinking, knowing, doubting, and a power of moving, etc., do subsist, we have as clear a notion of the substance of spirit as we have of body: the one being supposed to be (without knowing what it is) the *substratum* to those simple ideas we have from without; and the other supposed (with a like ignorance of what it is) to be the *substratum* to those operations which we experiment in ourselves within. It is plain, then, that the idea of *corporeal substance* in matter is as remote from our conceptions and apprehensions as that of *spiritual substance,* or spirit; and therefore, from our not having any notion of the substance of spirit, we can no more conclude its nonexistence than we can, for the same reason, deny the existence of body: it being as rational to affirm there is no body, because we have no clear and distinct idea of the substance of matter, as to say there is no spirit, because we have no clear and distinct idea of the substance of a spirit.

Our ideas of particular sorts of substances. Whatever therefore be the secret and abstract nature of substance in general, all the ideas we have of particular, distinct sorts of substances, are nothing but several combinations of simple ideas coexisting in such, though unknown, cause of their union, as makes the whole subsist of itself. It is by such combinations of simple ideas, and nothing else, that we represent particular sorts of substances to ourselves; such are the ideas we have of their several species in our minds; and such only do we, by their specific names, signify to others, v.g., man, horse, sun, water, iron; upon hearing which words everyone who understands the language, frames in his mind a combination of those several simple ideas which he has usually observed or fancied to exist together under that denomination; all which he supposes to rest in, and be, as it were, adherent to, that unknown common subject, which inheres not in anything else. Though in the meantime it be manifest, and everyone upon inquiry into his own thoughts will find, that he has no other idea of any substance, v.g., let it be gold, horse, iron, man, vitriol, bread, but what he has barely of those sensible qualities which he supposes to inhere with a supposition of such a *substratum* as gives, as it were, a support to those qualities, or simple ideas, which he has observed to exist united together. Thus, the idea of the sun—what is it but an aggregate of those several simple ideas—bright, hot, roundish, having a constant regular motion, at a certain distance from us, and perhaps some other: as he who thinks and discourses of the sun has been more or less accurate in observing those sensible qualities, ideas, or properties which are in that thing which he calls the sun.

Power, a great part of our complex ideas of substances. For he has the perfectest idea of any of the particular sorts of substances who has gathered and put together most of those simple ideas which do exist in it, among which are to be reckoned its active powers and passive capacities; which, though not simple ideas, yet in this respect, for brevity's sake, may conveniently enough be reckoned amongst them. Thus, the power of drawing iron is one of the ideas of the complex one of that substance we call a loadstone, and a power to be so drawn is a part of the complex one we call iron; which powers pass for inherent qualities in those subjects. . . .

Three sorts of ideas make our complex ones of substances. The ideas that make our complex ones of corporeal substances are of these three sorts. First, the ideas of the primary qualities of things which are discovered by our senses, and are in them even when we perceive them not; such as the bulk, figure, number, situation, and motion of the parts of bodies, which are really in them, whether we take notice of them or no. Secondly, the sensible secondary qualities which, depending on these, are nothing but the powers those substances have to produce several ideas in us by our senses; which ideas are not in the things themselves otherwise than as anything is in its cause. Thirdly, the aptness we consider in any substance to give or receive such alterations of primary qualities as that the substance so altered should produce in us different ideas from what it did before; these are called active and passive powers: all which powers, as far as we have any notice or notion of them, terminate only in sensible simple ideas. . . .

Our faculties of discovery suited to our state. The infinitely wise contriver of us, and all things about us, hath fitted our senses, faculties, and organs, to the conveniences of life, and the business we have to do here. We are able, by our senses, to know and distinguish things; and to examine them so far, as to apply them to our uses, and several ways to accommodate the exigencies of this life. We have insight enough into their admirable contrivances and wonderful effects, to admire and magnify the wisdom, power, and goodness of their author. Such a knowledge as this, which is suited to our present condition, we want not faculties to attain. But it appears not that God intended we should have a perfect, clear, and adequate knowledge of them: that perhaps is not in the comprehension of any finite being. We are furnished with faculties (dull and weak as they are) to discover enough in the creatures to lead us to the knowledge of the Creator, and the knowledge of our duty; and we are fitted well enough with abilities to provide for the conveniences of living: these are our business in this world. . . .

Idea of God. If we examine the idea we have of the incomprehensible Supreme Being, we shall find that we come by it the same way; and that the complex ideas we have both of God and separate spirits are made of the simple ideas we receive from reflection: v.g., having, from what we experiment in ourselves, got the ideas of existence and duration, of knowledge and power, of pleasure and happiness, and of several other qualities and powers which it is better to have than to be without; when we would frame an idea the most suitable we can to the Supreme Being, we enlarge every one of these with our idea of infinity; and so, putting them together, make our complex idea of God.

If I find that I know some few things, and some of them, or all, perhaps, imperfectly; I can frame an idea of knowing twice as many, which I can double again as often as I can add to number; and thus enlarge my idea of knowledge, by extending its comprehension to all things existing or possible. The same also I can do of knowing them more perfectly, i.e., all their qualities, powers, causes, consequences, and relations, etc., till all be perfectly known that is in them, or can any way relate to them; and thus frame the idea of infinite or boundless knowledge. The same may also be done of power, till we come to that we call infinite; and also of the duration of existence without beginning or end; and so frame the idea of an eternal being. The degrees or extent, wherein we ascribe existence, power, wisdom, and all other perfections (which we can have any ideas of), to that Sovereign Being which we call God, being all boundless and infinite, we frame the best idea of Him our minds are capable of: all which is done, I say, by enlarging those simple ideas we have taken from the operations of our own minds by reflection, or by our senses from exterior things, to that vastness to which infinity can extend them. . . .

OF CAUSE AND EFFECT

Whence their ideas got. In the notice that our senses take of the constant vicissitude of things, we cannot but observe that several particular both qualities and substances begin to exist; and that they receive this their existence from the due application and operation of some other being. From this observation we get our ideas of cause and effect. *That which produces any simple or complex idea,* we denote by the general name *cause;* and *that which is produced, effect.* Thus finding that in that substance which we call "wax" fluidity, which is a simple idea that was not in it before, is constantly produced by the application of a certain degree of heat, we call the simple idea of heat, in relation to fluidity in wax, the cause of it, and fluidity the effect. So also finding that the substance, wood, which is a certain collection of simple ideas so called, by the application of fire is turned into another substance called ashes, i.e., another complex idea, consisting of a collection of simple ideas, quite different from that complex idea which we call wood, we consider fire, in relation to ashes, as cause, and the ashes, as effect. So that whatever is considered by us to conduce or operate to the producing any particular simple idea, or collection of simple ideas, whether substance or mode, which did not before exist, hath thereby in our minds the relation of a cause, and so is denominated by us. . . .

OF KNOWLEDGE IN GENERAL

Our knowledge conversant about our ideas only. Since the mind, in all its thoughts and reasonings, hath no other immediate object but its own ideas, which it alone does or can contemplate, it is evident that our knowledge is only conversant about them.

Knowledge is the perception of the agreement or disagreement of two ideas. Knowledge then seems to me to be nothing but the perception of the connection of and agreement, or disagreement and repugnancy, of any of our ideas. In this alone it consists. Where this perception is, there is knowledge; and where it is not, there, though we may fancy, guess, or believe, yet we always come short of knowledge. For, when we know that white is not black, what do we else but perceive that these two ideas do not agree? When we possess ourselves with the utmost security of the demonstration that the three angles of a triangle are equal to two right ones, what do we more but perceive that equality to two right ones does necessarily agree to, and is inseparable from, the three angles of a triangle? . . .

OF THE EXTENT OF HUMAN KNOWLEDGE

Knowledge, as has been said, lying in the perception of the agreement or disagreement of any of our ideas, it follows from hence that,

(i) *No farther than we have ideas.* First, we can have knowledge no farther than we have ideas.

(ii) *No farther than we can perceive their agreement or disagreement.* Secondly, that we can have no knowledge farther than we can have perception of that agreement or disagreement: which perception being (1) either by intuition, or the immediate comparing any two ideas, or (2) by reason, examining the agreement or disagreement of two ideas by the intervention of some others, or (3) by sensation, perceiving the existence of particular things; hence it also follows,

(iii) *Intuitive knowledge extends itself not to all the relations of all our ideas.* Thirdly, that we cannot have an intuitive knowledge that shall extend itself to all our ideas, and all that we would know about them; because we cannot examine and perceive all the relations they have one to another by juxtaposition, or an immediate comparison one with another. Thus having the ideas of an obtuse and an acute-angled triangle, both drawn from equal bases and between parallels, I can by intuitive knowledge perceive the one not to be the other, but cannot that way know whether they be equal or no: because their agreement or disagreement in equality can never be perceived by an immediate comparing them; the difference of figure makes their parts incapable of an exact immediate application; and therefore there is need of some intervening qualities to measure them by, which is demonstration or rational knowledge.

(iv) *Nor demonstrative knowledge.* Fourthly, it follows also, from what is above observed, that our rational knowledge cannot reach to the whole extent of our ideas: because between two different ideas we would examine, we cannot always find such mediums as we can connect one to another with an intuitive knowledge, in all the parts of the deduction; and wherever that fails, we come short of knowledge and demonstration.

(v) *Sensitive knowledge narrower than either.* Fifthly, sensitive knowledge, reaching no farther than the existence of things actually present to our senses, is yet much narrower than either of the former. . . .

OF THE REALITY OF HUMAN KNOWLEDGE

Objection. Knowledge placed in ideas may be all bare vision. I doubt not but my reader by this time may be apt to think that I have been all this while only building a castle in the air; and be ready to say to me, "To what purpose all this stir? 'Knowledge,' say you, 'is only the perception of the agreement or disagreement of our own ideas'; but who knows what those ideas may be? Is there anything so extravagant as the imaginations of men's brains? Where is the head that has no chimeras in it? Or if there be a sober and a wise man, what difference will there be, by your rules, between his knowledge, and that of the most extravagant fancy in the world? They both have their ideas, and perceive their agreement or disagreement one with another. If there be any difference between them, the advantage will be on the warm-headed man's side, as having the more ideas, and the more lively. And so, by your rules, he will be the more knowing. If it be true that all knowledge lies only in the perception of the agreement or disagreement of our own ideas, the visions of an enthusiast, and the reasonings of a sober man, will be equally certain. It is no matter how things are: so a man observe but the agreement of his own imaginations, and talk conformably, it is all truth, all certainty. Such castles in the air will be as strongholds of truth as the demonstrations of Euclid. That an harpy is not a centaur is by this way as certain knowledge, and as much a truth, as that a square is not a circle.

"But of what use is all this fine knowledge of men's own imaginations to a man that inquires after the reality of things? It matters not what men's fancies are, it is the knowledge of things that is only to be prized; it is this alone gives a value of our reasonings, and preference to one man's knowledge over another's, that it is of things as they really are, and not of dreams and fancies."

Answer. Not so, where ideas agree with things. To which I answer, that if our knowledge of our ideas terminate in them, and reach no farther, where there is something farther intended, our most serious thoughts will be of little more use than the reveries of a crazy brain; and the truths built thereon of no more weight than the discourses of a man who sees things clearly in a dream, and with great assurance utters them. But I hope before I have done to make it evident that this way of certainty, by the knowledge of our own ideas, goes a little farther than bare imagination; and I believe it will appear that all the certainty of general truths a man has lies in nothing else.

It is evident the mind knows not things immediately, but only by the intervention of the ideas it has of them. Our knowledge therefore is real only so far as there is a conformity between our ideas and the reality of things. But what shall be here the criterion? How shall the mind, when it perceives nothing but its own ideas, know that they agree with things themselves? This, though it seems not to want difficulty, yet I think there be two sorts of ideas that we may be assured agree with things.

As (i) *all simple ideas do.* First, the first are simple ideas, which since the mind, as has been showed, can by no means make to itself, must necessarily be the product of things operating on the mind in a natural way, and producing therein those perceptions which by the wisdom and will of our Maker they are ordained and adapted to. From whence it follows that simple ideas are not fictions of our fancies, but the natural and regular productions of things without us really operating upon us, and so carry with them all the conformity which is intended, or which our state requires; for they represent to us things under those appearances which they are fitted to produce in us, whereby we are enabled to distinguish the sorts of particular substances, to discern the states they are in, and so to take them for our necessities, and apply them to our uses. Thus the idea of whiteness or bitterness, as it is in the mind, exactly answering that power which is in any body to produce it there, has all the real conformity it can or ought to have with things without us. And this conformity between our simple ideas and the existence of things is sufficient for real knowledge.

(ii) *All complex ideas except of substances.* Secondly, all our complex ideas except those of substances being archetypes of the mind's own making, not intended to be the copies of anything, not referred to the existence of anything, as to their originals, cannot want any conformity necessary to real knowledge. For that which is not designed to represent anything but itself can never be capable of a wrong representation, nor mislead us from the true apprehension of anything by its dislikeness to it; and such, excepting those of substances, are all our complex ideas: which are combinations of ideas which the mind by its free choice puts together without considering any connection they have in nature. And hence it is, that in all these sorts the ideas themselves are considered as the archetypes, and things [not] otherwise regarded but as they are conformable to them. So that we cannot but be infallibly certain that all the knowledge we attain concerning these ideas is real, and reaches things themselves; because in all our thoughts, reasonings, and discourses of this kind, we intend things no farther than as they are conformable to our ideas. So that in these we cannot miss of a certain and undoubted reality. . . .

(iii) *Ideas of substances have their archetypes without us.* Thirdly, there is another sort of complex ideas, which being referred to archetypes without us may differ from them, and so our knowledge about them may come short of being real. Such are our ideas of substances, which consisting of a collection of simple ideas, supposed taken from the works of nature, may yet vary from them, by having more or different ideas united in them than are to be found united in the things themselves: from whence it comes to pass that they may and often do fail of being exactly conformable to things themselves.

So far as they agree with those, so far our knowledge concerning them is real. . . . But our ideas of substances, being supposed copies, and referred to archetypes without us, must still be taken from something that does or has existed; they must not consist of ideas put together at the pleasure of our thoughts without any real pattern they were taken from, though we can perceive no inconsistence in such a combination. The reason whereof is, because we knowing not what real constitution it is of substances whereon our simple ideas depend, and which really is the cause of the strict union of some of them one with another, and the exclusion of others; there are very few of them that we can be sure are or are not inconsistent in nature, any farther than experience and sensible observation reach. Herein, therefore, is founded the reality of our knowledge concerning substances, that all our complex ideas of them must be such, and such only, as are made up of such simple ones as have been discovered to coexist in nature. And our ideas, being thus true, though not perhaps very exact copies, are yet the subjects of real (as far as we have any) knowledge of them: which, as has been already showed, will not be found to reach very far; but so far as it does, it will still be real knowledge. Whatever ideas we have, the agreement we find they have with others will still be knowledge. If those ideas be abstract, it will be general knowledge. But to make it real concerning substances, the ideas must be taken from the real existence of things. Whatever simple ideas have been found to coexist in any substance, these we may with confidence join together again, and so make abstract ideas of substances. For whatever have once had an union in nature may be united again.

QUESTIONS

1. What does Locke mean by "experience"? Is his meaning for "experience" the same as, or at least compatible with, what we ordinarily mean by "experience"?
2. What kinds of ideas does Locke distinguish?
3. What is Locke's model of the mind? How is this model related to his account of the nature of our knowledge of the world? How can one tell whether his

way of conceiving the mind is correct or incorrect? For instance, is his account of the mind open to experimental confirmation? Why or why not?
4. How does Locke distinguish between "primary qualities" and "secondary qualities' ? What does this distinction tell us about his conception of real existence outside the mind?
5. What does Locke mean by "substance"? Does his conception of substance contradict the principle of empiricism as he formulated it? Why or why not?
6. State Locke's reply to the objection that his view of knowledge is useless to "a man that inquires after the reality of things," and give your reasons for thinking that his reply succeeded, or failed, in answering the objection.
7. Disregarding Locke's psychological account of the origin of knowledge, and considering only his criteria for deciding when we have true knowledge of the world, state the differences between his criteria and those of Descartes. Which set of criteria do you prefer and on what grounds?

2. GILBERT RYLE

(*b. 1900*)

Sensation and Observation

Gilbert Ryle is Waynflete Professor of Metaphysical Philosophy at Oxford. He is the editor of *Mind* and the author of *The Concept of Mind* (1949) and *Dilemmas* (1954).

This reading has both a critical and a constructive side. On the one hand, Ryle argues against Locke's description of knowing as having an idea in mind, as though knowing must be likened to having a sensation. On the other hand, Ryle argues for the view that knowing something is better understood as having an appropriate ability. For example, someone who knows a song can recognize it when he hears it; and someone who knows the difference between needles and pins will bring the right

thing when he is asked to fetch a needle from the sewing basket. Both Ryle's critical and constructive points depend on his analysis of the logic of observation words and the difference between their logic and the logic of sensation words. The reader must consider the accuracy of Professor Ryle's account of how we talk of observing and sensing, and decide whether an examination of the logic of observation and sensation words is an appropriate method for establishing the distinctiveness of observation.

This reading is drawn from *The Concept of Mind*, Chapter VII, "Sensation and Observation."

TALKING OF SENSATIONS

For obvious reasons we have constantly to refer to the sensations which are connected with the organs of sense, for we are constantly having to mention what we see and do not see, what we hear, smell, taste and feel. But we do not talk about these sensations 'neat'; we ordinarily mention them only in reference to the things or events which we are observing or trying or claiming to observe. People speak of having a glimpse, but only in such contexts as having a glimpse of a robin, or as having a glimpse of something moving. Nor do they break out of this habit, when asked to describe how something looked, or sounded, or tasted; they will normally say that it looked like a haystack, that it sounded like something humming, or that it tasted as if it had pepper in it.

This procedure of describing sensations by referring in a certain way to common objects like haystacks, things that hum, and pepper is of great theoretical importance. A haystack, for example, is something about the description of which everyone could agree. A haystack is something which any observers could observe, and we should expect their accounts of it to tally with one another, or at least to be capable of correction until they did tally. Its position, shape, size, weight, date of construction, composition and function are facts which anyone could establish by ordinary methods of observation and inquiry. But more than this. These methods would also establish how the haystack would look, feel and smell to ordinary observers in ordinary conditions of observation. When I say that something looks like a haystack, (though it may actually be a blanket on a clothes-line), I am describing how it looks in terms of what anyone might expect a haystack to look like, when observed from a suitable angle, in a suitable light and against a suitable background. I am, that is, comparing how the blanket looks to me here and now, not with some other particular glimpse had by me, or had by some other particular person in a particular situation, but with a *type* of glimpse such as any ordinary observers could expect to get in situations of certain sorts, namely in situations where they are in the proximity of haystacks in daylight.

Similarly, to say that something tastes peppery is to say that it tastes to me now as any peppered viands would taste to anybody with a normal palate. It has been suggested that I can never know that pepper-grains do give different people similar sensations, but for the present it is enough to point out that our ordinary ways of imparting information about our own sensations consist in making certain sorts of references to what we think could be established in anyone's observations of common objects. We describe what is personal to ourselves in neutral or impersonal terms. Indeed, our descriptions would convey nothing unless couched in such terms. These are, after all, the terms which we learned by being taught them by others. We do not and cannot describe haystacks in terms of this or that set of sensations. We describe our sensations by certain sorts of references to observers and things like haystacks.

We follow the same practice in describing organic sensations. When a sufferer describes a pain as a stabbing, a grinding or a burning pain, though he does not necessarily think that his pain is given to him by a stiletto, a drill or an ember, still he says what sort of a pain it is by likening it to the sort of pain that would be given to anyone by such instruments. The same account holds of such descriptions as 'there is a singing in my ears', 'my blood ran cold' and 'I saw stars'. Even to say that one's view is hazy is to liken one's view to the way that common objects look to any observer who is seeing them through an atmospheric haze.

The present point of mentioning these ways of describing our sensations is to show how and why there exists a linguistic difficulty in discussing the logic of concepts of sensation. We do not employ a 'neat' sensation vocabulary. We describe particular sensations by referring to how common objects regularly look, sound and feel to any normal person.

Epistemologists are fond of using words like 'pains', 'itches', 'stabs', 'glows' and 'dazzles' as if they were 'neat' sensation names. But this practice is doubly misleading. Not only do most of these words draw their significance from situations involving common objects like fleas, daggers and radiators, but they also connote that the person who has the sensations likes or dislikes, or might well like or dislike, having them. A pain in my knee is a sensation that I mind having; so 'unnoticed pain' is an absurd expression, where 'unnoticed sensation' has no absurdity.

OBSERVING, AND HAVING A SENSATION

This point can serve to introduce a conceptual distinction which will shortly turn out to be of cardinal importance, namely, that between having a sensation and observing. When a person is said to be watching, scanning or looking at something, listening to it or savouring it, a part, but only a part, of what is meant is that he is having visual, auditory or gustatory sensations. But to be observing something the observer must also at least be trying to find something out. His scrutiny is accordingly describable as careful or careless, cursory or sustained, methodical or haphazard, accurate or inaccurate, expert or amateurish. Observing is a task which can be one of some arduousness, and we can be more or less successful in it and more or less good at it. But none of these ways of characterising the exercises of one's powers of observation can be applied to the having of visual, auditory or gustatory sensations. One can listen carefully, but not have a singing in one's ears carefully; one can look systematically, but one cannot have a dazzle-sensation systematically; one can try to discriminate flavours, but one cannot try to have sensations of taste. Again we observe, very often, from inquisitiveness or obedience, but we do not have tickles from this or any other motive. We observe on purpose, but we do not have sensations on purpose, though we can induce them on purpose. We can make mistakes of observation, but it is nonsense to speak of either making or avoiding mistakes in sensation; sensations can be neither correct nor incorrect, veridical nor non-veridical. They are neither apprehensions nor misapprehensions. Observing is finding out, or trying to find out, something, but having a sensation is neither finding out, nor trying to find out, nor failing to find out, anything.

This set of contrasts enables us to say that though mention of the degree to which, the ways in which and the objects of which a person is observant or unobservant is a part of the description of his wits and character, mention of his sensory capacities and actual sensations is no part of that description. To use an objectionable phrase, there is nothing 'mental' about sensations. Deafness is not a species of stupidity, nor is a squint any sort of turpitude; the retriever's keenness of scent does not prove him intelligent; and we do not try to train or shame children out of colour-blindness or think of them as mentally defective. It is not for the moralist or the alienist, but for the oculist, to diagnose and prescribe for imperfect vision. Having a sensation is not an exercise of a quality of intellect or character. Hence we are not too proud to concede sensations to reptiles.

Whatever series of sensations an intelligent person may have, it is always conceivable that a merely sentient creature might have had a precisely similar series; and if by 'stream of consciousness' were meant 'series of sensations', then from a mere inventory of the contents of such a stream there would be no possibility of deciding whether the creature that had these sensations was an animal or a human being; an idiot, a lunatic or a sane man; much less whether he was an ambitious and argumentative philologist or a slow-witted but industrious magistrates' clerk.

THE PRIVACY OF SENSATIONS

However, these considerations will not satisfy the theorists who want to make the stream of a person's sensations, feelings and images the stuff of his mind, and thus to back up the dogma that minds are special-status things composed of a special stuff. They will urge, quite correctly, that though the oculist and the dentist can modify the patient's sensations by applying chemical or mechanical treatments to his bodily organs, yet they are debarred from observing the sensations themselves. They may observe what is physiologically amiss with the patient's eyes and gums, but they must rely on the patient's testimony for knowledge of what he sees and feels. Only the wearer knows where the shoe pinches. From this it is argued, plausibly but fallaciously, that there does indeed exist the hallowed antithesis between the public, physical world and the private, mental world, between the things and events which anyone may witness and the things or events which only their possessor may witness. Planets, microbes, nerves and eardrums are publicly observable things in the outside world; sensations, feelings and images are privately observable constituents of our several mental worlds.

I want to show that this antithesis is spurious. It is true that the cobbler cannot witness the tweaks that I feel when the shoe pinches. But it is false that I witness them. The reason why my tweaks cannot be witnessed by him is not that some Iron Curtain prevents them from being witnessed by anyone save myself, but that they are not the sorts of things of which it makes sense to say that they are witnessed or unwitnessed at all, even by me. I feel or have the tweaks, but I do not discover or peer at them; they are not things that I find out about by watching them, listening to them, or savouring them. In the sense in which a person may be said to have had a robin under observation, it would be nonsense to say that he has had a twinge under observation. There may be one or several witnesses of a road-accident; there cannot be several witnesses, or even one witness, of a qualm.

We know what it is like to have and to need observational aids like telescopes, stethoscopes and torches for the observation of planets, heart-beats and moths, but we cannot think what it would be like to apply such instruments to our sensations. Similarly, though we know well what sorts of handicaps impair or prevent our observation of common objects, namely handicaps like fogs, tingling fingers and singings in the ears, we cannot think of analogous impediments getting between us and such sensations as tingles and singings in the ears.

In saying that sensations are not the sorts of things that can be observed, I do not mean that they are unobservable in the way in which inframicroscopic bacteria, flying bullets, or the mountains on the other side of the moon, are unobservable, or that they are unobservable in the way in which the planets are unobservable to the blind. I mean something like this. Every word that can be written down, except words of one letter, has a spelling; some words are more difficult to spell than others and some words have several different spellings. Yet if we are asked how the letters of the alphabet are spelled, we have to answer that they cannot be spelled at all. But this 'cannot' does not mean that the task is one of insuperable difficulty, but only that the question, 'Of what letters arranged in what order does a given letter consist?' is an improper question. As letters are neither easy to spell, nor insuperably hard to spell, so, I argue, sensations are neither observable nor unobservable. Correspondingly, however, just as the fact that we may not even ask how a letter is spelled by no means precludes us from knowing perfectly well how letters are written, so the fact that we may not talk of the observation of sensations by no means precludes us from talking of the notice or heed that people can pay to their sensations, or of the avowals and reports that they can make of the sensations of which they have taken notice. Headaches cannot be witnessed, but they can be noticed, and while it is improper to advise a person not to peep at his tickle, it is quite proper to advise him not to pay any heed to it.

We have seen that observing entails having sensations; a man could not be described as watching a robin who had not got a single glimpse of it, or as smelling a cheese who had not caught a whiff. (I am pretending, what is not true, that words like 'glimpse' and 'whiff' stand for sensations. The fact that a glimpse can be characterised as 'clear' or 'unclear' shows that it is an observation-word and not a 'neat' sensation-word.) An object of observation, like a robin, or a cheese, must therefore be the sort of thing of which it is possible for observers to catch glimpses, or to get whiffs. But many theorists ask us to look away from such common objects as robins and cheeses towards such things as glimpses and whiffs, and we are asked to declare that I, though nobody else, can observe the glimpses and the whiffs that I get, and observe them in the same sense of 'observe' as that in which anyone can observe the robin or the cheese. But to grant this would be to grant that if, when I catch a glimpse of a robin, I can observe that glimpse, then, in doing so, I must get something like a glimpse or a whiff of that glimpse of the robin. If sensations are proper objects of observation, then observing them must carry with it the having of sensations of those sensations analogous to the glimpses of the robin without which I could not be watching the robin. And this is clearly absurd. There is nothing answering to the phrases 'a glimpse of a glimpse' or 'a whiff of a pain' or 'the sound of a tweak' or 'the tingle of a tingle', and if there was anything to correspond, the series would go on for ever.

Again, when a person has been watching a horse-race, it is proper to ask whether he had a good or a bad view of it, whether he watched it carefully or carelessly and whether he tried to see as much of it as he could. So, if it was correct to say that a person observes his sensations, it would be proper to ask whether his inspection of a tickle had been hampered or unhampered, close or casual and whether he could have discerned more of it, if he had tried. No one ever asks such questions, any more than anyone asks how the first letter in 'London' is spelled. There are no such questions to ask. This point is partially obscured by the fact that the word 'observe', though generally used to cover such processes as watching, listening and savouring, or else such achievements as descrying and detecting, is sometimes used as a synonym of 'pay heed to' and 'notice'. Watching and descrying do involve paying heed, but paying heed does not involve watching.

It follows from this that it was wrong from the start to contrast the common objects of anyone's observation, like robins and cheeses, with the supposed peculiar objects of my privileged observation, namely my sensations, since sensations are not objects of observation at all. We do not, consequently, have to rig up one theatre, called 'the outside world', to house the common objects of anyone's observation, and another, called 'the mind', to house the objects of some monopoly observations. The antithesis between 'public' and 'private' was in part a misconstruction of the antithesis between objects which can be looked at, handled and tasted, on the one hand, and sensations which are had but not looked at, handled or tasted, on the other. It is true and even tautologous that the cobbler cannot feel the shoe pinching me, unless the cobbler is myself, but this is not because he is excluded from a peep-show open only to me, but because it would make no sense to say that he was in my pain, and no sense, therefore, to say that he was noticing the tweak that I was having.

Further consequences follow. The properties which we ascertain by observation, or not without observation, to characterise the common objects of anyone's observation cannot be significantly ascribed to, or denied of, sensations. Sensations do not have sizes, shapes, positions, temperatures, colours or smells. In the sense in which there is always an answer to the question, 'Where is?' or 'Where was the robin?', there is no answer to the question, 'Where is?' or 'Where was your glimpse of the robin?' There is indeed a sense in which a tickle is quite properly said to be 'in my foot', or a stinging 'in my nose', but this is a different sense from that in which bones are in my foot, or pepper-grains are in my nose. So in the muddled sense of 'world' in which people say that 'the outside world' or 'the public world' contains robins and cheeses, the locations and connections of which in that world can be found out, there is not another world, or set of worlds, in which the locations and connections of sensations can be found out; nor does the reputed problem exist of finding out what are the connections between the occupants of the public world and those of any such private worlds. Further, while one common object, like a needle, can be inside or outside another, like a haystack, there is no corresponding antithesis of 'inside' to 'outside' applying to sensations. My tweak is not hidden from the cobbler because it is inside me, either as being literally inside my skin, or as being, metaphorically, in a place to which he has no access. On the contrary, it cannot be described, as needles can, as being either internal or external to a common object like myself, nor as being either hidden or unhidden. Nor can letters be classified as either nouns or verbs or adjectives, or described as either obeying or dis-obeying the rules of English syntax. It is, of course, true and important that I am the only person who can give a first-hand account of the tweaks given me by my ill-fitting shoe, and an oculist who cannot speak my language is without his best source of information about my visual sensations. But the fact that I alone can give first-hand accounts of my sensations does not entail that I have, what others lack, the opportunity of observing those sensations.

TWO FURTHER POINTS

Two further connected points must be made. First, there is a philo-sophically unexciting though important sense of 'private' in which of course my sensations are private or proprietary to me. Namely, just as you cannot, in logic, hold my catches, win my races, eat my meals, frown my frowns, or dream my dreams, so you cannot have my twinges, or my after-images. Nor can Venus have Neptune's satellites, or Poland have Bulgaria's history. This is simply a part of the logical force of those sentences in which the accusative to a transitive verb is a cognate accusative. Such transitive verbs do not signify relations. 'I held my catch' does not assert a relation between me and a catch, such that that catch might conceivably have been in that relation to you instead of to me. It is not like 'I stopped my bicycle'; you might well have anticipated me in stopping my bicycle.

Next, in saying that 'I had a twinge' does not assert a relation, as 'I had a hat' does, I am saying that the phrase 'my twinge' does not stand for any sort of a *thing* or 'term'. It does not even stand for an episode, though 'I had a twinge' asserts that an episode took place. This is part of the reason why it is nonsense to speak of observing, inspecting, witnessing or scrutinising sensations, since the objects proper to such verbs are things and episodes.

Yet when we theorise about sensations, we are forcibly tempted to talk of them as if they were elusive things or episodes. We inadvertently work on such models as that of a solitary man inside his tent who sees spots and patches of light and feels indentations in the inside of the canvas. He then, perhaps, wishes he could see and feel the torches and boots that made those patches of light and indentations in the canvas. But, alas, he can never see those torches, or feel those boots, as the canvas is always in the way. Now illuminated and indented bits of canvas are things; and the momentary illuminations and indentations of the canvas are episodes. So they are the sorts of objects which it is proper to describe as being watched, scrutinised and detected by a man inside his tent; and it is also proper to speak of them being there, but being unwatched and undetected. Moreover a man who can watch or detect illuminated or indented canvas could watch and detect torches and boots, if they were not screened from him. The situation of a man having sensations is, therefore, quite out of analogy with that of the man in the tent. Having sensations is not watching or detecting objects; and watching and detecting things and episodes is not having them in the sense in which one has sensations.

. . .

USES OF 'TO OBSERVE'

We use the verb 'to observe' in two ways. In one use, to say that someone is observing something is to say that he is trying, with or without success, to find out something about it by doing at least some looking, listening, savouring, smelling or feeling. In another use, a person is said to have observed something, when his exploration has been successful, i.e. that he has found something out by some such methods. Verbs of perception such as 'see', 'hear', 'detect', 'discriminate' and many others are generally used to record observational successes, while verbs like 'watch', 'listen', 'probe', 'scan' and 'savour' are used to record observational undertakings, the success of which may be still in question. Hence it is proper to speak of someone watching carefully and successfully, but not of his seeing carefully or successfully, of his probing systematically, but not of his discovering systematically, and so on. The simple-seeming assertion 'I see a linnet' claims a success, where 'I am trying to make out what is moving' reports only an investigation.

In our present inquiry it will sometimes be convenient to use the ambiguous word 'observe' just because it can be used as well to signify discovery as to signify search. The words 'perception' and 'perceive' which are often used as cardinal in these inquiries, are too narrow since they cover only achievements, as do the specific verbs of perception 'see', 'hear', 'taste', 'smell' and, in one sense, 'feel'.

It has already been remarked that observing entails having at least one sensation, though having sensations does not entail observing. We might now ask, 'What more is there in observing than having at least one sensation?' But this formulation of the question is misleading, since it suggests that visually observing a robin consists in both having at least one visual sensation and doing or having something else as well, i.e. in two states or processes coupled together, as humming and walking can be coupled together; and this need not be the case. . . . There is a crucial difference between doing something with heed and doing it, e.g. in absence of mind, but this difference does not consist in heeding being a concomitant act, occurring in another 'place'. So we should ask, not, 'What is an observer doing besides having sensations?', but, 'What does the description of an observer embody over and above the description of him as having those sensations?' This point will be important before long.

THE 'PRISONER' MODEL OF PERCEPTION

We should begin by dismissing a model which in one form or another dominates many speculations about perception. The beloved but spurious question, 'How can a person get beyond his sensations to apprehension of external realities?' is often posed as if the situation were like this. There is immured in a windowless cell a prisoner, who has lived there in solitary confinement since birth. All that comes to him from the outside world is flickers of light thrown upon his cell-walls and tappings heard through the stones; yet from these observed flashes and tappings he becomes, or seems to become, apprised of unobserved football-matches, flower-gardens and eclipses of the sun. How then does he learn the ciphers in which his signals are arranged, or even find out that there are such things as ciphers? How can he interpret the messages which he somehow deciphers, given that the vocabularies of those messages are the vocabularies of football and astronomy and not those of flickers and tappings?

. . . The use of this sort of model involves the explicit or implicit assumption that, much as the prisoner can see flickers and hear tappings, but cannot, unfortunately, see or hear football matches, so we can observe our visual and other sensations, but cannot, unfortunately, observe robins. But this is doubly to abuse the notion of observation. As has been shown, on the one hand, it is nonsense to speak of a person witnessing a sensation, and, on the other, the ordinary use of verbs like 'observe', 'espy', 'peer at' and so on is in just such contexts as 'observe a robin', 'espy a ladybird' and 'peer at a book'. Football matches are just the sorts of things of which we do catch glimpses; and sensations are the sorts of things of which it would be absurd to say that anyone caught glimpses. In other words, the prison model suggests that, in finding out about robins and football matches, we have to do something like inferring from sensations, which we do observe, to birds and games, which we never could observe; whereas in fact it is robins and games that we observe, and it is sensations that we never could observe. The question, 'How do we jump from descrying or inspecting sensations to becoming apprised of robins and football matches?' is a spurious how-question.

OBSERVATION MORE THAN HAVING SENSATIONS

Now there is no unique and central problem of perception. There is a range of partially overlapping questions, most of which will cease to be intriguing, the moment that a few of them have been cleared up. We can illustrate certain of the problems which belong to this range in this way. To describe someone as finding a thimble is to say something about his having visual, tactual or auditory sensations, but it is to say more than that. Similarly to describe someone as trying to make out whether what he sees is a chaffinch or a robin, a stick or a shadow, a fly on the window or a mote in his eye, is to say something about his visual sensations, but it is to say more than that. Finally, to describe someone as 'seeing' a snake that is not there, or as 'hearing' voices, where all is silent, seems to be saying something about his images, if not about his sensations, but it is to say more than that. What more is being said? Or, what is the specific force of such descriptions in respect of which they differ both from one another and from 'neat' descriptions of sensations, supposing that we could produce such descriptions? The questions, that is, are not questions of the para-mechanical form 'How do we see robins?', but questions of the form, 'How do we use such descriptions as "he saw a robin"?'

When we describe someone as having detected a mosquito in the room, what more are we saying than that there was a certain sort of singing in his ears? We begin by answering that he not only had a singing in his ears but also recognised or identified what he heard as the noise of a fairly adjacent mosquito; and we are inclined to go on to say in more generic terms that he was not only having a singing in his ears, but was also thinking certain thoughts; perhaps that he was subsuming the singing under a concept, or that he was coupling an intellectual process with his sensitive state. But in saying this sort of thing, though we have one foot on the right track, we also have one foot on the wrong track. We are beginning to go on the wrong track, when we say that there must have taken place such and such conceptual or discursive processes; since this is in effect, if not in intention, to say that detecting a mosquito could not happen, unless some special but unobserved ghostly wheels had gone round, wheels whose existence and functions only epistemologists are clever enough to diagnose. On the other hand, in saying this sort of thing we are also on the right track. It is certainly true that a man could not detect a mosquito if he did not know what mosquitoes were and what they sounded like; or if, through absent-mindedness, panic or stupidity, he failed to apply this knowledge to the present situation; for this is part of what 'detecting' means.

We do not, that is, want tidings or hypotheses about any other things which the listener may have privily done or undergone. Even if there had taken place three, or seventeen, such *entr'actes,* news about them would not explain how detecting a mosquito differs from having a shrill singing in the ears. What we want to know is how the logical behaviour of 'he detected a mosquito' differs from that of 'there was a singing in his ears', from that of 'he tried in vain to make out what was making the noise', and from that of 'he mistook it for the noise of the wind in the telephone wires'.

RECOGNISING A TUNE

Let us consider a slightly different situation in which a person would be described as not merely hearing something, and not merely listening to something, and not merely trying to make out what he was hearing, but as identifying or recognising what he heard, namely the case of a person who recognises a tune. For this situation to obtain, there must be notes played in his hearing, so he must not be deaf, or anaesthetised, or fast asleep. Recognising what he hears entails hearing. It also entails heeding; the absent-minded or distracted man is not following the tune. But more than this, he must have met this tune before; and he must not only have met it, but also have learned it and not forgotten it. If he did not in this sense already know the tune, he could not be said to recognise it on listening to it now.

What then is it for a person to know a tune, that is to have learned and not forgotten it? It certainly does not entail his being able to tell its name, for it may have no name; and even if he gave it the wrong name, he might still be said to know the tune. Nor does it entail his being able to describe the tune in words, or write it out in musical notation, for few of us could do that, though most of us can recognise tunes. He need not even be able to hum or whistle the tune, though if he can do so, he certainly knows the tune; and if he can hum or whistle plenty of other tunes, but cannot produce this one, even when prompted, we suspect that he does not know this tune. To describe him as knowing the tune is at the least to say that he is capable of recognising it, when he hears it; and he will be said to recognise it, when he hears it, if he does any, some or all of the following things: if, after hearing a bar or two, he expects those bars to follow which do follow; if he does not erroneously expect the previous bars to be repeated; if he detects omissions or errors in the performance; if, after the music has been switched off for a few moments, he expects it to resume about where it does resume; if, when several people are whistling different tunes, he can pick out who is whistling this tune; if he can beat time correctly; if he can accompany it by whistling or humming it in time and tune, and so on indefinitely. And when we speak of him expecting the notes which are due to follow and not expecting notes or bars which are not due to follow, we do not require that he be actually thinking ahead. Given that he is surprised, scornful or amused, if the due notes and bars do not come at their due times, then it is true to say that he was expecting them, even though it is false to say that he went through any processes of anticipating them.

In short, he is now recognising or following the tune, if, knowing how it goes, he is now using that knowledge; and he uses that knowledge not just by hearing the tune, but by hearing it in a special frame of mind, the frame of mind of being ready to hear both what he is now hearing and what he will hear, or would be about to hear, if the pianist continues playing it and is playing it correctly. He knows how it goes and he now hears the notes as the progress of that tune. He hears them according to the recipe of the tune, in the sense that what he hears is what he is listening for. Yet the complexity of this description of him as both hearing the notes, as they come, and listening for, or being ready for, the notes that do, and the notes that should, come does not imply that he is going through a complex of operations. He need not, for example, be coupling with his hearing of the notes any silent or murmured prose-moves, or 'subsuming' what he hears 'under the concept of the tune'. Indeed, if he were told to think the thought of 'Lillibullero', without producing, imagining or actually listening to the tune itself, he would say that there was nothing left for him to think; and if he were told that the fact that he could recognise the tune, even though played in various ways in various situations, meant that he had a Concept, or Abstract Idea, of the tune, he would properly object that he could not think what it would be like to be considering or applying the Abstract Idea of 'Lillibullero', unless this meant merely that he could recognise the tune, when he heard it, detect mistakes and omissions in it, hum snatches from it and so on.

This enables us to reconsider what was said earlier, namely, that a person who recognises what he hears is not only having auditory sensations, but is also thinking. It is not true that a person following a familiar tune need be thinking thoughts such that there must be an answer to the question, 'What thoughts has he been thinking?' or even 'What general concepts has he been applying?' It is not true that he must have been pondering or declaring propositions to himself, or to the company, in English or French; and it is not true that he must have been marshalling any visual or auditory images. What is true is that he must have been in some degree vigilant, and the notes that he heard must have fallen as he expected them to fall, or shocked him by not doing so. He was neither merely listening, as one might listen to an unfamiliar air, nor yet was he necessarily coupling his listening with some other process; he was just listening according to the recipe.

To clarify further the senses in which following a known tune is and is not 'thinking', let us consider the case of a person hearing a waltz for the first time. He does not know how this tune goes, but since he knows how some other waltz tunes go, he knows what sorts of rhythms to expect. He is partially but not fully prepared for the succeeding bars, and he can partially but not completely place the notes already heard and now being heard. He is wondering just how the tune goes, and in wondering he is trying to piece out the arrangement of the notes. At no moment is he quite ready for the note that is due next. That is, he is thinking in the special sense of trying to puzzle something out.

But, in contrast with him, the person who already knows the tune follows the tune without any business of puzzling or trying to make out how the tune goes. It is completely obvious to him all the time. There need be no activity, not even a very swift and very easy activity, of trying to resolve uncertainties, for there are no uncertainties. He is not listening in a worrying-out way; he is just listening. Yet he is not merely hearing notes, for he is hearing 'Lillibullero'. Not only are the notes clearly audible to him (perhaps they are not), but the tune is quite obvious to him; and the obviousness of the tune is not a fact about his auditory sensitiveness, it is a fact about what he has learned and not forgotten and his present application of those lessons.

Finally, though following a familiar tune entails having become familiarised with it, it does not require going through any operations of reminiscence. Memories of past hearings of the tune need not well up, or be called up. The sense of 'thinking' in which a person following a familiar tune can be said to be thinking what he is hearing, is not that thoughts of past auditions are occurring to him. He has not forgotten how it goes, but he is not recalling how it formerly went.

Roughly, to know how a tune goes is to have acquired a set of auditory expectation propensities, and to recognise or follow a tune is to be hearing expected note after expected note. And this does not entail the occurrence of any other exercises of expectation than listening for what is being heard and what is due to be heard. The description of a person hearing expected notes is indeed different from that of a person hearing unexpected notes and from that of a person who hears notes without any expectations at all, (like a person who is hearing but not listening); but this does not mean that there is something extra going on in the first person which is not going on in the second or the third. It means that the hearing is going on in a different way, the description of which difference involves, not a report of extra occurrences, but only the characterisation of his hearing as specially schooled hearing. That a person is following a tune is, if you like, a fact both about his ears and about his mind; but it is not a conjunction of one fact about his ears and another fact about his mind, or a conjoint report of one incident in his sensitive life and another incident in his intellectual life. . . .

RECOGNISING A THIMBLE

We can now turn to consider some of the kinds of perceptual episodes which are ordinarily taken as the standard models of perceptual recognition. We shall see that they are in many important respects of a piece with the recognition of a tune. I chose to start with the example of someone following a familiar tune, because this is a protracted occupation. We can see a gate-post in a flash, but we cannot hear 'Lillibullero' in a flash. There is here, consequently, no temptation to postulate the occurrence of lightning intellectual processes, processes too rapid to be noticed, but intellectual enough to execute all the Herculean labours demanded by epistemologists.

When a person is described as having seen the thimble, part of what is said is that he has had at least one visual sensation, but a good deal more is said as well. Theorists commonly construe this as meaning that a description of a person as having seen the thimble both says that he had at least one visual sensation and says that he did or underwent something else as well; and they ask accordingly, 'What else did the finder of the thimble do or undergo, such that he would not have found the thimble if he had not done or undergone these extra things?' Their queries are then answered by stories about some very swift and unnoticed inferences, or some sudden and unrememberable intellectual leaps, or some fetching up of concepts and clapping them upon the heads of the visual data. They assume, that is, that because the proposition 'he espied the thimble' has a considerable logical complexity, it therefore reports a considerable complication of processes. And as these processes are not witnessed going on, it is postulated that they must be going on in a place where they cannot be witnessed, namely, in the finder's stream of consciousness.

Our analysis of what we have in mind, when we say that someone recognises a tune, can be applied to the new case. Certainly a person who espies the thimble is recognising what he sees, and this certainly entails not only that he has a visual sensation, but also that he has already learned and not forgotten what thimbles look like. He has learned enough of the recipe for the looks of thimbles to recognise thimbles, when he sees them in ordinary lights and positions at ordinary distances and from ordinary angles. When he espies the thimble on this occasion, he is applying his lesson; he is actually doing what he has learned to do. Knowing how thimbles look, he is ready to anticipate, though he need not actually anticipate, how it will look, if he approaches it, or moves away from it; and when, without having executed any such anticipations, he does approach it, or move away from it, it looks as he was prepared for it to look. When the actual glimpses of it that he gets are got according to the thimble recipe, they satisfy his acquired expectation-propensities; and this is his espying the thimble.

As with the tune, so with the thimble; if the recognition is impeded by no difficulties, if, that is, the thimble is obvious to the observer from the first glance, then no extra thinking or pondering, no puzzlings or reminiscences need to be performed. He need not say anything in English or in French, to himself or to the world; he need not marshal memory images or fancy images; he need not wonder, make conjectures, or take precautions; he need not recall past episodes; he need do nothing that would be described as the thinking of thoughts, though, if linguistically equipped, he can be expected to be ready to do some of these things, if there arises any call to do so. The sense in which he is thinking and not merely having a visual sensation, is that he is having a visual sensation in a thimble-seeing frame of mind. Just as a person who recognises a tune from the first few bars is prepared both retrospectively for those already heard and those now being heard and prospectively for the bars that are to follow, though he goes through no additional operations of preparing for them, so a person who recognises a cow at sight is prepared for a multifarious variety of sights, sounds and smells, of none of which need the thought actually occur to him.

SENSATIONS ARE NOT CLUES

The difficulty will probably be felt that even if this sort of account of the visual obviousness of thimbles and the auditory obviousness of tunes is true, the real question remains unanswered. How do we learn that there are thimbles in the first place? How can a person who starts with mere sensations reach the stage of finding out that there are physical objects? But this is a queer sort of how-question, since, construing it in one way, we all know the answer perfectly well. We know how infants come to learn that some noises do, and others do not, belong to tunes; that some tuneless sequences of noises, like nursery rhymes, have recognisable rhythms; others, like clock-noises, have recognisable monotonies; while yet others, like rattle-noises, are random and disorderly. We know, too, the sorts of games and exercises by which mothers and nurses teach their infants lessons of these sorts. There is no more of an epistemological puzzle involved in describing how infants learn perception recipes than there is in describing how boys learn to bicycle. They learn by practice, and we can specify the sorts of practice that expedite this learning.

Now clearly stories about learning by practice will not be felt to give the solution of the how-question asked above. This question was not intended as a question about the stages through which capacities and interests develop, or about the aids and impediments to their development. What then was intended? Perhaps its poser might say something like this. 'There is, perhaps, no philosophical puzzle about how children learn tunes, or recognise them, when they have once learned them. Nor perhaps is there a puzzle about analogous learning of recipes in respect of sights, tastes and smells. But there is a big difference between learning a tune and finding out that there are such things as violins, thimbles, cows and gate-posts. Finding out that there are material objects requires, as learning tunes does not, getting beyond noises, sights, tastes and smells to public existents other than, and independent of, our personal sensations. And by the metaphorical expression 'getting beyond' is meant getting to know that such objects exist on the basis of originally knowing only that these sensations exist. Our puzzle is, therefore, in accordance with what principles, and from what premises, can a person validly conclude that cows and gate-posts exist? Or, if by some lucky instinct he correctly believes such things without inferences, by what inferences can he justify these instinctive beliefs?' That is, the how-question is to be construed as a Sherlock Holmes question of the type 'what evidence had the detective ascertained which enabled him to confirm his suspicion that the gamekeeper was the murderer?' And construing the question in this way, we can swiftly see that it is an improper question. When we speak of the evidence ascertained by the detective, we are thinking of things which he or his informants had observed or witnessed, such as fingerprints found on glasses and conversations overheard by eavesdroppers. But a sensation is not something which its owner observes or witnesses. It is not a clue. Listening to a conversation entails having auditory sensations, for listening is heedful hearing, and hearing entails getting auditory sensations. But having sensations is not discovering clues. We discover clues by listening to conversations and looking at fingerprints. If we could not observe some things, we should not have clues for other things, and conversations are just the sorts of things to which we do listen, as fingerprints and gate-posts are just the sorts of things at which we do look.

This improper how-question is tempting, partly because there is a tendency mistakenly to suppose that all learning is discovery by inference from previously ascertained evidence; and then a process of sensing sense data is cast for the role of ascertaining the initial evidence. In fact, of course, we learn how to make inferences from previously ascertained facts just as we learn how to play chess, ride bicycles, or recognise gate-posts; namely by practice, reinforced, maybe, by some schooling. The application of rules of inference is not a condition of learning by practice; it is just one of the countless things learned by practice.

As has been shown, listening and looking are not merely having sensations; nor, however, are they joint processes of observing sensations and inferring to common objects. A person listening or looking is doing something which he would not do, if he were deaf or blind; or, what is quite different, if he were absent-minded, distracted or quite uninterested; or, what is quite different again, if he had not learned to use his ears and eyes. Observing is using one's ears and eyes. But using one's ears and eyes does not entail using, in a different sense, one's visual and auditory sensations as clues. It makes no sense to speak of 'using' sensations. It will not even do to say that in watching a cow, I am finding out about the cow 'by means of' visual sensations, since this too would suggest that sensations are tools, objects which can be handled in the same sorts of ways as the things seen and heard can be handled. And this would be even more misleading than it would be to say that manipulating a hammer involves first manipulating my fingers, or that I control the hammer by dint of controlling my fingers.

SENSATIONS ARE NOT RAW MATERIALS

There is another favourite model for the description of sensations. As flour, sugar, milk, eggs and currants are among the raw materials out of which the confectioner concocts cakes, or as bricks and timber are among the raw materials of the builder, so sensations are often spoken of as the raw materials out of which we construct the world we know. As a counterblast to even more misleading stories this story had some important merits. But the notions of collecting, storing, sorting, unpacking, treating, assembling and arranging, which apply to the ingredients of cakes and the materials of houses do not apply to sensations. We can ask what a cake is made of, but not what knowledge is made of; we can ask what those ingredients are to be made into, but not what is going to be concocted or constructed out of the visual and auditory sensations which the child has recently been having.

CONCLUSION

We can conclude, then, that there is no difference of principle, though there are plenty of differences in detail, between recognising tunes and recognising gate-posts. One such difference may be mentioned, before we leave the subject. At a fairly early stage of infancy, the child learns to coordinate, for example, the sight recipes, the sound recipes and the feel recipes of things like rattles and kittens; and having begun to learn how things of particular sorts can be expected to look, sound and feel, he then begins to learn how they behave; when, for example, the rattle or the kitten makes a noise and when it makes none. He now observes things in an experimental way. But the relatively contemplative business of learning tunes does not, by itself, involve much co-ordination of looks with sounds, or give much room for experimentation. But this is a difference of degree, not one of kind.

One or two residual points should receive brief notice. First, in talking of a person learning a perception recipe, I am not talking of his discovering any causal laws, such as those of physiology, optics or mechanics. The observation of common objects is prior to the discovery of general correlations between special kinds of common objects. Next, in talking of a person knowing a perception recipe, e.g. knowing how common objects are due to look, sound and feel, I am not crediting him with the ability to formulate or impart this recipe. Somewhat as most people know how to tie a few different sorts of knots, but are quite incapable of describing those knots, or following spoken or printed descriptions of them, so we all know how to identify a cow at sight a very long time before we can tell the world anything about the visible marks by which we recognise it, and quite an appreciable time before we can draw, paint or even recognise pictures of cows. Indeed, if we did not learn to recognise things on sight or hearing, before we had learnt to talk about them, we could never start at all. Talking and understanding talk themselves involve recognising words on saying and hearing them.

Though I have drawn most of my instances of seeing according to perception recipes from cases of non-mistaken observation, such as espying a gate-post, where there is a gate-post, the same general account holds for mistaken observations such as 'espying' a huntsman, where there is really a pillar box, 'discerning' a stick, where there is really a shadow, or 'seeing' a snake on the eiderdown, when there is really nothing on the eiderdown. Getting a thing wrong entails what getting it right entails, namely, the use of a technique. A person is not careless, if he has not learned a method, but only if he has learned it and does not apply it properly. Only a person who can balance can lose his balance; only a person who can reason can commit fallacies; only a person who can discriminate huntsmen from pillar boxes can mistake a pillar box for a huntsman; and only a person who knows what snakes look like can fancy he sees a snake without realising that he is only fancying.

QUESTIONS

1. What is the theoretical importance of describing sensations by referring to common objects?
2. What does Professor Ryle mean when he says that we do not employ a "neat" sensation vocabulary?

3. What is the importance of Ryle's claim that observing is a task and having sensations is not?
4. How does Ryle argue against the claim that a person may observe his own sensations? Are his arguments convincing?
5. What is the importance of Ryle's distinguishing between my observing my sensations and my noticing them?
6. In what sense are my sensations private to me?
7. How sound is Ryle's argument that sensations are neither things nor episodes?
8. What two uses of "to observe" does Ryle notice?
9. What is the "prisoner" model of perception and how does Ryle criticize it?
10. What more is there to observation besides having at least one sensation?
11. How does Ryle's discussion of recognizing a tune illuminate other instances of successful observing?
12. How does Ryle argue against the claim that our knowledge of objects is built up from our knowledge of our sensations?
13. What does Ryle mean by a perception recipe, and what is the relevance of this notion to the question "How does someone come to know that there are violins, thimbles, cows, and gate-posts?"
14. Do you think Ryle's discussion as a whole completely undercuts the view that the objects of knowledge are ideas in the mind of the knower (Locke and Berkeley)?

3. FRIEDRICH WAISMANN

(1896–1959)

Facts and Language

Friedrich Waismann was born in Vienna, Austria. He was educated at the University of Vienna, and began his teaching career there. Forced to flee Austria when the Nazis took over the country, he went to England. He taught first at Cambridge, and then at Oxford, where he was Senior Lecturer in the Philosophy of Mathematics at the time of his death. He had a remarkable command of English idioms, and, as in this selection, he often drew on this knowledge for philosophical insights. He was the author of a number of papers, and of *Introduction to Mathematical Thinking* (1936) and

The Principles of Linguistic Philosophy, published posthumously (1965).

Waismann's topic here is the relation of facts and language. In Locke's theory of knowledge, the observer's mind is characterized as a white paper innocently open to whatever impress the world outside cares to make upon it. In contrast with Locke's views, Waismann considers a wide range of examples which illustrate how an observer's way of looking at things has a bearing on what he finds. Under Waismann's careful scrutiny the innocent recipient of impressions evaporates, and the independence of a world of facts appears to be not all that independent. Yet Waismann offers no simple rule for assessing the impingement of "the world of words" on "the world of facts." Rather the wide range of examples is intended to alert the reader to the variety and extent of the relation between language and fact.

This selection is drawn from Part III of the essay "Verifiability."

From "Verifiability," *Aristotelian Society Supplementary Volume 19,* by Friedrich Waismann, Harrison & Sons, Ltd., London, 1945. Reprinted by permission of the Aristotelian Society.

People are inclined to think that there is a world of facts as opposed to a world of words which describe these facts. I am not too happy about that. Consider an example. We are accustomed to see colour as a "quality" of objects. That is, colour cannot subsist by itself, but must inhere in a thing. This conception springs from the way we express ourselves. When colour is rendered by an adjective, colour is conceived as an attribute of things, i.e. as something that can have no independent existence. That, however, is not the only way of conceiving colour. There are languages such as Russian, German, Italian, which render colour by means of verbs. If we were to imitate this usage in English by allowing some such form as "The sky blues," we should come face to face with the question, Do I mean the same fact when I say "The sky blues" as when I say "The sky is blue"? I don't think so. We say "The sun shines," "Jewels glitter," "The river shimmers," "Windows gleam," "Stars twinkle," etc.; that is, in the case of phenomena of lustre we make use of a verbal mode of expression. Now in rendering colour phenomena by verbs we assimilate them more closely to the phenomena of lustre; and in doing so we alter not only our manner of speaking but our entire way of apprehending colour. We *see* the blue differently now—a hint that language affects our whole mode of apprehension. In the word "blueing" we are clearly aware of an active, verbal element. On that account "being blue" is not quite equivalent to "blueing," since it lacks what is peculiar to the verbal mode of expression. The sky which "blues" is seen as something that continually brings forth blueness—it radiates blueness, so to speak; blue does not inhere in it as a mere quality, rather is it felt as the vital pulse of the sky; there is a faint suggestion of the operating of some force behind the phenomenon. It's hard to get the feel of it in English; perhaps it may help you to liken this mode of expression to the impressionist way of painting which is at bottom a new way of seeing: the impressionist sees in colour an immediate manifestation of reality, a free agent no longer bound up with things.

There are, then, different linguistic means of rendering colour. When this is done by means of adjectives, colour is conceived as an attribute of things. The learning of such a language involves for everyone who speaks it his being habituated to see colour as a "quality" of objects. This conception becomes thus incorporated into his picture of the world. The verbal mode of expression detaches colour from things: it enables us to see colour as a phenomenon with a life of its own. Adjective and verb thus represent two different worlds of thought.

There is also an adverbial way of talking about colour. Imagine a language with a wealth of expressions for all shades of lustre, but without adjectives for colours; colours, as a rule, are ignored; *when* they are expressed, this is done by adding an adverb to the word that specifies the sort of lustre. Thus the people who use this sort of language would say, "The sea is glittering golden in the sunshine," "The evening clouds glow redly," "There in the depth a shadow greenly gleams." In such phrases colour would lose the last trace of independence and be reduced to a mere modification of lustre. Just as we in our language cannot say "That's very," but only some such thing as "That's very brilliant," so in the language considered we could not say "That's bluish," but only, e.g., "That's shining bluishly." There can be little doubt that, owing to this circumstance, the users of such language would find it very hard to see colour as a quality of things. For them it would not be the *things* that are coloured, rather colour would reside in the lustre as it glows and darkens and changes—evidence that they would see the world with different eyes.

"But isn't it still true to say that I have the same experience whenever I look up at the sky?" You would be less happy if you were asked, "Do you have the same experience when you look at a picture puzzle and see a figure in it as before, when you didn't see it?" You may, perhaps, say you see the same lines, though each time in a different arrangement. Now what exactly corresponds to this different arrangement in the case when I look up at the sky? One might say: we are aware of the blue, but this awareness is itself tinged and coloured by the whole linguistic background which brings into prominence, or weakens and hides certain analogies. In this sense language does affect the whole manner in which we become aware of a fact: the fact articulates itself differently, so to speak. In urging that you *must* have the same experience whenever you look at the sky you forget that the term "experience" is itself ambiguous: whether it is taken, e.g., to include or to exclude all the various analogies which a certain mode of expression calls up. . . .

I have observed that when the clock strikes in the night and I, already half asleep, am too tired to count the strokes, I am seized by an impression that the sequence will never end—as though it would go on, stroke after stroke, in an unending measureless procession. The whole thing vanishes as soon as I *count*. Counting frees me, as it were, from the dark formlessness impending over me. (Is this not a parable of the rational?) It seems to me that one could say here that counting *alters* the quality of the experience.

Now is it the same fact which I perceive when counting and when not counting?

Again, suppose there is a tribe whose members count "one, two, three, a few, many." Suppose a man of this tribe looking at a flock of birds said "A few birds" whereas I should say "Five birds"—is it the same fact for him as it is for me? If in such a case I pass to a language of a different structure, I can no longer describe "the same" fact, but only another one more or less resembling the first. What, then, is the objective reality supposed to be described by language?

What rebels in us against such a suggestion is the feeling that the fact is there objectively no matter in which way we render it. I perceive something that exists and put it into words. From this it seems to follow that fact is something that exists independent of, and prior to language; language merely serves the end of communication. What we are liable to overlook here is that the way we see a fact—i.e. what we emphasize and what we disregard—is *our* work. "The sun-beams trembling on the floating tides" (Pope). Here a fact is something that emerges out from, and takes shape against a background. The background may be, e.g., my visual field; something that rouses my attention detaches itself from this field, is brought into focus and apprehended linguistically; that is what we call a fact. A fact is noticed; and by being noticed it becomes a fact. "Was it then no fact before you noticed it?" It was, if I *could* have noticed it. In a language in which there is only the number series "one, two, three, a few, many," a fact such as "There are five birds" is imperceptible.

To make my meaning still clearer consider a language in which description does not take the form of sentences. Examples of such a description would be supplied by a map, a picture language, a film, the musical notation. A map, for instance, should not be taken as a conjunction of single statements each of which describes a separate fact. For what, would you say, is the boundary of a fact? Where does the one end and the other begin? If we think of such types of description, we are no longer tempted to say, that a country, or a story told in a film, or a melody must consist of "facts." Here we begin to see how confusing the idea is according to which the world is a cluster of facts—just as if it were a sort of mosaic made up of little coloured stones. Reality is undivided. What we may have in mind is perhaps that *language* contains units, viz. *sentences*. In describing reality, by using sentences, we draw, as it were, lines through it, limit a part and call what corresponds with such a sentence a fact. In other words, language is the knife with which we cut out facts. (This account is oversimplified as it doesn't take notice of *false* statements.)

Reality, then, is not made up of facts in the sense in which a plant is made up of cells, a house of bricks, a stone of molecules; rather, if you want a simile, a fact is present, in much the same sense in which a character manifests itself in a face. Not that I invent the character and read it into the face; no, the character is somehow written on the face but no one would on that account say that a face is "made up" of features symbolic of such-and-such traits. Just as we have to interpret a face, so we have to interpret reality. The elements of such an interpretation, without our being aware of it, are already present in language—for instance, in such moulds as the notion of thinghood, of causality, of number, or again in the way we render colour, etc.

Noticing a fact may be likened to seeing a face in a cloud, or a figure in an arrangement of dots, or suddenly becoming aware of the solution of a picture puzzle: one views a complex of elements as one, reads a sort of unity into it, etc. Language supplies us with a means of comprehending and categorizing; and different languages categorize differently.

"But surely noticing a face in a cloud is not inventing it?" Certainly not; only you might not have noticed it unless you had already had the experience of human faces somewhere else. Does this not throw a light on what constitutes the noticing of facts? I would not dream for a moment of saying that I *invent* them; I might, however, be unable to perceive them if I had not certain moulds of comprehension ready at hand. These forms I borrow from language. Language, then, *contributes to the formation and participates in the constitution* of a fact; which, of course, does not mean that it *produces* the fact.

QUESTIONS

1. What does Waismann mean by "fact"? Does "fact" have any other meanings?
2. How does Waismann argue against the claim that there is a world of facts in opposition to a world of words which describe these facts?
3. Evaluate the advantages and disadvantages of Waismann's account of reality. For instance, does Waismann fail to appreciate our desire that reality have a certain permanence?
4. Is Waismann's account of the relation of facts and language damaged by posing the dilemma: Which came first, facts or the forms of language?

SUGGESTED FURTHER READING

INTRODUCTORY STUDIES

Austin, J. L., *Sense and Sensibilia,* Oxford University Press, New York, 1962.

Ayer, A. J., *The Problem of Knowledge,* Penguin Books, Harmondsworth, Middlesex, Eng., 1956. Especially Chaps. 1, "Philosophy and Knowledge"; 2, "Scepticism and Certainty"; and 3, "Perception."

Chisholm, Roderick M., *Theory of Knowledge,* Prentice-Hall, Englewood Cliffs, N. J., to be published.

Hirst, R. J., ed., *Perception and the External World,* Macmillan, New York, 1965. (Anthology.)

Hospers, John, *An Introduction to Philosophical Analysis,* Prentice-Hall, Englewood Cliffs, N. J., 1953. Chap. 6, "Perceiving the World."

Ryle, Gilbert, *Dilemmas,* Cambridge University Press, London, 1954. "Perception."

Woozley, A. D., *Theory of Knowledge,* Hutchinson's University Library, London, 1949.

ADVANCED STUDIES

Armstrong, D. M., *Perception and the Physical World,* Routledge and Kegan Paul, London, 1961.

Chisholm, Roderick M., *Perceiving: A Philosophical Study,* Cornell University Press, Ithaca, N. Y., 1957.

Hamlyn, D. W., *Sensation and Perception,* Routledge and Kegan Paul, London, 1961.

Lean, Martin E., *Sense-Perception and Matter,* Routledge and Kegan Paul, London, 1953.

Lewis, C. I., *Mind and the World Order,* Scribner's, New York, 1929.

Sellars, Wilfrid, *Science, Perception and Reality,* Routledge and Kegan Paul, London, 1963.

Chapter 2. Knowing and Stating One's Knowledge

When someone wishes to communicate to other persons his knowledge of violets or Napoleon or the square root of minus one, he makes statements about what he knows. Making statements is certainly not the only use to which language may be put; but it is probably the use which philosophers have most often studied. They have tried to sort statements according to how their truth or falsity is to be ascertained. As we shall see, this has not been a simple task, but its consequences are of the greatest importance. For philosophers have thought that the status of mathematics, history, the natural and social sciences, metaphysics, ethics, aesthetics, and theology as *knowledge* is to be determined by finding out how the truth or falsity of their statements may be known.

Philosophers of the Seventeenth and Eighteenth Centuries, stimulated by contemporary advances in mathematics and the natural sciences, were especially interested in the communication of knowledge, and in elucidating the grounds for belief. They wished that everyone hearing (or reading) a statement might know at least in principle the way in which its truth is established. Leibniz (1646–1716), for example, distinguished two different kinds of statements, calling them truths of reason and truths of fact. "Truths of reasoning are necessary and their opposite is impossible; those of fact are contingent and their opposite is possible." [1]

We may take Leibniz's rule as a starting point for a brief survey of the ways for distinguishing statements that have been proposed by philosophers. Consider the two statements, "A bachelor is a man of marriageable age who

[1] *The Monadology*, Para. 33.

has not married," and "Harry is a bachelor." We count the first statement as a truth of reason, for in Leibniz's phrase, its "opposite is impossible," that is, we should never call a man who is now married or who was once married a bachelor, for a bachelor can only be a man who has not married. We might go on to say that the truth of the statement we are considering is necessary, because it states just what we mean by "bachelor"; and so long as we stick to our meaning, the opposite could never be true. That is, the opposite is necessarily false or self-contradictory. This account of truths of reason would make their subject matter largely definitions or statements that are the consequences of definitions. For example, "A bachelor is a man of marriageable age who has not married" is a definition; and "No bachelor has a mother-in-law" is a statement which is a true consequence of that definition.

We count "Harry is a bachelor" as a truth of fact, for we cannot ascertain its truth or falsity unless we have some acquaintance with Harry and his past. The opposite of "Harry is a bachelor" is possible, and we must look to see whether Harry is or is not one. This is what is meant by saying that a truth of fact is contingent. To put the point negatively, "Harry is a bachelor" is not a truth of reason, for it is not a definition and we cannot find out its truth or falsity only by consulting the meaning of the words in it.

The first reading in this chapter is a discussion by David Hume of these two kinds of statements. Hume's terminology differs from Leibniz's, but what Hume calls relations-of-ideas statements correspond to Leibniz's truths of reason, and what Hume calls matters-of-fact statements correspond to Leibniz's truths of fact. Having distinguished these two kinds of statement, Hume goes on to offer what has become the classic analysis of our grounds for belief in matters of fact.

Hume held that the distinction between relations of ideas and matters of fact is exhaustive, and every sentence that is a statement must be about one or the other. Immanuel Kant, who respected Hume's work, argued nonetheless that there is a third kind of statement which is neither a contingent, matter-of-fact statement nor a necessary, relation-of-ideas statement. This third kind of statement is a necessary, matter-of-fact statement. Readers acquainted with the Descartes selection that opens Part One of this book may recall that after Descartes rejected, for skeptical reasons, both (1) knowledge gained by or through the senses and (2) the sort of knowledge of which arithmetic and geometry are examples, he found a sort of knowledge that he regarded as indubitably true: "I am, I exist is necessarily true each time that I pronounce it, or that I mentally conceive it." "I am, I exist" is certainly about existence, or a matter of fact, and would appear to be contingent; but Descartes calls this assertion necessarily true. We have here, then, a necessary, matter-of-fact statement, the third kind of statement which Kant argues for.

Kant's terminology for the classification of statements differs from that of both Leibniz and Hume. Kant takes into account both the forms of statements and the ways in which their truth or falsity is established. In form a statement may be either analytic or synthetic. An analytic statement is one whose predicate adds nothing new to the subject, but merely develops an idea already present in the subject. "A bachelor is a man of marriageable age who has not married" is, thus, an analytic statement, for "a man of mar-

riageable age who has not married" is identical with "bachelor" and is in that sense but a development, or expansion of it. In contrast with analytic, a synthetic statement is one whose predicate *adds* a new idea to the subject. "Harry is a bachelor" is synthetic in that it tells us something new about Harry. In Kantian terminology, the predicate is added to and not found in the subject.

Kant's distinction regarding the ways in which the truth of statements is established is marked by the terms "a priori" and "a posteriori." "A posteriori" means "by or through experience"; "a priori" means "without appeal to experience." An example of a statement whose truth is established a priori is "A bachelor is a man of marriageable age who has not married." An example of a statement whose truth is established a posteriori is "Harry is a bachelor."

For Kant, then, Leibniz's truths of reason (and Hume's relations-of-idea statements) are analytic and a priori, and Leibniz's truths of fact (and Hume's matter-of-fact statements) are synthetic and a posteriori. In addition to these two kinds of statements, the third sort for which Kant argues is, in his terminology, synthetic and a priori. Contrary to both Leibniz and Hume, Kant argues that mathematics affords examples of statements that are both synthetic and a priori. Other examples of synthetic a priori statements are to be found, according to Kant, in metaphysics and ethics. Kant's exposition and justification of his classification of statements forms the second reading in this chapter. The third reading, "A Defense of Synthetic Necessary Truth" by Stephen Toulmin is a modern consideration and justification of Kant's claims for this third sort of statement.

4. DAVID HUME

(1711–76)

Relations of Ideas and Matters of Fact

David Hume was born in Edinburgh, Scotland, and educated at the University of Edinburgh. At the age of 23, he went to France where he lived for three years; it was during this period that he wrote his great philosophical work, *A Treatise of Human Nature.* Although this was to become one of the most famous and influential books ever written in philosophy, it did not attract much attention during Hume's life, and his fame rested more on his *History of England* and his writings on religion. His principal philosophical writings are: *A Treatise of Human Nature* (1738–40); *An Enquiry Concerning Human Understanding* (1748; a restatement of the material of Book I of the *Treatise*); *An Enquiry Concerning the Principles of Morals* (1751; a restatement of the material of Book III of the *Treatise*); *The Natural History of Religion* (1757); and *Dialogues Concerning Natural Religion* (published posthumously).

Hume divides all knowledge into two fundamentally different kinds, which he calls "relations of ideas" and "matters of fact." The reader may best understand Hume's distinction between these two kinds of knowledge if he thinks of it as a way of classifying two different kinds of statements: those which express relations of ideas and those which express matters of

fact. A statement that expresses a relation of ideas is either a definition or one whose truth or falsity depends on a definition. For example, the statement "A bachelor is a man who has not married" is a definition or, to use Hume's terms, expresses a "relation of ideas." Thus the word "bachelor" is interchangeable with the phrase "a man who has not married," and hence is not interchangeable with the phrase "married man." An important consequence follows from any agreement about the definition of words, which may be illustrated by means of what has just been said about "bachelor." If someone says, "Harry is a bachelor," then we know immediately that the statement "Harry has not married" is true, for this is what "bachelor" means. No one can say first, "Harry is a bachelor," and then say, "Harry is married," because he would be contradicting himself, i.e., making two incompatible statements. For if one abides by the definition of "bachelor," one cannot say that someone is both a bachelor and married. The most important area in which relations of ideas figure is mathematical knowledge, and Hume's examples are drawn from mathematics. When he says that "The square of the hypotenuse is equal to the sum of the squares of the other two sides" (The Pythagorean Theorem) is demonstratively certain, he means that it follows undeniably from the original definitions, axioms and postulates, and the preceding theorems of Euclidean geometry, in the same way that "Harry has no mother-in-law" follows from "Harry is a bachelor."

In contrast with statements which express relations of ideas, statements which express matters of fact depend for their truth or falsity not on our definitions of words, but on our experience of the world. For example, if someone tells us that he has a friend named "Harry," we may think of Harry as being tall or short, thin or fat, married or unmarried; for until we know more about Harry we may think of him in any way we like. Without either being told about Harry or meeting and talking with him, we have no way of deciding whether, for instance, "Harry is married" or its contrary "Harry is not married" is true. Hence, these statements are examples of statements which express matters of fact.

The distinction between relations of ideas and matters of fact is of enormous importance to Hume; for he argues that our knowledge of the world, which he analyzes as our knowledge of causes and their effects, is a knowledge of matters of fact. Hence, we learn the truth of such causal generalizations as "Fire burns," by experience; but when we meet each new instance of fire, we cannot know without approaching it whether it might burn us. For each of the ideas, "it will burn" and "it will not burn," is equally compatible with fire, and only experience will enable us to decide between them. Our past experience may incline us to *expect* a fire to burn us, but we can only *know* that it will in a present experience. So, "Fire burns" and similar statements which summarize our knowledge of the world must never

be thought of as definitions or the consequences of definitions, which cannot be false. Unlike mathematical knowledge, our knowledge of the world is not demonstratively certain. Or to use another of Hume's phrases to express this notion, our knowledge of the world is not a priori, i.e., known without experience.

Hume's analysis of our knowledge of cause and effect includes a discussion of what has come to be known as *the principle of the uniformity of nature,* which deserves special notice because of Hume's influence on later philosophy. The principle of the uniformity of nature is also known as *the principle of induction,* for it is assumed whenever we make generalizations about the world on the basis of our experience of particulars. When we conclude "All wood burns" as an (inductive) inference from "This wood burned," "That wood burned," "The other wood burned," etc., we do so only on the assumption that the future will resemble the past. For "All wood burns" is a statement about the wood which we shall experience in the future as well as about the wood which we have experienced in the past.

The question which Hume then asks is: What reasons do we have which could validate the principle of uniformity (that similar causes have similar effects) or of induction (that the future will resemble the past)? He argues that the principle cannot be established as true a priori, and he argues that it cannot be established empirically. (The reader is invited to discover for himself the argument Hume gives in each case.) Since these are the only two ways of knowing, Hume concludes that we must assume this principle without having any reason which justifies our doing so. But even though there are no rational or empirical grounds for making this assumption, we must nevertheless make it whenever we gain knowledge about the world. Hume can only offer us a psychological explanation of how it is that we come to make this assumption, and with this explanation the reading ends.

Hume's skepticism consists in his belief that all of our knowledge of the world rests on a principle which we have no way of verifying or confirming. Ever since Hume raised this point, philosophers have struggled with the fundamental questions it poses concerning the reasonableness of empirical knowledge. The most famous attempt to answer these questions is that of Immanuel Kant in the next selection.

This reading is from Sections IV and V of *An Enquiry Concerning Human Understanding.*

SCEPTICAL DOUBTS CONCERNING THE OPERATIONS OF THE UNDERSTANDING

I

All the objects of human reason or enquiry may naturally be divided into two kinds, to wit, *Relations of Ideas,* and *Matters of Fact.* Of the first kind are the sciences of Geometry, Algebra, and Arithmetic; and in short, every affirmation which is either intuitively or demonstratively certain. *That the square of the hypotenuse is equal to the square of the two sides,* is a proposition which expresses a relation between these figures. *That three times five is equal to the half of thirty,* expresses a relation between these numbers. Propositions of this kind are discoverable by the mere operation of thought, without dependence on what is anywhere existent in the universe. Though there never were a circle or triangle in nature, the truths demonstrated by Euclid would for ever retain their certainty and evidence.

Matters of fact, which are the second objects of human reason, are not ascertained in the same manner; nor is our evidence of their truth, however great, of a like nature with the foregoing. The contrary of every matter of fact is still possible; because it can never imply a contradiction, and is conceived by the mind with the same facility and distinctness, as if ever so conformable to reality. *That the sun will not rise to-morrow* is no less intelligible a proposition, and implies no more contradiction than the affirmation, *that it will rise.* We should in vain, therefore, attempt to demonstrate its falsehood. Were it demonstratively false, it would imply a contradiction, and could never be distinctly conceived by the mind.

It may, therefore, be a subject worthy of curiosity, to enquire what is the nature of that evidence which assures us of any real existence and matter of fact, beyond the present testimony of our senses, or the records of our memory. This part of philosophy, it is observable, has been little cultivated, either by the ancients or moderns; and therefore our doubts and errors, in the prosecution of so important an enquiry, may be the more excusable; while we march through such difficult paths without any guide or direction. They may even prove useful, by exciting curiosity, and destroying that implicit faith and security, which is the bane of all reasoning and free enquiry. The discovery of defects in the common philosophy, if any such there be, will not, I presume, be a discouragement, but rather an incitement, as is usual, to attempt something more full and satisfactory than has yet been proposed to the public.

All reasonings concerning matter of fact seem to be founded on the relation of *Cause and Effect.* By means of that relation alone we can go beyond the evidence of our memory and senses. If you were to ask a man, why he believes any matter of fact, which is absent; for instance, that his friend is in the country, or in France; he would give you a reason; and this reason would be some other fact; as a letter received from him, or the knowledge of his former resolutions and promises. A man finding a watch or any other machine in a desert island, would conclude that there had once been men in that island. All our reasonings concerning fact are of the same nature. And here it is constantly supposed that there is a connexion between the present fact and that which is inferred from it. Were there nothing to bind them together, the inference would be entirely precarious. The hearing of an articulate voice and rational discourse in the dark assures us of the presence of some person: Why? because these are the effects of the human make and fabric, and closely connected with it. If we anatomize all the other reasonings of this nature, we shall find that they are founded on the relation of cause and effect, and that this relation is either near or remote, direct or collateral. Heat and light are collateral effects of fire, and the one effect may justly be inferred from the other.

If we would satisfy ourselves, therefore, concerning the nature of that evidence, which assures us of matters of fact, we must enquire how we arrive at the knowledge of cause and effect.

I shall venture to affirm, as a general proposition, which admits of no exception, that the knowledge of this relation is not, in any instance, attained by reasonings *a priori;* but arises entirely from experience, when we find that any particular objects are constantly conjoined with each other. Let an object be presented to a man of ever so strong natural reason and abilities; if that object be entirely new to him, he will not be able, by the most accurate examination of its sensible qualities, to discover any of its causes or effects. Adam, though his rational faculties be supposed, at the very first, entirely perfect, could not have inferred from the fluidity and transparency of water that it would suffocate him, or from the light and warmth of fire that it would consume him. No object ever discovers, by the qualities which appear to the senses, either the causes which produced it, or the effects which will arise from it; nor can our reason, unassisted by experience, ever draw any inference concerning real existence and matter of fact.

This proposition, *that causes and effects are discoverable, not by reason but by experience,* will readily be admitted with regard to such objects, as we remember to have once been altogether unknown to us; since we must be conscious of the utter inability, which we then lay under, of foretelling what would arise from them. Present two smooth pieces of marble to a man who has no tincture of natural philosophy; he will never discover that they will adhere together in such a manner as to require great force to separate them in a direct line, while they make so small a resistance to a lateral pressure. Such events, as bear little analogy to the common course of nature, are also readily confessed to be known only by experience; nor does any man imagine that the explosion of gunpowder, or the attraction of a loadstone, could ever be discovered by arguments *a priori.* In like manner, when an effect is supposed to depend upon an intricate machinery or secret structure of parts, we make no difficulty in attributing all our knowledge of it to experience. Who will assert that he can give the ultimate reason, why milk or bread is proper nourishment for a man, not for a lion or a tiger?

But the same truth may not appear, at first sight, to have the same evidence with regard to events, which have become familiar to us from our first appearance in the world, which bear a close analogy to the whole course of nature, and which are supposed to depend on the simple qualities of objects, without any secret structure of parts. We are apt to imagine that we could discover these effects by the mere operation of our reason, without experience. We fancy, that were we brought on a sudden into this world, we could at first have inferred that one Billiard-ball would communicate motion to another upon impulse; and that we needed not to have waited for the event, in order to pronounce with certainty concerning it. Such is the influence of custom, that, where it is strongest, it not only covers our natural ignorance, but even conceals itself, and seems not to take place, merely because it is found in the highest degree.

But to convince us that all the laws of nature, and all the operations of bodies without exception, are known only by experience, the following reflections may, perhaps, suffice. Were any object presented to us, and were we required to pronounce concerning the effect which will result from it, without consulting past observation; after what manner, I beseech you, must the mind proceed in this operation? It must invent or imagine some event, which it ascribes to the object as its effect; and it is plain that this invention must be entirely arbitrary. The mind can never possibly find the effect in the supposed cause, by the most accurate scrutiny and examination. For the effect is totally different from the cause, and consequently can never be discovered in it. Motion in the second Billiard-ball is a quite distinct event from motion in the first; nor is there anything in the one to suggest the smallest hint of the other. A stone or piece of metal raised into the air, and left without any support, immediately falls: but to consider the matter *a priori,* is there anything we discover in this situation which can beget the idea of a downward, rather than an upward, or any other motion, in the stone or metal?

And as the first imagination or invention of a particular effect, in all natural operations, is arbitrary, where we consult not experience; so must we also esteem the supposed tie or connexion between the cause and effect, which binds them together, and renders it impossible that any other effect could result from the operation of that cause. When I see, for instance, a Billiard-ball moving in a straight line towards another; even suppose motion in the second ball should by accident be suggested to me, as the result of their contact or impulse; may I not conceive, that a hundred different events might as well follow from that cause? May not both these balls remain at absolute rest? May not the first ball return in a straight line, or leap off from the second in any line or direction? All these suppositions are consistent and conceivable. Why then should we give the preference to one, which is no more consistent or conceivable than the rest? All our reasonings *a priori* will never be able to show us any foundation for this preference.

In a word, then, every effect is a distinct event from its cause. It could not, therefore, be discovered in the cause, and the first invention or conception of it, *a priori,* must be entirely arbitrary. And even after it is suggested, the conjunction of it with the cause must appear equally arbitrary; since there are always many other effects, which, to reason, must seem fully as consistent and natural. In vain, therefore, should we pretend to determine any single event, or infer any cause or effect, without the assistance of observation and experience.

Hence we may discover the reason why no philosopher, who is rational and modest, has ever pretended to assign the ultimate cause of any natural operation, or to show distinctly the action of that power, which produces any single effect in the universe. It is confessed, that the utmost effort of human reason is to reduce the principles, productive of natural phenomena, to a greater simplicity, and to resolve the many particular effects into a few general causes, by means of reasonings from analogy, experience, and observation. But as to the causes of these general causes, we should in vain attempt their discovery; nor shall we ever be able to satisfy ourselves, by any particular explication of them. These ultimate springs and principles are totally shut up from human curiosity and enquiry. Elasticity, gravity, cohesion of parts, communication of motion by impulse; these are probably the ultimate causes and principles which we shall ever discover in nature; and we may esteem ourselves sufficiently happy, if, by accurate enquiry and reasoning, we can trace up the particular phenomena to, or near to, these general principles. The most perfect philosophy of the natural kind only staves off our ignorance a little longer: as perhaps the most perfect philosophy of the moral or metaphysical kind serves only to discover larger portions of it. Thus the observation of human blindness and weakness is the result of all philosophy, and meets us at every turn, in spite of our endeavours to elude or avoid it.

Nor is geometry, when taken into the assistance of natural philosophy, ever able to remedy this defect, or lead us into the knowledge of ultimate causes, by all that accuracy of reasoning for which it is so justly celebrated. Every part of mixed mathematics proceeds upon the supposition that certain laws are established by nature in her operations; and abstract reasonings are employed, either to assist experience in the discovery of these laws, or to determine their influence in particular instances, where it depends upon any precise degree of distance and quantity. Thus, it is a law of motion, discovered by experience, that the moment or force of any body in motion is in the compound ratio or proportion of its solid contents and its velocity; and consequently, that a small force may remove the greatest obstacle or raise the greatest weight, if, by any contrivance or machinery, we can increase the velocity of that force, so as to make it an overmatch for its antagonist. Geometry assists us in the application of this law, by giving us the just dimensions of all the parts and figures which can enter into any species of machine; but still the discovery of the law itself is owing merely to experience, and all the abstract reasonings in the world could never lead us one step towards the knowledge of it. When we reason *a priori,* and consider merely any object or cause, as it appears to the mind, independent of all observation, it never could suggest to us the notion of any distinct object, such as its effect; much less, show us the inseparable and inviolable connexion between them. A man must be very sagacious who could discover by reasoning that crystal is the effect of heat, and ice of cold, without being previously acquainted with the operation of these qualities.

II

But we have not yet attained any tolerable satisfaction with regard to the question first proposed. Each solution still gives rise to a new question as difficult as the foregoing, and leads us on to farther enquiries. When it is asked, *What is the nature of all our reasonings concerning matter of fact?* the proper answer seems to be, that they are founded on the relation of cause and effect. When again it is asked, *What is the foundation of all our reasonings and conclusions concerning that relation?* it may be replied in one word, Experience. But if we still carry on our sifting humour, and ask, *What is the foundation of all conclusions from experience?* this implies a new question, which may be of more difficult solution and explication. Philosophers, that give themselves airs of superior wisdom and sufficiency, have a hard task when they encounter persons of inquisitive dispositions, who push them from every corner to which they retreat, and who are sure at last to bring them to some dangerous dilemma. The best expedient to prevent this confusion, is to be modest in our pretensions; and even to discover the difficulty ourselves before it is objected to us. By this means, we may make a kind of merit of our very ignorance.

I shall content myself, in this section, with an easy task, and shall pretend only to give a negative answer to the question here proposed. I say then, that, even after we have experience of the operations of cause and effect, our conclusions from that experience are *not* founded on reasoning, or any process of the understanding. This answer we must endeavour both to explain and to defend.

It must certainly be allowed, that nature has kept us at a great distance from all her secrets, and has afforded us only the knowledge of a few superficial qualities of objects; while she conceals from us those powers and principles on which the influence of those objects entirely depends. Our senses inform us of the colour, weight, and consistence of bread; but neither sense nor reason can ever inform us of those qualities which fit it for the nourishment and support of a human body. Sight or feeling conveys an idea of the actual motion of bodies; but as to that wonderful force or power, which would carry on a moving body for ever in a continued change of place, and which bodies never lose but by communicating it to others; of this we cannot form the most distant conception. But notwithstanding this ignorance of natural powers [1] and principles, we always presume, when we see like sensible qualities, that they have like secret powers, and expect that effects, similar to those which we have experienced, will follow from them. If a body of like colour and consistence with that bread, which we have formerly eat, be presented to us, we make no scruple of repeating the experiment, and foresee, with certainty, like nourishment and support. Now this is a process of the mind or thought, of which I would willingly know the foundation. It is allowed on all hands that there is no known connexion between the sensible qualities and the secret powers; and consequently, that the mind is not led to form such a conclusion concerning their constant and regular conjunction, by anything which it knows of their nature. As to past *Experience,* it can be allowed to give *direct* and *certain* information of those precise objects only, and that precise period of time, which fell under its cognizance: but why this experience should be extended to future times, and to other objects, which for aught we know, may be only in appearance similar; this is the main question on which I would insist. The bread, which I formerly eat, nourished me; that is, a body of such sensible qualities was, at that time, endued with such secret powers: but does it follow, that other bread must also nourish me at another time, and that like sensible qualities must always be attended with like secret powers? The consequence seems nowise necessary. At least, it must be acknowledged that there is here a consequence drawn by the mind; that there is a certain step taken; a process of thought, and an inference, which wants to be explained. These two propo-

---

[1] The word, Power, is here used in a loose and popular sense. The more accurate explication of it would give additional evidence to this argument.

sitions are far from being the same, *I have found that such an object has always been attended with such an effect,* and *I foresee, that other objects, which are, in appearance, similar, will be attended with similar effects.* I shall allow, if you please, that the one proposition may justly be inferred from the other: I know, in fact, that it always is inferred. But if you insist that the inference is made by a chain of reasoning, I desire you to produce that reasoning. The connexion between these propositions is not intuitive. There is required a medium, which may enable the mind to draw such an inference, if indeed it be drawn by reasoning and argument. What that medium is, I must confess, passes my comprehension; and it is incumbent on those to produce it, who assert that it really exists, and is the origin of all our conclusions concerning matter of fact.

This negative argument must certainly, in process of time, become altogether convincing, if many penetrating and able philosophers shall turn their enquiries this way and no one be ever able to discover any connecting proposition or intermediate step, which supports the understanding in this conclusion. But as the question is yet new, every reader may not trust so far to his own penetration, as to conclude, because an argument escapes his enquiry, that therefore it does not really exist. For this reason it may be requisite to venture upon a more difficult task; and enumerating all the branches of human knowledge, endeavour to show that none of them can afford such an argument.

All reasonings may be divided into two kinds, namely, demonstrative reasoning, or that concerning relations of ideas, and moral reasoning, or that concerning matter of fact and existence. That there are no demonstrative arguments in the case seems evident; since it implies no contradiction that the course of nature may change, and that an object, seemingly like those which we have experienced, may be attended with different or contrary effects. May I not clearly and distinctly conceive that a body, falling from the clouds, and which, in all other respects, resembles snow, has yet the taste of salt or feeling of fire? Is there any more intelligible proposition than to affirm, that all the trees will flourish in December and January, and decay in May and June? Now whatever is intelligible, and can be distinctly conceived, implies no contradiction, and can never be proved false by any demonstrative argument or abstract reasoning *a priori.*

If we be, therefore, engaged by arguments to put trust in past experience, and make it the standard of our future judgment, these arguments must be probable only, or such as regard matter of fact and real existence, according to the division above mentioned. But that there is no argument of this kind, must appear, if our explication of that species of reasoning be admitted as solid and satisfactory. We have said that all arguments concerning existence are founded on the relation of cause and effect; that our knowledge of that relation is derived entirely from experience; and that all our experimental conclusions proceed upon the supposition that the future will be conformable to the past. To endeavour, therefore, the proof of this last supposition by probable arguments, or arguments regarding existence, must be evidently going in a circle, and taking that for granted, which is the very point in question.

In reality, all arguments from experience are founded on the similarity which we discover among natural objects, and by which we are induced to expect effects similar to those which we have found to follow from such objects. And though none but a fool or madman will ever pretend to dispute the authority of experience, or to reject that great guide of human life, it may surely be allowed a philosopher to have so much curiosity at least as to examine the principle of human nature, which gives this mighty authority to experience, and makes us draw advantage from that similarity which nature has placed among different objects. From causes which appear *similar* we expect similar effects. This is the sum of all our experimental conclusions. Now it seems evident that, if this conclusion were formed by reason, it would be as perfect at first, and upon one instance, as after ever so long a course of experience. But the case is far otherwise. Nothing so like as eggs; yet no one, on account of this appearing similarity, expects the same taste and relish in all of them. It is only after a long course of uniform experiments in any kind, that we attain a firm reliance and security with regard to a particular event. Now where is that process of reasoning which, from one instance, draws a conclusion, so different from that which it infers from a hundred instances that are nowise different from that single one? This question I propose as much for the sake of information, as with an intention of raising difficulties. I cannot find, I cannot imagine any such reasoning. But I keep my mind still open to instruction, if any one will vouchsafe to bestow it on me.

Should it be said that, from a number of uniform experiments, we *infer* a connexion between the sensible qualities and the secret powers; this, I must confess, seems the same difficulty, couched in different terms. The question still recurs, on what process of argument this *inference* is founded? Where is the medium, the interposing ideas, which join propositions so very wide of each other? It is confessed that the colour, consistence, and other sensible qualities of bread appear not, of themselves, to have any connexion with the secret powers of nourishment and support. For otherwise we could infer these secret powers from the first appearance of these sensible qualities, without the aid of experience; contrary to the sentiment of all philosophers, and contrary to plain matter of fact. Here, then, is our natural state of ignorance with regard to the powers and influence of all objects. How is this remedied by experience? It only shows us a number of uniform effects, resulting from certain objects, and teaches us that those particular objects, at that particular time, were endowed with such powers and forces. When a new object, endowed with similar sensible qualities, is produced, we expect similar powers and forces, and look for a like effect. From a body of like colour and consistence with bread we expect like nourishment and support. But this surely is a step or progress of the mind, which wants to be explained. When a man says, *I have found, in all past instances, such sensible qualities conjoined with such secret powers:* And when he says, *Similar sensible qualities will always be conjoined with similar secret powers,* he is not guilty of a tautology, nor are these propositions in any respect the same. You say that the one proposition is an inference from the other. But you must confess that the inference is not intuitive; neither is it demonstrative: Of what nature is it, then? To say it is experimental, is begging the question. For all inferences from experience suppose, as their foundation, that the future will resemble the past, and that similar powers will be conjoined with similar sensible qualities. If there be any suspicion that the course of nature may change, and that the past may be no rule for the future, all experience becomes useless, and can give rise to no inference or conclusion. It is impossible, therefore, that any arguments from experience can prove this resemblance of the past to the future; since all these arguments are founded on the supposition of that resemblance. Let the course of things be allowed hitherto ever so regular; that alone, without some new argument or inference, proves not that, for the future, it will continue so. In vain do you pretend to have learned the nature of bodies from your past experience. Their secret nature, and consequently all their effects and influence, may change, without any change in their sensible qualities. This happens sometimes, and with regard to some objects: Why may it not happen always, and with regard to all objects? What logic, what process of argument secures you against this supposition? My practice, you say, refutes my doubts. But you mistake the purport of my question. As an agent, I am quite satisfied in the point; but as a philosopher, who has some share of curiosity, I will not say scepticism, I want to learn the foundation of this inference. No reading, no enquiry has yet been able to remove my difficulty, or give me satisfaction in a matter of such importance. Can I do better than propose the difficulty to the public, even though, perhaps, I have small hopes of obtaining a solution? We shall at least, by this means, be sensible of our ignorance, if we do not augment our knowledge.

. . .

Sceptical Solution of These Doubts

Suppose a person, though endowed with the strongest faculties of reason and reflection, to be brought on a sudden into this world; he would, indeed, immediately observe a continual succession of objects, and one event following another; but he would not be able to discover anything farther. He would not, at first, by any reasoning, be able to reach the idea of cause and effect; since the particular powers, by which all natural operations are performed, never appear to the senses; nor is it reasonable to conclude, merely because one event, in one instance, precedes another, that therefore the one is the cause, the other the effect. Their conjunction may be arbitrary and causal. There may be no reason to infer the existence of one from the appearance of the other. And in a word, such a person, without more experience, could never employ his conjecture or reasoning concerning any matter of fact, or be assured of anything beyond what was immediately present to his memory and senses.

Suppose, again, that he has acquired more experience, and has lived so long in the world as to have observed familiar objects or events to be constantly conjoined together; what is the consequence of this experience? He immediately infers the existence of one object from the appearance of the other. Yet he has not, by all his experience, acquired any idea or knowledge of the secret power by which the one object produces the other; nor is it, by any process of reasoning, he is engaged to draw this inference. But still he finds himself determined to draw it: And though he should be convinced that his understanding has no part in the operation, he would nevertheless continue in the same course of thinking. There is some other principle which determines him to form such a conclusion.

This principle is Custom or Habit. For wherever the repetition of any particular act or operation produces a propensity to renew the same act or operation, without being impelled by any reasoning or process of the understanding, we always say, that this propensity is the effect of *Custom*. By employing that word, we pretend not to have given the ultimate reason of such a propensity. We only point out a principle of human nature, which is universally acknowledged, and which is well known by its effects. Perhaps we can push our enquiries no farther, or pretend to give the cause of this cause; but must rest contented with it as the ultimate principle, which we can assign, of all our conclusions from experience. It is sufficient satisfaction, that we can go so far, without repining at the narrowness of our faculties because they will carry us no farther. And it is certain we here advance a very intelligible proposition at least, if not a true one, when we assert that, after the constant conjunction of two objects—heat and flame, for instance, weight and solidity—we are determined by custom alone to expect the one from the appearance of the other. This hypothesis seems even the only one which explains the difficulty, why we draw, from a thousand instances, an inference which we are not able to draw from one instance, that is, in no respect, different from them. Reason is incapable of any such variation. The conclusions which it draws from considering one circle are the same which it would form upon surveying all the circles in the universe. But no man, having seen only one body move after being impelled by another, could infer that every other body will move after a like impulse. All inferences from experience, therefore, are effects of custom, not of reasoning.

Custom, then, is the great guide of human life. It is that principle alone which renders our experience useful to us, and makes us expect, for the future, a similar train of events with those which have appeared in the past. Without the influence of custom, we should be entirely ignorant of every matter of fact beyond what is immediately present to the memory and senses. We should never know how to adjust means to ends, or to employ our natural powers in the production of any effect. There would be an end at once of all action, as well as of the chief part of speculation.

But here it may be proper to remark, that though our conclusions from experience carry us beyond our memory and senses, and assure us of matters of fact which happened in the most distant places and most remote ages, yet some fact must always be present to the senses or memory, from which we may first proceed in drawing these conclusions. A man, who should find in a desert country the remains of pompous buildings, would conclude that the country had, in ancient times, been cultivated by civilized inhabitants; but did nothing of this nature occur to him, he could never form such an inference. We learn the events of former ages from history; but then we must peruse the volumes in which this instruction is contained, and thence carry up our inferences from one testimony to another, till we arrive at the eyewitnesses and spectators of these distant events. In a word, if we proceed not upon some fact, present to the memory or senses, our reasonings would be merely hypothetical; and however the particular links might be connected with each other, the whole chain of inferences would have nothing to support it, nor could we ever, by its means, arrive at the knowledge of any real existence. If I ask why you believe any particular matter of fact, which you relate, you must tell me some reason; and this reason will be some other fact, connected with it. But as you cannot proceed after this manner, *in infinitum,* you must at last terminate in some fact, which is present to your memory or senses; or must allow that your belief is entirely without foundation.

What, then, is the conclusion of the whole matter? A simple one; though, it must be confessed, pretty remote from the common theories of philosophy. All belief of matter of fact or real existence is derived merely from some object, present to the memory or senses, and a customary conjunction between that and some other object. Or in other words; having found, in many instances, that any two kinds of objects—flame and heat, snow and cold—have always been conjoined together; if flame or snow be presented anew to the senses, the mind is carried by custom to expect heat or cold, and to *believe* that such a quality does exist, and will discover itself upon a nearer approach. This belief is the necessary result of placing the mind in such circumstances. It is an operation of the soul, when we are so situated, as unavoidable as to feel the passion of love, when we receive benefits; or hatred, when we meet with injuries. All these operations are a species of natural instincts, which no reasoning or process of the thought and understanding is able either to produce or to prevent.

QUESTIONS

1. Explain in your own words the difference between "relations of ideas" and "matters of fact." Why is the latter *empirical* knowledge, and not the former? Why does all knowledge of matters of fact rest on the assumption of the uniformity of nature (that similar causes will lead to similar effects)?

2. Are the following statements about relations of ideas or matters of fact? Give reasons for classifying each statement as you do.
    a. One-half of twelve is twice three.
    b. Two gloves, one made for the right hand and the other for the left, and which are of the same size, color, and pattern, make a pair.
    c. My two gloves are a pair.
    d. Sheep are wool-bearing mammals.
    e. My sheep bear wool.
    f. My sheep bear silk.
    g. The woman was wearing a silk dress made out of wool.
    h. The Eiffel Tower is in Washington, D. C.
    i. If you strike a match on the moon, it will not light.
    j. If one is to live, it is necessary for one to eat.
    k. There is no helium in water as it is chemically defined.
    l. My chocolate ice cream looks and tastes like vanilla.
    m. There are twelve inches in a linear foot.
    n. In baseball, three strikes and the batter is out.
    o. Every effect has a cause.
    p. When I push the button, the bell rings.
    q. When I push the button, I push the button.
    r. Fire burns.
    s. Every body perseveres in its state of rest, or of uniform motion in a right line, unless it is compelled to change that state by forces impressed thereon. (Newton)
    t. Whatever I conceive clearly and distinctly exists. (Descartes)

3. What is Hume's argument to show that the principle of the uniformity of nature is not true a priori? What is his argument to show that the principle is not true a posteriori (i.e., is not empirically true)? If you think there are flaws in these arguments, state what they are. If you do not think there are flaws in these arguments, state why you agree, or disagree, with the claim: "Hume has shown us that all empirical science rests on a blind faith that the future will be like the past."

4. What does Hume mean by his frequent references to ultimate springs and principles, and to secret qualities and powers in nature? Given Hume's views, how legitimate are these references?

5. IMMANUEL KANT

(1724–1804)

Analytic and Synthetic

Immanuel Kant was born in Königsberg, Germany, where he lived all his life. He attended the University of Königsberg and in 1755 received the degree of doctor of philosophy there. He became a lecturer at the University, and finally professor of metaphysics and logic. Kant's philosophical works have had a profound influence on all fields of philosophy since his time. He is perhaps most famous for his *Critique of Pure Reason* (1781). Kant wrote his *Prolegomena to Any Future Metaphysics* (1783), from which the present reading is taken, as a more readable and concise version of the *Critique of Pure Reason*. In these works he presents his theory of knowledge. Much of the lively discussion among contemporary philosophers concerning the nature of knowledge stems directly from these works. Similarly, Kant's writings in moral philosophy have had a powerful impact on the study of ethics today. The moral philosophy which Kant expounded in his *Fundamental Principles of the Metaphysic of Morals* (1785) and in his *Critique of Practical Reason* (1788) is still of vital concern to all who are interested in the problem of moral knowledge. The greater part of the *Fundamental Principles of the Metaphysic of Morals* is contained in Chapter 10 in this book.

In the *Critique of Pure Reason* and the *Prolegomena to Any Future Metaphysics,* Kant's chief purpose is to give an account of the meaning of metaphysical statements and the way their truth is ascertained. As a necessary preliminary to his consideration of these statements, he offers a general account of the different sorts of statements, or as he calls them, judgments. Kant classifies judgments in two ways. The first classification of judgments is as either *analytical* or *synthetical,* the second as either *a priori* or *a posteriori.* The first classification is concerned with the *meaning* of judgments, the second with the kinds of grounds on which judgments are *justified.*

A judgment is made up of a subject and a predicate. In order to understand what a judgment means, we must understand both the subject and the predicate. Let us suppose we do understand the subject and predicate of a given judgment. Then we can tell whether the judgment is analytical or synthetical in the following way. If in understanding the predicate we merely make explicit one of the ideas already contained in our idea of the subject, the judgment is analytical (i.e., its meaning is an analysis of a complex idea). If in understanding the predicate we add a new idea to our idea of the subject, then the judgment is synthetical (i.e., its meaning is a synthesis of different ideas). Let us take an example. The judgment, "A person six feet tall is taller than a person five feet tall," is analytical since the predicate "being taller than" does not add any new idea to the idea of the relation of a six-footer to a five-footer. But the judgment, "Christopher Columbus was six feet tall," is a synthetical judgment since we can know who Christopher Columbus was without knowing that he was six feet tall. (Indeed, he might not have been six feet tall, but this would not mean he was not Christopher Columbus.) Kant uses the following example. Every time we think of a physical body, we must think of it as taking up some space. Thus in the judgment, "All bodies are extended," the predicate does not add any new idea to the subject, but is already contained in the subject. Therefore the judgment is analytical. But when we think of a physical body we do not have to think of it as having weight (for instance, when we think of it as "floating" in space outside the gravitational pull of any celestial body). Thus the judgment, "All bodies have weight," is a synthetical judgment because the idea of weight adds something to the idea of a body.

Let us turn to the second classification of judgments, according to which judgments are either *a priori* or *a posteriori*. A judgment is a priori (or, as it is sometimes said, a judgment is true a priori or false a priori) when we can know that it is true or false without relying upon the evidence of experience. We can know it by pure reason alone and our knowledge of it is absolutely certain. In every case of an a priori judgment, the judgment is necessarily true or necessarily false. In Kant's terminology, the judgment is "apodictic." A judgment is a posteriori (true a posteriori or false a posteriori) when we can know that it is true or false only

empirically, that is, only by appealing to the evidence of our experience. Thus we may call an a posteriori judgment simply an empirical judgment. A posteriori judgments correspond to Hume's "matters of fact"; a priori judgments to his "relations of ideas."

Now there are four possible combinations of the different kinds of judgments: (1) analytical a priori, (2) analytical a posteriori, (3) synthetical a posteriori, and (4) synthetical a priori. Kant says that all analytical judgments are a priori, and therefore there are no such things as judgments of type (2). But he believes that synthetical judgments may be either a posteriori or a priori. Synthetical a posteriori judgments are all the empirical judgments of the sciences. Synthetical a priori judgments belong to two branches of knowledge: mathematics and metaphysics. Kant explains to his own satisfaction why mathematical propositions are synthetical and a priori. He then propounds his principal thesis: *If there is such a thing as metaphysical knowledge it must consist of synthetical a priori judgments.* His argument assumes that the task of legitimate metaphysical knowledge is to give us information about the world by means of purely rational (nonempirical) judgments which possess absolute certainty and necessity. If metaphysics claims to give us knowledge of a reality beyond all possible experience, it is mere speculation and not legitimate knowledge at all. But if it claims to give us knowledge about a reality within the limits of possible experience, then it must be knowledge derived a priori from pure reason; for otherwise it would yield the merely probable a posteriori judgments of the empirical sciences.

In our present reading Kant is setting up the problem which he later tries to solve in the main body of the

Prolegomena and the *Critique of Pure Reason*. The problem is this: How is legitimate metaphysical knowledge possible? And we have seen that this means: How is it possible to gain a priori knowledge of the world of experience?

We may briefly summarize the solution which Kant offers in the main body of his works. We can derive from reason alone, by means of a "deduction," the necessary conditions of all possible experience. Legitimate metaphysical knowledge is knowledge of the a priori presuppositions of all possible experience (and hence of all empirical knowledge). These presuppositions are the formal concepts imposed by the rational mind upon the manifold material supplied by our sensations. We can experience (and thus know) the world only through the union of rational form (concepts) and empirical matter (percepts).

This selection begins with Kant's account of the disorders in metaphysics. Kant sets the stage for his classification of judgments, which he believes will point the way to orderly metaphysical thinking. The reader may be helped in his study of this reading by comparing it with Professor S. Toulmin's selection which follows it, and by reading "True and False in Metaphysics" by Professor W. H. Walsh, in Chapter 3.

This reading is from Kant's own Introduction and Preamble to the *Prolegomena to Any Future Metaphysics*. The translation from the German is by Lewis White Beck. Kant's own section titles are used.

INTRODUCTION

My purpose is to persuade all those who think metaphysics worth studying that it is absolutely necessary to pause a moment and, regarding all that has been done as though undone, to propose first the preliminary question, "Whether such a thing as metaphysics be even possible at all?"

If it be science, how is it that it cannot, like other sciences, obtain universal and lasting recognition? If not, how can it maintain its pretensions and keep the human mind in suspense with hopes never ceasing, yet never fulfilled? Whether then we demonstrate our knowledge or our ignorance in this field, we must come once for all to a definite conclusion respecting the nature of this so-called science, which cannot possibly remain on its present footing. It seems almost ridiculous, while every other science is continually advancing, that in this, which pretends to be wisdom incarnate, for whose oracle everyone inquires, we should constantly move round the same spot, without gaining a single step. And so its votaries having melted away, we do not find men confident of their ability to shine in other sciences venturing their reputation here, where everybody, however ignorant in other matters, presumes to deliver a final verdict, because in this domain there is actually as yet no standard weight and measure to distinguish sound knowledge from shallow talk.

After all it is nothing extraordinary in the elaboration of a science that, when men begin to wonder how far it has advanced, the question should at last occur whether and how such a science is possible at all. Human reason so delights building that it has several times built up a tower and then razed it to see how the foundation was laid. It is never too late to become reasonable and wise; but if the knowledge comes late, there is always more difficulty in starting a reform. . . .

Since the *Essays* of Locke and Leibniz, or rather since the origin of metaphysics so far as we know its history, nothing has ever happened which could have been more decisive to its fate than the attack made upon it by David Hume. He threw no light on this species of knowledge, but he certainly struck a spark by which light might have been kindled had it caught some inflammable substance and had its smouldering fire been carefully nursed and developed.

Hume started chiefly from a single but important concept in metaphysics, namely, that of the connection of cause and effect (including its derivatives force and action, and so on). He challenged reason, which pretends to have given birth to this concept of herself, to answer him by what right she thinks anything could be so constituted that if that thing be posited, something else also must necessarily be posited; for this is the meaning of the concept of cause. He demonstrated irrefutably that it was perfectly impossible for reason to think, *a priori* and by means of concepts, such a combination, for it implies necessity. We cannot at all see why, in consequence of the existence of one thing, another must necessarily exist or how the concept of such a combination can arise *a priori*. Hence he inferred that reason was altogether deluded with reference to this concept, which she erroneously considered as one of her own children, whereas in reality it was nothing but a bastard of imagination, impregnated by experience, which subsumed certain representations under the law of association and mistook a subjective necessity (habit) for an objective necessity arising from insight. Hence he inferred that reason had no power to think such combinations, even in general, because her concepts would then be purely fictitious and all her pretended *a priori* cognitions nothing but common experiences marked with a false stamp. In plain language, this means that there is not and cannot be any such thing as metaphysics at all.

However hasty and mistaken Hume's inference may appear, it was at least founded upon investigation, and this investigation deserved the concentrated attention of the brighter spirits of his day as well as determined efforts on their part to discover, if possible, a happier solution of the problem in the sense proposed by him, all of which would have speedily resulted in a complete reform of the science.

But Hume suffered the usual misfortune of metaphysicians, of not being understood. It is positively painful to see how utterly his opponents, Reid, Oswald, Beattie, and lastly Priestley, missed the point of the problem; for while they were ever taking for granted that which he doubted, and demonstrating with zeal and often with impudence that which he never thought of doubting, they so misconstrued his valuable suggestion that everything remained in its old condition, as if nothing had happened. The question was not whether the concept of cause was right, useful, and even indispensable for our knowledge of nature, for this Hume had never doubted; but whether that concept could be thought by reason *a priori,* and consequently whether it possessed an inner truth, independent of all experience, implying a perhaps more extended use not restricted merely to objects of experience. This was Hume's problem. It was solely a question concerning the *origin,* not concerning the *indispensable* need of using the concept. Were the former decided, the conditions of the use and the sphere of its valid application would have been determined as a matter of course.

But to satisfy the conditions of the problem, the opponents of the great thinker should have penetrated very deeply into the nature of reason, so far as it is concerned with pure thinking—a task which did not suit them. They found a more convenient method of being defiant without any insight, namely, the appeal to *common sense*. It is indeed a great gift of God to possess right or (as they now call it) plain common sense. But this common sense must be shown in action by well-considered and reasonable thoughts and words, not by appealing to it as an oracle when no rational justification for one's position can be advanced. To appeal to common sense when insight and science fail, and no sooner—this is one of the subtile discoveries of modern times, by means of which the most superficial ranter can safely enter the lists with the most thorough thinker and hold his own. But as long as a particle of insight remains, no one would think of having recourse to this subterfuge. Seen clearly, it is but an appeal to the opinion of the multitude, of whose applause the philosopher is ashamed, while the popular charlatan glories and boasts in it. I should think that Hume might fairly have laid as much claim to common sense as Beattie and, in addition, to a critical reason (such as the latter did not possess), which keeps common sense in check and prevents it from speculating, or, if speculations are under discussion, restrains the desire to decide because it cannot satisfy itself concerning its own premises. By this means alone can common sense remain sound. Chisels and hammers may suffice to work a piece of wood, but for etching we require an etcher's needle. Thus common sense and speculative understanding are each serviceable, but each in its own way: the former in judgments which apply immediately to experience; the latter when we judge universally from more concepts, as in metaphysics, where that which calls itself, in spite of the inappropriateness of the name, sound common sense, has no right to judge at all.

I openly confess my recollection of David Hume was the very thing which many years ago first interrupted my dogmatic slumber and gave my investigations in the field of speculative philosophy a quite new direction. I was far from following him in the conclusions at which he arrived by regarding, not the whole of his problem, but a part, which by itself can give us no information. If we start from a well-founded, but undeveloped, thought which another has bequeathed to us, we may well hope by continued reflection to advance farther than the acute man to whom we owe the first spark of light.

I therefore first tried whether Hume's objection could not be put into a general form, and soon found that the concept of the connection of cause and effect was by no means the only concept by which the understanding thinks the connection of things *a priori,* but rather that metaphysics consists altogether of such concepts. I sought to ascertain their number; and when I had satisfactorily succeeded in this by starting from a single principle, I proceeded to the deduction of these concepts, which I was now certain were not derived from experience, as Hume had attempted to derive them, but sprang from the pure understanding. This deduction (which seemed impossible to my acute predecessor, which had never even occurred to anyone else, though no one had hesitated to use the concepts without investigating the basis of their objective validity) was the most difficult task which ever could have been undertaken in the service of metaphysics; and the worst was that metaphysics, such as it is, could not assist me in the least because this deduction alone can render metaphysics possible. But as soon as I had succeeded in solving Hume's problem, not merely in a particular case, but with respect to the whole faculty of pure reason, I could proceed safely, though slowly, to determine the whole sphere of pure reason completely and from universal principles, in its boundaries as well as in its contents. This was required for metaphysics in order to construct its system according to a safe plan. . . .

PREAMBLE ON THE PECULIARITIES OF ALL METAPHYSICAL KNOWLEDGE

Of the Sources of Metaphysics

First, as concerns the sources of metaphysical knowledge, its very concept implies that they cannot be empirical. Its principles (including not only its maxims but its basic notions) must never be derived from experience. It must not be physical but metaphysical knowledge, namely, knowledge lying beyond experience. It can therefore have for its basis neither external experience, which is the source of physics proper, nor internal, which is the basis of empirical psychology. It is therefore *a priori* knowledge, coming from pure understanding and pure reason. . . .

Concerning the Kind of Knowledge Which Can Alone Be Called Metaphysical

On the Distinction between Analytical and Synthetical Judgments in General. The peculiarity of its sources demands that metaphysical knowledge must consist of nothing but *a priori* judgments. But whatever be their origin or their logical form, there is a distinction in judgments, as to their content, according to which they are either merely *explicative,* adding nothing to the content of knowledge, or *expansive,* increasing the given knowledge. The former may be called *analytical,* the latter *synthetical,* judgments.

Analytical judgments express nothing in the predicate but what has been already actually thought in the concept of the subject, though not so distinctly or with the same (full) consciousness. When I say: "All bodies are extended," I have not amplified in the least my concept of body, but have only analyzed it, as extension was really thought to belong to that concept before the judgment was made, though it was not expressed. This judgment is therefore analytical. On the contrary, this judgment, "All bodies have weight," contains in its predicate something not actually thought in the universal concept of body; it amplifies my knowledge by adding something to my concept, and must therefore be called synthetical.

The Common Principle of All Analytical Judgments Is the Law of Contradiction. All analytical judgments depend wholly on the law of contradiction, and are in their nature *a priori* cognitions, whether the concepts that supply them with matter be empirical or not. For the predicate of an affirmative analytical judgment is already contained in the concept of the subject, of which it cannot be denied without contradiction. In the same way its opposite is necessarily denied of the subject in an analytical, but negative, judgment, by the same law of contradiction. Such is the nature of the judgments: "All bodies are extended," and "No bodies are unextended (that is, simple)."

For this very reason all analytical judgments are *a priori* even when the concepts are empirical, as, for example, "Gold is a yellow metal"; for to know this I require no experience beyond my concept of gold as a yellow metal. It is, in fact, the very concept, and I need only analyze it without looking beyond it.

Synthetical Judgments Require a Different Principle from the Law of Contradiction. There are synthetical *a posteriori* judgments of empirical origin; but there are also others which are certain *a priori,* and which spring from pure understanding and reason. Yet they both agree in this, that they cannot possibly spring from the principle of analysis, namely, the law of contradiction, alone. They require a quite different principle from which they may be deduced, subject, of course, always to the law of contradiction, which must never be violated, even though everything cannot be deduced from it. I shall first classify synthetical judgments.

Judgments of Experience are always synthetical. For it would be absurd to base an analytical judgment on experience, as our concept suffices for the purpose without requiring any testimony from experience. That body is extended is a judgment established *a priori,* and not an empirical judgment. For before appealing to experience, we already have all the conditions of the judgment in the concept, from which we have but to elicit the predicate according to the law of contradiction, and thereby to become conscious of the necessity of the judgment, which experience could not in the least teach us.

Mathematical Judgments are all synthetical. This fact seems hitherto to have altogether escaped the observation of those who have analyzed human reason; it even seems directly opposed to all their conjectures, though it is incontestably certain and most important in its consequences. For as it was found that the conclusions of mathematicians all proceed according to the law of contradiction (as is demanded by all apodictic certainty), men persuaded themselves that the fundamental principles were known from the same law. This was a great mistake, for a synthetical proposition can indeed be established by the law of contradiction, but only by presupposing another synthetical proposition from which it follows, but never by that law alone.

First of all, we must observe that all strictly mathematical judgments are *a priori,* and not empirical, because they carry with them necessity, which cannot be obtained from experience. But if this be not conceded to me, very good; I shall confine my assertion to *pure mathematics,* the very notion of which implies that it contains pure *a priori* and not empirical knowledge.

It must at first be thought that the proposition $7 + 5 = 12$ is a mere analytical judgment, following from the concept of the sum of seven and five, according to the law of contradiction. But on closer examination it appears that the concept of the sum of $7 + 5$ contains merely their union in a single number, without its being at all thought what the particular number is that unites them. The concept of twelve is by no means thought by merely thinking of the combination of seven and five; and, analyze this possible sum as we may, we shall not discover twelve in the concept. We must go beyond these concepts, by calling to our aid some intuition which corresponds to one of the concepts—that is, either our five fingers or five points (as Segner has it in his *Arithmetic*)—and we must add successively the units of the five given in the intuition to the concept of seven. Hence our concept is really amplified by the proposition $7 + 5 = 12$, and we add to the first concept a second concept not thought in it. Arithmetical judgments are therefore synthetical, and the more plainly according as we take larger numbers; for in such cases it is clear that, however closely we analyze our concepts without calling intuition to our aid, we can never find the sum by such mere dissection.

Just as little is any principle of geometry analytical. That a straight line is the shortest path between two points is a synthetical proposition. For my concept of straight contains nothing of quantity, but only a quality. The concept "shortest" is therefore altogether additional and cannot be obtained by any analysis of the concept "straight line." Here, too, intuition must come to aid us. It alone makes the synthesis possible. What usually makes us believe that the predicate of such apodictic judgments is already contained in our concept, and that the judgment is therefore analytical, is the duplicity of the expression. We must think a certain predicate as attached to a given concept, and necessity indeed belongs to the concepts. But the question is not what we must join in thought *to* the given concept, but what we actually think together with and in it, though obscurely; and so it appears that the predicate belongs to this concept necessarily indeed, yet not directly but indirectly by means of an intuition which must be present.

Some other principles, assumed by geometers, are indeed actually analytical, and depend on the law of contradiction; but they only serve, as identical propositions, as a method of concatenation, and not as principles—for example $a = a$, the whole is equal to itself, or $a + b > a$, the whole is greater than its part. And yet even these, though they are recognized as valid from mere concepts, are admitted in mathematics only because they can be represented in some intuition.

The essential and distinguishing feature of pure mathematical knowledge among all other *a priori* knowledge is that it cannot at all proceed from concepts, but only by means of the construction of concepts. As therefore in its propositions it must proceed beyond the concept to that which its corresponding intuition contains, these propositions neither can, nor ought to, arise analytically, by dissection of the concept, but are all synthetical.

I cannot refrain from pointing out the disadvantage resulting to philosophy from the neglect of this easy and apparently insignificant observation. Hume being prompted to cast his eye over the whole field of *a priori* cognitions in which human understanding claims such mighty possessions (a calling he felt worthy of a philosopher) heedlessly severed from it a whole, and indeed its most valuable, province, namely, pure mathematics; for he imagined its nature or, so to speak, the state constitution of this empire depended on totally different principles, namely, on the law of contradiction alone; and although he did not divide judgments in this manner formally and universally as I have done here, what he said was equivalent to this: that mathematics contains only analytical, but metaphysics synthetical, *a priori* propositions. In this, however, he was greatly mistaken, and the mistake had a decidedly injurious effect upon his whole conception. But for this, he would have extended his question concerning the origin of our synthetical judgments far beyond the metaphysical concept of causality and included in it the possibility of mathematics *a priori* also, for this latter he must have assumed to be equally synthetical. And then he could not have based his metaphysical propositions on mere experience without subjecting the axioms of mathematics equally to experience, a thing which he was far too acute to do. The good company into which metaphysics would thus have been brought would have saved it from the danger of a contemptuous ill-treatment, for the thrust intended for it must have reached mathematics, which was not and could not have been Hume's intention. Thus that acute man would have been led into considerations which must needs be similar to those that now occupy us, but which would have gained inestimably by his inimitably elegant style.

Metaphysical Judgments, properly so called, are all synthetical. We must distinguish judgments pertaining to metaphysics from metaphysical judgments properly so called. Many of the former are analytical, but they only afford the means for metaphysical judgments, which are the whole end of the science and which are always synthetical. For if there be concepts pertaining to metaphysics (as, for example, that of substance), the judgments springing from simple analysis of them also pertain to metaphysics, as, for example, substance is that which only exists as subject, etc.; and by means of several such analytical judgments we seek to approach the definition of the concepts. But as the analysis of a pure concept of the understanding (the kind of concept pertaining to metaphysics) does not proceed in any different manner from the dissection of any other, even empirical, concepts, not belonging to metaphysics (such as, air is an elastic fluid, the elasticity of which is not destroyed by any known degree of cold), it follows that the concept indeed, but not the analytical judgment, is properly metaphysical. This science has something peculiar in the production of its *a priori* cognitions, which must therefore be distinguished from the features it has in common with other rational knowledge. Thus the judgment that all the substance in things is permanent is a synthetical and properly metaphysical judgment.

If the *a priori* concepts which constitute the materials and tools of metaphysics have first been collected according to fixed principles, then their analysis will be of great value; it might be taught as a particular part (as a *philosophia definitiva*), containing nothing but analytical judgments pertaining to metaphysics, and could be treated separately from the synthetical which constitute metaphysics proper. For indeed these analyses are not of much value except in metaphysics, that is, as regards the synthetical judgments which are to be generated by these previously analyzed concepts.

The conclusion drawn in this section then is that metaphysics is properly concerned with synthetical propositions *a priori,* and these alone constitute its end, for which it indeed requires various dissections of its concepts, namely, analytical judgments, but wherein the procedure is not different from that in every other kind of knowledge, in which we merely seek to render our concepts distinct by analysis. But the generation of *a priori* knowledge by intuition as well as by concepts, in fine, of synthetical propositions *a priori,* especially in philosophical knowledge, constitutes the essential subject of metaphysics. . . .

The General Problem: How Is Knowledge
from Pure Reason Possible?

We have already learned the significant distinction between analytical and synthetical judgments. The possibility of analytical propositions was easily comprehended, being entirely founded on the law of contradiction. The possibility of synthetical *a posteriori* judgments, of those which are gathered from experience, also requires no particular explanations, for experience is nothing but a continued synthesis of perceptions. There remain therefore only synthetical propositions a *priori,* of which the possibility must be sought or investigated, because they must depend upon other principles than the law of contradiction.

But here we need not first establish the possibility of such propositions so as to ask whether they are possible. For there are enough of them which indeed are of undoubted certainty; and, as our present method is analytical, we shall start from the fact that such synthetical but purely rational knowledge actually exists; but we must now inquire into the ground of this possibility and ask *how* such knowledge is possible, in order that we may, from the principles of its possibility, be enabled to determine the conditions of its use, its sphere and its limits. The real problem upon which all depends, when expressed with scholastic precision, is therefore: "How are synthetic propositions *a priori* possible?"

For the sake of popular understanding I have above expressed this problem somewhat differently, as an inquiry into purely rational knowledge, which I could do for once without detriment to the desired insight, because, as we have only to do here with metaphysics and its sources, the reader will, I hope, after the foregoing reminders, keep in mind that when we speak of knowing by pure reason we do not mean analytical but synthetical knowledge.

Metaphysics stands or falls with the solution of this problem; its very existence depends upon it. Let anyone make metaphysical assertions with ever so much plausibility, let him overwhelm us with conclusions; but if he has not previously proved able to answer this question satisfactorily, I have a right to say: This is all vain, baseless philosophy and false wisdom. You speak through pure reason and claim, as it were, to create cognitions *a priori* not only by dissecting given concepts, but also by asserting connections which do not rest upon the law of contradiction, and which you claim to conceive quite independently of all experience; how do you arrive at this, and how will you justify such pretensions? . . .

All metaphysicians are therefore solemnly and legally suspended from their occupations till they shall have adequately answered the question, "How are synthetic cognitions *a priori* possible?" For the answer contains the only credentials which they must show when they have anything to offer us in the name of pure reason. But if they do not possess these credentials, they can expect nothing else of reasonable people, who have been deceived so often, than to be dismissed without further inquiry.

If they, on the other hand, desire to carry on their business, not as a science, but as an art of wholesome persuasion suitable to the common sense of man, this calling cannot in justice be denied them. They will then speak the modest language of a rational belief; they will grant that they are not allowed even to conjecture, far less to know, anything which lies beyond the bounds of all possible experience, but only to assume (not for speculative use, which they must abandon, but for practical use only) the existence of something possible and even indispensable for the guidance of the understanding and of the will in life. In this manner alone can they be called useful and wise men, and the more so as they renounce the title of metaphysicians. For the latter profess to be speculative philosophers; and since, when judgments *a priori* are under discussion, poor probabilities cannot be admitted (for what is declared to be known *a priori* is thereby announced as necessary), such men cannot be permitted to play with conjectures, but their assertion must be either science or nothing at all. . . .

QUESTIONS

1. What is metaphysics, according to Kant? What is his diagnosis of the ills of metaphysics? What is his remedy?
2. For Kant, what kind of judgment is analytical? What kind of judgment is synthetical?
3. How does Kant use the terms "a priori" and "a posteriori"? Give examples of (a) analytical, (b) synthetical a posteriori, and (c) synthetical a priori judgments.
4. The crucial question about Kant's program to show that metaphysics is possible is "Can one make synthetical a priori judgments?" How would you answer this question?
5. Kant says that "7 + 5 = 12" is a synthetical judgment. Yet it has been argued that in his terms such an arithmetical equation expresses "nothing in the predicate but what has been already actually thought in the concept of the subject." State why you think he was, or was not, mistaken about his classification of "7 + 5 = 12."
6. Kant says that "All bodies have weight" is a synthetical judgment. Yet it has been argued that we would not call something a body if it were weightless. State why you think he was, or was not, mistaken about the classification of the above statement.
7. Using Kant's classes of synthetical and analytical judgments, how would you classify the following judgments? Give your reasons for classifying them as you do. Are any of them synthetical a priori judgments?
   a. Things equal to the same thing are equal to each other.
   b. A pair of gloves is two matching gloves, one of which is for the right hand and the other for the left.
   c. If I am wearing a pair of gloves, then I am wearing two gloves.

    d. Every effect has a cause.
    e. Every event has a cause.
    f. Water is wet.
    g. At sea level, water freezes when the temperature is 32° F.
    h. At sea level, water freezes when it gets cold enough.
    i. This is a hot day. (A judgment made by someone when the temperature is 80° F.)
    j. A room is warm at 60° F. (A private judgment.)
    k. A room is warm at 60° F. (A legal definition in a city ordinance governing landlords who are responsible for providing heat in their buildings.)
    l. All red objects are red.
    m. Every body perseveres in its state of rest, or of uniform motion in a right line, unless it is compelled to change that state by forces impressed thereon. (Newton)

8. Read the selection by David Hume. Kant claims that Hume's philosophy is an attack on metaphysics. State why you agree or disagree with this claim. Is Hume himself writing metaphysics? What do you think Hume would say about the possibility of synthetical a priori judgments?

6. STEPHEN TOULMIN

(b. 1922)

A Defence of "Synthetic Necessary Truth"

Stephen Toulmin is Professor of the History of Ideas and Philosophy at Brandeis University. He has been a Research Fellow at King's College, Cambridge, Professor and Head of the Department of Philosophy at Leeds University, and Lecturer in the Philosophy of Science at Oxford. He was also the director of The Nuffield Foundation Unit for the History of Ideas. His works are *Examination of The Place of Reason in Ethics* (1950), *Philosophy of Science, An Introduction* (1953), *Uses of Argument* (1958), and *Foresight and Understanding* (1961). With June Goodfield, he has written *The Fabric of the Heavens* (1962) and *The Architecture of Matter* (1963).

In this paper Professor Toulmin offers a fresh justification of Kant's claim that in the class of necessary propositions we may distinguish some that are analytic and others that are synthetic. The claim must be established in the face of the opposing view that all necessary propositions must be analytic. Standard examples of synthetic, necessary propositions are "Seven and five make twelve," and "Nothing can be red and green all over." To give these propositions a neutral name, Professor Toulmin calls them "Type-Q propositions."

Type-Q propositions are generally agreed to be necessary, that is "the accumulation of evidence from experiments or observation is neither required for, nor relevant to, the establishment of their truth or falsity." But are they analytically necessary or synthetically necessary? If they are analytically necessary, then they are true by definition or by linguistic convention. If they are synthetically necessary, their truth does not follow simply from the definitions of the terms involved. It is this last alternative which Professor Toulmin supports, by showing that in determining the truth or falsity of Type-Q propositions what we must understand, in addition to the definitions of their terms, is the nature of their subject matter. Using the example of the organization of a regatta as a knockout competition, where we can say of it, "The first two crews in the draw can't both get into the final," Professor Toulmin shows that there are synthetic, necessary propositions, and that their truth is established by logical procedures open to all. He denies that any "intuition of the truth of a Type-Q proposition" is needed. In denying this, he is opposing a number of philosophers who have held that the mind can gain a direct knowledge of the truth of synthetic a priori propositions by an immediate apprehension which yields intellectual certainty. Professor Toulmin does not believe that any such intuitive deliverance of a mysterious "inner eye" is necessary for establishing the truth of synthetic a priori propositions.

From "A Defence of 'Synthetic Necessary Truth,'" *Mind*, Vol. 58, by Stephen Toulmin, April, 1949, pp. 164–77. Reprinted by permission of the author and the editor of *Mind*.

I

There is a certain class of propositions (which, in order to avoid begging any questions, I shall refer to as 'Type-Q' propositions) about whose logical status contemporary philosophers have come to hold radically-opposed opinions, opinions separated by an apparently unbridgeable gulf. Typically of the class are the two propositions,

"Seven and five make twelve" and
"Nothing can be both red and green all over" [1]

Others which have at one time or another been suggested as belonging to the class are the propositions,

"Such and such a type of intention or emotion would necessarily be fitting (or unfitting) to such and such a kind of situation", [2] and
"One ought always so to choose that the same volition shall comprehend the maxims of one's choice as a universal law". [3]

[1] See A. C. Ewing on "The Linguistic Theory of *A Priori* Propositions", *Proc. Aristot. Soc.*, 1939–40, pp. 207–44.
[2] C. D. Broad, *Five Types of Ethical Theory*, p. 282.
[3] Immanuel Kant, *Fundamental Principles of the Metaphysics of Morals*, tr. Abbott, p. 71.

It is generally agreed that the most typical propositions of this class are 'necessary', *i.e.,* that the accumulation of evidence from experiments or observations is neither required for, nor relevant to the establishment of their truth or falsity; but beyond this point there is no general agreement. Some philosophers hold that they are 'synthetic', *i.e.,* that their truth does not follow from the definitions of the terms involved alone, and that they are known by *'a priori* insight',[4] 'immediate apprehension',[5] or 'intuitive induction'.[6] (This opinion I shall refer to as the 'Synthetic Theory'.) Such philosophers find nothing obnoxious in the idea of propositions which are both 'synthetic' and 'necessary'. Their opponents, on the other hand, seem to regard the phrase 'synthetic necessary proposition' as a contradiction in terms; for they hold it to be demonstrable that there can be no such propositions, and *a fortiori* that 'type-Q' propositions are not both synthetic and necessary. Any necessary proposition which seems on a superficial examination to be also 'synthetic', they declare, will be found on closer inspection to be 'analytic'—true 'by definition', or by 'linguistic convention'—after all:

> "Our knowledge that no observation can ever confute the proposition '7 + 5 = 12' depends simply on the fact that the symbolic expression '7 + 5' is synonymous with '12', just as our knowledge that every oculist is an eye-doctor depends on the fact that the symbol 'eye-doctor' is synonymous with 'oculist'. And the same explanation holds good for every other *a priori* truth." [7]

(This opinion I shall call the 'Analytic Theory'.)

In this paper, I want to reconcile these opposing views. I shall argue that there is nothing self-contradictory in talking of 'synthetic necessary propositions'. With the help of an example more familiar in everyday life than in philosophical discussions, I shall try to throw fresh light on to the logical status of 'type-Q' propositions. I shall point out that the issue has been given a delusive sharpness by the introduction of certain irrelevant 'epistemological' arguments; namely, attempts to answer the conundrum, "How do we 'know' synthetic necessary truths?", as though it were like the question, "How do cats see in the dark?" Leaving these aside, I shall attempt to reconstruct the source of the Analytic Theory's plausibility, and at the same time to discover why supporters of the Synthetic Theory are led to get so hot under the collar at the prospect of the Analytic Theory ("a doctrine which must encourage the widespread depreciation of reason in so far as it has any influence at all".[8])

---

[4] See, for example, Ewing, p. 213.
[5] See, for example, D. D. Raphael, *The Moral Sense,* p. 34.
[6] Broad, *loc. cit.;* Raphael, p. 193, etc.
[7] A. J. Ayer, *Language, Truth and Logic,* 1st ed., p. 115.
[8] Ewing, p. 209.

II

The Analytic Theory, or at any rate the most usually published form of it, as interpreted in the most natural and literal senses of the terms employed, has defects which supporters of the Synthetic Theory have pointed out ably and at length: these defects I intend only to summarise. To begin with, although it can be agreed that the truth of type-Q propositions "depends wholly on the meaning of the terms used"[9]—supporters of the Synthetic Theory neither need to, nor do dispute this—this is not the same as saying that they are true or false in virtue of the *definitions* of the terms used. Their truth certainly does not depend on anything which anyone but a philosopher with an axe to grind would call 'definitions' or linguistic 'rules': books of grammar and dictionaries[10] do not suffice to establish typical type-Q propositions any more than they do matters of fact. Further, it is quite certain that, whatever language a type-Q proposition were expressed in, it must always remain logically unaffected: it must be as true or as false in Chinese, Afghan or Malay as it is when expressed in languages we can understand.[11] This fact is concealed by those who claim that the truth of type-Q propositions is based on 'linguistic conventions'; and the use of this phrase also gives such propositions a misleading air of arbitrariness ('conventionality'), which supporters of the Synthetic Theory understandably find offensive.[12]

Now it seems to me that supporters of the Analytic Theory ought to grant that these are perfectly valid objections to their view, certainly in the forms in which it has been expressed up to now. Indeed, I suspect that they only hesitate to grant this because they believe that to do so must commit them to the Synthetic Theory *as a whole*. Such a belief is mistaken: they can quite well afford to allow that there is some value in Kant's division of necessary propositions into 'analytic' and 'synthetic', and even agree to say, for the purposes of argument, that there can be such things as 'synthetic necessary propositions', without finding themselves forced to swallow, willy-nilly, all that seems to them unpalatable in the usual expositions of the Synthetic Theory. For what is pernicious in these expositions is, surely, not so much the decision to apply the title 'synthetic necessary proposition' to certain propositions, as the doctrine that, granted the existence of 'synthetic necessary truths', we must 'know' them by 'intuition', by *'a priori* insight', by a 'rational faculty of immediate apprehension' ("Something accompanying and behind all the senses, [which] receives *some* new ideas by itself and without the medium of sensation"[13]). This doctrine I shall refer to as 'the Doctrine of the Inner Eye'.

[9] *Cf., Ibid.,* pp. 231–32.
[10] *Ibid.,* p. 213.
[11] *Ibid.,* pp. 217–19.
[12] *Ibid.,* pp. 209, 232, 240–41.
[13] Raphael, pp. 2–3, 34, etc.

It is my first task to show that behind Kant's division of necessary propositions there lies an indisputable distinction, which is conveniently marked by the use of his terms, 'analytic' and 'synthetic'; but that to grant this is not necessarily to grant the Doctrine of the Inner Eye.

III

I can best do this with the help of examples taken from an everyday activity, that of running a regatta, consisting of a number of 'knock-out' competitions. Here (away from the blinding dust of the philosophical arena) we can recognise the distinction between 'synthetic' and 'analytic necessaries' without getting entangled in epistemological side-issues; and we can carry back the lessons learnt when we return and reconsider the more complicated and contentious 'type-Q' propositions.

Suppose, then, that eight crews enter for the Visitors' Challenge Cup, and that the draw comes out as follows:—

King's			
Lady Margaret	Heat 1	First	
Jesus		Semi-Final	
Christ Church	Heat 2		Final
Oriel	Heat 3		
New College		Second	
Corpus Christi	Heat 4	Semi-Final	
Pembroke			

I may now have occasion to say:

(a) "King's can't get into the final",
(b) "King's can't get into the second semi-final", or
(c) "King's and Lady Margaret can't both get into the final".

Of these propositions, (a) is unquestionably 'empirical'. If called upon to justify my belief I shall appeal to past form as evidence, saying "Their stroke is too short", "Their blade-work is ragged", or "The other crews in the top half of the draw are too fast for them". No such considerations are, on the other hand, relevant to the truth of (b) and (c).

There are, however, other grounds on which (b) and (c) may be called 'empirical', for King's and Lady Margaret might very well have been drawn elsewhere. (By exchanging King's and any of the four bottom crews, you falsify both (b) and (c).) In order to discount this empirical element—what we call 'the luck of the draw'—let us consider instead the two propositions,

(d) "The first crew in the draw can't get into the second semi-final", and

(e) "The first two crews in the draw can't both get into the final".

These propositions, I suggest, can fairly be called both 'necessary' and 'synthetic'.

In order to confirm that (*d*) and (*e*) are necessary, notice that no observation or experience could ever confute them. We do not need to go to more and more and more regattas in order to make sure of their truth: we know very well that they are true without that. If, for instance, a semi-final in which the first crew in the draw competed took place later in time than that between crews from the bottom half, that would not falsify (*d*). It would only show that the 'second semi-final' had been rowed before the 'first semi-final'.

But, granted that the propositions (*d*) and (*e*) are 'necessary', are they not perhaps also 'analytic'? I think it would be an unnatural extension of the term to call them 'analytic'. It would certainly be an unnatural extension of the terms 'definition' and 'convention' to say that they were true 'by definition' or 'by linguistic convention'. Nothing which it would be at all natural to give as 'definitions' of the terms 'crew', 'draw', 'heat', 'final', etc., (*e.g.*, the definitions in the *Oxford English Dictionary*) would be sufficient to establish the truth of (*d*) and (*e*). In protesting against the Analytic Theory on these grounds, supporters of the Synthetic Theory, such as Dr. Ewing,[14] seem to me to be entirely in the right. If it *is* from 'conventions' or 'rules' that the truth of (*d*) and (*e*) follows, it is not from 'linguistic' rules or conventions: it is from *the rules for running a regatta;* and these are something quite different from the definitions of 'crew', 'draw', 'heat', 'final', etc.

Advocates of the Analytic Theory may, of course, reply that to say this is only to make the truth of (*d*) and (*e*) follow, in addition, from the definitions of the terms 'knock-out competition' and 'regatta', and in a sense this is true; but, at the same time, it both is true in a misleading way and concedes the crucial point. To explain this: it is conceivable that one might come across people engaged in an activity closely resembling that which we call 'running a regatta', who denied the propositions (*d*) and (*e*). It might be that we found, for example, that among these people the race between the first two crews in the draw was taken as the 'decider' (so falsifying (*e*) in a practical manner), the winner of this race being given the prize and treated as 'the champion crew'. And, if this were to happen, we should no doubt want to say (according to the circumstances) that what they were running was 'a misconducted regatta', 'a different kind of regatta', or even 'not a regatta at all', certainly 'not what *we* call a regatta'. But suppose that considerations like these were held to show that the truth of the propositions (*d*) and (*e*) does, after all, depend on 'definitions' or 'linguistic conventions' (since their being true is part of what we should require before agreeing to apply the terms 'knock-out competition' and 'regatta' to any activity); then we must give a two-fold answer:—

(i) The 'definitions' at issue are not those of the terms involved in

14 *Cf.,* Ewing, quoted above.

(*d*) and (*e*) *alone,* for the words 'regatta' and 'knock-out competition' do not occur in either of these propositions. That fact alone, on the definition of 'synthetic' adopted in this paper, is enough to justify calling them 'synthetic': the crucial point is therefore conceded.

(ii) Even granted that the truth of (*d*) and (*e*) follows from all these 'definitions' taken together, the 'definition' of 'regatta' to which we must appeal is no arbitrary one. There is all the difference in the world between saying, "That's not what we call a 'regatta': the word for that is 'raffle' ", (so asserting a purely linguistic matter) and saying, "That's not what we call a regatta; that's hardly more than a raffle!", meaning, "That kind of competition is no test of the skill of the competitors: winning it is hardly more than a matter of pure chance, so it doesn't serve the purpose of a regatta at all!" The distinction between the *usages* of the terms 'regatta' and 'raffle' may be a linguistic convention, but it is (to put it at the best) hopelessly misleading to talk of the difference in *purpose* between a raffle and a regatta either as 'conventional' or as 'a matter of words'.

Let me sum up the lessons to be learnt from this example. There is an indisputable distinction to be drawn between necessary propositions of two kinds: those like "An oculist is an eye-doctor", whose truth follows from the definitions of the terms involved alone, and those like "The first two crews in the draw can't both get into the final", which cannot be proved true without a further appeal. This distinction is conveniently marked by calling propositions of the first kind 'analytic' and those of the second 'synthetic'. (I shall argue in a moment that this use of the terms 'synthetic' and 'analytic' reflects Kant's own practice, if not perhaps his intentions, and that, in adopting it, we shall be doing him more justice than do the advocates of the Doctrine of the Inner Eye.) Those philosophers, such as Ayer, who have in the past supported a 'purely analytic' theory of necessary propositions, need not be afraid of recognising this distinction; for, in order to justify what on these standards we shall call 'synthetic necessary propositions', we need not appeal to the evidence of any mysterious 'sixth sense', 'insight' or 'intuition', but only to our understanding of the nature of the subject-matter under discussion, that is, to the 'logical type' of the concepts involved. Still, the definitions of the terms involved are, by themselves, not enough. In order, for instance, to prove the truth of (*d*) and (*e*), we have to know not only the definitions of 'crew', 'final', 'draw', etc.: we have also to know (and, it is important to note, in considerable detail) what it is to run a 'regatta', as opposed to a 'sweepstake', a 'championship competition', etc. If we are to prove (*d*) and (*e*), "we must", to use Kant's own words, "advance beyond the cognition of the objects to a critical examination of the subject".[15]

[15] Kant, *loc. cit.*

IV

It is interesting to find Kant making a remark like this. His intentions are often obscure, and the way in which he uses terms like 'subject' is, as a result, consistently ambiguous. (Does he mean 'thinker' or 'subject-matter'?) If, however, we discount the mock-psychological façade, and examine the logical structure behind it, we shall find that his position is not widely different from ours.

Consider, for example, his 'principle of the autonomy of the will', the 'synthetical and necessary proposition' in elucidating which he makes the remark just quoted. This principle he states in the words,

> "Always so to choose that the same volition shall comprehend the maxims of our choice as a universal law." [16]

After stripping away the psychological trappings, I want to reinterpret it in the form,

> (*f*) "The only principles to which one ought to appeal in justification of one's decisions and actions are ones which apply universally—not to me rather than you, now rather than another time, etc."

(This may not be what Kant said, but it seems to me to have something very closely to do with what Kant said, and to be a proposition well worth discussing.)

Proposition (*f*) is, in my sense of the phrase, a 'synthetic necessary' proposition. We do not discover its truth by observation or experiment, as we go along: it is 'necessary' or nothing. At the same time, its truth could hardly be said to follow from anything one would naturally give as 'definitions' of the terms involved *alone*: it is, therefore, 'synthetic'. But, bearing in mind the lessons of the regatta example, it is not hard to discover what else it is that the truth of (*f*) *does* depend on. For, just as in the case of (*d*) and (*e*) it is taken for granted that we are talking about a 'knock-out competition' and a 'regatta', so (*f*) has to be understood as referring to the 'moral' justification of our decisions and actions. It is true that, if people stopped talking about what they ought 'morally speaking' to do, that is, if they ceased to take 'moral' considerations into account in making up their minds, the truth of (*f*) might be forgotten or denied. But, if that were to happen, we should have to say that they were no longer talking about the same kind of thing as before; that it was appeals to 'privilege', to 'expediency', to 'authority', with which they were concerned, rather than appeals to 'morality'; and this would make nonsense of (*f*), rather than falsifying it, since, in the absence of any qualification, we understand 'ought' as meaning 'ought (morally speaking)'.

[16] *Ibid.*

The truth of (*f*) depends, therefore, not only on the definitions of the terms involved, but in addition on what we mean by 'morality', as opposed to 'privilege', 'expediency', etc. Appealing to universal principles is a part of what we mean by 'appealing to morality', and by 'speaking morally'. Once again, we cannot question the truth of the synthetic necessary proposition (*f*), so long as we understand and accept the nature of the subject-matter under discussion; namely, that it is a question of 'morality'. And, once again, to claim that this proposition is true 'by linguistic convention', or 'by definition', after all (even if it does not actually follow from the definitions of the terms involved alone) is hopelessly misleading: the distinction we draw between 'morality' and 'privilege' is in most situations more than 'a matter of words'.

Before leaving Kant, may I interject a few remarks about the *Critique of Pure Reason?* When Kant declares that we cannot help thinking in terms of spatial, temporal and causal notions, he seems to be concerning himself with a kind of super-empirical psychology; and this raises endless problems. But there is logical backing for what he says, as we can recognise if we recall his preoccupation with the question, "How is knowledge possible?" [17]

Consider the proposition,

(*g*) "One cannot help thinking in terms of spatial, temporal and causal notions".

As it is expressed, this is certainly no analytic truism; but, if we add the clause, "If it's knowledge one is after", we can trace the source of its necessary truth. If you forswore the use of all spatial, temporal and causal notions, nothing which you said would be very informative, or would communicate anything which could properly be called 'knowledge'. It is true that you might still be able to say, "Something happened to me somewhere sometime". Yet even this might have to be ruled out, since the words 'somewhere' and 'sometime' could only be used correctly by one who understood words like 'here' and 'now'; in which case you could only exclaim, "Man!", or "Ow!", or "Hurrah!". Now, supposing that this *were* all that you could say to me, I should be entitled to reply, "That's not 'knowledge'!" By this I should mean, not "The word for that is 'rumour' or 'hokum' or 'exclamation', not 'knowledge' ", but rather, "That gives me none of the kind of help needed in this situation, such as you would have given me by saying, 'A tall man in a mackintosh jumped out from behind the gate as I was walking past it five minutes ago and struck me on the head, breaking my spectacles'." One might, therefore, argue very plausibly that proposition (*g*) is both true, and necessarily true, though its proof requires us to appeal not only to the definitions of the terms involved, but also to the nature of the subject at issue; that is, to the distinction between what can and what cannot properly be called 'knowledge'.

[17] This was pointed out to me by Professor von Wright in discussion.

V

It should now be possible to explain both the source of the Analytic Theory's plausibility, and the horror which it so often arouses in opponents.

First, then, what is it that has led philosophers to advocate the Analytic Theory, despite the comparatively obvious fallacies involved? Recall the lessons of the examples we have examined. There is a slightly eccentric sense of 'follow' such that type-Q propositions may be said to follow from certain 'definitions', or rather from the nature of certain distinctions which we are in the habit of making (and for very good reasons); such as that between a 'regatta' and a 'raffle', that between 'morality' and 'privilege', and that between what can and what cannot properly be called 'knowledge'. (These distinctions, however, define not the terms but the logical type, or the nature of the subject-matter of the type-Q propositions concerned.) In consequence, there is another class of propositions with which type-Q propositions may easily be confused. This class is made up as follows: for every type-Q proposition, we may construct a corresponding proposition in which the nature of the subject-matter is made explicit. In place of

(*e*) "The first two crews in the draw can't both get into the final",

we may consider

(*e'*) "In a 'knock-out competition' in a 'regatta', the first two crews in the 'draw' can't both get into the 'final' ".

In place of

(*f*) "The only principles to which one ought to appeal are universal ones . . .",

we may consider

(*f'*) "When taking 'moral' considerations into account, the only 'principles' to which we 'ought' to appeal are universal ones . . ."

In place of

(*g*) "One cannot help thinking in terms of spatial, temporal and causal notions",

we may consider

(*g'*) "If one is to obtain 'knowledge', one cannot help thinking in terms of spatial, temporal and causal notions".

And likewise, in place of

(*h*) "Seven and five make twelve",

we may consider

> (*h'*) "In 'the arithmetic of natural numbers', seven and five make twelve".

It is reasonable enough to call the propositions (*e'*) to (*h'*) 'analytic necessaries'. And, since these propositions only make explicit what is already implicit in the type-Q propositions (*e*) to (*h*), the advocates of the Analytic Theory may have argued that (*e*) to (*h*) must therefore also be classed as 'analytic necessaries'. "In any case", they may say, "we know nowadays how much more complicated definitions may be than used to be suspected: it is therefore pardonable to confuse, or rather to ignore the differences between the two classes of proposition." But, whatever may be said in their defence, and however much one may sympathise with them in their distaste for the Doctrine of the Inner Eye, the differences between the propositions (*e*) to (*h*) and the propositions (*e'*) to (*h'*) remain; and it remains an extension of the notion of a 'definition' far beyond its everyday limits to pack into it everything needed to prove the truth of type-Q propositions from the 'definitions' of their terms alone, for this means including in every 'definition' all those things which distinguish a notion of one type from notions of *other* logical types as well as everything marking it off from other notions of the *same* type, all those things which make red a 'colour' as well as everything marking it off from green, blue, brown, etc.

So much for the fallacies behind the Analytic Theory. But what makes it seem to so many of its opponents not just false but outrageous? One of the lessons of the regatta example was the difference between two similar-looking classes of propositions:—

> (i) "That's not a 'regatta'; that's a 'raffle' ".
> "That's not an 'oculist': that's an 'optician' ".

(The issue in these cases is purely 'linguistic'. The proposition is intended to correct someone's usage, and the second half can in each case be read as "the word for that is 'raffle', 'optician', etc.".)

> (ii) "That's not a regatta: that's hardly more than a raffle!"
> "That's not an appeal to morality: that's an appeal to privilege!"
> "You can't call that knowledge!"
> "That's a funny kind of arithmetic!"

(The issue in these cases is far from being purely linguistic. The proposition is intended not just to correct someone's usage, but to make him think and behave very differently. The issue can, therefore, hardly be called either 'conventional' or 'a matter of words'.)

Quite apart from confusing the propositions (*e*) to (*h*) and (*e'*) to (*h'*), advocates of the Analytic Theory have to assimilate all the members of class (ii) to class (i). Only by treating the members of class (ii) as 'matters of words', like those in class (i), can they justify themselves in calling type-Q propositions 'analytic', true 'by definition', true 'by linguistic convention'. And to do this is clearly to misrepresent both the nature of class (ii) propositions, and that of the type-Q propositions dependent on them. In view of this, we need hardly be surprised at the feelings of outrage which supporters of the Synthetic Theory express when faced with the Analytic Theory. (Even so, we may feel that they are hardly justified in suggesting that belief in the truth of the Analytic Theory should lead one to abandon discussion in favour of violence as a means of settling disputes! [18])

VI

A few remarks, in conclusion, about the Doctrine of the Inner Eye, since this is the real bone of contention between supporters of the two theories. It should be clear by now that the existence of 'synthetic necessary' propositions and the 'synthetic' nature of type-Q propositions are questions wholly independent of this doctrine. There is not much temptation to invoke any 'intuition' or other 'rational faculty' to justify one's certainty of the truth of the proposition (*e*), "The first two crews in the draw can't both get into the final": it is clear, in this case, that a knowledge of what it is 'to run a regatta' is all that we need to appeal to. The question we now have to ask is why this independence should be any less obvious in the case of more typical type-Q propositions. How is it, then, that so many philosophers have come to think that some special 'faculty', 'insight' or 'intuition' was needed to inform us of the truth of type-Q propositions?

I can, at the moment, suggest only the beginnings of an answer to this question. Notice to begin with two kinds of proposition of which it is possible to be 'absolutely certain'. On the one hand, (1) there are those propositions (for example, "The ace of hearts is in my hand") of whose truth we are certain without there being any question of our adducing 'reasons': if challenged, we can only appeal to 'the evidence of our senses'. On the other hand, (2) there are those propositions whose truth we cannot question if we understand the nature of the subject-matter at all. Type-Q (synthetic necessary) propositions belong, as I have been trying to explain, to the second class: advocates of the Doctrine of the Inner Eye talk as though they belonged to the first.

Consider the following passage written by a supporter of the Synthetic Theory (incidentally, by one who claims [19] not to 'postulate some mysterious faculty' to explain our knowledge of synthetic necessary truths) :—

"It is surely plain that some *a priori* propositions, *e.g.* everything which has shape has size, a thing cannot be both red and green, if one thing

[18] See Ewing, pp. 240–41.
[19] *Ibid.*, p. 243.

is above another and the second is above a third the first is above the third, all three-sided rectilinear figures have three angles, could be seen to be true without the use of language. A person who was capable of forming visual images might quite well see the truth of any of these propositions without having to put them into words, and therefore their truth cannot possibly depend on the structure of language." [20]

The crucial and ensnaring phrases in this passage are 'seen to be true' and 'see the truth of'. Certainly, when talking about propositions of class (1), we are accustomed to using phrases of the form 'seeing the ace of hearts in my hand', 'seeing that the ace of hearts is in my hand', 'seeing that the proposition "The ace of hearts is in my hand" is true' and 'seeing the truth of the proposition "The ace of hearts is in my hand"', interchangeably. But this practice can be extended to propositions of class (2) only through a misunderstanding. If this *is* done, however, the Doctrine of the Inner Eye acquires considerable plausibility. For then, having noticed that seeing the ace of hearts in your hand is much the same as seeing the truth of the proposition, "The ace of hearts is in my hand", you may all too easily begin looking for the experience whose description is interchangeable with the phrase 'seeing the truth of the proposition, "Nothing can be both red and green all over"'.

Once begun, this search need never end, for no answer can be at all satisfactory. No experience will do for the propositions, "Nothing can be both red and green all over" and "The first two crews in the draw can't both get into the final", what seeing the ace of hearts in your hand does for the proposition, "The ace of hearts is in my hand". "Use your eyes", is a fair answer to the question, "How am I to know that the ace of hearts is in my hand?": the answers to the questions, "How am I to know that the first two crews can't both get into the final?" and "How am I to know that nothing can be both red and green all over?" are to be given, not by any appeal to a 'sixth sense' or to 'visual imagery', but by reference to the way in which regattas are run, the purpose of regattas, etc., and to the nature of colour-concepts, the purpose of classification by colours, etc. One can conjure up a visual image of the ace of hearts in one's hand, and to do this is (if you like to call it that) 'to see what is meant by the words "The ace of hearts is in my hand"'. But, conjure up what visual images you choose, you will never find one which shows you 'what is meant by the words "Nothing can be both red and green all over"': all you can imagine is *red and green objects*. Nor is visualising three dots, one above the other, in any sense the same as 'seeing the truth of the proposition, "If one thing is above another, and the second is above a third, the first is above the third"': the most such a visual image could ever be said to do would be to *remind* you or to *convince* you of the truth of that proposition.

To resort to 'intuition', 'rational faculties', 'visual images' and so on is to

[20] *Ibid.*, p. 217.

overlook or forget the fact that 'seeing the truth of a type-Q proposition' is not a matter of 'having the right experiences', as it would be if type-Q propositions belonged to class (1), but is a matter of 'understanding the nature of the subject-matter'. And understanding the nature of the subject-matter is (to adapt Professor Ryle's illuminating distinction [21]) as much 'knowing how. . . .' or 'knowing what it is to. . . .' as it is 'knowing that. . . .' The natural thing, for example, to say about a man who knows that seven and five make twelve is that (unlike some) he knows 'how to count'; not that he has access, which others are denied, to certain mysteriously ultimate and ineluctable facts about the universe (or what Dr. Ewing inscrutably calls 'the real' [22]). Likewise, the man who knows that p and q together entail r is a man who knows 'how to make inferences'.

What we commonly call 'insight' may help mathematicians like Fermat and Ramanujan and logicians like Russell to get their answers more quickly than other people, and even to get answers which they would not have reached without it; but it is no substitute for a proof. '*A priori* insight', again, might *help* one to see the truth of complicated type-Q propositions; but it is no substitute for a discursive analysis of the types of situation and activity in connexion with which the propositions are used, and the functions they perform in those situations. Intuition, visual imagery, insight and what-you-like may be short cuts to confidence in the truth of synthetic necessary propositions, but they cannot constitute a proof.

QUESTIONS

1. What does Professor Toulmin mean by "necessary," "synthetic," and "analytic" as they are used to describe propositions?
2. What are Type-Q propositions and what is at issue between the Analytic Theory and the Synthetic Theory as accounts of the meaning and truth of this kind of proposition?
3. What is the Doctrine of the Inner Eye and why is it pernicious? How does Professor Toulmin argue against this doctrine?
4. What is the argument to establish that "The first two crews in the draw can't both get into the final" is a synthetic, necessary proposition?
5. Explain the claim that the propositions "An oculist is an eye-doctor" and "The first two crews can't both get into the final" represent two distinct kinds of necessary proposition. What is the importance of this distinction for Professor Toulmin's argument?
6. What does Professor Toulmin mean by understanding the nature of the subject matter of Type-Q propositions, and what is the importance to his argument of appeals to this kind of understanding?
7. Give three examples of your own of Type-Q propositions, which are *not* taken from situations of contest or games, and state why you think Professor Toulmin would consider them Type-Q propositions.

[21] See G. Ryle, "Knowing How and Knowing That", *Proc. Aristot. Soc.*, 1945–46, pp. 1–16.
[22] Ewing, p. 211.

8. Attack or defend the following thesis:
   The principle of induction, or the uniformity of nature (i.e., The future will resemble the past) is a Type-Q proposition and is a true one.
9. Make a detailed comparison between Professor Toulmin's view of synthetic, necessary propositions and Kant's view of synthetic a priori judgments. Which view do you consider the more correct, and why?

SUGGESTED FURTHER READING

INTRODUCTORY STUDIES

Barker, Stephen F., *Philosophy of Mathematics,* Prentice-Hall, Englewood Cliffs, N. J., 1964.

Hospers, John, *An Introduction to Philosophical Analysis,* Prentice-Hall, Englewood Cliffs, N.J., 1953. Especially Chaps. 2, "Necessary Knowledge"; 3, "Empirical Knowledge"; 4, "Law, Cause and Freedom"; and 6, "Perceiving the World."

MacNabb, D. G. C., *David Hume, His Theory of Knowledge and Morality,* Hutchinson's University Library, London, 1951.

Pears, D. F., ed., *David Hume: A Symposium,* Macmillan, London, 1963.

Sprague, Elmer, *What Is Philosophy?* Oxford University Press, New York, 1961. Chap. 2, "Philosophy and Man: Intellectual Powers."

Weldon, Thomas D., *Introduction to Kant's Critique of Pure Reason,* Clarendon Press, Oxford, 1945.

ADVANCED STUDIES

Benacerraf, Paul, and Hilary Putnam, eds., *Philosophy of Mathematics,* Prentice-Hall, Englewood Cliffs, N. J., 1964. (Anthology.)

Blanshard, Brand, *Reason and Analysis,* Allen & Unwin, London, 1962. Chaps. VI, X, and XI.

Feigl, Herbert, and Wilfrid Sellars, eds., *Readings in Philosophical Analysis,* Appleton-Century-Crofts, New York, 1949.

Lewis, C. I., *Mind and the World Order,* Scribner's, New York, 1929. Chap. VIII, "The Nature of the A Priori, and the Pragmatic Element in Knowledge."

Pap, Arthur, *Semantics and Necessary Truth,* Yale University Press, New Haven, 1958.

Parkinson, G. H. R., "Necessary Propositions and 'A Priori' Knowledge in Kant," *Mind,* 69:391–97, 1960.

Ryle, G., K. Popper, C. Lewy, "Why Are the Calculuses of Arithmetic and Logic Applicable to Reality?" *Aristotelian Society Supplementary Volume XX,* Harrison & Sons, Ltd., London, 1946.

Sesonske, Alexander, and Noel Fleming, eds., *Human Understanding: Studies in the Philosophy of David Hume,* Wadsworth, Belmont, Calif., 1965. (Anthology.)

Waismann, Friedrich, *Principles of Linguistic Philosophy,* ed. by R. Harre, St. Martin's, New York, 1966.

SELECTED ARTICLES ON THE ANALYTIC-SYNTHETIC DISTINCTION

Black, Max, "Necessary Statements and Rules" and "The Analysis of Rules," *Models and Metaphors,* Cornell University Press, Ithaca, N. Y., 1962.

Ebersole, F. B., "On Certain Confusions in the Analytic-Synthetic Distinction," *The Journal of Philosophy,* 53:485–94, August 2, 1956.

Grice, H. P., and P. Strawson, "In Defence of a Dogma," *The Philosophical Review*, 65:141–58, April, 1956.

Heinemann, F. H., "Truths of Reason and Truth of Fact," *The Philosophical Review*, 17:485 ff., 1948; and "Are There Only Two Kinds of Truth?", *Philosophy and Phenomenological Research*, 16:367–79, 1956.

Pears, D. F., "Synthetic Necessary Truth," *Mind*, 59:199–208, April, 1950. (A criticism of Stephen Toulmin's article.)

Quine, W. V., "Two Dogmas of Empiricism," *From a Logical Point of View*, Harvard University Press, Cambridge, Mass., 1953.

Chapter 3. Metaphysics

Metaphysics may be described in several different ways, and one of the live controversies in philosophy is over which description is the proper one, or at least over what is the correct degree of emphasis to be placed on each of the various descriptions. According to what may be the most widespread view, metaphysics is a report of the reality which lies behind appearances. The world with which our senses acquaint us is but an ever-shifting series of appearances, and behind them there must stand some sort of reality which lends stability and order to what we perceive. The task of metaphysics is to give an account of this imperceptible but somehow knowable ordering principle. An example of this sort of metaphysical doctrine is Locke's account of substance: "The unknown support of those qualities we find existing, which we imagine cannot subsist . . . without something to support them." Similarly, Berkeley and Russell, in the first readings in this chapter, argue for two quite different inferences that we may draw with respect to the reality that lies behind appearance.

Another view of metaphysics is that the metaphysician's task is to make an inventory of what there is. This aspect of metaphysics is given the name "ontology"—"the science of being" or "the study of what there is." The metaphysician's inventory is of a special sort, for it is not merely an indiscriminate listing of the things he finds in existence or thinks of as existing. Rather his task is to decide on the fundamental or ultimate kinds of things that there are; many metaphysicians do this by establishing theories of knowledge. For example, in Berkeley's theory of knowledge, anything which we know by way of our senses is ultimately a collection of ideas. Berkeley finds an apple, for example,

to be a collection of ideas of "a certain colour, taste, smell, figure and consistence." But as ideas exist by being known, there must be something that exists by knowing ideas, namely the mind. So for Berkeley the fundamental kinds of things are minds and ideas. In contrast with Berkeley, Russell allows that minds may know physical objects as well as ideas; so his theory of knowledge permits the existence of at least one more thing than Berkeley's does.

Yet a third view is that the metaphysician's task is not to describe the world, but to report his insight into the character of the world, an insight which underlies all true descriptions of the various parts of the world, and which makes our knowledge of the various parts cohere in an intelligible whole. For example, the insight which Berkeley offers might be summarized in the slogan "To be is to perceive or to be perceived." The claim here is that whatever is, is either a mind or something dependent on a mind. This is the basic tenet of the metaphysical theory (or system) known as Idealism. Opposed to it is Realism, the view that there is at least one sort of thing in the world that is neither mind nor dependent on a mind for its existence. Since the third ultimate sort of thing Russell argues for is matter, his Realism is a statement of Materialism. For the Materialist, if Matter is assumed, then much that is otherwise inexplicable can be explained. Some materialists believe that there is only one ultimate kind of thing, matter. Russell, on the other hand, believes that minds and their ideas exist as well as matter, and that these are not reducible to matter.

One way of coming to understand the nature of metaphysics is by considering the actual theories propounded by metaphysicians. Another way is to consider the objections which have been advanced by some philosophers against the whole enterprise of metaphysics. In "The Elimination of Metaphysics," Professor A. J. Ayer argues that metaphysical assertions are meaningless. His argument turns on the claim that there are only two kinds of meaningful statements—analytic (Hume's "relations of ideas") and synthetic (Hume's "matters of fact"). According to Ayer, since metaphysical assertions fit into neither of these classifications, they must be meaningless. In answer to this line of reasoning, Professor W. H. Walsh argues in "True and False in Metaphysics" that Ayer limits the possible kinds of statements too narrowly and that there is a third sort of meaningfulness that encompasses metaphysical assertions. This controversy over the logical status of metaphysical assertions shows the way to yet another characterization of metaphysics: Metaphysics is distinguished from other systems of thought by the way in which the truth or falsity of metaphysical assertions is to be ascertained.

The metaphysical issues treated in this anthology arise in a number of other chapters as well as in this one. In particular, there are two other topics which have received prolonged consideration by metaphysicians in their quest for the reality behind appearance, and which should be especially noticed as extensions of topics discussed in this chapter: the Self, in Chapter 5, and God, in Chapters 6, 7, and 8.

7. GEORGE BERKELEY

(1685–1753)

The Principles of Human Knowledge

George Berkeley was born in Ireland and educated at Trinity College, Dublin. He held a number of ecclesiastical positions in the Anglican Church, and finally became Bishop of Cloyne (County Cork, Ireland). His chief works are: *An Essay toward a New Theory of Vision* (1709); *A Treatise Concerning the Principles of Human Knowledge* (1710); and *Three Dialogues between Hylas and Philonous* (1713).

Like Locke, Berkeley believes that all our knowledge comes either from the outward data of our sense experience (colors, sounds, shapes, smells, touch sensations, etc.) or from the inward data of our thoughts and feelings. All of these data are called by Berkeley "ideas," and he makes a sharp distinction between them and the mind which perceives them. Ideas are those things which are perceived; minds are those things which do the perceiving. After stating these principles, Berkeley is ready to propound his famous thesis: That houses, mountains, rivers, and all perceivable objects exist only in our minds. "For," he says, "what are the forementioned objects but the things we perceive by sense? and what do we perceive besides our own ideas and sensations?" This thesis is Berkeley's statement of the kind of metaphysics called "Idealism."

Berkeley's metaphysics is open to two interpretations. One is that Berkeley is claiming that the only things which exist are minds. Objects that we perceive, such as houses and mountains, tables and chairs, are nothing but groups of ideas in our minds. Therefore nothing exists outside our minds. The other view is that Berkeley is not denying the existence of what are ordinarily called "material objects" at all. He is instead telling us that philosophers use the word "matter" entirely differently from the way it is used by the ordinary man. For the philosopher, "matter" refers to *substance* in which an object's sensible qualities are supposed to inhere, but which cannot itself be perceived by the senses. Substance is that part of an object which provides a "home," as it were, for an object's perceptible qualities. If substance were itself perceptible, then it too would need a "home." Because such a supposition would involve philosophers in an infinite regress of substances underlying substances, those philosophers who talk about substance define it as unperceivable. Since Berkeley believes that only the perceivable exists, he cannot count the philosopher's matter or substance as existing. In contrast with the philosopher's use of "matter," in ordinary life we use the word to refer to objects which are perceivable by the senses. Berkeley says that he does not deny the existence of matter in the latter sense, but only in the former sense. "The only thing whose existence we deny is that which *philosophers* call Matter or corporeal substance." (Berkeley's italics.) Here Berkeley is in direct opposition to Locke, who supposed that *substance* as the imperceptible support of perceptible qualities does exist. Thus, Berkeley's various arguments against the existence of a material world external to the mind may be interpreted in two ways—as the claim that nothing exists outside our minds, and as the denial of the existence of *substance*.

It is to be noted that Berkeley denies the distinction made by Locke between primary and secondary qualities, according to which only our ideas of primary qualities correspond to the actual properties of real material objects. In order to explain where our ideas of perceivable objects come from and why it is that they do not depend on our will, Berkeley says that there must be a supreme and all powerful mind which puts the ideas in our minds. The reading concludes with Berkeley's defense of his views against four objections.

The reading is from Sections 1–4, 6–11, 14–16, 18–20, 23, 25, 26, 28–35, 50, 51, 58, and 59 of *A Treatise Concerning the Principles of Human Knowledge,* second edition.

It is evident to any one who takes a survey of the *objects* of human knowledge, that they are either ideas actually imprinted on the senses; or else such as are perceived by attending to the passions and operations of the mind; or lastly, ideas formed by help of memory and imagination—either compounding, dividing, or barely representing those originally perceived in the aforesaid ways. By sight I have the ideas of light and colours, with their several degrees and variations. By touch I perceive hard and soft, heat and cold, motion and resistance, and of all these more and less either as to quantity or degree. Smelling furnishes me with odours; the palate with tastes; and hearing conveys sounds to the mind in all their variety of tone and composition. And as several of these are observed to accompany each other, they come to be marked by one name, and so to be reputed as one thing. Thus, for example, a certain colour, taste, smell, figure and consistence having been observed to go together, are accounted one distinct thing, signified by the name *apple;* other collections of ideas constitute a stone, a tree, a book, and the like sensible things—which as they are pleasing or disagreeable excite the passions of love, hatred, joy, grief, and so forth.

But, besides all that endless variety of ideas or objects of knowledge, there is likewise something which knows or perceives them, and exercises divers operations, as willing, imagining, remembering, about them. This perceiving, active being is what I call *mind, spirit, soul,* or *myself.* By which words I do not denote any one of my ideas, but a thing entirely distinct from them, wherein, they exist, or, which is the same thing, whereby they are perceived—for the existence of an idea consists in being perceived.

That neither our thoughts, nor passions, nor ideas formed by the imagination, exist without the mind, is what everybody will allow. And it seems no less evident that the various sensations or ideas imprinted on the sense, however blended or combined together (that is, whatever objects they compose), cannot exist otherwise than in a mind perceiving them—I think an intuitive knowledge may be obtained of this by any one that shall attend to what is meant by the term *exists,* when applied to sensible things. The table I write on I say exists, that is, I see and feel it; and if I were out of my study I should say it existed—meaning thereby that if I was in my study I might perceive it, or that some other spirit actually does perceive it. There was an odour, that is, it was smelt; there was a sound, that is, it was heard; a colour or figure, and it was perceived by sight or touch. This is all that I can understand by these and the like expressions. For as to what is said of the absolute existence of unthinking things without any relation to their being perceived, that seems perfectly unintelligible. Their *esse* is *percipi,* nor is it possible they should have any existence out of the minds or thinking things which perceive them.

It is indeed an opinion, strangely prevailing amongst men, that houses, mountains, rivers, and in a word all sensible objects, have an existence, natural or real, distinct from their being perceived by the understanding. But, with how great an assurance and acquiescence soever this principle may be entertained in the world, yet whoever shall find in his heart to call it in question may, if I mistake not, perceive it to involve a manifest contradiction. For, what are the forementioned objects but the things we perceive by sense?

and what do we perceive besides our own ideas or sensations? and is it not plainly repugnant that any one of these, or any combination of them, should exist unperceived? . . .

Some truths there are so near and obvious to the mind that a man need only open his eyes to see them. Such I take this important one to be, viz., that all the choir of heaven and furniture of the earth, in a word all those bodies which compose the mighty frame of the world, have not any subsistence without a mind, that their *being* is to be perceived or known; that consequently so long as they are not actually perceived by me, or do not exist in my mind or that of any other created spirit, they must either have no existence at all, or else subsist in the mind of some Eternal Spirit—it being perfectly unintelligible, and involving all the absurdity of abstraction, to attribute to any single part of them an existence independent of a spirit. To be convinced of which, the reader need only reflect, and try to separate in his own thoughts the *being* of a sensible thing from its *being perceived*.

From what has been said it follows there is not any other Substance than *Spirit,* or that which perceives. But, for the fuller proof of this point, let it be considered the sensible qualities are colour, figure, motion, smell, taste, etc., *i.e.* the ideas perceived by sense. Now, for an idea to exist in an unperceiving thing is a manifest contradiction, for to have an idea is all one as to perceive; that therefore wherein colour, figure, and the like qualities exist must perceive them; hence it is clear there can be no unthinking substance or *substratum* of those ideas.

But, say you, though the ideas themselves do not exist without the mind, yet there may be things like them, whereof they are copies or resemblances, which things exist without the mind in an unthinking substance. I answer, an idea can be like nothing but an idea; a colour or figure can be like nothing but another colour or figure. If we look but never so little into our thoughts, we shall find it impossible for us to conceive a likeness except only between our ideas. Again, I ask whether those supposed originals or external things, of which our ideas are the pictures or representations, be themselves perceivable or no? If they are, then they are ideas and we have gained our point; but if you say they are not, I appeal to any one whether it be sense to assert a colour is like something which is invisible; hard or soft, like something which is intangible; and so of the rest.

Some there are who make a distinction betwixt *primary* and *secondary* qualities. By the former they mean extension, figure, motion, rest, solidity or impenetrability, and number; by the latter they denote all other sensible qualities, as colours, sounds, tastes, and so forth. The ideas we have of these they acknowledge not to be the resemblances of anything existing without the mind, or unperceived, but they will have our ideas of the primary qualities to be patterns or images of things which exist without the mind, in an unthinking substance which they call Matter. By Matter, therefore, we are to understand an inert, senseless substance, in which extension, figure, and motion do actually subsist. But it is evident, from what we have already shown, that extension, figure, and motion are only ideas existing in the mind, and that an idea can be like nothing but another idea, and that consequently neither they nor their archetypes can exist in an unperceiving substance. Hence, it is plain that the very notion of what is called *Matter* or *corporeal substance* involves a contradiction in it.

They who assert that figure, motion, and the rest of the primary or original qualities do exist without the mind in unthinking substances, do at the same time acknowledge that colours, sounds, heat, cold, and suchlike secondary qualities, do not—which they tell us are sensations existing in the mind alone, that depend on and are occasioned by the different size, texture, and motion of the minute particles of matter. This they take for an undoubted truth, which they can demonstrate beyond all exception. Now, if it be certain that those original qualities are inseparably united with the other sensible qualities, and not, even in thought, capable of being abstracted from them, it plainly follows that they exist only in the mind. But I desire any one to reflect and try whether he can, by any abstraction of thought, conceive the extension and motion of a body without all other sensible qualities. For my own part, I see evidently that it is not in my power to frame an idea of a body extended and moving, but I must withal give it some colour or other sensible quality which is acknowledged to exist only in the mind. In short, extension, figure, and motion, abstracted from all other qualities, are inconceivable. Where therefore the other sensible qualities are, there must these be also, to wit, in the mind and nowhere else.

Again, *great* and *small, swift* and *slow,* are allowed to exist nowhere without the mind, being entirely relative, and changing as the frame or position of the organs of sense varies. The extension therefore which exists without the mind is neither great nor small, the motion neither swift nor slow, that is, they are nothing at all. . . . Without extension solidity cannot be conceived; since therefore it has been shewn that extension exists not in an unthinking substance, the same must also be true of solidity. . . .

I shall farther add, that, after the same manner as modern philosophers prove certain sensible qualities to have no existence in Matter, or without the mind, the same thing may be likewise proved of all other sensible qualities whatsoever. Thus, for instance, it is said that heat and cold are affections only of the mind, and not at all patterns of real beings, existing in the corporeal substances which excite them, for that the same body which appears cold to one hand seems warm to another. Now, why may we not as well argue that figure and extension are not patterns or resemblances of qualities existing in Matter, because to the same eye at different stations, or eyes of a different texture at the same station, they appear various, and cannot therefore be the images of anything settled and determinate without the mind? Again, it is proved that sweetness is not really in the sapid thing, because the thing remaining unaltered the sweetness is changed into bitter, as in case of a fever or otherwise vitiated palate. Is it not as reasonable to say that motion is not without the mind, since if the succession of ideas in the mind become swifter, the motion, it is acknowledged, shall appear slower without any alteration in any external object?

In short, let any one consider those arguments which are thought manifestly to prove that colours and taste exist only in the mind, and he shall find they may with equal force be brought to prove the same thing of extension, figure, and motion. Though it must be confessed this method of arguing does not so much prove that there is no extension or colour in an outward object, as that we do not know by sense which is the true extension or colour of the object. But the arguments foregoing plainly show it to be impossible that any colour or extension at all, or other sensible quality whatsoever, should exist in an unthinking subject without the mind, or in truth, that there should be any such thing as an outward object.

But let us examine a little the received opinion. It is said extension is a mode or accident of Matter, and that Matter is the *substratum* that supports it. Now I desire that you would explain to me what is meant by Matter's *supporting* extension. Say you, I have no idea of Matter and therefore cannot explain it. I answer, though you have no positive, yet, if you have any meaning at all, you must at least have a relative idea of Matter; though you know not what it is, yet you must be supposed to know what relation it bears to accidents, and what is meant by its supporting them. It is evident "support" cannot here be taken in its usual or literal sense—as when we say that pillars support a building; in what sense therefore must it be taken? . . .

But, though it were possible that solid, figured, movable substances may exist without the mind, corresponding to the ideas we have of bodies, yet how is it possible for us to know this? Either we must know it by sense or by reason. As for our senses, by them we have the knowledge only of our sensations, ideas, or those things that are immediately perceived by sense, call them what you will: but they do not inform us that things exist without the mind, or unperceived, like to those which are perceived. This the materialists themselves acknowledge. It remains therefore that if we have any knowledge at all of external things, it must be by reason, inferring their existence from what is immediately perceived by sense. But what reason can induce us to believe the existence of bodies without the mind, from what we perceive, since the very patrons of Matter themselves do not pretend there is any necessary connexion betwixt them and our ideas? I say it is granted on all hands (and what happens in dreams, phrensies, and the like, puts it beyond dispute) that it is possible we might be affected with all the ideas we have now, though there were no bodies existing without resembling them. Hence, it is evident the supposition of external bodies is not necessary for the producing our ideas; since it is granted they are produced sometimes, and might possibly be produced always in the same order, we see them in at present, without their concurrence.

But, though we might possibly have all our sensations without them, yet perhaps it may be thought easier to conceive and explain the manner of their production, by supposing external bodies in their likeness rather than otherwise; and so it might be at least probable there are such things as bodies that excite their ideas in our minds. But neither can this be said; for, though we give the materialists their external bodies, they by their own confession are never the nearer knowing how our ideas are produced; since they own themselves unable to comprehend in what manner body can act upon spirit, or how it is possible it should imprint any idea in the mind. Hence it is evident the production of ideas or sensations in our minds can be no reason why we should suppose Matter or corporeal substances, since that is acknowledged to remain equally inexplicable with or without this supposition. If therefore it were possible for bodies to exist without the mind, yet to hold they do so, must needs be a very precarious opinion; since it is to suppose, without any reason at all, that God has created innumerable beings that are entirely useless, and serve to no manner of purpose.

In short, if there were external bodies, it is impossible we should ever come to know it; and if there were not, we might have the very same reasons to think there were that we have now. Suppose—what no one can deny possible—an intelligence without the help of external bodies, to be affected with the same train of sensations or ideas that you are, imprinted in the same order and with like vividness in his mind. I ask whether that intelligence hath not all the reason to believe the existence of corporeal substances, represented by his ideas, and exciting them in his mind, that you can possibly have for believing the same thing? Of this there can be no question—which one consideration were enough to make any reasonable person suspect the strength of whatever arguments he may think himself to have, for the existence of bodies without the mind. . . .

But, say you, surely there is nothing easier than for me to imagine trees, for instance, in a park, or books existing in a closet, and nobody by to perceive them. I answer, you may so, there is no difficulty in it; but what is all this, I beseech you, more than framing in your mind certain ideas which you call books and trees, and the same time omitting to frame the idea of any one that may perceive them? But do not you yourself perceive or think of them all the while? This therefore is nothing to the purpose; it only shews you have the power of imagining or forming ideas in your mind: but it does not shew that you can conceive it possible the objects of your thought may exist without the mind. To make out this, it is necessary that you conceive them existing unconceived or unthought of, which is a manifest repugnancy. When we do our utmost to conceive the existence of external bodies, we are all the while only contemplating our own ideas. But the mind taking no notice of itself, is deluded to think it can and does conceive bodies existing unthought of or without the mind, though at the same time they are apprehended by or exist in itself. A little attention will discover to any one the truth and evidence of what is here said, and make it unnecessary to insist on any other proofs against the existence of *material substance.* . . .

All our ideas, sensations, notions, or the things which we perceive, by whatsoever names they may be distinguished, are visibly inactive—there is nothing of power or agency included in them. So that one idea or object of thought cannot produce or make any alteration in another. To be satisfied of the truth of this, there is nothing else requisite but a bare observation of our ideas. For, since they and every part of them exist only in the mind, it follows that there is nothing in them but what is perceived: but whoever shall attend to his ideas, whether of sense or reflection, will not perceive in them any power or activity; there is, therefore, no such thing contained in them. A little attention will discover to us that the very being of an idea implies passiveness and inertness in it, insomuch that it is impossible for an idea to do anything, or, strictly speaking, to be the cause of anything: neither can it be the resemblance or pattern of any active being. Whence it plainly follows that extension, figure, and motion cannot be the cause of our sensations. To say, therefore, that these are the effects of powers resulting from the configuration, number, motion, and size of corpuscles, must certainly be false.

We perceive a continual succession of ideas, some are anew excited, others are changed or totally disappear. There is therefore some cause of these ideas, whereon they depend, and which produces and changes them. That this cause cannot be any quality or idea or combination of ideas is clear from the preceding [paragraph]. It must therefore be a substance; but it has been shewn that there is no corporeal or material substance: it remains therefore that the cause of ideas is an incorporeal active substance or Spirit. . . .

I find I can excite ideas in my mind at pleasure, and vary and shift the scene as oft as I think fit. It is no more than willing, and straightway this or that idea arises in my fancy; and by the same power it is obliterated and makes way for another. This making and unmaking of ideas doth very properly denominate the mind active. Thus much is certain and grounded on experience; but when we think of unthinking agents or of exciting ideas exclusive of volition, we only amuse ourselves with words.

But, whatever power I may have over my own thoughts, I find the ideas actually perceived by Sense have not a like dependence on my will. When in broad daylight I open my eyes, it is not in my power to choose whether I shall see or no, or to determine what particular objects shall present themselves to my view; and so likewise as to the hearing and other senses; the ideas imprinted on them are not creatures of my will. There is therefore some *other* Will or Spirit that produces them.

The ideas of Sense are more strong, lively, and distinct than those of the imagination; they have likewise a steadiness, order, and coherence, and are not excited at random, as those which are the effects of human wills often are, but in a regular train or series, the admirable connexion whereof sufficiently testifies the wisdom and benevolence of its Author. Now the set rules or established methods, wherein the Mind we depend on excites in us the ideas of sense, are called the *laws of nature;* and these we learn by experience, which teaches us that such and such ideas are attended with such and such other ideas, in the ordinary course of things.

This gives us a sort of foresight which enables us to regulate our actions for the benefit of life. And without this we should be eternally at a loss; we could not know how to act anything that might procure us the least pleasure, or remove the least pain of sense. That food nourishes, sleep refreshes, and fire warms us; that to sow in the seed-time is the way to reap in the harvest; and in general that to obtain such or such ends, such or such means are conducive—all this we know, not by discovering any necessary connexion between our ideas, but only by the observation of the settled laws of nature, without which we should be all in uncertainty and confusion, and a grown man no more know how to manage himself in the affairs of life than an infant just born.

And yet this consistent uniform working, which so evidently displays the goodness and wisdom of that Governing Spirit whose Will constitutes the laws of nature, is so far from leading our thoughts to Him, that it rather sends them wandering after second causes. For, when we perceive certain ideas of Sense constantly followed by other ideas and we know this is not of our own doing, we forthwith attribute power and agency to the ideas themselves, and make one the cause of another, than which nothing can be more absurd and unintelligible. Thus, for example, having observed that when we perceive by sight a certain round luminous figure we at the same time perceive by touch the idea or sensation called heat, we do from thence conclude the sun to be the cause of heat. And in like manner perceiving the motion and collision of bodies to be attended with sound, we are inclined to think the latter the effect of the former.

The ideas imprinted on the Senses by the Author of nature are called *real things;* and those excited in the imagination being less regular, vivid, and constant, are more properly termed *ideas,* or *images of things,* which they copy and represent. But then our sensations, be they never so vivid and distinct, are nevertheless ideas, that is, they exist in the mind, or are perceived by it, as truly as the ideas of its own framing. The ideas of Sense are allowed to have more reality in them, that is, to be more strong, orderly, and coherent than the creatures of the mind; but this is no argument that they exist without the mind. They are also less dependent on the spirit, or thinking substance which perceives them, in that they are excited by the will of another and more powerful spirit; yet still they are *ideas,* and certainly no idea, whether faint or strong, can exist otherwise than in a mind perceiving it.

Before we proceed any farther it is necessary we spend some time in answering objections which may probably be made against the principles we have hitherto laid down. In doing of which, if I seem too prolix to those of quick apprehensions, I hope it may be pardoned, since all men do not equally apprehend things of this nature, and I am willing to be understood by every one.

First, then, it will be objected that by the foregoing principles all that is real and substantial in nature is banished out of the world, and instead thereof a chimerical scheme of *ideas* takes place. All things that exist, exist only in the mind, that is, they are purely notional. What therefore becomes of the sun, moon and stars? What must we think of houses, rivers, mountains, trees, stones; nay, even of our own bodies? Are all these but so many chimeras and illusions on the fancy? To all which, and whatever else of the same sort may be objected, I answer, that by the principles premised we are not deprived of any one thing in nature. Whatever we see, feel, hear, or anywise conceive or understand remains as secure as ever, and is as real as ever. There is a *rerum natura,* and the distinction between realities and chimeras retains its full force. We have shewn what is meant by *real things* in opposition to *chimeras* or ideas of our own framing; but then they both equally exist in the mind, and in that sense they are alike *ideas.*

I do not argue against the existence of any one thing that we can apprehend either by sense or reflexion. That the things I see with my eyes and touch with my hands do exist, really exist, I make not the least question. The only thing whose existence we deny is that which *philosophers* call Matter or corporeal substance. And in doing of this there is no damage done to the rest of mankind, who, I dare say, will never miss it. The Atheist indeed will want the colour of an empty name to support his impiety; and the Philosophers may possibly find they have lost a great handle for trifling and disputation. . . .

[*Secondly,*] you will say there have been a great many things explained by matter and motion; take away these and you destroy the whole corpuscular philosophy, and undermine those mechanical principles which have been applied with so much success to account for the phenomena. In short, whatever advances have been made, either by ancient or modern philosophers, in the study of nature do all proceed on the supposition that corporeal substance or Matter doth really exist. To this I answer that there is not any one phenomenon explained on that supposition which may not as well be explained without it, as might easily be made appear by an induction of particulars. To explain the phenomena, is all one as to shew why, upon such and such occasions, we are affected with such and such ideas. But how Matter should operate on a Spirit, or produce any idea in it, is what no philosopher will pretend to explain; it is therefore evident there can be no use of Matter in natural philosophy. Besides, they who attempt to account for things do it not by corporeal substance, but by figure, motion, and other qualities, which are in truth no more than mere ideas, and, therefore, cannot be the cause of anything, as hath been already shewn.

[*Thirdly,*] it will upon this be demanded whether it does not seem absurd to take away natural causes, and ascribe everything to the immediate operation of Spirits? We must no longer say upon these principles that fire heats, or water cools, but that a Spirit heats, and so forth. Would not a man be deservedly laughed at, who should talk after this manner? I answer, he would so; in such things we ought to "think with the learned, and speak with the vulgar." They who to demonstration are convinced of the truth of the Copernican system do nevertheless say "the sun rises," "the sun sets," or "comes to the meridian"; and if they affected a contrary style in common talk it would without doubt appear very ridiculous. A little reflexion on what is here said will make it manifest that the common use of language would receive no manner of alteration or disturbance from the admission of our tenets. . . .

[*Fourthly,*] it will be objected that the notions we advance are inconsistent with several sound truths in philosophy and mathematics. For example, the motion of the earth is now universally admitted by astronomers as a truth grounded on the clearest and most convincing reasons. But, on the foregoing principles, there can be no such thing. For, motion being only an idea, it follows that if it be not perceived it exists not; but the motion of the earth is not perceived by sense. I answer, that tenet, if rightly understood, will be found to agree with the principles we have premised; for, the question whether the earth moves or no amounts in reality to no more than this, to wit, whether we have reason to conclude, from what has been observed by astronomers, that if we were placed in such and such circumstances, and such or such a position and distance both from the earth and sun, we should perceive the former to move among the choir of the planets, and appearing in all respects like one of them; and this, by the established rules of nature which we have no reason to mistrust, is reasonably collected from the phenomena.

We may, from the experience we have had of the train and succession of ideas in our minds, often make, I will not say uncertain conjectures, but sure and well-grounded predictions concerning the ideas we shall be affected with pursuant to a great train of actions, and be enabled to pass a right judgment of what would have appeared to us, in case we were placed in circumstances very different from those we are in at present. Herein consists the knowledge of nature, which may preserve its use and certainty very consistently with what hath been said. It will be easy to apply this to whatever objections of the like sort may be drawn from the magnitude of the stars, or any other discoveries in astronomy or nature.

QUESTIONS

1. Why does Berkeley believe that there are only two kinds of things that make up the real world: minds and their ideas?
2. How does Berkeley criticize the doctrine of primary and secondary qualities?

3. According to Berkeley, what part does God play in our knowledge of the world? Does the place of God in Berkeley's philosophy resemble the place of God in Descartes' philosophy? Explain your answer.
4. Does Berkeley's belief in the existence of minds, as things which are "entirely distinct from" ideas, contradict the principle of empiricism? Why or why not?
5. State why you think Berkeley's philosophy does, or does not, contradict the findings of physics and chemistry concerning the material world.
6. The following argument has been raised against Berkeley:
   "According to Berkeley, we can only know the ideas in our minds. But he claims to have knowledge about what is beyond our minds, since he claims to know that there are no such things as material substances. For to know this, he would have to get beyond the ideas in our minds and somehow see that there are no material objects there, and this contradicts his empiricism. He ought to have said, 'I do not know whether there are any material substances,' instead of saying, 'There are no material substances.'"
   State why you think this is, or is not, a valid criticism.
7. In Boswell's *Life of Johnson,* the following passage appears:
   After we came out of the church, we stood talking for some time together of Bishop Berkeley's ingenious sophistry to prove the nonexistence of matter, and that everything in the universe is merely ideal. I observed, that though we are satisfied his doctrine is not true, it is impossible to refute it. I never shall forget the alacrity with which Johnson answered, striking his foot with mighty force against a large stone, till he rebounded from it, "I refute it *thus.*" [1]
   State why you think Dr. Johnson did, or did not, successfully refute Berkeley's doctrine.
8. How might Berkeley's account of perception be criticized in the light of "Sensation and Observation," by Professor Ryle?

[1] James Boswell, *Life of Johnson,* Oxford University Press (Oxford Standard Edition), New York, Vol. 1, 1953, p. 315.

8. BERTRAND RUSSELL

(*b. 1872*)

The Nature and Existence of Matter

Bertrand Russell, the third Earl Russell, philosopher and mathematician, is a member of the Order of Merit and a winner of the Nobel Prize for Literature. He is the author of a long list of books, from which we may appropriately cite here *Our Knowledge of the External World* (1914), *Mysticism and Logic, and Other Essays* (1917), *An*
Analysis of Matter (1927), and *Human Knowledge, Its Scope and Limits* (1948).

In this reading, Lord Russell defends a Materialistic version of realism. Whereas Idealism holds that the existence of things depends on their being known, and thus that ultimately everything is mind-dependent (see the pre-

ceding selection by Berkeley), the Real-
ist position is that existing is not to be
equated with being known, and that
there are things which exist independently of someone's knowing them. In
answer to the question, "What is the
nature of that which exists independently of its being known?" some Realists answer, "It is matter." These Realists are then also Materialists, and Lord
Russell is to be counted among them.

Russell moves with the greatest care
in advancing the claim that matter exists independently of being known. He

first distinguishes between appearance
and reality, and sensation and sense-
data. Then he cautiously advances arguments for our making an inferential
step from sense-data to physical objects.
The last part of the reading is Russell's
account of what matter might be like
as it exists beyond appearance.

This reading is drawn from *The
Problems of Philosophy,* Chapter I,
"Appearance and Reality"; Chapter II,
"The Existence of Matter"; and Chap-
ter III, "The Nature of Matter."

From *The Problems of Philosophy,* by Bertrand Russell,
Oxford University Press, London, 1912.
Reprinted by permission of the publisher.

APPEARANCE AND REALITY

. . .

In daily life, we assume as certain many things which, on a closer
scrutiny, are found to be so full of apparent contradictions that only a great
amount of thought enables us to know what it is that we really may believe.
In the search for certainty, it is natural to begin with our present experiences,
and in some sense, no doubt, knowledge is to be derived from them. But
any statement as to what it is that our immediate experiences make us know
is very likely to be wrong. It seems to me that I am now sitting in a chair,
at a table of a certain shape, on which I see sheets of paper with writing or
print. By turning my head I see out of the window buildings and clouds and
the sun. I believe that the sun is about ninety-three million miles from the
earth; that it is a hot globe many times bigger than the earth; that, owing
to the earth's rotation, it rises every morning, and will continue to do so for
an indefinite time in the future. I believe that, if any other normal person
comes into my room, he will see the same chairs and tables and books and
papers as I see, and that the table which I see is the same as the table which
I feel pressing against my arm. All this seems to be so evident as to be hardly
worth stating, except in answer to a man who doubts whether I know anything. Yet all this may be reasonably doubted, and all of it requires much
careful discussion before we can be sure that we have stated it in a form
that is wholly true.

To make our difficulties plain, let us concentrate attention on the table.

To the eye it is oblong, brown and shiny, to the touch it is smooth and cool and hard; when I tap it, it gives out a wooden sound. Any one else who sees and feels and hears the table will agree with this description, so that it might seem as if no difficulty would arise; but as soon as we try to be more precise our troubles begin. Although I believe that the table is 'really' of the same colour all over, the parts that reflect the light look much brighter than the other parts, and some parts look white because of reflected light. I know that, if I move, the parts that reflect the light will be different, so that the apparent distribution of colours on the table will change. It follows that if several people are looking at the table at the same moment, no two of them will see exactly the same distribution of colours, because no two can see it from exactly the same point of view, and any change in the point of view makes some change in the way the light is reflected.

For most practical purposes these differences are unimportant, but to the painter they are all-important: the painter has to unlearn the habit of thinking that things seem to have the colour which common sense says they 'really' have, and to learn the habit of seeing things as they appear. Here we have already the beginning of one of the distinctions that cause most trouble in philosophy—the distinction between 'appearance' and 'reality', between what things seem to be and what they are. The painter wants to know what things seem to be, the practical man and the philosopher want to know what they are; but the philosopher's wish to know this is stronger than the practical man's, and is more troubled by knowledge as to the difficulties of answering the question.

To return to the table. It is evident from what we have found, that there is no colour which preeminently appears to be *the* colour of the table, or even of any one particular part of the table—it appears to be of different colours from different points of view, and there is no reason for regarding some of these as more really its colour than others. And we know that even from a given point of view the colour will seem different by artificial light, or to a colour-blind man, or to a man wearing blue spectacles, while in the dark there will be no colour at all, though to touch and hearing the table will be unchanged. This colour is not something which is inherent in the table, but something depending upon the table and the spectator and the way the light falls on the table. When, in ordinary life, we speak of *the* colour of the table, we only mean the sort of colour which it will seem to have to a normal spectator from an ordinary point of view under usual conditions of light. But the other colours which appear under other conditions have just as good a right to be considered real; and therefore, to avoid favouritism, we are compelled to deny that, in itself, the table has any one particular colour.

The same thing applies to the texture. With the naked eye one can see the grain, but otherwise the table looks smooth and even. If we looked at it through a microscope, we should see roughnesses and hills and valleys, and all sorts of differences that are imperceptible to the naked eye. Which of these is the 'real' table? We are naturally tempted to say that what we see through the microscope is more real, but that in turn would be changed by a still more powerful microscope. If, then, we cannot trust what we see with the naked eye, why should we trust what we see through a microscope? Thus, again, the confidence in our senses with which we began deserts us.

The *shape* of the table is no better. We are all in the habit of judging as to the 'real' shapes of things, and we do this so unreflectingly that we come to think we actually see the real shapes. But, in fact, as we all have to learn if we try to draw, a given thing looks different in shape from every different point of view. If our table is 'really' rectangular, it will look, from almost all points of view, as if it had two acute angles and two obtuse angles. If opposite sides are parallel, they will look as if they converged to a point away from the spectator; if they are of equal length, they will look as if the nearer side were longer. All these things are not commonly noticed in looking at a table, because experience has taught us to construct the 'real' shape from the apparent shape, and the 'real' shape is what interests us as practical men. But the 'real' shape is not what we see; it is something inferred from what we see. And what we see is constantly changing in shape as we move about the room; so that here again the senses seem not to give us the truth about the table itself, but only about the appearance of the table.

Similar difficulties arise when we consider the sense of touch. It is true that the table always gives us a sensation of hardness, and we feel that it resists pressure. But the sensation we obtain depends upon how hard we press the table and also upon what part of the body we press with; thus the various sensations due to various pressures or various parts of the body cannot be supposed to reveal *directly* any definite property of the table, but at most to be *signs* of some property which perhaps *causes* all the sensations, but is not actually apparent in any of them. And the same applies still more obviously to the sounds which can be elicited by rapping the table.

Thus it becomes evident that the real table, if there is one, is not the same as what we immediately experience by sight or touch or hearing. The real table, if there is one, is not *immediately* known to us at all, but must be an inference from what is immediately known. Hence, two very difficult questions at once arise; namely, (1) Is there a real table at all? (2) If so, what sort of object can it be?

It will help us in considering these questions to have a few simple terms of which the meaning is definite and clear. Let us give the name of 'sense-data' to the things that are immediately known in sensation: such things as colours, sounds, smells, hardnesses, roughnesses, and so on. We shall give the name 'sensation' to the experience of being immediately aware of these things. Thus, whenever we see a colour, we have a sensation *of* the colour, but the colour itself is a sense-datum, not a sensation. The colour is that *of* which we are immediately aware, and the awareness itself is the sensation.

It is plain that if we are to know anything about the table, it must be by means of the sense-data—brown colour, oblong shape, smoothness, etc.— which we associate with the table; but, for the reasons which have been given, we cannot say that the table *is* the sense-data, or even that the sense-data are directly properties of the table. Thus a problem arises as to the relation of the sense-data to the real table, supposing there is such a thing.

The real table, if it exists, we will call a 'physical object.' Thus we have to consider the relation of sense-data to physical objects. The collection of all physical objects is called 'matter.' Thus our two questions may be re-stated as follows: (1) Is there any such thing as matter? (2) If so, what is its nature?

THE EXISTENCE OF MATTER

The problem we have to consider is this: Granted that we are certain of our own sense-data, have we any reason for regarding them as signs of the existence of something else, which we can call the physical object? When we have enumerated all the sense-data which we should naturally regard as connected with the table, have we said all there is to say about the table, or is there still something else—something not a sense-datum, something which persists when we go out of the room? Common sense unhesitatingly answers that there is. What can be bought and sold and pushed about and have a cloth laid on it, and so on, cannot be a *mere* collection of sense-data. If the cloth completely hides the table, we shall derive no sense-data from the table, and therefore, if the table were merely sense-data, it would have ceased to exist, and the cloth would be suspended in empty air, resting, by a miracle, in the place where the table formerly was. This seems plainly absurd; but whoever wishes to become a philosopher must learn not to be frightened by absurdities.

One great reason why it is felt that we must secure a physical object in addition to the sense-data, is that we want the *same* object for different people. When ten people are sitting round a dinner-table, it seems preposterous to maintain that they are not seeing the same tablecloth, the same knives and forks and spoons and glasses. But the sense-data are private to each separate person; what is immediately present to the sight of one is not immediately present to the sight of another: they all see things from slightly different points of view, and therefore see them slightly differently. Thus, if there are to be public neutral objects, which can be in some sense known to many different people, there must be something over and above the private and particular sense-data which appear to various people. What reason, then, have we for believing that there are such public neutral objects?

The first answer that naturally occurs to one is that, although different people may see the table slightly differently, still they all see more or less similar things when they look at the table, and the variations in what they see follow the laws of perspective and reflection of light, so that it is easy to arrive at a permanent object underlying all the different people's sense-data. I bought my table from the former occupant of my room; I could not buy *his* sense-data, which died when he went away, but I could and did buy the confident expectation of more or less similar sense-data. Thus it is the fact that different people have similar sense-data, and that one person in a given place at different times has similar sense-data, which makes us suppose that over and above the sense-data there is a permanent public object which underlies or causes the sense-data of various people at various times.

Now in so far as the above considerations depend upon supposing that there are other people besides ourselves, they beg the very question at issue. Other people are represented to me by certain sense-data, such as the sight of them or the sound of their voices, and if I had no reason to believe that there were physical objects independent of my sense-data, I should have no reason to believe that other people exist except as part of my dream. Thus, when we are trying to show that there must be objects independent of our own sense-data, we cannot appeal to the testimony of other people, since this testimony itself consists of sense-data, and does not reveal other people's experiences unless our own sense-data are signs of things existing independently of us. We must therefore, if possible, find, in our own purely private experiences, characteristics which show, or tend to show, that there are in the world things other than ourselves and our private experiences.

In one sense it must be admitted that we can never *prove* the existence of things other than ourselves and our experiences. No logical absurdity results from the hypothesis that the world consists of myself and my thoughts and feelings and sensations, and that everything else is mere fancy. In dreams a very complicated world may seem to be present, and yet on waking we find it was a delusion; that is to say, we find that the sense-data in the dream do not appear to have corresponded with such physical objects as we should naturally infer from our sense-data. (It is true that, when the physical world is assumed, it is possible to find physical causes for the sense-data in dreams: a door banging, for instance, may cause us to dream of a naval engagement. But although, in this case, there is a physical *cause* for the sense-data, there is not a physical object *corresponding* to the sense-data in the way in which an actual naval battle would correspond.) There is no logical impossibility in the supposition that the whole of life is a dream, in which we ourselves create all the objects that come before us. But although this is not logically impossible, there is no reason whatever to suppose that it is true; and it is, in fact, a less simple hypothesis, viewed as a means of accounting for the facts of our own life, than the common-sense hypothesis that there really are objects independent of us, whose action on us causes our sensations.

The way in which simplicity comes in from supposing that there really are physical objects is easily seen. If the cat appears at one moment in one part of the room, and at another in another part, it is natural to suppose that it has moved from the one to the other, passing over a series of intermediate positions. But if it is merely a set of sense-data, it cannot have ever been in any place where I did not see it; thus we shall have to suppose that it did not exist at all while I was not looking, but suddenly sprang into being in a new place. If the cat exists whether I see it or not, we can understand from our own experience how it gets hungry between one meal and the next; but if it does not exist when I am not seeing it, it seems odd that appetite should grow during non-existence as fast as during existence. And if the cat consists only of sense-data, it cannot be *hungry,* since no hunger but my own can be a sense-datum to me. Thus the behaviour of the sense-data which represent the cat to me, though it seems quite natural when regarded as an expression of hunger, becomes utterly inexplicable when regarded as mere movements and changes of patches of colour, which are as incapable of hunger as a triangle is of playing football.

But the difficulty in the case of the cat is nothing compared to the difficulty in the case of human beings. When human beings speak—that is, when we hear certain noises which we associate with ideas, and simultaneously see certain motions of lips and expressions of face—it is very difficult to suppose that what we hear is not the expression of a thought, as we know it would be if we emitted the same sounds. Of course similar things happen in dreams, where we are mistaken as to the existence of other people. But dreams are more or less suggested by what we call waking life, and are capable of being more or less accounted for on scientific principles if we assume that there really is a physical world. Thus every principle of simplicity urges us to adopt the natural view, that there really are objects other than ourselves and our sense-data which have an existence not dependent upon our perceiving them.

Of course it is not by argument that we originally come by our belief in an independent external world. We find this belief ready in ourselves as soon as we begin to reflect: it is what may be called an *instinctive* belief. We should never have been led to question this belief but for the fact that, at any rate in the case of sight, it seems as if the sense-datum itself were instinctively believed to be the independent object, whereas argument shows that the object cannot be identical with the sense-datum. This discovery, however—which is not at all paradoxical in the case of taste and smell and sound, and only slightly so in the case of touch—leaves undiminished our instinctive belief that there *are* objects *corresponding* to our sense-data. Since this belief does not lead to any difficulties, but on the contrary tends to simplify and systematize our account of our experiences, there seems no good reason for rejecting it. We may therefore admit—though with a slight doubt derived from dreams—that the external world does really exist, and is not wholly dependent for its existence upon our continuing to perceive it.

The argument which has led us to this conclusion is doubtless less strong than we could wish, but it is typical of many philosophical arguments, and it is therefore worth while to consider briefly its general character and validity. All knowledge, we find, must be built up upon our instinctive beliefs, and if these are rejected, nothing is left. But among our instinctive beliefs some are much stronger than others, while many have, by habit and association, become entangled with other beliefs, not really instinctive, but falsely supposed to be part of what is believed instinctively.

Philosophy should show us the hierarchy of our instinctive beliefs, beginning with those we hold most strongly, and presenting each as much isolated and as free from irrelevant additions as possible. It should take care to show that, in the form in which they are finally set forth, our instinctive beliefs do not clash, but form a harmonious system. There can never be any reason for rejecting one instinctive belief except that it clashes with others; thus, if they are found to harmonize, the whole system becomes worthy of acceptance.

It is of course *possible* that all or any of our beliefs may be mistaken, and therefore all ought to be held with at least some slight element of doubt. But we cannot have *reason* to reject a belief except on the ground of some other belief. Hence, by organizing our instinctive beliefs and their consequences, by considering which among them is most possible, if necessary, to modify or abandon, we can arrive, on the basis of accepting as our sole data what we instinctively believe, at an orderly systematic organization of our knowledge, in which, though the *possibility* of error remains, its likelihood is diminished by the interrelation of the parts and by the critical scrutiny which has preceded acquiescence.

This function, at least, philosophy can perform. Most philosophers, rightly or wrongly, believe that philosophy can do much more than this— that it can give us knowledge, not otherwise attainable, concerning the universe as a whole, and concerning the nature of ultimate reality. Whether this be the case or not, the more modest function we have spoken of can certainly be performed by philosophy, and certainly suffices, for those who have once begun to doubt the adequacy of common sense, to justify the arduous and difficult labours that philosophical problems involve.

THE NATURE OF MATTER

. . . we agreed, though without being able to find demonstrative reasons, that it is rational to believe that our sense-data—for example, those which we regard as associated with my table—are really signs of the existence of something independent of us and our perceptions. That is to say, over and above the sensations of colour, hardness, noise, and so on, which make up the appearance of the table to me, I assume that there is something else, *of* which these things are appearances. The colour ceases to exist if I shut my eyes, the sensation of hardness ceases to exist if I remove my arm from contact with the table, the sound ceases to exist if I cease to rap the table with my knuckles. But I do not believe that when all these things cease the table ceases. On the contrary, I believe that it is because the table exists continuously that all these sense-data will reappear when I open my eyes, replace my arm, and begin again to rap with my knuckles. The question we have to consider in this chapter is: What is the nature of this real table, which persists independently of my perception of it?

To this question physical science gives an answer, somewhat incomplete it is true, and in part still very hypothetical, but yet deserving of respect so far as it goes. Physical science, more or less unconsciously, has drifted into the view that all natural phenomena ought to be reduced to motions. Light and heat and sound are all due to wave-motions, which travel from the body emitting them to the person who sees light or feels heat or hears sound. That which has the wave-motion is either aether or 'gross matter', but in either case is what the philosopher would call matter. The only properties which science assigns to it are position in space, and the power of motion according to the laws of motion. Science does not deny that it *may* have other properties; but if so, such other properties are not useful to the man of science, and in no way assist him in explaining the phenomena.

It is sometimes said that 'light *is* a form of wave-motion', but this is misleading, for the light which we immediately see, which we know directly by means of our senses, is *not* a form of wave-motion, but something quite different—something which we all know if we are not blind, though we cannot describe it so as to convey our knowledge to a man who is blind. A wave-motion, on the contrary, could quite well be described to a blind man, since he can acquire a knowledge of space by the sense of touch; and he can experience a wave-motion by a sea voyage almost as well as we can. But this, which a blind man can understand, is not what we mean by *light:* we mean by *light* just that which a blind man can never understand, and which we can never describe to him.

Now this something, which all of us who are not blind know, is not, according to science, really to be found in the outer world: it is something caused by the action of certain waves upon the eyes and nerves and brain of the person who sees the light. When it is said that light *is* waves, what is really meant is that waves are the physical cause of our sensations of light. But light itself, the thing which seeing people experience and blind people do not, is not supposed by science to form any part of the world that is independent of us and our senses. And very similar remarks would apply to other kinds of sensations.

It is not only colours and sounds and so on that are absent from the scientific world of matter, but also *space* as we get it through sight or touch. It is essential to science that its matter should be in *a* space, but the space in which it is cannot be exactly the space we see or feel. To begin with, space as we see it is not the same as space as we get it by the sense of touch; it is only by experience in infancy that we learn how to touch things we see, or how to get a sight of things which we feel touching us. But the space of science is neutral as between touch and sight; thus it cannot be either the space of touch or the space of sight.

Again, different people see the same object as of different shapes, according to their point of view. A circular coin, for example, though we should always *judge* it to be circular, will *look* oval unless we are straight in front of it. When we judge that it *is* circular, we are judging that it has a real shape which is not its apparent shape, but belongs to it intrinsically apart from its appearance. But this real shape, which is what concerns science, must be in a real space, not the same as anybody's *apparent* space. The real space is public, the apparent space is private to the percipient. In different people's *private* spaces the same object seems to have different shapes; thus the real space, in which it has its real shape, must be different from the private spaces. The space of science, therefore, though *connected* with the spaces we see and feel, is not identical with them, and the manner of its connexion requires investigation.

We agreed provisionally that physical objects cannot be quite like our sense-data, but may be regarded as *causing* our sensations. These physical objects are in the space of science, which we may call 'physical' space. It is important to notice that, if our sensations are to be caused by physical objects, there must be a physical space containing these objects and our sense-organs and nerves and brain. We get a sensation of touch from an object when we are in contact with it; that is to say, when some part of our body occupies a place in physical space quite close to the space occupied by the object. We see an object (roughly speaking) when no opaque body is between the object and our eyes in physical space. Similarly, we only hear or smell or taste an object when we are sufficiently near to it, or when it touches the tongue, or has some suitable position in physical space relatively to our body. We cannot begin to state what different sensations we shall derive from a given object under different circumstances unless we regard the object and our body as both in one physical space, for it is mainly the relative positions of the object and our body that determine what sensations we shall derive from the object.

Now our sense-data are situated in our private spaces, either the space of sight or the space of touch or such vaguer spaces as other senses may give us. If, as science and common sense assume, there is one public all-embracing physical space in which physical objects are, the relative positions of physical objects in physical space must more or less correspond to the relative positions of sense-data in our private spaces. There is no difficulty in supposing this to be the case. If we see on a road one house nearer to us than another, our other senses will bear out the view that it is nearer; for example, it will be reached sooner if we walk along the road. Other people will agree that the house which looks nearer to us is nearer; the ordnance map will take the same view; and thus everything points to a spatial relation between the houses corresponding to the relation between the sense-data which we see when we look at the houses. Thus we may assume that there is a physical space in which physical objects have spatial relations corresponding to those which the corresponding sense-data have in our private spaces. It is this physical space which is dealt with in geometry and assumed in physics and astronomy.

Assuming that there is physical space, and that it does thus correspond to private spaces, what can we know about it? We can know *only* what is required in order to secure the correspondence. That is to say, we can know nothing of what it is like in itself, but we can know the sort of arrangement of physical objects which results from their spatial relations. We can know, for example, that the earth and moon and sun are in one straight line during an eclipse, though we cannot know what a physical straight line is in itself, as we know the look of a straight line in our visual space. Thus we come to know much more about the *relations* of distances in physical space than about the distances themselves; we may know that one distance is greater than another, or that it is along the same straight line as the other, but we cannot have that immediate acquaintance with physical distances that we have with distances in our private spaces, or with colours or sounds or other sense-data. We can know all those things about physical space which a man born blind might know through other people about the space of sight; but the kind of things which a man born blind could never know about the space of sight we also cannot know about physical space. We can know the properties of the relations required to preserve the correspondence with sense-data, but we cannot know the nature of the terms between which the relations hold.

With regard to time, our *feeling* of duration or of the lapse of time is notoriously an unsafe guide as to the time that has elapsed by the clock. Times when we are bored or suffering pain pass slowly, times when we are agreeably occupied pass quickly, and times when we are sleeping pass almost as if they did not exist. Thus, in so far as time is constituted by duration, there is the same necessity for distinguishing a public and a private time as there was in the case of space. But in so far as time consists in an *order* of before and after, there is no need to make such a distinction; the time-order which events seem to have is, so far as we can see, the same as the time-order which they do have. At any rate no reason can be given for supposing that the two orders are not the same. The same is usually true of space: if a regiment of men are marching along a road, the *shape* of the regiment will look different from different points of view, but the men will appear arranged in the same *order* from all points of view. Hence we regard the *order* as true also in physical space, whereas the shape is only supposed to correspond to the physical space so far as is required for the preservation of the order.

In saying that the time-order which events *seem to have* is the same as the time-order which they *really have,* it is necessary to guard against a possible misunderstanding. It must not be supposed that the various states of different physical objects have the same time-order as the sense-data which constitute the perceptions of those objects. Considered as physical objects, the thunder and lightning are simultaneous; that is to say, the lightning is simultaneous with the disturbance of the air in the place where the disturbance begins, namely, where the lightning is. But the sense-datum which we call hearing the thunder does not take place until the disturbance of the air has travelled as far as to where we are. Similarly, it takes about eight minutes for the sun's light to reach us; thus, when we see the sun we are seeing the sun of eight minutes ago. So far as our sense-data afford evidence as to the physical sun they afford evidence as to the physical sun of eight minutes ago; if the physical sun had ceased to exist within the last eight minutes, that would make no difference to the sense-data which we call 'seeing the sun.' This affords a fresh illustration of the necessity of distinguishing between sense-data and physical objects.

What we have found as regards space is much the same as what we find in relation to the correspondence of the sense-data with their physical counterparts. If one object looks blue and another red, we may reasonably presume that there is some corresponding difference between the physical objects: if two objects both look blue, we may presume a corresponding similarity. But we cannot hope to be acquainted directly with the quality in the physical object which makes it look blue or red. Science tells us that this quality is a certain sort of wave-motion, and this sounds familiar, because we think of wave-motions in the space we see. But the wave-motions must really be in physical space, with which we have no direct acquaintance; thus the real wave-motions have not that familiarity which we might have supposed them to have. And what holds for colours is closely similar to what holds for other sense-data. Thus we find out, although the *relations* of physical objects have all sorts of knowable properties, derived from their correspondence with the relations of sense-data, the physical objects themselves remain unknown in their intrinsic nature, so far at least as can be discovered by means of the senses. The question remains whether there is any other method of discovering the intrinsic nature of physical objects.

The most natural, though not ultimately the most defensible, hypothesis to adopt in the first instance, at any rate as regards visual sense-data, would be that, though physical objects cannot, for the reasons we have been considering, be *exactly* like sense-data, yet they may be more or less like. According to this view, physical objects will, for example, really have colours, and we might, by good luck, see an object as of the colour it really is. The colour which an object seems to have at any given moment will in general be very similar, though not quite the same, from many different points of view; we might thus suppose the 'real' colour to be a sort of medium colour, intermediate between the various shades which appear from the different points of view.

Such a theory is perhaps not capable of being definitely refuted, but it can be shown to be groundless. To begin with, it is plain that the colour we see depends only upon the nature of the light-waves that strike the eye, and is therefore modified by the medium intervening between us and the object, as well as by the manner in which light is reflected from the object in the direction of the eye. The intervening air alters colours unless it is perfectly clear, and any strong reflection will alter them completely. Thus the colour we see is a result of the ray as it reaches the eye, and not simply a property of the object from which the ray comes. Hence, also, provided certain waves reach the eye, we shall see a certain colour, whether the object from which the waves start has any colour or not. Thus it is quite gratuitous to suppose that physical objects have colours, and therefore there is no justification for making such a supposition. Exactly similar arguments will apply to other sense-data.

QUESTIONS

1. How does Russell's discussion of the qualities of a table illustrate the distinction between appearance and reality? What is the justification for this distinction? Make a list of the different ways in which we use "real" and "reality" in talking about things we encounter in everyday life. Is "reality" always used in opposition to "appearance"?
2. What does Russell mean by "sense-data" and "sensation"? Compare his use of these terms with Berkeley's use of the term "idea" in the preceding reading.
3. What are Russell's two arguments for inferring the existence of physical objects from sense-data? How does Russell think that his first argument may be refuted? How successfully might Berkeley criticize Russell's second argument?
4. What is meant by Russell's claim that "There is no logical impossibility in the supposition that the whole of life is a dream, in which we ourselves create all the objects that come before us"? Is "create" being used in any of its ordinary senses here? If not, does the claim still make sense?
5. What account does Russell give of "physical objects in the space of science"? Is this account any more or less legitimate than Berkeley's account of ideas in the mind of God? What is your criterion of legitimacy in answering this last question?
6. Can I know real things without either making an inferential step from sense-data to physical objects or without adopting the Idealist account of real things? Might a third way be found by paying attention to our ordinary use of "real"?
7. How might Russell's arguments for Materialism be criticized in the light of Professor Ryle's essay, "Sensation and Observation," in Chapter 2.

9. A. J. AYER

(b. 1910)

The Elimination of Metaphysics

Alfred Jules Ayer is Wykeham Professor of Logic in Oxford University. He is the editor of the *Pelican Philosophy Series* and the author of *Language, Truth and Logic* (1936), *The Foundations of Empirical Knowledge* (1940), *Philosophical Essays* (1954), *The Problem of Knowledge* (1956), and *Concept of a Person, and Other Essays* (1963).

This reading is from *Language, Truth and Logic,* Professor Ayer's statement of the doctrines of the Vienna Circle, a group of philosophers active at the University of Vienna between the years 1922 and 1938. They were primarily interested in introducing into philosophy the clarity and logical rigor of the sciences. In this reading, Professor Ayer describes the Vienna Circle's chief philosophical tool, the verification principle, and shows its use in one of the Circle's early objectives, the elimination of metaphysics. In the Preface to the first edition of *Language, Truth and Logic,* Professor Ayer makes certain observations about the origin of the verification principle, which will help the reader place it in the history of philosophy. He writes:

The views which are put forward in this treatise derive from the doctrines of Bertrand Russell and Wittgenstein, which are themselves the logical outcome of the empiricism of Berkeley and David Hume. Like Hume, I divide all genuine proposi-

tions into two classes: those which, in his terminology, concern "relations of ideas," and those which concern "matters of fact." The former class comprises the *a priori* propositions of logic and pure mathematics, and these I allow to be necessary and certain only because they are analytic. That is, I maintain that the reason why these propositions cannot be confuted in experience is that they do not make any assertion about the empirical world, but simply record our determination to use symbols in a certain fashion. Propositions concerning empirical matters of fact, on the other hand, I hold to be hypotheses, which can be probable but never certain. And in giving an account of the method of their validation I claim also to have explained the nature of truth.

To test whether a sentence expresses a genuine empirical hypothesis, I adopt what may be called a modified verification principle. For I require of an empirical hypothesis, not indeed that it should be conclusively verifiable, but that some possible sense-experience should be relevant to the determination of its truth or falsehood. If a putative proposition fails to satisfy this principle, and is not a tautology, then I hold that it is metaphysical, and that, being metaphysical, it is neither true nor false but literally senseless. It will be found that much of what ordinarily passes for philosophy is metaphysical according to this criterion, and, in particular, that it can not be significantly asserted that there is a nonempirical world of values, or that men have immortal souls, or that there is a transcendent God.

Professor Ayer makes use of the term "tautology" in the above quotation to mean any statement which is necessarily and always true, such as a mathematical equation or a geometrical theorem. The denial of a tautology would be self-contradictory. In the terminology of David Hume, a tautology is a statement expressing a "relation of ideas." (See the selection by Hume in Chapter 2.) In the terminology of Immanuel Kant, a tautology is an "analytical judgment." (See the selection by Kant in Chapter 2.)

This selection has been divided into three parts. Part One is a discussion of metaphysics as "knowledge of a reality transcending the world of science and common sense." Examples of metaphysics in this sense are the selection by Berkeley and possibly the selection by Russell in this chapter, and most of the writings by theologians in Chapters 6, 7, and 8. Part Two of this selection is a statement of the verification principle and a discussion of the way in which it is to be used in distinguishing between meaningful statements and nonsense sentences. This passage reveals what admirers of the Vienna Circle have always regarded as their strong point, and their critics have always regarded as their most serious error, namely, their parsimony about what they will permit philosophers to say. Part Three is an account of what leads philosophers to make metaphysical assertions. Professor Ayer argues that through misunderstanding the structure and function of sentences, metaphysicians believe they can say more than the semantical rules of a language permit them to say. When they violate those rules, their sentences become nonsense.

The reader's first task is to learn what Professor Ayer believes metaphysics to be, then what the verification principle is and how it is to be used. He may then consider for himself whether its use eliminates metaphysics, and whether it places proper limits on the meaningfulness of sentences.

This reading is from Chapter I of *Language, Truth and Logic*.

From *Language, Truth and Logic,* by Alfred Jules Ayer, reprinted through permission by the author and by Dover Publications, Inc., New York 10, N. Y. ($1.25, paperbound).

1

The traditional disputes of philosophers are, for the most part, as unwarranted as they are unfruitful. The surest way to end them is to establish beyond question what should be the purpose and method of a philosophical enquiry. And this is by no means so difficult a task as the history of philosophy would lead one to suppose. For if there are any questions which science leaves it to philosophy to answer, a straightforward process of elimination must lead to their discovery.

We may begin by criticising the metaphysical thesis that philosophy affords us knowledge of a reality transcending the world of science and common sense. Later on, when we come to define metaphysics and account for its existence, we shall find that it is possible to be a metaphysician without believing in a transcendent reality; for we shall see that many metaphysical utterances are due to the commission of logical errors, rather than to a conscious desire on the part of their authors to go beyond the limits of experience. But it is convenient for us to take the case of those who believe that it is possible to have knowledge of a transcendent reality as a starting-point for our discussion. The arguments which we use to refute them will subsequently be found to apply to the whole of metaphysics.

One way of attacking a metaphysician who claimed to have knowledge of a reality which transcended the phenomenal world would be to enquire from what premises his propositions were deduced. Must he not begin, as other men do, with the evidence of his senses? And if so, what valid process of reasoning can possibly lead him to the conception of a transcendent reality? Surely from empirical premises nothing whatsoever concerning the properties, or even the existence, of anything super-empirical can legitimately be inferred. But this objection would be met by a denial on the part of the metaphysician that his assertions were ultimately based on the evidence of his senses. He would say that he was endowed with a faculty of intellectual intuition which enabled him to know facts that could not be known through sense-experience. And even if it could be shown that he was relying on empirical premises, and that his venture into a nonempirical world was therefore logically unjustified, it would not follow that the assertions which he made concerning this nonempirical world could not be true. For the fact that a conclusion does not follow from its putative premise is not sufficient to show that it is false. Consequently one cannot overthrow a system of transcendent metaphysics merely by criticising the way in which it comes into being. What is required is rather a criticism of the nature of the actual statements which comprise it. And this is the line of argument which we shall, in fact, pursue. For we shall maintain that no statement which refers to a "reality" transcending the limits of all possible sense-experience can possibly have any literal significance; from which it must follow that the labours of those who have striven to describe such a reality have all been devoted to the production of nonsense.

It may be suggested that this is a proposition which has already been proved by Kant. But although Kant also condemned transcendent metaphysics, he did so on different grounds. For he said that the human understanding was so constituted that it lost itself in contradictions when it ventured out beyond the limits of possible experience and attempted to deal with things in themselves. And thus he made the impossibility of a transcendent metaphysic not, as we do, a matter of logic, but a matter of fact. He asserted, not that our minds could not conceivably have had the power of penetrating beyond the phenomenal world, but merely that they were in fact devoid of it. And this leads the critic to ask how, if it is possible to know only what lies within the bounds of sense-experience, the author can be justified in asserting that real things do exist beyond, and how he can tell what are the boundaries beyond which the human understanding may not venture, unless he succeeds in passing them himself. As Wittgenstein says, "In order to draw a limit to thinking, we should have to think both sides of this limit," [1] a truth to which Bradley gives a special twist in maintaining that the man who is ready to prove that metaphysics is impossible is a brother metaphysician with a rival theory of his own. [2]

Whatever force these objections may have against the Kantian doctrine, they have none whatsoever against the thesis that I am about to set forth. It cannot here be said that the author is himself overstepping the barrier he maintains to be impassable. For the fruitlessness of attempting to transcend the limits of possible sense-experience will be deduced, not from a psychological hypothesis concerning the actual constitution of the human mind, but from the rule which determines the literal significance of language. Our charge against the metaphysician is not that he attempts to employ the understanding in a field where it cannot profitably venture, but that he produces sentences which fail to conform to the conditions under which alone a sentence can be literally significant. Nor are we ourselves obliged to talk nonsense in order to show that all sentences of a certain type are necessarily devoid of literal significance. We need only formulate the criterion which enables us to test whether a sentence expresses a genuine proposition about a matter of fact, and then point out that the sentences under consideration fail to satisfy it. And this we shall now proceed to do. We shall first of all formulate the criterion in somewhat vague terms, and then give the explanations which are necessary to render it precise.

II

The criterion which we use to test the genuineness of apparent statements of fact is the criterion of verifiability. We say that a sentence is factually significant to any given person, if, and only if, he knows how to verify the proposition which it purports to express—that is, if he knows what observations would lead him, under certain conditions, to accept the proposition as being true, or reject it as being false. If, on the other hand, the putative proposition is of such a character that the assumption of its truth, or falsehood, is consistent with any assumption whatsoever concerning the nature

[1] *Tractatus Logico-Philosophicus,* Preface.
[2] Bradley, *Appearance and Reality,* 2nd ed., p. 1.

of his future experience, then, as far as he is concerned, it is, if not a tautology, a mere pseudo-proposition. The sentence expressing it may be emotionally significant to him; but it is not literally significant. And with regard to questions the procedure is the same. We enquire in every case what observations would lead us to answer the question, one way or the other; and, if none can be discovered, we must conclude that the sentence under consideration does not, as far as we are concerned, express a genuine question, however strongly its grammatical appearance may suggest that it does.

. . . This procedure needs to be examined in detail.

In the first place, it is necessary to draw a distinction between practical verifiability, and verifiability in principle. Plainly we all understand, in many cases believe, propositions which we have not in fact taken steps to verify. Many of these are propositions which we could verify if we took enough trouble. But there remain a number of significant propositions, concerning matters of fact, which we could not verify even if we chose; simply because we lack the practical means of placing ourselves in the situation where the relevant observations could be made. A simple and familiar example of such a proposition is the proposition that there are mountains on the farther side of the moon.[3] No rocket has yet been invented which would enable me to go and look at the farther side of the moon, so that I am unable to decide the matter by actual observation. But I do know what observations would decide it for me, if, as is theoretically conceivable, I were once in a position to make them. And therefore I say that the proposition is verifiable in principle, if not in practice, and is accordingly significant. On the other hand, such a metaphysical pseudo-proposition as "The Absolute enters into, but is itself incapable of, evolution and progress"[4] is not even in principle verifiable. For one cannot conceive of an observation which would enable one to determine whether the Absolute did, or did not, enter into evolution and progress. Of course it is possible that the author of such a remark is using English words in a way in which they are not commonly used by English-speaking people, and that he does, in fact, intend to assert something which could be empirically verified. But until he makes us understand how the proposition that he wishes to express would be verified, he fails to communicate anything to us. And if he admits, as I think the author of the remark in question would have admitted, that his words were not intended to express either a tautology or a proposition which was capable, at least in principle, of being verified, then it follows that he has made an utterance which has no literal significance even for himself.

A further distinction which we must make is the distinction between the "strong" and the "weak" sense of the term "verifiable." A proposition is said to be verifiable, in the strong sense of the term, if, and only if, its truth could be conclusively established in experience. But it is verifiable, in the weak

---

[3] This example has been used by Professor Schlick to illustrate the same point.
[4] A remark taken at random from *Appearance and Reality*, by F. H. Bradley.

sense, if it is possible for experience to render it probable. In which sense are we using the term when we say that a putative proposition is genuine only if it is verifiable?

It seems to me that if we adopt conclusive verifiability as our criterion of significance, as some positivists have proposed,[5] our argument will prove too much. Consider, for example, the case of general propositions of law—such propositions, namely, as "Arsenic is poisonous"; "All men are mortal"; "A body tends to expand when it is heated." It is of the very nature of these propositions that their truth cannot be established with certainty by any finite series of observations. But if it is recognised that such general propositions of law are designed to cover an infinite number of cases, then it must be admitted that they cannot, even in principle, be verified conclusively. And then, if we adopt conclusive verifiability as our criterion of significance, we are logically obliged to treat these general propositions of law in the same fashion as we treat the statements of the metaphysician.

In face of this difficulty, some positivists [6] have adopted the heroic course of saying that these general propositions are indeed pieces of nonsense, albeit an essentially important type of nonsense. But here the introduction of the term "important" is simply an attempt to hedge. It serves only to mark the authors' recognition that their view is somewhat too paradoxical, without in any way removing the paradox. Besides, the difficulty is not confined to the case of general propositions of law, though it is there revealed most plainly. It is hardly less obvious in the case of propositions about the remote past. For it must surely be admitted that, however strong the evidence in favour of historical statements may be, their truth can never become more than highly probable. And to maintain that they also constituted an important, or unimportant, type of nonsense would be unplausible, to say the very least. Indeed, it will be our contention that no proposition, other than a tautology, can possibly be anything more than a probable hypothesis. And if this is correct, the principle that a sentence can be factually significant only if it expresses what is conclusively verifiable is self-stultifying as a criterion of significance. For it leads to the conclusion that it is impossible to make a significant statement of fact at all.

Nor can we accept the suggestion that a sentence should be allowed to be factually significant if, and only if, it expresses something which is definitely confutable by experience.[7] Those who adopt this course assume that, although no finite series of observations is ever sufficient to establish the truth of a hypothesis beyond all possibility of doubt, there are crucial cases in which a single observation, or series of observations, can definitely confute it. But, as we shall show later on, this assumption is false. A hypothesis cannot be con-

[5] E.g., M. Schlick, "Positivismus und Realismus," *Erkenntnis*, Vol. I, 1930. F. Waismann, "Logische Analyse des Warscheinlichkeitsbegriffs," *Erkenntnis*, Vol. I, 1930.
[6] E.g., M. Schlick, "Die Kausalität in der gegenwärtigen Physik," *Naturwissenschaft*, Vol. 19, 1931.
[7] This has been proposed by Karl Popper in his *Logik der Forschung*.

clusively confuted any more than it can be conclusively verified. For when we take the occurrence of certain observations as proof that a given hypothesis is false, we presuppose the existence of certain conditions. And though, in any given case, it may be extremely improbable that this assumption is false, it is not logically impossible. We shall see that there need be no self-contradiction in holding that some of the relevant circumstances are other than we have taken them to be, and consequently that the hypothesis has not really broken down. And if it is not the case that any hypothesis can be definitely confuted, we cannot hold that the genuineness of a proposition depends on the possibility of its definite confutation.

Accordingly, we fall back on the weaker sense of verification. We say that the question that must be asked about any putative statement of fact is not, Would any observations make its truth or falsehood logically certain? but simply, Would any observations be relevant to the determination of its truth or falsehood? And it is only if a negative answer is given to this second question that we conclude that the statement under consideration is nonsensical.

To make our position clearer, we may formulate it in another way. Let us call a proposition which records an actual or possible observation an experiential proposition. Then we may say that it is the mark of a genuine factual proposition, not that it should be equivalent to an experiential proposition, or any finite number of experiential propositions, but simply that some experiential propositions can be deduced from it in conjunction with certain other premises without being deducible from those other premises alone.

This criterion seems liberal enough. In contrast to the principle of conclusive verifiability, it clearly does not deny significance to general propositions or to propositions about the past. Let us see what kinds of assertion it rules out.

A good example of the kind of utterance that is condemned by our criterion as being not even false but nonsensical would be the assertion that the world of sense-experience was altogether unreal. It must, of course, be admitted that our senses do sometimes deceive us. We may, as the result of having certain sensations, expect certain other sensations to be obtainable which are, in fact, not obtainable. But, in all such cases, it is further sense-experience that informs us of the mistakes that arise out of sense-experience. We say that the senses sometimes deceive us, just because the expectations to which our sense-experiences give rise do not always accord with what we subsequently experience. That is, we rely on our senses to substantiate or confute the judgements which are based on our sensations. And therefore the fact that our perceptual judgements are sometimes found to be erroneous has not the slightest tendency to show that the world of sense-experience is unreal. And, indeed, it is plain that no conceivable observation, or series of observations, could have any tendency to show that the world revealed to us by sense-experience was unreal. Consequently, anyone who condemns the sensible world as a world of mere appearance, as opposed to reality, is saying something which, according to our criterion of significance, is literally non-sensical.

An example of a controversy which the application of our criterion obliges us to condemn as fictitious is provided by those who dispute concerning the number of substances that there are in the world. For it is admitted both by monists, who maintain that reality is one substance, and by pluralists, who maintain that reality is many, that it is impossible to imagine any empirical situation which would be relevant to the solution of their dispute. But if we are told that no possible observation could give any probability either to the assertion that reality was one substance or to the assertion that it was many, then we must conclude that neither assertion is significant. There are genuine logical and empirical questions involved in the dispute between monists and pluralists. But the metaphysical question concerning "substance" is ruled out by our criterion as spurious.

A similar treatment must be accorded to the controversy between realists and idealists, in its metaphysical aspect. A simple illustration, which I have made use of in a similar argument elsewhere,[8] will help to demonstrate this. Let us suppose that a picture is discovered and the suggestion made that it was painted by Goya. There is a definite procedure for dealing with such a question. The experts examine the picture to see in what way it resembles the accredited works of Goya, and to see if it bears any marks which are characteristic of a forgery; they look up contemporary records for evidence of the existence of such a picture, and so on. In the end, they may still disagree, but each one knows what empirical evidence would go to confirm or discredit his opinion. Suppose, now, that these men have studied philosophy, and some of them proceed to maintain that this picture is a set of ideas in the perceiver's mind, or in God's mind, others that it is objectively real. What possible experience could any of them have which would be relevant to the solution of this dispute one way or the other? In the ordinary sense of the term "real," in which it is opposed to "illusory," the reality of the picture is not in doubt. The disputants have satisfied themselves that the picture is real, in this sense, by obtaining a correlated series of sensations of sight and sensations of touch. Is there any similar process by which they could discover whether the picture was real, in the sense in which the term "real" is opposed to "ideal"? Clearly there is none. But, if that is so, the problem is fictitious according to our criterion. This does not mean that the realist-idealist controversy may be dismissed without further ado. For it can legitimately be regarded as a dispute concerning the analysis of existential propositions, and so as involving a logical problem which, as we shall see, can be definitively solved. What we have just shown is that the question at issue between idealists and realists becomes fictitious when, as is often the case, it is given a metaphysical interpretation.

There is no need for us to give further examples of the operation of our

---

[8] Vide "Demonstration of the Impossibility of Metaphysics," *Mind,* 1934, p. 339.

criterion of significance. For our object is merely to show that philosophy, as a genuine branch of knowledge, must be distinguished from metaphysics. We are not now concerned with the historical question how much of what has traditionally passed for philosophy is actually metaphysical. We shall, however, point out later on that the majority of the "great philosophers" of the past were not essentially metaphysicians, and thus reassure those who would otherwise be prevented from adopting our criterion by considerations of piety.

. . . All propositions which have factual content are empirical hypotheses; and the function of an empirical hypothesis is to provide a rule for the anticipation of experience. And this means that every empirical hypothesis must be relevant to some actual, or possible, experience, so that a statement which is not relevant to any experience is not an empirical hypothesis, and accordingly has no factual content. But this is precisely what the principle of verifiability asserts.

It should be mentioned here that the fact that the utterances of the metaphysician are nonsensical does not follow simply from the fact that they are devoid of factual content. It follows from that fact, together with the fact that they are not *a priori* propositions. . . . *A priori* propositions, which have always been attractive to philosophers on account of their certainty, owe this certainty to the fact that they are tautologies. We may accordingly define a metaphysical sentence as a sentence which purports to express a genuine proposition, but does, in fact, express neither a tautology nor an empirical hypothesis. And as tautologies and empirical hypotheses form the entire class of significant propositions, we are justified in concluding that all metaphysical assertions are nonsensical. Our next task is to show how they come to be made.

III

The use of the term "substance," to which we have already referred, provides us with a good example of the way in which metaphysics mostly comes to be written. It happens to be the case that we cannot, in our language, refer to the sensible properties of a thing without introducing a word or phrase which appears to stand for the thing itself as opposed to anything which may be said about it. And, as a result of this, those who are infected by the primitive superstition that to every name a single real entity must correspond assume that it is necessary to distinguish logically between the thing itself and any, or all, of its sensible properties. And so they employ the term "substance" to refer to the thing itself. But from the fact that we happen to employ a single word to refer to a thing, and make that word the grammatical subject of the sentences in which we refer to the sensible appearances of the thing, it does not by any means follow that the thing itself is a "simple entity," or that it cannot be defined in terms of the totality of its appearances.

It is true that in talking of "its" appearances we appear to distinguish the thing from the appearances, but that is simply an accident of linguistic usage. Logical analysis shows that what makes these "appearances" the "appearances of" the same thing is not their relationship to an entity other than themselves, but their relationship to one another. The metaphysician fails to see this because he is misled by a superficial grammatical feature of his language.

A simpler and clearer instance of the way in which a consideration of grammar leads to metaphysics is the case of the metaphysical concept of Being. The origin of our temptation to raise questions about Being, which no conceivable experience would enable us to answer, lies in the fact that, in our language, sentences which express existential propositions and sentences which express attributive propositions may be of the same grammatical form. For instance, the sentences "Martyrs exist" and "Martyrs suffer" both consist of a noun followed by an intransitive verb, and the fact that they have grammatically the same appearance leads one to assume that they are of the same logical type. It is seen that in the proposition "Martyrs suffer," the members of a certain species are credited with a certain attribute, and it is sometimes assumed that the same thing is true of such a proposition as "Martyrs exist." If this were actually the case, it would, indeed, be as legitimate to speculate about the Being of martyrs as it is to speculate about their suffering. But, as Kant pointed out,[9] existence is not an attribute. For, when we ascribe an attribute to a thing, we covertly assert that it exists: so that if existence were itself an attribute, it would follow that all positive existential propositions were tautologies, and all negative existential propositions self-contradictory; and this is not the case.[10] So that those who raise questions about Being which are based on the assumption that existence is an attribute are guilty of following grammar beyond the boundaries of sense.

A similar mistake has been made in connection with such propositions as "Unicorns are fictitious." Here again the fact that there is a superficial grammatical resemblance between the English sentences "Dogs are faithful" and "Unicorns are fictitious," and between the corresponding sentences in other languages, creates the assumption that they are of the same logical type. Dogs must exist in order to have the property of being faithful, and so it is held that unless unicorns in some way existed they could not have the property of being fictitious. But, as it is plainly self-contradictory to say that fictitious objects exist, the device is adopted of saying that they are real in some nonempirical sense—that they have a mode of real being which is different from the mode of being of existent things. But since there is no way of testing whether an object is real in this sense, as there is for testing whether it is real in the ordinary sense, the assertion that fictitious objects have a special nonempirical mode of real being is devoid of all literal significance.

[9] Vide *The Critique of Pure Reason*, "Transcendental Dialectic," Book II, Chapter iii, section 4.

[10] This argument is well stated by John Wisdom, *Interpretation and Analysis*, pp. 62, 63.

It comes to be made as a result of the assumption that being fictitious is an attribute. And this is a fallacy of the same order as the fallacy of supposing that existence is an attribute, and it can be exposed in the same way.

In general, the postulation of real nonexistent entities results from the superstition, just now referred to, that, to every word or phrase that can be the grammatical subject of a sentence, there must somewhere be a real entity corresponding. For as there is no place in the empirical world for many of these "entities," a special nonempirical world is invoked to house them. To this error must be attributed, not only the utterances of a Heidegger, who bases his metaphysics on the assumption that "Nothing" is a name which is used to denote something peculiarly mysterious,[11] but also the prevalence of such problems as those concerning the reality of propositions and universals whose senselessness, though less obvious, is no less complete.

These few examples afford a sufficient indication of the way in which most metaphysical assertions come to be formulated. They show how easy it is to write sentences which are literally nonsensical without seeing that they are nonsensical. And thus we see that the view that a number of the traditional "problems of philosophy" are metaphysical, and consequently fictitious, does not involve any incredible assumptions about the psychology of philosophers.

Among those who recognise that if philosophy is to be accounted a genuine branch of knowledge it must be defined in such a way as to distinguish it from metaphysics, it is fashionable to speak of the metaphysician as a kind of misplaced poet. As his statements have no literal meaning, they are not subject to any criteria of truth or falsehood: but they may still serve to express, or arouse, emotion, and thus be subject to ethical or aesthetic standards. And it is suggested that they may have considerable value, as means of moral inspiration, or even as works of art. In this way, an attempt is made to compensate the metaphysician for his extrusion from philosophy.

I am afraid that this compensation is hardly in accordance with his deserts. The view that the metaphysician is to be reckoned among the poets appears to rest on the assumption that both talk nonsense. But this assumption is false. In the vast majority of cases the sentences which are produced by poets do have literal meaning. The difference between the man who uses language scientifically and the man who uses it emotively is not that the one produces sentences which are incapable of arousing emotion, and the other sentences which have no sense, but that the one is primarily concerned with the expression of true propositions, the other with the creation of a work of art. Thus, if a work of science contains true and important propositions, its value as a work of science will hardly be diminished by the fact that they are inelegantly expressed. And similarly, a work of art is not necessarily the worse for the fact that all the propositions comprising it are literally false. But to say that many literary works are largely composed of

[11] Vide *Was ist Metaphysik?* by Heidegger.

falsehoods, is not to say that they are composed of pseudo-propositions. It is, in fact, very rare for a literary artist to produce sentences which have no literal meaning. And where this does occur, the sentences are carefully chosen for their rhythm and balance. If the author writes nonsense, it is because he considers it most suitable for bringing about the effects for which his writing is designed.

The metaphysician, on the other hand, does not intend to write nonsense. He lapses into it through being deceived by grammar, or through committing errors of reasoning, such as that which leads to the view that the sensible world is unreal. But it is not the mark of a poet simply to make mistakes of this sort. There are some, indeed, who would see in the fact that the metaphysician's utterances are senseless a reason against the view that they have aesthetic value. And, without going so far as this, we may safely say that it does not constitute a reason for it.

It is true, however, that although the greater part of metaphysics is merely the embodiment of humdrum errors, there remain a number of metaphysical passages which are the work of genuine mystical feeling; and they may more plausibly be held to have moral or aesthetic value. But, as far as we are concerned, the distinction between the kind of metaphysics that is produced by a philosopher who has been duped by grammar, and the kind that is produced by a mystic who is trying to express the inexpressible, is of no great importance: what is important to us is to realise that even the utterances of the metaphysician who is attempting to expound a vision are literally senseless; so that henceforth we may pursue our philosophical researches with as little regard for them as for the more inglorious kind of metaphysics which comes from a failure to understand the workings of our language.

QUESTIONS

1. What is the verification principle, and how is it to be used in distinguishing between meaningful statements and meaningless utterances?
2. Use the verification principle in deciding whether the following are meaningful:
   a. The universe contains other solar systems resembling our own.
   b. Darkest Africa contains wild animals unknown to modern science.
   c. New York City is the capital of the United States.
   d. The woman wore a blue dress that was yellow all over.
   e. The round tower is square.
   f. How high is up?
   g. Electricity is running through the cord of my lighted desk lamp.
   h. Please shake hands with my invisible, intangible, inaudible friend, who has been waiting for you to greet him for the last fifteen minutes.
   i. The meaning of a statement is its method of verification.
   j. The world extends infinitely beyond our private consciousness, because it is the world of a universal mind. (Royce)
3. What does Professor Ayer mean by "metaphysics"? How does he believe that it can be eliminated?
4. Compare this selection by Professor Ayer with "The Emotive Theory," also

by him. How is his verification principle related to his "emotive theory" of ethics? Attack or defend the statement: "Professor Ayer destroys all philosophy by eliminating both metaphysics and ethics as rational attempts to solve genuine problems."

5. Professor Ayer claims that his views are "the logical outcome of the empiricism of Berkeley and David Hume." After reading either the selection by Berkeley in this chapter, or the selection by Hume in Chapter 2, or both, state why you agree or disagree with Professor Ayer's claim.

6. How might Professor Ayer reply to the following objection? Defend (or attack) the reply you construct as an adequate (or inadequate) answer to the objection.

"You say that those who have tried to describe a reality which transcends all sense experience have merely produced nonsense. But all you can justifiably assert from the failure of these attempts is that no one has yet gained knowledge of such a reality. You should say only that *we do not know* the nature of such a reality. You should not say that the attempt to describe it is nonsense."

7. Explain by means of examples the difference between "practical verifiability" and "verifiability in principle." What is the consequence of using this distinction in deciding whether sentences are meaningful or meaningless?

8. Explain by means of examples the difference between the "strong" and the "weak" sense of the term "verifiable." Which of the two senses does Professor Ayer adopt as a criterion of meaning, and why?

9. ". . . It is plain that no conceivable observation, or series of observations, could have any tendency to show that the world revealed to us by sense experience was unreal." Do you agree? Why or why not?

10. Show why the dispute whether reality is one substance or many substances is meaningless, when tested by the verification principle.

11. How are metaphysicians deceived by grammar, according to Professor Ayer? Explain what is meant by "grammar" in this discussion.

12. Are the metaphysics of Berkeley and Russell eliminated when their assertions are considered in the light of the verification principle? Is either Berkeley or Russell deceived by grammar, in the way that Ayer claims metaphysicians may be?

10. W. H. WALSH

(b. 1913)

True and False in Metaphysics

W. H. Walsh is Professor of Philosophy at the University of Edinburgh. He is the author of *Reason and Experience* (1947), *Introduction to Philosophy of History* (1951), and *Metaphysics* (1963).

In this essay, Professor Walsh wishes to give an account of metaphysics that does justice to the subject and at the same time meets certain criticisms that have been made against it. The principal criticism which he answers is the claim that metaphysical assertions cannot be true or false because they are compatible with any facts whatever; and since these assertions cannot be verified or falsified, they are nonsense. (See the preceding reading, "The Elimination of Metaphysics," by Professor A. J. Ayer.) Professor Walsh argues that metaphysicians are not asserting new facts as yet unnoticed by others. Rather, they are offering imaginative pictures of the world which may serve as guides for ordering already known facts in a comprehensive way. He then discusses the truth and falsity of metaphysical assertions in the light of this account of metaphysics.

To illustrate his account of metaphysics, Professor Walsh discusses three metaphysical systems: materialism, the metaphysics of Aristotle, and the metaphysics of Kant. The reader should pay careful attention to these examples, to see whether they bear out the claims (1) that metaphysical assertions are neither synthetic (about matters of fact) nor analytic (about relations of ideas) but are rather a third sort of assertion, namely, principles of categorial status, and (2) that one of the distinctive purposes of a metaphysics is to provide an imaginative picture of how reality is to be understood. The views which Professor Walsh advances in this article are argued at greater length in his book *Metaphysics*.[1]

From "True and False in Metaphysics," by W. H. Walsh, *Filosofia*, November, 1959. Reprinted by permission of the author and the editor of *Filosofia*.

1

'The Elimination of Metaphysics', as it was called in the first chapter of Ayer's *Language, Truth and Logic,* has been a continuing theme in modern thought. Already in the eighteenth century, in the writings of Voltaire for example, the term 'metaphysics' was a term of abuse: to call a man a metaphysician was something like calling him a charlatan. Metaphysicians, the suggestion was, stood to genuine enquirers (natural philosophers) in the same relations as witch-doctors stand to qualified practitioners: at best they might produce useful results by inspired guesswork, though the common effect of their labours was only to increase superstition and obscurantism. Kant's early description of metaphysics as 'this fictitious science with its accursed fertility'[2] may be taken as representative of the advanced thought of the age, even if it does not fully correspond to his considered view in the *Critique of Pure Reason*. Hume, of course, had expressed the same sentiment some years earlier in his famous passage about volumes of 'divinity and school metaphysics' which are to be 'consigned to the flames, as containing nothing but sophistry and illusion'.

[1] Harcourt, Brace & World, Inc., New York, 1963.
[2] Letter to Mendelssohn, 8 April, 1766, quoted by Popper, *The Open Society*, II, 237.

The analytic movement in twentieth-century philosophy has in effect been conspicuously anti-metaphysical, though the elimination of metaphysics did not figure explicitly in the original analytic programme. Russell in *Our Knowledge of the External World,* for example, objected to Bradley not because he was a metaphysician, but rather because he sought to do philosophy in the grand manner: sought, that is to say, to solve all philosophical problems at once, and to solve them by the armchair methods introduced by Parmenides and Plato. This, he said, could at best result in 'large untested generalities recommended only by a certain appeal to the imagination'. Against this Russell promised that the introduction of his own analytic method would produce 'piecemeal, detailed and verifiable results', modestly comparing his work to that of Galileo in physics.[3] Seen at a distance of forty years, the philosophy of logical atomism has a more speculative air than its founder suggested; Wittgenstein's *Tractatus,* which gave definitive expression to it, has itself been described recently as a metaphysical treatise. But though this description is in a certain sense just, it is not one which would have occurred to early admirers of the work, who saw in it a crushing exposé of metaphysical pretensions, a modern restatement of the anti-metaphysical position of Hume. The line of development which led from Russell and the early Wittgenstein to Carnap and Ayer was thus entirely natural: it was (or seemed at the time) only a short step from saying that the generalities propounded by the major philosophers of the past are untested to saying that they are untestable, or again from describing their work as having an appeal only to the imagination to maintaining that they contrived to say nothing of real significance. And while it is true that many propositions which seemed obvious to *avant-garde* thinkers in the 'thirties have been subjected to severe criticism by subsequent philosophers, the proposition that metaphysicians, generally speaking, talk nonsense continues to enjoy wide acceptance. There is some recognition of the subtlety and insight displayed by certain major metaphysical writers in analysing and connecting concepts, but little or no tendency to take the constructive side of their work seriously.

What I shall call the official view of metaphysics, the view which is still, I think, most widely accepted among English-speaking philosophers, has two main points to it. First, that metaphysicians seek to give us information about the reality which, they say, underlies appearances, or about what they hold to be the 'true' nature of things. This amounts, as Kant saw long ago, to a project to penetrate beyond what can be known by empirical methods to its alleged supersensible substrate, and so is a promise to bring us news from nowhere. Secondly, that metaphysicians get themselves into the position of thinking that their project is feasible, and even that they have succeeded in carrying it out, by making a series of logical mistakes. Examples of such mistakes are perhaps not so freely offered by supporters of the official account as we should expect, but the idea can be illustrated from the celebrated

[3] *Ibid.,* p. 14.

instance of Heidegger, first put forward by Carnap and somewhat oddly repeated by Ayer, who made play with the concept of 'The Nothing', and is said to have got away with it only because the logical grammar of the word 'nothing' is in certain respects like that of a proper name. Moore's case of the confusion inherent in the Ontological Argument, as a result of which a statement like 'Tigers exist' is interpreted as precisely parallel to 'Tigers are fierce', would be another, altogether more plausible, example.

Now I have no wish to deny that metaphysicians, like the rest of us, are liable to make logical mistakes, nor do I want to play down the importance of these mistakes when they occur. Admittedly, metaphysicians have on occasion resorted to logical equivocation to eke out otherwise unconvincing arguments, and so far as they have done so, whether consciously or not, their work must stand condemned. But it is one thing to say this and another to believe that logical equivocation is all there is to metaphysics. I find it very unplausible to suppose that any such thesis could be true when I think of the analytic powers and sensitivity to logical distinctions displayed by so many of the great metaphysical writers; by Aristotle, for example, or by Leibniz. Similarly with the view that the object of metaphysics is to bring us news from nowhere, to put us in touch with the Beyond. There have indeed been many metaphysicians, from Plato onwards, who have spoken as if this were precisely their object, as witness their talk of Forms, Monads or the Absolute, to say nothing of God and the immortal soul. But here again appearances, especially first appearances, may be misleading. It may well be that this reading of the metaphysical enterprise, on which it would indeed stand condemned, is not compulsive; that Kant's celebrated description of metaphysics as the supposed science of things super-sensible is radically mistaken.

One powerful reason for thinking that there might be more to metaphysics than bad logic and a futile striving after the unknowable is to be found in the effect which unprejudiced reading of metaphysical treatises continues to produce. Despite all that has been said about the empty character of metaphysical concepts and the unverifiability of metaphysical assertions, the fact remains that works like Spinoza's *Ethics,* Hegel's *Phenomenology of Mind* and even the *Monadology* of Leibniz have what I can only call a power to speak to us. One cannot go through the process of studying such writings and remain totally unaltered by the experience. And the alteration that occurs is not that one is, *per impossibile,* put in touch with things super-sensible, as if by some sort of intellectual spiritualism; it is rather that, after appreciating the author's point of view and grasping his system of ideas, one as it were sees familiar things with fresh eyes. Whatever the explanation, we have to admit that people find metaphysical works illuminating and revealing. To claim that they reveal what lies beyond experience would be to claim that they reveal the unrevealable. What then do they reveal?

In answering this question I should like to concentrate on a particular metaphysical view with which we are all familiar, namely materialism. Of course the word 'materialism' is used to mean different things in different contexts; quite often it is little more than a term of abuse, thanks to the common association of materialism with the preference for sensual pleasures over states and conditions which are widely thought to be more estimable. I want now, however, to disregard these moral overtones and to consider materialism solely as a system of speculative ideas. The point I am hoping to decide will be best approached by asking how the central doctrine of such a system should be expressed.

Will it do to say that a materialist is a man committed to a thesis about what there is, the thesis namely that nothing exists except matter and its modifications? It is certainly in this way that many people think of the subject, so far as they think of it at all. But this formulation would, if accepted, be open to immediate objections. Suppose in the first place that, in the statement that nothing exists except matter, we took the term 'matter' in what may be called the ordinary, non-controversial sense. The statement would on this interpretation be false, for there clearly are many things, for example thoughts and feelings, which are not material in this sense. But if the materialist in consequence shifts his ground and tells us that the matter of which he speaks is not the genus of which wood and stone are species, but is something totally distinct from anything we know immediately which lies behind and explains whatever falls within experience, he saves his thesis from falsity only at the cost of rendering it unverifiable. The Matter of which everything is now said to consist is as unaccessible as the Platonic world of Forms. No empirical considerations can count either for or against its existence, whose postulation is therefore entirely otiose.

But is it necessary to suppose that those who argue for or against metaphysical materialism are engaged in a dispute about what there is? It seems to me that a quite different account of the subject can and should be given. For when I wonder, as in point of fact I quite often do, whether materialism may not be true, I am not asking myself if it may not be the case that I am literally only a lump of matter, or even a lump of Matter. What I ask myself, put crudely, is rather whether natural scientists do not have the answers to all the important questions, with the result that I am, whatever my pretensions to the contrary, nothing more than a part of nature. Here what concerns me is the validity or invalidity of a particular way of taking things, not a question of fact in the narrow sense. I know that no limits can be set to the range of phenomena on which scientists can be expected to pronounce, and I find that on many topics what they say has an air of finality about it; the possibility I now face is whether they may not have the last word to say on all important issues. If they have, then the scientific way of taking things must be allowed to hold the field against all alternative ways, including those which see men as independent rational agents. The thesis that it does is the thesis of materialism, which I should accordingly formulate as holding that there is nothing that cannot be satisfactorily explained in scientific or natural terms.

There are many points in this formula which call for further comment. To begin with something relatively unimportant, I may be told that there is no such thing as a single scientific way of taking things. Contrary to what was once supposed, the sciences are a confederation of independent states, not a centrally controlled empire dominated by physics. I accept the possibility, but remark that it would, if correct, require me either to define the term 'materialism' more closely or allow that it was generic; it would not rule out the *kind* of definition I have given. In fact the formula supplied is sufficiently specific for several important conclusions to be drawn.

Materialism on this view of the matter is not a doctrine about what is to be found in the world, still less out of it. A materialist does not have to claim to know any existence propositions of which his opponents are ignorant; what he has to claim is ability to get into perspective, or understand, things with which everyone either is or could be familiar. It is true that the materialist position carries with it the denial of certain existence claims which have been made by other philosophers, for instance the Aristotelian claim that there exist purely spiritual beings. But the materialist can make this denial without having to presuppose any special insight into the Beyond: he makes it because he is convinced that the facts do not warrant any such assumption, in the same way as most of us deny the existence of fairies because we see that the facts do not justify our assuming it. He could, if he chose, stop short of absolute denial of a claim like Aristotle's, and say only that there was nothing to be said for it; to counter him, an opponent would have to point to *phenomena* which materialism leaves unexplained.

Materialism as I am understanding it is not itself a scientific thesis; it is a doctrine which asserts the omnicompetence of science. A materialist makes a pronouncement about science, but does not necessarily engage in any form of scientific activity himself. The results which scientists establish are of vital concern when we come to make up our minds about materialism, yet it would be quite wrong to suppose that materialists simply repeat those results. What they add can be brought out if we say that, whereas scientists assert their conclusions as true, materialists want to say that these conclusions embody *the* truth on the subject in question. The point can perhaps be elucidated further if we pay attention to the word 'satisfactorily' in the formula suggested above. A materialist may be said to be a man who finds the scientific explanation (I am assuming here that we can thus speak in the singular) of a situation or happening the convincing or satisfactory explanation, and who is persuaded that there is nothing which cannot be explained in a similar manner; and this at once differentiates him from the ordinary scientific enquirer and reveals the circumstances in which his theory is generated. A working scientist may well believe that there is nothing which cannot be considered from the scientific point of view, but he will not necessarily hold that this is all that can be said on the matter. Suppose, for example, that a physiologist establishes that thinking is always accompanied by certain electrical changes in the brain: he may then be ready to assert that, from his special point of view, thinking can be explained in terms of such changes. But if you ask him if his pronouncement is to be taken as ruling out, or diminishing the importance of, other sorts of approach to thinking, for instance that we make when we grade arguments as valid or invalid, he will probably reply that this question falls outside his competence: his is a departmental enquiry, concerned to investigate what may well be only a single aspect of a complex situation. But a materialist metaphysician shows no such caution or modesty, nor for that matter do his metaphysical rivals. They *start* from the conclusions the physiologist has established, consider these in the light of other ways of taking the situation which they are said to explain, and then presume to pronounce on which of these ways gives the true account. In taking this decision they will naturally not confine themselves to considering a single case, or even a single type of case: the strength of materialism springs not from any particular scientific achievement, but from the ability of scientists to say something striking and pertinent on a wide variety of unexpected and unconnected topics. It is when we take what physiology establishes about the brain, connect it with the achievement of cyberneticists and remember such things as the theories of Freud about religion and the work done by sociologists on the social conditioning of ideas that we are tempted to think that, whatever the difficulties, alternative ways of approaching the world must be given up and it must henceforth be allowed that scientists have the real answers.

If the case of materialism is typical of metaphysics (a question I shall consider at a later stage of this essay), we can perhaps put the general position as follows. There are times when human beings ask themselves what they are to make of the scheme of things entire, in what terms they are to take or seek to comprehend it. This is not a question which arises inside any particular discipline or form of activity; its origin is to be found in the puzzlement which thoughtful people experience when they reflect on the implications of what particular disciplines establish and the presuppositions with which particular activities are conducted. There is *prima facie* an incompatibility, to give an obvious example, between taking religion at its face value and accepting anything like a Freudian account of the subject; and though we can, if we choose, shut our eyes to one or the other, to do so leaves a feeling of acute intellectual discomfort. As if by a sort of instinct we hanker after a unitary reading of experience, a reading which will do justice to all the phenomena and enable everything to be seen in its place. It is readings of this kind which metaphysicians presume to offer. They present considerations (with what cogency I shall discuss later) in favour of this or that way of seeing the world and human experience as a whole. And the enlightenment which results when people are convinced by their arguments is similar to the enlightenment we get when someone explains to us a complicated literary text: we think we now see how each part of what is before us hangs together, and can get the whole into perspective.

There is a persistent tradition which connects metaphysics with the assertion of synthetic *a priori* truths. I think myself that the tradition is a correct one, though the 'truths' spoken of are very different from what traditional critics of metaphysics have supposed. The synthetic *a priori* 'truth' which lies at the basis of materialism might be stated in the words: it is out of the question that there should be anything which cannot be satisfactorily explained in natural terms. It is obvious enough when we think about the matter that we are not here dealing with a supposed truth of fact: no amount of scrutiny of the available evidence could establish a principle of such unrestricted generality. It is equally obvious that we are not dealing with an analytic proposition: no breach of the laws of logic is involved in its denial. A principle of this kind has a different status from either of these sorts of proposition; it is of a higher logical order than even the most general truth of fact, in so far as it embodies, or expresses, our fundamental approach to the facts. If we wish to characterise it as synthetic *a priori* (and there are some grounds for choosing this description, despite the many misunderstandings its use tends to provoke), we must think of it as, roughly at least, sharing the status of the synthetic *a priori* principles for which Kant argued in the second half of the Analytic. Like them, it has a function in ordering experience without being itself read out of experience. And like them it has no real significance except when brought to bear on empirical situations.[4]

It is idle to deny that metaphysicians are in a certain sense dogmatists. They show their cloven hooves in the confidence with which they advocate their particular points of view, and the incredulity with which they greet any suggestion that they might be mistaken. But we should not put too hasty a construction on these facts. It would be a mistake to contrast metaphysicians with empirical enquirers as men who have closed minds as opposed to men who have open minds and frame their theories to fit the evidence rather than the reverse. For in the first place it is by no means true that competent metaphysicians take up their positions without considering evidence: as I have suggested, metaphysical theories claim to do justice to all sides of experience, and any metaphysician worth his salt must be constantly considering whether his particular theory lives up to this pretension. Nor could it be claimed that theories of this kind are such that nothing that occurs can refute them, though the point is, as we shall see, a delicate one. What has to be admitted, and indeed stressed, is that a metaphysician is of his nature a man with a point of view to advance, and to advance a point of view in this context is in effect to issue a series of injunctions. A metaphysician is committed to the correctness of his point of view just as a moralist is committed to the correctness of the moral principles he urges on us. If we do not hold a

---

[4] See further my article *Categories* in "Kant-Studien", 1953–4.

moralist's confidence against him (how could he do his job at all if he did not believe in the principles he advocates?), no more should we reproach a metaphysician for advancing his position as finally true. You cannot at once assign categorial status to a principle and treat it as an everyday empirical hypothesis.

There is one further point about metaphysical theories on which it will be useful to remark at this stage, which can again be made most effectively if we consider the special case of materialism. A materialist not only offers a scheme of ideas inside which, as he says, sense can be made of whatever falls within human experience; he builds his scheme round a central point, the idea of the whole of reality operating as a vast unthinking machine. An idea of this kind is perhaps imaginative rather than strictly intellectual, providing as it does a sort of picture of what the metaphysician means to convey; but it should not for that reason be discounted. Not only can such an idea have a powerful effect on those who come into contact with the system; its place in the thought of the metaphysician himself is also all-important, since it constitutes the 'intuition' or 'insight' from which he starts and to which he constantly returns. Certainly if a metaphysician had nothing more to offer than such an idea we should scarcely call him a philosopher at all, but the value of his whole system can all the same not be assessed without taking its central idea into account. To isolate, and enter imaginatively into, its central insight is in consequence of extreme importance when we come to study any particular metaphysical system: to put it crudely, we need to know what makes the metaphysician in question 'tick', and failing such knowledge our criticisms of his work, however seemingly cogent, will in all likelihood strike its author as wholly wide of the mark.[5]

II

I should claim for the foregoing discussion at least the merit of being based on a concrete case instead of proceeding, as so many discussions of metaphysics have, entirely in the abstract. It remains, however, to ask whether an account of metaphysics which so obviously leans on a single instance can be satisfactorily extended to others, and in particular whether it can be extended to cover the classical systems. Needless to say, only the scrappiest observations on this subject can be made within the compass of an article.

Let me say at once that I agree with Professor Ryle that many metaphysicians at any rate have seen their task as being to 'assert the existence or occurrence of things unseen and give for these assertions purely philosophical or conceptual reasons'.[6] Plato answers this description, and so, no doubt, do theistic philosophers like Aquinas. There have, it is true, been

[5] Compare Russell on Bradley, or for that matter Bradley on Russell.
[6] *The Nature of Metaphysics,* ed. D. F. Pears (London, 1957), p. 144.

attempts to interpret Plato's philosophy in a way which plays down his apparent insistence on the existence of transcendent Forms and tries to re-interpret the latter as no more than limiting concepts, to be used in the judging of phenomena; just as there have been persons who have striven to eliminate all mention of the supersensible in religion, on the pretence that God is no more than the Eternal not ourselves which makes for Righteous-ness or (in a more modern version) that 'God exists' means roughly the same as 'Love one another'. It would, however, be only candid to allow that the first view has won no more support among Platonic scholars than has the second among theologians. Yet it would be wrong to fly to the other extreme and assume that because Plato and Aquinas had an undeniable be-lief in transcendent realities they were totally without interest in things em-pirical, when everything suggests that they saw an intimate connection between the two. It would be still more wrong to suppose that every meta-physician who uses a terminology with apparent ontological implications—I am thinking here of writers like Hegel or Bradley—is to be taken *au pied de la lettre* with the crudest literalness. No doubt metaphysicians are always apt to charm or bewitch their readers with language which suggests that they are revealing new facts; but if we study them with charity we need not always put that construction on their work.

I shall sketch here very briefly two cases in which a different sort of interpretation is at least plausible.[7]

The Metaphysics of Aristotle. It is well known that Aristotle described 'first philosophy' as the science of 'being as such', and that he said alter-natively (this time entitling it 'theology') that it was concerned with pure form. I think most readers find a real difficulty in connecting at any rate the first of these descriptions with the actual contents of the work now known as the *Metaphysics*. Nor is it altogether easy to trace the thread which links the multiform discussions of that far from simple book. I suggest that we must take account of the following features or factors if we are to grasp what is central in Aristotle's thought.

First and most obviously, the concept of substance: the Aristotelian world-picture is, in the first place, that of a plurality of substances or subjects to which things happen. By a substance Aristotle meant, initially at any rate, a self-subsistent entity, and if he had been asked for instances of such entities he would have pointed to particular men or horses. It is such things, as the argument of the *Categories* makes clear, which have properties or stand in

---

[7] Since I first gave the lecture on which this essay is based Professor J. N. Findlay has published his *Hegel: a Re-examination* (London, 1958), which is a sustained attempt to argue that Hegel's philosophy was 'this-worldly' rather than 'other-worldly'. Hegel, according to Findlay, was an 'empiricist' and an 'anti-metaphysician', in so far as he would have nothing to do with the transcendent. Findlay contrasts Hegel with Bradley, but I think myself that Bradley's concept of the Absolute can be interpreted along similar lines. See *Bradley et la Métaphysique,* forthcoming in "Les Études philo-sophiques".

relations. But not everything which can have properties and stand in relations is for Aristotle a substance: waterfalls, pieces of land and statues (all of them 'continuants' in the modern sense) might satisfy this requirement without qualifying as substances for Aristotle.

Second, the concept of nature, which modifies the Aristotelian concept of substance and explains the exceptions just noted. A substance is something which is self-subsistent or exists by nature. Now 'nature' has for Aristotle a sense which it no longer has for us: it is connected in his thought with the idea of growth or life. What exists by nature is what is alive and growing. And the proper way to look at growth is to see it as the making actual of what was previously only there potentially, or, more intelligibly, as the imposition on a certain matter of a form which the growing thing shares with other specimens of its kind.

Third, the doctrine of the four causes, which connects closely with the linked distinctions potentiality/actuality and matter/form. This doctrine, together with the doctrine of substance, embodies Aristotle's characteristic way of looking at the world and is thus the clue to his metaphysics. It offers a way, or perhaps one should say an interconnected set of ways, of explaining both why things are what they are and why they change as they do. The notions of formal and material causation help us to understand things from a static point of view, those of efficient and final causation serve to make change intelligible. And underlying the whole analysis is the model of a biological specimen which is to be seen as embodying a specific form which it realises more and more fully as it grows to maturity.

The ideas I have mentioned quite obviously colour, indeed constitute, Aristotle's thought on many subjects. Not only are they appealed to in his biological writings proper: he attempts to extend their use backwards into physics and chemistry (though it must be admitted with very little success), and forwards into psychology, morals and politics. His achievement in interpreting the details of experience clearly depends in no small measure on the bold, interpretative scheme which he seeks everywhere to apply. Because of this there is a massive impressiveness in Aristotelianism and a living quality which it retains today despite all that has happened in the scientific world since its ideas were first formulated.

What I am saying is that Aristotle's 'ontology', so far at least as we have considered it here, is a misnomer. It is not a doctrine of what there is, but a statement of how we are to take things. Its inspiration, as will be apparent, is biological, and it consists in essentials of an attempt to apply ideas which make sense in biology to all the phenomena of experience. That Aristotle himself applied these ideas with only limited success is not to the point: what is important is that he conceived the general notion and worked out the main lines of its application. Whatever its shortcomings, his scheme of concepts had the great merit of enabling him to connect a vast mass of diverse phenomena in a way which seemed convincing to many subsequent generations and has not entirely lost its appeal even today. It is for this reason more than any other that he deserves to be classed as a major metaphysician.

I should not dispute that this account of Aristotle's metaphysics is, even on its own level, historically incomplete. Aristotle no less than Plato believed in the existence of purely spiritual substances, and indeed suggested sometimes that 'first philosophy' was properly concerned only with questions about their existence and nature. And the reasons he offers for accepting their existence are conceptual reasons, even if it is in connection with his astronomy that he makes his most determined attempt to argue for them. To this extent Aristotle's metaphysics fit what I called the official account better than the one by which I have tried to replace it. Aristotle's commitment to the Unmoved Mover cannot be ignored, but equally it should not be overstressed. Whatever the truth about Plato, there can be no doubt of Aristotle's abiding interest in the here and now; it is with this world that he is in practice ultimately concerned even in speaking of pure form. To single out this interest and make it central in our interpretation of Aristotelianism is accordingly not inappropriate, and to this extent it may be said that he can be brought under the scheme outlined above.[8]

The Metaphysics of Kant. To put forward Kant as the author of a metaphysical system may well seem strange, in view of the devastating criticism he himself brought against metaphysics. I maintain nevertheless that Kant had a distinctive metaphysical point of view of his own, one which had, and continues to have, a considerable appeal. Perhaps the best approach to this is through the famous pronouncement in which he expressed his admiration for those two very different things, the starry heavens above and the moral law within. The point of Kant's philosophy was, of course, to do justice to both. He wanted in the first place to say that no limits could be set to the scientific enterprise of uncovering the secrets of nature: investigation of the starry heavens and of all the phenomena of the natural world must not only proceed without captious objections from moralists and theologians, but must be recognised as affording the possibility of discoveries about man himself of a new and surprising kind. To support, and indeed press, the claims of science, by arguing that nothing which fell within experience could be granted exemption from scientific scrutiny, was one of the two dominating motives in Kant's thought. The other was his desire to hold that all this could be done without any sacrifice of the moral point of view. Scientific investigation of man as a phenomenon could coexist with the treatment of man as a moral being, for morals was a matter of practice, of acting as if we were free of determination by natural causes, rather than of knowledge.

So far we have not metaphysics but metaphysical neutralism, a view,

---

[8] It may be useful to remember in this connection that one of Aristotle's aims was to refute materialism, which he had met with in the work of Empedocles and Democritus.

much favoured today, which holds that you can avoid the sort of choice with which I said the metaphysician was faced by distinguishing different uses of language, and arguing that nontheoretical uses have no theoretical implications. In Kant's official doctrine morals is practical and science theoretical, which means that no clash between the two need arise. But it may be doubted whether he wishes merely to juxtapose moral and scientific activity; he wishes also to explain the juxtaposition. It is for this reason that he introduces the contrast of phenomenon and noumenon, which are perhaps the key concepts of his philosophy. Man as an object of scientific scrutiny is said to be phenomenon, whereas when he acts morally he transfers himself to the noumenal world. And while Kant insists over and over again that we can know nothing of noumena, the fact remains that he thinks the concept of noumenon gets more than negative significance once we adopt the moral point of view. Kantian commentators have long been puzzled about how Kant can confine knowledge to appearances and still talk about things in themselves: the solution is, I suggest, that he believed there were things in themselves because he believed that moral agents were more than phenomena. We might not know about ourselves as noumena, but we were at least well assured that we were such. I do not see how sense can be made of Kant's complex position unless this is taken as true, unless, that is to say, we regard him as having believed, whatever his professions, that man *is* both phenomenon and noumenon, or, if you like, both flesh and spirit. Only on this hypothesis will his claim to have shown the falsity of materialism make sense; only with it can we explain his evident hankering after knowledge of the noumenal, coming out for instance in the surprising remark that the geometer would 'gladly exchange the whole of his science' for a solution of the problems propounded in the Antinomies.[9] The very choice of the terms 'phenomenal' and 'noumenal', with the implication that as the phenomenal is the apparent the noumenal must be the real, argues that for Kant metaphysical neutralism cannot be finally true.

If we are to class Kant as a metaphysician at all, we must set him down as a dualist. But it scarcely needs to be added that his is a dualism with a difference. He continuously urges on us that man is both phenomenon and more than phenomenon, but is just as insistent that nothing can be known about him in the latter capacity. It is only in moral contexts and in relation to moral experience that we can find real significance for the concept of the noumenal; and when we do so the result is not knowledge in the strict sense but 'pure practical belief'. It may be thought to be stretching language to describe this as a metaphysical point of view and say that it offers a framework inside which sense can be made of all sides of human experience. But that Kant thought of it in this way seems hard to deny. Nor could it be argued that the general scheme was peculiar to his narrow and unsympa-

[9] *Critique of Pure Reason* B 491/A 463.

thetic mind; on the contrary, it gave expression, as no other philosophy has done, to important elements in Protestantism. Whatever its shortcomings from the point of view of the speculatively-minded, it may nonetheless contain as many concessions to speculation as can reasonably be made.

III

Assuming now that the view of metaphysics argued for in the first part of this paper has been sufficiently if not fully authenticated, I want to conclude by asking if it can meet a criticism to which metaphysicians have been persistently subjected, the criticism that there are no criteria for deciding whether what they maintain is false or true. It is commonly said that whereas in science, mathematics, or even in history we know, in principle at any rate, what considerations will rule out a statement as unacceptable, there is really nothing comparable in the case of metaphysics. Metaphysical assertions are such that they are compatible with any facts whatsoever; a circumstance which would certainly make them empty of significance.

Before addressing ourselves to this problem it will be useful to consider just why we can get clear decisions about truth or falsity in science and mathematics. The answer is surely that investigators in these fields work inside a framework of rules which are not themselves thought to be open to question. Not only do science and mathematics have clearly defined tasks; in both there are agreed procedures for dealing with them. The procedures may change, even change radically, over a period of years, but the change is all the same a piecemeal one, in the sense that not everything is altered at once. As a result individual students of these subjects know what their colleagues are up to, and have relatively little difficulty in deciding when they are right.

The contrast between science and history is instructive in this connection. Many professional historians have claimed scientific status for their results, and their main ground for doing so would seem to be their conviction that historical questions are definitively decidable. Confront a competent historian with a problem and its solution, and he will be able to tell you whether the solution is correct, or at least whether it is hopelessly wide of the mark. But there is reason to think that this result can be attained, at any rate where something more than a simple question of fact is concerned, only when historians agree in their fundamental judgments of importance. In point of fact professional historians in Great Britain and America are virtually unanimous in their ideas about what is really important in history, with the result that philosophical doubts about the objectivity of history strike them as exceedingly far-fetched. If they lived in countries where Marxism, or even Roman Catholicism, had a greater intellectual impact, they might well be less sanguine. A liberal historian who was convinced of the correctness of his reading of, say, the French Revolution would be hard put to it to prove his point to a Marxist, just because of their differences in fundamentals.

Something of the same situation arises in morals, though here, of course, we are not concerned with assertions but with decisions. As modern philosophers are never tired of telling us, morals is a matter of practice, and this means that moral questions arise in a context where people are constantly making what are generally agreed to be right or wrong moves. Morals could not be the working system it is if the thing to do in a moral quandary could never be properly specified. But though the case for a general moral scepticism has been much exaggerated, it certainly seems to make better sense at some times than at others. It has a relatively high plausibility in conditions where there is much disagreement about fundamental moral rules, a relatively low one in societies where people are generally satisfied with established ways of going on. In the latter case people are apt to confuse moral judgments with judgments of fact, since the rules are clear and the only question is whether the case under judgment comes under them or not.

All this suggests that the comparison commonly made between scientific and metaphysical theories in respect to their claims to truth is at best seriously misleading. Clear decisions about whether to accept or reject a scientific proposition are possible because science is an activity which proceeds under agreed rules, rules which, among other things, specify what is to count as evidence for or against. In metaphysics, by contrast, we are not so much working under rules as advocating them, with the result that objective proof, proof that is to say which any right-thinking person would acknowledge, is impossible. In this context the dispute turns on what is meant by the phrase 'right-thinking person'.

It may be thought that this exaggerates the difficulties of metaphysics. After all, we can choose rationally between different sets of rules if we are clear about the requirements which a good set of rules must fulfil. Might it not be claimed that everybody acknowledges at least one such requirement in a set of metaphysical rules, namely that it should offer an explanation of *all* the facts? If there are obvious facts which a metaphysical system fails to cover, it is so far deficient.

Unhappily this test looks more promising in theory than it turns out to be in practice. To see this we have only to consider its application to materialism. Many people reject materialism on the ground that there are more things in heaven and earth than are dreamt of in this philosophy, but would a materialist agree that his philosophy left anything out? Suppose it were said that he failed to take account of, say, the phenomena of religious experience or the compelling character of the feeling of moral obligation. His comment would surely be that he not only mentioned these phenomena but explained them, and explained them in the only way which could make them intelligible. In the case of religion, for example, he showed how it was, i.e. in what physical, psychological and perhaps social conditions, people came to have what are commonly called religious experiences and why they were disposed to put a certain construction on those experiences. And if it were suggested to him that this explanation simply omits what is the essence of the matter, in so far as it says nothing about the cognitive content of such experiences, he would reply that it is an illusion to suppose that they have any such content. Having a religious experience is perhaps like being vividly aware of the presence of another person, with the difference that in this case there is no other person to be aware of. The important point, however, according to the materialist, is that we can see how the illusion develops and what purpose it serves.

The trouble about testing a theory like that of materialism by its capacity to cover all the facts is that there is no general agreement about what 'the facts' are. Facts exist, or perhaps we should say obtain, only from particular points of view, and here points of view are in dispute. The consequence of this is that the metaphysician is necessarily judge in his own case, for though he must admit to an obligation to take account of all the facts as he sees them, it is in the last resort for him to say what is fact and what not. His office confers on him the duty of giving an overall interpretation, but simultaneously allows him a veto on accepting anything which cannot be fitted into his scheme.

For these reasons I am altogether less confident than I once was that there can be objective tests of the truth or falsity of metaphysical structures. Yet I also feel that it would be absurd to treat acceptance or rejection of a metaphysical view as something which is wholly arbitrary, a matter of personal taste or particular liking. Such an account is just not true of actual metaphysical thinking, as anyone who has tried to make up his mind about materialism will witness. In such a case there certainly are considerations which will strengthen or weaken confidence in either sort of conclusion, considerations whose relevance to the problem will be acknowledged by materialist and anti-materialist alike even if their judgment of the lesson to be drawn from them varies. There are circumstances in which an honest man finds himself forced to accept or reject a theory of this sort, knows that, failing further developments, he for his part must acknowledge it to be true or false.

I suggest that in thinking about conviction and proof in metaphysics we ought to have in mind, not the relatively tight arguments of natural scientists, but the altogether looser procedures followed by critics of literature and the arts. We are all familiar with the situation where there exists a plurality of conflicting interpretations of a major work of literature like *Hamlet*. A critic who puts forward such an interpretation would certainly claim that there are considerations which make his own theory superior to those of his rivals; he is convinced, that is to say, that his is a reasoned case. But he might very well, if he were sensible, allow that there could be no knock-down demonstration of the correctness of his point of view. To the sceptic who persisted in finding his views unplausible he could give only one piece of advice: to go back to the text, make an honest effort to see it in the way recommended, and then see whether fresh enlightenment did not result. He would have no answer to a critic unwilling to make that experiment.

What is true of literary appreciation here is also true of metaphysics. Much metaphysical, like much literary, discussion turns on whether or not a theory avoids inconsistency, and this, of course, is a matter that can be definitively decided, once we can be certain that the concepts of the theory have been properly grasped by its critics. But there is another species of objection which people bring against metaphysicians, to the effect that their views are not sufficiently comprehensive or fail to cover the facts adequately. I have already explained why I think objections of this sort cannot be pushed home: there are no neutral data which a metaphysical theory has to cover on pain of being pronounced untrue. But it does not follow that the metaphysician criticised will be insensitive to objections of this sort, at least when they are put forward by critics who have made a real effort to see the world as he sees it; he will try to show that he can meet the points made, or will try to adjust his system to meet them. And if he can do neither he may even abandon it.

In the last resort the only test of truth which can be applied in metaphysics is a personal test: we have to try, by an effort which is imaginative as well as intellectual, to grasp for ourselves what the metaphysician is saying, to consider its application to the diverse sides of human experience, more particularly to those where its initial plausibility is at its lowest, and then finally to pronounce for ourselves on its adequacy. The arguments which others, including the metaphysician himself, bring to bear on the subject, may incline us to a certain conclusion, but they cannot necessitate our acceptance of it, as similar arguments can in the scientific field. Perhaps this is the real reason why metaphysics is misdescribed as the queen of the sciences: it is not a science at all, but belongs to the humanities.

QUESTIONS

1. What are the characteristics of metaphysics according to the official view?
2. What does Professor Walsh mean when he says that great metaphysical works have a power to speak to us?
3. Review the different formulations of materialism which Professor Walsh considers, and explain why he rejects the earlier ones and why he finds the last one acceptable. What makes the doctrine of materialism metaphysical, and, consequently, what are the defining characteristics of a metaphysical doctrine?
4. Would Professor Walsh consider the position advanced by Lord Russell in the second reading of this chapter a metaphysics or part of a metaphysics? Why or why not?
5. How do Professor Walsh's discussions of the metaphysics of Aristotle and of Kant illustrate the claims that metaphysical assertions are principles of categorial status, and metaphysicians are creators of imaginative pictures to guide us in taking a comprehensive view of the world?
6. What is ontology?

7. What are the differences in the tests for truth and falsity in science, history, morals, and metaphysics?
8. What are the similarities between metaphysics and the interpretation and criticism of works of literature?
9. How successfully does Professor Walsh meet the criticisms of metaphysics advanced by Professor Ayer in "The Elimination of Metaphysics"?
10. How might Professor Walsh respond to the following criticism: On your account of them, metaphysical assertions are rules for viewing the world. But all rules are analytic statements. Therefore there is no need to argue for a third class of statement to account for the truth or falsity of metaphysical assertions.
11. What similarities and what differences do you find between Professor Walsh's account of metaphysical assertions as categorial principles or rules, and the account of synthetic necessary truths given by Professor Toulmin in Chapter 2?

SUGGESTED FURTHER READING

INTRODUCTORY STUDIES

Chisholm, Roderick M., ed., *Realism and the Background to Phenomenology,* Free Press, Glencoe, Ill., 1960. (Anthology.)
Ewing, A. C., *Idealism,* Methuen, London, 1930.
———, ed., *Idealist Tradition from Berkeley to Blanshard,* Free Press, Glencoe, Ill., 1957. (Anthology.)
Munitz, Milton K., *The Mystery of Existence,* Appleton-Century-Crofts, New York, 1965.
Sprague, Elmer, *What Is Philosophy?* Oxford University Press, New York, 1961. Chap. 3, "Philosophy and the World."
Taylor, Richard, *Metaphysics,* Prentice-Hall, Englewood Cliffs, N. J., 1963.
Warnock, G. J., *Berkeley,* Penguin Books, Harmondsworth, Middlesex, Eng., 1953.

ADVANCED STUDIES

Bouwsma, O. K., *Philosophical Essays,* University of Nebraska Press, Lincoln, Nebr., 1965. "Naturalism."
Burtt, E. A., "Descriptive Metaphysics," *Mind,* 72:18–39, January, 1963.
Collingwood, R. G., *An Essay on Metaphysics,* Oxford University Press, London, 1940.
Lazerowitz, Morris, *The Structure of Metaphysics,* Routledge and Kegan Paul, London, 1955.
Malcolm, Norman, "The Verification Argument," *Knowledge and Certainty,* Prentice-Hall, Englewood Cliffs, N. J., 1963.
Moore, G. E., "The Refutation of Idealism," *Philosophical Studies,* Routledge and Kegan Paul, London, 1922.
———, "A Defence of Common Sense" and "Proof of an External World," *Philosophical Papers,* Macmillan, New York, 1959.
Quine, W. V., "On What There Is," *From a Logical Point of View,* Harvard University Press, Cambridge, Mass., 1953.
Stace, W. T., "The Refutation of Realism," in H. Feigl and W. Sellars, *Readings in Philosophical Analysis,* Appleton-Century-Crofts, New York, 1949.

Chapter 4. The Scientist's Knowledge

THE TWO KINDS
OF SCIENCES

All scientific knowledge may be divided into the empirical sciences and the formal sciences. Physics, chemistry, and biology are examples of empirical sciences. Arithmetic, geometry, and algebra are examples of formal sciences. The distinction between these kinds of sciences is based on the differences in the proof of their statements. In an empirical science, the proof of its statements is based on an appeal to experiences which show that the statements correctly describe the world. In a formal science, the proof of its statements is based on an appeal to their consistency with the science's initial assumptions and definitions. This distinction between empirical and formal sciences is similar to Hume's distinction between matters of fact and relations of ideas and Kant's distinction between synthetical and analytical judgments (see Chapter 2) with which the reader may already be familiar. When we speak of science or scientific knowledge here we shall mean the empirical sciences rather than the formal sciences. Having distinguished empirical and formal sciences, we must notice immediately an important connection between them. Mathematics, the principal family of formal sciences, is one of the tools regularly employed by the empirical scientist in his task of describing the world.

THE PROBLEM
OF
SCIENTIFIC KNOWLEDGE

The problem of scientific knowledge is part of the larger problem of our knowledge of the world. The scientific notion of proof involves an appeal to sense experience; and the claim that the sciences give us genuine knowledge rests on the assumption that our sense perceptions inform us of the nature of the world. Thus perceptual knowledge is the foundation of all scientific knowledge, and unless our senses can be shown to be reliable, the claim that the sciences provide knowledge of the world cannot be justified. The reliability of perceptual knowledge is explored in earlier chapters.

The questions about scientific knowledge considered in this chapter are these: What distinguishes a scientist's way of thinking about the world from other ways of thinking about it? What distinguishes scientific statements about the world from other kinds of statements? Besides perceptual knowledge, what other grounds does a scientist have for his knowledge, and are they good grounds? and, How does scientific knowledge of the world fit in with our everyday, or common sense, knowledge of the world? It is not the aim of this chapter to teach the reader a particular empirical science. Rather, its aim is to throw some light on the second-order question, "What is science?"

It may be profitable to work our way into the problem of scientific knowledge by reminding ourselves of some of the differences between common sense or a person's everyday knowledge of the world, and scientific knowledge. These differences may be only differences of degree, but nonetheless it will be instructive to notice them. The principal distinction between common sense knowledge and scientific knowledge appears to be that common sense is acquired in the ordinary business of living, but scientific knowledge must be pursued deliberately and systematically. This distinction gives rise to differences in point of view, in degree of refinement, and in method.

Despite its name, the viewpoint of common sense is individual; it varies according to person, place, and time. But the scientist aims at a universal point of view. He wants to describe the world in ways that are, in principle, comprehensible to anyone, anywhere, at any time. This difference in point of view is closely related to the difference in degree of refinement. Common sense is concerned with the obvious, with that which "leaps to the eye"; and, as a consequence, common sense knowledge can be expressed in words at the level of "earth," "air," "fire," "water," "animal," "vegetable," and "mineral." But the scientist in his search for a universal viewpoint must analyze the obvious and general by means of concepts that are sharply defined. As a consequence he requires a vocabulary of abstract words like "atom," "wave," "field," "element," "stratum," "cell," and "species." This difference in refinement leads us to say that common sense is vague while scientific knowledge is precise; and one aspect of the problem of scientific knowledge is a consideration of how its preciseness is obtained, and of the advantages and disadvantages of this preciseness.

The difference between common sense and scientific knowledge in degree of refinement is closely related to the presence of method in science and its absence in common sense. Scientists have established procedures for improving and increasing their knowledge of the world, so that yet another difference between science and common sense is one of controlled experiment against uncontrolled experience. The development of scientific knowledge is directed and systematic, while common sense just grows. Indeed, this methodological difference between common sense and science brings us back to the original distinction we noticed: Common sense knowledge seems just to come to us, but scientific knowledge must be pursued deliberately and systematically.

This comparison of scientific with common sense knowledge illuminates the questions which we said earlier characterize the problem of scientific knowledge. To get at the question of what distinguishes a scientist's way of thinking about the world, we must study scientific concepts and discover the ways in which they both differ from and resemble common sense concepts. To get at the question of what distinguishes scientific statements, we must examine the way in which the scientist uses his concepts to formulate his hypotheses. To get at the closely related question of the grounds for scientific statements, we must examine the scientist's method for confirming his hypotheses.

In the first selection that follows, "Hypothesis and Scientific Method," by Professors Morris R. Cohen and Ernest Nagel, the reader is introduced to the problems of hypothesis-making and hypothesis-confirming, and to the difficult question of what makes a good hypothesis. Professor Max Black's essay, "The Definition of Scientific Method," is first of all a consideration of what we are asking for, and what we may get, when we ask for definitions of science and scientific method. He then proceeds to sketch what he believes to be the most helpful definition of scientific method. In the last selection, "The Physicist and the World," Professor L. Susan Stebbing explores the relation between scientific knowledge of the world and the ordinary person's knowledge of the world.

She is especially interested in showing that the ordinary person's knowledge is not in principle inferior and mistaken when contrasted with scientific knowledge, and that the everyday, familiar world is not an illusory duplicate of a scientific world.

11. MORRIS R. COHEN *and* ERNEST NAGEL

(1880–1947)   *(b. 1901)*

Hypotheses and Scientific Method

Morris Cohen taught philosophy at the City College in New York City from 1912 until he retired in 1938. Ernest Nagel, one of Professor Cohen's former students, is a professor of philosophy at Columbia University. Both men are joint authors of *An Introduction to Logic and Scientific Method* from which this reading is taken, and each published separately books relevant to the problem of scientific knowledge. Professor Cohen is the author of *Reason and Nature, An Essay on the Meaning of Scientific Method* (1931); and Professor Nagel is the author of *Sovereign Reason, and Other Studies in the Philosophy of Science* (1954), and *The Structure of Science* (1961).

In this reading Cohen and Nagel discuss the invention and verification of hypotheses in the natural sciences. According to one view, our scientific knowledge consists of hypotheses about the natural world. The question for the reader then is: How are scientific hypotheses different from other kinds of statements? With regard to scientific hypotheses themselves the appropriate question is: What is a good hypothesis? Because they have taken the making and testing of hypotheses in the whole of natural science as their subject, the authors' remarks are necessarily very general. The reader who is acquainted with a particular natural science should both supplement what Cohen and Nagel have to say from his own knowledge, and test what they say against his own knowledge of the making and testing of hypotheses.

This reading is taken from *An Introduction to Logic and Scientific Method*, Chapter XI, "Hypotheses and Scientific Method," with slight omissions. The revised edition of 1936 has been used, and the authors' section headings have been retained.

"Those who refuse to go beyond fact rarely get as far as fact. . . . Almost every great step [in the history of science] has been made by the 'anticipation of nature,' that is, by the invention of hypotheses which, though verifiable, often had very little foundation to start with."—T. H. HUXLEY.

"How odd it is that anyone should not see that all observation must be for or against some view, if it is to be of any service."—CHARLES DARWIN.

THE OCCASION AND THE FUNCTION OF INQUIRY

In the second book of his fascinating *History*, Herodotus recounts the sights that met him on his travels to Egypt. The river Nile aroused his attention:

"Now the Nile, when it overflows, floods not only the Delta, but also the tracts of country on both sides the stream which are thought to belong to Libya and Arabia, in some places reaching to the extent of two days' journey from its banks, in some even exceeding that distance, but in others falling short of it.

"Concerning the nature of the river, I was not able to gain any information either from the priests or from others. I was particularly anxious to learn from them why the Nile, at the commencement of the summer solstice, begins to rise, and continues to increase for a hundred days—and why, as soon as that number is past, it forthwith retires and contracts its stream, continuing low during the whole of the winter until the summer solstice comes around again. On none of these points could I obtain any explanation from the inhabitants, though I made every inquiry, wishing to know what was commonly reported—they could neither tell me what special virtue the Nile has which makes it so opposite in its nature to all other streams, nor why, unlike every other river, it gives forth no breezes from its surface.

"Some of the Greeks, however, wishing to get a reputation for cleverness, have offered explanations of the phenomena of the river, for which they have accounted in three different ways. Two of these I do not think it worth while to speak of, further than simply to mention what they are. One pretends that the Etesian winds [the northwest winds blowing from the Mediterranean] cause the rise of the river by preventing the Nile-water from running off into the sea. But in the first place it has often happened, when the Etesian winds did not blow, that the Nile has risen according to its usual wont; and further, if the Etesian winds produced the effect, the other rivers which flow in a direction opposite to those winds ought to present the same phenomena as the Nile, and the more so as they are all smaller streams, and have a weaker current. But these rivers, of which there are many both in Syria and in Libya, are entirely unlike the Nile in this respect.

"The second opinion is even more unscientific than the one just mentioned, and also, if I may so say, more marvellous. It is that the Nile acts so strangely because it flows from the ocean, and that the ocean flows all round the earth.

"The third explanation, which is very much more plausible than either of the others, is positively the furthest from the truth; for there is really nothing in what it says, any more than in the other theories. It is that the inundation of the Nile is caused by the melting of snows. Now, as the Nile flows out of Libya [Central Africa], through Ethiopia into Egypt, how is it possible that it can be formed of melted snow, running, as it does, from the hottest regions of the world into cooler countries? Many are the proofs whereby anyone capable of reasoning on the subject may be convinced that it is most unlikely this should be the case. The first and strongest argument is furnished by the winds, which always blow hot from these regions. The second is that rain and frost are unknown there. Now, whenever snow falls, it must of necessity rain within five days; so that, if there were snow, there must be rain also in those parts. Thirdly, it is certain that the natives of the country are black with the heat, that the kites and the swallows remain there the whole year, and that the cranes, when they fly from the rigors of a Scythian winter, flock thither to pass the cold season. If then, in the country whence the Nile has its source, or in that through which it flows, there fell ever so little snow, it is absolutely impossible that any of these circumstances could take place.

"As for the writer who attributes the phenomenon to the ocean, his account is involved in such obscurity, that it is impossible to disprove it by argument. For my part I know of no river called Ocean, and I think that Homer, or one of the earlier poets, invented the name and introduced it into his poetry." [1]

Herodotus then goes on to state his own explanation of the behavior of the Nile.

Has the reader ever been guilty of believing or saying that the way to find out what the truth is, is to "study the facts" or to "let the facts speak for themselves"? Then let him examine this quotation for the light it may throw on the nature of the circumstances under which contributions to knowledge are made. Unless habitual beliefs are shaken into doubt by alterations in our familiar environment or by our curiosity, we either do no thinking at all, or our thinking, such as it is, has a routine character. We wish now to reinforce this suggestion and indicate its importance in understanding the nature of reflective or scientific method.

This excerpt from Herodotus illustrates clearly the Greek zest for scientific knowledge and speculation. But it also illustrates the great difference between the habit of simple acceptance of apparently stray, disconnected information, and the attitude that searches for some order in facts which are only superficially isolated. The observable inundation of the Nile was to many a brute fact, unconnected with other familiar but isolated facts. For

[1] *History,* tr. by George Rawlinson, 1859, 4 vols. Vol. II, pp. 24–29.

Herodotus, however, the behavior of the Nile was not simply a brute fact. It presented a *problem* that could be resolved only by finding some general *connection* between the periodic inundation of the Nile and *other* facts.

It is an utterly superficial view, therefore, that the truth is to be found by "studying the facts." It is superficial because no inquiry can even get under way until and unless *some difficulty is felt* in a practical or theoretical situation. It is the difficulty, or problem, which guides our search for some *order among the facts,* in terms of which the difficulty is to be removed. We could not possibly discover the *reasons* for the inundation of the Nile unless we first recognized in the inundation a *problem* demanding solution.

If some problem is the occasion for inquiry, the *solution* of the problem is the goal and function of the inquiry. What constitutes a satisfactory solution of a problem, and in particular of the problem: Why does the Nile overflow its banks? The sort of answer for which Herodotus was looking was the discovery of a connection between the fact of the Nile's behavior and *other* facts; in virtue of that connection, apparently isolated facts would be seen to be *ordered* facts. And in general, scientific investigations must begin with some problem, and aim at an order connecting what at first sight may seem unrelated facts. But the ability to perceive in some brute experience the occasion for a problem, and especially a problem *whose solution has a bearing on the solution of other problems,* is not a common talent among men. For no rule can be given by means of which men can learn to ask significant questions. It is a mark of scientific genius to be sensitive to difficulties where less gifted people pass by untroubled with doubt.

THE FORMULATION OF RELEVANT HYPOTHESES

How does such a search for an order among facts proceed? The reader must note in the first place that a problem cannot even be *stated* unless we are somewhat familiar with the subject matter in which we discover the problem. The Greeks found a problem in the behavior of the Nile because, among other reasons, they were acquainted with the behavior of other rivers, and because the behavior of these other rivers was known to them to be connected with such things as wind, snowfall, and evaporation.

In order to state some obscurely felt difficulty in the form of a determinate problem, we must be able to *pick out,* on the basis of *previous knowledge,* certain elements in the subject matter as *significant.* Thus Herodotus noted the *distance covered* by the overflowing waters, the *time* at which the inundation *begins,* the *time* at which the overflow reaches its *maximum,* and the absence of *breezes* at the river's surface. It was in terms of such distinguishable and repeatable elements in the total situation known as "the inundation of the Nile" that Herodotus stated his difficulty. But his attention was drawn to these elements, rather than to others, because he was familiar with certain *theories* dealing with the behavior of rivers. It was his familiarity with such theories which made him look to facts like the winds, snowfall, or evaporation, rather than to other facts in order to find a connection between them and the Nile's behavior.

We cannot take a single step forward in any inquiry unless we begin with a *suggested* explanation or solution of the difficulty which originated it. Such tentative explanations are suggested to us by something in the subject matter and by our previous knowledge. When they are formulated as propositions, they are called *hypotheses*.

The function of a hypothesis is to *direct* our search for the order among facts. The suggestions formulated in the hypothesis *may* be solutions to the problem. *Whether* they are, is the task of the inquiry. No one of the suggestions need necessarily lead to our goal. And frequently some of the suggestions are incompatible with one another, so that they cannot all be solutions to the same problem.

We shall discuss below the formal conditions a satisfactory hypothesis must fulfill. The reader should note at this point that Herodotus examined three hypotheses (besides his own) for solving the problem of the Nile's periodic inundation. He accepted his own, after rejecting the other three. As a matter of fact, all four explanations are false. Nevertheless, the procedure he followed in rejecting some hypotheses and accepting others is still a model of scientific method.

How important hypotheses are in directing inquiry will be seen clearly if we reflect once more on the frequent advice: "Let the facts speak for themselves." For what *are* the facts, and *which* facts should we study? Herodotus could have observed the rise and retreat of the Nile until the end of time without finding in that particular repeated fact the sort of connections he was looking for—the relations of the inundation to the rainfall in Central Africa, for example. His problem could receive a solution only with the discovery of an invariable connection between the overflow of the Nile and some other fact. But *what* other fact? The number of other facts is endless, and an undirected observation of the Nile may never reveal either the other facts or their mode of connection. Facts must be *selected* for study on the basis of a hypothesis.

In directing an inquiry, a hypothesis must of necessity regard some facts as *significant* and others as not. It would have been humanly impossible for Herodotus to examine the relations of the Nile to *every other* class of events. Such a task, however, would have been regarded by him as preposterous. For most of these other facts, such as the number of prayers offered by the Egyptians every day, or the number of travelers visiting Naucratis each season, were judged by him to be *irrelevant*.

What is meant by saying that some hypotheses express "relevant" connection of facts, and others do not? The melting of snows is a relevant fact for understanding the Nile's behavior, Herodotus might have explained, because *on the basis of previous knowledge* melting snow can be regarded as related more or less constantly and in some determinate manner with the volume of rivers. But the number of visitors in Naucratis each season is not relevant to the Nile's behavior, because no such relation is known to exist between changes in the visiting population of a city and variations in the volume of rivers. A hypothesis is believed to be relevant to a problem if it expresses determinate modes of connections between a set of facts, including the fact investigated; it is irrelevant otherwise.

No rules can be stated for "hitting upon" relevant hypotheses. A hypothesis may often be believed to be relevant which subsequent inquiry shows to be not so. Or we may believe that certain facts are irrelevant to a problem although subsequent inquiry may reveal the contrary. *In the absence of knowledge concerning a subject matter, we can make no well-founded judgments of relevance.*

It follows that the valuable suggestions for solving a problem can be made only by those who are familiar with the kinds of connections which the subject matter under investigation is capable of exhibiting. Thus the explanation of the Nile's periodic overflow as due to heavy rainfall would not be very likely to occur to anyone not already familiar with the relation between rain and swollen rivers. The hypotheses which occur to an investigator are therefore a function, in part at least, of his previous knowledge.

THE DEDUCTIVE DEVELOPMENT OF HYPOTHESES

Let us now reëxamine the procedure of Herodotus in terms of the distinctions already familiar.

The search for an explanation of the Nile's behavior was a search for a *general rule* which asserts a *universal* connection between facts of that kind and other facts of different kind. The task of Herodotus was to show that the general rule which was suggested to him in the form of a hypothesis *did truly and in fact* apply to the specific problem at hand. How did he perform it?

The argument which Herodotus employed to reject the first theory may be stated as follows: The defender of the theory offers the following argument:

If the Etesian winds blow, the Nile rises (*general rule*).
The Nile rises for one hundred days beginning with the summer solstice (*observed fact*).
∴ The Etesian winds blow, beginning with the summer solstice (*inferred event*).

The inference is, of course, invalid as a conclusive proof. But its proponent may claim that the reasoning is a *presumptive probable inference*, so that the conclusion is probable on the evidence. Herodotus shows that this is not the case. He points out that we can find an occasion when the Nile rises (*observed case*) and the Etesian winds do not blow. Such a case is obviously not explained by our general rule. He therefore concludes that the hypothesis of the winds will not *always* account for the inundation of the river. But he is not content with this, for the defender of the theory may perhaps be satisfied with an explanation of the overflow which is not invariable. Herodotus showed further that the logical consequences of the Etesian wind theory were *contrary* to the known facts. In order to do this, he had therefore to point out some of the other consequences of that theory by discovering what it *implied*.

His argument continues:

> If the blowing of the Etesian winds produced inundations, other rivers should behave as the Nile does (*elaborated rule*).
> These other rivers do not overflow their banks (*observed fact*).
> ∴. The blowing of the Etesian winds does not invariably produce inundations.

This inference is a valid mixed hypothetical syllogism. Herodotus has therefore shown that the Etesian-wind theory cannot be regarded as a satisfactory explanation of the problem.

In this rejection of the first theory, Herodotus was compelled to elaborate it deductively. The importance of this step can be seen even more clearly by considering his rejection of the third theory. This may be stated as follows: If there are periodic melting snows in the interior of Africa, then the Nile will inundate periodically. Herodotus rejects this explanation not because he can *actually observe* the absence of snow in Central Africa, but because he can observe what he believes to be the consequences of Central Africa's being a warm country. And since he rejects the possibility of snowfall in warm places, he also rejects the theory of melting snows as the cause of the Nile's behavior. Let us restate part of his argument:

> If hot winds blow from a region, then that region itself is hot (*general rule*).
> Hot winds blow from the interior of Africa (*observed fact*).
> ∴. The interior of Africa is hot (*inferred fact*).
> If snow falls in a region, then that region cannot have a hot climate (*rule*).
> The interior of Africa *is* hot (*inferred fact from the previous inference*).
> ∴. Snow does not fall in the interior of Africa (*inferred fact*).

From this analysis we may conclude that the deductive elaboration of a hypothesis must follow its formulation. For we can discover the full meaning of a hypothesis, whether it is relevant and whether it offers a satisfactory solution of the problem, only by discovering what it *implies*. It is worth noting that Herodotus rejected the second theory simply on the ground that it was obscurely stated, so that it was impossible to find out what it did imply.

We are therefore already in the position to appreciate how important the technique of deduction is for scientific method. By attending to a few more relatively simple examples the reader can appreciate the indispensability for scientific procedure of developing a hypothesis deductively.

Galileo's study on falling bodies is one of the most far-reaching in modern times. He had shown that if we neglect the resistance of air, the velocity with which bodies fall to the ground does not depend on their weight. It was known that bodies pick up speed as they approach the ground. But it was not known what the relation is between the velocity, the space traveled, and the time required for the fall. Of what general law could the fall of a body be regarded as an instance?

Galileo considered two hypotheses. According to the first, the increase in the velocity of a freely falling body is proportional to the *space* traversed. But Galileo argued (mistakenly, as we now know) that one consequence of this assumption is that a body should travel *instantaneously* through a portion of its path. He believed this was impossible, and therefore rejected the proposed law of the increase in velocity.

Galileo next considered the hypothesis that the change in velocity of a freely falling body during an interval of time is proportional to that interval. This assumption may be expressed in modern notation as: $v = at$, where v represents the velocity, a the velocity acquired in one second, and t the number of seconds the body has fallen. It may also be expressed by saying that the acceleration of a falling body (defined as the change in velocity during any unit interval of time) is constant.

But the assumption that the acceleration is constant could not be put to the test *directly*. Galileo was compelled to strengthen his argument by *deducing other consequences* from the acceleration hypothesis, and showing that these consequences were capable of direct verification. The argument was strengthened because these consequences had not previously been known to be true. For example, he deduced from the hypothesis $v = at$, the proposition: The distances freely falling bodies traverse are proportional to the square of the time of their fall.

Instances of this rule can be established experimentally. Thus a body which falls for two seconds travels four times as far as a body which falls only one second; and a body falling three seconds travels nine times as far as a body falling one second. This, therefore, strengthens the evidence for the hypothesis that bodies fall so that their acceleration is constant.

In a similar fashion, Galileo deduced other propositions from the acceleration hypothesis, all of which he could verify with much precision. In this way the evidence for that hypothesis was increased. *But it was possible to increase it only after exploring its directly verifiable implications.*

Nevertheless, the evidence for the acceleration hypothesis always remains only *probable*. The hypothesis is only probable on the evidence because it is always logically possible to find some other hypothesis from which all the verified propositions are consequences. Nevertheless, it shows itself the best available so long as it enables us to infer and discover an ever greater variety of true propositions. A comprehensive theory is established as true with a high probability by showing that various *samplings* from its logical consequences are empirically true.

Let us now summarize the general features of Galileo's procedure. We find that he *selected* some *portion* of his experiences for study. His experiments from the Tower of Pisa resolved some of his doubts. But the resolution of these doubts only raised others. If the behavior of freely falling bodies did not depend upon their weight, upon what did it depend? The ancients, as well as his own contemporaries, had already isolated some properties of bodies as *irrelevant* to their behavior in falling. The temperature, the smell, the color, the shapes of the bodies, were tacitly assumed to be irrelevant qualities. The ancients also regarded the distance and the duration of fall as unimportant. But this assumption Galileo refused to make. And he ventured to formulate hypotheses in which these properties of bodies were the determining factors of their behavior.

This selection of the relevant factors was in part based on his previous knowledge. Galileo, like the ancients, neglected the color and smell of bodies because general experience seemed to indicate that their color or smell could vary without corresponding changes in their behavior when falling. In part, however, the selection was based on a tentative guess that properties heretofore regarded as unimportant were in fact relevant. Galileo had already made successful researches in physics, in which the quantitative relations exclusively studied by the mathematics of his day played a fundamental rôle. He was also well read in ancient philosophy, and had an unbounded confidence that the "Book of Nature" was written in geometric characters. It was not, therefore, with an *unbiased* mind, it was not with a mind empty of strong convictions and interesting suggestions, that Galileo tried to solve for himself the problems of motion. It was a conviction with him that the only relevant factors in the study of motion were velocity, time, distance, and certain constant proportions.

We may thus distinguish two sets of ideas which Galileo employed in studying the motions of bodies. One set, by far the larger, consisted of his mathematical, physical, and philosophical convictions, which determined his choice of subjects and their relevant properties. The other set consisted of the *special* hypotheses he devised for discovering the relations between the relevant factors. The first set was a relatively stable collection of beliefs and prejudices. It is very likely Galileo would have held on to these, even if neither of his two hypotheses on falling bodies had been confirmed by experiment. The second set, especially at the stage of scientific development in Galileo's time, was a more unsettled collection of suggestions and beliefs. Thus Galileo might easily have sacrificed his very simple equations between velocity, time, distance, and acceleration for somewhat more complex ones if his experiments had demanded the latter.

It is these special assumptions which become formulated consciously as hypotheses or theories. And it is to a more careful study of the conditions which such hypotheses must meet that we now turn.

THE FORMAL CONDITIONS FOR HYPOTHESES

1. In the first place, a hypothesis must be formulated in such a manner that deductions can be made from it and that consequently a decision can be reached as to whether it does or does not explain the facts considered. This condition may be discussed from two points of view.

a. It is often the case—indeed the most valuable hypotheses of science are of this nature—that a hypothesis cannot be directly verified. We cannot establish directly by any simple observation that two bodies attract each other inversely as the square of their distances. The hypothesis must therefore be stated so that by means of the well-established techniques of logic and mathematics its implications can be clearly traced, and then subjected to experimental confirmation. Thus the hypothesis that the sun and the planet Mars attract each other proportionally to their masses, but inversely as the square of their distances, cannot be directly confirmed by observation. But one set of consequences from this hypothesis, that the orbit of Mars is an ellipse with the sun at the focus, and that therefore, given certain initial conditions, Mars should be observable at different points of the ellipse on stated occasions, is capable of being verified.

b. Unless each of the constituent terms of a hypothesis denotes a determinate experimental procedure, it is impossible to put the hypothesis to an experimental test. The hypothesis that the universe is shrinking in such a fashion that all lengths contract in the same ratio is empirically meaningless if it can have no consequences which are verifiable. In the same way the hypothesis that belief in a Providence is a stronger force making for righteous living than concern for one's fellow man can have no verifiable consequences unless we can assign an experimental process for measuring the relative strength of the "forces" involved.

2. A second, very obvious, condition which a hypothesis must satisfy is that it should provide the answer to the problem which generated the inquiry. Thus the theory that freely falling bodies fall with constant accelerations accounts for the known behavior of bodies near the surface of the earth.

Nevertheless, it would be a gross error to suppose that false hypotheses—that is, those whose logical consequences are not all in agreement with observation—are always useless. A false hypothesis may direct our attention to unsuspected facts or relations between facts, and so increase the evidence for other theories. The history of human inquiry is replete with hypotheses that have been rejected as false but which have had a useful purpose. The phlogiston theory in chemistry, the theory of caloric, or specific heat substance, the corpuscular theory of light, the one-fluid theory of electricity, the contract theory of the state, the associationist theory of psychology—these are a few examples of such useful hypotheses. A more obvious illustration is the following: The ancient Babylonians entertained many false notions about the magical properties of the number seven. Nevertheless, because of their belief that the heavenly bodies visible to the naked eye which move among the fixed stars had to be seven in number, they were led to look for and find the rarely seen planet Mercury. . . .

3. A very important further condition must be imposed upon hypotheses. As we have seen, Galileo's theory of acceleration enabled him not only to account for what he already knew when he formulated it, but also to *predict* that observation would reveal certain propositions to be true whose truth was not known or even suspected at the time the prediction was made. He was able to show, for example, that if the acceleration of a freely falling body was constant, then the path of projectiles fired from a gun inclined to the horizon would have to be a parabola. A hypothesis becomes *verified,* but of course *not proved* beyond every doubt, through the successful predictions it makes.

Let us change the illustration to make the point clearer. Let us imagine a very large bag which contains an enormous number of slips of paper. Each piece of paper, moreover, has a numeral written upon it. Suppose now we draw from the bag without replacing it one slip of paper at a time, and record the numeral we find written on each. The first numeral we draw, we continue to imagine, is 3, the second is 9. We are now offered a fortune if we can state what the five successive numerals beginning with the hundredth drawing will be.

What reply shall we give to the implied question? We may say, perhaps, that one answer is as good as another, because we suspect that the order in which the numerals appear is completely random. We may, however, entertain the hypothesis that the numeral we obtain on one drawing is *not* unrelated to the numeral we obtain on another drawing. We may then look for an *order* in which the numerals appear. On the *general* hypothesis that there is such an order we may then offer a *special* hypothesis to account for the sequence of the numerals. For it is clear that we can *try* to formulate such a law of sequence, even if in fact the numerals do not appear in any determinate sequence. The supposition we may make at this time, that the numerals appear in an ordered array, need not prevent us at some subsequent time from affirming, on the basis of better evidence, that they do not.

Let us accept the general hypothesis of order. The problem then is to find the *particular* order. Now the particular law or formula that we may entertain will be largely determined by our previous knowledge and our familiarity with mathematical series. On the basis of such familiarity it may appear plausible that the numeral drawn is connected with the *number of the drawing.* Other modes of connection may, of course, be entertained; the numerals drawn may be supposed connected with the *time* at which they are drawn, for example. Let us, however, accept the suggestion that the numeral is a function of the number of the drawing. Several formulae expressing this mode of connection will occur to everyone familiar with algebra. Thus we may offer as the law of the series the formula $y_1 = 3^n$, where n is the number of the drawing and y_1 the numeral drawn. When $n = 1$, y_1 is 3; and when $n = 2$, y_1 is 9. This hypothesis, therefore, completely accounts for the known facts.

But we know several other hypotheses which will also completely account for the known facts. $y_2 = 6n - 3$; $y_3 = \frac{3}{2}(n^2 + n)$; $y_4 = 2n^2 + 1$; $y_5 = (n^3/3) + (11n/3) - 1$, are four other formulae which will do so. And it is easy to show that an endless number of different expressions can be found which will perform the same function. If we reject this multitude of hypotheses without even a cursory examination, it is because we think we have some *relevant knowledge* for considering only these five.

But are all these five formulae equally "good"? If the discovery of an order determining the numerals *already drawn* were the only condition imposed upon a hypothesis, there would indeed be no reason for preferring one formula to another. However, we desire that our laws or formulae should be truly *universal:* they must express the *invariable* relations in which the numerals stand to one another. Hence the hypothesis to be preferred is the one which can *predict* what will happen, and from which we can infer what has *already* happened, even if we did not know what has happened when the hypothesis was formulated. Accordingly, we can calculate that if any one of these five formulae is universally applicable to the series of drawings, then on the third drawing from the bag we should obtain the following numerals: 27 if the first is true; 15 if the second is true; 18 if the third is true; 19 if the fourth is true; and 19 if the fifth is true.

It is extremely important to state the hypothesis and its consequences *before* any attempt at verification. For in the first place, until the hypothesis is stated we do not know what it is we are trying to verify. And in the second place, if we deliberately choose the hypothesis so that it will in fact be confirmed by a set of instances, we have no guarantee that it will be confirmed by other instances. In such a case we have not guarded against the fallacy of selection, and the "verification" is not a test or check upon the hypothesis so chosen. The logical function of prediction is to permit a genuine verification of our hypotheses by indicating, prior to the actual process of verification, instances which may verify them.

If, therefore, in our illustration the third numeral to be drawn should happen to be 19, the first three formulae would be eliminated. The remaining two would have faced the challenge of a larger body of experience. Nevertheless, we cannot be sure that these two formulae are the *only* two which could have expressed the order of the sequence of the numerals.

It becomes evident that a function of verification is to supply satisfactory evidence for eliminating some or all of the hypotheses we are considering. We are supposing we have been left with the two formulae: y_4 and y_5. Both have been imagined to be successful in predicting the third numeral. However, what we have said of what is necessary for a hypothesis to predict successfully applies not only to the third drawing, but to all subsequent drawings. If a hypothesis expresses a universal connection it must maintain itself and not be eliminated in the face of *every possible* attempt at verification. But since, as in our illustration, it is often the case that more than one hypothesis is left in the field after a finite number of verifications, we cannot affirm one such hypothesis to the *exclusion* of the others. We can *try*, however, by repeating the process, to eliminate all the relevant alternatives to some *one* hypothesis. This is an ideal which guides our inquiry, but it can rarely, if ever, be realized. And we are fortunate indeed if the hypotheses we had initially regarded as relevant are not all eliminated in the development of the inquiry.

To say that a hypothesis must be so formulated that its material consequences can be discovered means, then, that a hypothesis must be *capable of verification*. At the time a hypothesis is developed, it may be impossible to verify it actually because of practical or technical difficulties. The logical consequences of a hypothesis may be such that much time may have to elapse between the time of drawing the inference and the time of the predicted consequence. Thus a total eclipse of the sun was required for testing one of the consequences of the theory of relativity. But while a hypothesis is frequently incapable of immediate verification, and while it can never be *demonstrated* if it asserts a truly universal connection, it must be *verifiable*. Its consequences, as we have already observed, must be stated in terms of *determinate* empirical operations.

It follows that unless a hypothesis is explicitly or implicitly *differentiating* in the order it specifies, it cannot be regarded as adequate. A hypothesis must be *capable of being refuted* if it specifies one order of connection rather than another.

Consider the proposition *All men are mortal,* which is a hypothesis to account for the behavior of men. Is this a satisfactory formulation? If we should find a man who is two hundred years old, need this instance cast any doubt on the universality of the mortality theory of men? Certainly a defender of the theory would not have to think so. But what if we found a gentleman as old as one of the Struldbrugs? The defender of the theory could still maintain that his hypothesis is perfectly compatible with such an instance. We may reflect, however, that the hypothesis is so stated that *no matter how aged a man we could produce,* the hypothesis would not be refuted. The hypothesis, to be satisfactory, must be modified so that an experimental determination is possible between it and any contrary alternative.

A hypothesis, if it has verifiable consequences, cannot pretend to explain *no matter what* may happen: the consequences which are capable of being observed if the hypothesis is true cannot all be the same as the verifiable consequences of a contrary hypothesis. In our example, the hypothesis receives the proper modification if it is stated in the form *All men die before they reach the two-hundredth anniversary of their birth*. In this form, a five-hundred-year-old gentleman would definitely refute the hypothesis.

Many theories which have a wide popular appeal fail to meet the condition we have specified. Thus the theory that whatever happens is the work of Providence, or the will of the unconscious self, is unsatisfactory from the point of view we are now considering. For that theory is *not* verified, if *after* the "happening" we can interpret the event as the work of Providence or of the unconscious self. In fact, the theory is so poorly formulated that we cannot state what its logical consequences are, and therefore what should be the nature of some future event. The theory does not enable us to predict. It is not verifiable. It does not differentiate between itself and any apparently contrary theory, such as that whatever happens is fortuitous.

4. One further condition for satisfactory hypotheses remains to be considered. In our artificial illustration we found that after the third drawing, two hypotheses still remained in the field. How are we to decide between them? The answer seems not to be difficult in this case. Since the formula y_4 will yield a different numeral for $n = 4$ than will the formula y_5, the fourth drawing will enable us to verify one of them and eliminate the other, or perhaps eliminate both. But what if we should be dealing with two hypotheses of which all the consequences we can actually verify are the same?

We must distinguish two cases in which this may happen. Suppose, as the first case, that two investigators wish to determine the nature of a closed curved line they find traced on a piece of ground. One says it is a curve such that the distances from points on it to a certain fixed point are all equal. The other says the curve is such that the area inclosed by it is the largest one that can be inclosed by a curve of that length. It can be shown, however, that all the logical consequences of the first hypothesis are the same as those of the second. Indeed, the two hypotheses are not different logically. If the two investigators should quarrel about their respective theories, they would be quarreling either about words or about their esthetic preferences for the different formulations of what is essentially the same theory.

It may happen, however, that two theories are not logically equivalent although the consequences in which they differ are incapable of being tested experimentally. Such a situation may arise when our methods of observation are not sensitive enough to distinguish between the logically distinct consequences. For example, the Newtonian theory of gravitation asserts that two bodies attract each other inversely as the "second power" of their distances; an alternative theory may assert that the attraction is inversely proportional to the 2.00000008 power of their distances. We cannot detect experimentally the difference between the two theories. What further condition must be imposed so that we may be able to decide in such cases between rival hypotheses?

The answer we shall examine is that the *simpler* one of two hypotheses is the more satisfactory. We may cite as a familiar example the heliocentric theory formulated by Copernicus to account for the apparent motions of the sun, moon, and planets. The geocentric theory of Ptolemy had been formulated for the same purpose. Both theories enable us to account for these motions, and in the sixteenth century, apart from the question of the phases of Venus, neither theory permitted a prediction which could not be made by the other theory. Indeed, it has been shown that for many applications the two theories are mathematically equivalent. Moreover, the theory of Ptolemy had the advantage that it did not go counter to the testimony of the senses: men could "see" the sun rise in the east and sink in the west; the heliocentric view, from the point of view of "common sense," is a very sophisticated explanation. Nevertheless, Copernicus and many of his contemporaries found the heliocentric theory "simpler" than the ancient theory of Ptolemy, and therefore to be perferred. What are we to understand by this? We must try to analyze what is meant by "simplicity."

a. "Simplicity" is often confused with "familiarity." Those not trained in physics and mathematics doubtless find a geocentric theory of the heavens simpler than a heliocentric theory, since in the latter case we must revise habitual interpretations of what it is we are supposed to see with our eyes. The theory that the earth is flat is simpler than the theory that it is round, because the untutored man finds it difficult to conceive of people at the antipodes walking on the surface of the earth without falling off. But "simplicity" so understood can be no guide for choosing between rival hypotheses. A new and therefore unfamiliar hypothesis would never be chosen for its simplicity. What is simple to one person is not so to another. To say that Einstein's theory of relativity is simpler (in this sense) than Newton's physics is clearly absurd.

b. One hypothesis is said to be simpler than another if the number of independent types of elements in the first is smaller than in the second. Plane geometry may be said to be simpler than solid geometry, not merely because most people find the first easier to master than the second, but also because configurations in three independent dimensions are studied in the latter and only two are studied in the former. Plane projective geometry is simpler in this sense than plane metric geometry, because only those transformations are studied in the first which leave invariant the colinearity of points and the concurrence of lines, while in the second type of geometry there is added the study of transformations which leave invariant the congruence of segments, angles, and areas. So also theories of physics are simpler than theories of biology, and these latter simpler than the theories of the social sciences.

A theory of human behavior which postulates a single unlearned impulse, for example, sex desire, or self-preservation, is often believed to be simpler in this sense than a theory which assumes several independent unlearned impulses. But this belief is mistaken, because in theories of the first type it is necessary to introduce special assumptions or qualifications of the single impulse in order to account for the observed variety of types of human behavior. Unless, therefore, *all* the assumptions of a hypothesis are explicitly stated, together with the relations between them, it is impossible to say whether it is in fact simpler than another hypothesis.

c. We are thus led to recognize another sense of simplicity. Two hypotheses may be both capable of introducing order into a certain domain. But one theory may be able to show that various facts in the domain are related on the basis of the *systematic implications of its assumptions.* The second theory, however, may be able to formulate an order only on the basis of special assumptions formulated *ad hoc* which are unconnected in any systematic fashion. The first theory is then said to be simpler than the second. Simplicity in this sense is the *simplicity of system.* A hypothesis simple in this sense is characterized by *generality.* One theory will therefore be said to be more simple or general than another if the first can, while the second cannot, exhibit the connections it is investigating as *special instances* of the relations it takes as fundamental.

The heliocentric theory, especially as it was developed by Newton, is systematically simpler than the theory of Ptolemy. We can account for the succession of day and night and of the seasons, for solar and lunar eclipses, for the phases of the moon and of the interior planets, for the behavior of gyroscopes, for the flattening of the earth at the poles, for the precession of the equinoxes, and for many other events, in terms of the fundamental ideas of the heliocentric theory. While a Ptolemaic astronomy can also account for these things, *special* assumptions have to be made in order to explain some of them, and such assumptions are not systematically related to the type of relation taken as fundamental.

Systematic simplicity is the kind sought in the advanced stages of scientific inquiry. Unless we remember this, the changes that are taking place in science must seem to us arbitrary. For changes in theory are frequently made for the sole purpose of finding some more general theory which will explain what was heretofore explained by two different and unconnected theories. And when it is said we should prefer the simpler one of two theories, it is systematic simplicity which must be understood. As we shall see presently, it is not easy at an advanced stage in a science to find a satisfactory hypothesis in order to explain some difficulty. For not every hypothesis will do. The explanation demanded is one in terms of a theory *analogous* in certain ways to theories already recognized in other domains. Such a demand is clearly reasonable, because if it is satisfied we are one step nearer to the ideal of a coherent *system* of explanations for an extensive domain of facts. In this sense, Einstein's general theory of relativity, although its mathematics is more difficult than that of the Newtonian theory of gravitation, is simpler than the latter. Unlike the latter, it does not introduce forces *ad hoc.*

It must be said, however, that it is difficult to differentiate between the relative systematic simplicity of two theories at an advanced stage of science.

Is the Schrödinger wave theory more or less simple than the Heisenberg matrix theory of the atom? Here we must allow for an incalculable esthetic element in the choice between rival theories. But while there is an element of arbitrariness in thus choosing between very general theories, the arbitrariness is limited, for the theory chosen is still subject to the other formal conditions we have examined.

FACTS, HYPOTHESES, AND CRUCIAL EXPERIMENTS

Observation

A hypothesis, we have said, must be verifiable, and verification takes place through experiment or sense observation. Observation, however, is not so simple a matter as is sometimes believed. A study of what is involved in making observations will enable us to offer the *coup de grâce* to the utterly misleading view that knowledge can be advanced by merely collecting facts.

1. Even apparently random observation requires the use of hypothesis to interpret what it is we are sensing. We can claim, indeed, that we "see" the fixed stars, the earth eclipsing the moon, bees gathering nectar for honey, or a storm approaching. But we shall be less ready to maintain that we simply and literally *see* these things, unaided by any theory, if we remember how comparatively recent in human history are these explanations of *what* it is we see. Unless we identify observation with an immediate, ineffable experience, we must employ hypotheses even in observation. For the objects of our seeing, hearing, and so on, acquire meaning for us only when we link up what is directly given in experience with what is not. This brilliant white spot of light against the deep-blue background—it has an incommunicable quality; but it also *means* a star many light-years away. In significant observation we *interpret* what is immediately given in sense. We *classify* objects of perception (calling this a "tree," that a "star") in virtue of noted similarities between things, similarities which are believed to be significant because of the theories we hold. Thus, a whale is classified as a mammal, and not as a fish, in spite of certain superficial resemblances between whales and fish.

2. Observation may be erroneous. The contradictory testimony of witnesses claiming to have "seen" the same occurrence is a familiar theme of applied psychology. Every day in our courts of law men swear in good faith to having seen things which on cross-examination they admit they were not in a position to observe. This is satirized in Anatole France's *Penguin Island* in the replies given by the villagers of Alca when they were asked for the color of the dragon who had brought destruction in the darkness of the night before. They answered:

"Red."

"Green."

"Blue."

"Yellow."

"His head is bright green, his wings are brilliant orange tinged with pink, his limbs are silver grey, his hind-quarters and his tail are striped with brown and pink bands, his belly bright yellow spotted with black."

"His color? He has no color."

"His is the color of a dragon." [2]

No wonder, after hearing this testimony, the Elders remained uncertain as to what should be done! But if uninterpreted sense experience were observation, how could error ever arise?

3. The hypothesis which *directs* observation also determines in large measure what factors in the subject matter are noted. For this reason, unless the conditions under which an observation is made are known, the observation is very unreliable, if not worthless. Changes are most satisfactorily studied when only a single factor is varied at a time. Of what value, then, is an observation that a certain liquid boils at 80° C., if we do not also observe its density and the atmospheric pressure? But, clearly, only some theory will lead us to observe all the relevant factors; only a theory will indicate whether atmospheric pressure is a single factor, or whether it may be distinguished into several others, as force is into magnitude and direction.

4. All but primitive observations are carried on with the aid of specially devised instruments. The nature and limitations of such instruments must be known. Their readings must be "corrected" and interpreted in the light of a comprehensive theoretical system.

These points are made in a striking manner by the French physicist Pierre Duhem. "Enter a laboratory; approach the table crowded with an assortment of apparatus, an electric cell, copper wire covered with silk, small cups of mercury, spools of wire, an iron bar carrying a mirror; an experimenter is plugging into small openings the metal end of a pin whose head is ebony; the iron oscillates, and by means of a mirror which is attached to it, throws upon a celluloid scale a luminous band; the forward and backward motion of this luminous spot enables the physicist to observe minutely the oscillations of the iron bar. But ask him what he is doing. Will he answer, 'I am studying the oscillations of an iron bar which carries a mirror?' No, he will answer that he is measuring the electric resistance of the spools. If you are astonished, if you ask him what his words mean, what relation they have with the phenomena he has been observing and which you have noted at the same time as he, he will answer that your question requires a long explanation, and that you should take a course in electricity." [3]

Is it not imperative, therefore, that the sharp distinction frequently made between fact and hypothesis be overhauled? Facts, we have seen, are not obtained by simply using our organs of sense. What, then, are facts? Are

[2] Translation by A. W. Evans, Bk. II, Chap. VI.

[3] *La théorie physique,* p. 218.

they, as is sometimes asserted, hypotheses for which evidence is considerable?
But in that case does this evidence consist only of *other* hypotheses for which
the evidence is considerable, and so on *ad infinitum*?

Facts

We must, obviously, distinguish between the different senses of "fact."
It denotes at least four distinct things.

1. We sometimes mean by "facts" certain discriminated elements in sense
perception. That which is denoted by the expressions "This band of color lies
between those two bands," "The end of this pointer coincides with that mark
on the scale," are facts in this sense. But we must note that no inquiry *begins*
with facts so defined. Such sensory elements are *analytically sought out by us*,
for the purpose of finding reliable signs which will enable us to test the
inferences we make. All observation appeals ultimately to certain *isolable*
elements in sense experience. We search for such elements because concerning them universal agreement among all people is obtainable.

2. "Fact" sometimes denotes the propositions which *interpret* what is
given to us in sense experience. *This is a mirror, That sound is the dinner
bell, This piece of gold is malleable,* are facts in this sense. All inquiry must
take for granted a host of propositions of this sort, although we may be led
to reject some of them as false as the inquiry progresses.

3. "Fact" also denotes propositions which truly assert an invariable sequence or conjunction of characters. *All gold is malleable, Water solidifies at
zero degree Centigrade, Opium is a soporific,* are facts in this sense, while,
Woman is fickle, is not a fact, or at least is a disputed fact. What is *believed*
to be a fact in this (or even in the second) sense depends clearly upon the
evidence we have been able to accumulate; ultimately, upon facts in the first
sense noted, together with certain assumed universal connections between
them. Hence, whether a proposition shall be called a fact or a hypothesis
depends upon the state of our evidence. The proposition *The earth is round*
at one time had no known evidence in its favor; later, it was employed as a
hypothesis to *order* a host of directly observable events; it is now regarded
as a fact because to doubt it would be to throw into confusion other portions
of our knowledge.

4. Finally, "fact" denotes those things existing in space or time, together
with the relations between them, in virtue of which a proposition is true.
Facts in this sense are neither true nor false; they simply *are:* they can be
apprehended by us in part through the senses; they may have a career in
time, may push each other, destroy each other, grow, disappear; or they may
be untouched by change. Facts in this fourth sense are distinct from the
hypotheses we make about them. A hypothesis is true, and is a fact in the
second or third sense, when it does state *what* the fact in this fourth sense is.

Consequently, the distinction between fact and hypothesis is never sharp when by "fact" is understood a proposition which may indeed be true, but for which the evidence can never be complete. It is the function of a hypothesis to reach the facts in our fourth sense. However, at any stage of our knowledge this function is only partially fulfilled. Nevertheless, as Joseph Priestley remarked: "Very lame and imperfect theories are sufficient to suggest useful experiments which serve to correct those theories, and give birth to others more perfect. These, then, occasion farther experiments, which bring us still nearer to the truth; and in this method of *approximation,* we must be content to proceed, and we ought to think ourselves happy, if, in this slow method, we make any real progress." [4]

Crucial Experiments

In the light of these remarks on the distinction between fact and hypothesis, we must reconsider, and qualify, our previous discussion of the verification of hypotheses. It is a common belief that a *single crucial experiment* may often decide between two rival theories. For if one theory implies an experimentally certifiable proposition which contradicts a proposition implied by a second theory, by carrying out the experiment, the argument runs, we can definitely eliminate one of the theories.

Consider two hypotheses: H_1, the hypothesis that light consists of very small particles traveling with enormous speeds, and H_2, the hypothesis that light is a form of wave motion. Both hypotheses explain a class of events E, for example, the rectilinear propagation of light, the reflection of light, the refraction of light. But H_1 implies the proposition p_1 that the velocity of light in water is *greater* than in air; while H_2 implies the proposition p_2 that the velocity of light in water is *less* than in air. Now p_1 and p_2 cannot both be true. Here, apparently, is an ideal case for performing a crucial experiment. If p_2 should be confirmed by experiment, p_1 would be refuted, and we could then argue, *and argue validly,* that the hypothesis H_1 cannot be true. By 1850 experimental technique in physical optics had become very refined, and Foucault was able to show that light travels faster in air than in water. According to the doctrine of crucial experiments, the corpuscular hypothesis of light should have been banished to limbo once for all.

Unfortunately, matters are not so simple: contemporary physics has revived Newton's corpuscular hypothesis in order to explain certain optical effects. How can this be? What is wrong with the apparently impeccable logic of the doctrine of crucial experiments?

The answer is simple, but calls our attention once more to the intimate way in which observation and theory are interrelated. In order to deduce the proposition p_1 from H_1, and in order that we may be able to perform the experiment of Foucault, many *other* assumptions, K, must be made about the nature of light and the instruments we employ in measuring its velocity.

[4] *The History . . . of Discoveries Relating to Vision, Light, and Colours,* 1772, p. 181.

Consequently, it is not the hypothesis H_1 alone which is being put to the test by the experiment—it is H_1 and K. The logic of the crucial experiment therefore is as follows: If H_1 and K, then p_1; but p_1 is false; therefore either H_1 is false or K (in part or completely) is false. Now if we have good grounds for believing that K is not false, H_1 is refuted by the experiment. Nevertheless the experiment really tests both H_1 *and* K. If in the interest of the coherence of our knowledge it is found necessary to revise the assumptions contained in K, the crucial experiment must be reinterpreted, and it need not then decide against H_1.

Every experiment, therefore, tests not an isolated hypothesis, but the *whole body* of relevant knowledge logically involved. If the experiment is claimed to refute an isolated hypothesis, this is because the rest of the assumptions we have made are believed to be well founded. But this belief may be mistaken.

This point is important enough to deserve another illustration. Let us suppose we wish to discover whether our "space" is Euclidean, that is, whether the angle sum of a physical triangle is equal to two right angles. We select as vertices of such a triangle three fixed stars, and as its sides the paths of rays traveling from vertex to vertex. By making a series of measurements we can *calculate* the magnitude of the angles of this triangle and so obtain the angle sum. Suppose the sum is less than two right angles. *Must* we conclude that Euclidean geometry is not true? Not at all! There are at least three alternatives open to us:

1. We may explain the discrepancy between the theoretical and "observed" values of the angle sum on the hypothesis of errors in measurement.

2. We may conclude that Euclidean geometry is not physically true.

3. We may conclude that the "lines" joining the vertices of the triangle with each other and with our measuring instruments are not "really" straight lines; that is, Euclidean geometry is physically true, but light does not travel in Euclidean straight lines in stellar space.

If we accept the second alternative, we do so on the assumption that light is propagated rectilinearly, an assumption which, although supported by much evidence, is nevertheless not indubitable. If we accept the third alternative, it may be because we have some independent evidence for denying the rectilinear propagation of light; or it may be because a greater coherence or system is introduced into the body of our physical knowledge as a consequence of this denial.

"Crucial experiments," we must conclude, are crucial against a hypothesis only if there is a relatively stable set of assumptions which we do not wish to abandon. But no guarantees can be given, for reasons we have stated, that some portion of such assumptions will never be surrendered.

THE ROLE OF ANALOGY IN THE
FORMATION OF HYPOTHESES

The reader of this [essay], noticing that it is nearing its end, may perhaps finally lose his patience. "You have told me what a hypothesis means, how central a position it occupies in all inquiry, and what the requirements for a hypothesis are. For all this I thank you. But why don't you tell me how I am to discover a satisfactory hypothesis—what rules I should follow?"

. . . We must perhaps try the reader's patience still further, first, by quoting what a great wit replied to a similar question, and second, by considering critically a piece of advice that is sometimes given as an aid in discovering hypotheses. The wit is De Morgan. "A hypothesis must have been started," he wrote, "not by rule, but by that sagacity of which no description can be given, precisely because the very owners of it do not act under laws perceptible to themselves. The inventor of hypothesis, if pressed to explain his method, must answer as did Zerah Colburn [a Vermont calculating boy of the early nineteen-hundreds] when asked for his mode of instantaneous calculation. When the poor boy had been bothered for some time in this manner, he cried out in a huff, 'God put it into my head, and I can't put it into yours.' " [5]

The advice is that analogies or resemblances should be noted between the facts we are trying to explain and other facts whose explanation we already know. But which analogies, we are tempted to ask? We can always find *some* resemblances, although not all of them are significant. What we have already said about relevance is applicable here. Nevertheless, it is true enough that if previously established knowledge can be used in new settings, analogies must be noted and exploited.

It is a mistake, however, to suppose that we always explicitly notice precise analogies and then rationally develop their consequences. We generally begin with an unanalyzed feeling of vague resemblance, which is discovered to involve an explicit analogy in structure or function *only by a careful inquiry*. We do not *start* by noting the structural identity in the bend of a human arm and the bend of a pipe, and then go on to characterize the latter as an "elbow." Nor do we notice first the slant of the eyes and thinness of the lips of Orientals, and then conclude that they look alike. Usually it is rather the other way.

Moreover, considerations of analogy are not always on hand when we wish to formulate a satisfactory hypothesis. For though a hypothesis is generally satisfactory only when it does have certain *structural analogies* to other well-established theories, it is not easy to formulate hypotheses which meet this condition. When we study the behavior of gases, we wish to find

[5] *A Budget of Paradoxes,* Vol. I, p. 86.

a theory analogous to those *already* established to account for the behavior of matter in motion. This is not an easy task, as the history of the kinetic theory of gases shows. The analogy of a hypothesis to others is therefore a *condition we impose* upon it, in the interest of the systematic simplicity of all our knowledge, before such analogy can aid in any discovery. And when we succeed in formulating a hypothesis analogous to others, this is an *achievement,* and the starting-point of further inquiry.

QUESTIONS

1. Why is the view that scientific truth is to be found by "studying the facts" a superficial one?
2. How does a scientific hypothesis differ from any other kind of statement? What makes a given hypothesis *relevant* to a problem? Why is it indispensable for scientific procedure to develop a hypothesis deductively? Name and illustrate the authors' four formal conditions for a scientific hypothesis. Explain the importance of each of these conditions.
3. What is a fact in science? Consider whether Bertrand Russell accurately represents the relation of facts to scientific hypotheses when he writes:

    . . . Science, though it starts from observation of the particular, is not concerned essentially with the particular, but with the general. A fact, in science, is not a mere fact, but an instance.[6]
4. Which of the following statements are facts, or hypotheses, or both? Explain how you are using the words "fact" and "hypothesis." Can you distinguish different kinds of facts, or different degrees of sophistication in hypotheses, or both? Perhaps you can use some of the following statements to illustrate the distinctions you may wish to make in answering this last question.
    a. The sun shines.
    b. The sun is a luminous body.
    c. The sun is a mass of burning gases.
    d. The sun is a mass of radiant energy.
    e. The sun is a process in which hydrogen is converted to helium.
    f. On earth, night follows day.
    g. The earth rotates on its axis.
    h. The earth revolves around the sun.
    i. The sun goes around the earth.
    j. The earth is flat.
    k. The earth is a sphere.
5. Hiero, the ruler of Syracuse, ordered Archimedes to discover, without destroying the crown, whether a gold crown contained silver alloy. Archimedes noticed one day while taking a bath that his body seemed lighter, and it occurred to him that any body immersed in a liquid loses a weight equal to the weight of the displaced liquid.

    Show that this suggestion is sufficient to solve the problem put to Archimedes. (From Cohen and Nagel)
6. Before the eighteenth century, heat was regarded as an "imponderable fluid" or caloric, which lodged in the pores of substances. According to this, when an object gets colder the caloric fluid flows out, and conversely it flows in when the object gets warmer. This theory accounted for all known facts about heat.

[6] Bertrand Russell, *The Scientific Outlook,* Norton, New York, 1931, pp. 57–58.

But an alternative theory of heat was suggested, according to which heat is a form of motion. This theory also explained the known facts. At the beginning of the nineteenth century, however, Sir Humphry Davy performed an experiment which was allegedly crucial between the two theories. The experiment consisted in rubbing together two pieces of ice which were isolated from all sources of heat. The ice melted, and according to the caloric theory it must have combined with the caloric fluid to produce water. The caloric theory, however, could not explain the source of this caloric. On the other hand, the melting of the ice was easily explained on the kinetic theory of heat. Hence Davy's experiment is regarded as a crucial one.

In what sense does this claim hold? (From Cohen and Nagel)

7. Show that an important condition for hypotheses is not fulfilled by the part of Freud's theory discussed in the following:

[Freud declares that] "the *libido is regularly and lawfully of a masculine nature, be it in the man or in the woman; and if we consider its object, this may be either the man or the woman.*" . . . Those individuals whose sex life seeks an object he calls the anaclitic type, and this is essentially a masculine type, since it is originally the woman who tends the infant. . . . *Later on he states that where woman is anaclitic or object-loving in her makeup, in that degree is she masculine.* This is a perfect example of the unassailable position, and has its analogs in much of male estimation of woman. Woman is primarily unintelligent, many men from Plato's time have said. But if they are shown a woman who is intelligent, their answer is, well, in that respect she is masculine! [7] (From Cohen and Nagel)

[7] Abraham Myerson, "Freud's Theory of Sex," in *Sex in Civilization,* ed. by V. F. Calverton and S. D. Schmalhausen, 1929, pp. 519, 520.

12. MAX BLACK

(*b. 1909*)

The Definition of Scientific Method

Max Black is Susan Linn Sage Professor of Philosophy in Cornell University. He is the author of *Language and Philosophy* (1949), *Problems of Analysis* (1954), *Models and Metaphors* (1962), and *A Companion to Wittgenstein's Tractatus* (1964).

In this reading Professor Black discusses what sort of task it is to define terms like "science" and "scientific method." He examines persuasive definitions, essential definitions, and range definitions, which are catalogues of the various uses of a term. It is this last sort of definition which he believes to be appropriate for "science," because it will reveal the "overlapping and interacting criteria" we have for applying the term to a range of entities. We shall thus be warned not to regard the term as the name of a single, immutable thing.

In noticing the several factors to be taken into account in defining "science," Professor Black discusses the philosophy of science of Claude Bernard (1813–78), the French physiologist. He considers particularly Bernard's insistence on the falsifiability of any scientific statement, while at the same time, through his adherence to determinism, believing in the orderliness of the world. This tension between skepticism and faith in Bernard's thought serves to illuminate the claim that the scientist cannot make observations or conduct experiments without having some conception of how the world must be; but should the observations or the experiments tell against the scientist's conceptions, then they must be abandoned without regret. Beyond its immediate usefulness in helping us to understand science, Professor Black's essay serves as a model for the kind of philosophical thinking that must be done to provide a range definition for a term.

My object in this essay is to clarify some of the problems involved in attempting to define scientific method. I shall argue that most writers who have tried to define scientific method have been working with a notion of definition which is too narrow for the task. I shall try to outline a pattern of definition which would be more adequate and discuss some criteria which any satisfactory definition of scientific method must satisfy. The purpose will therefore be to clear away some of the difficulties which have impeded the search for a satisfactory definition, rather than to provide a definition of my own.

Let us begin by considering some of the motives which lead us, as it has led so many philosophers and scientists in the past, to search for a definition of scientific method—or, for what is nearly the same thing, science itself.

The laziest answer will invoke that "intellectual curiosity" which so conveniently explains an interest in truth for its own sake. No doubt a thinker of precise intellectual habits will find it distasteful to be constantly using a term like "science" without having an explicit analysis of its connotation; the problem of definition may challenge his ingenuity as a chess problem might, and its solution will provide a satisfaction similar in kind. Disinterested philosophical lexicography is a harmless pursuit not to be sneered at in a world in which so few occupations are innocent. Nevertheless, we shall misconstrue the nature of our problem if we treat the definition of scientific method as a mere intellectual exercise.

When a term has a relatively well-determined denotation or application, the analysis of its connotation will, it is true, have little effect upon practice. Carpenters will continue to make tables, in happy ignorance of the epistemologist's inability to define the term "table." The case is different when the term to be defined has controversial or problematic application. To define such a term as "justice" is to engage in a hazardous occupation, as Socrates long ago discovered. Men are firmly convinced that justice is an excellent thing, while agreeing neither in the application of the term nor on the criteria which ought to determine its use. In these circumstances, the practice of those who use the term "justice" is likely to be as inconsistent as their thought is confused, and a good philosophical analysis runs the risk of bringing such inconsistencies to public notice. To anybody who continues to believe in justice, any shift in the term's application, induced by philosophical definition, threatens to bring about a redirection of his interests. And in general, *any* definition removing inconsistencies or involving a redistribution of emphasis will redirect the interests of those who use the term, provided they can understand the definition, and have sufficient intelligence to be moved by rational considerations.

The importance of such "persuasive definitions," as they have come to be called,[1] is being increasingly recognized. We can see today, more clearly than in the past, that definition of difficult terms is usually a process not regulated simply by the character of the concept to be defined.[2] The adequacy of a persuasive definition has also to be judged in relation to the soundness of the interests which it is designed to serve; the criticism of persuasive definitions is a proceeding partly normative in character, involving considerations of an ethical as well as of a methodological and logical character. This view, if correct, raises some difficult questions of procedure, some of which must be considered later in this essay.

Now I wish to maintain that the attempt to define scientific method or to analyze science is a search for a *persuasive* definition. I hold this to be true because I believe that the term "science" has no definite and unambiguous application. No doubt we should all agree that physics is a science par excellence, and that the atomic physicists use scientific method, whatever scientific method may prove to be. But we shall hardly agree with the remark attributed to Lord Rutherford that science consists of "physics and stamp collecting"— if this is taken to imply that nothing but physics is a science in the strict sense. Is chemistry science? Of course. But is psychology a science or the mere hope of a science? Is history a science? Or mathematics? Or ethics? Or sociology? Such questions have no answer *because they have no clear sense;* and they are asked, paradoxically enough, just *because* clear sense is lacking. For the

[1] "A 'persuasive' definition is one which gives a new conceptual meaning to a familiar word without substantially changing its emotive meaning, and which is used with the conscious or unconscious purpose of changing, by this means, the direction of people's interests" (C. L. Stevenson in *Mind*, 47 [1938]: 331). I would want to change this definition of "persuasive definition" in some respects, however. The reference to "emotive meaning," for instance, commits users of the term "persuasive" to a controversial and, in my judgment, mistaken analysis of meaning.

[2] Strictly speaking there is no determinate "concept" in such a case.

term "science" is eulogistic, whatever science may prove to be after analysis; and these requests for classification are also clamorous demands for the recognition and material rewards which await the application of the honorific label.

If this view of the situation is correct and we are looking for a persuasive definition, the search for a definition of scientific method will require the following combination of descriptive and normative procedures.

Instances of modes of investigation provisionally identified as eminently "scientific" will be collated and compared with the hope of determining common characteristics. The instances must be such as will not be seriously disputed—and this is perhaps why a few stock instances like Kepler's investigations into planetary motion reappear so often in textbook discussions of scientific method. So long as agreement about the scientific character of the instructive examples can be preserved, the process of comparison and analysis can be treated as non-normative and descriptive; the collation of undisputed instances of scientific method is, in principle, as "objective" as taxonomy. Unfortunately, the generalizations resulting from the examination of such undisputed instances are too indefinite to be of much use; the definitions of scientific method produced at this level are little better than banalities, and just because they codify what is commonly accepted, such definitions help not at all in resolving the burning questions of the applicability of scientific method to disputed cases. To be told that "perhaps science is after all only organized common sense, preferably derived from experiment and preferably organized on a quantitative basis" [3] helps not at all to decide whether psychical research is scientific or ethics extra-scientific. The formula elicits general agreement because it is so vague; and the vagueness covers a multitude of omissions. It is not unfair to say that the more those who write about scientific method agree, the less there is *about which* they agree.

Once we leave the area of universal agreement, we find ourselves compelled to choose criteria which are not clearly exemplified in acceptable instances: the instances are as problematic as the criteria to be employed. Our choice has to be made in the light of an interest we find to be good and is thus determined by normative considerations. It cannot be otherwise, since in this area of wider but uncertain application there is no definite denotation of the term to be analyzed. Let me make this plainer by an extreme illustration. Suppose my interest in science were to be confined exclusively to its chances of making me some financial profit (an attitude which is not altogether unheard of); in that case I might define as scientific only those investigations which, while conforming to the vague specifications achieved at our first level of analysis, *also* showed prospects of profitable exploitation by myself. The choice of my own financial interest as my *summum bonum* would be normative; but the implications of that choice would be non-

[3] James Bryant Conant, "The Advancement of Learning in the United States in the Post-War World," *Science*, 99 (February 4, 1944): 91.

normative or, in the language I have been using, descriptive. If the instance seems grotesque, it is so because we know in advance that we should refuse to accept the profit motive of a single person as determining our own interests in science. But the emphasis of theorists, from Bacon onward, on science as yielding power and mastery is not so remote from the grotesque hypothesis I have just considered. Those who single out technology for special emphasis in the definition of scientific method are committed to regarding technological advance, in that context, as a pre-eminent good. My point is that there must *be* a choice if the definition is to be worth having; it will be valuable *because* it is controversial. (The question of how such choices and value commitments are to be validated raises some of the most difficult problems of philosophy and cannot be discussed here.)

The regularizing of their own procedures is among the enduring interests of scientists. There is, in science, as in other creative human activities, a continual tension between the conservative demands of the tradition and the revolutionary activities of those who transform the tradition by revolting against it. There is something lawless in the creative process itself, and the scientists whom scientists have most wished to honor have made their discoveries by means as mysterious to themselves as to their contemporaries. But if their results are to be useful they must be communicable to those who are not themselves geniuses. Thus what begins as a brilliant discovery, as incoherent as it is dazzling, is eventually converted into a routine which the mere artisan of science can master and apply. In this way the new tradition is created but for which the later pioneers would have nothing to rebel against.

In some ways the progress of science, as here depicted, smacks too much of the marvelous and the unpredictable for comfort; and the hope has never been abandoned of reducing the process of discovery itself to a routine that can be communicated and taught. This hope has inspired investigators of scientific method from Aristotle to Descartes and from Bacon to Eddington. In one version of the legend of the Holy Grail those who sought it hoped to find a "self-acting, food-providing, talisman" [4] and this is precisely what such men as Bacon have hoped to discover. We can write off such a project as illusory and no more likely to succeed than the quest of the Grail itself; but it would be rash to assume that there are no principles relevant to the practice of research. However much we stress the final mystery of the art of creation, we have to admit that even the genius learns; and all learning is, necessarily, the learning of something general, reproducible, and, in theory at least, communicable. There are principles which assist the process of discovery, however insufficient in themselves to yield novel results; and if even this is not conceded, it will perhaps be granted that there are erroneous principles which constrict and hinder scientific progress. The study of scientific method may help at least to remove some of the obstacles to the develop-

[4] *Encyclopaedia Britannica,* 11th ed., 12: 320.

ment and extension of scientific thought. This alone would be sufficient justification for the most careful attempts to provide satisfactory analyses of scientific method.

I hope I have said enough to indicate something of the motives leading men to formulate definitions of scientific method; I have explained my interpretation of the procedure in which they were engaged. Now anybody who is persuaded of the importance of this enterprise may well feel some disappointment upon examining the analyses and definitions which invite his acceptance. Consider, for instance, the ancient tradition which identifies what is "really" or "pre-eminently" or "essentially" scientific with what is mathematical. This Pythagorean attitude recurs constantly in the philosophy of science; it has deep roots in Platonic metaphysics, was strong in Kepler and Galileo, Leibniz and Descartes; it was stated with unequivocal definiteness by Kant and is a living force today. Such a view can certainly not be accused of triteness or banality; it appears rather as a wild paradox which only "a fool or an advanced thinker" would seriously defend. A position which regards mathematics as the queen of the sciences, relegating the fact-finding activities of the observer and the experimenter to the role of "mere" auxiliaries, is certainly in need of a good deal of argument to render it plausible. Yet the curious inquirer, naïvely wondering at the boldness of the abstraction involved, will search in vain for such defense. What he is likely to discover instead is a claim that science is *essentially* mathematical, in spite of all appearance to the contrary.

I suppose that very few who use such language would admit that they were in search of an *essence,* in some Aristotelian sense. Yet I think it plausible that some of the defects of any definition as abstract as this are due to the use of a pattern of definition which is Aristotelian in origin. For until recent times nearly all textbooks of logic have echoed Aristotle's doctrine of definition.[5] Those who would shudder at professing Aristotelian or Thomist metaphysics continue to look for definitions *per genus et differentiam* as if no other mode of definition were conceivable.

I shall not try to make much of the point that modern generalizations of traditional logic show definition by division to be only one among many conceivable forms of definition. For this is not of much importance here, except as helping to encourage an attitude of sensible irreverence in respect of any claims of finality for Aristotelian logical doctrine.

What is more important to stress is that definition by genus and dif-

---

[5] "The traditional theory of definition is based upon the theory of the predicables. It can be summed up in the rule: definition should be *per genus et differentiam* (i.e., by assigning the genus and the distinguishing characteristic). This rule expresses Aristotle's view that definition states the essence of what is defined. . . . Everything, it is assumed, has a determinate essence and there is one and only one definition appropriate to it, viz., that which expresses the essence" (L. S. Stebbing, *A Modern Introduction to Logic* [1st ed.; New York, 1930], p. 432).

ferentia is always definition of a *determinate* and *immutable species*. What we define in this manner is a *kind* of thing, capable of having repeated instances alike in character; and the kind of thing that we define must have precise and constant boundaries. So long as this type of definition is used, it is impossible to define the name of a unique entity, say "Napoleon"; nor can we define a general term such as "bald" which, being vague, admits of a fringe of borderline cases; nor a term such as "music" whose criteria change in time. Definition is of something generic, determinate, and unchanging; and it follows that definitions are final, in the sense of never calling for revision. We may make a mistake in defining "science" or "scientific method," but if we find the correct definition it will stand for all time; to characterize a definition as "provisional" or "approximate" is to talk nonsense. Again, if "science" is a vague term, the boundaries of which are *not* precisely determined, it is insofar recalcitrant to this kind of definition: the best we can do is to substitute for the vague term some more precise substitute which *can* be defined. If the progress of science is in some respects a unique historical phenomenon, definition is impossible; if the "nature" of science is not constant, there is nothing that we can properly define.

These assumptions of the generality, definiteness, and constancy of the object of definition will seem to most people too obvious to be questioned; and we may as well grant that definition is most easily accomplished where the assumptions are justified. I wish to urge, however, that when the object of definition is "science" or "scientific method" we are not justified in postulating generality, definiteness, and constancy. We ought at least to consider seriously the possibility that the "scientific method" which is worth defining is in some respects historically unique, is continuous with its contraries, and is appreciably variable with time.

If serious account is taken of the uniqueness, indeterminateness, and variability of scientific method, it will be a matter of relative unimportance whether the process of analysis is called "definition." For those who conform most faithfully to the Aristotelian canons of definition will permit *some* kind of investigation into the connotation of individual, indeterminate, or variable terms. Rather than talk of definition in such cases they may prefer to say that the individual can be *described,* the indeterminate can be rendered determinate (by elimination of vagueness), and the variable can be subsumed under unchanging laws of change. Such ways of describing the task to be performed are not to be recommended; for they blur the important point that what we have to do is not so much to describe an object or to invent a new notation *as to clarify the language we now have and the thoughts we express by means of it.* I see no good reason not to call this "definition." Whether it can be effectively practiced remains to be seen.

My quarrel with the traditional mode of definition is, in short, that it takes for granted certain conditions of generality, definiteness, and fixity which are not always, or always completely, satisfied; that rigid adherence to these assumptions narrowly limits the range of what can be "properly" defined; and entails that "scientific method," *qua* unique, indeterminate, and subject to change, is indefinable.

So far, you may complain, no shred of evidence has been given of the contention that "science" and "scientific method" are recalcitrant to definition in the Aristotelian mode. I can think of no better means of persuasion than to invite you to contemplate in imagination the totality of the activities involved in and relevant to what we call "science."

Consider, if you will, the vast variety of activities of a scientific character which must have occurred yesterday—the glass blowing and the dissecting; the manipulation of rulers, stop watches, test tubes, bunsen burners, cyclotrons, questionnaires; men fishing in swamps, solving differential equations, polishing lenses, composing manuscripts, developing photographic plates, writing a polemic against vitalism, modifying an axiom system; handling, manufacturing, observing, experimenting, calculating, theorizing, speculating. Is not the resulting impression one of the extreme diversity, not to say heterogeneity, of the activities which we are naturally inclined to regard as scientific? Yet there is something more than a mere aggregate here; we know that this congeries of observations, manipulations, experimentations, explanations, calculations, predictions, speculations is unified by an extremely fine network of relationships. There *is* a pattern, but an extremely complex one.

The activities I have distinguished are not conducted independently and in isolation; the prosperity of one depends upon the success of all: calculation is performed for the sake of experimental and observational test; experiment is conducted in the service of generalization, which in turn uses theory, which provokes speculation, which invites systematization, which is controlled by experiment . . . and so on, without end, in a maze of cross connections and mutual dependencies. Science is an organic system of activities; and the pattern of its development is also organic.

We have imagined ourselves taking the latest cross section of scientific activity. To do justice to our subject we must extend our survey in imagination to cover the history and development of scientific activity no less than its present condition. We shall then see that this vast symphony of activities displays superordinate rhythms of development and change; there will be brought vividly to our notice the striking variety of motives and circumstances which have fostered or hindered the progress of science, the changes in instruments, modes of calculation, theories, underlying methodologies, and philosophies. For sheer complexity of texture and incident, science is like life itself and as little to be reduced to formula.

Some scientists regard an interest in the history of their subject as mere antiquarianism, and it may be that the very remote past consists largely of mistakes to be avoided. But it deserves to be remembered that the history of any scientific discipline intimately determines the current modes of investigation. The frames of reference which appear eligible to any given epoch, the instruments accepted as respectable, and the types of "fact" taken to have evidential value are historically conditioned. To pretend otherwise is to claim for human reason, as manifested in scientific progress, a universality and fixity it has never manifested. We may justly call the pattern of development organic, since the causal pattern is not analyzable into a set of independent causal strands; there is constant interaction across the temporal dimension.

A lively awareness of the complexity of science, regarded as a historical phenomenon, will make it seem unlikely that we shall succeed in finding a relatively simple and immutable essence underlying the confusing procession of accidents. We seem to have not a coherent nexus of well-defined and fully cognizable universals, but rather a concentration and overlapping of characteristics of variable degree. None of the characters which we recognize in the scientific process are independently necessary or sufficient, but all, supporting and jointly reinforcing one another, give rise to the unique historical phenomenon.

Neither observation, nor generalization, nor the hypothetico-deductive use of assumptions, nor measurement, nor the use of instruments, nor mathematical construction—nor all of them together—can be regarded as essential to science. For branches of science can easily be found where any one of these criteria is either absent or has so little influence as to be negligible. Astronomy makes no experiments, mathematics uses no observation, geography is mainly descriptive, archaeology hardly uses measurement, much taxonomy frames no abstract generalizations, and biology is hardly beginning to use mathematical idealization and formalization. The characters mentioned are neither necessary nor sufficient, but they may be present in higher or lower degree and they contribute to what we recognize as science. Their diminution removes from an activity the feature we apprehend as scientific; their joint presence in high degree creates conditions recognized as preeminently scientific.

This line of thought will lead us to abandon the search for a timeless and immutable essence in favor of the identification of a system of overlapping and interacting criteria. I propose to call this "range definition." [6] I am proposing, in fact, that we take seriously the organic and historical aspects of science. I propose that we treat "scientific method" as a historical expression meaning, among other things, "those procedures which, as a matter of historical fact, have proved most fruitful in the acquisition of systematic and comprehensive knowledge." On this approach, the methodological problems involved in the definition of scientific method closely parallel those arising in an attempt to define Napoleon, the industrial revolution, slavery, or any other person or institution having historical actuality. In each such case, what we recognize as the idiosyncrasy of the unique historical phenomenon is

[6] For further discussion of this kind of definition, see the second essay in *Problems of Analysis,* by Max Black, Cornell University Press, Ithaca, N. Y., 1954.—Eds.

constituted by a growing together, a concrescence, of variable factors, interacting to produce the degree of unification and contrast with an environment which leads us to recognize a distinct entity.

The technical problems which arise in range definitions are similar in character to those encountered in the specification of biological or psychological "types." And logicians have already begun to consider the methods of formalization appropriate.[7] To provide a satisfactory range definition we shall need (a) a description of the main factors engaged, (b) determination of their relative "weight" or importance, and (c) an account of their mode of interaction.

In trying to carry out such a program as this the pervasive difficulty will be that of choosing a proper level of abstraction. The greater formal complexity of range definition will not exempt it automatically from the danger of overabstraction; the result of our labors may still prove to be a sterile formula, unable, for all its complexity, to influence practice. There is, however, a kind of formulation of principle which is able to avoid this danger. I shall try to show how this happens by considering an illuminating illustration of the formulation of principles of scientific method.

Claude Bernard's *Introduction to the Study of Experimental Medicine,* first published in 1865,[8] is a classic of the philosophy of science which deserves to be better known in the English-speaking countries. Its title may have misled readers into expecting a technical treatise on physiology; it is in fact an essay on method not unworthy to be classed with that of Descartes. We shall not find here the pretensions to system, arrangement, and thoroughness of more elaborate treatises on scientific method. Here everything is said directly, simply, without pretentiousness or pseudo profundity; we can almost hear the harpsichord playing in the background. But there is nothing forced or contrived in this elegance; every page is informed with the judgment and educated memory of a superb experimenter. We seem to be always in the presence of a *person,* meditating upon a lifetime's experience of creative research.

The reflections of such a man deserve respect. I shall select for special attention two aspects of his doctrine which are directly relevant to my present purpose. First, Bernard's fallibilism [9] with respect to scientific theory—a doctrine held by many but never, to my knowledge stated better—will point the way for a more radical fallibilism with respect to the principles of scientific method. Second, Bernard's use of determinism as an instrument of criticism and discovery may throw light upon the manner in which principles of method can, in favorable cases, contribute to the progress and extension of science.

[7] See C. G. Hempel and P. Oppenheim, *Der Typusbegriff im Lichte der neuen Logik* (Leyden, 1936).

[8] I shall quote from H. D. Greene's translation, published by Macmillan in 1927.

[9] The term is Peirce's. See *Collected Papers of Charles Sanders Peirce,* ed. Charles Hartshorne and Paul Weiss (6 vols.; Cambridge, 1931–35), 1: 13, 141–52.

Bernard's views about the uncertainty of all scientific theory arise from his analysis of the distinction between experiment and observation and of the part played in both by hypothesis. Experiment, he says, differs from observation in demanding artificially induced variation for the sake of comparison and reasoning.[10] Experiment is relatively active, observation relatively passive; but the most elaborately artificial experiment terminates in simple observation, a submission to the verdict of experience. It is important to notice that because the experimenter *interrogates* nature, every experiment is based upon a "preconceived idea," a hypothesis to be tested.[11] But once the experimental conditions have been set up, the scientist must turn passive again. "Observers, then, must be photographers of phenomena; their observations must accurately represent nature. We must observe without any preconceived idea; the observer's mind must be passive, must hold its peace; it listens to nature and writes at its dictation." [12] Without hypotheses or "preconceived ideas" we should never discover the observations—so that even an erroneous theory is better than none at all.[13] But we must always "be ready to abandon, to alter or to supplant" [14] the hypothesis in the light of the decisive judgment of the observations by which it is tested.

To a generation successfully weaned from Baconian empiricism, Bernard's insistence upon the primacy of fact and the need for theoretical "preconceptions" in research may seem too elementary to call for praise. But a successful marriage of rationalism and empiricism is hard to arrange; and it is of great interest to see how Bernard manages to reconcile his great respect for fact with a thorough belief in the intelligibility of phenomena. He is a rationalist to the finger tips; observation, he says, is *always* made for the sake of generalization and explanation; the disproof of a theory must always be an incentive to theoretical explanation of the discrepancy—"negative facts when considered alone never teach us anything." [15] So it is that, in spite of his confidence in the senses,[16] he does not hesitate to outlaw a fact, if necessary. He says, of a particular instance, "The irrationality of the fact, there-

[10] "We give the name observer to the man who applies methods of investigation, whether simple or complex, to the study of phenomena which he does not vary and which he therefore gathers as nature offers them. We give the name experimenter to the man who applies methods of investigation, whether simple or complex, so as to make natural phenomena vary, or so as to alter them with some purpose or other, and to make them present themselves in circumstances or conditions in which nature does not show them." Bernard, *Experimental Medicine,* p. 15.

[11] "It is impossible to devise an experiment without a preconceived idea; devising an experiment, we said, is putting a question; we never conceive a question without an idea which invites an answer" (*ibid.,* p. 23).

[12] *Ibid.,* p. 22. See p. 192: "We must never go beyond facts and must be, as it were, photographers of nature."

[13] "Even mistaken hypotheses and theories are of use in leading to discoveries. . . . It seems, indeed a necessary weakness of our mind to be able to reach truth only across a multitude of errors and obstacles" (*ibid.,* 170).

[14] *Ibid.,* p. 23.

[15] *Ibid.,* p. 174.

[16] *Ibid.,* p. 177.

fore, led me to see *a priori* that it must be false, and that it could not be used as a basis for scientific reasoning." [17] Yet faith in the ultimate intelligibility and rationality of the universe is controlled and moderated in him by an abiding scepticism concerning *particular* explanations and reasons. Because every theory is an imperfect, and partly arbitrary, extrapolation from observation, we must never place unqualified trust in *any* theory. "When we propound a general theory in our sciences, we are sure only that, literally speaking, all such theories are false." [18] "Even when we have a theory that seems sound, it is never more than relatively sound, and it always includes a certain proportion of the unknown." [19] This paradoxical attitude of active scepticism, of an undogmatic and corrigible faith, Bernard sums up in a striking phrase: "We must have robust faith," he says, "and not believe." [20] We must not believe wholeheartedly in any body of scientific theory; the object of our robust faith is determinism. Determinism, he says, "is the absolute principle of science" [21] and to abandon it is to renounce the hope of being scientific. "In science we must firmly believe in principles, but must question formulae; on the one hand, indeed, we are sure that determinism exists, but we are never certain we have attained it." [22]

It might be supposed that a determinism such as Bernard espoused would be too pliable to serve as a guide and a stimulant to research. It has often been pointed out that determinism, construed as the principle that laws exist of no matter what degree of complexity, is irrefutable in principle. Faced with no matter how much confusion and irregularity of appearance, a determinist can always continue to *look* for laws. Is Bernard's major principle anything more than an expression of his determination to continue to look and to theorize? Does his determinism do any work, or is it merely a regrettable lapse into metaphysics?

Now I am inclined to think that Bernard's determinism, *as he used it,* can be shown to have been an active instrument of research and criticism. His practice repeatedly shows his faith in ultimate rationality lighting the path to original discovery. When the physicians of his day invoked the tact and intuition of the medical practitioner, Bernard counters with a stubborn

[17] *Ibid.,* p. 179.
[18] *Ibid.,* p. 36.
[19] *Ibid.,* p. 162.
[20] *Ibid.,* p. 168. We may be reminded here of Huxley's notion of "tätige skepsis" that he adapted from Goethe. For a similar more recent statement see Morris R. Cohen, *Studies in Philosophy and Science* (New York, 1949), p. 50: "We may define science as a self-corrective system . . . *science invites doubt.* It can grow or make progress, not only because it is fragmentary, but also because no one proposition in it is in itself absolutely certain, and so the process of correction can operate when we find more adequate evidence. But note, however, that the doubt and the correction are always in accordance with the canons of the scientific method, so that the latter is the bond of continuity."
[21] Bernard, *Experimental Medicine,* p. 39.
[22] *Ibid.,* p. 168.

search for causal sequences; when other theorists hid their ignorance of biological laws by appealing to some mysterious "vitality" or vital force, he condemns them for irrationality and continues to experiment; and in more specific contexts where less clearheaded experimenters blunder, Bernard's robust faith in a deterministic order of nature fortifies him in a laborious but successful search for rational explanation. Belief in determinism was, to him, a light for the darkness, not a mere obeisance to an imputed order of nature.

Such an interpretation might easily be wrong; and it is conceivable, though I find myself unable to believe it, that Bernard read his philosophical principles back into earlier researches which at the time of their performance required no better support than the luck and cunning of the investigator. Those who prefer to think that the experimenter is guided mainly by intuition may do so if they can persuade themselves that the term is something better than a disguise for our own ignorance of the creative process. But the general point is sound, and could be supported by ample illustrations from the history of science. As the individual experiment itself would be nothing without a preconceived idea, however crude and faulty in detail, so would the whole course of research be a mere random succession of fumbles but for the co-ordination of leading ideas. It seems implausible to me that any regulative principle as abstract as determinism in its most general formulation can have decisive influences upon research; and I think it demonstrable that in any epoch of experimental research the leading ideas take more specific forms, varying with the climate of philosophical opinion and the earlier fortunes of the science.[23]

I have been citing Claude Bernard's philosophy of science in support of my contention that cautious extrapolation of methodological principles may be a valuable guide to scientific research. There is, however, much in Bernard's doctrines themselves that would seem open to serious objection.

His conception of the fact of observation as simply given, the observer himself acting as a passive photographer of nature, is hardly adequate. The image itself betrays the intention; for a photograph is not an identical reproduction of the scene it portrays and must itself be correctly interpreted if it is to be a suitable datum for inference. The insistence upon the primacy of what is presented is valuable, but it must be reconciled with the principle of opposite tendency, to the effect that there is no observation without interpretation; pure observation is a myth. What shall *count* as a fact in any well-developed science is already largely determined by theory embodied in the disposition of the scientific instruments, the selection of "competent"

---

[23] I take this to explain in part Bernard's success in using determinism. Given the special context of physiological experiment in the last century, I think he had robust faith, not in general determinism, but rather in the existence of laws and explanations of *a certain kind*.

scientists, and the postures of "correct" observation. That Bernard needed to take no account of such complications is explained by the simplicity of his observations.

We cannot share, today, his unqualified faith in determinism. If we are to continue to search for laws, we must be prepared to find them complex beyond all the expectations of earlier scientists. Bernard's distrust of statistical generalization—thoroughly justified in his own context—must seem old-fashioned to a generation educated in statistical physics. We must be prepared to mix a little more scepticism with our faith than Bernard was prepared for.

One of the major contributions of this century's philosophy of science has been the clarification and analysis of the symbolic aspects of science. We are beginning to understand how very far from being a literal generalization about observable features of observable phenomena the theories of any advanced science must be taken to be. The more advanced the science, the greater the part played in its theories by unobservables; and the more urgent the task of elucidating the deductive paths connecting such abstruse and recondite entities with the experiences to which, however indirectly, they refer. A well-developed philosophy of science will have much to say in this chapter of its investigations.

We can now begin to see some hope of solving our problem about the choice of overlapping criteria for a definition of science. It will be remembered that I claimed that science, as a historical process, resembled an organism in being a manifestation of variable, interacting factors. Now we have to add that analysis of the character of this process, as it shows itself in the formulation of an explicit methodology, may itself become a factor in the further development. Principles abstracted from the past history may be put to work to help determine its future and themselves become subjected in this way to continuing experimental test. And the same holds for the goals, standards, and ideals which determine the choice, acceptance, and rejection of principles in the light of continuing experimental tests. Looking back at the history of science, we choose such principles of method as will seem to answer best to the search for knowledge of the world—as in the light of that examination we feel constrained to envisage what we now call the world and knowledge of it. If our choice is wise, the principles can be set to work to assist in the acquisition of more knowledge; and if the application, however successful, changes our conceptions of what should be the right method—indeed, of what we should regard as "nature," "the world," "fact," "evidence," and the other terms of our philosophical discourse—that is no more than we should be wise to expect.

I am advocating an attitude of active scepticism, of faith without belief, toward the very principles of investigation themselves. No doubt, to renounce the support of determinism or any other immutable theoretical certainty is to call for an attitude of mind difficult to sustain. There will be some to object that in the absence of some such underpinning the program is condemned to a futile relativism and, if it be wholehearted, a complete scepticism. "What," it will be said, "in the last analysis, justifies your choice of standards, ideals, criteria, and principles? If the justification lies in the future, then your choice of a scientific method is no better *now* than a blind guess. To be rational *now*, it must itself be based on rational first principles necessarily incapable of justification empirically. You want the advantage of a metaphysics while shirking the labor required to establish it."

The question is too large to be argued fully here. Let me be content to affirm that in the last analysis there is *no* last analysis. If the search for a definition of scientific method is more than an exercise in platitudinous verity or epigrammatic falsity, it is a serious attempt to clarify the relation of our culture to its past in order to bring into sharper focus our commitments to its future. This means starting from the standpoint not of a detached rational being exempt from the influence of his history but from our own standpoint in space and time. We start with given notions, preconceptions, and prejudices about knowledge, evidence, method, and science which it is mere folly to pretend to ignore. What we can do is to render these philosophical preconceptions more rational by testing them against past history and future experience. This is as far removed from blind guessing as the calculations of the meteorologist are from the casual weather predictions of the man in the street. But the philosopher of science may be sufficiently humble to expect no higher ratio of success than the weather forecaster; his one advantage in the long run over the advocate of intuition or guesswork is that he may hope to learn from his mistakes.

Since we have introduced the salutary virtue of humility, let me repeat that at best we have here the mere outline of a program. The detailed execution of the program, by which its merits must eventually be judged, is by far the harder undertaking. When we compare our present conception of scientific method with those of Herschel, Whewell, Jevons, Bernard, John Stuart Mill, and the other nineteenth-century writers we may take pride in having made marked advances. Certainly we have a much sounder grasp of the character and importance of the symbolic aspects of scientific method; our conceptions of statistical method, the nature of mathematics, of measurement, and the use of nonobservable theoretical entities have advanced in a way which would astound our not-so-distant predecessors. It would be self-deception, however, to pretend that light shines everywhere in those intensely cultivated regions, and it is safe to predict that theorists who venture already to lay down definite prescriptions for research in economics, psychology, or the still embryonic social sciences will seem entertainingly doctrinaire to their not-so-distant successors. The wisest philosophers of science have shown their wisdom not least in shrouding their first principles in protective ambiguity. The best we can hope for is some useful second principles that will prove to be not so vague as to be exempt from refutation by experience still to come, or so hopelessly wrong as to deserve outright rejection when science has suffered its next benign convulsion.

So much ground has been covered in this paper that a summary may be welcome. I began by characterizing definitions of "scientific method" as "persuasive," in a technical sense of that term. "Scientific method," it was contended, is a term of such controversial application that a definition universally acceptable can be expected to be platitudinous. A useful definition will be a controversial one, determined by a choice made, more or less wisely, in the hope of codifying and influencing scientific procedures. It is too much to expect infallible recipes for conducting research, but most definitions in the literature fail to satisfy the more modest demand of helping to determine the development and extension of scientific method. A common defect is excessive abstraction; it was suggested that this arises from conformity to a pattern of definition Aristotelian in origin. The search for an immutable and determinate essence underlying the plentitude of the historical process can result only in epigrammatic paradox. We may do better, I urged, to think of science as a concrescence, a growing together of variable, interacting, mutually reinforcing factors contributing to a development organic in character. The type of definition appropriate takes the form of a description of the constitutive factors, together with an indication of their relative weight or importance and their mutual relationships.

For further light upon the kind of definition that would be satisfactory I turned to Claude Bernard's philosophy of science. He was found to be advocating a blend of rationalism and empiricism, marked by submission to the authority of the results of observation, and an unflagging confidence in the causal structure of the universe. His scepticism with regard to the finality of scientific theory was congenial to the more radical fallibilism advocated in this paper. Though his robust faith in determinism cannot be shared without reservation, the use he made of it as an instrument of criticism encouraged us to hope that methodological principles might have a useful regulative function.

My own contention was that the very principles of scientific method are themselves to be regarded as provisional and subject to later correction, so that a definition of "scientific method" would be verifiable, in some wide sense of the term. To the degree that the definition is framed in the light of our best reflection about past knowledge-seeking activities, with the intention that it shall guide our further pursuit of knowledge in the future, we can properly claim that the procedure is rational. For to be rational is to be always in a position to learn more from experience.

QUESTIONS

1. What sort of term calls for a persuasive definition? How do persuasive definitions differ from nonpersuasive definitions?

2. What are the difficulties in the way of defining "science" and "scientific method," and why do these difficulties imply that the terms will lend themselves to persuasive definitions?

3. What is a definition *per genus et differentiam,* and what are the limitations on its usefulness? Why cannot such a definition be given of "science"?

4. What is a range definition? What must someone who offers a range definition of "science" take into account?

5. What is fallibilism and what does it have to do with scientific theory? How does Bernard's philosophy of science exemplify fallibilism?

6. What is the doctrine of scientific determinism and how does Bernard make use of it?

7. What is the symbolic aspect of science, and why must it be taken into account in the definition of scientific method?

8. Give a brief summary of Professor Black's recommendations for defining "science." How might his procedures in defining "science" serve as a model for the definition of "the social sciences," "the humanities," "art," "religion," "government," and "poetry"?

13. L. SUSAN STEBBING

(1885–1943)

The Physicist and the World

L. Susan Stebbing was born near Wimbledon, England. She read history at Cambridge and took an advanced degree in Philosophy at London University. She taught philosophy at Cambridge, and for the last ten years of her life she was Professor of Philosophy in London University. Her best-known books are *A Modern Introduction to Logic* (1930), *Philosophy and the Physicists* (1937), *Thinking to Some Purpose* (1939), and *Ideals and Illusions* (1941).

Impressed by what the scientist can say about the world, ordinary people may disparage their own knowledge of the world and, at the same time, be mystified about the relation between scientific knowledge and the everyday, familiar world. Professor Stebbing's

topic, here, is the relation between what the physical scientist can say about the world and what can be said about it from an everyday point of view. She explores this theme by examining passages from the popular writings of the physicist Sir Arthur Eddington (1882–1944).

Eddington, distinguished in his own field, was the author of such genuinely scientific works as *Mathematical Theory of Relativity* (1923) and *Relativity Theory of Protons and Electrons* (1936). But in other writings such as *The Nature of the Physical World* (1928), he tried to convey to the common reader a scientific view of the world couched in popular terms. Professor Stebbing finds two large faults in Eddington's writings. She objects to his use of an indiscriminate, and consequently misleading, mixture of everyday language and scientific language, as well as to his argument that from a scientific point of view, the everyday world is illusory and in our thinking may be eliminated in favor of a "scientific" world. Professor Stebbing uses her criticism of Eddington as the vehicle for two positive points. (1) Our everyday way of talking about the world is not grossly and inherently mistaken, and need not be dropped in favor of speaking "scientifically." Each way of talking has its appropriate occasion. (2) The purpose of scientific knowledge is to enable us to understand the familiar, everyday world, not to persuade us that it is somehow defective or nonexistent.

From *Philosophy and the Physicists,* by L. Susan Stebbing, Dover Publications, Inc., New York. Reprinted by permission of the publisher. ($1.65) Permission also granted by Methuen & Co., Ltd., London.

'Roused by the shock he started from his trance—
The cold white light of morning, the blue moon
Low in the west, the clear and garish hills,
The distant valley and the vacant woods,
Spread round him where he stood. Whither have fled
The hues of heaven that canopied his bower
Of yesternight? The sounds that soothed his sleep,
The mystery and the majesty of Earth,
The joy, the exultation?'—WORDSWORTH

I enter my study and see the blue curtains fluttering in the breeze, for the windows are open. I notice a bowl of roses on the table; it was not there when I went out. Clumsily I stumble against the table, bruising my leg against its hard edge; it is a heavy table and scarcely moves under the impact of my weight. I take a rose from the bowl, press it to my face, feel the softness of the petals, and smell its characteristic scent. I rejoice in the beauty of the graded shading of the crimson petals. In short—I am in a familiar room, seeing, touching, smelling familiar things, thinking familiar thoughts, experiencing familiar emotions.

In some such way might any common reader describe his experiences in the familiar world that he inhabits. With his eyes shut he may recognize a rose from its perfume, stumble against a solid obstacle and recognize it to be a table, and feel the pain from its contact with his comparatively yielding flesh. You, who are reading this may pause and look around you. Perhaps you are in your study, perhaps seated on the seashore, or in a cornfield, or on board ship. Wherever you may be, you will see objects distinguishable one from another, differing in colour and in shape; probably you are hearing various sounds. You can see the printed marks on this page, and notice that they are black marks on a whitish background. That you are perceiving something coloured and shaped you will not deny; that your body presses against something solid you are convinced; that, if you wish, you can stop reading this book, you know quite well. It may be assumed that you have some interest in philosophy; otherwise you would not be reading *this*. Perhaps you have allowed yourself to be persuaded that the page is not 'really coloured', that the seat upon which you are sitting is not 'really solid'; that you hear only 'illusory sounds'. If so, it is for such as you that this chapter is written.

Imagine the following scene. You are handed a dish containing some apples—rosy-cheeked, green apples. You take the one nearest to you, and realize that you have been 'had'. The 'apple' is too hard and not heavy enough to be really an apple; as you tap it with your finger-nail it gives out a sound such as never came from tapping a 'real' apple. You admire the neatness of the imitation. To sight the illusion is perfect. It is quite sensible to contrast this ingenious fake with a 'real' apple, for a 'real' apple just is an object that *really* is an apple, and not only *seems* to be one. This fake is an object that looks to your eyes to be an apple, but neither feels nor tastes as an apple does. As soon as you pick it up you know that it is not an apple; there is no need to taste it. We should be speaking in conformity with the rules of good English if we were to say that the dish contained real apples and imitation apples. But this mode of speaking does not lead us to suppose that there are two varieties of *apples,* namely real and imitation apples, as there are Bramley Seedlings and Blenheim pippins. Again, a shadow may be thrown on a wall, or an image may be thrown through a lantern on to a screen. We distinguish the shadow from the object of which it is the shadow, the image from that of which it is the image. Shadow and image are apprehensible only by sight; they really are visual, i.e. *seeable, entities*. I can see a man, and I can see his shadow; but there is not both a *real* man and a *shadow* man; there is just the shadow of the man.

This point may seem to have been unduly laboured. It is, however, of great importance. The words "real" and "really" are familiar words; they are variously used in every-day speech, and are not, as a rule, used ambiguously. The opposition between a *real* object and an *imitation* of a real object is clear. So, too, is the opposition between 'really seeing a man' and having an illusion.[1] We can speak sensibly of the distinction between 'the real size' and 'the apparent size' of the moon, but we know that both these expressions are extremely elliptical. The significance of the words "real" and "really" can be determined only by reference to the context in which they are used. Nothing but confusion can result if, in one and the same sentence, we mix up language used appropriately for the furniture of earth and our daily dealings with it with language used for the purpose of philosophical and scientific discussion.

---

[1] *Cf.* 'How easy is that bush supposed a bear!'

A peculiarly gross example of such a linguistic mixture is provided by one of Eddington's most picturesque passages:

> I am standing on a threshold about to enter a room. It is a complicated business. In the first place I must shove against an atmosphere pressing with a force of fourteen pounds on every square inch of my body. I must make sure of landing on a plank travelling at twenty miles a second round the sun—a fraction of a second too early or too late, the plank would be miles away. I must do this whilst hanging from a round planet head outward into space, and with a wind of aether blowing at no one knows how many miles a second through every interstice of my body. The plank has no solidity of substance. To step on it is like stepping on a swarm of flies. Shall I not slip through? No, if I make the venture one of the flies hits me and gives me a boost up again; I fall again and am knocked upwards by another fly; and so on. I may hope that the net result will be that I remain steady; but if unfortunately I should slip through the floor or be boosted too violently up to the ceiling the occurrence would be, not a violation of the laws of Nature, but a rare coincidence. (N.Ph.W. 342.)

Whatever we may think of Eddington's chances of slipping through the floor, we must regard his usage of language in this statement as gravely misleading to the common reader. I cannot doubt that it reveals serious confusion in Eddington's own thinking about 'the nature of the physical world'. Stepping on a plank is not in the least like 'stepping on a swarm of flies'. This language is drawn from, and is appropriate to, our daily intercourse with the familiar furniture of earth. We understand well what it is like to step on to a solid plank; we can also imagine what it would be like to step on to a swarm of flies. We know that two such experiences would be quite different. The plank is solid. If it be securely fixed, it will support our weight. What, then, are we to make of the comparison of stepping on to a plank with stepping on to a swarm of flies? What can be meant by saying that 'the plank has no solidity of substance'?

Again, we are familiar with the experience of shoving against an obstacle, and with the experience of struggling against a strong head-wind. We know that we do not have 'to shove against an atmosphere' as we cross the threshold of a room. We can imagine what it would be like to jump on to a moving plank. We may have seen in a circus an equestrian acrobat jump from the back of a swiftly moving horse on to the back of another horse moving with approximately the same speed. We know that no such acrobatic feat is required to cross the threshold of a room.[2]

I may seem too heavy-handed in my treatment of a picturesque passage, and thus to fall under the condemnation of the man who cannot see a joke

---

[2] Eddington's words suggest that he is standing on a stationary plank and has to land on to another plank that is moving, relatively to himself, with a speed of twenty miles a second. It would be charitable to regard this as a slip, were it not that its rectification would spoil this part of his picture. There is an equally gross absurdity in the statement that he is 'hanging head outward into space'.

and needs to be 'in contact with merry-minded companions'[3] in order that he may develop a sense of humour. But the picturesqueness is deceptive; the passage needs serious criticism since Eddington draws from it a conclusion that is important. 'Verily,' he says, 'it is easier for a camel to pass through the eye of a needle than for a scientific man to pass through a door. And whether the door be barn door or church door it might be wiser that he should consent to be an ordinary man and walk in rather than wait until all the difficulties involved in a really scientific ingress are resolved.' It is, then, suggested that an ordinary man has no difficulty in crossing the threshold of a room but that 'a really scientific ingress' presents difficulties.[4] The suggested contrast is as absurd as the use of the adjective 'scientific' prefixed to 'ingress', in this context, is perverse. Whatever difficulties a scientist, by reason of his scientific knowledge, may encounter in becoming a member of a spiritual church, these difficulties bear no comparison with the difficulties of the imagined acrobatic feat. Consequently, they are not solved by the consideration that Eddington, no less than the ordinary man, need not hesitate to cross the threshold of his room. . . .

If Eddington had drawn this picture for purely expository purposes, it might be unobjectionable. The scientist who sets out to give a popular exposition of a difficult and highly technical subject must use what means he can devise to convey to his readers what it is all about. At the same time, if he wishes to avoid being misunderstood, he must surely warn his readers that, in the present stage of physics, very little can be conveyed to a reader who lacks the mathematical equipment required to understand the methods by which results are obtained and the language in which these results can alone find adequate expression. Eddington's picture seems to me to be open to the objection that the image of a swarm of flies used to explain the electronic structure of matter is more appropriate to the old-fashioned classical conceptions that found expression in a model than to the conceptions he is trying to explain. Consequently, the reader may be misled unless he is warned that nothing resembling the spatial relations of flies in a swarm can be found in the collection of electrons. No concepts drawn from the level of common-sense thinking are appropriate to sub-atomic, i.e. microphysical, phenomena. Consequently, the language of common sense is not appropriate

---

[3] See *The Nature of the Physical World*. 336.

[4] In the article 'The Domain of Physical Science' (*Science, Religion and Reality*) a similar passage begins as follows:

'The learned physicist and the man in the street were standing together on the threshold about to enter a room.

The man in the street moved forward without trouble, planted his foot on a solid unyielding plank at rest before him, and entered.

The physicist was faced with an intricate problem.' (There follows much the same account of the difficulties as in the passage quoted.)

Eddington here goes on to suggest that the physicist may be 'content to follow *the same crude conception* of his task that presented itself to the mind of his unscientific colleague' (my italics).

to the descrption of such phenomena. Since, however, the man in the street tends to think in pictures and may desire to know something about the latest developments of physics, it is no doubt useful to provide him with some rough picture. The danger arises when the scientist uses the picture for the purpose of making explicit denials, and expresses these denials in common-sense language used in such a way as to be devoid of sense. This, unfortunately, is exactly what Eddington has done in the passage we are considering, and indeed, in many other passages as well.

It is worth while to examine with some care what exactly it is that Eddington is denying when he asserts that 'the plank has no solidity of substance'. What are we to understand by "solidity"? Unless we do understand it we cannot understand what the denial of solidity to the plank amounts to. But we can understand "solidity" only if we can truly say that the plank is solid. For "solid" just is the word we use to describe a certain respect in which a plank of wood resembles a block of marble, a piece of paper, and a cricket ball, and in which each of these differs from a sponge, from the interior of a soap-bubble, and from the holes in a net. We use the word "solid" sometimes as the opposite of "empty", sometimes as the opposite of "hollow", sometimes as the opposite of "porous". We may also, in a very slightly technical usage, contrast "solid" with "liquid" or with "gaseous". There is, no doubt, considerable variation in the precise significance of the word "solid" in various contexts. Further, as is the case with all words, "solid" may be misused, and may also be used figuratively. But there could not be a *misuse,* nor a *figurative* use, unless there were some correct and literal usages. The point is that the common usage of language enables us to attribute a meaning to the phrase "a solid plank"; but there is no common usage of language that provides a meaning for the word "solid" that would make sense to say that the plank on which I stand is not *solid.* We oppose the solidity of the walls of a house to the emptiness of its unfurnished rooms; we oppose the solidity of a piece of pumice-stone to the porous loofah sponge. We do not deny that the pumice-stone is to some degree porous, that the bricks of the wall have chinks and crevices. But we do not know how to use a word that has no sensible opposite. If the plank is non-solid, then what does "solid" *mean?* In the companion passage to the one quoted above, and to which reference was made in a preceding footnote, Eddington depicts the physicist, about to enter a room, as reflecting that 'the plank is not what it appears to be—a continuous support for his weight'. This remark is absurd. The plank appears to be capable of supporting his weight, and, as his subsequent entry into the room showed, it *was* capable of supporting his weight. If it be objected that the plank is 'a support for his weight' but not 'a *continuous* support', I would reply that the word "continuous" is here used without any assigned meaning. The plank appears *solid* in that sense of the word "solid" in which the plank is, in fact, solid. It is of the utmost importance to press the question: If the plank appears to be *solid,* but is really *non-solid,* what does "solid" mean? If "solid" has no assignable meaning, then "non-solid" is also without sense. If the plank is non-solid, then where can we find an example to show us what "solid" means? The pairs of words, "solid"—"empty", "solid"—"hollow", "solid"—"porous", belong to the vocabulary of common-sense language; in the case of each pair, if one of the two is without sense, so is the other.

This nonsensical denial of solidity is very common in popular expositions of the physicist's conception of material objects. The author of a recently published book says: 'A table, a piece of paper, no longer possess that solid reality which they appear to possess; they are both of them porous, and consist of very small electrically charged particles, which are arranged in a peculiar way.'[5] How are we to understand the statement that the table *no longer* possesses 'the solid reality' which it appears to possess? The context of the statement must be taken into account. The sentence quoted occurs in a summary of the view of the physical world according to classical physics. It immediately follows the statement: 'This picture formed by the physicists has one great drawback as compared with the picture formed by the non-scientific man in the street. It is much more abstract.' . . . Here we are concerned . . . with the suggestion that the non-scientific man forms one 'picture' of the material world and the scientist another. There are, then, two pictures. Of what, we must ask, are they pictures? Where are we to find application for the words "solid reality", which we may not use with reference to the table? Again we must ask: If the table is non-solid, what does "solid" mean?

No doubt the author had in mind the nineteenth-century view of the ultra-microscopic world as consisting of solid, absolutely hard, indivisible billiard-ball-like atoms, which were assumed to be solid and hard in a perfectly straightforward sense of the words "solid" and "hard". If so, it would be more appropriate to say that the modern physicist no longer believes that the table *consists* of solid atomic balls, than to say that 'the table no longer possesses solid reality'. There is, indeed, a danger in talking about *the table* at all, for the physicist is not, in fact, concerned with tables. The recent habit of talking as though he were is responsible for much confusion of thought. It leads Eddington into the preposterous nonsense of the 'two tables'. This view will be familiar to every one who is interested in the philosophy of the physicists. Nevertheless, it is desirable to quote a considerable part of Eddington's statement, since it is important to examine his view in some detail.

---

[5] Ernst Zimmer: *The Revolution of Physics,* trans. by H. Stafford Hatfield, 1936, p. 51. I have not been able to consult the German original, so I am unable to determine whether 'solid reality' is a good rendering of Zimmer's meaning. Certainly the juxtaposition of the two words is unfortunate, but is evidently judged to be appropriate at least by his translator.

I have settled down to the task of writing these lectures and have drawn up my chairs to my two tables. Two tables! Yes; there are duplicates of every object about me—two tables, two chairs, two pens. . . . One of them has been familiar to me from earliest years. It is a commonplace object of that environment which I call the world. How shall I describe it? It has extension; it is comparatively permanent; it is coloured; above all, it is *substantial*. . . . Table No. 2 is my scientific table. It is a more recent acquaintance and I do not feel so familiar with it. . . . My scientific table is mostly emptiness. Sparsely scattered in that emptiness are numerous electric charges rushing about with great speed; but their combined bulk amounts to less than a billionth of the bulk of the table itself. Notwithstanding its strange construction it turns out to be an entirely efficient table. It supports my writing paper as satisfactorily as table No. 1; for when I lay the paper on it the little electric particles with their headlong speed keep on hitting the underside, so that the paper is maintained in shuttlecock fashion at a nearly steady level. If I lean upon this table I shall not go through; or, to be strictly accurate, the chance of my scientific elbow going through my scientific table is so excessively small that it can be neglected in practical life . . . There is nothing *substantial* about my second table. It is nearly all empty space—space pervaded it is true by fields of force, but these are assigned to the categories of 'influences', not of 'things'.[6]

There is so much to criticize in this passage that it is difficult to know where to begin. Probably Eddington's defence against any criticism would be that this is one of the passages in which he 'was leading the reader on'[7] (presumably—to put it vulgarly—'up the garden path'), and that consequently it must not be taken as giving 'explicit statements' of his philosophical ideas. But he has nowhere expounded his philosophical ideas in non-popular language. Moreover, the mistakes are so frequently repeated in his writings and seem to be so inextricably bound up with his philosophical conclusions, that it is inevitable that these mistakes should be submitted to detailed criticism.

Perhaps the first comment that should be made is that Eddington takes quite seriously the view that there are *two tables;* one belongs to 'the external world of physics,' the other to 'a world of familiar acquaintance in human consciousness.' Eddington's philosophy may be regarded as the outcome of a sustained attempt to answer the question: How are the two tables related to one another? It never seems to occur to him that the form of the question is absurd. In answering the question he is hampered from the start by his initial assumption that the tables are *duplicates* of each other, i.e. that it really isn't nonsensical to speak of two *tables*. I hazard the conjecture that Eddington is an inveterate visualizer,[8] and that once he has committed him-

---

[6] *N.Ph.W.* xi, xii, xiii. I assume the reader's familiarity with the rest of the chapter in which this passage occurs.

[7] *New Pathways in Science.* 291.

[8] The following passage is significant: 'When I think of an electron there rises to my mind a hard, red, tiny ball; the proton similarly is neutral grey. Of course the

self to the language of 'two tables' he cannot avoid thinking of one as the shadow and of the other as the substance. (In this sentence, I have used the word "substance" simply as the correlative of "shadow." This usage has undoubtedly influenced Eddington's thinking on this topic.) It is evident that the scientific table is to be regarded as the shadow. There are statements that conflict with this interpretation, but Eddington does not leave us in doubt that, whenever he is using the language of *shadowing,* it is the scientific table that is a shadow of the familiar table. It is true that he says, 'I need not tell you that modern physics has by delicate test and remorseless logic assured me that my second scientific table is the only one which is really there—wherever "there" may be'. Elsewhere he says, 'Our conception of the familiar table was an illusion' (*N.Ph.W.* 323). These discrepancies result from the deep-seated confusions out of which his philosophy springs. . . . At present we are concerned with the view—in conflict with the statements just quoted—that the scientific table is a shadow. 'In the world of physics', he says, 'we watch a shadowgraph performance of the drama of familiar life. The shadow of my elbow rests on the shadow table as the shadow ink flows over the shadow paper. It is all symbolic, and as a symbol the physicist leaves it' (xvi). Elsewhere he suggests that physicists would generally say that 'the matter of this familiar table is *really* a curvature of space', but that is a view difficult to reconcile with either of the statements we are considering now.

Certainly there is much in the passage about the two tables that seems to conflict with the view of the scientific table as a shadow. It is said to be 'mostly emptiness', but scattered in the emptiness are numerous electric charges whose 'combined bulk' is compared in amount with 'the bulk of the table itself'. Is 'the table itself' the familiar table? I think it must be. But the comparison of the *two* bulks is surely nonsensical. Moreover, a shadow can hardly be said to have *bulk.* Yet Eddington insists that the two tables are 'parallel'—an odd synonym, no doubt, for a 'shadow'. He contrasts the scientific *table,* which has a familiar *table* parallel to it, with the scientific electron, quantum, or potential, which have no familiars that are parallel. Of the latter he says that the physicist is scrupulously careful to guard them 'from contamination by conceptions borrowed from the other [i.e., the familiar] world.' But if electrons, belonging to world No. 2, are to be scrupulously guarded from contamination by world No. 1, how can it make sense to say that they 'keep on hitting the underside' of a sheet of paper that, indubitably,

colour is absurd—perhaps not more absurd than the rest of the conception—but I am incorrigible' (*N.Ph.W.* xviii).

Cf. also, 'I am liable to visualize a Test-Match in Australia as being played upside down' (*N.P.Sc.* 314). Perhaps this habit is responsible for the queer statement (quoted above, p. 260) that the feat of entering his study has to be accomplished whilst he is hanging from a round planet head outward into space.' Only, in that case, he has forgotten that his study would be hanging outward the same way. What is more important is that he has created a difficulty out of a mode of speech.

is part of the familiar furniture of earth? It is Eddington who reintroduces contamination when he talks in this fashion, and he does so because he supposes that there is a scientific table parallel to the familiar table. I venture to suggest that it is as absurd to say that there is a scientific table as to say that there is a familiar electron or a familiar quantum, or a familiar potential. Eddington insists upon the lack of familiar parallels in the latter cases; surely he is justified in doing so. What is puzzling is his view that there are parallel *tables*. It suggests a return to the days when physicists demanded a model; 'the physicist,' says Eddington, 'used to borrow the raw material of his world from the familiar world, but he does so no longer' (xv). But if the 'scientific table' is to be regarded as the product of the 'raw material of the scientific world,' how can it be regarded as parallel to the familiar table? Eddington seems unable to free himself from the conviction that the physicist is concerned with things of the same nature as the things of the familiar world; hence, *tables* are to be found in both world No. 1 and world No. 2. There is a statement in his exposition of 'The Downfall of Classical Physics' that shows how deep-rooted this conviction is. 'The atom,' he says, 'is as porous as the solar system. If we eliminated all the unfilled space in a man's body and collected his protons and electrons into one mass, the man would be reduced to a speck just visible with a magnifying glass' (*N.Ph.W.* 1–2). The comparison is useful enough; the absurdity comes from speaking of the speck as a *man*. If this statement stood alone, it might well be regarded as an expository device. But the constant cropping up of the parallel tables shows that Eddington does not regard it as absurd to think of the reduction as still leaving a *man*. When, later in the book, he is expounding the conception of space required by relativity theory, he points out that our difficulty in conceiving it is due to the fact that we are 'using a conception of space which must have originated many millions of years ago and has become rather firmly embedded in human thought' (81). He adds: 'But the space of physics ought not to be dominated by this creation of the dawning mind of an enterprising ape.' It seems to me that in allowing himself to speak of the speck as a man, Eddington is allowing himself to be thus dominated. It is true that, in the statement just quoted, Eddington was speaking of relativity physics, but I do not think that 'the creation of the dawning mind of an enterprising ape' is any more appropriate to the conception of space in atomic physics. . . . It must suffice at the moment to insist that a *man* is an object belonging to the familiar world, and has no duplicate in 'the scientific world'.

Perhaps we may be convinced of the absurdity of the notion that there are 'duplicates of every object' in the familiar world, if we return to the consideration of the description of a familiar scene with which this chapter opened. I spoke there of 'blue curtains', of a crimson and scented rose, of a bruised leg. Neglecting at present the consideration of the bruised leg, which

—judging by Eddington's account of the adventures of an elephant [9]—is beneath the notice of a scientist, we may ask what duplicate of *blue* is to be found in the scientific world. The answer is that there is no duplicate. True that it has a 'counterpart', but that is a very different matter. The counterpart of colour is 'its scientific equivalent electromagnetic wave-length' (88). 'The wave,' says Eddington, 'is the reality—or the nearest we can get to a description of reality; the colour is mere mind-spinning. The beautiful hues which flood our consciousness under stimulation of the waves have no relevance to the objective reality.' It is obvious that here Eddington is regarding the scientific world as 'the objective reality'; the familiar world is subjective. This does not square with the view that the scientific world is the shadow of the familiar world, but it is hopeless to attempt to extract from Eddington any consistent view of their relation. With this difficulty, however, we are not at the moment concerned. The point is that Eddington firmly extrudes *colour* from the scientific world, and rightly so. But the *rose* is coloured, the *table* is coloured, the *curtains* are coloured. How, then, can that which is not coloured duplicate the rose, the curtains, the table? To say that an electromagnetic wave-length is coloured would be as nonsensical as to say that symmetry is coloured. Eddington does not say so. But he has failed to realize that a coloured object could be *duplicated* only by something with regard to which it would not be meaningless to say that it was coloured.

It seems to me that in his theory of the duplicate worlds Eddington has fallen into the error of which Berkeley accused the Newtonians. Berkeley was strongly convinced that the sensible world [10] was pre-eminently a *seeable* world. No doubt he over-stressed the sense of sight at the expense of the other senses, but in the climate of opinion in which he was living this over-emphasis served a useful purpose. Consider the following passage:

> How vivid and radiant is the lustre of the fixed stars! how magnificent and rich that negligent profusion, with which they appear to be scattered throughout the whole azure vault! Yet if you take the telescope, it brings into your sight a new host of stars that escape the naked eye. . . . Is not the whole system immense, beautiful, glorious beyond expression and beyond thought? What treatment then do those philosophers deserve, who would deprive these noble and delightful scenes of all reality? How should those principles be entertained, that lead us to think all the visible beauty of the creation a false imaginary glare? [11]

It seemed to Berkeley that the metaphysics of Descartes and Newton resulted in the description of a 'real world' that had all the properties of the sensible

---

[9] *N.Ph.W.* 251–52.
[10] I use the phrase "sensible world" here with the same denotative reference as Eddington's phrase "familiar world".
[11] *Three Dialogues between Hylas and Philonous* (Second Dialogue).

world except the vital property of being seeable. 'Ask a Cartesian,' he said,[12] 'whether he is wont to imagine his globules without colour. Pellucidness is a colour. The colour of ordinary light of the sun is white. Newton in the right in assigning colour to the rays of light.[13] A man born blind would not imagine Space as we do. We give it always some dilute, or duskish, or dark colour—in short, we imagine it as visible, or intromitted by the eye, which he would not do.' *Black* also is, in the sense required, a *colour;* a 'dark world' is no less a world apprehensible only by sight than a 'bright world' is. But the pure mathematician cannot take note of colour. Hence, under the influence of the *Mathematical Principles of Natural Philosophy* and of the rapidly developing science of optics, Berkeley's contemporaries looked to the principles of optics to account for the *seeability* of things. It is Berkeley's merit to have realized that the Cartesian–Newtonian philosophers, seeking to account for a *seeable* world, succeeded only in substituting a world that could in no sense be *seen.* He realized that they had substituted a theory of optics for a theory of visual perception. The outcome of this mistake is a duplication of worlds—the Image-World, sensibly perceived by men, the Real-World apprehended only by God. Newton is quite explicit on this point:

> Was the Eye contrived without Skill in Opticks, and the Ear without Knowledge of Sounds? . . . Is not the sensory of Animals that place to which the sensitive Substance is present, and into which the sensible Species of Things are carried through the Nerves and Brain, that there they may be perceived by their immediate presence to that Substance? And these things being rightly dispatch'd, does it not appear from Phaenomena that there is a Being incorporeal, living, intelligent, omnipresent, who in infinite Space, as it were in his Sensory, sees the things themselves intimately, and thoroughly perceives them, and comprehends them wholly by their immediate presence to himself: Of which things the Images only carried through the Organs of Sense into our little Sensoriums, are there seen and beheld by that which in us perceives and thinks.[14]

Berkeley saw the absurdity of this duplication; he failed to realize that it was rendered necessary only by the confusion of the theory of optics with the theory of vision. He saw that the question—How is perception possible? —is devoid of sense; he saw that it is no less absurd to look to physics for an answer to the question. Unfortunately he accepted the account of objects of sight that was provided by the Optical Theory, and thus abolished the duplication of worlds only by locating (however indirectly) 'the things by me perceived' in the Mind of the Infinite Spirit. Newton had transferred colours from *things seen* into 'our little Sensoriums'; he conceived them as optical Images; accordingly, there were still required the things in them-

---

[12] *Commonplace Book,* ed. by G. A. Johnston, p. 50.
[13] But see below, p. 269.
[14] *Opticks,* Query 28. (Edition reprinted 1931, p. 370.)

selves *of which* they were Images. These things must be found in the Sensory of God. Berkeley abolished the Images but only by carrying to a conclusion the absurdities initiated by the use of the language of Optics.

The achievement of Newton in the theory of Optics was that by his discovery of differently refrangible rays he discovered *measurable correlates of colour;* he thereby made the use of quantitative methods possible in a domain which would otherwise be excluded from the scope of physics. His extremely confused metaphysics is the result of his refusal to admit that there is anything in the perceived world except the measurable correlates, which ought, accordingly, to be regarded as the correlates of nothing. Newton saved himself from this manifest contradiction by having resort to a transmissive theory of Nature, and thus to a causal theory of perception. Allowing for the difference of phraseology we may surely see in the following quotation from Newton an anticipation of Eddington's theory of the sensible world.

> The homogeneal Light and Rays which appear red, or rather make Objects appear so, I call Rubrifick or Red-making; those which make Objects appear yellow, green, blue, and violet, I call Yellow-making, Green-making, Blue-making, Violet-making, and so of the rest. And if at any time I speak of Light and Rays as coloured or endued with Colours, I would be understood to speak not philosophically and properly, but grossly, and accordingly to such Conceptions as vulgar People in seeing all these experiments would be apt to frame. For the Rays to speak properly are not coloured. In them there is nothing else than a certain Power and Disposition to stir up a Sensation of this or that Colour. For as Sound in a Bell or musical String, or other sounding Body, is nothing but a trembling Motion, and in the Air nothing but that motion propagated from the Object, and in the Sensorium 'tis a Sense of that Motion under the Form of Sound; so Colours in the Object are nothing but a Disposition to reflect this or that sort of Rays more copiously than the Rest; in the Rays they are nothing but their Dispositions to propagate this or that Motion into the Sensorium, and in the Sensorium they are Sensations of those Motions under the Forms of Colours.[15]

This wholly fallacious argument has been strangely persuasive to physicists. Sensible qualities have no place in the world; they are *nothing but* 'dispositions to propagate this or that motion into the Sensorium'. There they undergo a transformation, not in the mathematical sense of that word, but a strange transformation indeed—a metamorphosis of 'the external world of physics' into 'a world of familiar acquaintance in human consciousness'.[16] The transformation remains inexplicable. Small wonder that Mr. Joad, reflecting upon the philosophical consequences of 'modern physics', exclaimed in perplexity, 'But, if I never know directly events in the external world, but only their alleged effects on my brain, and if I never know my

[15] *Opticks,* Bk. I, Pt. II (1931 ed., pp. 124–5).
[16] See *N.Ph.W.* xiv.

brain except in terms of its alleged effects on my brain, I can only reiterate in bewilderment my original questions: "What sort of thing is it that I know?" and "Where is it?" ' [17] Such perplexity can be resolved only by reconsidering the assumptions that led to the asking of these unanswerable questions. We shall find that the problem of perception, in this form, arose only because we have allowed the physicists to speak of a 'real world' that does not contain any of the qualities relevant to perception. To adopt the striking phrase of Professor E. A. Burtt, we have allowed the physicists 'to make a metaphysic out of a method'. In so doing they have forgotten, and philosophers do not seem to remember, that their method has been designed to facilitate investigations originating from a study of 'the furniture of the earth'.

QUESTIONS

1. What distinctions are marked by the contrast between (a) real and imitation, (b) real and false, and (c) real and illusory?
2. Catalogue the linguistic mix-ups in the passage from Eddington near the beginning of this selection. What is the objection to representing the electronic structure of matter as a swarm of flies?
3. What critical point is made by asking, "If the plank appears to be *solid,* but is really *nonsolid,* what does 'solid' mean?"
4. How does Professor Stebbing criticize the view that there are two tables, one belonging "to the world of familiar acquaintance in human consciousness" and another belonging "to the external world of physics"? Are her criticisms the result of empirical observation or conceptual analysis?
5. What is the "theory of duplicate worlds" and how may it be criticized?
6. If we think of curtains and electromagnetism as part of the same world, why is it (or is it not) nonsense to ask, "If curtains are colored, why isn't electromagnetism colored?"

SUGGESTED FURTHER READING

INTRODUCTORY STUDIES

Bridgman, Percy W., *The Logic of Modern Physics,* Macmillan, New York, 1927.
Conant, James Bryant, ed., *Harvard Case Studies in Experimental Science,* Harvard University Press, Cambridge, Mass., 1957, 2 vols.
Einstein, Albert, and Leopold Infeld, *The Evolution of Physics,* Cambridge University Press, London, 1947.
Hempel, Carl, *Philosophy of Natural Science,* Prentice-Hall, Englewood Cliffs, N. J., to be published.
Holton, Gerald, *Introduction to Concepts and Theories in Physical Science,* Addison-Wesley, Reading, Mass., 1953. Especially Chaps. 8, "The Nature of Scientific Theory"; 12, "Concepts"; 13, "The Growth of Science"; 14, "Laws."
Ryle, Gilbert, *Dilemmas,* Cambridge University Press, London, 1954. Chap. V,

---

[17] *Aristotelian Society:* Supp. Vol. IX, p. 137.

"The World of Science and the Everyday World"; Chap. VI, "Technical and Untechnical Concepts."

Toulmin, Stephen, *The Philosophy of Science,* Hutchinson's University Library, London, 1953.

ADVANCED STUDIES

Burtt, Edwin A., *The Metaphysical Foundations of Modern Physical Science,* rev. ed., Doubleday, New York, 1955.

Feigl, Herbert, and Wilfrid Sellars, eds., *Readings in Philosophical Analysis,* Appleton-Century-Crofts, New York, 1949.

Feigl, Herbert, and May Brodbeck, eds., *Readings in the Philosophy of Science,* Appleton-Century-Crofts, New York, 1953.

————, *et al., Minnesota Studies in the Philosophy of Science,* University of Minnesota Press, Minneapolis, Vol. I, 1956; Vol. II, 1958; Vol. III, 1962.

Hanson, Norwood Russell, *Patterns of Discovery,* Cambridge University Press, London, 1958.

Kneale, William, *Probability and Induction,* Oxford University Press, New York, 1949.

Kuhn, Thomas S., *The Structure of Scientific Revolutions,* University of Chicago Press, Chicago, 1963.

Mach, Ernst, *The Science of Mechanics: A Critical and Historical Account of Its Development,* 5th ed., Open Court, La Salle, Ill., 1942.

Nagel, Ernest, ed., *John Stuart Mill's Philosophy of Scientific Method,* Hafner, New York, 1950.

————, *The Structure of Science,* Harcourt, Brace & World, New York, 1961.

Schlick, Moritz, *Philosophy of Nature,* Philosophical Library, New York, 1949.

Toulmin, Stephen, "Contemporary Scientific Mythology," *Metaphysical Beliefs, Three Essays,* by S. Toulmin, R. W. Hepburn, A. MacIntyre, Student Christian Movement Press, London, 1957.

Chapter 5. Mind, Body, Self, and Immortality

One of the questions which Descartes asked in his *Meditations* was "What am I?" He concluded that he was a mind, but a mind that is both related to his body and still separable from it. While he spoke only of himself, he expected that his findings would serve as an account of all persons. Our acquaintance with the *Meditations,* then, has already given us reason to ask how we are to understand the terms "mind" and "body," and what account we are to give of the relationship of mind and body. In this chapter we shall take up these questions anew, as we consider some of the answers which philosophers have given to the question, "What is a person?"

Earlier readings have dealt with persons as knowers; and the consideration of what can be known led us in the chapters on metaphysics and scientific knowledge to consider the status of things in general. Now we are considering that special kind of thing, a person, and we are asking how persons fit into the scheme of things. As we shall see, much turns on the way the scheme of things is conceived. The authors of the first two readings in this chapter both turn to nature for clues to understanding the relation of mind and body. Yet Bishop Butler finds that we may suppose the mind, or soul, to be separable from the body, and therefore immortal, while Baron d'Holbach finds the mind to be dependent on the body, and concludes that human mortality is indubitable. The difference between these men appears to turn on Butler's arguing for a distinction between nature and a realm above nature, while Holbach understands nature to encompass all that there is. Thus, Butler is a dualist, someone who argues that the world consists of two fundamentally different sorts of things, neither of which can be

reduced to the other. By contrast, Holbach is a monist, someone who argues that everything is ultimately reducible to one sort of thing. For Holbach the fundamental sort of thing is matter; so his is a materialistic monism. This difference in metaphysical viewpoint between Butler and Holbach would seem to make it impossible to reconcile their opposing views; and the reader must consider what light this irreconcilability throws on the differences between their views of persons.

As well as trying to construe persons as some kind of relationship of mind and body, philosophers have also tried to answer the question, "What is a person?" by considering the nature of the self. The last two readings in this chapter are on this topic. Hume admits that his account of the self is abortive; but it is nonetheless interesting. For he is determined to resist accounts of the self as an unchanging substance underlying all our perceptions and indispensable to their occurrence. He insists, however, that the mind is a bundle of perceptions, in which nothing but the individual and separable perceptions are discoverable. Given this starting point, he can find nothing in the bundle whose persistence justifies the continuity which we usually attribute to minds.

An antidote for Humean despair at our ever accounting for the self is to be found in the reading by Professor Gilbert Ryle. He agrees with the Humean rejection of the substantive theory of the self, and argues that a true understanding of the self is to be achieved by attending to what we say when we talk of ourselves. As well as offering substantive conclusions, the readings in this chapter are methodological examples of the care which must be taken in order to talk sense about such topics as person, body, mind, soul, the self, and life and death.

We have already noticed the relation of this chapter to earlier ones. Chapter 9, "Freedom of the Will," and Chapter 10, "Moral Knowledge," are also relevant to a philosophical understanding of the notion of person.

14. JOSEPH BUTLER

(1692–1752)

Of a Future Life

Joseph Butler was born at Wantage, England, educated at Oxford, and ordained in the Church of England. He rose to be Bishop of Bristol and later became Bishop of Durham. He is the author of *Fifteen Sermons* (1726), which is really a series of essays on moral philosophy; and *The Analogy of Religion, Natural and Revealed, to the Course and Constitution of Nature* (1736), an essay in natural theology.

Butler does not argue for our immortality so much as he argues against our mortality. Thus, his essay is not an account of a future life, but an estimate of the probability of our continuing life. He begins by examining the claim, and rejecting the evidence usually given in support of it, that death may have some effect on what he calls the "living being." He then considers the distinctness of the self or "living being" from the body, and the way in which the self might survive the death of the body. The large question to be asked about Butler's conclusions is, "Are these conclusions empirical or are they the result of the previously agreed-upon definitions of his terms?"

The selection here is the first chapter of *The Analogy*.

. . . let us consider what the analogy of nature, and the several changes which we know we may undergo without being destroyed, suggest, as to the effect which death may, or may not, have upon us; and whether it be not from thence probable, that we may survive this change, and exist in a future state of life and perception.

From our being born into the present world in the helpless imperfect state of infancy, and having arrived from thence to mature age, we find it to be a general law of nature in our own species, that the same creatures, the same individuals, should exist in degrees of life and perception, with capacities of action, of enjoyment and suffering, in one period of their being, greatly different from those appointed them in another period of it. And in other creatures the same law holds. For the difference of their capacities and states of life at their birth (to go no higher) and in maturity; the change of worms into flies, and the vast enlargement of their locomotive powers by such change: and birds and insects bursting the shell of their habitation, and by this means entering into a new world, furnished with new accommodations for them, and finding a new sphere of action assigned them; these are instances of this general law of nature. Thus all the various and wonderful transformations of animals are to be taken into consideration here.

But the states of life in which we ourselves existed formerly in the womb and in our infancy, are almost as different from our present in mature age, as it is possible to conceive any two states or degrees of life can be. Therefore, that we are to exist hereafter in a state as different (suppose) from our present, as this is from our former, is but according to the analogy of nature; according to a natural order or appointment of the very same kind, with what we have already experienced.

We know we are endued with capacities of action, of happiness and misery: for we are conscious of acting, of enjoying pleasure and suffering pain. Now that we have these powers and capacities before death, is a presumption that we shall retain them through and after death; indeed a probability of it abundantly sufficient to act upon, unless there be some positive reason to think that death is the destruction of those living powers: because there is in every case a probability, that all things will continue as we experience they are, in all respects, except those in which we have some reason to think they will be altered. This is that *kind* [1] of presumption or probability from analogy, expressed in the very word *continuance,* which seems our only natural reason for believing the course of the world will continue to-morrow, as it has done so far as our experience or knowledge of history can carry us back. Nay, it seems our only reason for believing, that any one substance now existing will continue to exist a moment longer; the self-existent substance only excepted. Thus if men were assured that the unknown event, death, was not the destruction of our faculties of perception and of action, there would be no apprehension, that any other power or event unconnected with this of death, would destroy these faculties just at the instant of each creature's death; and therefore no doubt but that they would remain after it: which shows the high probability that our living powers will continue after death, unless there be some ground to think that death is their destruction. [2]

[1] I say *kind* of presumption or probability; for I do not mean to affirm that there is the same *degree* of conviction, that our living powers will continue after death, as there is, that our substances will.

[2] *Destruction of living powers* is a manner of expression unavoidably ambiguous; and may signify either *the destruction of a living being, so as that the same living being shall be uncapable of ever perceiving or acting again at all:* or *the destruction of those*

For, if it would be in a manner certain that we should survive death, provided it were certain that death would not be our destruction, it must be highly probable we shall survive it, if there be no ground to think death will be our destruction.

Now though I think it must be acknowledged, that prior to the natural and moral proofs of a future life commonly insisted upon, there would arise a general confused suspicion, that in the great shock and alteration which we shall undergo by death, we, i.e. our living powers, might be wholly destroyed; yet even prior to those proofs, there is really no particular distinct ground or reason for this apprehension at all, so far as I can find. If there be, it must arise either from *the reason of the thing,* or from *the analogy of nature.*

But we cannot argue from *the reason of the thing,* that death is the destruction of living agents, because we know not at all what death is in itself; but only some of its effects, such as the dissolution of flesh, skin, and bones. And these effects do in no wise appear to imply the destruction of a living agent. And besides, as we are greatly in the dark, upon what the exercise of our living powers depends, so we are wholly ignorant what the powers themselves depend upon; the powers themselves as distinguished, not only from their actual exercise, but also from the present capacity of exercising them; and as opposed to their destruction: for sleep, or however a swoon, shows us, not only that these powers exist when they are not exercised, as the passive power of motion does in inanimate matter; but shows also that they exist, when there is no present capacity of exercising them: or that the capacities of exercising them for the present, as well as the actual exercise of them, may be suspended, and yet the powers themselves remain undestroyed. Since then we know not at all upon what the existence of our living powers depends, this shows further, there can no probability be collected from the reason of the thing, that death will be their destruction: because their existence may depend upon somewhat in no degree affected by death; upon somewhat quite out of the reach of this king of terrors. So that there is nothing more certain, than that *the reason of the thing* shows us no connection between death, and the destruction of living agents.

Nor can we find any thing throughout the whole *analogy of nature,* to afford us even the slightest presumption, that animals ever lose their living powers; much less, if it were possible, that they lose them by death: for we

means and instruments by which it is capable of its present life, of its present state of perception and of action. It is here used in the former sense. When it is used in the latter, the epithet *present* is added. The loss of a man's eye is a destruction of living powers in the latter sense. But we have no reason to think the destruction of living powers, in the former sense, to be possible. We have no more reason to think a being endued with living powers, ever loses them during its whole existence, than to believe that a stone ever acquires them.

have no faculties wherewith to trace any beyond or through it, so as to see what becomes of them. This event removes them from our view. It destroys the *sensible* proof, which we had before their death, of their being possessed of living powers, but does not appear to afford the least reason to believe that they are, then, or by that event, deprived of them.

And our knowing, that they were possessed of these powers, up to the very period to which we have faculties capable of tracing them, is itself a probability of their retaining them, beyond it. And this is confirmed, and a sensible credibility is given to it, by observing the very great and astonishing changes which we have experienced; so great, that our existence in another state of life, of perception and of action, will be but according to a method of providential conduct, the like to which has been already exercised even with regard to ourselves; according to a course of nature, the like to which we have already gone through.

However, as one cannot but be greatly sensible, how difficult it is to silence imagination enough to make the voice of reason even distinctly heard in this case; as we are accustomed, from our youth up, to indulge that forward delusive faculty, ever obtruding beyond its sphere; of some assistance indeed to apprehension, but the author of all error: as we plainly lose ourselves in gross and crude conceptions of things, taking for granted that we are acquainted with, what indeed we are wholly ignorant of: it may be proper to consider the imaginary presumptions, that death will be our destruction, arising from these kinds of early and lasting prejudices; and to show how little they can really amount to, even though we cannot wholly divest ourselves of them. And,

All presumption of death's being the destruction of living beings, must go upon supposition that they are compounded; and so, discerptible. But since consciousness is a single and indivisible power, it should seem that the subject in which it resides must be so too. For were the motion of any particle of matter absolutely one and indivisible, so as that it should imply a contradiction to suppose part of this motion to exist, and part not to exist, i.e. part of this matter to move, and part to be at rest; then its power of motion would be indivisible; and so also would the subject in which the power inheres, namely, the particle of matter: for if this could be divided into two, one part might be moved and the other at rest, which is contrary to the supposition. In like manner it has been argued,[3] and, for any thing appearing to the contrary, justly, that since the perception or consciousness, which we have of our own existence, is indivisible, so as that it is a contradiction to suppose one part of it should be here and the other there; the

---

[3] See Dr. Clarke's Letter to Mr. Dodwell, and the defences of it.

perceptive power, or the power of consciousness, is indivisible too: and conse-quently the subject in which it resides; i.e. the conscious being.

Now upon supposition that living agent each man calls himself, is thus a single being, which there is at least no more difficulty in conceiving than in conceiving it to be a compound, and of which there is the proof now men-tioned; it follows, that our organized bodies are no more ourselves or part of ourselves, than any other matter around us. And it is as easy to conceive, how matter, which is no part of ourselves, may be appropriated to us in the manner which our present bodies are; as how we can receive impressions from, and have power over any matter. It is as easy to conceive, that we may exist out of bodies, as in them; that we might have animated bodies of any other organs and senses wholly different from these now given us, and that we may hereafter animate these same or new bodies variously modified and organized; as to conceive how we can animate such bodies as our present. And lastly, the dissolution of all these several organized bodies, supposing ourselves to have successively animated them, would have no more con-ceivable tendency to destroy the living beings ourselves, or deprive us of living faculties, the faculties of perception and of action, than the dissolution of any foreign matter, which we are capable of receiving impressions from, and making use of for the common occasions of life.

The simplicity and absolute oneness of a living agent cannot indeed, from the nature of the thing, be properly proved by experimental obser-vations. But as these *fall in* with the supposition of its unity, so they plainly lead us to *conclude* certainly, that our gross organized bodies, with which we perceive the objects of sense, and with which we act, are no part of ourselves; and therefore show us, that we have no reason to believe their destruction to be ours: even without determining whether our living sub-stances be material or immaterial. For we see by experience, that men may lose their limbs, their organs of sense, and even the greatest part of these bodies, and yet remain the same living agents. And persons can trace up the existence of themselves to a time, when the bulk of their bodies was ex-tremely small, in comparison of what it is in mature age: and we cannot but think, that they might then have lost a considerable part of that small body, and yet have remained the same living agents; as they may now lose great part of their present body, and remain so.

And it is certain, that the bodies of all animals are in a constant flux, from that never-ceasing attrition, which there is in every part of them. Now things of this kind unavoidably teach us to distinguish, between these living agents ourselves, and large quantities of matter, in which we are very nearly interested: since these may be alienated, and actually are in a daily course of succession, and changing their owners; whilst we are assured, that each living agent remains one and the same permanent being. And this general observation leads us on to the following ones.

First, That we have no way of determining by experience, what is the certain bulk of the living being each man calls himself: and yet, till it be determined that it is larger in bulk than the solid elementary particles of matter, which there is no ground to think any natural power can dissolve, there is no sort of reason to think death to be the dissolution of it, of the living being, even though it should not be absolutely indiscerptible.

Secondly, From our being so nearly related to and interested in certain systems of matter, suppose our flesh and bones, and afterwards ceasing to be at all related to them, the living agents ourselves remaining all this while undestroyed notwithstanding such alienation; and consequently these systems of matter not being ourselves: it follows further, that we have no ground to conclude any other, suppose *internal systems* of matter, to be the living agents ourselves; because we can have no ground to conclude this, but from our relation to and interest in such other systems of matter: and therefore we can have no reason to conclude, what befalls those systems of matter at death, to be the destruction of the living agents. We have already several times over lost a great part or perhaps the whole of our body, according to certain common established laws of nature; yet we remain the same living agents: when we shall lose as great a part, or the whole, by another common established law of nature, death; why may we not also remain the same? That the alienation has been gradual in one case, and in the other will be more at once, does not prove any thing to the contrary. We have passed undestroyed through those many and great revolutions of matter, so peculiarly appropriated to us ourselves; why should we imagine death will be so fatal to us?

Nor can it be objected, that what is thus alienated or lost, is no part of our original solid body, but only adventitious matter; because we may lose entire limbs, which must have contained many solid parts and vessels of the original body: or if this be not admitted, we have no proof, that any of these solid parts are dissolved or alienated by death. Though, by the way, we are very nearly related to that extraneous or adventitious matter, whilst it continues united to and distending the several parts of our solid body. But after all; the relation a person bears to those parts of his body, to which he is the most nearly related; what does it appear to amount to but this, that the living agent, and those parts of the body, mutually affect each other? And the same thing, the same thing in kind though not in degree, may be said of *all foreign* matter, which gives us ideas, and which we have any power over. From these observations the whole ground of the imagination is removed, that the dissolution of any matter, is the destruction of a living agent, from the interest he once had in such matter.

Thirdly, If we consider our body somewhat more distinctly, as made up of organs and instruments of perception and of motion, it will bring us to the same conclusion. Thus the common optical experiments show, and even the observation how sight is assisted by glasses shows, that we see with our eyes in the same sense as we see with glasses. Nor is there any reason to believe, that we see with them in any other sense; any other, I mean, which would lead us to think the eye itself a percipient. The like is to be said of hearing: and our feeling distant solid matter by means of somewhat in our hand, seems an instance of the like kind, as to the subject we are considering. All these are instances of foreign matter, or such as is no part of our body, being instrumental in preparing objects for, and conveying them to, the perceiving power, in a manner similar or like to the manner in which our organs of sense prepare and convey them. Both are in a like way instruments of our receiving such ideas from external objects, as the Author of nature appointed those external objects to be the occasions of exciting in us. However, glasses are evidently instances of this; namely of matter which is no part of our body, preparing objects for and conveying them towards the perceiving power, in like manner as our bodily organs do. And if we see with our eyes only in the same manner as we do with glasses, the like may justly be concluded, from analogy, of all our other senses. It is not intended, by any thing here said, to affirm, that the whole apparatus of vision, or of perception by any other of our senses, can be traced through all its steps, quite up to the living power of seeing, or perceiving: but that so far as it can be traced by experimental observations, so far it appears, that our organs of sense prepare and convey on objects, in order to their being perceived, in like manner as foreign matter does, without affording any shadow of appearance, that they themselves perceive.

And that we have no reason to think our organs of sense percipients, is confirmed by instances of persons losing some of them, the living beings themselves, their former occupiers, remaining unimpaired. It is confirmed also by the experienec of dreams; by which we find we are at present possessed of a latent, and, what would otherwise be, an unimagined unknown power of perceiving sensible objects, in as strong and lively a manner without our external organs of sense as with them.

So also with regard to our power of moving, or directing motion by will and choice: upon the destruction of a limb, this active power remains, as it evidently seems, unlessened; so as that the living being, who has suffered this loss, would be capable of moving as before, if it had another limb to move with. It can walk by the help of an artificial leg; just as it can make use of a pole or a lever, to reach towards itself and to move things, beyond the length and the power of its natural arm: and this last it does in the same manner as it reaches and moves, with its natural arm, things nearer and of less weight. Nor is there so much as any appearance of our limbs being endued with a power of moving or directing themselves; though they are adapted, like the several parts of a machine, to be the instruments of motion to each other; and some parts of the same limb, to be instruments of motion to other parts of it.

Thus a man determines, that he will look at such an object through a microscope; or being lame suppose, that he will walk to such a place with a staff a week hence. His eyes and his feet no more determine in these cases, than the microscope and the staff. Nor is there any ground to think they any more put the determination in practice; or that his eyes are the seers or his feet the movers, in any other sense than as the microscope and the staff are. Upon the whole then, our organs of sense and our limbs are certainly instruments, which the living persons ourselves make use of to perceive and move with: there is not any probability, that they are any more; nor consequently, that we have any other kind of relation to them, than what we may have to any other foreign matter formed into instruments of perception and motion, suppose into a microscope or a staff; (I say any other kind of relation, for I am not speaking of the degree of it;) nor consequently is there any probability, that the alienation or dissolution of these instruments is the destruction of the perceiving and moving agent.

And thus our finding, that the dissolution of matter, in which living beings were most nearly interested, is not their dissolution; and that the destruction of several of the organs and instruments of perception and of motion belonging to them, is not their destruction; shows demonstratively, that there is no ground to think that the dissolution of any other matter, or destruction of any other organs and instruments, will be the dissolution or destruction of living agents, from the like kind of relation. And we have no reason to think we stand in any other kind of relation to any thing which we find dissolved by death.

But it is said these observations are equally applicable to brutes: and it is thought an insuperable difficulty, that they should be immortal, and by consequence capable of everlasting happiness. Now this manner of expression is both invidious and weak: but the thing intended by it, is really no difficulty at all, either in the way of natural or moral consideration. For first, Suppose the invidious thing, designed in such a manner of expression, were really implied, as it is not in the least, in the natural immortality of brutes; namely, that they must arrive at great attainments, and become rational and moral agents; even this would be no difficulty: since we know not what latent powers and capacities they may be endued with. There was once, prior to experience, as great presumption against human creatures, as there is against the brute creatures, arriving at that degree of understanding, which we have in mature age. For we can trace up our own existence to the same original with theirs. And we find it to be a general law of nature, that creatures endued with capacities of virtue and religion should be placed in a condition of being, in which they are altogether without the use of them, for a considerable length of their duration; as in infancy and childhood. And great part of the human species go out of the present world, before they come to the exercise of these capacities in any degree at all. But then, secondly, The natural immortality of brutes does not in the least imply, that they are endued with any latent capacities of a rational or moral nature. And the economy of the universe might require, that there should be living creatures without any capacities of this kind.

And all difficulties as to the manner how they are to be disposed of are so apparently and wholly founded in our ignorance, that it is wonderful they should be insisted upon by any, but such as are weak enough to think they are acquainted with the whole system of things. There is then absolutely nothing at all in this objection, which is so rhetorically urged, against the greatest part of the natural proofs or presumptions of the immortality of human minds: I say the greatest part; for it is less applicable to the following observation, which is more peculiar to mankind:

That as it is evident our *present* powers and capacities of reason, memory, and affection, do not depend upon our gross body in the manner in which perception by our organs of sense does; so they do not appear to depend upon it at all in any such manner, as to give ground to think, that the dissolution of this body will be the destruction of these our *present* powers of reflection, as it will of our powers of sensation; or to give ground to conclude, even that it will be so much as a suspension of the former.

Human creatures exist at present in two states of life and perception, greatly different from each other; each of which has its own peculiar laws, and its own peculiar enjoyments and sufferings. When any of our senses are affected or appetites gratified with the objects of them, we may be said to exist or live in a state of sensation. When none of our senses are affected or appetites gratified, and yet we perceive, and reason, and act; we may be said to exist or live in a state of reflection. Now it is by no means certain, that any thing which is dissolved by death, is any way necessary to the living being in this its state of reflection, after ideas are gained. For, though, from our present constitution and condition of being, our external organs of sense are necessary for conveying in ideas to our reflecting powers, as carriages, and levers, and scaffolds are in architecture: yet when these ideas are brought in, we are capable of reflecting in the most intense degree, and of enjoying the greatest pleasure, and feeling the greatest pain, by means of that reflection, without any assistance from our senses; and without any at all, which we know of, from that body which will be dissolved by death. It does not appear then, that the relation of this gross body to the reflecting being is, in any degree, necessary to thinking; to our intellectual enjoyments or sufferings: nor, consequently, that the dissolution or alienation of the former by death, will be the destruction of those present powers, which render us capable of this state of reflection.

Further, there are instances of mortal diseases, which do not at all affect our present intellectual powers; and this affords a presumption, that those diseases will not destroy these present powers. Indeed, from the observations made above, it appears, that there is no presumption, from their mutually affecting each other, that the dissolution of the body is the destruction of the living agent. And by the same reasoning, it must appear too, that there is no presumption, from their mutually affecting each other, that the dissolution of the body is the destruction of our present reflecting powers: but instances of their not affecting each other, afford a presumption of the contrary. Instances of mortal diseases not impairing our present reflecting powers, evidently turn our thoughts even from imagining such diseases to be the destruction of them. Several things indeed greatly affect all our living powers, and at length suspend the exercise of them; as for instance drowsiness, increasing till it ends in sound sleep: and from hence we might have imagined it would destroy them, till we found by experience the weakness of this way of judging. But in the diseases now mentioned, there is not so much as this shadow of probability, to lead us to any such conclusion, as to the reflecting powers which we have at present. For in those diseases, persons the moment before death appear to be in the highest vigour of life. They discover apprehension, memory, reason, all entire; with the utmost force of affection; sense of a character, of shame and honour; and the highest mental enjoyments and sufferings, even to the last gasp: and these surely prove even greater vigour of life than bodily strength does. Now what pretence is there for thinking, that a progressive disease when arrived to such a degree, I mean that degree which is mortal, will destroy those powers, which were not impaired, which were not affected by it, during its whole progress quite up to that degree? And if death by diseases of this kind is not the destruction of our present reflecting powers, it will scarce be thought that death by any other means is.

It is obvious that this general observation may be carried on further: and there appears so little connection between our bodily powers of sensation, and our present powers of reflection, that there is no reason to conclude, that death, which destroys the former, does so much as suspend the exercise of the latter, or interrupt our *continuing* to exist in the like state of reflection which we do now. For suspension of reason, memory, and the affections which they excite, is no part of the idea of death, nor is implied in our notion of it. And our daily experiencing these powers to be exercised, without any assistance, that we know of, from those bodies, which will be dissolved by death; and our finding often, that the exercise of them is so lively to the last; these things afford a sensible apprehension, that death may not perhaps be so much as a discontinuance of the exercise of these powers, nor of the enjoyments and sufferings which it implies.[4] So that our posthumous life, whatever there may be in it additional to our present, yet may not be entirely beginning anew; but going on.

Death may, in some sort, and in some respects, answer to our birth; which is not a suspension of the faculties which we had before it, or a total change of the state of life in which we existed when in the womb; but a continuation of both, with such and such great alterations.

Nay, for ought we know of ourselves, of our present life and of death; death may immediately, in the natural course of things, put us into a higher and more enlarged state of life, as our birth does; a state in which our capacities, and sphere of perception and of action, may be much greater than at present. For as our relation to our external organs of sense, renders us capable of existing in our present state of sensation; so it may be the only natural hindrance to our existing, immediately and of course, in a higher state of reflection. The truth is, reason does not at all show us, in what state death naturally leaves us.

But were we sure, that it would suspend all our perceptive and active powers; yet the suspension of a power and the destruction of it, are effects so totally different in kind, as we experience from sleep and a swoon, that we cannot in any wise argue from one to the other; or conclude even to the lowest degree of probability, that the same kind of force which is sufficient to suspend our faculties, though it be increased ever so much, will be sufficient to destroy them.

These observations together may be sufficient to show, how little presumption there is, that death is the destruction of human creatures. However, there is the shadow of an analogy, which may lead us to imagine it is; the supposed likeness which is observed between the decay of vegetables, and of living creatures. And this likeness is indeed sufficient to afford the poets very

---

[4] There are three distinct questions, relating to a future life, here considered: Whether death be the destruction of living agents; if not, Whether it be the destruction of their *present* powers of reflection, as it certainly is the destruction of their present powers of sensation; and if not, Whether it be the suspension, or discontinuance of the exercise, of these present reflecting powers. Now, if there be no reason to believe the last, there will be, if that were possible, less for the next, and less still for the first.

apt allusions to the flowers of the field, in their pictures of the frailty of our present life. But in reason, the analogy is so far from holding, that there appears no ground even for the comparison, as to the present question: because one of the two subjects compared is wholly void of that, which is the principal and chief thing in the other, the power of perception and of action; and which is the only thing we are inquiring about the continuance of. So that the destruction of a vegetable is an event not similar or analogous to the destruction of a living agent.

But if, as was above intimated, leaving off the delusive custom of substituting imagination in the room of experience, we would confine ourselves to what we do know and understand; if we would argue only from that, and from that form our expectations; it would appear at first sight, that as no probability of living beings ever ceasing to be so, can be concluded from the reason of the thing; so none can be collected from the analogy of nature; because we cannot trace any living beings beyond death. But as we are conscious that we are endued with capacities of perception and of action, and are living persons; what we are to go upon is, that we shall continue so, till we foresee some accident or event, which will endanger those capacities, or be likely to destroy us: which death does in no wise appear to be.

And thus, when we go out of this world, we may pass into new scenes, and a new state of life and action, just as naturally as we came into the present. And this new state may naturally be a social one. And the advantages of it, advantages of every kind, may naturally be bestowed, according to some fixed general laws of wisdom, upon every one in proportion to the degrees of his virtue. And though the advantages of that future natural state should not be bestowed, as these of the present in some measure are, by the will of the society; but entirely by his more immediate action, upon whom the whole frame of nature depends: yet this distribution may be just as natural, as their being distributed here by the instrumentality of men. And indeed, though one were to allow any confused undetermined sense, which people please to put upon the word *natural*, it would be a shortness of thought scarce credible, to imagine, that no system or course of things can be so, but only what we see at present: especially whilst the probability of a future life, or the natural immortality of the soul, is admitted upon the evidence of reason; because this is really both admitting and denying at once, a state of being different from the present to be natural. But the only distinct meaning of that word is, *stated, fixed,* or *settled*: since what is natural, as much requires and presupposes an intelligent agent to render it so, i.e. to effect it continually, or at stated times; as what is supernatural or miraculous does to effect it for once. And from hence it must follow, that persons' notion of what is natural, will be enlarged in proportion to their greater knowledge of the works of God, and the dispensations of his Providence. Nor is there any absurdity in supposing, that there may be beings in the universe, whose capacities, and knowledge, and views, may be so extensive, as that the whole Christian dispensation may to them appear natural, i.e. analogous or conformable to God's dealings with other parts of his creation; as natural as the visible known course of things appears to us. For there seems scarce any other possible sense to be put upon the word, but that only in which it is here used; similar, stated, or uniform.

This credibility of a future life, which has been here insisted upon, how little soever it may satisfy our curiosity, seems to answer all the purposes of religion, in like manner as a demonstrative proof would. Indeed a proof, even a demonstrative one, of a future life, would not be a proof of religion. For, that we are to live hereafter, is just as reconcilable with the scheme of atheism, and as well to be accounted for by it, as that we are now alive is: and therefore nothing can be more absurd than to argue from that scheme, that there can be no future state. But as religion implies a future state, any presumption against such a state, is a presumption against religion. And the foregoing observations remove all presumptions of that sort, and prove, to a very considerable degree of probability, one fundamental doctrine of religion; which, if believed, would greatly open and dispose the mind seriously to attend to the general evidence of the whole.

QUESTIONS

1. What is the analogy of nature? What does it imply about the effect which death may have on men? How does Butler's account of "presumption, or probability from analogy" compare with Hume's account of our knowledge of matters of fact in Chapter 2?
2. What is an argument "from the reason of the thing"? Why can this kind of argument not be used to establish that death is the destruction of living agents? Why can the analogy of nature not be used to establish that conclusion, either?
3. How does Butler argue for the simplicity of consciousness? How tenable is the claim that the simplicity of consciousness implies that living beings are not discerptible? What is meant by "living being" here?
4. When Butler says, ". . . our organized bodies are no more ourselves or part of ourselves, than any other matter around us," what does he mean by "self," "body," and "matter"? Evaluate the arguments which he advances to establish the above claim.
5. Examine critically Butler's claim that human beings exist in two states of life: sensation and reflection.
6. Evaluate Butler's arguments against our inferring the death of human beings from the decay of vegetables and living creatures. What meaning does Butler give to "death" in this reading?
7. How might Hume criticize the definition of "natural" and the account of our knowledge of the natural which is offered in the last part of this reading?

15. BARON d'HOLBACH

(1723–89)

Nature, Man, and Immortality

Paul Heinrich Dietrich, Baron d'Holbach, was born at Heidelsheim in the Palatinate. He settled in Paris, where he was the friend and collaborator of the Encyclopedists, Diderot and d'Alembert. Holbach prepared articles on chemistry and mineralogy, translated largely from German sources, for the *Encyclopédie*. The work which established his fame was *The System of Nature* (1770), an often impassioned statement of the materialistic consequences which Holbach drew from the theories of the Encyclopedists.

This selection is from *The System of Nature,* and is intended to introduce the reader to Holbach's view of man in nature, and his consequent opposition to the notion of human immortality. For Holbach, "nature" is a comprehensive metaphysical term, so that no sense can be made of the claim that there is anything outside of nature. Thus, "supernatural" is a meaningless

term. His view of man may be stated in sentences of slogan-like character: *Man is a work of nature. Man is a purely physical being. Man is a machine subject to the laws of nature.* The question for the reader to consider is whether these doctrines are (1) generalizations drawn from Holbach's study of men or (2) a priori recommendations of the way we should view men. Starting from his materialistic account of man then, Holbach is able to argue against mankind's possessing immaterial souls, and, consequently, against the possibility of human immortality. The soundness of these views is directly dependent on the tenability of his account of the place of man in nature.

This reading is drawn from *The System of Nature,* Volume I, Chapters I, VI, VII, VIII, and XIII. The translation from the French is by H. D. Robinson.

MAN IN NATURE

Men will always deceive themselves by abandoning experience to follow imaginary systems. Man is the work of Nature: he exists in Nature: he is submitted to her laws: he cannot deliver himself from them; nor can he step beyond them even in thought. It is in vain his mind would spring forward beyond the visible world, an imperious necessity always compels his return. For a being formed by Nature, and circumscribed by her laws, there exists nothing beyond the great whole of which he forms a part, of which he experiences the influence. The beings which he pictures to himself as above nature, or distinguished from her, are always chimeras formed after that which he has already seen, but of which it is impossible he should ever form any correct idea, either as to the place they occupy, or of their manner of acting. There is not, there can be nothing out of that Nature which includes all beings.

Instead, therefore, of seeking out of the world he inhabits for beings who can procure him a happiness denied to him by Nature, let man study this Nature, let him learn her laws, contemplate her energies, observe the immutable rules by which she acts:—let him apply these discoveries to his own felicity and submit in silence to her mandates, which nothing can alter:—let him cheerfully consent to ignore causes hid from him by an impenetrable veil:—let him without murmuring yield to the decrees of a universal necessity, which can never be brought within his comprehension, nor ever emancipate him from those laws imposed on him by his essence.

The distinction which has been so often made between the *physical* and the *moral* man is evidently an abuse of terms. Man is a being purely physical: the moral man is nothing more than this physical being considered under a certain point of view, that is to say, with relation to some of his modes of action, arising out of his particular organization. But is not this organization itself the work of Nature? The motion or impulse to action of which he is susceptible, is that not physical? His visible actions, as well as the invisible motion interiorly excited by his will or his thoughts, are equally the natural effects, the necessary consequences, of his peculiar mechanism, and the impulse he receives from those beings by whom he is surrounded. All that the human mind has successively invented with a view to change or perfect his being, and to render himself more happy, was only a necessary consequence of man's peculiar essence, and that of the beings who act upon him. The object of all his institutions, of all his reflections, of all his knowledge, is only to procure that happiness towards which he is incessantly impelled by the peculiarity of his nature. All that he does, all that he thinks, all that he is, all that he will be, is nothing more than what Universal Nature has made him. His ideas, his will, his actions, are the necessary effects of those qualities infused into him by Nature, and of those circumstances in which she has placed him. In short, *art* is nothing but Nature acting with the tools she has made.

Nature sends man naked and destitute into this world which is to be his abode: he quickly learns to cover his nakedness, to shelter himself from the inclemency of the weather, first with rude huts and the skins of the beasts of the forest; by degrees he mends their appearance, renders them more convenient: he establishes manufactories of cloth, of cotton, of silk; he digs clay, gold, and other fossils from the bowels of the earth, converts them into bricks for his house, into vessels for his use, gradually improves their shape, augments their beauty. To a being elevated above our terrestrial globe, who should contemplate the human species through all the changes he undergoes in his progress towards civilization, man would not appear less subjected to the laws of Nature when naked in the forest painfully seeking his sustenance, then when living in civilized society surrounded with comforts; that is to say, enriched with greater experience, plunged in luxury, where he every day invents a thousand new wants and discovers a thousand new modes of satisfying them. All the steps taken by man to regulate his existence, ought only to be considered as a long succession of causes and effects, which are nothing more than the development of the first impulse given him by nature.

The same animal by virtue of his organization passes successively from the most simple to the most complicated wants; it is nevertheless the consequence of his nature. The butterfly whose beauty we admire, whose colours are so rich, whose appearance is so brilliant, commences as an inanimate unattractive egg; from this, heat produces a worm, this becomes a chrysalis, then changes into that winged insect decorated with the most vivid tints: arrived at this stage he reproduces, he propagates: at last despoiled of his ornaments he is obliged to disappear, having fulfilled the task imposed on him by Nature, having described the circle of mutation marked out for beings of his order.

The same progress, the same change takes place in vegetables. It is by a succession of combinations originally interwoven with the energies of the aloe, that this plant is insensibly regulated, gradually expanded, and at the end of a great number of years produces those flowers which announce its dissolution.

It is equally so with man, who in all his motion, all the changes he undergoes, never acts but according to laws peculiar to his organization, and to the matter of which he is composed.

. . .

MAN, MORAL AND PHYSICAL

Man occupies a place amidst that crowd, that multitude of beings, of which nature is the assemblage. His essence, that is to say, the peculiar manner of existence by which he is distinguished from other beings, renders him susceptible of various modes of action, of a variety of motion, some of which are simple and visible, others concealed and complicated. His life itself is nothing more than a long series, a succession of necessary and connected motion, which operates perpetual and continual changes in his machine; which has for its principle either causes contained within himself, such as blood, nerves, fibres, flesh, bones, in short, the matter, as well solid as fluid, of which his body is composed—or those exterior causes, which, by acting upon him, modify him diversely; such as the air with which he is encompassed, the aliments by which he is nourished, and all those objects from which he receives any impulse whatever by the impression they make on his senses.

Man, like all other beings in nature, tends to his own preservation—he experiences inert force—he gravitates upon himself—he is attracted by objects that are analogous, and repelled by those that are contrary to him—he seeks after some—he flies or endeavours to remove himself from others. It is this variety of action, this diversity of modification of which the human being is susceptible, that has been designated under such different names, by such varied nomenclature. It will be necessary, presently, to examine these closely and in detail.

However marvellous, however hidden, however complicated, may be the modes of action which the human frame undergoes, whether interiorly or exteriorly; whatever may be, or appear to be the impulse he either receives or communicates, examined closely, it will be found that all his motion, all his operations, all his changes, all his various states, all his revolutions, are constantly regulated by the same laws, which nature has prescribed to all the beings she brings forth—which she develops—which she enriches with faculties—of which she increases the bulk—which she conserves for a season —which she ends by decomposing or destroying—thus obliging them to change their form.

Man, in his origin, is an imperceptible point, a speck, of which the parts are without form; of which the mobility, the life, escapes his senses; in short in which he does not perceive any sign of those qualities called *sentiment, feeling, thought, intelligence, force, reason,* etc. Placed in the womb suitable to his expansion, this point unfolds, extends, increases by the continual addition of matter he attracts that is analogous to his being, which consequently assimilates itself with him. Having quitted this womb, so appropriate to conserve his existence, to unfold his qualities, to strengthen his habit; so competent to give, for a season, consistence to the weak rudiments of his frame; he becomes adult: his body has then acquired a considerable extension of bulk, his motion is marked, his action is visible, he is sensible in all his parts; he is a living, an active mass; that is to say, he feels, thinks, and fulfils the functions peculiar to beings of his species. But how has he become sensible? Because he has been by degrees nourished, enlarged, repaired by the continual attraction that takes place within himself of that kind of matter which is pronounced inert, insensible, inanimate; although continually combining itself with his machine, of which it forms an active whole, that is living, that feels, judges, reasons, wills, deliberates, chooses, elects; with a capability of labouring, more or less efficaciously, to his own individual preservation; that is to say, to the maintenance of the harmony of his natural existence.

All the motion and changes that man experiences in the course of his life, whether it be from exterior objects, or from those substances contained within himself, are either favourable or prejudicial to his existence; either maintain its order, or throw it into confusion; are either in conformity with, or repugnant to the essential tendency of his peculiar mode of being. He is compelled by nature to approve of some, to disapprove of others; some of necessity render him happy, others contribute to his misery; some become the objects of his most ardent desire, others of his determined aversion: some elicit his confidence, others make him tremble with fear.

In all the phenomena man presents, from the moment he quits the womb of his mother, to that wherein he becomes the inhabitant of the silent tomb, he perceives nothing but a succession of necessary causes and effects, which are strictly conformable to those laws common to all the beings in nature. All his modes of action—all his sensations—all his ideas—all his passions—every act of his will—every impulse he either gives or receives, are the necessary consequences of his own peculiar properties, and those which he finds in the various beings by whom he is moved. Every thing he does—every thing that passes within himself, are the effects of inert force— of self-gravitation—of the attractive or repulsive powers contained in his machine—of the tendency he has, in common with other beings, to his own individual preservation; in short, of that energy which is the common property of every being he beholds. Nature, in man, does nothing more than show, in a decided manner, what belongs to the peculiar nature by which he is distinguished from the beings of a different system or order.

The source of those errours into which man has fallen when he has contemplated himself, has its rise, as will presently be shown, in the opinion he has entertained, that he moved by himself—that he always acts by his own natural energy—that in his actions, in the will that gave him impulse, he was independent of the general laws of nature, and of those objects which, frequently without his knowledge, and always in spite of him, are, in obedience to these laws, continually acting upon him. If he had examined himself attentively, he must have acknowledged, that none of the motion he underwent was spontaneous—he must. have discovered, that even his birth depended on causes wholly out of the reach of his own powers—that it was without his own consent he entered into the system in which he occupies a place—that, from the moment in which he is born, until that in which he dies, he is continually impelled by causes which, in spite of himself, influence his frame, modify his existence, dispose of his conduct. Would not the slightest reflection have sufficed to prove to him, that the fluids and the solids of which his body is composed, as well as that concealed mechanism, which he believes to be independent of exterior causes, are, in fact, perpetually under the influence of these causes; that without them he would find himself in a total incapacity to act? Would he not have seen, that his temperament, his constitution, did in nowise depend on himself—that his passions are the necessary consequence of this temperament—that his will is influenced—his actions determined by these passions; and consequently by opinions which he has not given to himself? His blood more or less heated or abundant, his nerves more or less braced, his fibres more or less relaxed, give him dispositions either transitory or durable, which are at every moment decisive of his ideas, of his desires, of his fears, of his motion, whether visible or concealed. And the state in which he finds himself, does it not necessarily depend on the air which surrounds him diversely modified; on the various properties of the aliments which nourish him; of the secret combinations that form themselves in his machine, which either preserve its order, or throw it into confusion? In short, had man fairly studied himself, every thing must have convinced him, that in every moment of his duration, he was nothing more than a passive instrument in the hands of necessity.

Thus it must appear, that where all the causes are linked one to the other, where the whole forms but one immense chain, there cannot be any independent, any isolated energy; any detached power. It follows, then, that nature, always in action, marks out to man each point of the line he is bound to describe. It is nature that elaborates, that combines the elements of which he must be composed.—It is nature that gives him his being, his tendency, his peculiar mode of action.—It is nature that develops him, expands him, strengthens him, and preserves him for a season, during which he is obliged to fulfil the task imposed on him.—It is nature, that in his journey through life, strews on the road those objects, those events, those adventures, that modify him in a variety of ways, and give him impulses which are sometimes agreeable and beneficial, at others prejudicial and disagreeable.—It is nature, that in giving him feeling, has endowed him with capacity to choose the means, and to take those methods that are most conducive to his conservation.—It is nature, who, when he has finished his career, conducts him to his destruction, and thus obliges him to undergo the constant, the universal law, from the operation of which nothing is exempted. It is thus, also, motion brings man forth out of the womb, sustains him for a season, and at length destroys him, or obliges him to return into the bosom of nature, who speedily reproduces him, scattered under an infinity of forms, in which each of his particles will, in the same manner, run over again the different stages, as necessarily as the whole had before run over those of his preceding existence.

The beings of the human species, as well as all other beings, are susceptible of two sorts of motion: the one, that of the mass, by which an entire body, or some of its parts, are visibly transferred from one place to another; the other, internal and concealed, of some of which man is sensible, while some takes place without his knowledge, and is not even to be guessed at but by the effect it outwardly produces. In a machine so extremely complex as man, formed by the combination of such a multiplicity of matter, so diversified in its properties, so different in its proportions, so varied in its modes of action, the motion necessarily becomes of the most complicated kind; its dullness, as well as its rapidity, frequently escapes the observation of those themselves in whom it takes place.

Let us not, then, be surprised, if when man would account to himself for his existence, for his manner of acting, finding so many obstacles to encounter, he invented such strange hypotheses to explain the concealed spring of his machine—if when this motion appeared to him to be different from that of other bodies, he conceived an idea that he moved and acted in a manner altogether distinct from the other beings in nature. He clearly perceived that his body, as well as different parts of it, did act; but, frequently, he was unable to discover what brought them into action: he then conjectured he contained within himself a moving principle distinguished from his machine, which secretly gave an impulse to the springs which set this machine in motion; that moved him by its own natural energy; and that consequently he acted according to laws totally distinct from those which regulated the motion of other beings. He was conscious of certain internal motion which he could not help feeling; but how could he conceive that this invisible motion was so frequently competent to produce such striking effects? How could he comprehend that a fugitive idea, an imperceptible act of thought, could frequently bring his whole being into trouble and confusion? He fell into the belief, that he perceived within himself a substance distinguished from that self, endowed with a secret force, in which he supposed existed qualities distinctly differing from those of either the visible causes that acted on his organs, or those organs themselves. He did not sufficiently understand, that the primitive causes which make a stone fall, or his arm move, are perhaps as difficult of comprehension, as arduous to be explained, as those internal impulses of which his thought or his will are the effects. Thus, for want of meditating nature—of considering her under her true point of view—of remarking the conformity and noticing the simultaneity of the motion of this fancied motive-power with that of his body and of his material organs—he conjectured he was not only a distinct being, but that he was set apart, with different energies, from all the other beings in nature; that he was of a more simple essence, having nothing in common with any thing that he beheld.[1]

It is from thence his notions of *spirituality, immateriality, immortality,* have successively sprung; in short, all those vague unmeaning words he has invented by degrees, in order to subtilize and designate the attributes of the unknown power which he believes he contains within himself, and which he

---

[1] "We must," says an anonymous writer, "define life, before we can reason upon the soul: but this is what I esteem impossible, because there are things in nature so simple that imagination cannot divide them, nor reduce them to any thing more simple than themselves: such is *life, whiteness,* and *light,* which we have not been able to define but by their effects."—See *Miscellaneous Dissertations, Printed at Amsterdam,* 1740, p. 232. —Life is the assemblage of motion natural to an organized being, and motion can only be a property of matter.

conjectures to be the concealed principle of all his visible actions. To crown the bold conjectures he ventured to make on this internal motive-power, he supposed that different from all other beings, even from the body that served to envelop it, it was not bound to undergo dissolution; that such was its perfect simplicity, that it could not be decomposed, nor even change its form; in short, that it was by its essence exempted from those revolutions to which he saw the body subjected, as well as all the compound beings with which nature is filled.

Thus man became double; he looked upon himself as a whole, composed by the inconceivable assemblage of two distinct natures, which had no point of analogy between themselves: he distinguished two substances in himself; one evidently submitted to the influence of gross beings, composed of coarse inert matter: this he called *body:*—the other, which he supposed to be simple, and of a purer essence, was contemplated as acting from itself, and giving motion to the body with which it found itself so miraculously united: this he called *soul or spirit:* The functions of the one he denominated *physical, corporeal, material;* the functions of the other he styled *spiritual, intellectual.* Man, considered relatively to the first, was termed the *physical man;* viewed with relation to the last, he was designated the *moral man.*

These distinctions, although adopted by the greater number of the philosophers of the present day, are only founded on gratuitous suppositions. Man has always believed he remedied his ignorance of things by inventing words to which he could never attach any true sense or meaning. He imagined he understood matter, its properties, its faculties, its resources, its different combinations, because he had a superficial glimpse of some of its qualities: he has, however, in reality done nothing more than obscure the faint ideas he has been capacitated to form of this matter, by associating it with a substance much less intelligible than itself. It is thus speculative man, in forming words, in multiplying beings, has only plunged himself into greater difficulties than those he endeavoured to avoid, and thereby placed obstacles to the progress of his knowledge: whenever he has been deficient of facts, he has had recourse to conjecture, which he quickly changed into fancied realities. Thus, his imagination no longer guided by experience, was lost, without hope of return, in the labyrinth of an ideal and intellectual world, to which he had himself given birth; it was next to impossible to withdraw him from this delusion, to place him in the right road of which nothing but experience can furnish him the clue. Nature points out, that in man himself, as well as in all those objects which act upon him, there is nothing more than matter endowed with various properties, diversely modified, and acting by reason of these properties: that man is an organized whole, composed of a variety of matter; that, like all the other productions of nature, he follows general and known laws, as well as those laws or modes of action which are peculiar to himself, and unknown.

Thus, when it shall be inquired, what is man?

We say, he is a material being, organized after a peculiar manner; conformed to a certain mode of thinking, of feeling, capable of modification in certain modes peculiar to himself, to his organization, to that particular combination of matter which is found assembled in him.

. . .

OF THE SOUL

Man, after having gratuitously supposed himself composed of two distinct independent substances, having no common properties relatively with each other, has pretended, as we have seen, that that which actuated him interiorly, that motion which is invisible, that impulse which is placed within himself, is essentially different from those which act exteriorly. The first he designated, as we have already said, by the name of a *spirit,* or a *soul.* If, however, it be asked, what is a spirit? the moderns will reply, that the whole fruit of their metaphysical researches is limited to learning that this motive-power, which they state to be the spring of man's action, is a substance of an unknown nature, so simple, so indivisible, so deprived of extent, so invisible, so impossible to be discovered by the senses, that its parts cannot be separated, even by abstraction or thought. But how can we conceive such a substance, which is only the negation of every thing of which we have a knowledge? How form to ourselves an idea of a substance void of extent, yet acting on our senses; that is to say, on material organs which have extent? How can a being without extent be moveable and put matter in action? How can a substance, devoid of parts, correspond successively with different parts of space?

At any rate all men are agreed in this position, that motion is the successive change of the relations of one body with other bodies, or with the different parts of space. If that, which is called *spirit,* be susceptible of communicating or receiving motion; if it acts—if it gives play to the organs or body—to produce these effects it necessarily follows, that this being changes successively its relation, its tendency, its correspondence, the position of its parts, either relatively to the different points of space, or to the different organs of the body which it puts in action; but to change its relation with space and with the organs to which it gives impulse, this spirit must have extent, solidity, consequently distinct parts: whenever a substance possesses these qualities, it is what we call *matter,* and can no longer be regarded as a simple pure being in the sense attached to it by the moderns.

Thus it will be seen that those who have supposed in man an immaterial substance, distinguished from his body, have not thoroughly understood themselves; indeed they have done nothing more than imagined a negative quality of which they cannot have any correct idea: matter alone is capable of acting on our senses, and without this action nothing would be capable of making itself known to us. They have not seen that a being without extent, is neither in a capacity to move itself, nor has the capability of communicating motion to the body, since such a being, having no parts, has not the faculty of changing its relation, or its distance, relatively to other bodies, nor of exciting motion in the human body, which is itself material. That which is called our soul, moves itself with us; now motion is a property of matter—this soul gives impulse to the arm; the arm, moved by it, makes an impression, a blow, that follows the general law of motion: in this case, the force remaining the same, if the mass was twofold, the blow would be double. This soul again evinces its materiality in the invincible obstacles it encounters on the part of the body. If the arm be moved by its impulse when nothing opposes it, yet this arm can no longer move when it is charged with a weight beyond its strength. Here then is a mass of matter that annihilates the impulse given by a spiritual cause, which spiritual cause having no analogy with matter, ought not to find more difficulty in moving the whole world than in moving a single atom, nor an atom than the universe. From this it is fair to conclude that such a substance is a chimera; a being of the imagination: nevertheless such is the being the metaphysicians have made the contriver and the author of nature!!

As soon as I feel an impulse or experience motion, I am under the necessity to acknowledge extent, solidity, density, impenetrability in the substance I see move, or from which I receive impulse: thus, when action is attributed to any cause whatever, I am obliged to consider it *material*. I may be ignorant of its individual nature, of its mode of action, of its generic properties; but I cannot deceive myself in general properties which are common to all matter: besides this ignorance will only be increased, when I shall take that for granted of a being of which I am precluded from forming any idea, which moreover deprives it completely of the faculty of moving and acting. Thus, a spiritual substance, that moves itself, that gives an impulse to matter, that acts, implies a contradiction, which necessarily infers a total impossibility.

The partizans of spirituality believe they answer the difficulties they have themselves accumulated, by saying, *"The soul is entire, is whole under each point of its extent."* If an absurd answer will solve difficulties, they have done it; for after all it will be found, that this point, which is called soul, however insensible, however minute, must yet remain something. But if as much solidity had appeared in the answer as there is a want of it, it must be acknowledged, that in whatever manner the spirit or the soul finds itself in its extent, when the body moves forward, the soul does not remain behind; if so, it has a quality in common with the body peculiar to matter, since it is transferred from place to place jointly with the body. Thus, if even the soul should be immaterial, what conclusion must be drawn? Entirely submitted to the motion of the body, without this body it would remain dead and inert. This soul would only be part of a twofold machine, necessarily impelled forward by a concatenation or connexion with the whole. It would resemble a bird, which a child conducts at its pleasure by the string with which it is bound.

Thus, it is for want of consulting experience, and by not attending to reason, that man has obscured his ideas upon the concealed principle of his motion. If, disentangled from prejudice, he would contemplate his soul, or the moving principle that acts within him, he would be convinced that it forms part of his body; that it cannot be distinguished from it but by abstraction; and that it is only the body itself considered relatively with some of its functions, or with those faculties of which its nature and its peculiar organization renders it susceptible. He will also perceive that this soul is obliged to undergo the same changes as the body; that it is born and expands itself with it; that, like the body, it passes through a state of infancy, a period of weakness, a season of inexperience; that it enlarges and strengthens itself in the same progression; that, like the body, it arrives at an adult age, reaches maturity; that it is then it obtains the faculty of fulfilling certain functions, enjoys reason, and displays more or less wit, judgment, and manly activity; that like the body, it is subject to those vicissitudes which exterior causes oblige it to undergo by their influence; that, conjointly with the body, it suffers, enjoys, partakes of its pleasures, shares its pains, is sound when the body is healthy, diseased when the body is oppressed with sickness; that, like the body, it is continually modified by the different degrees of density in the atmosphere; by the variety of the seasons; by the various properties of the aliments received into the stomach: in short, he would be obliged to acknowledge that at some periods, it manifests visible signs of torpor, decrepitude, and death.

· · ·

PHYSICAL BASIS OF INTELLECT

To convince ourselves that the faculties called *intellectual,* are only certain modes of existence, or determinate manners of acting which result from the peculiar organization of the body, we have only to analyze them: we shall then see, that all the operations which are attributed to the soul, are nothing more than certain modifications of the body, of which a substance that is without extent, that has no parts, that is immaterial, is not susceptible.

The first faculty we behold in the living man, that from which all his others flow, is *feeling:* however inexplicable this faculty may appear on a first view, if it be examined closely, it will be found to be a consequence of the essence, a result of the properties of organized beings; the same as *gravity, magnetism, elasticity, electricity,* etc. result from the essence or nature of some others; and we shall also find that these last phenomena are not less inexplicable than that of feeling. Nevertheless, if we wish to define to ourselves a precise idea of it, we shall find that feeling is a particular manner of being moved peculiar to certain organs of animated bodies, occasioned by the presence of a material object that acts upon these organs, and which transmits the impulse of shock to the brain.

Man only feels by the aid of nerves dispersed through his body, which is itself, to speak correctly, nothing more than a great nerve; or may be said to resemble a large tree, of which the branches experience the action of the root communicated through the trunk. In man the nerves unite and loose themselves in the brain; that intestine is the true seat of feeling: like the spider suspended in the centre of his web, it is quickly warned of all the changes that happen to the body, even at the extremities to which it sends its filaments and branches. Experience enables us to ascertain that man ceases to feel in those parts of his body of which the communication with the brain is intercepted; he feels very little, or not at all, whenever this organ is itself deranged or affected in too lively a manner.

However this may be, the sensibility of the brain, and of all its parts, is a fact. If it be asked, whence comes this property? We shall reply, it is the result of an arrangement, of a combination, peculiar to the animal; insomuch, that coarse and insensible matter ceases to be so by animalizing itself, that is to say, by combining and identifying itself with the animal. It is thus that milk, bread, wine, change themselves in the substance of man, who is a sensible being: this insensible matter becomes sensible in combining itself with a sensible whole. Some philosophers think that sensibility is a universal quality of matter: in this case it would be useless to seek from whence this property is derived, as we know it by its effects. If this hypothesis be admitted, in like manner as two kinds of motion are distinguished in nature, the one called *live* force, the other *dead,* or *inert* force, two sorts of sensibility will be distinguished—the one active or live, the other inert or dead. Then to animalize a substance, is only to destroy the obstacles that prevent its being active or sensible. In fact, sensibility is either a quality which communicates itself like motion, and which is acquired by combination; or this sensibility is a property inherent in all matter: in both, or either case, an unextended being, without parts, such as the human soul is said to be, can neither be the cause of it, nor submitted to its operation.

. . .

OF THE IMMORTALITY OF THE SOUL

Nothing is more popular than the doctrine of the *immortality of the soul;* nothing is more universally diffused than the expectation of another life. Nature having inspired man with the most ardent love for his existence, the desire of preserving himself for ever was a necessary consequence: this desire was presently converted into certainty; from that desire of existing eternally, which nature has implanted in him, he made an argument to prove that man would never cease to exist. Abbadie says: "Our soul has no useless desires, it desires naturally an eternal life"; and by a very strange logic he concludes, that this desire could not fail to be fulfilled. However this may be, man, thus disposed, listened with avidity to those who announced to him systems so conformable with his wishes. Nevertheless, he ought not to regard as supernatural the desire of existing, which always was, and always will be, of the essence of man; it ought not to excite surprise if he received with eagerness an hypothesis that flattered his hopes, by promising that his desire would one day be gratified; but let him beware how he concludes, that this desire itself is an indubitable proof of the reality of this future life, with which, for his present happiness, he seems to be far too much occupied. The passion for existence, is in man only a natural consequence of the tendency of a sensible being, whose essence it is to be willing to conserve himself: in the human being, it follows the energy of his soul or keeps pace with the force of his imagination, always ready to realize that which he strongly desires. He desires the life of the body, nevertheless this desire is frustrated; wherefore should not the desire for the life of the soul be frustrated like the other?

The most simple reflection upon the nature of his soul, ought to convince man that the idea of its immortality is only an illusion of the brain. Indeed, what is his soul, save the principle of sensibility? What is it to think, to enjoy, to suffer; is it not to feel? What is life, except it be the assemblage of modifications, the congregation of motion, peculiar to an organized being? Thus, as soon as the body ceases to live, its sensibility can no longer exercise itself; therefore it can no longer have ideas, nor in consequence thoughts. Ideas, as we have proved, can only reach man through his senses; now, how will they have it, that once deprived of his senses, he is yet capable of receiving sensations, of having perceptions, of forming ideas? As they have made the soul of man a being separated from the animated body, wherefore have they not made life a being distinguished from the living body? Life in a body is the totality of its motion; feeling and thought make a part of this motion: thus, in the dead man, these motions will cease like all the others.

Indeed, by what reasoning will it be proved, that this soul, which cannot feel, think, will, or act, but by aid of man's organs, can suffer pain, be susceptible of pleasure, or even have a consciousness of its own existence, when the organs which should warn it of their presence, are decomposed or destroyed? Is it not evident that the soul depends on the arrangement of the various parts of the body, and on the order with which these parts conspire to perform their functions or motions? Thus the organic structure once destroyed, can it be doubted the soul will be destroyed also? Is it not seen, that during the whole course of human life, this soul is stimulated, changed, deranged, disturbed, by all the changes man's organs experience? And yet it will be insisted that this soul acts, thinks, subsists, when these same organs have entirely disappeared!

An organized being may be compared to a clock, which, once broken, is no longer suitable to the use for which it was designed. To say, that the soul shall feel, shall think, shall enjoy, shall suffer, after the death of the body, is to pretend, that a clock, shivered into a thousand pieces, will continue to strike the hour, and have the faculty of marking the progress of time. Those who say, that the soul of man is able to subsist notwithstanding the destruction of the body, evidently support the position, that the modification of a body will be enabled to conserve itself, after the subject is destroyed: but this is completely absurd.

It will be said, that the conservation of the soul after the death of the body, is an effect of the divine omnipotence: but this is supporting an absurdity by a gratuitous hypothesis. It surely is not meant by divine omnipotence, of whatever nature it may be supposed, that a thing shall exist and not exist at the same time: that a soul shall feel and think without the intermediates necessary to thought.

Let them, then, at least forbear asserting, that reason is not wounded by the doctrine of the immortality of the soul, or by the expectation of a future life. These notions, formed to flatter man, or to disturb the imagination of the uninformed who do not reason, cannot appear either convincing or probable to enlightened minds. Reason, exempted from the illusions of prejudice, is, without doubt, wounded by the supposition of a soul that feels, that thinks, that is afflicted, that rejoices, that has ideas, without having organs; that is to say, destitute of the only known and natural means by which it is possible for it to feel sensations, have perceptions, or form ideas. If it be replied, that other means are able to exist, which are *supernatural* or *unknown;* it may be answered, that these means of transmitting ideas to the soul separated from the body, are not better known to, or more within the reach of those who suppose it than they are of other men.

QUESTIONS

1. Is "Man is a work of nature" a statement of fact or an expression of faith? Explain the consequences of your classification of the sentence.
2. Compare Holbach's conception of nature with that of Joseph Butler, the author of the preceding selection. To what extent are their views compatible? Does Holbach's personification of nature tell against the tenability of his views?
3. What is the distinction between moral man and physical man, and why does Holbach think that "moral man" is an abuse of terms?
4. Is Holbach's claim that man is a machine an inductive generalization or is it a recommendation that we look at man in a certain way? What are the consequences of your answer?
5. How does Holbach's claim that man is subject to the laws of nature lead to the view that human actions are determined? How comprehensive is Holbach's determinism? Try to construct a refutation of his determinism.
6. How does Holbach criticize the notion of a human soul? How may his criticisms be answered?

7. How does Holbach argue against the notion of human immortality? How might Butler criticize Holbach's views? Is the issue decidable by making some additional observations? What does your answer to this last question imply about the issue of human immortality?

16. DAVID HUME

(1711–76)

The Self

(A general introductory note on Hume may be found on page 116.)

The problem of personal identity is the problem of explaining how the self, or mind, remains the same, so that throughout the many changes which someone undergoes, we may still say that he is the same person. Hume states the problem in accordance with his own philosophical viewpoint, and the defects in his solution of the problem, defects which Hume himself recognizes, are directly attributable to that viewpoint.

Hume, in a restatement of Locke's theory of knowledge, holds that our knowledge amounts ultimately to sense impressions and ideas that are copies of sense impressions. Hume believes that for a word to be meaningful it must stand for an impression or set of impressions or for an idea that can ultimately be traced back to impres-

sions. When he searches for the meaning of "self," however, he can find no distinctive self-perception. Therefore, he concludes, there is no self. The reader is invited to subject this whole procedure to a critical examination.

Unsuccessful in his search for the self, Hume tries to account for our belief in a persistent self. However, starting from his description of the mind as an assemblage of ever-changing, always different perceptions, he fails by his own admission to offer an intelligible account of personal identity. The following selection contains both Hume's effort to account for personal identity and his own later commentary on it.

This reading is drawn from *A Treatise of Human Nature,* Book I, Part IV, Section VI, "Of Personal Identity," and the Appendix.

OF PERSONAL IDENTITY

There are some philosophers, who imagine we are every moment intimately conscious of what we call our SELF; that we feel its existence and its continuance in existence; and are certain, beyond the evidence of a demonstration, both of its perfect identity and simplicity. The strongest sensation, the most violent passion, say they, instead of distracting us from this view, only fix it the more intensely, and make us consider their influence on *self* either by their pain or pleasure. To attempt a farther proof of this were to weaken its evidence; since no proof can be deriv'd from any fact, of which we are so intimately conscious; nor is there any thing, of which we can be certain, if we doubt of this.

Unluckily all these positive assertions are contrary to that very experience, which is pleaded for them, nor have we any idea of *self,* after the manner it is here explain'd. For from what impression cou'd this idea be deriv'd? This question 'tis impossible to answer without a manifest contradiction and absurdity; and yet 'tis a question, which must necessarily be answer'd, if we wou'd have the idea of self pass for clear and intelligible. It must be some one impression, that gives rise to every real idea. But self or person is not any one impression, but that to which our several impressions and ideas are suppos'd to have a reference. If any impression gives rise to the idea of self, that impression must continue invariably the same, thro' the whole course of our lives; since self is suppos'd to exist after that manner. But there is no impression constant and invariable. Pain and pleasure, grief and joy, passions and sensations succeed each other, and never all exist at the same time. It cannot, therefore, be from any of these impressions, or from any other, that the idea of self is deriv'd; and consequently there is no such idea.

But farther, what must become of all our particular perceptions upon this hypothesis? All these are different, and distinguishable, and separable from each other, and may be separately consider'd, and may exist separately, and have no need of any thing to support their existence. After what manner, therefore, do they belong to self; and how are they connected with it? For my part, when I enter most intimately into what I call *myself,* I always stumble on some particular perception or other, of heat or cold, light or shade, love or hatred, pain or pleasure. I never can catch *myself* at any time without a perception, and never can observe any thing but the perception. When my perceptions are remov'd for any time, as by sound sleep; so long am I insensible of *myself,* and may truly be said not to exist. And were all my perceptions remov'd by death, and cou'd I neither think, nor feel, nor see, nor love, nor hate after the dissolution of my body, I shou'd be entirely annihilated, nor do I conceive what is farther requisite to make me a perfect non-entity. If any one upon serious and unprejudic'd reflexion, thinks he has a different notion of *himself,* I must confess I can reason no longer with him. All I can allow him is, that he may be in the right as well as I, and that we are essentially different in this particular. He may, perhaps, perceive something simple and continu'd, which he calls *himself;* tho' I am certain there is no such principle in me.

But setting aside some metaphysicians of this kind, I may venture to affirm of the rest of mankind, that they are nothing but a bundle or collection of different perceptions, which succeed each other with an inconceivable rapidity, and are in a perpetual flux and movement. Our eyes cannot turn in their sockets without varying our perceptions. Our thought is still more variable than our sight; and all our other senses and faculties contribute to this change; nor is there any single power of the soul, which remains un-alterably the same, perhaps for one moment. The mind is a kind of theatre, where several perceptions successively make their appearance; pass, re-pass, glide away, and mingle in an infinite variety of postures and situations. There is properly no *simplicity* in it at one time, nor *identity* in different; whatever natural propension we may have to imagine that simplicity and identity. The comparison of the theatre must not mislead us. They are the successive perceptions only, that constitute the mind; nor have we the most distant notion of the place, where these scenes are represented, or of the materials, of which it is compos'd.

[Having sought the self as something simple and continued, and finding only perceptions in perpetual flux, Hume tries to account for our attributing identity to the changing bundle of perceptions. He reminds us that we attribute identity through time to an object which we see at different times, even though, since we are ignorant of what happens during the intervening times, we ought to say no more than that we have seen a series of similar objects. The great similarity in the members of the series, however, makes it easy for the imagination to pass from one member to another; and we say, of the object we see at different times, that it is the same object at all times. Hume then argues that this sort of identity, albeit fictitious, is the kind which we attribute to the successive perceptions that constitute the mind.]

We now proceed to explain the nature of *personal identity,* which has become so great a question in philosophy, especially of late years in *England,* where all the abstruser sciences are study'd with a peculiar ardour and appli-cation. And here 'tis evident, the same method of reasoning must be con-tinu'd, which has so successfully explain'd the identity of plants, and animals, and ships, and houses, and of all the compounded and changeable produc-tions either of art or nature. The identity, which we ascribe to the mind of man, is only a fictitious one, and of a like kind with that which we ascribe to vegetables and animal bodies. It cannot, therefore, have a different origin, but must proceed from a like operation of the imagination upon like objects.

But lest this argument shou'd not convince the reader; tho' in my opinion perfectly decisive; let him weigh the following reasoning, which is still closer and more immediate. 'Tis evident, that the identity, which we attribute to the human mind, however perfect we may imagine it to be, is not able to run the several different perceptions into one, and make them lose their characters of distinction and difference, which are essential to them. 'Tis still true, that every distinct perception, which enters into the composition of the mind, is a distinct existence, and is different, and distinguishable, and separable from every other perception, either contemporary or successive. But, as, notwithstanding this distinction and separability, we suppose the whole train of perceptions to be united by identity, a question naturally arises concerning this relation of identity; whether it be something that really binds our several perceptions together, or only associates their ideas in the imagination. That is, in other words, whether in pronouncing concerning the identity of a person, we observe some real bond among his perceptions, or only feel one among the ideas we form of them. This question we might easily decide, if we wou'd recollect what has been already prov'd at large, that the understanding never observes any real connexion among objects, and that even the union of cause and effect, when strictly examin'd, resolves itself into a customary association of ideas. For from thence it evidently follows, that identity is nothing really belonging to these different perceptions, and uniting them together; but is merely a quality, which we attribute to them, because of the union of their ideas in the imagination, when we reflect upon them. Now the only qualities, which can give ideas an union in the imagination, are these three relations above-mention'd.[1] These are the uniting principles in the ideal world, and without them every distinct object is separable by the mind, and may be separately consider'd, and appears not to have any more connexion with any other object, than if disjoin'd by the greatest difference and remoteness. 'Tis, therefore, on some of these three relations of resemblance, contiguity and causation, that identity depends; and as the very essence of these relations consists in their producing an easy transition of ideas; it follows, that our notions of personal identity, proceed entirely from the smooth and uninterrupted progress of the thought along a train of connected ideas, according to the principles above-explain'd.

The only question, therefore, which remains, is, by what relations this uninterrupted progress of our thought is produc'd, when we consider the successive existence of a mind or thinking person. And here 'tis evident we must confine ourselves to resemblance and causation, and must drop contiguity, which has little or no influence in the present case.

To begin with *resemblance;* suppose we cou'd see clearly into the breast of another, and observe that succession of perceptions, which constitutes his mind or thinking principle, and suppose that he always preserves the memory of a considerable part of past perceptions; 'tis evident that nothing cou'd more contribute to the bestowing a relation on this succession amidst all its variations. For what is the memory but a faculty, by which we raise up the images of past perceptions? And as an image necessarily resembles its object, must not the frequent placing of these resembling perceptions in the chain of thought, convey the imagination more easily from one link to another, and make the whole seem like the continuance of one object? In this particular, then, the memory not only discovers the identity, but also contributes to its production, by producing the relation of resemblance among the perceptions. The case is the same whether we consider ourselves or others.

---

[1] Resemblance, Contiguity, and Causation.—Eds.

As to *causation;* we may observe, that the true idea of the human mind, is to consider it as a system of different perceptions or different existences, which are link'd together by the relation of cause and effect, and mutually produce, destroy, influence, and modify each other. Our impressions give rise to their correspondent ideas; and these ideas in their turn produce other impressions. One thought chaces another, and draws after it a third, by which it is expell'd in its turn. In this respect, I cannot compare the soul more properly to any thing than to a republic or commonwealth, in which the several members are united by the reciprocal ties of government and subordination, and give rise to other persons, who propagate the same republic in the incessant changes of its parts. And as the same individual republic may not only change its members, but also its laws and constitutions; in like manner the same person may vary his character and disposition, as well as his impressions and ideas, without losing his identity. Whatever changes he endures, his several parts are still connected by the relation of causation. And in this view our identity with regard to the passions serves to corroborate that with regard to the imagination, by the making our distant perceptions influence each other, and by giving us a present concern for our past or future pains or pleasures.

As memory alone acquaints us with the continuance and extent of this succession of perceptions, 'tis to be consider'd, upon that account chiefly, as the source of personal identity. Had we no memory, we never shou'd have any notion of causation, nor consequently of that chain of causes and effects, which constitute our self or person. But having once acquir'd this notion of causation from the memory, we can extend the same chain of causes, and consequently the identity of our persons beyond our memory, and can comprehend times, and circumstances, and actions, which we have entirely forgot, but suppose in general to have existed. For how few of our past actions are there, of which we have any memory? Who can tell me, for instance, what were his thoughts and actions on the first of *January* 1715, the 11th of *March* 1719, and the 3d of *August* 1733? Or will he affirm, because he has entirely forgot the incidents of these days, that the present self is not the same person with the self of that time; and by that means overturn all the most establish'd notions of personal identity? In this view, therefore, memory does not so much *produce* as *discover* personal identity, by shewing us the relation of cause and effect among our different perceptions. 'Twill be incumbent on those, who affirm that memory produces entirely our personal identity, to give a reason why we can thus extend our identity beyond our memory.

The whole of this doctrine leads us to a conclusion, which is of great importance in the present affair, *viz.* that all the nice and subtile questions concerning personal identity can never possibly be decided, and are to be regarded rather as grammatical than as philosophical difficulties. Identity depends on the relations of ideas; and these relations produce identity, by means of that easy transition they occasion. But as the relations, and the easiness of the transition may diminish by insensible degrees, we have no just standard, by which we can decide any dispute concerning the time, when they acquire or lose a title to the name of identity. All the disputes concerning the identity of connected objects are merely verbal, except so far as the relation of parts gives rise to some fiction or imaginary principle of union, as we have already observ'd.

What I have said concerning the first origin and uncertainty of our notion of identity, as apply'd to the human mind, may be extended with little or no variation to that of *simplicity*. An object, whose different co-existent parts are bound together by a close relation, operates upon the imagination after much the same manner as one perfectly simple and indivisible, and requires not a much greater stretch of thought in order to its conception. From this similarity of operation we attribute a simplicity to it, and feign a principle of union as the support of this simplicity, and the center of all the different parts and qualities of the object.

[After Hume had published the above argument, he doubted that he had given sufficient weight to the distinctiveness and separability of each perception from all others. These characteristics of perceptions seemed to tell so strongly against his argument for personal identity that he felt compelled to include in the Appendix to the *Treatise* the following critical examination of his account of our belief in personal identity.]

I had entertain'd some hopes, that however deficient our theory of the intellectual world might be, it wou'd be free from those contradictions, and absurdities, which seem to attend every explication, that human reason can give of the material world. But upon a more strict review of the section concerning *personal identity,* I find myself involv'd in such a labyrinth, that, I must confess, I neither know how to correct my former opinions, nor how to render them consistent. If this be not a good *general* reason for scepticism, 'tis at least a sufficient one (if I were not already abundantly supplied) for me to entertain a diffidence and modesty in all my decisions. I shall propose the arguments on both sides, beginning with those that induc'd me to deny the strict and proper identity and simplicity of a self or thinking being.

When we talk of *self* or *substance,* we must have an idea annex'd to these terms, otherwise they are altogether unintelligible. Every idea is deriv'd from preceding impressions; and we have no impression of self or substance, as something simple and individual. We have, therefore, no idea of them in that sense.

Whatever is distinct, is distinguishable; and whatever is distinguishable, is separable by the thought or imagination. All perceptions are distinct. They are, therefore, distinguishable, and separable, and may be conceiv'd as separately existent, and may exist separately, without any contradiction or absurdity.

When I view this table and that chimney, nothing is present to me but particular perceptions, which are of a like nature with all the other perceptions. This is the doctrine of philosophers. But this table, which is present to me, and that chimney, may and do exist separately. This is the doctrine of the vulgar, and implies no contradiction. There is no contradiction, therefore, in extending the same doctrine to all the perceptions.

In general, the following reasoning seems satisfactory. All ideas are borrow'd from preceding perceptions. Our ideas of objects, therefore, are deriv'd from that source. Consequently no proposition can be intelligible or consistent with regard to objects, which is not so with regard to perceptions. But 'tis intelligible and consistent to say, that objects exist distinct and independent, without any common *simple* substance or subject of inhesion. This proposition, therefore, can never be absurd with regard to perceptions.

When I turn my reflexion on *myself,* I never can perceive this *self* without some one or more perceptions; nor can I ever perceive any thing but the perceptions. 'Tis the composition of these, therefore, which forms the self.

We can conceive a thinking being to have either many or few perceptions. Suppose the mind to be reduc'd even below the life of an oyster. Suppose it to have only one perception, as of thirst or hunger. Consider it in that situation. Do you conceive any thing but merely that perception? Have you any notion of *self* or *substance?* If not, the addition of other perceptions can never give you that notion.

The annihilation, which some people suppose to follow upon death, and which entirely destroys this self, is nothing but an extinction of all particular perceptions; love and hatred, pain and pleasure, thought and sensation. These therefore must be the same with self; since the one cannot survive the other.

Is *self* the same with *substance?* If it be, how can that question have place, concerning the subsistence of self, under a change of substance? If they be distinct, what is the difference betwixt them? For my part, I have a notion of neither, when conceiv'd distinct from particular perceptions.

Philosophers begin to be reconcil'd to the principle, *that we have no idea of external substance, distinct from the ideas of particular qualities.* This must pave the way for a like principle with regard to the mind, *that we have no notion of it, distinct from the particular perceptions.*

So far I seem to be attended with sufficient evidence. But having thus loosen'd all our particular perceptions, when I proceed to explain the principle of connexion, which binds them together, and makes us attribute to them a real simplicity and identity; I am sensible, that my account is very defective, and that nothing but the seeming evidence of the precedent reasonings cou'd have induc'd me to receive it. If perceptions are distinct existences, they form a whole only by being connected together. But no connexions among distinct existences are ever discoverable by human understanding. We only *feel* a connexion or determination of the thought, to pass from one object to another. It follows, therefore, that the thought alone finds personal identity, when reflecting on the train of past perceptions, that compose a mind, the ideas of them are felt to be connected together, and naturally introduce each other. However extraordinary this conclusion may seem, it need not surprize us. Most philosophers seem inclin'd to think, that personal identity *arises* from consciousness; and consciousness is nothing but a reflected thought or perception. The present philosophy, therefore, has so far a promising aspect. But all my hopes vanish, when I come to explain the principles, that unite our successive perceptions in our thought or consciousness. I cannot discover any theory, which gives me satisfaction on this head.

In short there are two principles, which I cannot render consistent; nor is it in my power to renounce either of them, viz. *that all our distinct perceptions are distinct existences,* and *that the mind never perceives any real connexion among distinct existences.* Did our perceptions either inhere in something simple and individual, or did the mind perceive some real connexion among them, there wou'd be no difficulty in the case. For my part, I must plead the privilege of a sceptic, and confess, that this difficulty is too hard for my understanding. I pretend not, however, to pronounce it absolutely insuperable. Others, perhaps, or myself, upon more mature reflexions, may discover some hypothesis, that will reconcile those contradictions.

QUESTIONS

1. What is Hume looking for when he looks for the self? What is his method of looking, and how may it be criticized?
2. What does Hume mean when he says, "I never can catch *myself* at any time without a perception, and never can observe anything but the perception"? What account is to be given of "I" in Hume's statement?
3. How may Hume's account of the self as "a bundle or collection of different perceptions" be criticized?
4. In Hume's account of the identity of the mind, what part is played by resemblance, and what part by causation? How tenable is Hume's model of the mind as a republic or commonwealth?
5. What part is played by memory in the production of personal identity?
6. What is Hume's distinction between grammatical and philosophical difficulties?
7. Evaluate the following objection to Hume's account of our belief in personal identity: I believe that the car I am driving today is the same car I drove yesterday because the "two" cars resemble each other strongly. But the perceptions of the mind are so varied that there can be nothing like as strong a resemblance or even similarity among them. Therefore, how can Hume cite resemblance among perceptions as a source of personal identity?
8. Why does Hume find the principle that all our distinct perceptions are distinct existences an embarrassment to his account of the self?
9. What is the substance theory of the self? Why does Hume find it unsatisfactory, and on what grounds does he believe that it may be abandoned?
10. Evaluate the following objection to Hume's account of the self: Hume reduces the self, or mind, to a bundle of perceptions. But he does not see that the word "perceptions" implies a perceiver; and he fails utterly to account for the perceiver of that bundle of perceptions.

17 . GILBERT RYLE

(b. 1900)

The Self and the Systematic Elusiveness of "I"

(For a brief biographical note on Professor Ryle see page 89.)

In this reading, Professor Ryle argues that there is no mysteriously undiscoverable entity called the self. He explains our urge to hunt for such an entity, by our thinking of the word "I" as a name. But when we do hunt for the entity which "I" names, we find the "I" of our talk about ourselves systematically eluding us. He dispels this mystery by showing that our knowledge of ourselves is like our knowledge of other people, but requiring greater sophistication in its acquisition. The reader will find that the sophistication in our acquiring knowledge of ourselves both explains the elusiveness of "I" and shows it to be necessary.

THE SELF

Not only theorists but also quite unsophisticated people, including young children, find perplexities in the notion of 'I'. Children sometimes puzzle their heads with such questions as, 'What would it be like if I became you and you became me?' and 'Where was I before I began?' Theologians have been exercised over the question 'What is it in an individual which is saved or damned?', and philosophers have speculated whether 'I' denotes a peculiar and separate substance and in what consists my indivisible and continuing identity.   .   .   .

The enigmas that I have in mind all turn on what I shall call the 'systematic elusiveness' of the concept of 'I'. When a child, like Kim, having no theoretical commitments or equipment, first asks himself, 'Who or What am I?' he does not ask it from a desire to know his own surname, age, sex, nationality or position in the form. He knows all his ordinary personalia. He feels that there is something else in the background for which his 'I' stands, a something which has still to be described after all his ordinary personalia have been listed. He also feels, very vaguely, that whatever it is that his 'I' stands for, it is something very important and quite unique, unique in the sense that neither it, nor anything like it, belongs to anyone else. There *could* only be one of it. Pronouns like 'you', 'she' and 'we' feel quite unmystifying, while 'I' feels mystifying. And it feels mystifying, anyhow in part, because the more the child tries to put his finger on what 'I' stands for, the less does he succeed in doing so. He can catch only its coat-tails; it itself is always and obdurately a pace ahead of its coat-tails. Like the shadow of one's own head, it will not wait to be jumped on. And yet it is never very far ahead; indeed, sometimes it seems not to be ahead of the pursuer at all. It evades capture by lodging itself inside the very muscles of the pursuer. It is too near even to be within arm's reach.

Theorists have found themselves mocked in a similar way by the concept of 'I'. Even Hume confesses that, when he has tried to sketch all the items of his experience, he has found nothing there to answer to the word 'I', and yet he is not satisfied that there does not remain something more and something important, without which his sketch fails to describe his experience.

Other epistemologists have felt similar qualms. Should I, or should I not, put my knowing self down on my list of the sorts of things that I can have knowledge of? If I say 'no', it seems to reduce my knowing self to a theoretically infertile mystery, yet if I say 'yes', it seems to reduce the fishing-net to one of the fishes which it itself catches. It seems hazardous either to allow or to deny that the judge can be put into the dock.

I shall try before long to explain this systematic elusiveness of the notion of 'I' and with it the apparent non-parallelism between the notion of 'I' and the notions of 'you' and 'he'. But it is expedient first to consider some points which hold good of all personal pronouns alike.

People, including philosophers, tend to raise their questions about what constitutes a self by asking what the words 'I' and 'you' are the names of. They are familiar with the river of which 'Thames' is the name and with the dog called 'Fido'. They are also familiar with the persons of whom their acquaintances' and their own surnames are the surnames. They then feel vaguely that since 'I' and 'you' are not public surnames, they must be names of another and queer sort and must in consequence be the names of some extra individuals hidden away behind or inside the persons who are known abroad by their ordinary surnames and Christian names. As pronouns are not registered at Somerset House, their owners must be different, somehow, from the owners of the Christian and surnames which are registered there. But this way of broaching the question is mistaken from the start. Certainly 'I' and 'you' are not regular proper names like 'Fido' and 'Thames', but they are not irregular proper names either. They are not proper names, or names at all, any more than 'today' is an ephemeral name of the current day. Gratuitous mystification begins from the moment that we start to peer around for the beings named by our pronouns. Sentences containing pronouns do, of course, mention identifiable people, but the way in which the people mentioned are identified by pronouns is quite different from the way in which they are identified by proper names.

This difference can be provisionally indicated in the following manner. There is a class of words (which for ease of reference may be called 'index words') that indicate to the hearer or reader the particular thing, episode, person, place or moment referred to. Thus 'now' is an index word which indicates to the hearer of the sentence 'the train is now going over the bridge' the particular moment of the crossing. The word 'now' can, of course, be used at any moment of any day or night, but it does not mean what is meant by 'at any moment of any day or night'. It indicates that particular moment at which the hearer is intended to hear the word 'now' being uttered. The moment at which the train crosses the bridge is indicated by the utterance at that moment of the word 'now'. The moment at which 'now' is breathed is the moment which it indicates. In a partly similar way the word 'that' is often used to indicate the particular thing at which the speaker's index finger is pointing at the moment when he breathes out the word 'that'. 'Here' indicates, sometimes, that particular place from which the speaker propagates the noise 'here' into the surrounding air; and the page indicated by the phrase 'this page' is the page of which the printed word 'this' occupies a part. Other index words indicate indirectly. 'Yesterday' indicates the day before that on which it is uttered, or printed in a newspaper; 'then', in certain uses, indicates a moment or period standing in a specified relation with that in which it is heard or read.

Now pronouns like 'I' and 'you' are, anyhow sometimes, direct index words, while others, like 'he' and 'they' and, in some uses, 'we' are indirect index words. 'I' can indicate the particular person from whom the noise 'I', or the written mark 'I', issues; 'you' can indicate the one person who hears me say 'you', or it can indicate that person, whoever he is (and there may be several) who reads the 'you' that I write, or have printed. In all cases the physical occurrence of an index word is bodily annexed to what the word indicates. Hence 'you' is not a queer name that I and others sometimes give you; it is an index word which, in its particular conversational setting, indicates to you just who it is to whom I am addressing my remarks. 'I' is not an extra name for an extra being; it indicates, when I say or write it, the same individual who can also be addressed by the proper name 'Gilbert Ryle'. 'I' is not an alias for 'Gilbert Ryle'; it indicates the person whom 'Gilbert Ryle' names, when Gilbert Ryle uses 'I'.

But this is far from being the whole story. We have now to notice that we use our pronouns, as well as our proper names, in a wide variety of different ways. Further mystifications have arisen from the detection, without the comprehension of contrasts between such different uses of 'I' and, to a lesser extent, of 'you' and 'he'.

In the sentence 'I am warming myself before the fire', the word 'myself' could be replaced by 'my body' without spoiling the sense; but the pronoun

'I' could not be replaced by 'my body' without making nonsense. Similarly the sentence 'Cremate me after I am gone' says nothing self-annihilating, since the 'me' and the 'I' are being used in different senses. So sometimes we can, and sometimes we cannot, paraphrase the first personal pronoun by 'my body'. There are even some cases where I can talk about a part of my body, but cannot use 'I' or 'me' for it. If my hair were scorched in a fire, I could say 'I was not scorched; only my hair was', though I could never say 'I was not scorched; only my face and hands were'. A part of the body which is insensitive and cannot be moved at will is mine, but it is not part of me. Conversely, mechanical auxiliaries to the body, such as motor-cars and walking-sticks, can be spoken of with 'I' and 'me'; as in 'I collided with the pillar-box', which means the same thing as 'the car which I was driving (or which I owned and was having driven for me in my presence) collided with the pillar-box'.

Let us now consider some contexts in which 'I' and 'me' can certainly not be replaced by 'my body' or 'my leg'. If I say 'I am annoyed that I was cut in the collision', while I might accept the substitution of 'my leg was cut' for 'I was cut', I should not allow 'I am annoyed' to be reconstructed in any such way. It would be similarly absurd to speak of 'my head remembering', 'my brain doing long division', or 'my body battling with fatigue'. Perhaps it is because of the absurdity of such collocations that so many people have felt driven to describe a person as an association between a body and a non-body.

However, we are not yet at the end of our list of elasticities in the uses of 'I' and 'me'; for we find further contrasts breaking out between uses of the first personal pronoun in which none can be paraphrased by mere references to the body. It makes perfect sense to say that I caught myself just beginning to dream, but not that I caught my body beginning to dream, or that my body caught me doing so; and it makes sense to say that a child is telling himself a fairy-story, but nonsense to make his body either narrator or auditor.

Contrasts of these types, perhaps above all the contrasts advertised in descriptions of exercises of self-control, have induced many preachers and some thinkers to speak as if an ordinary person is really some sort of committee or team of persons, all laced together inside one skin; as if the thinking and vetoing 'I' were one person, and the greedy or lazy 'I' were another. But this sort of picture is obviously of no use. Part of what we mean by 'person' is someone who is capable of catching himself beginning to dream, of telling himself stories and of curbing his own greed. So the suggested reduction of a person to a team of persons would merely multiply the number of persons without explaining how it is that one and the same person can be both narrator and auditor, or both vigilant and dreamy, both scorched and amazed at being scorched. The beginning of the required explanation is that in such a statement as 'I caught myself beginning to dream', the two pronouns are not names of different persons, since they are not names at all, but that they are index words being used in different senses in different sorts of context, just as we saw was the case with the statement 'I am warming myself by the fire' (though this is a different difference of sense from the other). In case it seems unplausible to say that inside one sentence the twice used first personal pronoun can both indicate the same person and also have two different senses, it is enough for the moment to point out that the same thing can happen even with ordinary proper names and personal titles. The sentence 'after her wedding Miss Jones will no longer be Miss Jones' does not say that the particular woman will cease to be herself, or cease to be the sort of person she now is, but only that she will have changed her name and status; and the sentence 'after Napoleon returned to France, he was Napoleon no longer' might mean only that his qualities of generalship had altered, and is obviously analogous to the familiar expression 'I am not myself'. The statements 'I was just beginning to dream' and 'I caught myself just beginning to dream' are statements of logically different types, and it follows from their being of different types that the pronoun 'I' is being used with a different logical force in the two sentences.

In considering specifically human behaviour—behaviour, that is, which is unachieved by animals, infants and idiots—we should for several reasons notice the fact that some sorts of actions are in one way or another concerned with, or are operations upon, other actions. When one person retaliates upon another, scoffs at him, replies to him or plays hide-and-seek with him, his actions have to do, in one way or another, with certain actions on the part of the other; in a sense to be specified later, the performance of the former involves the thought of the latter. An action on the part of one agent could not be one of spying or applauding, unless it had to do with the actions of another agent; nor could I behave as a customer, unless you or someone else behaved as a seller. One man must give evidence if another is to cross-examine him; some people must be on the stage, if others are to be dramatic critics. It will sometimes be convenient to use the title 'higher order actions' to denote those the descriptions of which involve the oblique mention of other actions.

Some, but not all, higher order actions influence the agent dealt with. If I merely comment on your actions behind your back, my comment has to do with your actions in the sense that my performance of my act involves the thought of your performance of yours; but it does not modify your actions. This is especially clear where the commentator or critic is operating after the death of the agent on whose doings he passes his judgments. The historian cannot change Napoleon's conduct of the battle of Waterloo. On the other hand, the moment and the methods of my attacking do affect the timing and the techniques of your defence, and what I sell has a lot to do with what you buy.

Next, when I speak of the actions of one agent having to do with those of another, I do not exclude those actions which are performed under the mistaken impression that the other is doing something which he is not really doing. The child who applauds my skill in pretending to be asleep, though I have in fact really fallen asleep, is doing something which, in the required sense, presupposes that I am pretending; and Robinson Crusoe really is having conversationally to do with his parrot, if he believes, or half believes, that the bird follows what he says, even if this belief is false.

Finally, there are many kinds of dealings which are concerned with subsequent, or even merely possible, or probable, actions. When I brive you to vote for me, your voting has not yet taken place and may never take place. A reference to your vote enters into the description of my bribe, but the reference must be of the pattern 'that you shall vote for me', and not of the pattern 'because you did vote', or 'because I thought that you did vote for me'. In the same way my talking to you presupposes only in this way your understanding and agreeing with me, namely that I talk in order that you may understand and agree with me.

So when John Doe counters, detects, reports, parodies, exploits, applauds, mocks, abets, copies or interprets something done by Richard Roe, any description of his action would have to embody an oblique mention of the thing done, or supposed to be done, by Richard Roe; whereas no such description of John Doe's behaviour would have to enter into the description of that of Richard Roe. To talk about John Doe's detection or mockery would involve, but not be involved in, talking about what he had been detecting or mocking, and this is what is meant by saying that John Doe's action is of a higher order than that of Richard Roe. By 'higher' I do not mean 'loftier'. Blackmailing a deserter is of a higher order than his desertion, and advertising is of a higher order than selling. Recollecting the doing of a kindness is not nobler than the doing of it, but it is of a higher order.

It may be hygienic to remember that though the actions of reporting or commenting on the actions of others behind their backs is one species of higher order action, it has no special priority over the other ways of dealing with these actions. Keeping an academic tally of what Richard Roe does is only one way in which John Doe takes steps about Richard Roe's steps. The construction and public or private use of sentences in the indicative is not, as intellectualists love to think, either John Doe's indispensable first move or his Utopian last move. But this point requires us to consider the sense in which performing a higher order action 'involves the thought of' the corresponding lower order action. It does not mean that if, for example, I am to mimic your gestures, I must do two things, namely both verbally describe your gestures to myself and produce gestures complying with the terms employed in that description. Telling myself about your gestures would in itself be a higher order performance, and one which would equally involve the thought of your gestures. The phrase 'involve the thought of' does not signify a causal transaction, or the concomitance of a process of one sort with a process of another sort. As commenting on your gestures, to be commenting, must itself *be* thinking in a certain way of your gestures, so mimicking them, to be mimicry and not mere replica, must itself *be* thinking in a certain way of your gestures. But of course this is a strained sense of 'thinking'; it does not denote any sort of pondering or entail the enunciation of any propositions. It means that I must know what I am doing and, since what I am doing is mimicking, I must know the gestures you made and be using that knowledge, using it in the mimicking way and not in the reporting or commenting way.

Higher order actions are not instinctive. Any one of them can be done efficiently or inefficiently, appropriately or inappropriately, intelligently or stupidly. Children have to learn how to perform them. They have to learn how to resist, parry and retaliate, how to forestall, give way and co-operate, how to exchange and haggle, reward and punish. They have to learn to make jokes against others and to see some jokes against themselves, to obey orders and give them, make requests and grant them, receive marks and award them. They have to learn to compose and follow reports, descriptions and commentaries; to understand and to give criticisms, to accept, reject, correct and compose verdicts, catechise and be catechised. Not least (and also not soonest) they have to learn to keep to themselves things which they are inclined to divulge. Reticence is of a higher order than unreticence.

My object in drawing attention to these truisms of the playroom and the schoolroom can now be seen. At a certain stage the child discovers the trick of directing higher order acts upon his own lower order acts. Having been separately victim and author of jokes, coercions, catechisms, criticisms and mimicries in the inter-personal dealings between others and himself, he finds out how to play both roles at once. He has listened to stories before, and he has told stories before, but now he tells stories to his own enthralled ear. He has been detected in insincerities and he has detected the insincerities of others, but now he applies the techniques of detection to his own insincerities. He finds that he can give orders to himself with such authority that he sometimes obeys them, even when reluctant to do so. Self-suasion and self-dissuasion become more or less effective. He learns in adolescence to apply to his own behaviour most of those higher order methods of dealing with the young that are regularly practised by adults. He is then said to be growing up.

Moreover, just as he had earlier acquired not only the ability, but also the inclination to direct higher order acts upon the acts of others, so he now becomes prone, as well as competent, to do the same upon his own behaviour; and just as he had earlier learned to cope not only with the particular performances of others, but also with their dispositions to conduct such performances, so he now becomes in some degree both able and ready to take steps, theoretical and practical, about his own habits, motives and abilities. Nor are his own higher order performances, or his dispositions to perform them, in any way exempted from just the same treatment. For any performance of any order, it is always possible that there should be performed a variety of higher order actions about it. If I ridicule something done by you, or by myself, I can, but usually do not go on to pass a verbal comment on my amusement, apologise for it, or let others into the joke; and then I can go on to applaud or reproach myself for doing so, and make a note in my diary that I have done this.

. . .

THE SYSTEMATIC ELUSIVENESS OF 'I'

We are now in a position to account for the systematic elusiveness of the notion of 'I', and the partial non-parallelism between it and the notion of 'you' or 'he'. To concern oneself about oneself in any way, theoretical or practical, is to perform a higher order act, just as it is to concern oneself about anybody else. To try, for example, to describe what one has just done, or is now doing, is to comment upon a step which is not itself, save *per accidens*, one of commenting. But the operation which is the commenting is not, and cannot be, the step on which that commentary is being made. Nor can an act of ridiculing be its own butt. A higher order action cannot be the action upon which it is performed. So my commentary on my performances must always be silent about one performance, namely itself, and this performance can be the target only of another commentary. Self-commentary, self-ridicule and self-admonition are logically condemned to eternal penultimacy. Yet nothing that is left out of any particular commentary or admonition is privileged thereby to escape comment or admonition for ever. On the contrary it may be the target of the very next comment or rebuke.

The point may be illustrated in this way. A singing-master might criticize the accents or notes of a pupil by mimicking with exaggerations each word that the pupil sang; and if the pupil sang slowly enough, the master could parody each word sung by the pupil before the next came to be uttered. But then, in a mood of humility, the singing-master tries to criticise his own singing in the same way, and more than that to mimic with exaggerations each word that he utters, including those that he utters in self-parody. It is at once clear, first, that he can never get beyond the very earliest word of his song and, second, that at any given moment he has uttered one noise which has yet to be mimicked—and it makes no difference how rapidly he chases his notes with mimicries of them. He can, in principle, never catch more than the coat-tails of the object of his pursuit, since a word cannot be a parody of itself. None the less, there is no word that he sings which remains unparodied; he is always a day late for the fair, but every day he reaches the place of yesterday's fair. He never succeeds in jumping on to the shadow of his own head, yet he is never more than one jump behind.

An ordinary reviewer may review a book, while a second order reviewer criticises reviews of the book. But the second order review is not a criticism of itself. It can only be criticised in a further third order review. Given complete editorial patience, any review of any order could be published, though at no stage would all the reviews have received critical notices. Nor can every act of a diarist be the topic of a record in his diary; for the last entry made in his diary still demands that the making of it should in its turn be chronicled.

This, I think, explains the feeling that my last year's self, or my yesterday's self, could in principle be exhaustively described and accounted for, and that your past or present self could be exhaustively described and accounted for by me, but that my today's self perpetually slips out of any hold of it that I tried to take. It also explains the apparent non-parallelism between the notion of 'I' and that of 'you', without construing the elusive residuum as any kind of ultimate mystery.

. . .

This general conclusion that any performance can be the concern of a higher order performance, but cannot be the concern of itself, is connected with what was said earlier about the special functioning of index words, such as 'now', 'you' and 'I'. An 'I' sentence indicates whom in particular it is about by being itself uttered or written by someone in particular. 'I' indicates the person who utters it. So, when a person utters an 'I' sentence, his utterance of it may be part of a higher order performance, namely one, perhaps of self-reporting, self-exhortation or self-commiseration, and this performance itself is not dealt with in the operation which it itself is. Even if the person is, for special speculative purposes, momentarily concentrating on the Problem of the Self, he has failed and knows that he has failed to catch more than the flying coat-tails of that which he was pursuing. His quarry was the hunter.

To conclude, there is nothing mysterious or occult about the range of higher order acts and attitudes, which are apt to be inadequately covered by the umbrella-title 'self-consciousness'. They are the same in kind as the higher order acts and attitudes exhibited in the dealings of people with one another. Indeed the former are only a special application of the latter and are learned first from them. If I perform the third order operation of commenting on a second order act of laughing at myself for a piece of manual awkwardness, I shall indeed use the first personal pronoun in two different ways. I say to myself, or to the company, 'I was laughing at myself for being butterfingered'. But so far from this showing that there are two 'Mes' in my skin, not to speak, yet, of the third one which is still commenting on them, it shows only that I am applying the public two-pronoun idiom in which we talk of her laughing at him; and I am applying this linguistic idiom, because I am applying the method of inter-personal transaction which the idiom is ordinarily employed to describe.

QUESTIONS

1. What does Professor Ryle mean by the term "index word"? What is the difference between direct and indirect index words?
2. Why are pronouns index words and not names? What mysteries are dissolved when pronouns are regarded as index words?
3. What does Ryle mean by higher order action? What does my being capable of higher order action have to do with my self-knowledge? Why is "I" systematically elusive?
4. Compare Ryle's account of the self with Hume's efforts to account for the self. Are they talking about the same thing? If they are, why does Ryle succeed where Hume failed?

SUGGESTED FURTHER READING

INTRODUCTORY STUDIES

Anderson, Alan Ross, ed., *Minds and Machines,* Prentice-Hall, Englewood Cliffs, N. J., 1964. (Anthology.)
Ayer, A. J., *Concept of a Person,* St Martin's, New York, 1963.
Chappell, V. C., ed., *The Philosophy of Mind,* Prentice-Hall, Englewood Cliffs, N. J., 1962. (Anthology.)
Ducasse, C. J., *Nature, Mind and Death,* Open Court, La Salle, Ill., 1951.
Flew, Antony, ed., *Body, Mind and Death,* Macmillan, New York, 1964. (Anthology.)
Gustafson, D. F., ed., *Essays in Philosophical Psychology,* Doubleday, Garden City, N. J., 1964.
Lange, F. A., *History of Materialism,* Routledge and Kegan Paul, London, 1925.
Watson, John B., *Behaviorism,* Routledge and Kegan Paul, London, 1931.

ADVANCED STUDIES

Broad, C. D., *The Mind and Its Place in Nature,* Routledge and Kegan Paul, London, 1925.
Hampshire, Stuart, *Thought and Action,* Chatto and Windus, London, 1959.
Hook, Sidney, ed., *Dimensions of Mind,* New York University Press, New York, 1960. (Anthology.)
Shoemaker, Sidney, *Self-Knowledge and Self-Identity,* Cornell University Press, Ithaca, N. Y., 1963.
Shwayder, David S., *Stratification of Behavior,* Routledge and Kegan Paul, London, 1965.
Strawson, P. F., *Individuals,* Methuen, London, 1959.

Part Two

PHILOSOPHY
AND THE
KNOWLEDGE
OF GOD

We may introduce the problem of knowledge of God by asking the reader to consider the following religious statements. In the Twenty-third Psalm King David says, "The Lord is my shepherd; I shall not want." In many Christian churches the members of the congregation say together, "I believe in God the Father, Creator of Heaven and Earth. . . ." These are statements about God, and are examples of the most important variety of religious statement. Now the philosopher's questions about religious statements are the questions which he asks about any statement: What are the grounds for believing it? and, Do we have good grounds for believing it? But because of the nature of religion, the philosopher's questions must be qualified in certain ways.

First, we must notice that we are confronted not with religion, but with religions. What is more, unlike the sciences, these religions cannot be harmonized in the way in which chemistry and physics support one another. Nor do they treat of different subject matters as geology and biology do. Rather, the relation of religions appears to be such that if someone accepts one, he must reject the others. Because of the magnitude of the subject, we can do nothing here to examine the claims of any one religion over all others. Hence we have thought it best to confine ourselves to the problem of knowledge of God as it has arisen in connection with Christianity and Judaism, the religions which we suppose are most likely to interest our readers.

Judaism and Christianity are theistic, indeed monotheistic religions. A theistic religion is based on a belief in a god or gods. A monotheistic religion is based on a belief in a single god. There are also nontheistic religions, of which Buddhism is an example. By limiting ourselves to the problem of the knowledge of God as it has arisen in connection with Judaism and Christianity, we refrain from the philosophical consideration of the doctrines of other monotheistic religions (such as Islam) and of all polytheistic and nontheistic religions. In addition, we shall limit ourselves to the examination of the problem of knowledge of God as it occurs in those forms of Judaism and Christianity which are based on a belief in a *transcendent* god, that is, a god who is thought of as prior to and apart from the world, who in some sense created the world and can bring about changes in it. Finally, we shall confine our philosophical study to theists' claims to have knowledge of a transcendent god's existence and of the relation of this god to the world. By limiting our study to these claims we are focusing our attention upon the central philosophical problems of theistic religion.

Our first question, then, concerns the way in which statements of a transcendent theistic religion are to be believed. Are they to be believed on grounds similar to those for our belief that $2 + 2 = 4$? Or on grounds similar to those for our belief that fire burns? Or on grounds similar to those for our belief that the earth revolves around the sun? Or are religious statements to be believed on grounds that are neither definitional, nor empirical, nor scientific, but of some fourth kind? The traditional answer to questions about the grounds for religious statements is that for some statements the ground is a divine revelation, and for others the grounds may be reason as well as revelation. The nature of reason and revelation, their relationship in religion, and the range of their use in support of religious statements are examined in the readings by Aquinas and Locke in Chapter 6, "Revelation and Reason." The chapter ends with a modern discussion of the meaning and truth of statements about God.

Proving the existence of a god, and the relationship of that god to the world, are the themes of Chapters 7 and 8. These themes are treated from the point of view of natural, rather than revealed, theology; that is, all conclusions are advanced or rejected by an appeal to reasonable argument rather than to divine revelation. While all of the authors in these chapters appeal to reason, they are not in agreement about the scope of reason in religion. Thus, the reader must consider not only their conclusions about the existence of God, the occurrence of miracles, and the implications of evil, but also their assumptions about what makes a sound argument on these topics.

Chapter 6. Revelation and Reason

When reason is considered as a ground of religious knowledge, the word "reason" is used to mean any attempt by the human mind alone, without divine assistance, to know the truth of a religious statement. It means knowing that a religious statement is true by an inference from either our experience of the world, our conception of God, or our conception of the world. Giving reason a place in religion raises these questions: Can my religious beliefs be confirmed (or disproved) by my experience of the world? and, Can my religious beliefs be proved (or disproved) on the basis of my conceptions of God or of the world?

When we turn to revelation as a basis for religious knowledge, the following questions confront us: What is revelation? How does one know that an experience of one's own or of someone else is a revelation? and, What is the relation of reason to revelation? In this chapter these questions are considered by St. Thomas Aquinas, and John Locke.

Many Christians, who want to find a place for reason in religion, regard Aquinas as the most persuasive defender of the view that reason may support at least some religious truths. Indeed, Aquinas' advocacy of reason is often regarded as the crucial demonstration of the possibility of natural theology, the discovery of truths about God by human faculties alone. Aquinas argues for the possibility of natural theology by pointing out that reason as well as revelation is a gift of God. Its origin, then, is a guarantee of reason's reliability, and we are justified in using it to establish the truth of the statement, "God exists," and of certain statements about God's nature. The success of Aquinas' introduction of reason into religion turns largely on his claim that reason and revelation will never be incompatible because reason cannot be used to determine the authenticity of an alleged revelation. This is the point at which Locke may be found to be in opposition to Aquinas.

Locke holds that when any religious statement is offered to us as a revelation, we may at the very least use reason to ascertain whether the statement is in origin a revelation. What is more, he believes that if the content of the statement is contrary to reason, we have a sufficient case for not counting it as a revelation because God is too good to be the author of unreason. Locke believes that there may be some religious truths above reason, but we leave it to the reader to decide whether truths above reason would be intelligible by Locke's standards of meaningfulness.

The last reading in this chapter, the symposium "Theology and Falsification" by Antony Flew, R. M. Hare, and Basil Mitchell, is a contemporary discussion of the meaningfulness of theological statements. Professor Flew argues that if a theological statement is meaningful it should be possible to specify the sort of state of affairs whose existence would prove the statement false. By this test, theological statements are meaningless. Mr. Hare and Mr. Mitchell argue that Professor Flew's test for the meaningfulness of these statements is too narrow, and they offer more sympathetic accounts of the meaning of theological statements. This discussion is a modern addendum to the old debate over whether religious beliefs may be tested by reason, and what constitutes a reasonable test.

326

18. ST. THOMAS AQUINAS
(1225?–74)

The Ways of Knowing Divine Truths

Thomas Aquinas was a Dominican friar. The Dominican order, founded to preach Christianity throughout the world, was confirmed by Pope Honorius III in 1216; Thomas joined it in 1244, when the order was in its twenty-eighth year. These dates are mentioned to place Aquinas' writings in the context of his order and its missionary purposes. His great works are the *Summa Contra Gentiles,* written during the years 1259 to 1264, and the *Summa Theologica,* begun in 1265 and left unfinished at his death. The "summa" in the titles means "summary" or "compendium." The "gentiles" against whom the first summa is written are those who do not believe in Christianity. Both of the summas are comprehensive surveys of Christian doctrine, but each is written from a different point of view. The *Summa Contra Gentiles* is written to convince non-Christian readers of the truth of Christianity on reasonable grounds. It contains the sort of material which a Christian missionary would find useful in preaching to nonbelievers. The *Summa Theologica* is written for the benefit of those who are already believers. A preacher would find it useful in his task of offering orderly expositions of Christian beliefs to his congregation. In both of the summas, however, Aquinas adheres to his opinion

that reason, as well as faith, has a place in religion.

Aquinas is one of the most notable members of a philosophical movement called "Scholasticism," which flourished among the Christian clergy of Western Europe from the ninth through the fourteenth centuries. The Scholastics' program was to use reason to organize, harmonize, and justify Christian doctrines. One of the principal causes of interest in such a program was the clergy's new knowledge of Greek philosophy. Greek philosophy presented an intellectual challenge to Christian belief, which the Scholastics proposed to meet by rationalizing Christianity. Aquinas was particularly interested in this aspect of the Scholastic program, and he endeavored to carry it out in a remarkable way. He adapted the philosophy of the pagan, but supremely reasonable, Aristotle to the support of a Christianity which Aquinas believed was consistent with reason.

In this reading, Aquinas justifies his attempt to write a reasonable exposition of Christianity. Aquinas' case depends on his being able to show that there are two kinds of truths about God (truths which exceed human reason, and truths which can be known by reason), and that these truths are not inconsistent. This selection may also be read as a preface to Aquinas' proofs of God's existence; for these proofs are one of the fruits of his conviction that reason can confirm religion.

This reading is drawn from the *Summa Contra Gentiles,* Book I, Chap-

ters 3 through 8. The original chapter titles are used as subtitles in this reading. The translation from the Latin is by Professor Anton C. Pegis.

ON THE WAY IN WHICH DIVINE TRUTH IS TO BE MADE KNOWN

The way of making truth known is not always the same, and, as the Philosopher has very well said, "it belongs to an educated man to seek such certitude in each thing as the nature of that thing allows." But, since such is the case, we must first show what way is open to us in order that we may make known the truth which is our object.

There is a twofold mode of truth in what we profess about God. Some truths about God exceed all the ability of the human reason. Such is the truth that God is triune. But there are some truths which the natural reason also is able to reach. Such are that God exists, that He is one, and the like. In fact, such truths about God have been proved demonstratively by the philosophers, guided by the light of the natural reason.[1]

That there are certain truths about God that totally surpass man's ability appears with the greatest evidence. Since, indeed, the principle of all knowledge that the reason perceives about some thing is the understanding of the very substance of that being (for according to Aristotle "what a thing is" is

---

[1] In the *Summa Contra Gentiles,* Book I, Chapter 2, Aquinas qualifies the use of natural reason in divine matters in the following way:

"To proceed against individual errors is a difficult business, and this for two reasons. In the first place, it is difficult because the sacrilegious remarks of individual men who have erred are not so well known to us so that we may use what they say as the basis of proceeding to a refutation of their errors. This is, indeed, the method that the ancient Doctors of the Church used in the refutation of the errors of the Gentiles. For they could know the positions taken by the Gentiles since they themselves had been Gentiles, or at least had lived among the Gentiles and had been instructed in their teaching. In the second place, it is difficult because some of them, such as the Mohammedans and the pagans, do not agree with us in accepting the authority of any Scripture, by which they may be convinced of their error. Thus, against the Jews we are able to argue by means of the Old Testament, while against heretics we are able to argue by means of the New Testament. But the Mohammedans and the pagans accept neither the one nor the other. We must, therefore, have recourse to the natural reason, to which all men are forced to give their assent. However, it is true, in divine matters the natural reason has its failings."—Eds.

the principle of demonstration), it is necessary that the way in which we understand the substance of a thing determines the way in which we know what belongs to it. Hence, if the human intellect comprehends the substance of some thing, for example, that of a stone or of a triangle, no intelligible characteristic belonging to that thing surpasses the grasp of the human reason. But this does not happen to us in the case of God. For the human intellect is not able to reach a comprehension of the divine substance through its natural power. For, according to its manner of knowing in the present life, the intellect depends on the sense for the origin of knowledge; and so those things that do not fall under the senses cannot be grasped by the human intellect except in so far as the knowledge of them is gathered from sensible things. Now, sensible things cannot lead the human intellect to the point of seeing in them the nature of the divine substance; for sensible things are effects that fall short of the power of their cause. Yet, beginning with sensible things, our intellect is led to the point of knowing about God that He exists, and other such characteristics that must be attributed to the First Principle. There are, consequently, some intelligible truths about God that are open to the human reason; but there are others that absolutely surpass its power.

. . .

THAT THE TRUTH ABOUT GOD TO WHICH THE NATURAL REASON REACHES IS FITTINGLY PROPOSED TO MEN FOR BELIEF

Since, therefore, there exists a twofold truth concerning the divine being, one to which the inquiry of the reason can reach, the other which surpasses the whole ability of the human reason, it is fitting that both of these truths be proposed to man divinely for belief. This point must first be shown concerning the truth that is open to the inquiry of the reason; otherwise, it might perhaps seem to someone that, since such a truth can be known by the reason, it was uselessly given to men through a supernatural inspiration as an object of belief.

Yet, if this truth were left solely as a matter of inquiry for the human reason, three awkward consequences would follow.

The first is that few men would possess the knowledge of God. For there are three reasons why most men are cut off from the fruit of diligent inquiry which is the discovery of truth. Some do not have the physical disposition for such work. As a result, there are many who are naturally not fitted to pursue knowledge; and so, however much they tried, they would be unable to reach the highest level of human knowledge which consists in knowing God. Others are cut off from pursuing this truth by the necessities imposed upon them by their daily lives. For some men must devote themselves to taking care of temporal matters. Such men would not be able to give so much time to the leisure of contemplative inquiry as to reach the highest peak at which human investigation can arrive, namely, the knowledge of God. Finally, there are some who are cut off by indolence. In order to know the things that the reason can investigate concerning God, a knowledge of many things must already be possessed. For almost all of philosophy is directed towards the knowledge of God, and that is why metaphysics, which deals with divine things, is the last part of philosophy to be learned. This means that we are able to arrive at the inquiry concerning the aforementioned truth only on the basis of a great deal of labor spent in study. Now, those who wish to undergo such a labor for the mere love of knowledge are few, even though God has inserted into the minds of men a natural appetite for knowledge.

The second awkward effect is that those who would come to discover the abovementioned truth would barely reach it after a great deal of time. The reasons are several. There is the profundity of this truth, which the human intellect is made capable of grasping by natural inquiry only after a long training. Then, there are many things that must be presupposed, as we have said. There is also the fact that, in youth, when the soul is swayed by the various movements of the passions, it is not in a suitable state for the knowledge of such lofty truth. On the contrary, "one becomes wise and knowing in repose," as it is said in the *Physics*.[2] The result is this. If the only way open to us for the knowledge of God were solely that of the reason, the human race would remain in the blackest shadows of ignorance. For then the knowledge of God, which especially renders men perfect and good, would come to be possessed only by a few, and these few would require a great deal of time in order to reach it.

The third awkward effect is this. The investigation of the human reason for the most part has falsity present within it, and this is due partly to the weakness of our intellect in judgment, and partly to the admixture of images. The result is that many, remaining ignorant of the power of demonstration, would hold in doubt those things that have been most truly demonstrated. This would be particularly the case since they see that, among those who are reputed to be wise men, each one teaches his own brand of doctrine. Furthermore, with the many truths that are demonstrated, there sometimes is mingled something that is false, which is not demonstrated but rather asserted on the basis of some probable or sophistical argument, which yet has the credit of being a demonstration. This is why it was necessary that the unshakable certitude and pure truth concerning divine things should be presented to men by way of faith.[3]

---

[2] Aristotle, *Physics*, VII, 3 (247b 9).

[3] Although St. Thomas does not name Maimonides or his *Guide for the Perplexed* (*Dux neutrorum*), there are evident points of contact between the Catholic and the Jewish theologian. On the reasons for revelation given here, on our knowledge of God,

Beneficially, therefore, did the divine Mercy provide that it should instruct us to hold by faith even those truths that the human reason is able to investigate. In this way, all men would easily be able to have a share in the knowledge of God, and this without uncertainty and error.

Hence it is written: "Henceforward you walk not as also the Gentiles walk in the vanity of their mind, having their understanding darkened" (Eph. 4:17–18). And again: "All thy children shall be taught of the Lord" (Isa. 54:13).

THAT THE TRUTHS THE HUMAN REASON IS NOT ABLE TO INVESTIGATE ARE FITTINGLY PROPOSED TO MEN FOR BELIEF

Now, perhaps some will think that men should not be asked to believe what the reason is not adequate to investigate, since the divine Wisdom provides in the case of each thing according to the mode of its nature. We must therefore prove that it is necessary for man to receive from God as objects of belief even those truths that are above the human reason.

No one tends with desire and zeal towards something that is not already known to him. But men are ordained by the divine Providence towards a higher good than human fragility can experience in the present life. That is why it was necessary for the human mind to be called to something higher than the human reason here and now can reach, so that it would thus learn to desire something and with zeal tend towards something that surpasses the whole state of the present life. This belongs especially to the Christian religion, which in a unique way promises spiritual and eternal goods. And so there are many things proposed to men in it that transcend human sense. The Old Law, on the other hand, whose promises were of a temporal character, contained very few proposals that transcended the inquiry of the human reason. Following this same direction, the philosophers themselves, in order that they might lead men from the pleasure of sensible things to virtue, were concerned to show that there were in existence other goods of a higher nature than these things of sense, and that those who gave themselves to the active or contemplative virtues would find much sweeter enjoyment in the taste of these higher goods.

It is also necessary that such truth be proposed to men for belief so that they may have a truer knowledge of God. For then only do we know God truly when we believe Him to be above everything that it is possible for man to think about Him; for the divine substance surpasses the natural knowl-

on creation and the eternity of the world, and on Aristotelianism in general, St. Thomas has Maimonides in mind both to agree and to disagree with him. By way of background for *SCG*, I, the reader can usefully consult the references to Maimonides in E. Gilson, *History of Christian Philosophy in the Middle Ages* [Random House], New York, 1955, pp. 649–51.—A. C. Pegis edge of which man is capable. Hence, by the fact that some things about God are proposed to man that surpass his reason, there is strengthened in man the view that God is something above what he can think.

Another benefit that comes from the revelation to men of truths that exceed the reason is the curbing of presumption, which is the mother of error. For there are some who have such a presumptuous opinion of their own ability that they deem themselves able to measure the nature of everything; I mean to say that, in their estimation, everything is true that seems to them so, and everything is false that does not. So that the human mind, therefore, might be freed from this presumption and come to a humble inquiry after truth, it was necessary that some things should be proposed to man by God that would completely surpass his intellect.

A still further benefit may also be seen in what Aristotle says in the *Ethics*. There was a certain Simonides who exhorted people to put aside the knowledge of divine things and to apply their talents to human occupations. He said that "he who is a man should know human things, and he who is mortal, things that are mortal." Against Simonides Aristotle says that "man should draw himself towards what is immortal and divine as much as he can." And so he says in the *De animalibus* that, although what we know of the higher substances is very little, yet that little is loved and desired more than all the knowledge that we have about less noble substances. He also says in the *De caelo et mundo* that when questions about the heavenly bodies can be given even a modest and merely plausible solution, he who hears this experiences intense joy. From all these considerations it is clear that even the most imperfect knowledge about the most noble realities brings the greatest perfection to the soul. Therefore, although the human reason cannot grasp fully the truths that are above it, yet, if it somehow holds these truths at least by faith, it acquires great perfection for itself.

Therefore it is written: "For many things are shown to thee above the understanding of men" (Ecclus. 3:25). Again: "So the things that are of God no man knoweth but the Spirit of God. But to us God hath revealed them by His Spirit" (I Cor. 2:11, 10).

THAT TO GIVE ASSENT TO THE TRUTHS OF FAITH IS NOT FOOLISHNESS EVEN THOUGH THEY ARE ABOVE REASON

Those who place their faith in this truth, however, "for which the human reason offers no experimental evidence," do not believe foolishly, as though "following artificial fables" (II Peter 1:16). For these "secrets of divine Wisdom" (Job 11:6) the divine Wisdom itself, which knows all things to the full, has deigned to reveal to men. It reveals its own presence, as well as the truth of its teaching and inspiration, by fitting arguments; and in order to confirm those truths that exceed natural knowledge, it gives visible manifestation to works that surpass the ability of all nature. Thus, there are the wonderful cures of illnesses, there is the raising of the dead, and the wonderful immutation in the heavenly bodies; and what is more wonderful, there is the inspiration given to human minds, so that simple and untutored persons, filled with the gift of the Holy Spirit, come to possess instantaneously the highest wisdom and the readiest eloquence. When these arguments were examined, through the efficacy of the abovementioned proof, and not the violent assault of arms or the promise of pleasures, and (what is most wonderful of all) in the midst of the tyranny of the persecutors, an innumerable throng of people, both simple and most learned, flocked to the Christian faith. In this faith there are truths preached that surpass every human intellect; the pleasures of the flesh are curbed; it is taught that the things of the world should be spurned. Now, for the minds of mortal men to assent to these things is the greatest of miracles, just as it is a manifest work of divine inspiration that, spurning visible things, men should seek only what is invisible. Now, that this has happened neither without preparation nor by chance, but as a result of the disposition of God, is clear from the fact that through many pronouncements of the ancient prophets God had foretold that He would do this. The books of these prophets are held in veneration among us Christians, since they give witness to our faith.

The manner of this confirmation is touched on by St. Paul: "Which," that is, human salvation, "having begun to be declared by the Lord, was confirmed unto us by them that hear Him: God also bearing them witness of signs, and wonders, and divers miracles, and distributions of the Holy Ghost" (Heb. 2:3-4).

This wonderful conversion of the world to the Christian faith is the clearest witness of the signs given in the past; so that it is not necessary that they should be further repeated, since they appear most clearly in their effect. For it would be truly more wonderful than all signs if the world had been led by simple and humble men to believe such lofty truths, to accomplish such difficult actions, and to have such high hopes. Yet it is also a fact that, even in our own time, God does not cease to work miracles through His saints for the confirmation of the faith.

On the other hand, those who founded sects committed to erroneous doctrines proceeded in a way that is opposite to this. The point is clear in the case of Mohammed. He seduced the people by promises of carnal pleasure to which the concupiscence of the flesh goads us. His teaching also contained precepts that were in conformity with his promises, and he gave free rein to carnal pleasure. In all this, as is not unexpected, he was obeyed by carnal men. As for proofs of the truth of his doctrine, he brought forward only such as could be grasped by the natural ability of anyone with a very modest wisdom. Indeed, the truths that he taught he mingled with many fables and with doctrines of the greatest falsity. He did not bring forth any signs produced in a supernatural way, which alone fittingly gives witness to divine inspiration; for a visible action that can be only divine reveals an invisibly inspired teacher of truth. On the contrary, Mohammed said that he was sent in the power of his arms—which are signs not lacking even to robbers and tyrants. What is more, no wise men, men trained in things divine and human, believed in him from the beginning. Those who believed in him were brutal men and desert wanderers, utterly ignorant of all divine teaching, through whose numbers Mohammed forced others to become his followers by the violence of his arms. Nor do divine pronouncements on the part of preceding prophets offer him any witness. On the contrary, he perverts almost all the testimonies of the Old and New Testaments by making them into fabrications of his own, as can be seen by anyone who examines his law. It was, therefore, a shrewd decision on his part to forbid his followers to read the Old and New Testaments, lest these books convict him of falsity. It is thus clear that those who place any faith in his words believe foolishly.

THAT THE TRUTH OF REASON IS NOT OPPOSED TO THE TRUTH OF THE CHRISTIAN FAITH

Now, although the truth of the Christian faith which we have discussed surpasses the capacity of the reason, nevertheless that truth that the human reason is naturally endowed to know cannot be opposed to the truth of the Christian faith. For that with which the human reason is naturally endowed is clearly most true; so much so, that it is impossible for us to think of such truths as false. Nor is it permissible to believe as false that which we hold by faith, since this is confirmed in a way that is so clearly divine. Since, therefore, only the false is opposed to the true, as is clearly evident from an examination of their definitions, it is impossible that the truth of faith should be opposed to those principles that the human reason knows naturally.

Furthermore, that which is introduced into the soul of the student by the teacher is contained in the knowledge of the teacher—unless his teaching is fictitious, which it is improper to say of God. Now, the knowledge of the principles that are known to us naturally has been implanted in us by God; for God is the Author of our nature. These principles, therefore, are also contained by the divine Wisdom. Hence, whatever is opposed to them is opposed to the divine Wisdom, and, therefore, cannot come from God. That which we hold by faith as divinely revealed, therefore, cannot be contrary to our natural knowledge.

. . .

HOW THE HUMAN REASON IS RELATED
TO THE TRUTH OF FAITH

There is also a further consideration. Sensible things, from which the human reason takes the origin of its knowledge, retain within themselves some sort of trace of a likeness to God. This is so imperfect, however, that it is absolutely inadequate to manifest the substance of God. For effects bear within themselves, in their own way, the likeness of their causes, since an agent produces its like; yet an effect does not always reach to the full likeness of its cause. Now, the human reason is related to the knowledge of the truth of faith (a truth which can be most evident only to those who see the divine substance) in such a way that it can gather certain likenesses of it, which are yet not sufficient so that the truth of faith may be comprehended as being understood demonstratively or through itself. Yet it is useful for the human reason to exercise itself in such arguments, however weak they may be, provided only that there be present no presumption to comprehend or to demonstrate. For to be able to see something of the loftiest realities, however thin and weak the sight may be, is, as our previous remarks indicate, a cause of the greatest joy.

The testimony of Hilary agrees with this. Speaking of this same truth, he writes as follows in his *De Trinitate:* "Enter these truths by believing, press forward, persevere. And though I may know that you will not arrive at an end, yet I will congratulate you in your progress. For, though he who pursues the infinite with reverence will never finally reach the end, yet he will always progress by pressing onward. But do not intrude yourself into the divine secret, do not, presuming to comprehend the sum total of intelligence, plunge yourself into the mystery of the unending nativity; rather, understand that these things are incomprehensible."

QUESTIONS
1. What are the two kinds of truth about God which Aquinas distinguishes? Try to extend his list of examples of these two kinds of truth.
2. What does Aquinas mean by "the natural reason"? Why does he believe that it is possible to know that God exists by the natural reason?
3. What awkward consequences would follow if truths about God knowable by reason could not be "proposed to man divinely for belief"?
4. What does Aquinas mean by a truth about God which exceeds "all the ability of the human reason"?
5. How does Aquinas seek to show that it is not foolish to believe a truth about God which is above human reason? On what grounds can one accept (or reject) his criterion of foolishness?

6. Why does Aquinas believe that what is known about God by reason cannot be opposed by what is accepted on faith? In what respects does his account of the relation between faith and reason resemble (or differ from) the account of Locke?

19. JOHN LOCKE
(1632–1704)

Faith and Reason: Their Distinct Provinces

(A general introductory note on Locke may be found on page 70.)

It is generally known that Locke's contributions to the theory of knowledge have given him a secure place in the history of philosophy, but it is not always remembered that the implications of his epistemology for the problem of religious knowledge have also earned him a small but significant place in the history of religion, particularly in the history of the Christianity of the English-speaking world. Locke believed that reason has a place in religion. He assigned it the task of certifying the divine origin of revelations, and of guaranteeing their content against unreasonableness. Whether any revelation can survive such a scrutiny by reason

is a question which we leave to the reader. Locke claims that faith and reason are not opposed to each other, and this claim depends largely on his view that there are some propositions whose content is "above reason" but not "contrary to reason." Without such propositions the religious person would of course have nothing to believe on faith. Whether Locke succeeds in leaving room for such propositions is an additional question which we leave to the reader's consideration.

This selection is drawn from Locke's *Essay Concerning Human Understanding* (1690), Book IV, Chapters 16, 17, and 18. The original chapter titles have been retained as subtitles in this selection.

The bare testimony of revelation is the highest certainty.   There is one sort of propositions that challenge the highest degree of our assent upon bare testimony, whether the thing proposed agree or disagree with common experience and the ordinary course of things, or no. The reason whereof is, because the testimony is of such an one, as cannot deceive, nor be deceived, and that is God himself. This carries with it an assurance beyond doubt, evidence beyond exception. This is called by a peculiar name, revelation; and our assent to it, faith; which as absolutely determines our minds, and as perfectly excludes all wavering, as our knowledge itself; and we may as well doubt of our own being, as we can, whether any revelation from God be true. So that faith is a settled and sure principle of assent and assurance, and leaves no manner of room for doubt or hesitation. Only we must be sure that it be a divine revelation, and that we understand it right: else we shall expose ourselves to all the extravagancy of enthusiasm, and all the error of wrong principles, if we have faith and assurance in what is not divine revelation. And therefore in those cases, our assent can be rationally no higher than the evidence of its being a revelation, and that this is the meaning of the expressions it is delivered in. If the evidence of its being a revelation, or that this is its true sense, be only on probable proofs: our assent can reach no higher than an assurance or diffidence, arising from the more or less apparent probability of the proofs. But of faith, and the precedency it ought to have before other arguments of persuasion, I shall speak more hereafter, where I treat of it, as it is ordinarily placed, in contradistinction to reason; though in truth it be nothing else but an assent founded on the highest reason.

OF REASON

Various significations of the word reason. The word "reason" in the English language has different significations: sometimes it is taken for true and clear principles; sometimes for clear and fair deductions from those principles; and sometimes for the cause, and particularly the final cause. But the consideration I shall have of it here is in a signification different from all these; and that is, as it stands for a faculty in man, that faculty whereby man is supposed to be distinguished from beasts, and wherein it is evident he much surpasses them.

Wherein reasoning consists. If general knowledge, as has been shown, consists in a perception of the agreement or disagreement of our own ideas, and the knowledge of the existence of all things without us (except only of a God, whose existence every man may certainly know and demonstrate to himself from his own existence) be had only by our senses: what room is there for the exercise of any other faculty, but outward sense and inward perception? What need is there of reason? Very much; both for the enlargement of our knowledge, and regulating our assent; for it hath to do both in knowledge and opinion, and is necessary and assisting to all our other intellectual faculties, and indeed contains two of them, viz., sagacity and illation. By the one, it finds out; and by the other, it so orders the intermediate ideas, as to discover what connection there is in each link of the chain, whereby the extremes are held together; and thereby, as it were, to draw into view the truth sought for, which is that which we call illation or inference, and consists in nothing but the perception of the connection there is between the ideas, in each step of the deduction, whereby the mind comes to see either the certain agreement or disagreement of any two ideas, as in demonstration, in which it arrives at knowledge; or their probable connection, on which it gives or withholds its assent, as in opinion. Sense and intuition reach but a very little way. The greatest part of our knowledge depends upon deductions and intermediate ideas: and in those cases, where we are fain to substitute assent instead of knowledge, and take propositions for true, without being certain they are so, we have need to find out, examine, and compare the grounds of their probability. In both these cases, the faculty which finds out the means, and rightly applies them to discover certainty in the one, and probability in the other, is that which we call reason. For as reason perceives the necessary and indubitable connection of all the ideas or proofs one to another, in each step of any demonstration that produces knowledge: so it likewise perceives the probable connection of all the ideas or proofs one to another, in every step of a discourse, to which it will think assent due. This is the lowest degree of that which can be truly called reason. For where the mind does not perceive this probable connection, where it does not discern whether there be any such connection or no; there men's opinions are not the product of judgment, or the consequence of reason, but the effects of chance and hazard, of a mind floating at all adventures, without choice and without direction.

Its four parts. So that we may in reason consider these four degrees; the first and highest is the discovering and finding out of truths; the second, the regular and methodical disposition of them, and laying them in a clear and fit order, to make their connection and force be plainly and easily perceived; the third is the perceiving their connection; and the fourth, a making a right conclusion. . . .

Above, contrary, and according to reason. By what has been before said of reason, we may be able to make some guess at the distinction of things, into those that are according to, above, and contrary to reason. (1) According to reason are such propositions, whose truth we can discover by examining and tracing those ideas we have from sensation and reflection: and by natural deduction find to be true or probable. (2) Above reason are such propositions, whose truth or probability we cannot by reason derive from those principles. (3) Contrary to reason are such propositions, as are inconsistent with, or irreconcilable to, our clear and distinct ideas. Thus the existence of one God is according to reason; the existence of more than one God, contrary to reason; the resurrection of the dead above reason. Farther, as above reason may be taken in a double sense, viz., either as signifying above probability, or above certainty; so in that large sense also, contrary to reason is, I suppose, sometimes taken.

Reason and faith not opposite. There is another use of the word reason, wherein it is opposed to faith; which though it be in itself a very improper way of speaking, yet common use has so authorized it, that it would be folly either to oppose or hope to remedy it: only I think it may not be amiss to take notice that however faith be opposed to reason, faith is nothing but a firm assent of the mind: which if it be regulated, as is our duty, cannot be afforded to anything but upon good reason; and so cannot be opposite to it. He that believes, without having any reason for believing, may be in love with his own fancies; but neither seeks truth as he ought, nor pays the obedience due to his Maker, who would have him use those discerning faculties he has given him, to keep him out of mistake and error. He that does not this to the best of his power, however he sometimes lights on truth, is in the right but by chance; and I know not whether the luckiness of the accident will excuse the irregularity of his proceeding. This at least is certain, that he must be accountable for whatever mistakes he runs into: whereas he that makes use of the light and faculties God has given him, and seeks sincerely to discover truths by those helps and abilities he has, may have this satisfaction in doing his duty as a rational creature, that, though he should miss truth, he will not miss the reward of it. For he governs his assent right, and places it as he should, who, in any case or matter whatsoever, believes or disbelieves, according as reason directs him. He that doth otherwise transgresses against his own light, and misuses those faculties which were given him to no other end, but to search and follow the clearer evidence and greater probability. But, since reason and faith are by some men opposed, we will so consider them in the following chapter.

OF FAITH AND REASON, AND THEIR DISTINCT PROVINCES

Necessary to know their boundaries. It has been above shown: (1) That we are of necessity ignorant, and want knowledge of all sorts, where we want ideas. (2) That we are ignorant, and want rational knowledge, where we want proofs. (3) That we want certain knowledge and certainty, as far as we want clear and determined specific ideas. (4) That we want probability to direct our assent in matters where we have neither knowledge of our own, nor testimony of other men, to bottom our reason upon.

From these things thus premised, I think we may come to lay down the measures and boundaries between faith and reason; the want whereof may possibly have been the cause, if not of great disorders, yet at least of great disputes, and perhaps mistakes in the world. For till it be resolved, how far we are to be guided by reason, and how far by faith, we shall in vain dispute, and endeavor to convince one another in matters of religion.

Faith and reason what, as contradistinguished. I find every sect, as far as reason will help them, make use of it gladly; and where it fails them, they cry out, it is matter of faith, and above reason. And I do not see how they can argue with anyone, or ever convince a gainsayer who makes use of the same plea, without setting down strict boundaries between faith and reason; which ought to be the first point established in all questions, where faith has anything to do.

Reason, therefore, here, as contradistinguished to faith, I take to be the discovery of the certainty or probability of such propositions or truths, which the mind arrives at by deduction made from such ideas, which it has got by the use of its natural faculties, viz., by sensation or reflection.

Faith, on the other side, is the assent to any proposition, not thus made out by the deductions of reason; but upon the credit of the proposer, as coming from God, in some extraordinary way of communication. This way of discovering truths to men we call revelation.

No new simple idea can be conveyed by traditional revelation. First, then, I say that no man inspired by God can by any revelation communicate to others any new simple ideas, which they had not before from sensation or reflection. For whatsoever impressions he himself may have from the immediate hand of God, this revelation, if it be of new simple ideas, cannot be conveyed to another, either by words, or any other signs. Because words, by their immediate operation on us, cause no other ideas, but of their natural sounds: and it is by the custom of using them for signs, that they excite and revive in our minds latent ideas; but yet only such ideas as were there before. For words, seen or heard, recall to our thoughts those ideas only, which to us they have been wont to be signs of; but cannot introduce any perfectly new and formerly unknown simple ideas. The same holds in all other signs, which cannot signify to us things, of which we have before never had any idea at all. Thus whatever things were discovered to St. Paul, when he was rapt up into the third heaven, whatever new ideas his mind there received, all the description he can make to others of that place is only this, that there are such things, "as eye hath not seen, nor ear heard, nor hath it entered into the heart of man to conceive." And supposing God should discover to anyone, supernaturally, a species of creatures inhabiting, for example, Jupiter or Saturn (for that it is possible there may be such, nobody can deny), which had six senses; and imprint on his mind the ideas conveyed to theirs by that sixth sense; he could no more, by words, produce in the minds of other men those ideas, imprinted by that sixth sense, than one of us could convey the idea of any color by the sounds of words into a man who, having the other four senses perfect, had always totally wanted the fifth of seeing. For our simple ideas then, which are the foundation and sole matter of all our notions and knowledge, we must depend wholly on our reason, I mean our natural faculties; and can by no means receive them, or any of them, from traditional revelation; I say, traditional revelation, in distinction to original revelation. By the one, I mean that first impression, which is made immediately by God, on the mind of any man, to which we cannot set any bounds; and by the other, those impressions delivered over to others in words, and the ordinary ways of conveying our conceptions one to another.

Traditional revelation may make us know propositions knowable also by reason, but not with the same certainty that reason doth. Secondly, I say that the same truths may be discovered, and conveyed down from revelation, which are discoverable to us by reason, and by those ideas we naturally may have. So God might, by revelation, discover the truth of any proposition of Euclid; as well as men, by the natural use of their faculties, come to make the discovery themselves. In all things of this kind, there is little need or use of revelation, God having furnished us with natural and surer means to arrive at the knowledge of them. For whatsoever truth we come to the clear discovery of, from the knowledge and contemplation of our own ideas, will always be certainer to us than those which are conveyed to us by traditional revelation. For the knowledge we have, that this revelation came at first from God, can never be so sure as the knowledge we have from the clear and distinct perception of the agreement or disagreement of our own ideas; v. g., if it were revealed some ages since, that the three angles of a triangle were equal to two right ones, I might assent to the truth of that proposition, upon the credit of the tradition that it was revealed; but that would never amount to so great a certainty as the knowledge of it, upon the comparing and measuring my own ideas of two right angles, and the three angles of a triangle. The like holds in matter of fact knowable by our senses; v. g., the history of the deluge is conveyed to us by writings, which had their original from revelation: and yet nobody, I think, will say he has as certain and clear a knowledge of the flood, as Noah that saw it; or that he himself would have had, had he then been alive and seen it. For he has no greater assurance than that of his senses, that it is writ in the book supposed writ by Moses inspired: but he has not so great an assurance that Moses writ that book, as if he had seen Moses write it. So that the assurance of its being a revelation is less still than the assurance of his senses.

Revelation cannot be admitted against the clear evidence of reason. In propositions then, whose certainty is built upon the clear perception of the agreement or disagreement of our ideas, attained either by immediate intuition as in self-evident propositions, or by evident deductions of reason in demonstrations, we need not the assistance of revelation as necessary to gain our assent, and introduce them into our minds. Because the natural ways of knowledge could settle them there, or had done it already; which is the greatest assurance we can possibly have of anything, unless where God immediately reveals it to us: and there too our assurance can be no greater than our knowledge is that it is a revelation from God. But yet nothing, I think, can, under that title, shake or overrule plain knowledge; or rationally prevail with any man to admit it for true, in a direct contradiction to the clear evidence of his own understanding. For since no evidence of our faculties, by which we receive such revelations, can exceed, if equal, the certainty of our intuitive knowledge, we can never receive for a truth anything that is directly contrary to our clear and distinct knowledge; v. g., the ideas of one body, and one place, do so clearly agree, and the mind has so evident a perception of their agreement, that we can never assent to a proposition that affirms the same body to be in two distant places at once, however it should pretend to the authority of a divine revelation: since the evidence, first, that we deceive not ourselves in ascribing it to God; secondly, that we understand it right; can never be so great as the evidence of our own intuitive knowledge, whereby we discern it impossible for the same body to be in two places at once. And therefore no proposition can be received for divine revelation, or obtain the assent due to all such, if it be contradictory to our clear intuitive knowledge. Because this would be to subvert the principles and foundations of all knowledge, evidence, and assent whatsoever: and there would be left no difference between truth and falsehood, no measures of credible and incredible in the world, if doubtful propositions shall take place before self-evident; and what we certainly know give way to what we may possibly be mistaken in. In propositions therefore contrary to the clear perception of the agreement or disagreement of any of our ideas, it will be in vain to urge them as matters of faith. They cannot move our assent, under that or any other title whatsoever. For faith can never convince us of anything that contradicts our knowledge. Because though faith be founded on the testimony of God (who cannot lie) revealing any proposition to us, yet we cannot have an assurance of the truth of its being a divine revelation, greater than our own knowledge: since the whole strength of the certainty depends upon our knowledge that God revealed it, which in this case, where the proposition supposed revealed contradicts our knowledge or reason, will always have this objection hanging to it, viz., that we cannot tell how to conceive that to come from God, the bountiful Author of our being, which, if received for true, must overturn all the principles and foundations of knowledge he has given us; render all our faculties useless; wholly destroy the most excellent part of his workmanship, our understandings; and put a man in a condition, wherein he will have less light, less conduct than the beast that perisheth. For if the mind of man can never have a clearer (and perhaps not so clear) evidence of anything to be a divine revelation, as it has of the principles of its own reason, it can never have a ground to quit the clear evidence of its reason, to give a place to a proposition, whose revelation has not a greater evidence than those principles have.

Traditional revelation much less. Thus far a man has use of reason, and ought to hearken to it, even in immediate and original revelation, where it is supposed to be made to himself: but to all those who pretend not to immediate revelation, but are required to pay obedience, and to receive the truths revealed to others, which by the tradition of writings, or word of mouth, are conveyed down to them, reason has a great deal more to do, and is that only which can induce us to receive them. For matter of faith being only divine revelation, and nothing else, faith, as we use the word (called commonly divine faith) has to do with no propositions, but those which are supposed to be divinely revealed. So that I do not see how those, who make revelation alone the sole object of faith, can say that it is a matter of faith, and not of reason, to believe that such or such a proposition, to be found in such or such a book, is of divine inspiration; unless it be revealed that that proposition, or all in that book, was communicated by divine inspiration. Without such a revelation, the believing, or not believing, that proposition or book to be of divine authority can never be matter of faith, but matter of reason; and such as I must come to an assent to, only by the use of my reason, which can never require or enable me to believe that which is contrary to itself: it being impossible for reason ever to produce any assent to that which to itself appears unreasonable.

In all things, therefore, where we have clear evidence from our ideas, and those principles of knowledge I have above mentioned, reason is the proper judge; and revelation, though it may in consenting with it confirm its dictates, yet cannot in such cases invalidate its decrees: nor can we be obliged, where we have the clear and evident sentence of reason, to quit it for the contrary opinion, under a pretence that it is matter of faith; which can have authority against the plain and clear dictates of reason.

Things above reason. But, thirdly, there being many things, wherein we have very imperfect notions, or none at all; and other things, of whose past, present, or future existence, by the natural use of our faculties, we can have no knowledge at all: these, as being beyond the discovery of our natural faculties, and above reason, are, when revealed, the proper matter of faith. Thus, that part of the angels rebelled against God, and thereby lost their first happy state; and that the dead shall rise, and live again: these, and the like, being beyond the discovery of reason, are purely matters of faith; with which reason has directly nothing to do.

Or not contrary to reason, if revealed, are matter of faith. But since God in giving us the light of reason has not thereby tied up his own hands from affording us, when he thinks fit, the light of revelation in any of those matters, wherein our natural faculties are able to give a probable determination; revelation, where God has been pleased to give it, must carry it against the probable conjectures of reason. Because the mind, not being certain of the truth of that it does not evidently know but only yielding to the probability that appears in it, is bound to give up its assent to such a testimony; which, it is satisfied, comes from one who cannot err, and will not deceive.

But yet it still belongs to reason to judge of the truth of its being a revelation, and of the signification of the words wherein it is delivered. Indeed, if anything shall be thought revelation, which is contrary to the plain principles of reason, and the evident knowledge the mind has of its own clear and distinct ideas; there reason must be hearkened to, as to a matter within its province: since a man can never have so certain a knowledge that a proposition, which contradicts the clear principles and evidence of his own knowledge, was divinely revealed, or that he understands the words rightly wherein it is delivered; as he has that the contrary is true: and so is bound to consider and judge of it as a matter of reason, and not swallow it, without examination, as a matter of faith.

Revelation in matters where reason cannot judge, or but probably, ought to be hearkened to. First, whatever proposition is revealed, of whose truth our mind, by its natural faculties and notions, cannot judge; that is purely matter of faith, and above reason.

Secondly, all propositions, whereof the mind, by the use of its natural faculties, can come to determine and judge from naturally acquired ideas, are matter of reason; with this difference still, that in those concerning which it has but an uncertain evidence, and so is persuaded of their truth only upon probable grounds, which still admit a possibility of the contrary to be true, without doing violence to the certain evidence of its own knowledge, and overturning the principles of its own reason; in such probable propositions, I say, an evident revelation ought to determine our assent even against probability. For where the principles of reason have not evidenced a proposition to be certainly true or false, there clear revelation as another principle of truth, and ground of assent, may determine; and so it may be matter of faith, and be also above reason. Because reason, in that particular matter, being able to reach no higher than probability, faith gave the determination where reason came short; and revelation discovered on which side the truth lay.

In matters where reason can afford certain knowledge that is to be hearkened to. Thus far the dominion of faith reaches, and that without any violence or hindrance to reason, which is not injured or disturbed, but assisted and improved, by new discoveries of truth coming from the eternal fountain of all knowledge. Whatever God hath revealed is certainly true; no doubt can be made of it. This is the proper object of faith: but whether it be a divine revelation or no, reason must judge; which can never permit the mind to reject a greater evidence to embrace what is less evident, nor allow it to entertain probability in opposition to knowledge and certainty. There can be no evidence that any traditional revelation is of divine original, in the words we receive it, and in the sense we understand it, so clear and so certain, as that of the principles of reason: and therefore nothing that is contrary to, and inconsistent with, the clear and self-evident dictates of reason has a right to be urged or assented to as a matter of faith, wherein reason hath nothing to do. Whatsoever is divine revelation ought to overrule all our opinions, prejudices, and interest, and hath a right to be received with full assent. Such a submission as this, of our reason to faith, takes not away the landmarks of knowledge: this shakes not the foundations of reason, but leaves us that use of our faculties, for which they were given us.

If the boundaries be not set between faith and reason, no enthusiasm or extravagancy in religion can be contradicted. If the provinces of faith and reason are not kept distinct by these boundaries, there will, in matters of religion, be no room for reason at all; and those extravagant opinions and ceremonies that are to be found in the several religions of the world will not deserve to be blamed. For, to this crying up of faith, in opposition to reason, we may, I think, in good measure ascribe those absurdities that fill almost all the religions which possess and divide mankind. For men, having been principled with an opinion that they must not consult reason in the things of religion, however apparently contradictory to common sense and the very principles of all their knowledge, have let loose their fancies and natural superstition; and have been by them let into so strange opinions, and extravagant practices in religion, that a considerate man cannot but stand amazed at their follies, and judge them so far from being acceptable to the great and wise God, that he cannot avoid thinking them ridiculous, and offensive to a sober good man. So that in effect religion, which should most distinguish us from beasts, and ought most peculiarly to elevate us, as rational creatures, above brutes, is that wherein men often appear most irrational and more senseless than beasts themselves. *"Credo, quia impossibile est,"* I believe, because it is impossible, might in a good man pass for a sally of zeal; but would prove a very ill rule for men to choose their opinions or religion by.

QUESTIONS

1. What does Locke mean by "reason" and by "faith"? How does he show that in religion reason and faith are not opposed?
2. What is Locke's distinction between propositions which are "above reason" and those which are "contrary to reason"? Illustrate the distinction with examples. Using these categories, how would you classify the following propositions (explain your answers):
   a. The dead man came to life again.
   b. Triangles do not have three sides.
3. When Locke says that "the existence of more than one God [is] contrary to reason," does he speak as a reasonable man, or as a believing Christian, or both? Explain your answer.
4. What does Locke mean by "revelation"? In what areas does he allow reason to be the critic of revelation? On what matters can revelation be independent of reason? How does Locke answer the question of whether someone's revelation about a matter independent of reason can be intelligible to another person?
5. In what respects is it a just (or unjust) criticism of Locke to say that while he permits us to have original revelations if we can, he assures us that we can

never understand anyone else's revelation whose subject is God's nature or will; so he makes it impossible for religion to be discussed?

6. Consider the following argument:

"If the boundary between what can be known by reason and what must be believed on faith is drawn by reason, then reason is the arbiter of faith. But for the limits of faith to be defined by reason is a contradiction which destroys faith. On the other hand, if the boundary between faith and reason is drawn by faith, then faith is the arbiter of reason. But it is a manifest contradiction for the nonreasonable to define the reasonable. Thus a man can be either reasonable or faithful, but he can never be both."

State your own reasons for accepting, or rejecting, the above argument. How do you think that Locke or Aquinas would reply to this argument?

20. ANTONY FLEW, R. M. HARE,
and
BASIL MITCHELL

Theology and Falsification

The following symposium on the logic of theological statements was originally published in the British journal, *University*, in 1950–51. The participants in the symposium are Antony Flew, Professor of Philosophy at the University of Keele, England; R. M. Hare, Fellow of Balliol College, Oxford; and Basil Mitchell, Fellow of Keble College, Oxford.

Professor Flew opens the discussion by arguing that no utterance—not even a declarative sentence—can express an assertion unless the speaker is willing to admit that there is something which is being *denied* by his utterance. In other words, unless the speaker acknowledges that the occurrence of some set of conditions in existence would count as evidence against the truth of his utterance, he is not making an assertion at all. For if his statement is consistent with every possible set of conditions, there is nothing that it denies,

and if it denies nothing then it asserts nothing.

Now when we look at certain theological statements, we find that no facts about the world or about human life are allowed to count as a disproof of, or even as evidence against, the statements. Therefore, Professor Flew concludes, the person who makes such statements is not really asserting anything and cannot claim that what he says is true.

The second participant in the symposium, Mr. Hare, admits that Professor Flew is completely victorious on his own grounds. But there is another way of looking at religious statements, according to Mr. Hare's theory of *bliks*. Whether a person does or does not believe in a religion, Mr. Hare argues, there are certain basic assumptions in terms of which each person reacts to the world and by means of which he interprets and explains what happens in the world. These basic assumptions make up the person's *blik*. Depending on the particular *blik* a person has, it is appropriate for him to take certain attitudes toward the world and to have certain expectations about what will occur in it. Thus a person's *blik* may be thought of as the conceptual framework by which he understands what happens to him in his everyday experiences. It serves as a guide to his actions as well as the background for his deepest feelings, longings, hopes, and fears.

An example of a *blik* is a person's religion, which underlies the way he understands and reacts to the world. But the scientist as well as the religious believer has a *blik*, which is shown by his expectation of order in the world and by his commitment to the validity of the rules of inductive logic, according to which he carries on all his reasoning. A psychotic paranoid also has a *blik*, in terms of which he interprets all his relationships with other people. In each case, a person's *blik* is compatible with whatever happens in the world, since it sets the rules of thought by which whatever happens is to be understood. Thus the statements in which a person expresses his *blik* are not asser-

tions capable of being disproved or falsified. Nor are they assertions capable of verification by experience. Instead, they are ultimate ways of thinking and feeling about any experience.

Mr. Mitchell replies to Professor Flew's attack on theological utterances in a different way. He denies that the religious believer is unwilling to count anything as evidence against his assertions. A clear example of just such evidence is the fact of innocent people suffering, which the religious believer finds to be a reason against the statement that God loves and cares for men. But even though the believer accepts this as a reason against the statement, he does not think it falsifies the statement since he does not consider it to be *conclusive* evidence against it. The religious believer may accordingly have serious doubts about various statements made in his religion just because there is evidence against them. Yet his faith is such that none of this evidence by itself is seen to constitute a final disproof of the religion. Mr. Mitchell then contrasts his view of religion with Mr. Hare's concept of a *blik*. The concluding remarks by Professor Flew are replies to the arguments of Mr. Hare and Mr. Mitchell.

Reprinted with permission of The Macmillan Company from *New Essays in Philosophical Theology,* edited by Antony Flew and Alasdair MacIntyre. First published, 1955. Permission also granted by Student Christian Movement Press, Ltd., London.

A

Antony Flew

Let us begin with a parable. It is a parable developed from a tale told by John Wisdom in his haunting and revelatory article 'Gods'.[1] Once upon a time two explorers came upon a clearing in the jungle. In the clearing

[1] *P.A.S.,* 1944–45, reprinted as Ch. X of *Logic and Language,* Vol. I (Blackwell, 1951), and in his *Philosophy and Psychoanalysis* (Blackwell, 1953).

were growing many flowers and many weeds. One explorer says, 'Some
gardener must tend this plot'. The other disagrees, 'There is no gardener'.
So they pitch their tents and set a watch. No gardener is ever seen. 'But
perhaps he is an invisible gardener.' So they set up a barbed-wire fence. They
electrify it. They patrol with bloodhounds. (For they remember how H. G.
Wells's *The Invisible Man* could be both smelt and touched though he could
not be seen.) But no shrieks ever suggest that some intruder has received a
shock. No movements of the wire ever betray an invisible climber. The
bloodhounds never give cry. Yet still the Believer is not convinced. 'But
there is a gardener, invisible, intangible, insensible to electric shocks, a gardener who has no scent and makes no sound, a gardener who comes secretly
to look after the garden which he loves.' At last the Sceptic despairs, 'But
what remains of your original assertion? Just how does what you call an
invisible, intangible, eternally elusive gardener differ from an imaginary
gardener or even from no gardener at all?'

In this parable we can see how what starts as an assertion, that something exists or that there is some analogy between certain complexes of phenomena, may be reduced step by step to an altogether different status, to an
expression perhaps of a 'picture preference'.[2] The Sceptic says there is no
gardener. The Believer says there is a gardener (but invisible, etc.). One
man talks about sexual behaviour. Another man prefers to talk of Aphrodite
(but knows that there is not really a superhuman person additional to, and
somehow responsible for, all sexual phenomena).[3] The process of qualification may be checked at any point before the original assertion is completely
withdrawn and something of that first assertion will remain (Tautology).
Mr. Wells's invisible man could not, admittedly, be seen, but in all other
respects he was a man like the rest of us. But though the process of qualification may be, and of course usually is, checked in time, it is not always
judiciously so halted. Someone may dissipate his assertion completely without noticing that he has done so. A fine brash hypothesis may thus be killed
by inches, the death by a thousand qualifications.

And in this, it seems to me, lies the peculiar danger, the endemic evil,
of theological utterance. Take such utterances as 'God has a plan', 'God
created the world', 'God loves us as a father loves his children'. They look at
first sight very much like assertions, vast cosmological assertions. Of course,
this is no sure sign that they either are, or are intended to be, assertions.

---

[2] Cf. J. Wisdom, 'Other Minds', *Mind*, 1940; reprinted in his *Other Minds* (Blackwell,
1952).

[3] Cf. Lucretius, *De Rerum Natura*, II, 655–60,

> Hic siquis mare Neptunum Cereremque vocare
> Constituet fruges et Bacchi nomine abuti
> Mavolat quam laticis proprium proferre vocamen
> Concedamus ut hic terrarum dictitet orbem
> Esse deum matrem dum vera re tamen ipse
> Religione animum turpi contingere parcat.

But let us confine ourselves to the cases where those who utter such sentences intend them to express assertions. (Merely remarking parenthetically that those who intend or interpret such utterances as crypto-commands, expressions of wishes, disguised ejaculations, concealed ethics, or as anything else but assertions, are unlikely to succeed in making them either properly orthodox or practically effective).

Now to assert that such and such is the case is necessarily equivalent to denying that such and such is not the case.[4] Suppose then that we are in doubt as to what someone who gives vent to an utterance is asserting, or suppose that, more radically, we are sceptical as to whether he is really asserting anything at all, one way of trying to understand (or perhaps it will be to expose) his utterance is to attempt to find what he would regard as counting against, or as being incompatible with, its truth. For if the utterance is indeed an assertion, it will necessarily be equivalent to a denial of the negation of that assertion. And anything which would count against the assertion, or which would induce the speaker to withdraw it and to admit that it had been mistaken, must be part of (or the whole of) the meaning of the negation of that assertion. And to know the meaning of the negation of an assertion, is as near as makes no matter, to know the meaning of that assertion.[5] And if there is nothing which a putative assertion denies then there is nothing which it asserts either: and so it is not really an assertion. When the Sceptic in the parable asked the Believer, 'Just how does what you call an invisible, intangible, eternally elusive gardener differ from an imaginary gardener or even from no gardener at all?' he was suggesting that the Believer's earlier statement had been so eroded by qualification that it was no longer an assertion at all.

Now it often seems to people who are not religious as if there was no conceivable event or series of events the occurrence of which would be admitted by sophisticated religious people to be a sufficient reason for conceding 'There wasn't a God after all' or 'God does not really love us then'. Someone tells us that God loves us as a father loves his children. We are reassured. But then we see a child dying of inoperable cancer of the throat. His earthly father is driven frantic in his efforts to help, but his Heavenly Father reveals no obvious sign of concern. Some qualification is made— God's love is 'not a merely human love' or it is 'an inscrutable love', perhaps —and we realize that such sufferings are quite compatible with the truth of the assertion that 'God loves us as a father (but, of course, . . .)'. We are reassured again. But then perhaps we ask: what is this assurance of God's (appropriately qualified) love worth, what is this apparent guarantee really a guarantee against? Just what would have to happen not merely (morally and wrongly) to tempt but also (logically and rightly) to entitle us to say 'God does not love us' or even 'God does not exist'? I therefore put to the

[4] For those who prefer symbolism: $p \equiv \sim \sim p$.
[5] For by simply negating $\sim p$ we get p : $\sim \sim p \equiv p$.

succeeding symposiasts the simple central questions, 'What would have to occur or to have occurred to constitute for you a disproof of the love of, or of the existence of, God?'

B

R. M. Hare

I wish to make it clear that I shall not try to defend Christianity in particular, but religion in general—not because I do not believe in Christianity, but because you cannot understand what Christianity is, until you have understood what religion is.

I must begin by confessing that, on the ground marked out by Flew, he seems to me to be completely victorious. I therefore shift my ground by relating another parable. A certain lunatic is convinced that all dons want to murder him. His friends introduce him to all the mildest and most respectable dons that they can find, and after each of them has retired, they say, 'You see, he doesn't really want to murder you; he spoke to you in a most cordial manner; surely you are convinced now?' But the lunatic replies 'Yes, but that was only his diabolical cunning; he's really plotting against me the whole time, like the rest of them; I know it I tell you'. However many kindly dons are produced, the reaction is still the same.

Now we say that such a person is deluded. But what is he deluded about? About the truth or falsity of an assertion? Let us apply Flew's test to him. There is no behaviour of dons that can be enacted which he will accept as counting against his theory; and therefore his theory, on this test, asserts nothing. But it does not follow that there is no difference between what he thinks about dons and what most of us think about them—otherwise we should not call him a lunatic and ourselves sane, and dons would have no reason to feel uneasy about his presence in Oxford.

Let us call that in which we differ from this lunatic, our respective *bliks*. He has an insane *blik* about dons; we have a sane one. It is important to realize that we have a sane one, not no *blik* at all; for there must be two sides to any argument—if he has a wrong *blik,* then those who are right about dons must have a right one. Flew has shown that a *blik* does not consist in an assertion or system of them; but nevertheless it is very important to have the right *blik*.

Let us try to imagine what it would be like to have different *bliks* about other things than dons. When I am driving my car, it sometimes occurs to me to wonder whether my movements of the steering-wheel will always continue to be followed by corresponding alterations in the direction of the car. I have never had a steering failure, though I have had skids, which must be similar. Moreover, I know enough about how the steering of my car is made, to know the sort of thing that would have to go wrong for the steering to fail—steel joints would have to part, or steel rods break, or something—but how do I know that this won't happen? The truth is, I don't know; I just have a *blik* about steel and its properties, so that normally I trust the steering of my car; but I find it not at all difficult to imagine what it would be like to lose this *blik* and acquire the opposite one. People would say I was silly about steel; but there would be no mistaking the reality of the difference between our respective *bliks*—for example, I should never go in a motor-car. Yet I should hesitate to say that the difference between us was the difference between contradictory assertions. No amount of safe arrivals or bench-tests will remove my *blik* and restore the normal one; for my *blik* is compatible with any finite number of such tests.

It was Hume who taught us that our whole commerce with the world depends upon our *blik* about the world; and that differences between *bliks* about the world cannot be settled by observation of what happens in the world. That was why, having performed the interesting experiment of doubting the ordinary man's *blik* about the world, and showing that no proof could be given to make us adopt one *blik* rather than another, he turned to backgammon to take his mind off the problem. It seems, indeed, to be impossible even to formulate as an assertion the normal *blik* about the world which makes me put my confidence in the future reliability of steel joints, in the continued ability of the road to support my car, and not gape beneath it revealing nothing below; in the general non-homicidal tendencies of dons; in my own continued well-being (in some sense of that word that I may not now fully understand) if I continue to do what is right according to my lights; in the general likelihood of people like Hitler coming to a bad end. But perhaps a formulation less inadequate than most is to be found in the Psalms: 'The earth is weak and all the inhabiters thereof: I bear up the pillars of it'.

The mistake of the position which Flew selects for attack is to regard this kind of talk as some sort of *explanation,* as scientists are accustomed to use the word. As such, it would obviously be ludicrous. We no longer believe in God as an Atlas—*nous n'avons pas besoin de cette hypothèse.* But it is nevertheless true to say that, as Hume saw, without a *blik* there can be no explanation; for it is by our *bliks* that we decide what is and what is not an explanation. Suppose we believed that everything that happened, happened by pure chance. This would not of course be an assertion; for it is compatible with anything happening or not happening, and so, incidentally, is its contradictory. But if we had this belief, we should not be able to explain or predict or plan anything. Thus, although we should not be *asserting* anything different from those of a more normal belief, there would be a great difference between us; and this is the sort of difference that there is between those who really believe in God and those who really disbelieve in him.

The word 'really' is important, and may excite suspicion. I put it in, because when people have had a good Christian upbringing, as have most of those who now profess not to believe in any sort of religion, it is very hard to discover what they really believe. The reason why they find it so easy to think that they are not religious, is that they have never got into the frame of mind of one who suffers from the doubts to which religion is the answer. Not for them the terrors of the primitive jungle. Having abandoned some of the more picturesque fringes of religion, they think that they have abandoned the whole thing—whereas in fact they still have got, and could not live without, a religion of a comfortably substantial, albeit highly sophisticated, kind, which differs from that of many 'religious people' in little more than this, that 'religious people' like to sing Psalms about theirs—a very natural and proper thing to do. But nevertheless there may be a big difference lying behind—the difference between two people who, though side by side, are walking in different directions. I do not know in what direction Flew is walking; perhaps he does not know either. But we have had some examples recently of various ways in which one can walk away from Christianity, and there are any number of possibilities. After all, man has not changed biologically since primitive times; it is his religion that has changed, and it can easily change again. And if you do not think that such changes make a difference, get acquainted with some Sikhs and some Mussulmans of the same Punjabi stock; you will find them quite different sorts of people.

There is an important difference between Flew's parable and my own which we have not yet noticed. The explorers do not *mind* about their garden; they discuss it with interest, but not with concern. But my lunatic, poor fellow, minds about dons; and I mind about the steering of my car; it often has people in it that I care for. It is because I mind very much about what goes on in the garden in which I find myself, that I am unable to share the explorers' detachment.

C

Basil Mitchell

Flew's article is searching and perceptive, but there is, I think, something odd about his conduct of the theologian's case. The theologian surely would not deny that the fact of pain counts against the assertion that God loves men. This very incompatibility generates the most intractable of theological problems—the problem of evil. So the theologian *does* recognize the fact of pain as counting against Christian doctrine. But it is true that he will not allow it—or anything—to count decisively against it; for he is committed by his faith to trust in God. His attitude is not that of the detached observer, but of the believer.

Perhaps this can be brought out by yet another parable. In time of war in an occupied country, a member of the resistance meets one night a stranger who deeply impresses him. They spend that night together in conversation. The Stranger tells the partisan that he himself is on the side of the resistance —indeed that he is in command of it, and urges the partisan to have faith in him no matter what happens. The partisan is utterly convinced at that meeting of the Stranger's sincerity and constancy and undertakes to trust him.

They never meet in conditions of intimacy again. But sometimes the Stranger is seen helping members of the resistance, and the partisan is grateful and says to his friends, 'He is on our side'.

Sometimes he is seen in the uniform of the police handing over patriots to the occupying power. On these occasions his friends murmur against him: but the partisan still says, 'He is on our side'. He still believes that, in spite of appearances, the Stranger did not deceive him. Sometimes he asks the Stranger for help and receives it. He is then thankful. Sometimes he asks and does not receive it. Then he says, 'The Stranger knows best'. Sometimes his friends, in exasperation, say 'Well, what *would* he have to do for you to admit that you were wrong and that he is not on our side?' But the partisan refuses to answer. He will not consent to put the Stranger to the test. And sometimes his friends complain, 'Well, if *that's* what you mean by his being on our side, the sooner he goes over to the other side the better'.

The partisan of the parable does not allow anything to count decisively against the proposition 'The Stranger is on our side'. This is because he has committed himself to trust the Stranger. But he of course recognizes that the Stranger's ambiguous behaviour *does* count against what he believes about him. It is precisely this situation which constitutes the trial of his faith.

When the partisan asks for help and doesn't get it, what can he do? He can (*a*) conclude that the stranger is not on our side or; (*b*) maintain that he is on our side, but that he has reasons for withholding help.

The first he will refuse to do. How long can he uphold the second position without its becoming just silly?

I don't think one can say in advance. It will depend on the nature of the impression created by the Stranger in the first place. It will depend, too, on the manner in which he takes the Stranger's behaviour. If he blandly dismisses it as of no consequence, as having no bearing upon his belief, it will be assumed that he is thoughtless or insane. And it quite obviously won't do for him to say easily, 'Oh, when used of the Stranger the phrase "is on our side" *means* ambiguous behaviour of this sort'. In that case he would be like the religious man who says blandly of a terrible disaster 'It is God's will'. No, he will only be regarded as sane and reasonable in his belief, if he experiences in himself the full force of the conflict.

It is here that my parable differs from Hare's. The partisan admits that many things may and do count against his belief: whereas Hare's lunatic who has a *blik* about dons doesn't admit that anything counts against his *bliḳ*. Nothing *can* count against *bliḳs*. Also the partisan has a reason for having in the first instance committed himself, viz. the character of the Stranger; whereas the lunatic has no reason for his *bliḳ* about dons—because, of course, you can't have reasons for *bliḳs*.

This means that I agree with Flew that theological utterances must be assertions. The partisan is making an assertion when he says, 'The Stranger is on our side'.

Do I want to say that the partisan's belief about the Stranger is, in any sense, an explanation? I think I do. It explains and makes sense of the Stranger's behaviour: it helps to explain also the resistance movement in the context of which he appears. In each case it differs from the interpretation which the others put upon the same facts.

'God loves men' resembles 'the Stranger is on our side' (and many other significant statements, e.g. historical ones) in not being conclusively falsifiable. They can both be treated in at least three different ways: (1) As provisional hypotheses to be discarded if experience tells against them; (2) As significant articles of faith; (3) As vacuous formulae (expressing, perhaps, a desire for reassurance) to which experience makes no difference and which make no difference to life.

The Christian, once he has committed himself, is precluded by his faith from taking up the first attitude: 'Thou shalt not tempt the Lord thy God'. He is in constant danger, as Flew has observed, of slipping into the third. But he need not; and, if he does, it is a failure in faith as well as in logic.

D

Antony Flew

It has been a good discussion: and I am glad to have helped to provoke it. But now—at least in *University*—it must come to an end: and the Editors of *University* have asked me to make some concluding remarks. Since it is impossible to deal with all the issues raised or to comment separately upon each contribution, I will concentrate on Mitchell and Hare, as representative of two very different kinds of response to the challenge made in 'Theology and Falsification'.

The challenge, it will be remembered, ran like this. Some theological utterances seem to, and are intended to, provide explanations or express assertions. Now an assertion, to be an assertion at all, must claim that things stand thus and thus; *and not otherwise*. Similarly an explanation, to be an explanation at all, must explain why this particular thing occurs; *and not something else*. Those last clauses are crucial. And yet sophisticated religious people—or so it seemed to me—are apt to overlook this, and tend to refuse to allow, not merely that anything actually does occur, but that anything conceivably could occur, which would count against their theological assertions and explanations. But in so far as they do this their supposed explanations are actually bogus, and their seeming assertions are really vacuous.

Mitchell's response to this challenge is admirably direct, straightforward, and understanding. He agrees 'that theological utterances must be assertions'. He agrees that if they are to be assertions, there must be something that would count against their truth. He agrees, too, that believers are in constant danger of transforming their would-be assertions into 'vacuous formulae'. But he takes me to task for an oddity in my 'conduct of the theologian's case. The theologian surely would not deny that the fact of pain counts against the assertion that God loves men. This very incompatibility generates the most intractable of theological problems, the problem of evil'. I think he is right. I should have made a distinction between two very different ways of dealing with what looks like evidence against the love of God: the way I stressed was the expedient of qualifying the original assertion; the way the theologian usually takes, at first, is to admit that it looks bad but to insist that there is—there must be—some explanation which will show that, in spite of appearances, there really is a God who loves us. His difficulty, it seems to me, is that he has given God attributes which rule out all possible saving explanations. In Mitchell's parable of the Stranger it is easy for the believer to find plausible excuses for ambiguous behaviour: for the Stranger is a man. But suppose the Stranger is God. We cannot say that he would like to help but cannot: God is omnipotent. We cannot say that he would help if he only knew: God is omniscient. We cannot say that he is not responsible for the wickedness of others: God creates those others. Indeed an omnipotent, omniscient God must be an accessory before (and during) the fact to every human misdeed; as well as being responsible for every non-moral defect in the universe. So, though I entirely concede that Mitchell was absolutely right to insist against me that the theologian's first move is to look for an *explanation,* I still think that in the end, if relentlessly pursued, he will have to resort to the avoiding action of *qualification.* And there lies the danger of that death by a thousand qualifications, which would, I agree, constitute 'a failure in faith as well as in logic'.

Hare's approach is fresh and bold. He confesses that 'on the ground marked out by Flew, he seems to me to be completely victorious'. He therefore introduces the concept of *blik*. But while I think that there is room for some such concept in philosophy, and that philosophers should be grateful to Hare for his invention, I nevertheless want to insist that any attempt to analyse Christian religious utterances as expressions or affirmations of a *blik* rather than as (at least would-be) assertions about the cosmos is fundamentally misguided. *First,* because thus interpreted they would be entirely unorthodox. If Hare's religion really is a *blik,* involving no cosmological assertions about the nature and activities of a supposed personal creator, then surely he is not a Christian at all? *Second,* because thus interpreted, they could scarcely do the job they do. If they were not even intended as assertions then many religious activities would become fraudulent, or merely silly. If 'You ought *because* it is God's will' asserts no more than 'You ought', then the person who prefers the former phraseology is not really giving a reason, but a fraudulent substitute for one, a dialectical dud cheque. If 'My soul must be immortal *because* God loves his children, etc.' asserts no more than 'My soul must be immortal', then the man who reassures himself with theological arguments for immortality is being as silly as the man who tries to clear his overdraft by writing his bank a cheque on the same account. (Of course neither of these utterances would be distinctively Christian: but this discussion never pretended to be so confined.) Religious utterances may indeed express false or even bogus assertions: but I simply do not believe that they are not both intended and interpreted to be or at any rate to presuppose assertions, at least in the context of religious practice; whatever shifts may be demanded, in another context, by the exigencies of theological apologetic.

One final suggestion. The philosophers of religion might well draw upon George Orwell's last appalling nightmare *1984* for the concept of *double-think*. 'Doublethink means the power of holding two contradictory beliefs simultaneously, and accepting both of them. The party intellectual knows that he is playing tricks with reality, but by the exercise of *doublethink* he also satisfies himself that reality is not violated'. Perhaps religious intellectuals too are sometimes driven to doublethink in order to retain their faith in a loving God in face of the reality of a heartless and indifferent world. But of this more another time, perhaps.

QUESTIONS

1. What is the philosophical point of the Parable of the Invisible Gardener, cited by Professor Flew?
2. What reasoning leads Professor Flew to claim that, if such utterances as "God created the world" and "God loves us" do not deny anything, they cannot be assertions? Is this reasoning sound? Defend your answer.
3. Suppose that, in answer to the question, "Just what would have to happen to entitle us to say that God does not love us?" a religious believer replies, "Nothing could possibly happen to entitle us to say that, since it is false to say it." What comments would Professor Flew make about such a reply?
4. What does Mr. Hare mean by a *blik?* Give examples of *bliks* other than those mentioned by Mr. Hare, and explain why they are *bliks*.
5. Mr. Hare states, "Flew has shown that a *blik* does not consist in an assertion or system of them." What reasons does he have for saying this?
6. Defend or attack the following thesis: "*Bliks* are neither true nor false because it is they that determine the criteria of truth and falsity for any statement." Would Mr. Hare accept this thesis? Answer by referring to passages from Mr. Hare's discussion.
7. Does it follow from Mr. Hare's view that every person has a religion, whether or not he is willing to call it by that name? Why or why not?
8. How does Mr. Mitchell reply to Professor Flew's challenge to the religious believer? State why you think his reply is, or is not, successful.

9. What is the philosophical point of the Parable of the Stranger, given by Mr. Mitchell?
10. Mr. Mitchell argues that the statement "God loves men" can be treated in three different ways. Explain in detail what each of these ways is, and show why, in your opinion, each of these ways does or does not necessarily exclude the other two. Can you think of a fourth way, which might be acceptable to a religious believer? Which way would be most acceptable to St. Thomas Aquinas?
11. Assess the strengths and weaknesses of Professor Flew's final replies to the arguments given by Mr. Hare and Mr. Mitchell.
12. How does Professor Walsh's account of the nature of metaphysical assertions in "True and False in Metaphysics" (Chapter 3) tend to support Mr. Hare's account of the nature of religious assertions?

SUGGESTED FURTHER READING

Alston, W. P., ed., *Religious Belief and Philosophical Thought,* Harcourt, Brace & World, New York, 1963. (Anthology.)

Barth, Karl, *The Word of God and the Word of Man,* Harper, New York, 1957.

Bendall, K., and F. Ferre, *Exploring the Logic of Faith,* Association Press, New York, 1962.

Copleston, F. C., *Aquinas,* Penguin Books, Harmondsworth, Middlesex, Eng., 1955.

Dewey, John, *A Common Faith,* Yale University Press, New Haven, 1935.

Dods, Marcus, ed., *The Works of Aurelius Augustine,* Vol. 9, *On Christian Doctrine; The Enchiridion; On Catechising, and On Faith and the Creed.* T. & T. Clark, Edinburgh, 1892.

Ferré, F., *Language, Logic and God,* Harper, New York, 1961.

Flew, Antony, and Alasdair MacIntyre, eds., *New Essays in Philosophical Theology,* Macmillan, New York, 1955.

Gosse, Edmund, *Father and Son: A Study of Two Temperaments,* Scribner's, New York, 1907. (Autobiographical account of religious experience.)

Hepburn, Ronald, *Christianity and Paradox,* Humanities Press, New York, 1958.

Hick, John, *Faith and Knowledge,* Cornell University Press, Ithaca, 1957.

———, ed., *Philosophers and Faith,* Macmillan, London, 1964. (Anthology.)

———, *Philosophy of Religion,* Prentice-Hall, Englewood Cliffs, N. J., 1963.

James, William, *Varieties of Religious Experience,* 1902. Many publishers, many editions.

Kaufmann, Walter, *Critique of Religion and Philosophy,* Harper, New York, 1958.

Kimpel, Ben F., *Language and Religion,* Philosophical Library, New York, 1957.

Lewis, H. D., *Our Experience of God,* Macmillan, New York, 1959.

MacIntyre, Alasdair, "The Logical Status of Religious Belief," *Metaphysical Beliefs: Three Essays,* by S. E. Toulmin, R. W. Hepburn, and A. MacIntyre, Student Christian Movement Press, London, 1957.

Martin, C. B., *Religious Belief,* Cornell University Press, Ithaca, N. Y. 1959.

McCarthy, Mary, *Memories of a Catholic Girlhood,* Harcourt, Brace & World, New York, 1957. (Autobiographical account of religious experience.)

Mitchell, Basil, ed., *Faith and Logic,* Allen & Unwin, London, 1957.

Robinson, Richard, *An Atheist's Values,* Oxford University Press, London, 1964.

Russell, Bertrand, *Religion and Science,* Oxford University Press, Oxford, 1935.

———, *Why I Am Not a Christian,* Allen & Unwin, London, 1957.

Spinoza, Benedict de, *Tractatus Theologico-Politicus,* 1670. Many publishers, many editions.

Sprague, Elmer, *What Is Philosophy?,* Oxford University Press, New York, 1961. Chap. 4, "Philosophy and God."

Stace, W. T., *Mysticism and Philosophy,* Macmillan, London, 1961.

———, ed., *The Teachings of the Mystics,* New American Library, New York, 1960.

Underhill, Evelyn, *Mysticism,* Macmillan, London, 1930.

Wisdom, John, "Gods," *Proceedings of the Aristotelian Society,* 1944. Reprinted in *Philosophy and Psycho-Analysis,* by John Wisdom, Blackwell, Oxford, 1957; and in *Logic and Language, First Series,* ed. by Antony Flew, Blackwell, Oxford, 1951.

Chapter 7. Proving God's Existence

Notice the sort of question which the question "Is there a God?" is not like. It is not like the question "Are there okapis?" For this question can be finally answered by showing the questioner an okapi. But if, as many theists suppose (and here we shall follow their supposition), God is outside the world, is a transcendent being, then we cannot look for God in the world. So we cannot answer the question "Is there a God?" by pointing to something in the world, as we can answer the question "Are there okapis?" by pointing to an okapi.

How then do theists who believe in a transcendent God prove his existence? In this chapter we offer examples of their efforts which may be classified under three heads: Proofs from the Nature of God, Proofs from the Nature of the World, and the Proof by Analogy. Proofs from the nature of God are designed to show that God's nature is such that once we understand it, we can see it implies his existence. Proofs from the nature of the world show that the world has some quality (motion, beauty, order, etc.) which it could not have given itself and which implies the existence of a source, namely, God. The proof by analogy is designed to show that there is a resemblance between the world and machines and that just as machines have inventors so the world must have a maker, who is God. In this chapter we offer Anselm's proof from the nature of God, Aquinas' proofs from the nature of the world, and

Hume's discussion of the proof by analogy. Just after each of these ways of proving by reason that God exists, the reader will find an equally reasonable criticism which may be leveled against the proof.

Anselm believes as a matter of faith that God exists. But he tries to *prove* that God exists as a matter of intellectual curiosity. We say as a matter of intellectual curiosity, because his success is in no way crucial to his belief. Whether he succeeds or fails, he will continue to believe on faith. Guanilo's criticisms of Anselm's argument may sting; but they will never shake his belief, because it is not dependent on the argument.

Aquinas, too, believes as a matter of faith that God exists. But he tries to prove by reason that God exists, so that he may convince nonbelievers by undeniable arguments that they ought to believe in God's existence.

Hume does not believe that God's existence can be proved by reason, and he uses reason to demolish those arguments which are supposed to prove that God exists. Aquinas and Hume are, of course, working in direct contradiction, the one expecting to support the statement "God exists" by reason, the other expecting to show its untenability on reasonable grounds. Whether these attempts to argue for or against God's existence on the grounds of reason alone are misdirected or inappropriate is a question which the reader must consider for himself.

21. ST. ANSELM

(1033?–1109)

Faith Seeking Understanding

Anselm was first Prior and then Abbot of the Monastery of Bec, in Normandy, which was in his time the greatest center of learning in all Europe. He spent the last six years of his life as Archbishop of Canterbury in England. We remember him today as a Scholastic theologian. His most famous contribution to religious thought is probably his proof of God's existence based on God's nature (or being), and his statement of this proof is the subject of the reading before us. This proof is commonly called the ontological argument (from "ontology," the science of being) and it owes much to the theology of the early Christian writer, St. Augustine (354–430 A.D.). Augustine's theology in turn owes much to the philosophy of Plato. Anselm is, however, to be credited with making the definitive statement of the ontological argument, and everyone turns to him to read the argument in its original form.

A typical example of a proof of God's existence by arguing from his nature follows. The clue to God's nature is the way we talk about him, and we say that God is a perfect being. Now, it is an imperfection not to exist. But God is perfect; so he has no imperfections. Therefore, since he is perfect, he must exist.

The reader must see that this argument turns on unpacking the word "perfect." It is being used in an equivocal way, that is, with several meanings, one of which is "existent." Thus, when we say that God is perfect, we are also saying that God exists. The critical questions, then, which may be asked about this argument are these: Must we say that "perfect" means "existent"? and, Must we say that God is perfect? As Aquinas points out in his criticism of this kind of argument, we need say neither of these things. So, the appeal of any proof of God's existence by an inference from his nature is strictly limited to those who are willing to talk of God as the argument prescribes. But there is yet a more serious question to be asked about any proof of God's existence drawn from his nature: Isn't it an effort to define God into existence? The fact that we know how to talk about unicorns, and could identify one if we saw it in the garden, does not mean that we should ever expect to see one. As Aquinas remarks, it is one thing to define a word; it is a separate and independent move to claim that what the word can be used to talk about exists. So, we may define "God" as meaning "a perfect being," but it is another thing to claim that God exists. Of course, the theists, who take the proof of God's existence from his nature seriously, point out that God is unique in being the one entity, the inconceivability of whose nonexistence is shown as soon as his nature is properly conceived. But this is a contention whose value we must leave the reader to consider for himself.

This selection is drawn from the *Proslogion* (1077–78), Preface and Chapters I through IV. The original chapter titles are retained as subtitles in this reading. The translation from the Latin is by Professor Eugene R. Fairweather.

From *A Scholastic Miscellany,* by Eugene R. Fairweather,
editor and translator, The Westminster Press, Phila., 1956.
Used by permission.

PREFACE

Some time ago, at the urgent request of some of my brethren, I published a brief work,[1] as an example of meditation on the grounds of faith. I wrote it in the role of one who seeks, by silent reasoning with himself, to learn what he does not know. But when I reflected on this little book, and saw that it was put together as a long chain of arguments, I began to ask myself whether *one* argument might possibly be found, resting on no other argument for its proof, but sufficient in itself to prove that God truly exists, and that he is the supreme good, needing nothing outside himself, but needful for the being and well-being of all things. I often turned my earnest attention to this problem, and at times I believed that I could put my finger on what I was looking for, but at other times it completely escaped my mind's eye, until finally, in despair, I decided to give up searching for something that seemed impossible to find. But when I tried to put the whole question out of my mind, so as to avoid crowding out other matters, with which I might make some progress, by this useless preoccupation, then, despite my unwillingness and resistance, it began to force itself on me more persistently than ever. Then, one day, when I was worn out by my vigorous resistance to the obsession, the solution I had ceased to hope for presented itself to me, in the very turmoil of my thoughts, so that I enthusiastically embraced the idea which, in my disquiet, I had spurned.

I thought that the proof I was so glad to find would please some readers if it were written down. Consequently, I have written the little work that follows, dealing with this and one or two other matters, in the role of one who strives to raise his mind to the contemplation of God and seeks to understand what he believes. Neither this essay nor the other one I have already mentioned really seemed to me to deserve to be called a book or to bear an author's name; at the same time, I felt that they could not be pub-

[1] The *Monologion,* probably Anselm's first work, was written at Bec in the second half of 1076 (cf. Landgraf, *Einführung,* 53). Text in Schmitt, I, 7–87.—E. R. Fairweather

lished without some title that might encourage anyone into whose hands they fell to read them, and so I gave each of them a title. The first I called *An Example of Meditation on the Grounds of Faith,* and the second *Faith Seeking Understanding.*

But when both of them had been copied under these titles by a number of people, I was urged by many people—and especially by Hugh, the reverend archbishop of Lyons, apostolic legate in Gaul, who ordered this with apostolic authority—to attach my name to them. In order to do this more fittingly, I have named the first *Monologion* (or *Soliloquy*), and the second *Proslogion* (or *Address*).

THE AWAKENING OF THE MIND TO THE CONTEMPLATION OF GOD

Now then, little man, for a short while fly from your business; hide yourself for a moment from your turbulent thoughts. Break off now your troublesome cares, and think less of your laborious occupations. Make a little time for God, and rest for a while in him. Enter into the chamber of your mind, shut out everything but God and whatever helps you to seek him, and, when you have shut the door, seek him. Speak now, O my whole heart, speak now to God: "I seek thy face; thy face, Lord, do I desire." [2]

And do thou, O Lord my God, teach my heart where and how to seek thee, where and how to find thee. Lord, if thou art not here, where shall I seek thee who art absent? But if thou art everywhere, why do I not see thee who art present? . . . Let me receive thy light, even from afar, even from the depths. Teach me to seek thee, and when I seek thee show thyself to me, for I cannot seek thee unless thou teach me, or find thee unless thou show me thyself. Let me seek thee in my desire, let me desire thee in my seeking. Let me find thee by loving thee, let me love thee when I find thee.

I acknowledge, O Lord, with thanksgiving, that thou hast created this thy image in me, so that, remembering thee, I may think of thee, may love thee. But this image is so effaced and worn away by my faults, it is so obscured by the smoke of my sins, that it cannot do what it was made to do, unless thou renew and reform it. I am not trying, O Lord, to penetrate thy loftiness, for I cannot begin to match my understanding with it, but I desire in some measure to understand thy truth, which my heart believes and loves. For I do not seek to understand in order to believe, but I believe in order to understand. For this too I believe, that "unless I believe, I shall not understand."

[2] Ps. 26:8 (P.B.V., 27:9); not an exact quotation.—E. R. Fairweather

GOD TRULY IS

And so, O Lord, since thou givest understanding to faith, give me to understand—as far as thou knowest it to be good for me—that thou dost exist, as we believe, and that thou art what we believe thee to be. Now we believe that thou art a being than which none greater can be thought. Or can it be that there is no such being, since "the fool hath said in his heart, 'There is no God' "? But when this same fool hears what I am saying—"A being than which none greater can be thought"—he understands what he hears, and what he understands is in his understanding, even if he does not understand that it exists. For it is one thing for an object to be in the understanding, and another thing to understand that it exists. When a painter considers beforehand what he is going to paint, he has it in his understanding, but he does not suppose that what he has not yet painted already exists. But when he has painted it, he both has it in his understanding and understands that what he has now produced exists. Even the fool, then, must be convinced that a being than which none greater can be thought exists at least in his understanding, since when he hears this he understands it, and whatever is understood is in the understanding. But clearly that than which a greater cannot be thought cannot exist in the understanding alone. For if it is actually in the understanding alone, it can be thought of as existing also in reality, and this is greater. Therefore, if that than which a greater cannot be thought is in the understanding alone, this same thing than which a greater cannot be thought is that than which a greater can be thought. But obviously this is impossible. Without doubt, therefore, there exists, both in the understanding and in reality, something than which a greater cannot be thought.

GOD CANNOT BE THOUGHT OF AS NONEXISTENT

And certainly it exists so truly that it cannot be thought of as nonexistent. For something can be thought of as existing, which cannot be thought of as not existing, and this is greater than that which *can* be thought of as not existing. Thus, if that than which a greater cannot be thought can be thought of as not existing, this very thing than which a greater cannot be thought is *not* that than which a greater cannot be thought. But this is contradictory. So, then, there truly is a being than which a greater cannot be thought—so truly that it cannot even be thought of as not existing.

And *thou* art this being, O Lord our God. Thou so truly art, then, O Lord my God, that thou canst not even be thought of as not existing. And this is right. For if some mind could think of something better than thou, the creature would rise above the Creator and judge its Creator; but this is altogether absurd. And indeed, whatever is, except thyself alone, can be thought of as not existing. Thou alone, therefore, of all beings, hast being in the truest and highest sense, since no other being so truly exists, and thus every other being has less being. Why, then, has "the fool said in his heart, 'There is no God,'" when it is so obvious to the rational mind that, of all beings, thou dost exist supremely? Why indeed, unless it is that he is a stupid fool?

HOW THE FOOL HAS SAID IN HIS HEART WHAT CANNOT BE THOUGHT

But how did he manage to say in his heart what he could not think? Or how is it that he was unable to think what he said in his heart? After all, to say in one's heart and to think are the same thing. Now if it is true—or, rather, since it is true—that he thought it, because he said it in his heart, but did not say it in his heart, since he could not think it, it is clear that something can be said in one's heart or thought in more than one way. For we think of a thing, in one sense, when we think of the word that signifies it, and in another sense, when we understand the very thing itself. Thus, in the first sense God can be thought of as nonexistent, but in the second sense this is quite impossible. For no one who understands what God is can think that God does not exist, even though he says these words in his heart—perhaps without any meaning, perhaps with some quite extraneous meaning. For God is that than which a greater cannot be thought, and whoever understands this rightly must understand that he exists in such a way that he cannot be nonexistent even in thought. He, therefore, who understands that God thus exists cannot think of him as nonexistent.

Thanks be to thee, good Lord, thanks be to thee, because I now understand by thy light what I formerly believed by thy gift, so that even if I were to refuse to believe in thy existence, I could not fail to understand its truth.

QUESTIONS

1. How does Anselm endeavor to prove that God exists? Do the steps in his proof appear to be statements of fact, or definitions, or some third kind of statement? If you accept (or reject) the steps in Anselm's proof, what are your grounds for doing so? (The reader may find it easier to answer these questions if he writes out the steps of the proof in 1, 2, 3 order.)
2. What bearing does Anselm's prefacing his proof of God's existence with a prayer have on its validity?
3. How does Anselm account for a "fool's" trying to reject his argument?
4. How would Anselm reply to a person who said:
   "I can think of the most perfect society, a Utopia, but that does not mean that a perfect society exists anywhere in the world; therefore, just because I think of a perfect being, namely, God, that does not mean that God exists."?

22. GUANILO

(Eleventh Century)

In Behalf of the Fool

Guanilo, a monk of Marmoutier in Touraine and a contemporary of Anselm, wrote a reply to Anselm's argument proving God's existence. Guanilo makes a sharp distinction between someone's being able to think of a thing and that thing's existing; hence, he argues against our being able to infer the existence of something from our being able to think of it.

The selection by Guanilo is drawn from "In Behalf of the Fool." The translation from the Latin is by Sidney Norton Deane.

From *St. Anselm: Basic Writings,* trans. by S. N. Deane, 2nd ed., with an introduction by Charles Hartshorne, The Open Court Publishing Co., La Salle, Illinois, 1961.

The fool might make this reply:

This being is said to be in my understanding already, only because I understand what is said. Now could it not with equal justice be said that I have in my understanding all manner of unreal objects, having absolutely no existence in themselves, because I understand these things if one speaks of them, whatever they may be?

Unless indeed it is shown that this being is of such a character that it cannot be held in concept like all unreal objects, or objects whose existence is uncertain: and hence I am not able to conceive of it when I hear of it, or to hold it in concept; but I must understand it and have it in my understanding; because, it seems, I cannot conceive of it in any other way than by understanding it, that is, by comprehending in my knowledge its existence in reality.

But if this is the case, in the first place there will be no distinction between what has precedence in time—namely, the having of an object in the understanding—and what is subsequent in time—namely, the understanding that an object exists; as in the example of the picture, which exists first in the mind of the painter, and afterwards in his work.

Moreover, the following assertion can hardly be accepted: that this being, when it is spoken of and heard of, cannot be conceived not to exist in the way in which even God can be conceived not to exist. For if this is impossible, what was the object of this argument against one who doubts or denies the existence of such a being?

Finally, that this being so exists that it cannot be perceived by an understanding convinced of its own indubitable existence, unless this being is afterwards conceived of—this should be proved to me by an indisputable argument, but not by that which you have advanced: namely, that what I understand, when I hear it, already is in my understanding. For thus in my understanding, as I still think, could be all sorts of things whose existence is uncertain, or which do not exist at all, if some one whose words I should understand mentioned them. And so much the more if I should be deceived, as often happens, and believe in them: though I do not yet believe in the being whose existence you would prove.

.   .   .

But that this being must exist, not only in the understanding but also in reality, is thus proved to me:

If it did not so exist, whatever exists in reality would be greater than it. And so the being which has been already proved to exist in my understanding, will not be greater than all other beings.

I still answer: if it should be said that a being which cannot be even conceived in terms of any fact, is in the understanding, I do not deny that this being is, accordingly, in my understanding. But since through this fact it can in no wise attain to real existence also, I do not yet concede to it that existence at all, until some certain proof of it shall be given.

For he who says that this being exists, because otherwise the being which is greater than all will not be greater than all, does not attend strictly enough to what he is saying. For I do not yet say, no, I even deny or doubt that this being is greater than any real object. Nor do I concede to it any other existence than this (if it should be called existence) which it has when the mind, according to a word merely heard, tries to form the image of an object absolutely unknown to it.

How, then, is the veritable existence of that being proved to me from the assumption, by hypothesis, that it is greater than all other beings? For I should still deny this, or doubt your demonstration of it, to this extent, that I should not admit that this being is in my understanding and concept even in the way in which many objects whose real existence is uncertain and doubtful, are in my understanding and concept. For it should be proved first that this being itself really exists somewhere; and then, from the fact that it is greater than all, we shall not hesitate to infer that it also subsists in itself.

For example: it is said that somewhere in the ocean is an island, which, because of the difficulty, or rather the impossibility, of discovering what does not exist, is called the lost island. And they say that this island has an inestimable wealth of all manner of riches and delicacies in greater abundance than is told of the Islands of the Blest; and that having no owner or inhabitant, it is more excellent than all other countries, which are inhabited by mankind, in the abundance with which it is stored.

Now if some one should tell me that there is such an island, I should easily understand his words, in which there is no difficulty. But suppose that he went on to say, as if by a logical inference: "You can no longer doubt that this island which is more excellent than all lands exists somewhere, since you have no doubt that it is in your understanding. And since it is more excellent not to be in the understanding alone, but to exist both in the understanding and in reality, for this reason it must exist. For if it does not exist, any land which really exists will be more excellent than it; and so the island already understood by you to be more excellent will not be more excellent."

If a man should try to prove to me by such reasoning that this island truly exists, and that its existence should no longer be doubted, either I should believe that he was jesting, or I know not which I ought to regard as the greater fool: myself, supposing that I should allow this proof; or him, if he should suppose that he had established with any certainty the existence of this island. For he ought to show first that the hypothetical excellence of this island exists as a real and indubitable fact, and in no wise as any unreal object, or one whose existence is uncertain, in my understanding.

. . .

QUESTIONS

1. How does Guanilo attack the claim that the being which is greater than all must be in my understanding already, because I understand what is said?
2. How does Guanilo attack the claim that the being which is greater than all must exist in order to be greater than all?
3. How is Guanilo's Lost Island Argument a refutation of Anselm's argument to prove the existence of a being greater than all?

23. ST. ANSELM

(1033?–1109)

Anselm's Apologetic

In his reply to Guanilo, Anselm argues that the distinction between the conceivability of something and its real existence applies to everything except a being whose nature is such that a greater cannot be thought. Thus, his argument about God's existence, he claims, escapes Guanilo's strictures.

This selection is drawn from "Anselm's Apologetic." The translation from the Latin is by Sidney Norton Deane.

From *St. Anselm: Basic Writings,* trans. by S. N. Deane,
2nd ed., with an introduction by Charles Hartshorne,
The Open Court Publishing Co., La Salle, Illinois, 1961.

You say—whosoever you may be, who say that a fool is capable of making these statements—that a being than which a greater cannot be conceived is not in the understanding in any other sense than that in which a being that is altogether inconceivable in terms of reality, is in the understanding. You say that the inference that this being exists in reality, from the fact that it is in the understanding, is no more just than the inference that a lost island most certainly exists, from the fact that when it is described the hearer does not doubt that it is in his understanding.

But I say: if a being than which a greater is inconceivable is not understood or conceived, and is not in the understanding or in concept, certainly either God is not a being than which a greater is inconceivable, or else he is not understood or conceived, and is not in the understanding or in concept. But I call on your faith and conscience to attest that this is most false. Hence, that than which a greater cannot be conceived is truly understood and conceived, and is in the understanding and in concept. Therefore either the grounds on which you try to controvert me are not true, or else the inference which you think to base logically on those grounds is not justified.

But you hold, moreover, that supposing that a being than which a greater cannot be conceived is understood, it does not follow that this being is in the understanding; nor, if it is in the understanding, does it therefore exist in reality.

In answer to this, I maintain positively: if that being can be even conceived to be, it must exist in reality. For that than which a greater is inconceivable cannot be conceived except as without beginning. But whatever can be conceived to exist, and does not exist, can be conceived to exist through a beginning. Hence what can be conceived to exist, but does not exist, is not the being than which a greater cannot be conceived. Therefore, if such a being can be conceived to exist, necessarily it does exist.

Furthermore: if it can be conceived at all, it must exist. For no one who denies or doubts the existence of a being than which a greater is inconceivable, denies or doubts that if it did exist, its non-existence, either in reality or in the understanding, would be impossible. For otherwise it would not be a being than which a greater cannot be conceived. But as to whatever can be conceived, but does not exist—if there were such a being, its non-existence, either in reality or in the understanding, would be possible. Therefore if a being than which a greater is inconceivable can be even conceived, it cannot be non-existent.

But let us suppose that it does not exist, even if it can be conceived. Whatever can be conceived, but does not exist, if it existed, would not be a being than which a greater is inconceivable. If, then, there were a being a greater than which is inconceivable, it would not be a being than which a greater is inconceivable: which is most absurd. Hence, it is false to deny that a being than which a greater cannot be conceived exists, if it can be even conceived; much the more, therefore, if it can be understood or can be in the understanding.

. . .

But, you say, it is as if one should suppose an island in the ocean, which surpasses all lands in its fertility, and which, because of the difficulty, or rather the impossibility, of discovering what does not exist, is called a lost island; and should say that there can be no doubt that this island truly exists in reality, for this reason, that one who hears it described easily understands what he hears.

Now I promise confidently that if any man shall devise anything existing either in reality or in concept alone (except that than which a greater cannot be conceived) to which he can adapt the sequence of my reasoning, I will discover that thing, and will give him his lost island, not to be lost again.

But it now appears that this being than which a greater is inconceivable cannot be conceived not to be, because it exists on so assured a ground of truth; for otherwise it would not exist at all.

Hence, if any one says that he conceives this being not to exist, I say that at the time when he conceives of this either he conceives of a being than which a greater is inconceivable, or he does not conceive at all. If he does not conceive, he does not conceive of the non-existence of that of which he does not conceive. But if he does conceive, he certainly conceives of a being which cannot be even conceived not to exist. For if it could be conceived not to exist, it could be conceived to have a beginning and an end. But this is impossible.

He, then, who conceives of this being conceives of a being which cannot be even conceived not to exist; but he who conceives of this being does not conceive that it does not exist; else he conceives what is inconceivable. The non-existence, then, of that than which a greater cannot be conceived is inconceivable.

QUESTIONS

1. How does Anselm argue against Guanilo's claim that a being, a greater than which cannot be conceived, can be thought of and still not exist?
2. How does Anselm meet Guanilo's Lost Island Argument? If you can pick a winner in the dispute between Guanilo and Anselm, whom do you pick and why?

24. ST. THOMAS AQUINAS

(1225?–74)

The Demonstration of God's Existence

(A general introductory note on Aquinas may be found on page 327.)

This selection contains both Aquinas' defense of the claim that it is possible to demonstrate by reason that God exists, and his statement of the five arguments which prove that God exists as given in the *Summa Theologica.* In the *Summa Contra Gentiles,* Aquinas acknowledges his debt to Aristotle for the first four of these arguments, and to both St. John Damascene (d. before 754), a theologian of the Greek Church, and Averroës (1126–98), an Arab philosopher, for the fifth. What is more, all of the arguments owe much to Aristotle's doctrine of the four kinds of causes. Thus, to aid the reader, we have appended to this selection a short statement of Aristotle's doctrine of causes taken from his *Metaphysics.*

To appreciate proofs of God's existence from the nature of the world, of which Aquinas' five are the most notable examples, the reader ought to like detective stories, for these proofs are essays in detection. As a reminder of the hazards of detective investigations, it will be helpful to examine the kind of reasoning which occurs in the following situation. When a firm's office manager arrived at his office one morning, he discovered that the door of the office safe had been blown from its hinges, and the safe had been emptied

of its contents. Believing that only robbers blow open safes, he immediately telephoned his employer to report the robbery. The employer, however, greeted the manager's news with laughter. For, wanting to get into the safe the previous night and not being able to wait for the time lock to operate, the employer himself had blown open the safe. Disappointed at the evaporation of the robber, the manager reviewed his reasoning to discover his mistake. The exploded safe door undeniably exists, and he was surely right in believing that safes do not blow themselves open. But, the manager noticed, the exploded safe implies the existence of a robber only if one looks at it with robbers in mind, that is, only if one employs the rule of reasoning: "Only robbers blow open safes." Mindful of his new rule, "Employers can blow open safes too," the manager resolved to be more careful in the future about reasoning from what exists to what might exist.

Now theists who try to prove God's existence from the nature of the world argue very much like our manager who argued from the exploded safe door to robbers. The theist who argues from the nature of the world to God's existence points out that the world possesses some characteristic which it could not have given itself. But since the world has the characteristic, it must have been given it by some entity which does have it. Therefore this entity, which the theist calls God, must exist. We may illustrate the strength and weakness of this kind of proof by an argument from what the theist regards as the most basic of the world's characteristics: its existence. Consider the fact that the world exists, a fact which we all accept as indubitably true. The world, however, could not have brought itself into existence. Therefore there must be some source of the existence of the world which is beyond or outside the world. This source of existence we call God.

The reader should notice that for someone to accept this argument he must agree to make two assumptions, without which the conclusion cannot be guaranteed. These assumptions are that the world could not bring itself into existence, and that there is a source of existence which is outside the world and always in existence itself, and which could bring the world into existence. These assumptions work to prove God's existence in the same way that the manager's rules, "Safes do not explode themselves," and "Only robbers blow open safes," worked to prove the existence of a robber. There are, however, certain difficulties in the theist's assumptions. The chief difficulty is that if the success of this argument turns on these assumptions, why must we accept them? For instance, why should we accept the assumption, "The world could not bring itself into existence," rather than the assumption, which is in effect the contradictory of the theist's assumption, "The world has always existed"? To make this last assumption is, of course, to deny that there is any problem about explaining the world's existence, which requires a transcendent God for its answer. Or,

consider the difficulties inherent in the theist's second assumption, "There is a source of existence which is outside the world and always in existence; and which could bring the world into existence." First, notice that in the light of the theist's postulating an ultimate source of existence, his opponent's postulating that the world has always existed may not seem too radical a move. Second, when the theist postulates an ultimate source of existence as part of his argument, he seems to assume what he intends to prove, namely, that God exists.

Whether the difficulties listed above render proving God's existence from the nature of the world a hopeless enterprise is a question which we leave to the reader's consideration. David Hume thought that difficulties like these do irreparable damage to theistic proofs from the nature of the world. Indeed he called such proofs "a priori," meaning to point out that their conclusion is assumed in the very statement of the argument. Aquinas, however, regarded the theistic proofs from the nature of the world as a posteriori, that is, as genuine inferences from experience. If they are genuine inferences from experience, then the reader should, of course, be able to conceive the kind of experience that would falsify them. We must add that Aquinas counted the proof of God's existence from his nature as a priori. The reader would do well to scrutinize Aquinas' own arguments for the existence of God based on the nature of the world, to see whether he commits any of the errors in reasoning which he discovers in proofs based on the nature of God.

This selection is the Second and Third Articles of Question II in the First Part of the *Summa Theologica.* The title of each article is a question.

In each article Aquinas first reports as objections the answers given to the title question by those authorities with whom he differs. Then he states his own answer to the question and finishes the article by offering his refutations of the objections.

From *Summa Theologiae:* Volume 2, *Existence and Nature of God,* by St. Thomas Aquinas. Copyright © Blackfriars, 1964. Used by permission of the Publisher, McGraw-Hill Book Company.

CAN IT BE MADE EVIDENT THAT THERE IS A GOD?

1. That God exists cannot, it seems, be made evident. For that God exists is an article of faith, and since, as St Paul says, faith is concerned with *the unseen,*[1] its propositions cannot be demonstrated, that is made evident. It is therefore impossible to demonstrate that God exists.

2. Moreover, the central link of demonstration is a definition. But Damascene[2] tells us that we cannot define what God is, but only what he is not. Hence we cannot demonstrate that God exists.

3. Moreover, if demonstration of God's existence were possible, this could only be by arguing from his effects. Now God and his effects are incommensurable; for God is infinite and his effects finite, and the finite cannot measure the infinite. Consequently, since effects incommensurate with their cause cannot make it evident, it does not seem possible to demonstrate that God exists.

ON THE OTHER HAND, St Paul tells us that *the hidden things of God can be clearly understood from the things that he has made.*[3] If so, one must be able to demonstrate that God exists from the things that he has made, for knowing whether a thing exists is the first step towards understanding it.

REPLY: There are two types of demonstration. One, showing 'why', follows the natural order of things among themselves, arguing from cause to effect; the other, showing 'that', follows the order in which we know things, arguing from effect to cause (for when an effect is more apparent to us than its cause, we come to know the cause through the effect). Now any effect of a cause demonstrates that that cause exists, in cases where the effect is better known to us, since effects are dependent upon causes, and can only occur if the causes already exist. From effects evident to us, therefore, we can demonstrate what in itself is not evident to us, namely, that God exists.

[1] *Hebrews* II, I.
[2] *De Fide Orthodoxa* I, 4. PG 94, 800.
[3] *Romans* I, 20.

Hence: 1. The truths about God which St Paul says we can know by our natural powers of reasoning [4]—that God exists, for example—are not numbered among the articles of faith, but are presupposed to them. For faith presupposes natural knowledge, just as grace does nature and all perfections that which they perfect. However, there is nothing to stop a man accepting on faith some truth which he personally cannot demonstrate, even if that truth in itself is such that demonstration could make it evident.

2. When we argue from effect to cause, the effect will take the place of a definition of the cause in the proof that the cause exists; and this especially if the cause is God. For when proving anything to exist, the central link is not what that thing is (we cannot even ask what it is until we know that it exists), but rather what we are using the name of the thing to mean. Now when demonstrating from effects that God exists, we are able to start from what the word 'God' means, for, as we shall see, the names of God are derived from these effects.

3. Effects can give comprehensive knowledge of their cause only when commensurate with it: but, as we have said, any effect whatever can make it clear that a cause exists. God's effects, therefore, can serve to demonstrate that God exists, even though they cannot help us to know him comprehensively for what he is.

IS THERE A GOD?

1. It seems that there is no God. For if, of two mutually exclusive things, one were to exist without limit, the other would cease to exist. But by the word 'God' is implied some limitless good. If God then existed, nobody would ever encounter evil. But evil is encountered in the world. God therefore does not exist.

2. Moreover, if a few causes fully account for some effect, one does not seek more. Now it seems that everything we observe in this world can be fully accounted for by other causes, without assuming a God. Thus natural effects are explained by natural causes, and contrived effects by human reasoning and will. There is therefore no need to suppose that a God exists.

ON THE OTHER HAND, the book of *Exodus* represents God as saying, *I am who am.*[5]

REPLY: There are five ways in which one can prove that there is a God.

The first and most obvious way is based on change. Some things in the world are certainly in process of change: this we plainly see. Now anything in process of change is being changed by something else. This is so because it is characteristic of things in process of change that they do not yet have

---

[4] *Romans* I, 19–20.
[5] *Exodus* 3, 14.

the perfection towards which they move, though able to have it; whereas it is characteristic of something causing change to have that perfection already. For to cause change is to bring into being what was previously only able to be, and this can only be done by something that already is: thus fire, which is actually hot, causes wood, which is able to be hot, to become actually hot, and in this way causes change in the wood. Now the same thing cannot at the same time be both actually x and potentially x, though it can be actually x and potentially y: the actually hot cannot at the same time be potentially hot, though it can be potentially cold. Consequently, a thing in process of change cannot itself cause that same change; it cannot change itself. Of necessity therefore anything in process of change is being changed by something else. Moreover, this something else, if in process of change, is itself being changed by yet another thing; and this last by another. Now we must stop somewhere, otherwise there will be no first cause of the change, and, as a result, no subsequent causes. For it is only when acted upon by the first cause that the intermediate causes will produce the change: if the hand does not move the stick, the stick will not move anything else. Hence one is bound to arrive at some first cause of change not itself being changed by anything, and this is what everybody understands by God.

The second way is based on the nature of causation. In the observable world causes are found to be ordered in series; we never observe, nor ever could, something causing itself, for this would mean it preceded itself, and this is not possible. Such a series of causes must however stop somewhere; for in it an earlier member causes an intermediate and the intermediate a last (whether the intermediate be one or many). Now if you eliminate a cause you also eliminate its effects, so that you cannot have a last cause, nor an intermediate one, unless you have a first. Given therefore no stop in the series of causes, and hence no first cause, there would be no intermediate causes either, and no last effect, and this would be an open mistake. One is therefore forced to suppose some first cause, to which everyone gives the name 'God'.

The third way is based on what need not be and on what must be, and runs as follows. Some of the things we come across can be but need not be, for we find them springing up and dying away, thus sometimes in being and sometimes not. Now everything cannot be like this, for a thing that need not be, once was not; and if everything need not be, once upon a time there was nothing. But if that were true there would be nothing even now, because something that does not exist can only be brought into being by something already existing. So that if nothing was in being nothing could be brought into being, and nothing would be in being now, which contradicts observation. Not everything therefore is the sort of thing that need not be; there has got to be something that must be. Now a thing that must be, may or may not owe this necessity to something else. But just as we must stop somewhere in a series of causes, so also in the series of things which must be and owe this to other things. One is forced therefore to suppose something which must be, and owes this to no other thing than itself; indeed it itself is the cause that other things must be.

The fourth way is based on the gradation observed in things. Some things are found to be more good, more true, more noble, and so on, and other things less. But such comparative terms describe varying degrees of approximation to a superlative; for example, things are hotter and hotter the nearer they approach what is hottest. Something therefore is the truest and best and most noble of things, and hence the most fully in being; for Aristotle says that the truest things are the things most fully in being.[6] Now *when many things possess some property in common, the one most fully possessing it causes it in the others: fire,* to use Aristotle's example, *the hottest of all things, causes all other things to be hot.*[7] There is something therefore which causes in all other things their being, their goodness, and whatever other perfection they have. And this we call 'God'.

The fifth way is based on the guidedness of nature. An orderedness of actions to an end is observed in all bodies obeying natural laws, even when they lack awareness. For their behaviour hardly ever varies, and will practically always turn out well; which shows that they truly tend to a goal, and do not merely hit it by accident. Nothing however that lacks awareness tends to a goal, except under the direction of someone with awareness and with understanding; the arrow, for example, requires an archer. Everything in nature, therefore, is directed to its goal by someone with understanding, and this we call 'God'.

Hence: 1. As Augustine says, *Since God is supremely good, he would not permit any evil at all in his works, unless he were sufficiently almighty and good to bring good even from evil.*[8] It is therefore a mark of the limitless goodness of God that he permits evils to exist, and draws from them good.

2. Natural causes act for definite purposes under the direction of some higher cause, so that their effects must also be referred to God as the first of all causes. In the same manner contrived effects must likewise be referred back to a higher cause than human reasoning and will, for these are changeable and can cease to be, and, as we have seen, all changeable things and things that can cease to be require some first cause which cannot change and of itself must be.

[6] Metaphysics II, I. 993b30.
[7] Metaphysics II, I. 993b25.
[8] Enchiridion II, PL 40, 236. St. Augustine of Hippo, died 430.

ARISTOTLE
Cause

APPENDIX TO AQUINAS:
THE DEMONSTRATION OF GOD'S EXISTENCE

(A general introductory note on Aristotle may be found on page 506.)

Aristotle recognizes four types of determining factors or causes. In the *Metaphysics* his account of the four kinds of causes is stated as a four-part definition of the word "cause." The four kinds of causes are usually called by philosophers "the material cause," "the formal cause," "the efficient cause," and "the final cause." These four names correspond to the four denotations of the word "cause" below. The translation from the Greek is by John Warrington.

From Aristotle's *Metaphysics,* edited and translated by John Warrington. Revisions, © by J. M. Dent & Sons, Ltd. Everyman's Library. Reprinted by permission of E. P. Dutton & Co., Inc. Permission also granted by J. M. Dent & Sons, Ltd., London.

"Cause" denotes:

1. That from which (as immanent material) a thing comes into being; e.g. the bronze of a statue, the silver of a drinking-bowl, and the classes [1] to which bronze and silver belong.

2. The form or pattern of a thing (i.e. the formula of its essence), the classes to which it belongs,[2] and its own parts.

3. The starting-point of change or rest. Thus an adviser is the cause of an action, and a father of his child. In general, the maker is the cause of the thing made, and that which changes of that which suffers change.

4. The end, i.e. that for the sake of which a thing is. For example, health is the cause of walking: in answer to the question, Why does one walk? we reply "In order to be healthy"; and in saying so we believe we have assigned the cause. The same is true of all the means which lead from an independent source of motion to its end. Thus, slimming, purging, medicines, surgical appliances, all lead to health; all of them exist for the sake of the end, though they differ one from another in that some of them are instruments and others acts.

---

[1] Metal, mineral, etc.

[2] Thus the ratio 2:1 and number in general is the cause of the octave.

There you have practically all the meanings of "cause"; and because the word has a variety of meanings, it follows that a single thing has several causes, and in no accidental sense. Sculptor and bronze are both causes of a statue considered not under two different aspects, but *qua* statue. The two, however, are not causes *in the same way:* bronze is the material, sculptor the efficient cause.

What *causes* a thing in one sense may be its *effect* in another. Thus exercise is the cause of physical fitness, and the latter again of exercise; but *not in the same way,* for in the first case the cause is efficient and in the second final.

Again, a single cause may have opposite effects. That which when present causes one thing is sometimes, when absent, denounced as the cause of the opposite. For instance, we assign the pilot's absence as the cause of a ship-wreck, whereas his presence is admitted as the cause of the vessel's safety; so that in either case, whether present or absent, he is the (efficient) cause.

QUESTIONS

1. State as carefully as you can the steps in Aquinas' first argument to prove God's existence. Then, state as carefully as you can the assumptions or presuppositions on which the first argument depends. Refer to Aristotle where he may be helpful. All arguments depend on assumptions, so it is no criticism of Aquinas to point out that his do too. The proper question then is this: Is there any way in which one of Aquinas' assumptions invalidates his argument by assuming what is to be proved? For instance, when Aquinas follows Aristotle and supposes that one may ask of anything including the world, "What is its efficient cause?" is this a way of assuming God's existence in the premises of his argument? (The reader may examine Aquinas' other arguments in the way outlined above.)

2. When Aquinas promises that "the existence of God . . . can be demonstrated from those of His effects which are known to us," what assumption lies behind the phrase "His effects"? How could Aquinas answer the judgment that such an assumption is unwarranted?

3. When Aquinas says that God's existence can be demonstrated, what does he mean by "demonstration"? (Hint: He does not mean by "demonstration" what the vacuum cleaner salesman means when he asks permission to demonstrate his machine.)

4. In what respects do Aquinas' first three arguments follow the same pattern? Can you show that this pattern is also discoverable in the last two arguments?

5. What other characteristics of the world can you think of which might be used as the basis for arguments similar to Aquinas' to prove that God exists? For example, beauty and the moral consciousness of man are two additional characteristics of the world on which arguments to prove God's existence have been based. What are the criteria for choosing a characteristic of the world as a basis for a proof of God's existence? If there are any characteristics which cannot be used in such a proof, what are they, and why can they not be used?

    (Additional questions about Aquinas' arguments to prove God's existence may be found after the selection in which David Hume criticizes theistic proofs from the nature of the world.)

25. DAVID HUME

(1711–76)

God's Existence Cannot Be Demonstrated

(A general introductory note on Hume may be found on page 116.)

In this reading Hume attacks efforts like those of Aquinas in the preceding selection to demonstrate that God exists. Hume means by the term "demonstration" an argument whose conclusion cannot be doubted. A typical example of a demonstration would be the proof of a theorem in Euclidean geometry. In such a proof one is shown that one must accept the theorem because it follows from the definitions, axioms, postulates, and preceding theorems which one has already accepted. To deny the theorem which follows from all that has gone before would land one in a self-contradiction. But Hume's claim about demonstrative arguments is that a demonstration can never be used to prove existence. For when the conclusion of an argument is "God exists," Hume claims that there is no self-contradiction in someone's saying "God does not exist." Hence, the argument cannot be a demonstration, and its conclusion, "God exists," can never be regarded as proved beyond doubt.

To make Hume's meaning perfectly clear we should add that when he says

that demonstrative arguments are a priori, he means that the indubitability of their conclusions derives from the assumptions which one makes prior to framing the argument. Thus, any proof in Euclidean geometry is a priori because the proof of a theorem turns on the definitions, axioms, postulates, and sometimes the previous theorems which are accepted prior to framing the proof in question.

In determining whether Hume's criticism makes arguments like Aquinas' untenable, the reader must decide whether Hume's rule, "Whatever we conceive as existent, we can also conceive as nonexistent," applies to a subject like God. What prospect is there for a theist's exempting God from the rule? And what would be the consequences for the status of God, if he did?

This selection is drawn from Part IX of the *Dialogues Concerning Natural Religion* (1779). The speakers in the dialogues are Cleanthes, a theist who believes that God's existence can be proved by an appeal to experience, Demea, a theist who believes God's existence can be proved only by a priori reasoning, and Philo, who is a skeptic.

From *Dialogues Concerning Natural Religion,* by David Hume, edited with introduction by Henry D. Aiken, Hafner Library of Classics, Hafner Publishing Co., Inc., New York, 1957.

The argument, [said] Demea, which I would insist on is the common one. Whatever exists must have a cause or reason of its existence, it being absolutely impossible for anything to produce itself or be the cause of its own existence. In mounting up, therefore, from effects to causes, we must either go on in tracing an infinite succession, without any ultimate cause at all, or must at last have recourse to some ultimate cause that is *necessarily* existent. Now that the first supposition is absurd may be thus proved. In the infinite chain or succession of causes and effects, each single effect is determined to exist by the power and efficacy of that cause which immediately preceded; but the whole eternal chain or succession, taken together, is not determined or caused by anything, and yet it is evident that it requires a cause or reason, as much as any particular object which begins to exist in time. The question is still reasonable why this particular succession of causes existed from eternity, and not any other succession or no succession at all. If there be no necessarily existent being, any supposition which can be formed is equally possible; nor is there any more absurdity in *nothing's* having existed from eternity than there is in that succession of causes which constitutes the universe. What was it, then, which determined *something* to exist rather than *nothing,* and bestowed being on a particular possibility, exclusive of the rest? *External causes,* there are supposed to be none. *Chance* is a word without a meaning. Was it *nothing?* But that can never produce anything. We must, therefore, have recourse to a necessarily existent Being who carries the *reason* of his existence in himself, and who cannot be supposed not to exist, without an express contradiction. There is, consequently, such a Being—that is, there is a Deity.

I shall not leave it to Philo, said Cleanthes, though I know that the starting objections is his chief delight, to point out the weakness of this metaphysical reasoning. It seems to me so obviously ill-grounded, and at the same time of so little consequence to the cause of true piety and religion, that I shall myself venture to show the fallacy of it.

I shall begin with observing that there is an evident absurdity in pretending to demonstrate a matter of fact, or to prove it by any arguments *a priori.* Nothing is demonstrable unless the contrary implies a contradiction. Nothing that is distinctly conceivable implies a contradiction. Whatever we conceive as existent, we can also conceive as nonexistent. There is no being, therefore, whose nonexistence implies a contradiction. Consequently there is no being whose existence is demonstrable. I propose this argument as entirely decisive, and am willing to rest the whole controversy upon it.

It is pretended that the Deity is a necessarily existent being; and this necessity of his existence is attempted to be explained by asserting that, if we knew his whole essence or nature, we should perceive it to be as impossible for him not to exist, as for twice two not to be four. But it is evident that this can never happen, while our faculties remain the same as at present. It will still be possible for us, at any time, to conceive the nonexistence of what we formerly conceived to exist; nor can the mind ever lie under a necessity of supposing any object to remain always in being; in the same manner as we lie under a necessity of always conceiving twice two to be four. The words, therefore, *necessary existence* have no meaning or, which is the same thing, none that is consistent.

But further, why may not the material universe be the necessarily existent Being, according to this pretended explication of necessity? We dare not affirm that we know all the qualities of matter; and, for aught we can determine, it may contain some qualities which, were they known, would make its nonexistence appear as great a contradiction as that twice two is five. I find only one argument employed to prove that the material world is not the necessarily existent Being; and this argument is derived from the contingency both of the matter and the form of the world. "Any particle of matter," it is said, "may be *conceived* to be annihilated, and any form may be *conceived* to be altered. Such an annihilation or alteration, therefore, is not impossible." But it seems a great partiality not to perceive that the same argument extends equally to the Deity, so far as we have any conception of him, and that the mind can at least imagine him to be nonexistent or his attributes to be altered. It must be some unknown, inconceivable qualities which can make his nonexistence appear impossible or his attributes unalterable; and no reason can be assigned why these qualities may not belong to matter. As they are altogether unknown and inconceivable, they can never be proved incompatible with it.

Add to this that in tracing an eternal succession of objects it seems absurd to inquire for a general cause or first author. How can anything that exists from eternity have a cause, since that relation implies a priority in time and a beginning of existence?

In such a chain, too, or succession of objects, each part is caused by that which preceded it, and causes that which succeeds it. Where then is the difficulty? But the *whole,* you say, wants a cause. I answer that the uniting of these parts into a whole, like the uniting of several distinct countries into one kingdom, or several distinct members into one body, is performed merely by an arbitrary act of the mind, and has no influence on the nature of things. Did I show you the particular causes of each individual in a collection of twenty particles of matter, I should think it very unreasonable should you afterwards ask me what was the cause of the whole twenty. This is sufficiently explained in explaining the cause of the parts.

Though the reasonings which you have urged, Cleanthes, may well excuse me, said Philo, from starting any further difficulties, yet I cannot forbear insisting still upon another topic. It is observed by arithmeticians that the products of 9 compose always either 9 or some lesser product of 9 if you add together all the characters of which any of the former products is composed. Thus, of 18, 27, 36, which are products of 9, you make 9 by adding 1 to 8, 2 to 7, 3 to 6. Thus 369 is a product also of 9; and if you add 3, 6, and 9, you make 18, a lesser product of 9. To a superficial observer so wonderful a regularity may be admired as the effect either of chance or design; but a skilful algebraist immediately concludes it to be the work of necessity, and demonstrates that it must for ever result from the nature of these numbers. Is it not probable, I ask, that the whole economy of the universe is conducted by a like necessity, though no human algebra can furnish a key which solves the difficulty? And instead of admiring the order of natural beings, may it not happen that, could we penetrate into the intimate nature of bodies, we should clearly see why it was absolutely impossible they could ever admit of any other disposition? So dangerous is it to introduce this idea of necessity into the present question! and so naturally does it afford an inference directly opposite to the religious hypothesis!

But dropping all these abstractions, continued Philo, and confining ourselves to more familiar topics, I shall venture to add an observation that the argument *a priori* has seldom been found very convincing, except to people of a metaphysical head who have accustomed themselves to abstract reasoning, and who, finding from mathematics that the understanding frequently leads to truth through obscurity, and contrary to first appearances, have transferred the same habit of thinking to subjects where it ought not to have place. Other people, even of good sense and the best inclined to religion, feel always some deficiency in such arguments, though they are not perhaps able to explain distinctly where it lies—a certain proof that men ever did and ever will derive their religion from other sources than from this species of reasoning.

QUESTIONS

1. Why does Hume believe that a matter of fact, such as that God exists, cannot be demonstrated? What are the consequences of regarding (and not regarding) God's existence as a matter of fact? (If the reader is not already acquainted with Hume's account of our knowledge of matters of fact, he may wish to consult the selection in Chapter 2.)
2. In what way does the acceptance of Hume's rule, "Whatever we conceive as existent, we can also conceive as nonexistent," make Aquinas' arguments to prove God's existence untenable? Is there any way in which a theist might exempt the concept of God from Hume's rule? Could the theist escape the charge of making an a priori assumption if he did exempt the concept of God from Hume's rule? Can Hume's rule be objected to on the grounds that it is a priori?
3. What is Hume's argument that the material universe may be necessarily existent? What does this argument show about the character of arguments that God must necessarily exist?
4. What are the consequences for religion of Hume's criticism of arguments like Aquinas' to prove that God exists? If Hume succeeds in showing that religion cannot be founded on reasonable grounds, as Aquinas supposed, what has religion gained (or lost)?

26. DAVID HUME

(1711–76)

An Analysis of the Argument from Design

(A general introductory note on Hume may be found on page 116.)

In this reading Hume both states, and offers his refutation of, the argument from design. This argument depends on our regarding the universe as a great machine. The possibility of regarding the universe in this way is an outgrowth of the scientific interest in giving mechanistic accounts of physical phenomena, as, for example, Newton's mechanistic account of planetary motion. When the parts of the universe are thought of as machine-like, and all the parts are thought of as fitting together in one vast machine, an interesting analogy follows. If the universe is like a machine, then it must have a characteristic which all machines possess. It must have been made. So, just as a watch implies the existence of a watchmaker, the existence of a universe-machine implies the existence of a universe-machine maker.

Against this argument Hume raises two points which we must leave to the reader's consideration. His first point is that if there is no analogy there is no argument, and Hume finds the resemblance between the universe and a machine too weak to guarantee that God exists. So the first question for the reader is this: Does the universe resemble a machine? Hume's second point is that even if the argument from design rested on a good analogy, the consequent supposition of a resemblance between human machine-makers and God would make our conception of God too absurd to be entertained by any religious person. So the second question for the reader is this: Are the ridiculous consequences which Hume draws from the theistic proof by analogy so devastating that nothing can be salvaged? The reader should notice that Hume's attack on that proof calls into question the very possibility of our having any conception of God at all.

This selection is taken from the *Dialogues Concerning Natural Religion* (1779). Part I of this selection is drawn from Part II of the original *Dialogues;* and Part II of this selection is drawn from Part V of the original. The speakers in the dialogues are Cleanthes, a theist who believes that God's existence can be proved by an appeal to experience, Demea, a theist who believes God's existence can be proved only by a priori reasoning, and Philo, who is a skeptic.

From *Dialogues Concerning Natural Religion,* by David Hume, edited with introduction by Henry D. Aiken, Hafner Library of Classics, Hafner Publishing Co., Inc., New York, 1957.

PART I

Not to lose any time in circumlocutions, said Cleanthes, addressing himself to Demea, much less in replying to the pious declamations of Philo, I shall briefly explain how I conceive this matter. Look round the world, contemplate the whole and every part of it: you will find it to be nothing but one great machine, subdivided into an infinite number of lesser machines, which again admit of subdivisions to a degree beyond what human senses and faculties can trace and explain. All these various machines, and even their most minute parts, are adjusted to each other with an accuracy which ravishes into admiration all men who have ever contemplated them. The curious adapting of means to ends, throughout all nature, resembles exactly, though it much exceeds, the productions of human contrivance—of human design, thought, wisdom, and intelligence. Since therefore the effects resemble each other, we are led to infer, by all the rules of analogy, that the causes also resemble, and that the Author of nature is somewhat similar to the mind of man, though possessed of much larger faculties, proportioned to the grandeur of the work which he has executed. By this argument *a posteriori,* and by this argument alone, do we prove at once the existence of a Deity and his similarity to human mind and intelligence.

I shall be so free, Cleanthes, said Demea, as to tell you that from the beginning I could not approve of your conclusion concerning the similarity of the Deity to men; still less can I approve of the mediums by which you endeavour to establish it. What! No demonstration of the Being of God! No abstract arguments! No proofs *a priori!* Are these which have hitherto been so much insisted on by philosophers all fallacy, all sophism? Can we reach no farther in this subject than experience and probability? I will not say that this is betraying the cause of a Deity; but surely, by this affected candour, you give advantages to atheists which they never could obtain by the mere dint of argument and reasoning.

What I chiefly scruple in this subject, said Philo, is not so much that all religious arguments are by Cleanthes reduced to experience, as that they appear not to be even the most certain and irrefragable of that inferior kind. That a stone will fall, that fire will burn, that the earth has solidity, we have observed a thousand and a thousand times; and when any new instance of this nature is presented, we draw without hesitation the accustomed inference. The exact similarity of the cases gives us a perfect assurance of a similar event, and a stronger evidence is never desired nor sought after. But wherever you depart, in the least, from the similarity of the cases, you diminish proportionably the evidence, and may at last bring it to a very weak *analogy,* which is confessedly liable to error and uncertainty. After having experienced the circulation of the blood in human creatures, we make no doubt that it takes place in Titius and Maevius; but from its circulation in frogs and fishes it is only a presumption, though a strong one, from analogy that it takes place in men and other animals. The analogical reasoning is much weaker when we infer the circulation of the sap in vegetables from our experience that the blood circulates in animals; and those who hastily followed that imperfect analogy are found, by more accurate experiments, to have been mistaken.

If we see a house, Cleanthes, we conclude, with the greatest certainty, that it had an architect or builder because this is precisely that species of effect which we have experienced to proceed from that species of cause. But surely you will not affirm that the universe bears such a resemblance to a house that we can with the same certainty infer a similar cause, or that the analogy is here entire and perfect. The dissimilitude is so striking that the utmost you can here pretend to is a guess, a conjecture, a presumption concerning a similar cause; and how that pretension will be received in the world, I leave you to consider.

It would surely be very ill received, replied Cleanthes; and I should be deservedly blamed and detested did I allow that the proofs of a Deity amounted to no more than a guess or conjecture. But is the whole adjustment of means to ends in a house and in the universe so slight a resemblance? the economy of final causes? the order, proportion, and arrangement of every part? Steps of a stair are plainly contrived that human legs may use them in mounting; and this inference is certain and infallible. Human legs are also contrived for walking and mounting; and this inference, I allow, is not altogether so certain because of the dissimilarity which you remark; but does it, therefore, deserve the name only of presumption or conjecture?

Good God! cried Demea, interrupting him, where are we? Zealous defenders of religion allow that the proofs of a Deity fall short of perfect evidence! And you, Philo, on whose assistance I depended in proving the adorable mysteriousness of the Divine Nature, do you assent to all these extravagant opinions of Cleanthes? For what other name can I give them?

You seem not to apprehend, replied Philo, that I argue with Cleanthes in his own way, and, by showing him the dangerous consequences of his tenets, hope at last to reduce him to our opinion. But what sticks most with you, I observe, is the representation which Cleanthes has made of the argument *a posteriori;* and, finding that that argument is likely to escape your hold and vanish into air, you think it so disguised that you can scarcely believe it to be set in its true light. Now, however much I may dissent, in other respects, from the dangerous principle of Cleanthes, I must allow that he has fairly represented that argument, and I shall endeavour so to state the matter to you that you will entertain no further scruples with regard to it.

Were a man to abstract from everything which he knows or has seen, he would be altogether incapable, merely from his own ideas, to determine what kind of scene the universe must be, or to give the preference to one state or situation of things above another. For as nothing which he clearly conceives could be esteemed impossible or implying a contradiction, every chimera of his fancy would be upon an equal footing; nor could he assign any just reason why he adheres to one idea or system, and rejects the others which are equally possible.

Again, after he opens his eyes and contemplates the world as it really is, it would be impossible for him at first to assign the cause of any one event, much less of the whole of things, or of the universe. He might set his fancy a rambling, and she might bring him in an infinite variety of reports and representations. These would all be possible, but, being all equally possible, he would never of himself give a satisfactory account for his preferring one of them to the rest. Experience alone can point out to him the true cause of any phenomenon.

Now, according to this method of reasoning, Demea, it follows (and is, indeed, tacitly allowed by Cleanthes himself) that order, arrangement, or the adjustment of final causes, is not of itself any proof of design, but only so far as it has been experienced to proceed from that principle. For aught we can know *a priori,* matter may contain the source or spring of order originally within itself, as well as mind does; and there is no more difficulty in conceiving that the several elements, from an internal unknown cause, may fall into the most exquisite arrangement, than to conceive that their ideas, in the great universal mind, from a like internal unknown cause, fall into that arrangement. The equal possibility of both these suppositions is allowed. But, by experience, we find (according to Cleanthes) that there is a difference between them. Throw several pieces of steel together, without shape or form, they will never arrange themselves so as to compose a watch. Stone and mortar and wood, without an architect, never erect a house. But the ideas in a human mind, we see, by an unknown, inexplicable economy, arrange themselves so as to form the plan of a watch or house. Experience, therefore, proves that there is an original principle of order in mind, not in matter. From similar effects we infer similar causes. The adjustment of means to ends is alike in the universe, as in a machine of human contrivance. The causes, therefore, must be resembling.

I was from the beginning scandalized, I must own, with this resemblance which is asserted between the Deity and human creatures, and must conceive it to imply such a degradation of the Supreme Being as no sound theist could endure. With your assistance, therefore, Demea, I shall endeavour to defend what you justly call the adorable mysteriousness of the Divine Nature, and shall refute this reasoning of Cleanthes, provided he allows that I have made a fair representation of it.

When Cleanthes had assented, Philo, after a short pause, proceeded in the following manner.

That all inferences, Cleanthes, concerning fact are founded on experience, and that all experimental reasonings are founded on the supposition that similar causes prove similar effects, and similar effects similar causes, I shall not at present much dispute with you. But observe, I entreat you, with what extreme caution all just reasoners proceed in the transferring of experiments to similar cases. Unless the cases be exactly similar, they repose no perfect confidence in applying their past observation to any particular phenomenon. Every alteration of circumstances occasions a doubt concerning the event; and it requires new experiments to prove certainly that the new circumstances are of no moment or importance. A change in bulk, situation, arrangement, age, disposition of the air, or surrounding bodies—any of these particulars may be attended with the most unexpected consequences. And unless the objects be quite familiar to us, it is the highest temerity to expect with assurance, after any of these changes, an event similar to that which before fell under our observation. The slow and deliberate steps of philosophers here, if anywhere, are distinguished from the precipitate march of the vulgar, who, hurried on by the smallest similitude, are incapable of all discernment or consideration.

But can you think, Cleanthes, that your usual phlegm and philosophy have been preserved in so wide a step as you have taken when you compared to the universe houses, ships, furniture, machines, and, from their similarity in some circumstances, inferred a similarity in their causes? Thought, design, intelligence, such as we discover in men and other animals, is no more than one of the springs and principles of the universe, as well as heat or cold, attraction or repulsion, and a hundred others which fall under daily observation. It is an active cause by which some particular parts of nature, we find, produce alterations on other parts. But can a conclusion, with any propriety, be transferred from parts to the whole? Does not the great disproportion bar all comparison and inference? From observing the growth of a hair, can we learn anything concerning the generation of a man? Would the manner of a leaf's blowing, even though perfectly known, afford us any instruction concerning the vegetation of a tree?

But allowing that we were to take the *operations* of one part of nature upon another for the foundation of our judgment concerning the *origin* of the whole (which never can be admitted), yet why select so minute, so weak, so bounded a principle as the reason and design of animals is found to be upon this planet? What peculiar privilege has this little agitation of the brain which we call *thought,* that we must thus make it the model of the whole universe? Our partiality in our own favour does indeed present it on all occasions, but sound philosophy ought carefully to guard against so natural an illusion.

So far from admitting, continued Philo, that the operations of a part can afford us any just conclusion concerning the origin of the whole, I will not allow any one part to form a rule for another part if the latter be very remote from the former. Is there any reasonable ground to conclude that the inhabitants of other planets possess thought, intelligence, reason, or anything similar to these faculties in men? When nature has so extremely diversified her manner of operation in this small globe, can we imagine that she incessantly copies herself throughout so immense a universe? And if thought, as we may well suppose, be confined merely to this narrow corner and has even there so limited a sphere of action, with what propriety can we assign it for the original cause of all things? The narrow views of a peasant who makes his domestic economy the rule for the government of kingdoms is in comparison a pardonable sophism.

But were we ever so much assured that a thought and reason resembling the human were to be found throughout the whole universe, and were its activity elsewhere vastly greater and more commanding than it appears in this globe, yet I cannot see why the operations of a world constituted, arranged, adjusted, can with any propriety be extended to a world which is in its embryo state, and is advancing towards that constitution and arrangement. By observation we know somewhat of the economy, action, and nourishment of a finished animal, but we must transfer with great caution that observation to the growth of a foetus in the womb, and still more to the formation of an animalcule in the loins of its male parent. Nature, we find, even from our limited experience, possesses an infinite number of springs and principles which incessantly discover themselves on every change of her position and situation. And what new and unknown principles would actuate her in so new and unknown a situation as that of the formation of a universe, we cannot, without the utmost temerity, pretend to determine.

A very small part of this great system, during a very short time, is very imperfectly discovered to us; and do we thence pronounce decisively concerning the origin of the whole?

Admirable conclusion! Stone, wood, brick, iron, brass, have not, at this time, in this minute globe of earth, an order or arrangement without human art and contrivance; therefore, the universe could not originally attain its order and arrangement without something similar to human art. But is a part of nature a rule for another part very wide of the former? Is it a rule for the whole? Is a very small part a rule for the universe? Is nature in one situation a certain rule for nature in another situation vastly different from the former?

And can you blame me, Cleanthes, if I here imitate the prudent reserve of Simonides, who, according to the noted story, being asked by Hiero, *What God was?* desired a day to think of it, and then two days more; and after that manner continually prolonged the term, without ever bringing in his definition or description? Could you even blame me if I had answered, at first, *that I did not know,* and was sensible that this subject lay vastly beyond the reach of my faculties? You might cry out sceptic and rallier, as much as you pleased; but, having found in so many other subjects much more familiar the imperfections and even contradictions of human reason, I never should expect any success from its feeble conjectures in a subject so sublime and so remote from the sphere of our observation. When two *species* of objects have always been observed to be conjoined together, I can *infer*, by custom, the existence of one wherever I *see* the existence of the other; and this I call an argument from experience. But how this argument can have place where the objects, as in the present case, are single, individual, without parallel or specific resemblance, may be difficult to explain. And will any man tell me with a serious countenance that an orderly universe must arise from some thought and art like the human because we have experience of it? To ascertain this reasoning it were requisite that we had experience of the origin of worlds; and it is not sufficient, surely, that we have seen ships and cities arise from human art and contrivance.

Philo was proceeding in this vehement manner, somewhat between jest and earnest, when he observed some signs of impatience in Cleanthes, and then immediately stopped short. What I had to suggest, said Cleanthes, is only that you would not abuse terms, or make use of popular expressions to subvert philosophical reasonings. You know that the vulgar often distinguish reason from experience, even where the question relates only to matter of fact and existence, though it is found, where that *reason* is properly analyzed, that it is nothing but a species of experience. To prove by experience the origin of the universe from mind is not more contrary to common speech than to prove the motion of the earth from the same principle. And a caviller might raise all the same objections to the Copernican system which you have urged against my reasonings. Have you other earths, might he say, which you have seen to move? Have . . .

Yes! cried Philo, interrupting him, we have other earths. Is not the moon another earth, which we see to turn round its centre? Is not Venus another earth, where we observe the same phenomenon? Are not the revolutions of the sun also a confirmation, from analogy, of the same theory? All the planets, are they not earths which revolve about the sun? Are not the satellites moons which move round Jupiter and Saturn, and along with these primary planets round the sun? These analogies and resemblances, with others which I have not mentioned, are the sole proofs of the Copernican system; and to you it belongs to consider whether you have any analogies of the same kind to support your theory.

In reality, Cleanthes, continued he, the modern system of astronomy is now so much received by all inquirers, and has become so essential a part even of our earliest education, that we are not commonly very scrupulous in examining the reasons upon which it is founded. It is now become a matter of mere curiosity to study the first writers on that subject who had the full force of prejudice to encounter, and were obliged to turn their arguments on every side in order to render them popular and convincing. But if we peruse Galileo's famous *Dialogues*[1] concerning the system of the world, we shall find that that great genius, one of the sublimest that ever existed, first bent

[1] *Dialogo dei due Massimi Sistemi del Mondo (1632)*—H. D. Aiken

all his endeavours to prove that there was no foundation for the distinction commonly made between elementary and celestial substances. The schools, proceeding from the illusions of sense, had carried this distinction very far; and had established the latter substances to be ingenerable, incorruptible, unalterable, impassible; and had assigned all the opposite qualities to the former. But Galileo, beginning with the moon, proved its similarity in every particular to the earth: its convex figure, its natural darkness when not illuminated, its density, its distinction into solid and liquid, the variations of its phases, the mutual illuminations of the earth and moon, their mutual eclipses, the inequalities of the lunar surface, etc. After many instances of this kind, with regard to all the planets, men plainly saw that these bodies became proper objects of experience, and that the similarity of their nature enabled us to extend the same arguments and phenomena from one to the other.

In this cautious proceeding of the astronomers you may read your own condemnation, Cleanthes, or rather may see that the subject in which you are engaged exceeds all human reason and inquiry. Can you pretend to show any such similarity between the fabric of a house and the generation of a universe? Have you ever seen nature in any such situation as resembles the first arrangement of the elements? Have worlds ever been formed under your eye, and have you had leisure to observe the whole progress of the phenomenon, from the first appearance of order to its final consummation? If you have, then cite your experience and deliver your theory.

PART II

But to show you still more inconveniences, continued Philo, in your anthropomorphism, please to take a new survey of your principles. *Like effects prove like causes.* This is the experimental argument; and this, you say too, is the sole theological argument. Now it is certain that the liker the effects are which are seen and the liker the causes which are inferred, the stronger is the argument. Every departure on either side diminishes the probability and renders the experiment less conclusive. You cannot doubt of the principle; neither ought you to reject its consequences.

All the new discoveries in astronomy which prove the immense grandeur and magnificence of the works of nature are so many additional arguments for a Deity, according to the true system of theism; but, according to your hypothesis of experimental theism, they become so many objections, by removing the effect still farther from all resemblance to the effects of human art and contrivance. . . .

The discoveries by microscopes, as they open a new universe in miniature, are still objections, according to you, arguments, according to me. The further we push our researches of this kind, we are still led to infer the universal cause of all to be vastly different from mankind, or from any object of human experience and observation.

And what say you to the discoveries in anatomy, chemistry, botany? . . . These surely are no objections, replied Cleanthes; they only discover new instances of art and contrivance. It is still the image of mind reflected on us from innumerable objects. Add a mind *like the human,* said Philo. I know of no other, replied Cleanthes. And the liker, the better, insisted Philo. To be sure, said Cleanthes.

Now, Cleanthes, said Philo, with an air of alacrity and triumph, mark the consequences. *First,* by this method of reasoning you renounce all claim to infinity in any of the attributes of the Deity. For, as the cause ought only to be proportioned to the effect, and the effect, so far as it falls under our cognizance, is not infinite, what pretensions have we, upon your suppositions, to ascribe that attribute to the Divine Being? You will still insist that, by removing him so much from all similarity to human creatures, we give in to the most arbitrary hypothesis, and at the same time weaken all proofs of his existence.

Secondly, you have no reason, on your theory, for ascribing perfection to the Deity, even in his finite capacity, or for supposing him free from every error, mistake, or incoherence, in his undertakings. There are many inexplicable difficulties in the works of nature which, if we allow a perfect author to be proved *a priori,* are easily solved, and become only seeming difficulties from the narrow capacity of man, who cannot trace infinite relations. But according to your method of reasoning, these difficulties become all real, and, perhaps, will be insisted on as new instances of likeness to human art and contrivance. At least, you must acknowledge that it is impossible for us to tell, from our limited views, whether this system contains any great faults or deserves any considerable praise if compared to other possible and even real systems. Could a peasant, if the *Aeneid* were read to him, pronounce that poem to be absolutely faultless, or even assign to it its proper rank among the productions of human wit, he who had never seen any other production?

But were this world ever so perfect a production, it must still remain uncertain whether all the excellences of the work can justly be ascribed to the workman. If we survey a ship, what an exalted idea must we form of the ingenuity of the carpenter who framed so complicated, useful, and beautiful a machine? And what surprise must we feel when we find him a stupid mechanic who imitated others, and copied an art which, through a long succcession of ages, after multiplied trials, mistakes, corrections, deliberations, and controversies, had been gradually improving? Many worlds might have been botched and bungled, throughout an eternity, ere this system was struck out; much labour lost, many fruitless trials made, and a slow but continued improvement carried on during infinite ages in the art of world-making. In such subjects, who can determine where the truth, nay, who can conjecture where the probability lies, amidst a great number of hypotheses which may be proposed, and a still greater which may be imagined?

And what shadow of an argument, continued Philo, can you produce from your hypothesis to prove the unity of the Deity? A great number of men join in building a house or ship, in rearing a city, in framing a commonwealth; why may not several deities combine in contriving and framing a world? This is only so much greater similarity to human affairs. By sharing the work among several, we may so much further limit the attributes of each, and get rid of that extensive power and knowledge which must be supposed in one deity, and which, according to you, can only serve to weaken the proof of his existence. And if such foolish, such vicious creatures as man can yet often unite in framing and executing one plan, how much more those deities or demons, whom we may suppose several degrees more perfect!

To multiply causes without necessity is indeed contrary to true philosophy, but this principle applies not to the present case. Were one deity antecedently proved by your theory who were possessed of every attribute requisite to the production of the universe, it would be needless, I own (though not absurd), to suppose any other deity existent. But while it is still a question whether all these attributes are united in one subject or dispersed among several independent beings, by what phenomena in nature can we pretend to decide the controversy? Where we see a body raised in a scale, we are sure that there is in the opposite scale, however concealed from sight, some counterpoising weight equal to it; but it is still allowed to doubt whether that weight be an aggregate of several distinct bodies or one uniform united mass. And if the weight requisite very much exceeds anything which we have ever seen conjoined in any single body, the former supposition becomes still more probable and natural. An intelligent being of such vast power and capacity as is necessary to produce the universe, or, to speak in the language of ancient philosophy, so prodigious an animal exceeds all analogy and even comprehension.

But further, Cleanthes: Men are mortal, and renew their species by generation; and this is common to all living creatures. The two great sexes of male and female, says Milton, animate the world. Why must this circumstance, so universal, so essential, be excluded from those numerous and limited deities? Behold, then, the theogeny of ancient times brought back upon us.

And why not become a perfect anthropomorphite? Why not assert the deity or deities to be corporeal, and to have eyes, a nose, mouth, ears, etc.? Epicurus maintained that no man had ever seen reason but in a human figure; therefore, the gods must have a human figure. And this argument, which is deservedly so much ridiculed by Cicero, becomes, according to you, solid and philosophical.

In a word, Cleanthes, a man who follows your hypothesis is able, perhaps, to assert or conjecture that the universe sometime arose from something like design; but beyond that position he cannot ascertain one single circumstance, and is left afterwards to fix every point of his theology by the utmost license of fancy and hypothesis. This world, for aught he knows, is very faulty and imperfect, compared to a superior standard, and was only the first rude essay of some infant deity who afterwards abandoned it, ashamed of his lame performance; it is the work only of some dependent, inferior diety, and is the object of derision to his superiors; it is the production of old age and dotage in some superannuated deity, and ever since his death has run on at adventures, from the first impulse and active force which it received from him. You justly give signs of horror, Demea, at these strange suppositions; but these, and a thousand more of the same kind, are Cleanthes' suppositions, not mine. From the moment the attributes of the Deity are supposed finite, all these have place. And I cannot, for my part, think that so wild and unsettled a system of theology is, in any respect, preferable to none at all.

These suppositions I absolutely disown, cried Cleanthes: they strike me, however, with no horror, especially when proposed in that rambling way in which they drop from you. On the contrary, they give me pleasure when I see that, by the utmost indulgence of your imagination, you never get rid of the hypothesis of design in the universe, but are obliged at every turn to have recourse to it. To this concession I adhere steadily; and this I regard as a sufficient foundation for religion.

QUESTIONS

1. What is the argument from design for God's existence? What part does analogy play in this argument? How does one measure the strength of an analogical argument?
2. What specific weaknesses does Hume (Philo) find in the analogy on which the argument from design is based? Do you think these are real weaknesses which undercut the whole argument, or do you think the analogy is still strong enough to give some plausibility to the argument? Defend your answer.
3. Suppose the world *was* very similar to a machine, so that there would be none of the weaknesses in the analogy which Hume (Philo) points out. On what additional grounds would he still challenge the argument from design as a legitimate proof of God's existence?
4. How can Hume (Philo) defend arguments by analogy as a way of learning about the nature of the world, but not about God?
5. Is Cleanthes right when he implies that Hume (Philo) can "never get rid of the hypothesis of design in the universe"? Is this hypothesis indispensable?

SUGGESTED FURTHER READING

Copleston, F. C., *Aquinas*, Penguin Books, Harmondsworth, Middlesex, Eng., 1955.

Creed, John Martin, and John Sandwith Boys Smith, eds., *Religious Thought in the Eighteenth Century, Illustrated from Writers of the Period,* Cambridge University Press, London, 1935.

Hick, John, ed., *The Existence of God,* Macmillan, New York, 1964. (Anthology.)

———, *The Philosophy of Religion,* Prentice-Hall, Englewood Cliffs, N. J., 1963.

Joyce, G. H., *The Principles of Natural Theology,* Longmans, Green, London and New York, 1951.

McGiffert, A. C., *Protestant Thought Before Kant,* Harper Torchbooks, New York, 1962. Chap. X, "Rationalism."

Matson, W. I., *The Existence of God,* Cornell University Press, Ithaca, N. Y., 1965.

Paley, William, *Natural Theology: or, Evidences of the Existence and Attributes of the Deity, Collected from the Appearances of Nature,* many publishers, many editions.

Plantinga, A., ed., *The Ontological Argument,* Doubleday, New York, 1965. (Anthology.)

Sprague, Elmer, *What Is Philosophy?* Oxford University Press, New York, 1961. Chap. 4, "Philosophy and God: Proving God's Existence."

Tennant, F. R., *Philosophical Theology,* Cambridge University Press, London, Vol. I, 1928, Vol. II, 1930.

Tillich, Paul, *Systematic Theology,* University of Chicago Press, Chicago, 1951–57.

Chapter 8. God and the Natural Order

The theist contends that while God is outside the world, he is nonetheless capable of intervening in the course of world events. Two of the problems which arise from this theistic contention are the problem of miracles and the problem of evil. The problem of miracles centers on the question of whether God does intervene in the world. The problem of evil centers on the question of why, if the world is God's creation and God can intervene in the world, there is evil. In this chapter these problems are discussed under the assumption that God exists. To deny God's existence is, of course, to deny these problems.

We have included in this chapter readings on the problem of miracles by Hume, who argues that miracles are impossible, and by Professor C. S. Lewis, who argues that miracles are possible. These authors mean by the word "miracle" any interruption of the order of nature which must be accounted for as a divine suspension of the laws of nature. The reader should be careful to distinguish this meaning of "miracle" from another common use of the word. "Miracle" is sometimes used to mean any natural event which causes wonder, any event which is, as we say, "improbable but not impossible"; people do sometimes say that God is the cause of events of this kind too. But this last sense of "miracle" is not the sense in which our authors are interested in the possibility of miracles.

Hume's argument against miracles is based on his conception of the character of our knowledge of the world. What we call the order of nature is the sum of our experiences of the world. Now when someone asks us to believe that a miracle, an interruption of the order of nature, has occurred, he is asking us to believe something which contradicts our experience of the world. Notice that we are not being asked to believe something that is simply unknown to us by experience but is nonetheless not incompatible with our experience, as if we were asked to believe that a certain man always walks on his hands, sleeps during the day and stays awake at night, and dines by eating nuts first and soup last. When we are asked to believe a miracle we are being asked to believe something on the order of a man's dying and then coming to life again, an alleged state of affairs that is contradictory to our experience. This very contradiction is its own disproof. So, Hume argues, every claim that a miracle has occurred requires our disbelief. In direct opposition to Hume we offer Professor C. S. Lewis' argument for miracles. Professor Lewis' case rests on a criticism of Hume's account of the improbability of miracles and his own defense of their probability. We leave to the reader the task of deciding between Hume and Professor Lewis.

Let us now turn to the second problem arising from the claim that God can enter into the world. This is the problem of evil, which has long perplexed the theist. Epicurus (342?–270 B.C.) is credited with inventing the following dilemma about God and evil: Either God would remove evil out of this world, and cannot; or he can, and will not; or he has not the power nor will; or, lastly, he has both the power and will. If he has the will, and not the power, this shows weakness, which is contrary to the nature of God. If he has the power, and not the will, it is malignity; and this is no less contrary to his nature. If he is neither able nor willing, he is both impotent and malignant, and consequently cannot be God. If he be both willing and able (which alone is consonant to the nature of God), whence comes evil, or why does he not prevent it?

If there is evil in the world it is

difficult for the theist to maintain the claim that God is benevolent. But if God is not benevolent, can he be God? In this chapter we offer two readings on the problem of evil, one by Leibniz and the other by Hume. Leibniz meets the theistic dilemma of evil in the world by questioning whether there *is* evil in the world, and thus saves the theist's belief in a benevolent God. Hume, on the other hand, is inclined to the view that "the original source

of all things" is indifferent to the propagation of either good or evil in the world. But such a view renders any ordinary sort of theism absurd.

The questions which lie behind the problem of evil are these: Can any observation of the world render theism false? Does the existence of evil render theism false? Would the absence of evil from the world render theism true? These are questions which we must leave to the reader's consideration.

27. DAVID HUME
(1711–76)

Can Miracles Be Known to Happen?

(A general introductory note on Hume may be found on page 116.)

Hume believed that our knowledge of the world is founded on experience. Thus, if we are to have any knowledge of miracles, it must be by experience. But, Hume asks, can we ever expect to experience a miracle? A miracle is defined as a violation of the laws of nature. Our knowledge of the laws of nature, however, is derived from experience. So to ask us to believe in a miracle is to ask us to believe in something that contradicts our experience. Whether Hume is correct in these

statements and whether his argument is sufficient to disprove the possibility of a miracle are questions we leave to the reader's consideration. In addition, we must remind the reader of the much more difficult question which underlies this selection: Is there any other theory of knowledge which both makes knowledge of the world possible and allows for the possibility of miracles?

This reading is drawn from Hume's *Enquiry Concerning Human Understanding* (1748), Section X.

. . . I flatter myself, that I have discovered an argument, which, if just, will, with the wise and learned, be an everlasting check to all kinds of superstitious delusion, and consequently, will be useful as long as the world endures. For so long, I presume, will the accounts of miracles and prodigies be found in all history, sacred and profane.

Though experience be our only guide in reasoning concerning matters of fact; it must be acknowledged, that this guide is not altogether infallible, but in some cases is apt to lead us into errors. One, who in our climate, should expect better weather in any week of June than in one of December, would reason justly, and conformably to experience; but it is certain, that he may happen, in the event, to find himself mistaken. However, we may observe, that, in such a case, he would have no cause to complain of experience; because it commonly informs us beforehand of the uncertainty, by that contrariety of events, which we may learn from a diligent observation. All effects follow not with like certainty from their supposed causes. Some events are found, in all countries and all ages, to have been constantly conjoined together: Others are found to have been more variable, and sometimes to disappoint our expectations; so that, in our reasonings concerning matter of fact, there are all imaginable degrees of assurance, from the highest certainty to the lowest species of moral evidence.

A wise man, therefore, proportions his belief to the evidence. In such conclusions as are founded on an infallible experience, he expects the event with the last degree of assurance, and regards his past experience as a full *proof* of the future existence of that event. In other cases, he proceeds with more caution: He weighs the opposite experiments: He considers which side is supported by the greater number of experiments: to that side he inclines, with doubt and hesitation; and when at last he fixes his judgement, the evidence exceeds not what we properly call *probability*. All probability, then, supposes an opposition of experiments and observations, where the one side is found to overbalance the other, and to produce a degree of evidence, proportioned to the superiority. A hundred instances or experiments on one side, and fifty on another, afford a doubtful expectation of any event; though a hundred uniform experiments, with only one that is contradictory, reasonably beget a pretty strong degree of assurance. In all cases, we must balance the opposite experiments, where they are opposite, and deduct the smaller number from the greater, in order to know the exact force of the superior evidence.

To apply these principles to a particular instance; we may observe, that there is no species of reasoning more common, more useful, and even necessary to human life, than that which is derived from the testimony of men, and the reports of eye-witnesses and spectators. This species of reasoning, perhaps, one may deny to be founded on the relation of cause and effect. I shall not dispute about a word. It will be sufficient to observe that our assurance in any argument of this kind is derived from no other principle than our observation of the veracity of human testimony, and of the usual conformity of facts to the reports of witnesses. It being a general maxim, that no objects have any discoverable connexion together, and that all the inferences, which we can draw from one to another, are founded merely on our experience of their constant and regular conjunction; it is evident, that we ought not to make an exception to this maxim in favour of human testimony, whose connexion with any event seems, in itself, as little necessary as any other. Were not the memory tenacious to a certain degree; had not men commonly an inclination to truth and a principle of probity; were they not sensible to shame, when detected in a falsehood: Were not these, I say, discovered by *experience* to be qualities, inherent in human nature, we should never repose the least confidence in human testimony. A man delirious, or noted for falsehood and villany, has no manner of authority with us.

And as the evidence, derived from witnesses and human testimony, is founded on past experience, so it varies with the experience, and is regarded either as a *proof* or a *probability,* according as the conjunction between any particular kind of report and any kind of object has been found to be constant or variable. There are a number of circumstances to be taken into consideration in all judgements of this kind; and the ultimate standard, by which we determine all disputes, that may arise concerning them, is always derived from experience and observation. Where this experience is not entirely uniform on any side, it is attended with an unavoidable contrariety in our judgements, and with the same opposition and mutual destruction of argument as in every other kind of evidence. We frequently hesitate concerning the reports of others. We balance the opposite circumstances, which cause any doubt or uncertainty; and when we discover a superiority on any side, we incline to it; but still with a diminution of assurance, in proportion to the force of its antagonist.

This contrariety of evidence, in the present case, may be derived from several different causes; from the opposition of contrary testimony; from the character or number of the witnesses; from the manner of their delivering their testimony; or from the union of all these circumstances. We entertain a suspicion concerning any matter of fact, when the witnesses contradict each other; when they are but few, or of a doubtful character; when they have an interest in what they affirm; when they deliver their testimony with hesitation, or on the contrary, with too violent asseverations. There are many other particulars of the same kind, which may diminish or destroy the force of any argument, derived from human testimony.

Suppose, for instance, that the fact, which the testimony endeavours to establish, partakes of the extraordinary and the marvellous; in that case, the evidence, resulting from the testimony, admits of a diminution, greater or less, in proportion as the fact is more or less unusual. The reason why we place any credit in witnesses and historians, is not derived from any *connexion,* which we perceive *a priori,* between testimony and reality, but because we are accustomed to find a conformity between them. But when the fact attested is such a one as has seldom fallen under our observation, here is a contest of two opposite experiences; of which the one destroys the other, as far as its force goes, and the superior can only operate on the mind by the force, which remains. The very same principle of experience, which gives us a certain degree of assurance in the testimony of witnesses, gives us also, in this case, another degree of assurance against the fact, which they endeavour to establish; from which contradiction there necessarily arises a counterpoize, and mutual destruction of belief and authority.

I should not believe such a story were it told me by Cato, was a proverbial saying in Rome, even during the lifetime of that philosophical patriot.[1] The incredibility of a fact, it was allowed, might invalidate so great an authority.

The Indian prince, who refused to believe the first relations concerning the effects of frost, reasoned justly; and it naturally required very strong testimony to engage his assent to facts, that arose from a state of nature, with which he was unacquainted, and which bore so little analogy to those events, of which he had had constant and uniform experience. Though they were not contrary to his experience, they were not conformable to it.[2]

But in order to encrease the probability against the testimony of witnesses, let us suppose, that the fact, which they affirm, instead of being only marvellous, is really miraculous; and suppose also, that the testimony considered apart and in itself, amounts to an entire proof; in that case, there is proof against proof, of which the strongest must prevail, but still with a diminution of its force, in proportion to that of its antagonist.

A miracle is a violation of the laws of nature; and as a firm and unalterable experience has established these laws, the proof against a miracle, from the very nature of the fact, is as entire as any argument from experience can possibly be imagined. Why is it more than probable, that all men must die; that lead cannot, of itself, remain suspended in the air; that fire consumes wood, and is extinguished by water; unless it be, that these events are found agreeable to the laws of nature, and there is required a violation of these laws, or in other words a miracle to prevent them? Nothing is esteemed a miracle, if it ever happen in the common course of nature. It is

---

[1] Plutarch, in vita Catonis.

[2] No Indian, it is evident, could have experience that water did not freeze in cold climates. This is placing nature in a situation quite unknown to him; and it is impossible for him to tell *a priori* what will result from it. It is making a new experiment, the consequence of which is always uncertain. One may sometimes conjecture from analogy what will follow; but still this is but conjecture. And it must be confessed, that, in the present case of freezing, the event follows contrary to the rules of analogy, and is such as a rational Indian would not look for. The operations of cold upon water are not gradual, according to the degrees of cold; but whenever it comes to the freezing point, the water passes in a moment, from the utmost liquidity to perfect hardness. Such an event, therefore, may be denominated *extraordinary,* and requires a pretty strong testimony, to render it credible to people in a warm climate: But still it is not *miraculous,* nor contrary to uniform experience of the course of nature in cases where all the circumstances are the same. The inhabitants of Sumatra have always seen water fluid in their own climate, and the freezing of their rivers ought to be deemed a prodigy: But they never saw water in Muscovy during the winter; and therefore they cannot reasonably be positive what would there be the consequence.

no miracle that a man, seemingly in good health, should die on a sudden: because such a kind of death, though more unusual than any other, has yet been frequently observed to happen. But it is a miracle, that a dead man should come to life; because that has never been observed in any age or country. There must, therefore, be a uniform experience against every miraculous event, otherwise the event would not merit that appellation. And as a uniform experience amounts to a proof, there is here a direct and full *proof,* from the nature of the fact, against the existence of any miracle; nor can such a proof be destroyed, or the miracle rendered credible, but by an opposite proof, which is superior.[3]

The plain consequence is (and it is a general maxim worthy of our attention), 'That no testimony is sufficient to establish a miracle, unless the testimony be of such a kind, that its falsehood would be more miraculous, than the fact, which it endeavours to establish; and even in that case there is a mutual destruction of arguments, and the superior only gives us an assurance suitable to that degree of force, which remains, after deducting the inferior.' When anyone tells me, that he saw a dead man restored to life, I immediately consider with myself, whether it be more probable, that this person should either deceive or be deceived, or that the fact, which he relates, should really have happened. I weigh the one miracle against the other; and according to the superiority, which I discover, I pronounce my decision, and always reject the greater miracle. If the falsehood of his testimony would be more miraculous, than the event which he relates; then, and not till then, can he pretend to command my belief or opinion.

In the foregoing reasoning we have supposed, that the testimony, upon which a miracle is founded, may possibly amount to an entire proof, and that the falsehood of that testimony would be a real prodigy: But it is easy to shew, that we have been a great deal too liberal in our concession, and that there never was a miraculous event established on so full an evidence.

---

[3] Sometimes an event may not, *in itself, seem* to be contrary to the laws of nature, and yet, if it were real, it might, by reason of some circumstances, be denominated a miracle; because, in *fact,* it is contrary to these laws. Thus if a person, claiming a divine authority, should command a sick person to be well, a healthful man to fall down dead, the clouds to pour rain, the winds to blow, in short, should order many natural events, which immediately follow upon his command; these might justly be esteemed miracles, because they are really, in this case, contrary to the laws of nature. For if any suspicion remain, that the event and command concurred by accident, there is no miracle and no transgression of the laws of nature. If this suspicion be removed, there is evidently a miracle, and a transgression of these laws; because nothing can be more contrary to nature than that the voice or command of a man should have such an influence. A miracle may be accurately defined, *a transgression of a law of nature by a particular volition of the Deity, or by the interposition of some invisible agent.* A miracle may either be discoverable by men or not. This alters not its nature and essence. The raising of a house or ship into the air is a visible miracle. The raising of a feather, when the wind wants ever so little of a force requisite for that purpose, is as real a miracle, though **not so sensible with regard to us.**

For *first,* there is not to be found, in all history, any miracle attested by a sufficient number of men, of such unquestioned good-sense, education, and learning, as to secure us against all delusion in themselves; of such undoubted integrity, as to place them beyond all suspicion of any design to deceive others; of such credit and reputation in the eyes of mankind, as to have a great deal to lose in case of their being detected in any falsehood; and at the same time, attesting facts performed in such a public manner and in so celebrated a part of the world, as to render the detection unavoidable: All which circumstances are requisite to give us a full assurance in the testimony of men.

Secondly. We may observe in human nature a principle which, if strictly examined, will be found to diminish extremely the assurance, which we might, from human testimony, have, in any kind of prodigy. The maxim, by which we commonly conduct ourselves in our reasonings, is, that the objects, of which we have no experience, resemble those, of which we have; that what we have found to be most usual is always most probable; and that where there is an opposition of arguments, we ought to give the preference to such as are founded on the greatest number of past observations. But though, in proceeding by this rule, we readily reject any fact which is unusual and incredible in an ordinary degree; yet in advancing farther, the mind observes not always the same rule; but when anything is affirmed utterly absurd and miraculous, it rather the more readily admits of such a fact, upon account of that very circumstance, which ought to destroy all its authority. The passion of *surprise* and *wonder,* arising from miracles, being an agreeable emotion, gives a sensible tendency towards the belief of those events, from which it is derived. And this goes so far, that even those who cannot enjoy this pleasure immediately, nor can believe those miraculous events, of which they are informed, yet love to partake of the satisfaction at second-hand or by rebound, and place a pride and delight in exciting the admiration of others.

· · ·

Thirdly. It forms a strong presumption against all supernatural and miraculous relations, that they are observed chiefly to abound among ignorant and barbarous nations; or if a civilized people has ever given admission to any of them, that people will be found to have received them from ignorant and barbarous ancestors, who transmitted them with that inviolable sanction and authority, which always attend received opinions.

· · ·

I may add as a *fourth* reason, which diminishes the authority of prodigies, that there is no testimony for any, even those which have not been expressly detected, that is not opposed by an infinite number of witnesses; so that not only the miracle destroys the credit of testimony, but the testimony destroys itself. To make this the better understood, let us consider, that, in matters of religion, whatever is different is contrary; and that it is impossible the religions of ancient Rome, of Turkey, of Siam, and of China should, all of them, be established on any solid foundation. Every miracle, therefore, pretended to have been wrought in any of these religions (and all of them abound in miracles), as its direct scope is to establish the particular system to which it is attributed; so has it the same force, though more indirectly, to overthrow every other system. In destroying a rival system, it likewise destroys the credit of those miracles, on which that system was established; so that all the prodigies of different religions are to be regarded as contrary facts, and the evidences of these prodigies, whether weak or strong, as opposite to each other. According to this method of reasoning, when we believe any miracle of Mahomet or his successors, we have for our warrant the testimony of a few barbarous Arabians: And on the other hand, we are to regard the authority of Titus Livius, Plutarch, Tacitus, and, in short, of all the authors and witnesses, Grecian, Chinese, and Roman Catholic, who have related any miracle in their particular religion; I say, we are to regard their testimony in the same light as if they had mentioned that Mahometan miracle, and had in express terms contradicted it, with the same certainty as they have for the miracle they relate. This argument may appear over subtile and refined; but is not in reality different from the reasoning of a judge, who supposes, that the credit of two witnesses, maintaining a crime against any one, is destroyed by the testimony of two others, who affirm him to have been two hundred leagues distant, at the same instant when the crime is said to have been committed.

* * *

Upon the whole, then, it appears, that no testimony for any kind of miracle has ever amounted to a probability, much less to a proof; and that, even supposing it amounted to a proof, it would be opposed by another proof; derived from the very nature of the fact, which it would endeavour to establish. It is experience only, which gives authority to human testimony; and it is the same experience, which assures us of the laws of nature. When, therefore, these two kinds of experience are contrary, we have nothing to do but substract the one from the other, and embrace an opinion, either on one side or the other, with that assurance which arises from the remainder. But according to the principle here explained, this substraction, with regard to all popular religions, amounts to an entire annihilation; and therefore we may establish it as a maxim, that no human testimony can have such force as to prove a miracle, and make it a just foundation for any such system of religion.

I beg the limitations here made may be remarked, when I say, that a miracle can never be proved, so as to be the foundation of a system of religion. For I own, that otherwise, there may possibly be miracles, or violations of the usual course of nature, of such a kind as to admit of proof from human testimony; though, perhaps, it will be impossible to find any such in all the records of history. Thus, suppose, all authors, in all languages, agree, that, from the first of January 1600, there was a total darkness over the whole earth for eight days: suppose that the tradition of this extraordinary event is still strong and lively among the people: that all travellers, who return from foreign countries, bring us accounts of the same tradition, without the least variation or contradiction: it is evident, that our present philosophers, instead of doubting the fact, ought to receive it as certain, and ought to search for the causes whence it might be derived. The decay, corruption, and dissolution of nature, is an event rendered probable by so many analogies, that any phenomenon, which seems to have a tendency towards that catastrophe, comes within the reach of human testimony, if that testimony be very extensive and uniform.

But suppose, that all the historians who treat of England, should agree, that, on the first of January 1600, Queen Elizabeth died; that both before and after her death she was seen by her physicians and the whole court, as is usual with persons of her rank; that her successor was acknowledged and proclaimed by the parliament; and that, after being interred a month, she again appeared, resumed the throne, and governed England for three years: I must confess that I should be surprised at the concurrence of so many odd circumstances, but should not have the least inclination to believe so miraculous an event. I should not doubt of her pretended death, and of those other public circumstances that followed it: I should only assert it to have been pretended, and that it neither was, nor possibly could be real. You would in vain object to me the difficulty, and almost impossibility of deceiving the world in an affair of such consequence; the wisdom and solid judgement of that renowned queen; with the little or no advantage which she could reap from so poor an artifice: All this might astonish me; but I would still reply, that the knavery and folly of men are such common phenomena, that I should rather believe the most extraordinary events to arise from their concurrence, than admit of so signal a violation of the laws of nature.

But should this miracle be ascribed to any new system of religion; men, in all ages, have been so much imposed on by ridiculous stories of that kind, that this very circumstance would be a full proof of a cheat, and sufficient, with all men of sense, not only to make them reject the fact, but even reject it without farther examination. Though the Being to whom the miracle is ascribed, be, in this case, Almighty, it does not, upon that account, become a whit more probable; since it is impossible for us to know the attributes or actions of such a Being, otherwise than from the experience which we have of his productions, in the usual course of nature. This still reduces us to past observation, and obliges us to compare the instances of the violation of truth in the testimony of men, with those of the violation of the laws of nature by miracles, in order to judge which of them is most likely and probable. As the violations of truth are more common in the testimony concerning religious miracles, than in that concerning any other matter of fact; this must diminish very much the authority of the former testimony, and make us form a general resolution, never to lend any attention to it, with whatever specious pretence it may be covered.

. . .

I am the better pleased with the method of reasoning here delivered, as I think it may serve to confound those dangerous friends or disguised enemies to the *Christian Religion,* who have undertaken to defend it by the principles of human reason. Our most holy religion is founded on *Faith,* not on reason; and it is a sure method of exposing it to put it to such a trial as it is, by no means, fitted to endure. To make this more evident, let us examine those miracles, related in scripture; and not to lose ourselves in too wide a field, let us confine ourselves to such as we find in the *Pentateuch,* which we shall examine, according to the principles of these pretended Christians, not as the word or testimony of God himself, but as the production of a mere human writer and historian. Here then we are first to consider a book, presented to us by a barbarous and ignorant people, written in an age when they were still more barbarous, and in all probability long after the facts which it relates, corroborated by no concurring testimony, and resembling those fabulous accounts, which every nation gives of its origin. Upon reading this book, we find it full of prodigies and miracles. It gives an account of a state of the world and of human nature entirely different from the present: Of our fall from that state: Of the age of man, extended to near a thousand years: Of the destruction of the world by a deluge: Of the arbitrary choice of one people, as the favourites of heaven; and that people the countrymen of the author: Of their deliverance from bondage by prodigies the most astonishing imaginable: I desire any one to lay his hand upon his heart, and after a serious consideration declare, whether he thinks that the falsehood of such a book, supported by such a testimony, would be more extraordinary and miraculous than all the miracles it relates; which is, however, necessary to make it be received, according to the measures of probability above established.

What we have said of miracles may be applied, without any variation, to prophecies; and indeed, all prophecies are real miracles, and as such only, can be admitted as proofs of any revelation. If it did not exceed the capacity of human nature to foretell future events, it would be absurd to employ any prophecy as an argument for a divine mission or authority from heaven. So that, upon the whole, we may conclude, that the *Christian Religion* not only was at first attended with miracles, but even at this day cannot be believed by any reasonable person without one. Mere reason is insufficient to convince us of its veracity: And whoever is moved by *Faith* to assent to it, is conscious of a continued miracle in his own person, which subverts all the principles of his understanding, and gives him a determination to believe what is most contrary to custom and experience.

QUESTIONS

1. What does Hume mean by "miracle"?
2. How do we obtain our knowledge of the order of nature? What is the difference between something we have never experienced and something which contradicts our experience? Answer this last question by citing examples. For instance, how would you classify the following examples:
    a. A person flies in a rocket to Mars.
    b. A person flies through the air without the help of a machine.
    c. A person turns lead into gold.
    d. A person has X-ray eyes, and can see through walls which everyone else finds opaque.
    e. A man stands on one finger of one hand.
    f. A man jumps ten feet into the air and remains there without any support for ten minutes.
    g. A magician makes a card disappear.
    h. It begins to snow, but the snow is colored red.
    i. A child is born with six toes on each foot.
    j. A child is born with the ability at birth to discuss Einstein's theory of relativity with physicists.
    k. A person dives backward, out of the water up onto the diving board (as appears to happen when a motion picture of diving is reversed).
    l. A man swallows a cupful of nails and broken glass and does not die.
    m. A cube of pure ice in a glass of pure water sinks to the bottom of the glass.
3. Why does Hume believe that a miracle is disproved if its description contradicts our experience of the order of nature?
4. What place does a consideration of evidence by testimony have in a discussion of the possibility of miracles?
5. How does Hume use the rule that "no testimony is sufficient to establish a miracle unless the testimony be of such a kind that its falsehood would be more miraculous than the fact which it endeavors to establish" to disprove the possibility of miracles?
6. Even if we ought not to believe another person's report of a miracle, can we on Hume's principles ever expect to experience a miracle ourselves? Why or why not?

28. C. S. LEWIS

(1898–1963)

The Reasonableness of Believing in Miracles

Clive Staples Lewis was Professor of Medieval and Renaissance English at Cambridge University. He was also the author of more than a half dozen books of Christian apologetics addressed to the common reader and noted for their clarity and intellectual vigor. Perhaps the best known of these books is *The Screwtape Letters* (1942).

In this reading Professor Lewis

makes a case for the probability of miracles, which is in part deliberately constructed in opposition to David Hume's case against miracles stated in the preceding selection. The reader should pay close attention to the premises on which Professor Lewis bases his case for miracles, both noticing his differences with Hume, and determining the grounds on which someone might choose between their views.

This reading is drawn from Chapters VIII and XIII of *Miracles: A Preliminary Study*, 1947. The original chapter titles are retained in this reading.

ON PROBABILITY

Probability is founded on the presumption of a resemblance between those objects of which we have had experience and those of which we have had none; and therefore it is impossible that this presumption can arise from probability.—HUME, *Treatise of Human Nature*, I, III, vi.

. . . Miracles are possible and . . . there is nothing antecedently ridiculous in the stories which say that God has sometimes performed them. This does not mean, of course, that we are committed to believing all stories of miracles. Most stories about miraculous events are probably false: if it comes to that, most stories about natural events are false. Lies, exaggerations, misunderstandings and hearsay make up perhaps more than half of all that is said and written in the world. We must therefore find a criterion whereby to judge any particular story of the miraculous.

In one sense, of course, our criterion is plain. Those stories are to be accepted for which the historical evidence is sufficiently good. But then . . . the answer to the question, "How much evidence should we require for this story?" depends on our answer to the question, "How far is this story intrinsically probable?" We must therefore find a criterion of probability.

The ordinary procedure of the modern historian, even if he admits the possibility of miracle, is to admit no particular instance of it until every possibility of "natural" explanation has been tried and failed. That is, he will accept the most improbable "natural" explanations rather than say that a miracle occurred. Collective hallucination, hypnotism of unconsenting spectators, widespread instantaneous conspiracy in lying by persons not otherwise known to be liars and not likely to gain by the lie—all these are known to be very improbable events: so improbable that, except for the special purpose of excluding a miracle, they are never suggested. But they are preferred to the admission of a miracle.

Such a procedure is, from the purely historical point of view, sheer mid-summer madness *unless* we start by knowing that any miracle whatever is more improbable than the most improbable natural event. Do we know this?

We must distinguish the different kinds of improbability. Since miracles are, by definition, rarer than other events, it is obviously improbable beforehand that one will occur at any given place and time. In that sense every miracle is improbable. But that sort of improbability does not make the story that a miracle *has* happened incredible; for in the same sense all events whatever were once improbable. It is immensely improbable beforehand that a pebble dropped from the stratosphere over London will hit any given spot, or that any one particular person will win a large lottery. But the report that the pebble has landed outside such and such a shop or that Mr. So-and-So has won the lottery is not at all incredible. When you consider the immense number of meetings and fertile unions between ancestors which were necessary in order that you should be born, you perceive that it was once immensely improbable that such a person as you should come to exist: but once you are here, the report of your existence is not in the least incredible. With probability of this kind—antecedent probability of chances—we are not here concerned. Our business is with historical probability.

Ever since Hume's famous *Essay* it has been believed that historical statements about miracles are the most intrinsically improbable of all historical statements. According to Hume, probability rests on what may be called the majority vote of our past experiences. The more often a thing has been known to happen, the more probable it is that it should happen again; and the less often the less probable. Now the regularity of Nature's course, says Hume, is supported by something better than the majority vote of past experiences: it is supported by their unanimous vote, or, as Hume says, by "firm and unalterable experience." There is, in fact, "uniform experience" against Miracle; otherwise, says Hume, it would not be Miracle. A Miracle is therefore the most improbable of all events. It is always more probable that the witnesses were lying or mistaken than that a Miracle occurred.

Now of course we must agree with Hume that if there is absolutely "uniform experience" against miracles, if in other words they have never happened, why then they never have. Unfortunately we know the experience against them to be uniform only if we know that all the reports of them are false. And we can know all the reports to be false only if we know already that miracles have never occurred. In fact, we are arguing in a circle.

There is also an objection to Hume which leads us deeper into our problem. The whole idea of Probability (as Hume understands it) depends on the principle of the Uniformity of Nature. Unless Nature always goes on in the same way, the fact that a thing had happened ten million times would not make it a whit more probable that it would happen again. And how do we know the Uniformity of Nature? A moment's thought shows that we do not know it by experience. We observe many regularities in Nature. But of course all the observations that men have made or will make while the race lasts cover only a minute fraction of the events that actually go on. Our observations would therefore be of no use unless we felt sure that Nature when we are not watching her behaves in the same way as when we are: in other words, unless we believed in the Uniformity of Nature. Experience therefore cannot prove uniformity, because uniformity has to be assumed before experience proves anything. And mere length of experience does not help matters. It is no good saying, "Each fresh experience confirms our belief in uniformity and therefore we reasonably expect that it will always be confirmed"; for that argument works only on the assumption that the future will resemble the past—which is simply the assumption of Uniformity under a new name. Can we say that Uniformity is at any rate very probable? Unfortunately not. We have just seen that all probabilities depend on *it*. Unless Nature is uniform, nothing is either probable or improbable. And clearly the assumption which you have to make before there is any such thing as probability cannot itself be probable.

The odd thing is that no man knew this better than Hume. His *Essay on Miracles* is quite inconsistent with the more radical, and honourable, scepticism of his main work.

The question, "Do miracles occur?" and the question, "Is the course of Nature absolutely uniform?" are the same question asked in two different ways. Hume by sleight of hand, treats them as two different questions. He first answers, "Yes," to the question whether Nature is absolutely uniform: and then uses this "Yes" as a ground for answering, "No," to the question, "Do miracles occur?" The single real question which he set out to answer is never discussed at all. He gets the answer to one form of the question by assuming the answer to another form of the same question.

Probabilities of the kind that Hume is concerned with hold inside the framework of an assumed Uniformity of Nature. When the question of miracles is raised we are asking about the validity or perfection of the frame itself. No study of probabilities inside a given frame can ever tell us how probable it is that the frame itself can be violated. Granted a school time-table with French on Tuesday morning at ten o'clock, it is really probable that Jones, who always skimps his French preparation, will be in trouble next Tuesday, and that he was in trouble on any previous Tuesday. But what does this tell us about the probability of the time-table's being altered? To find that out you must eavesdrop in the masters' common-room. It is no use studying the time-table.

If we stick to Hume's method, far from getting what he hoped (namely, the conclusion that all miracles are infinitely improbable) we get a complete deadlock. The only kind of probability he allows holds exclusively within the frame of uniformity. When uniformity is itself in question (and it is in question the moment we ask whether miracles occur) this kind of probability is suspended. And Hume knows no other. By his method, therefore, we cannot say that uniformity is either probable or improbable; and equally we cannot say that miracles are either probable or improbable. We have impounded *both* uniformity *and* miracles in a sort of limbo where probability and improbability can never come. This result is equally disastrous for the scientist and the theologian; but along Hume's lines there is nothing whatever to be done about it.

Our only hope, then, will be to cast about for some quite different kind of Probability. Let us for the moment cease to ask what right we have to believe in the Uniformity of Nature, and ask why in fact men do believe in it. I think the belief has three causes, two of which are irrational. In the first place we are creatures of habit. We expect new situations to resemble old ones. It is a tendency which we share with animals; one can see it working, often to very comic results, in our dogs and cats. In the second place, when we plan our actions, we have to leave out of account the theoretical possibility that Nature might not behave as usual to-morrow, because we can do nothing about it. It is not worth bothering about because no action can be taken to meet it. And what we habitually put out of our minds we soon forget. The picture of uniformity thus comes to dominate our minds without rival and we believe it. Both these causes are irrational and would be just as effective in building up a false belief as in building up a true one.

But I am convinced that there is a third cause. "In science," said the late Sir Arthur Eddington, "we sometimes have convictions which we cherish but cannot justify; we are influenced by some innate sense of the fitness of things." This may sound a perilously subjective and aesthetic criterion; but can one doubt that it is a principal source of our belief in Uniformity? A universe in which unprecedented and unpredictable events were at every moment flung into Nature would not merely be inconvenient to us: it would be profoundly repugnant. We will not accept such a universe on any terms whatever. It is utterly detestable to us. It shocks our "sense of the fitness of things." In advance of experience, in the teeth of many experiences, we are already enlisted on the side of uniformity. For of course science actually proceeds by concentrating not on the regularities of Nature but on her apparent irregularities. It is the apparent irregularity that prompts each new hypothesis. It does so because we refuse to acquiesce in irregularities: we never rest till we have formed and verified a hypothesis which enables us to say that they were not really irregularities at all. Nature as it comes to us looks at first like a mass of irregularities. The stove which lit all right yesterday won't light to-day; the water which was wholesome last year is poisonous this year. The whole mass of seemingly irregular experience could never have been turned into scientific knowledge at all unless from the very start we had brought to it a faith in uniformity which almost no number of disappointments can shake.

This faith—the preference—is it a thing we can trust? Or is it only the way our minds happen to work? It is useless to say that it has hitherto always been confirmed by the event. That is no good unless you (at least silently) add, "And therefore always will be": and you cannot add that unless you know already that our faith in uniformity is well grounded. And that is just what we are now asking. Does this sense of fitness of ours correspond to anything in external reality?

The answer depends on the Metaphysic one holds. If all that exists is Nature, the great mindless interlocking event, if our own deepest convictions are merely the bye-products of an irrational process, then clearly there is not the slightest ground for supposing that our sense of fitness and our consequent faith in uniformity tell us anything about a reality external to ourselves. Our convictions are simply a fact *about us*—like the colour of our hair. If Naturalism is true we have no reason to trust our conviction that Nature is uniform. It can be trusted only if quite a different Metaphysic is true. If the deepest thing in reality, the Fact which is the source of all other facthood, is a thing in some degree like ourselves—if it is a Rational Spirit and we derive our rational spirituality from it—then indeed our conviction can be trusted. Our repugnance to disorder is derived from Nature's Creator and ours. The disorderly world which we cannot endure to believe in is the disorderly world He would not have endured to create. Our conviction that the time-table will not be perpetually or meaninglessly altered is sound because we have (in a sense) eavesdropped in the Master's common-room.

The sciences logically require a metaphysic of this sort. Our greatest natural philosopher thinks it is also the metaphysic out of which they originally grew. Professor Whitehead points out [1] that centuries of belief in a God who combined "the personal energy of Jehovah" with "the rationality of a Greek philosopher" first produced that firm expectation of systematic order which rendered possible the birth of modern science. Men became scientific because they expected Law in Nature, and they expected Law in Nature because they believed in a Legislator. In most modern scientists this belief has died: it will be interesting to see how long their confidence in uniformity survives it. Two significant developments have already appeared —the hypothesis of a lawless subnature, and the surrender of the claim that science is true. We may be living nearer than we suppose to the end of the Scientific Age.

But if we admit God, must we admit Miracle? Indeed, indeed, you have no security against it. That is the bargain. Theology says to you in effect, "Admit God and with Him the risk of a few miracles, and I in return will ratify your faith in uniformity as regards the overwhelming majority of events." The philosophy which forbids you to make uniformity absolute is also the philosophy which offers you solid grounds for believing it to be

[1] *Science and the Modern World.* Chapter II.

general, to be *almost* absolute. The Being who threatens Nature's claim to omnipotence confirms her in her lawful occasions. Give us this ha'porth of tar and we will save the ship. The alternative is really much worse. Try to make Nature absolute and you find that her uniformity is not even probable. By claiming too much, you get nothing. Yet get the deadlock, as in Hume. Theology offers you a working arrangement, which leaves the scientist free to continue his experiments and the Christian to continue his prayers.

We have also, I suggest, found what we were looking for—a criterion whereby to judge the intrinsic probability of an alleged miracle. We must judge it by our "innate sense of the fitness of things," that same sense of fitness which led us to anticipate that the universe would be orderly. I do not mean, of course, that we are to use this sense in deciding whether miracles in general are possible: we know that they are on philosophical grounds. Nor do I mean that a sense of fitness will do instead of close inquiry into the historical evidence. As I have repeatedly pointed out, the historical evidence cannot be estimated unless we have first estimated the intrinsic probability of the recorded event. It is in making that estimate as regards each story of the miraculous that our sense of fitness comes into play.

If in giving such weight to the sense of fitness I were doing anything new, I should feel rather nervous. In reality I am merely giving formal acknowledgment to a principle which is always used. Whatever men may *say,* no one really thinks that the Christian doctrine of the Resurrection is exactly on the same level with some pious tittle-tattle about how Mother Egarée Louise miraculously found her second best thimble by the aid of St. Antony. The religious and the irreligious are really quite agreed on the point. The whoop of delight with which the sceptic would unearth the story of the thimble, and the "rosy pudency" with which the Christian would keep it in the background, both tell the same tale. Even those who think all stories of miracles absurd think some very much more absurd than others: even those who believe them all (if anyone does) think that some require a specially robust faith. The criterion which both parties are actually using is that of fitness. More than half the disbelief in miracles that exists is based on a sense of their *unfitness:* a conviction (due, as I have argued, to false philosophy) that they are unsuitable to the dignity of God or Nature or else to the indignity and insignificance of man.

MIRACLE AND THE LAWS OF NATURE

The question is whether Nature can be known to be of such a kind that supernatural interferences with her are impossible. She is already known to be, in general, regular: she behaves according to fixed laws, many of which have been discovered, and which interlock with one another. There is, in this discussion, no question of mere failure or inaccuracy to keep these laws on the part of Nature, no question of chancey or spontaneous variation.[2] The only question is whether, granting the existence of a Power outside Nature, there is any intrinsic absurdity in the idea of its intervening to produce within Nature events which the regular "going on" of the whole natural system would never have produced.

Three conceptions of the "Laws" of Nature have been held. (1) That they are mere brute facts, known only by observation, with no discoverable rhyme or reason about them. We know *that* Nature behaves thus and thus; we do not know why she does and can see no reason why she should not do the opposite. (2) That they are applications of the law of averages. The foundations of Nature are in the random and lawless. But the numbers of units we are dealing with are so enormous that the behaviour of these crowds (like the behaviour of very large masses of men) can be calculated with practical accuracy. What we call "impossible events" are events so overwhelmingly improbable—by actuarial standards—that we do not need to take them into account. (3) That the fundamental laws of Physics are really what we call "necessary truths" like the truths of mathematics—in other words, that if we clearly understand what we are saying we shall see that the opposite would be meaningless nonsense. Thus it is a "law" that when one billiard ball shoves another the amount of momentum lost by the first ball must exactly equal the amount gained by the second. People who hold that the laws of Nature are necessary truths would say that all we have done is to split up the single event into two halves (adventures of ball A, and adventures of ball B) and then discover that "the two sides of the account balance." When we understand this we see that of course they *must* balance. The fundamental laws are in the long run merely statements that every event is itself and not some different event.

It will at once be clear that the first of these three theories gives no assurance against Miracles—indeed no assurance that, even apart from Miracles, the "laws" which we have hitherto observed will be obeyed to-morrow. If we have no notion why a thing happens, then of course we know no reason why it should not be otherwise, and therefore have no certainty that it might not some day be otherwise. The second theory, which depends on the law of averages, is in the same position. The assurance it gives us is of the same general kind as our assurance that a coin tossed a thousand times will not give the same result, say, nine hundred times: and that the longer you toss it the more nearly the numbers of Heads and Tails will come to being equal. But this is so only provided the coin is an honest coin. If it is a loaded coin our expectations may be disappointed. But the people who believe in miracles are maintaining precisely that the coin *is* loaded. The expectations based on the law of averages will work only for *undoctored* Nature. And the question

[2] If any region of reality is in fact chancey or lawless then it is a region which, so far from admitting Miracle with special ease, renders the word "Miracle" meaningless throughout that region.

whether miracles occur is just the question whether Nature is ever doctored.

The third view (that Laws of Nature are necessary truths) seems at first sight to present an insurmountable obstacle to miracle. The breaking of them would, in that case, be a self-contradiction and not even Omnipotence can do what is self-contradictory. Therefore the Laws cannot be broken. And therefore, shall we conclude, no miracle can ever occur?

We have gone too quickly. It is certain that the billiard balls will behave in a particular way, just as it is certain that if you divide a shilling unequally between two recipients then A's share must exceed the half and B's share fall short of it by exactly the same amount. Provided, of course, that A does not by sleight of hand steal some of B's pennies at the very moment of the transaction. In the same way, you know what will happen to the two billiard balls —provided nothing interferes. If one ball encounters a roughness in the cloth which the other does not, their motion will not illustrate the law in the way you had expected. Of course what happens as a result of the roughness in the cloth will illustrate the law in some other way, but your original prediction will have been false. Or again, if I snatch up a cue and give one of the balls a little help, you will get a third result: and that third result will equally illustrate the laws of physics, and equally falsify your prediction. I shall have "spoiled the experiment." All interferences leave the law perfectly true. But every prediction of what will happen in a given instance is made under the proviso "other things being equal" or "if there are no interferences." Whether other things *are* equal in a given case and whether interferences may occur is another matter. The arithmetician, as an arithmetician, does not know how likely A is to steal some of B's pennies when the shilling is being divided; you had better ask a criminologist. The physicist, as a physicist, does not know how likely I am to catch up a cue and "spoil" his experiment with the billiard balls; you had better ask someone who knows *me*. In the same way the physicist, as such, does not know how likely it is that some supernatural power is going to interfere with them: you had better ask a metaphysician. But the physicist does know, just because he is a physicist, that if the billiard balls are tampered with by any agency, natural or supernatural, which he had not taken into account, then their behaviour must differ from what he expected. Not because the law is false, but because it is true. The more certain we are of the law, the more clearly we know that if new factors have been introduced the result will vary accordingly. What we do not know, as physicists, is whether Supernatural power might be one of the new factors.

If the laws of Nature are necessary truths, no miracle can break them: but then no miracle needs to break them. It is with them as with the laws of arithmetic. If I put six pennies into a drawer on Monday and six more on Tuesday, the laws decree that—*other things being equal*—I shall find twelve pennies there on Wednesday. But if the drawer has been robbed I may in fact find only two. Something will have been broken (the lock of the drawer or the laws of England) but the laws of arithmetic will not have been broken.

The new situation created by the thief will illustrate the laws of arithmetic just as well as the original situation. But if God comes to work miracles, He comes "like a thief in the night." Miracle is, from the point of view of the scientist, a form of doctoring, tampering, if you like, cheating. It introduces a new factor into the situation, namely supernatural force, which the scientist had not reckoned on. He calculates what will happen, or what must have happened on a past occasion, in the belief that the situation, at that point of space and time, is or was A. But if supernatural force has been added, then the situation really is or was AB. And no one knows better than the scientist that AB *cannot* yield the same result as A. The necessary truth of the laws, far from making it impossible that miracles should occur makes it certain that if the Supernatural is operating they must occur. For if the natural situation by itself, and the natural situation *plus* something else, yielded only the same result, it would be then that we should be faced with a lawless and unsystematic universe. The better you know that two and two make four, the better you know that two and three don't.

This perhaps helps to make a little clearer what the laws of Nature really are. We are in the habit of talking as if they caused events to happen; but they have never caused any event at all. The laws of motion do not set billiard balls moving: they analyse the motion after something else (say, a man with a cue, or a lurch of the liner, or, perhaps, supernatural power) has provided it. They produce no events: they state the pattern to which every event—if only it can be induced to happen—must conform, just as the rules of arithmetic state the pattern to which all transactions with money must conform—if only you can get hold of any money. Thus in one sense the laws of Nature cover the whole field of space and time; in another, what they leave out is precisely the whole real universe—the incessant torrent of actual events which makes up true history. That must come from somewhere else. To think the laws can produce it is like thinking that you can create real money by simply doing sums. For every law, in the last resort, says "If you have A, then you will get B." But first catch your A: the laws won't do it for you.

It is therefore inaccurate to define a miracle as something that breaks the laws of Nature. It doesn't. If I knock out my pipe I alter the position of a great many atoms: in the long run, and to an infinitesimal degree, of all the atoms there are. Nature digests or assimilates this event with perfect ease and harmonises it in a twinkling with all other events. It is one more bit of raw material for the laws to apply to, and they apply. I have simply thrown one event into the general cataract of events and it finds itself at home there and conforms to all other events. If God annihilates or creates or deflects a unit of matter He has created a new situation at that point. Immediately all Nature domiciles this new situation, makes it at home in her realm, adapts all other events to it. It finds itself conforming to all the laws. If God creates a miraculous spermatozoon in the body of a virgin, it does not proceed to break any laws. The laws at once take it over. Nature is ready. Pregnancy follows, according to all the normal laws, and nine months later a child is born. We see every day that physical nature is not in the least incommoded by the daily inrush of events from biological nature or from psychological nature. If events ever come from beyond Nature altogether, she will be no more incommoded by them. Be sure she will rush to the point where she is invaded, as the defensive forces rush to a cut in our finger, and there hasten to accommodate the newcomer. The moment it enters her realm it obeys all her laws. Miraculous wine will intoxicate, miraculous conception will lead to pregnancy, inspired books will suffer all the ordinary processes of textual corruption, miraculous bread will be digested. The divine art of miracle is not an art of suspending the pattern to which events conform but of feeding new events into that pattern. It does not violate the law's proviso, "If A, then B": it says, "But this time instead of A, A2," and Nature, speaking through all her laws, replies, "Then B2," and naturalises the immigrant, as she well knows how. She is an accomplished hostess.

A miracle is emphatically not an event without cause or without results. Its cause is the activity of God: its results follow according to Natural law. In the forward direction (i.e. during the time which follows its occurrence) it is interlocked with all Nature just like any other event. Its peculiarity is that it is not in that way interlocked backwards, interlocked with the previous history of Nature. And this is just what some people find intolerable. The reason they find it intolerable is that they start by taking Nature to be the whole of reality. And they are sure that all reality must be interrelated and consistent. I agree with them. But I think they have mistaken a partial system within reality, namely Nature, for the whole. That being so, the miracle and the previous history of Nature may be interlocked after all but not in the way the Naturalist expected: rather in a much more roundabout fashion. The great complex event called Nature, and the new particular event introduced into it by the miracle, are related by their common origin in God, and doubtless, if we knew enough, most intricately related in His purpose and design, so that a Nature which had had a different history, and therefore been a different Nature, would have been invaded by different miracles or by none at all. In that way the miracle and the previous course of Nature are as well interlocked as any other two realities, but you must go back as far as their common Creator to find the interlocking. You will not find it *within* Nature. The same sort of thing happens with any partial system. The behaviour of fishes which are being studied in a tank makes a relatively closed system. Now suppose that the tank is shaken by a bomb in the neighbourhood of the laboratory. The behaviour of the fishes will now be no longer fully explicable by what was going on in the tank before the bomb fell: there will be a failure of backward interlocking. This does not mean that the bomb and the previous history of events within the tank are totally and finally unrelated. It does mean that to find their relation you must go back to the much larger reality which includes both the tank and the bomb—the reality of war-time England in which bombs are falling but some laboratories are still at work. You would never find it within the history of the tank. In the same way, the miracle is not *naturally* interlocked in the backward direction. To find how it is interlocked with the previous history of Nature you must replace both Nature and the miracle in a larger context. Everything *is* connected with everything else: but not all things are connected by the short and straight roads we expected.

The rightful demand that all reality should be consistent and systematic does not therefore exclude miracles: but it has a very valuable contribution to make to our conception of them. It reminds us that miracles, if they occur, must, like all events, be revelations of the total harmony of all that exists. Nothing arbitrary, nothing simply "stuck on" and left unreconciled with the texture of total reality, can be admitted. By definition, miracles must of course interrupt the usual course of Nature; but if they are real they must, in the very act of so doing, assert all the more the unity and self-consistency of total reality at some deeper level. They will not be like unmetrical lumps of prose breaking the unity of a poem; they will be like that crowning metrical audacity which, though it may be paralleled nowhere else in the poem, yet, coming just where it does, and effecting just what it effects, is (to those who understand) the supreme revelation of the unity in the poet's conception. If what we call Nature is modified by supernatural power, then we may be sure that the capability of being so modified is of the essence of nature—that the total event, if we could grasp it, would turn out to involve, by its very character, the possibility of such modifications. If Nature brings forth miracles then doubtless it is as "natural" for her to do so when impregnated by the masculine force beyond her as it is for a woman to bear children to a man. In calling them miracles we do not mean that they are contradictions or outrages; we mean that, left to her own resources, she could never produce them.

QUESTIONS

1. What are the different senses of "natural law" which Professor Lewis notices? What does he mean by "miracle"? How does he show that a miracle is possible in each sense of "natural law" that he distinguishes?
2. How does Professor Lewis attempt to solve the theistic problem of accounting for the intervention in nature of a God who is above nature?
3. What is the difference between an event which "breaks the laws of nature" and an event which "interrupt[s] the usual course of nature"? Illustrate your answer with examples.
4. What is Hume's argument against miracles? (See preceding selection.) What argument does Professor Lewis advance against Hume? Decide who has the better case, and justify your decision.
5. How does Professor Lewis use the concept of "fitness" to account for the probability of miracles? What assumptions are required for someone to be able to use Professor Lewis' concept of "fitness" as he does?

29. G. W. LEIBNIZ

(1646–1716)

God and Evil: A Positive View

Leibniz is justly famous as a philosopher, a mathematician, and a theologian. But he is popularly remembered for providing Voltaire with the theme of *Candide* (1759): This is the best of all possible worlds. Whether Leibniz's doctrine is as untenable as Voltaire attempts to show is a question which the reader will be better able to decide after considering this selection. The topic which Leibniz considers here is that of God and evil. Does the existence of evil in the world count against the existence of God? Or, at the very least, does the existence of evil disprove God's benevolence? Leibniz answers both of these questions with a "No," and the reader must be careful to notice the principles which Leibniz believes guarantee his negative answers. The reader must decide whether Leibniz's principles are the only ones which may be invoked, and, further, he must consider the extremely difficult question of how one decides what principles to invoke here.

The first paragraph of this selection is taken from *Principles of Nature and of Grace, Founded on Reason* (1714). The remainder is the last half of *On the Ultimate Origination of Things* (1697). The translation is by Mary Morris.

From the book *Philosophical Writings*, by Leibniz.
Everyman's Library Series. Published by E. P. Dutton & Co., Inc.
Reprinted by permission of the publishers. Permission also
granted by J. M. Dent & Sons, Ltd., London.

It follows from the supreme perfection of God that in producing the universe He chose the best possible plan, containing the greatest variety together with the greatest order; the best arranged situation, place, and time; the greatest effect produced by the simplest means; the most power, the most knowledge, the most happiness and goodness in created things of which the universe admitted. For as all possible things have a claim to existence in the understanding of God in proportion to their perfections, the result of all these claims must be the most perfect actual world which is possible. Otherwise it would not be possible to explain why things have happened as they have rather than otherwise. . . .

. . . The ultimate reason of the reality both of essences and of existences in a Unity must certainly be greater, higher, and prior to the world itself, since through it alone not only the existent things, which the world contains, but also the things that are possible have their reality. It cannot be found except in one single source, because of the interconnection of all these things with one another. It is evident that from this source existent things are continually issuing and being produced, and have been produced, since it is not clear why one state of the world rather than another, yesterday's state rather than today's, should flow from the world itself. It is also evident how God acts not only physically but also freely; and how there lies in Him not only the efficient but also the final cause; and how from Him proceeds the reason not only of the greatness or potency that there is in the mechanism for the universe as now established, but also of the goodness or wisdom involved in the establishing of it.

In case someone may think that moral perfection or goodness is here being confused with metaphysical perfection or greatness, and may admit the latter while denying the former, it should be pointed out that it follows from what has been said not only that the world is the most perfect physically, or, if you prefer it, metaphysically, or in other words that that series of things will be forthcoming which in actual fact affords the greatest quantity of reality, but also that the world should be the most perfect morally, because true moral perfection is physical perfection in minds themselves. Hence the world is not only the most wonderful machine, but also in regard to minds it is the best commonwealth, by whose means there is bestowed on minds the greatest possible amount of felicity or joyfulness; and it is in this that their physical perfection consists.

But, you will say, we find in the world the very opposite of this. Often the worst of sufferings fall upon the best men; the innocent (I speak not only of the brutes, but of men also) are afflicted, and are slain even with tortures; indeed the world, especially if we look at the government of the human race, seems rather a confused chaos than an affair ordained by some supreme wisdom. So it appears at first sight, I allow: but on deeper examination it must be agreed that the opposite is the case. It is evident *a priori* from those very principles which I have adduced that without doubt there is secured in the world the highest perfection that there could possibly be of all things, and therefore of minds.

And indeed it is unreasonable, as the lawyers say, to give a judgment without inspecting the whole law. We have knowledge of a tiny part of that eternity which stretches out immeasurably. For how small a thing is the memory of the few thousand years which history hands down to us! And yet out of so little experience we rashly make judgments about the immeasurable and the eternal; just as men who had been born and bred in prison or in the subterranean salt-mines of Sarmatia might think that there was no other light in the world than the treacherous flicker of torches, which was hardly sufficient to guide their footsteps. Look at the most lovely picture, and then cover it up, leaving uncovered only a tiny scrap of it. What else will you see there, even if you look as closely as possible, and the more so as you look from nearer and nearer at hand, but a kind of confused medley of colours, without selection, without art! And yet when you remove the covering, and look upon the whole picture from the proper place, you will see that what previously seemed to you to have been aimlessly smeared on the canvas was in fact accomplished with the highest art by the author of the work. What happens to the eyes in painting is equally experienced by the ears in music. The great composers frequently mingle discords with harmonious chords so that the listener may be stimulated and pricked as it were, and may become eager to know what is going to happen; presently when all is restored to order he feels so much the more content. In the same way we may take pleasure in small dangers, or in the experience of ills, from the very sense or proof they give us of our own power or felicity. Or again at the spectacle of rope-walking or sword-dancing we are delighted by the very element of fear that is involved, and we ourselves in play with children hold them as if we were going to throw them out of the window, and half let them go—in very much the same way as the ape carried Christian, King of Denmark, when he was still an infant wrapped in long clothes, to the edge of the roof, and then, when everybody was in terror, turned it into jest and put him back into his cradle safe and sound. On the same principle it has an insipid effect if we always eat sweet things; sharp, acid, and even bitter things should be mixed in to stimulate the taste. He who has not tasted what is bitter has not earned what is sweet, nor will he appreciate it. This is the very law of enjoyment, that positive pleasure does not come from an even course; such things produce weariness, and make men dull, not joyful.

What I have said, however, about the possibility of a part being disturbed without upsetting the harmony of the whole must not be interpreted to mean that no account is taken of the parts; or that it is sufficient for the whole world to be completed at all points, even though it should turn out that the human race was wretched, and that there was in the universe no care for justice and no account was taken of us—as is maintained by some people whose judgment about the sum of things is ill-grounded. For the truth is that, just as in a well-regulated commonwealth care is taken that as far as possible things shall be to the interest of the individual, in the same way the universe would not be sufficiently perfect unless, as far as can be done without upsetting the universal harmony, the good of individual people is considered. Of this there could be established no better measure than the very law of justice itself, which dictates that each should have a part in the perfection of the universe and in his own happiness in proportion to his own virtue and to the extent to which his will is directed towards the common good; by which is fulfilled what we call the charity and love of God, in which alone, according to the judgment of wise theologians also, stands the whole force and power of the Christian religion. Nor ought it to seem remarkable that all this deference should be paid to minds in the universe, since they bear the closest resemblance to the image of the supreme Author, and their relation to Him is not that of machines to their artificer (like the rest of the world) but rather that of citizens to their prince; moreover they will endure as long as the universe itself, and they, in some manner, express and concentrate the whole in themselves; so that it might be said that minds are whole parts.

As for the afflictions of men, and especially of good men, we must hold ourselves assured that they contribute to the greater good of those who suffer them; and this is true not only theologically, but physically also, just as a grain of wheat cast into the earth must suffer before it bears fruit. And in general it is true to say that afflictions are for the time being evil, but in effect good, since they are short cuts to a greater perfection. Similarly in physics the liquids which ferment slowly are also more slowly purified, whereas those in which there is a more violent disturbance throw off the foreign parts with greater force and so more quickly become pure. You might fairly say that this is a case of taking a step back in order to make a stronger leap forward (*reculer pour mieux sauter*). These things must be allowed to be not only pleasant and consoling, but also most true. Indeed in general I hold that there is nothing truer than happiness, and nothing happier and sweeter than truth.

Further, we realize that there is a perpetual and a most free progress of the whole universe in fulfilment of the universal beauty and perfection of the works of God, so that it is always advancing towards a greater development. Thus, even now a great part of our earth has received cultivation, and will receive it more and more. And though it is true that there are times when some parts of it go back again to virgin forest, or are destroyed again and oppressed, this must be understood in the same sense as I just now interpreted the meaning of affliction, namely, that this very destruction and oppression contributes to achieve something greater, so that in some way we receive profit from our very loss.

To the objection that may perhaps be offered that if this were so the world would long ago have become a paradise, the answer is at hand: although many substances have already come to great perfection, yet owing to the infinite divisibility of what is continuous, there always remain in the abyss of things parts that are asleep, and these need to be awakened and to be driven forward into something greater and better—in a word, to a better development. Hence this progress does not ever come to an end.

QUESTIONS

1. What sort of thing does Leibniz count as evil? In general, how does one tell when something is evil? Does a judgment of what is evil depend on one's point of view? Explain your answer.

2. How does Leibniz argue that the presence of evil in the world disproves neither God's existence nor his benevolence?

3. In framing his arguments, does Leibniz ask us to accept principles which assume what he is trying to prove? Defend your answer.

30. DAVID HUME

(1711–76)

God and Evil: A Skeptical View

(A general introductory note on Hume may be found on page 116.)

Hume's contribution to the problem of whether the presence of evil in the world counts for (or against) either the existence or the benevolence of God takes the form of an examination of the following question: Starting solely from our knowledge of the world, is there anything about the world which would lead us to believe that it has been made by a benevolent God? Hume's answer to this question is "No." The reader must decide whether Hume has good grounds for answering this question as he does. In addition the reader ought to contrast Hume's discussion of God and evil with Leibniz's. For these selections represent opposing points of view about the same topic, and the reader should work out the assumptions on which each point of view depends, the better to see why anyone should choose one point of view rather than the other.

This selection is drawn from the *Dialogues Concerning Natural Religion* (1779), Part XI. It is part of a speech which Hume assigns to his skeptical character, Philo.

From *Dialogues Concerning Natural Religion,* by David Hume, edited with introduction by Henry D. Aiken, Hafner Library of Classics, Hafner Publishing Co., New York, 1957.

My sentiments, [said] Philo, are not worth being made a mystery of; and, therefore, without any ceremony, I shall deliver what occurs to me with regard to the present subject. It must, I think, be allowed that, if a very limited intelligence whom we shall suppose utterly unacquainted with the universe were assured that it were the production of a very good, wise, and powerful Being, however finite, he would, from his conjectures, form *beforehand* a different notion of it from what we find it to be by experience; nor would he ever imagine, merely from these attributes of the cause of which he is informed, that the effect could be so full of vice and misery and disorder, as it appears in this life. Supposing now that this person were brought into the world, still assured that it was the workmanship of such a sublime and benevolent Being, he might, perhaps, be surprised at the disappointment, but would never retract his former belief if founded on any very solid argument, since such a limited intelligence must be sensible of his own blindness and ignorance, and must allow that there may be many solutions of those phenomena which will forever escape his comprehension. But supposing, which is the real case with regard to man, that this creature is not antecedently convinced of a supreme intelligence, benevolent, and powerful, but is left to gather such a belief from the appearances of things—this entirely alters the case, nor will he ever find any reason for such a conclusion. He may be fully convinced of the narrow limits of his understanding, but this will not help him in forming an inference concerning the goodness of superior powers, since he must form that inference from what he knows, not from what he is ignorant of. The more you exaggerate his weakness and ignorance, the more diffident you render him, and give him the greater suspicion that such subjects are beyond the reach of his faculties. You are obliged, therefore, to reason with him merely from the known phenomena, and to drop every arbitrary supposition or conjecture.

Did I show you a house or palace where there was not one apartment convenient or agreeable, where the windows, doors, fires, passages, stairs, and the whole economy of the building were the source of noise, confusion, fatigue, darkness, and the extremes of heat and cold, you would certainly blame the contrivance, without any further examination. The architect would in vain display his subtilty, and prove to you that, if this door or that window were altered, greater ills would ensue. What he says may be strictly true: the alteration of one particular, while the other parts of the building remain, may only augment the inconveniences. But still you would assert in general that, if the architect had had skill and good intentions, he might have formed such a plan of the whole, and might have adjusted the parts in such a manner as would have remedied all or most of these inconveniences. His ignorance, or even your own ignorance of such a plan, will never convince you of the impossibility of it. If you find any inconveniences and deformities in the building, you will always, without entering into any detail, condemn the architect.

In short, I repeat the question: Is the world, considered in general and as it appears to us in this life, different from what a man or such a limited being would, *beforehand,* expect from a very powerful, wise, and benevolent Deity? It must be strange prejudice to assert the contrary. And from thence I conclude that, however consistent the world may be, allowing certain suppositions and conjectures with the idea of such a Deity, it can never afford us an inference concerning his existence. The consistency is not absolutely denied, only the inference. Conjectures, especially where infinity is excluded from the Divine attributes, may perhaps be sufficient to prove a consistency, but can never be foundations for any inference.

There seem to be *four* circumstances on which depend all or the greatest part of the ills that molest sensible creatures; and it is not impossible but all these circumstances may be necessary and unavoidable. We know so little beyond common life, or even of common life, that, with regard to the economy of a universe, there is no conjecture, however wild, which may not be just, nor any one, however plausible, which may not be erroneous. All that belongs to human understanding, in this deep ignorance and obscurity, is to be sceptical or at least cautious, and not to admit of any hypothesis whatever, much less of any which is supported by no appearance of probability. Now this I assert to be the case with regard to all the causes of evil and the circumstances on which it depends. None of them appear to human reason in the least degree necessary or unavoidable, nor can we suppose them such, without the utmost license of imagination.

The *first* circumstance which introduces evil is that contrivance or economy of the animal creation by which pains, as well as pleasures, are employed to excite all creatures to action, and make them vigilant in the great work of self-preservation. Now pleasure alone, in its various degrees, seems to human understanding sufficient for this purpose. All animals might be constantly in a state of enjoyment; but when urged by any of the necessities of nature, such as thirst, hunger, weariness, instead of pain, they might feel a diminution of pleasure by which they might be prompted to seek that object which is necessary to their subsistence. Men pursue pleasure as eagerly as they avoid pain; at least, they might have been so constituted. It seems, therefore, plainly possible to carry on the business of life without any pain. Why then is any animal ever rendered susceptible of such a sensation? If animals can be free from it an hour, they might enjoy a perpetual exemption from it, and it required as particular a contrivance of their organs to produce that feeling as to endow them with sight, hearing, or any of the senses. Shall we conjecture that such a contrivance was necessary, without any appearance of reason, and shall we build on that conjecture as on the most certain truth?

But a capacity of pain would not alone produce pain were it not for the *second* circumstance, viz., the conducting of the world by general laws; and this seems nowise necessary to a very perfect Being. It is true, if everything were conducted by particular volitions, the course of nature would be perpetually broken, and no man could employ his reason in the conduct of life. But might not other particular volitions remedy this inconvenience? In short, might not the Deity exterminate all ill, wherever it were to be found, and produce all good, without any preparation or long progress of causes and effects?

Besides, we must consider that, according to the present economy of the world, the course of nature, though supposed exactly regular, yet to us appears not so, and many events are uncertain, and many disappoint our expectations. Health and sickness, calm and tempest, with an infinite number of other accidents whose causes are unknown and variable, have a great influence both on the fortunes of particular persons and on the prosperity of public societies; and indeed all human life, in a manner, depends on such accidents. A being, therefore, who knows the secret springs of the universe might easily, by particular volitions, turn all these accidents to the good of mankind and render the whole world happy, without discovering himself in any operation. A fleet whose purposes were salutary to society might always meet with a fair wind. Good princes enjoy sound health and long life. Persons born to power and authority be framed with good tempers and virtuous dispositions. A few such events as these, regularly and wisely conducted, would change the face of the world, and yet would no more seem to disturb the course of nature or confound human conduct than the present economy of things where the causes are secret and variable and compounded. Some small touches given to Caligula's brain in his infancy might have converted him into a Trajan. One wave, a little higher than the rest, by burying Caesar and his fortune in the bottom of the ocean, might have restored liberty to a considerable part of mankind. There may, for aught we know, be good reasons why Providence interposes not in this manner, but they are unknown to us; and, though the mere supposition that such reasons exist may be sufficient to *save* the conclusion concerning the Divine attributes, yet surely it can never be sufficient to *establish* that conclusion.

If everything in the universe be conducted by general laws, and if animals be rendered susceptible of pain, it scarcely seems possible but some ill must arise in the various shocks of matter and the various concurrence and opposition of general laws; but this ill would be very rare were it not for the *third* circumstance which I proposed to mention, viz., the great frugality with which all powers and faculties are distributed to every particular being. So well adjusted are the organs and capacities of all animals, and so well fitted to their preservation, that, as far as history or tradition reaches, there appears not to be any single species which has yet been extinguished in the universe. Every animal has the requisite endowments, but these endowments are bestowed with so scrupulous an economy that any considerable diminution must entirely destroy the creature. Wherever one power is increased, there is a proportional abatement in the others. Animals which excel in swiftness are commonly defective in force. Those which possess both are either imperfect in some of their senses or are oppressed with the most craving wants. The human species, whose chief excellence is reason and sagacity, is of all others the most necessitous, and the most deficient in bodily advantages, without clothes, without arms, without food, without lodging, without any convenience of life, except what they owe to their own skill and industry. In short, nature seems to have formed an exact calculation of the necessities of her creatures, and, like a *rigid master,* has afforded them little more powers or endowments than what are strictly sufficient to supply those necessities.

An *indulgent parent* would have bestowed a large stock in order to guard against accidents, and secure the happiness and welfare of the creature in the most unfortunate concurrence of circumstances. Every course of life would not have been so surrounded with precipices that the least departure from the true path, by mistake or necessity, must involve us in misery and ruin. Some reserve, some fund, would have been provided to ensure happiness, nor would the powers and the necessities have been adjusted with so rigid an economy. The Author of nature is inconceivably powerful; his force is supposed great, if not altogether inexhaustible, nor is there any reason, as far as we can judge, to make him observe this strict frugality in his dealings with his creatures. It would have been better, were his power extremely limited, to have created fewer animals, and to have endowed these with more faculties for their happiness and preservation. A builder is never esteemed prudent who undertakes a plan beyond what his stock will enable him to finish.

In order to cure most of the ills of human life, I require not that man should have the wings of the eagle, the swiftness of the stag, the force of the ox, the arms of the lion, the scales of the crocodile or rhinoceros; much less do I demand the sagacity of an angel or cherubim. I am contented to take an increase in one single power or faculty of his soul. Let him be endowed with a greater propensity to industry and labour, a more vigorous spring and activity of mind, a more constant bent to business and application. Let the whole species possess naturally an equal diligence with that which many individuals are able to attain by habit and reflection, and the most beneficial consequences, without any allay of ill, is the immediate and necessary result of this endowment. Almost all the moral as well as natural evils of human life arise from idleness; and were our species, by the original constitution of their frame, exempt from this vice or infirmity, the perfect cultivation of land, the improvement of arts and manufactures, the exact execution of every office and duty, immediately follow; and men at once may fully reach that state of society which is so imperfectly attained by the best regulated government. But as industry is a power, and the most valuable of any, nature seems determined, suitably to her usual maxims, to bestow it on men with a very sparing hand, and rather to punish him severely for his deficiency in it than to reward him for his attainments. She has so contrived his frame that nothing but the most violent necessity can oblige him to labour; and she employs all his other wants to overcome, at least in part, the want of diligence, and to endow him with some share of a faculty of which she has thought fit naturally to bereave him. Here our demands may be allowed very humble, and therefore the more reasonable. If we required the endowments of superior penetration and judgment, of a more delicate taste of beauty, of a nicer sensibility to benevolence and friendship, we might be told that we impiously pretend to break the order of nature, that we want to exalt ourselves into a higher rank of being, that the presents which we require, not being suitable to our state and condition, would only be pernicious to us. But it is hard, I dare to repeat it, it is hard that, being placed in a world so full of wants and necessities, where almost every being and element is either our foe or refuses its assistance . . . we should also have our own temper to struggle with, and should be deprived of that faculty which can alone fence against these multiplied evils.

The *fourth* circumstance whence arises the misery and ill of the universe is the inaccurate workmanship of all the springs and principles of the great machine of nature. It must be acknowledged that there are few parts of the universe which seem not to serve some purpose, and whose removal would not produce a visible defect and disorder in the whole. The parts hang all together, nor can one be touched without affecting the rest, in a greater or less degree. But at the same time, it must be observed that none of these parts or principles, however useful, are so accurately adjusted as to keep precisely within those bounds in which their utility consists; but they are, all of them, apt, on every occasion, to run into the one extreme or the other. One would imagine that this grand production had not received the last hand of the maker—so little finished is every part, and so coarse are the strokes with which it is executed. Thus the winds are requisite to convey the vapours along the surface of the globe, and to assist men in navigation; but how often, rising up to tempests and hurricanes, do they become pernicious? Rains are necessary to nourish all the plants and animals of the earth; but how often are they defective? how often excessive? Heat is requisite to all life and vegetation, but is not always found in the due proportion. On the mixture and secretion of the humours and juices of the body depend the health and prosperity of the animal; but the parts perform not regularly their proper function. What more useful than all the passions of the mind, ambition, vanity, love, anger? But how often do they break their bounds and cause the greatest convulsions in society? There is nothing so advantageous in the universe but what frequently becomes pernicious, by its excess or defect; nor has nature guarded, with the requisite accuracy, against all disorder or confusion. The irregularity is never perhaps so great as to destroy any species, but is often sufficient to involve the individuals in ruin and misery.

On the concurrence, then, of these *four* circumstances does all or the greatest part of natural evil depend. Were all living creatures incapable of pain, or were the world administered by particular volitions, evil never could have found access into the universe; and were animals endowed with a large stock of powers and faculties, beyond what strict necessity requires, or were the several springs and principles of the universe so accurately framed as to preserve always the just temperament and medium, there must have been very little ill in comparison of what we feel at present. What then shall we pronounce on this occasion? Shall we say that these circumstances are not necessary, and that they might easily have been altered in the contrivance of the universe? This decision seems too presumptuous for creatures so blind and ignorant. Let us be more modest in our conclusions. Let us allow that, if the goodness of the Deity (I mean a goodness like the human) could be established on any tolerable reasons *a priori,* these phenomena, however untoward, would not be sufficient to subvert that principle, but might easily, in some unknown manner, be reconcilable to it. But let us still assert that, as this goodness is not antecedently established but must be inferred from the phenomena, there can be no grounds for such an inference while there are so many ills in the universe, and while these ills might so easily have been remedied, as far as human understanding can be allowed to judge on such a subject. I am sceptic enough to allow that the bad appearances, notwithstanding all my reasonings, may be compatible with such attributes as you suppose, but surely they can never prove these attributes. Such a conclusion cannot result from scepticism, but must arise from the phenomena, and from our confidence in the reasonings which we deduce from these phenomena.

Look round this universe. What an immense profusion of beings, animated and organized, sensible and active! You admire this prodigious variety and fecundity. But inspect a little more narrowly these living existences, the only beings worth regarding. How hostile and destructive to each other! How insufficient all of them for their own happiness! How contemptible or odious to the spectator! The whole presents nothing but the idea of a blind nature, impregnated by a great vivifying principle, and pouring forth from her lap, without discernment or parental care, her maimed and abortive children!

Here the Manichaean system occurs as a proper hypothesis to solve the difficulty; and, no doubt, in some respects it is very specious and has more probability than the common hypothesis, by giving a plausible account of the strange mixture of good and ill which appears in life. But if we consider, on the other hand, the perfect uniformity and agreement of the parts of the universe, we shall not discover in it any marks of the combat of a malevolent with a benevolent being. There is indeed an opposition of pains and pleasures in the feelings of sensible creatures; but are not all the operations of nature carried on by an opposition of principles, of hot and cold, moist and dry, light and heavy? The true conclusion is that the original Source of all things is entirely indifferent to all these principles, and has no more regard to good above ill than to heat above cold, or to drought above moisture, or to light above heavy.

There may *four* hypotheses be framed concerning the first causes of the universe: that they are endowed with perfect goodness; that they have perfect malice; that they are opposite and have both goodness and malice; that they have neither goodness nor malice. Mixed phenomena can never prove the two former unmixed principles; and the uniformity and steadiness of general laws seem to oppose the third. The fourth, therefore, seems by far the most probable.

What I have said concerning natural evil will apply to moral with little or no variation; and we have no more reason to infer that the rectitude of the Supreme Being resembles human rectitude than that his benevolence resembles the human. Nay, it will be thought that we have still greater cause to exclude from him moral sentiments, such as we feel them, since moral evil, in the opinion of many, is much more predominant above moral good than natural evil above natural good.

But even though this should not be allowed, and though the virtue which is in mankind should be acknowledged much superior to the vice, yet, so long as there is any vice at all in the universe, it will very much puzzle you anthropomorphites how to account for it. You must assign a cause for it, without having recourse to the first cause. But as every effect must have a cause, and that cause another, you must either carry on the progression *in infinitum* or rest on that original principle, who is the ultimate cause of all things. . . .

QUESTIONS

1. What does Hume mean by "evil"?
2. How does Hume show that "the original source of all things" is indifferent to good and evil? What assumptions are involved in his proof?
3. Does Hume's argument that "the original source of all things" is indifferent to good and evil depend on his initial assumptions or on what we can observe of the world? Explain your answer.
4. How do Hume and Leibniz differ in their views on God and evil? Can one decide between them? Why or why not? If one can, how does one justify one's choice?

SUGGESTED FURTHER READING

Flew, Antony, *Hume's Philosophy of Belief,* Humanities Press, New York, 1961. Chap. VIII, "Miracles and Methodology."

Lewis, C. S., *The Problem of Pain,* Macmillan, New York, 1962.

MacTaggart, J. M. E., *Dogmas of Religion,* Edward Arnold, London, 1906.

Matson, W. I., *The Existence of God,* Cornell University Press, Ithaca, N. Y., 1965. Part III, "Evil."

Mill, John Stuart, *Three Essays on Religion: Nature, The Utility of Religion, and Theism,* 1874. Many publishers, many editions.

Paine, Thomas, *The Age of Reason, Being an Investigation of True and Fabulous Theology,* many publishers, many editions.

Pike, Nelson, ed., *God and Evil,* Prentice-Hall, Englewood Cliffs, N.J., 1964. (Anthology.)

Sprague, Elmer, *What Is Philosophy?* Oxford University Press, New York, 1961. Chap. 4, "Philosophy and God."

Part Three

VALUES
AND THEIR
JUSTIFICATION

INTRODUCTION

Philosophical inquiry covers not only questions about knowledge and reality, God and the world, but also questions about values. Philosophy seeks to understand and account for the whole of human experience, and one fundamental aspect of man's experience is the making of value judgments and the striving to live up to a set of values. By "values" we shall mean the standards of evaluation and the rules of conduct that a person or a society has adopted as guides to its behavior and attitudes. Standards are sometimes called "norms," and the value judgments based on norms are sometimes referred to as "normative" judgments. When such judgments are made, the object being judged is called good or bad, depending on whether or not it fulfills the given standards to a certain degree. If it fulfills the standards to a very high degree, we call the object excellent, superb, magnificent, or great. When the degree of fulfillment is at a lower level, we judge the object to be fair, not bad, all right, or so-so. A similar variation occurs in our negative value judgments, depending on the extent to which an object fails to satisfy the conditions set by our standards.

In addition to our standards, there are rules of conduct that operate as the norms or principles underlying our value judgments. In this case we judge actions by whether they conform to or violate given rules that tell us what we ought or ought not to do in certain situations. Positive rules impose on us obligations or requirements. They prescribe certain kinds of acts, such as keeping our promises or paying our debts. Negative rules tell us what we are not to do, prohibiting or forbidding certain acts, such as stealing or murdering. When a person does an act required of him or when he refrains from doing something prohibited, we say that his act is right. We call an act wrong when it breaks a given rule of conduct.

Individuals and societies differ in the standards and rules they use in making value judgments, and this raises the philosophical questions: Can standards and rules be validated? Is there a method of reasoning by which a person can justify his adopting certain standards and rules and rejecting others? We can see how these questions arise on a simple level by noticing that even in one culture different standards are used not only for evaluating things of different kinds but also for evaluating things of the same kind. Thus the standards used for judging cars are completely different from those used in judging fountain pens. There is little disagreement over the standards or criteria of a good fountain pen, since there is one clear purpose for which pens are made and for which people use them: a good pen writes smoothly and clearly, does not leak, has the shape, size, and weight that make it easy to hold in a writing position, and so on. On the other hand, there may be considerable disagreement about the standards of a good car. Some people will use speed and power as their criteria; others will consider the appearance and design; still others will judge according to the car's social prestige as a status symbol. Furthermore, while the same combination of standards may be used by two people, they may each assign a different weight to a standard, one person placing more importance upon its fulfillment than the other. Hence a car judged to be good according to one person's standards will be judged bad (or not as good) according to another's standards. People will dispute, in other words, not only about what particular cars are good ones, but also about what makes a car a good car. Such arguments involve reasoning, and even on this comparatively trivial level of values, philosophy has its role to play. Its task is to examine critically the logical structure of reasoning used in disputes about values.

A completely general theory of value in philosophy would attempt to account for all types of standards and rules, analyzing the meanings of such value words as "good," "right," and "ought" as they occur in all sorts of value judgments, and examining the kinds of reasons given to justify the application of norms to particular objects in the making of such judgments. In the history of philosophy, however, there have been two areas of values which have been considered the most fundamental and important in human life and on which most philosophical thinking about values has been focused. They are the areas of ethical or moral values, and of aesthetic values or those that arise in the creation, appreciation, and criticism of the arts. Philosophical thinking about moral values is called "ethics" or "moral philosophy"; that concerned with aesthetic value is called "aesthetics" or "philosophy of art."

In Part Three of this book two chapters are devoted to some of the main problems in each of these divisions of the philosophy of value. In the chapter on ethics (Chapter 10) we are interested in the meaning and justification of certain types of moral judgment, in which the concepts of moral obligation or duty, right conduct, and the good life for man are central. The chapter on aesthetics (Chapter 11) deals with the concepts of beauty, artistic excellence, aesthetic experience, and the nature of a work of art. In both chapters the philosopher is investigating the logical foundations of value judgments by analyzing the concepts used in such judgments and by exploring the kinds of reasons and arguments by which such judgments are supported.

Another chapter, placed at the beginning of Part Three because it serves as a connecting link between the philosophy of value and those other areas of philosophy considered in Parts One and Two, is concerned with the idea of freedom of the will, which has been a subject of philosophical debate ever since philosophy began. As will be seen, discussions of free will involve references to determinism and causation, which connect this chapter with metaphysics, theory of knowledge, and the philosophy of science; the concept of "will" also brings up problems of philosophical psychology and the philosophy of mind. Moreover, the problem of free will takes on special significance in the light of theological beliefs about God and His relation to the world. Finally, since the problem of free will makes direct reference to the idea of moral responsibility, the entire chapter raises questions that are basic to ethics.

We are now ready to enter upon philosophical investigations into the meaning of value concepts, and upon philosophical studies of the rational basis of arguments about values. We shall thus round out our introductory exploration of the main branches of philosophy.

Chapter 9. Freedom of the Will

FREEDOM OF CHOICE AND MORAL RESPONSIBILITY

When we examine the grounds of our moral judgments about a person's actions, we find two beliefs always present: (1) the belief that a certain moral standard is applicable to the actions we judge, and (2) the belief that the person acted of his own free will. Our moral judgments rest on good grounds only if, first, we can justify the moral standard which we apply in making our judgments, and second, we can show that the person whom we judge actually did act of his own free will.

The problem of justifying a moral standard we have called "the problem of moral knowledge," and Chapter 10 is devoted to that problem. The problem of showing that a person acted of his own free will and can therefore be held responsible for what he did is the problem of freedom of the will. In order to see what is involved in the belief that a person must act from his own free will if he is to be held responsible for what he does, let us consider the actual conditions which must be satisfied when we hold a person responsible (or when a person holds himself responsible).

Suppose we were told that a person sitting alone on a beach did nothing to help someone who was drowning just off shore. We would certainly condemn the person on moral grounds. But if we then were informed that he was physically disabled and could neither walk nor swim, we would immediately withdraw our moral condemnation. Or, suppose we were told that a person in wartime disclosed military secrets to the enemy. If we then learned that he had betrayed his country only after he was tortured for a number of days, we would excuse his action and would not

blame him for what he did. Or, to take a third case, suppose we learned that a man who committed a murder had a form of insanity of such a nature that he was driven by an overwhelming inner compulsion which no amount of will power could control. We would then be doubtful about holding him responsible as a moral agent, and many of us would say that we should not condemn him at all. We retract our moral judgment in the first example because the person we are judging *lacked the ability* to do the right thing in the situation, in the second example because the person was *compelled by an external force or constraint* to do the wrong thing, in the third example because the person was *compelled by an internal force or constraint* to do the wrong thing.

When a person could not have done anything but what he did do, we say that he had no freedom of choice. By this we mean that although the person might have known of alternative actions to the one he finally did, these were not real alternatives either because the person lacked the ability to do them or because he was coerced by an external or internal force to do the act he finally did. In common speech we say of such situations that the person "had no alternative" or "could not have done otherwise." By reflecting on our examples it can now be seen that when a person has no freedom of choice we do not feel justified in doing any of the following things: (1) to praise or blame the person for what he did, (2) to reward or punish him for what he did, (3) to say that he ought to feel pride or guilt about what he did, or (4) to hold him responsible for what he did. We may sum up this argument in the statement: Freedom of choice is a necessary condition for moral responsibility.

FREEDOM OF CHOICE
AND THE CAUSES OF CHOICE

A thoughtful person may now raise the question whether it is only freedom of choice which is necessary for moral responsibility. Is there not some further requirement, especially in light of the fact that there are *causes* for a person's choice?

We have seen that a person has freedom of choice when he has the ability to do other acts than the one he chooses to do and he is not under external or internal constraint. We might describe such a situation by saying that the person's act followed from his own free choice. But what made him choose the way he did? If we explain his choice by saying that it resulted from his being the kind of person he was, we might then seek an explanation of why he was that kind of person. An adequate explanation could only be found in a psychological study of his personality development. Such a study would, point to certain factors in the person's heredity and environment, especially in the environment of his infancy and early childhood. It would show that there were many causes operating on the person which shaped his personality in such a way that, in the circumstances of a particular situation of choice, the person would be likely to choose to do one kind of act rather than another.

Now the advances being made in psychology and its related sciences seem to be giving greater and greater support to the assumption that if we knew *all* the causal factors in one's personality development, and if we knew *all* the circumstances in a situation of choice, we could know exactly how one would choose. And this would hold even in cases where one had freedom of choice as defined above. It is then that the question arises in our minds: Are we really justified in holding a person morally responsible for what he does, even when he has freedom of choice? For if we knew everything about the person's past we would see that he had to become just the kind of person he did become, and given the fact that he was that kind of person at the moment of choice, then we would see that his choice necessarily followed from his being that kind of person. It was, we might say, the only choice that kind of person could have made in the circumstances.

The consequences sometimes drawn from this line of thought are as follows. Granted the person at the moment of choice is able to do any of a number of alternative actions confronting him, and granted that he is not being forced by anyone nor is being constrained by any compulsive desire, nevertheless, he is not really free. His belief that he has a free choice among open possibilities is an illusion because, being the kind of person he is, he cannot choose otherwise than as he finally does choose. Therefore (the conclusion is then drawn) he cannot be held responsible for what he does.

Whether it is legitimate to draw this conclusion is one of the chief questions which constitute the problem of freedom of the will. There is no doubt that people sometimes do draw such a conclusion, and although they might be making a mistake in doing so, it is up to a thinking person to show whether a mistake actually is made and if so, where it lies.

A number of different positions have been taken with regard to the foregoing argument. We shall distinguish three, as representing the sharpest divergence of opinion on the matter. Whether there are possible intermediate positions or combinations among them are points left open for the reader to decide when he reads the selections included in this chapter. There is no agreement among philosophers as to what to call these three views, but perhaps the least misleading names are "mechanistic determinism," "indeterminism," and "nonmechanistic determinism."

MECHANISTIC DETERMINISM. From the point of view of the first position, the argument presented above is perfectly valid. The conclusion does follow from the premises, it is held, because we must accept the principle of determinism, specifically, a mechanistic principle of determinism. The principle of determinism is that everything that happens has a cause. Those who take this first point of view have a mechanistic conception of determinism, according to which the world is a vast machine in which everything that happens is due to the movement of various parts of the machine, these parts being moved by the movement of other parts, and so on. Just as material objects must behave exactly as they do because they are moved by physical forces which completely determine their movement, so human beings must behave just as they do because they are integral parts of the same mechanical universe. Our bodies are material objects which operate strictly in accordance with the laws of physics and chemistry. Our thoughts, our feelings, our "wills" are simply the result of certain physical processes taking place in our nervous systems, the nervous system being necessitated to react by the physical stimuli which impinge upon it.

The whole universe is thus seen as a closed system of causes and effects in which the causes compel the effects to follow. What will happen in the future will happen inevitably as the necessary consequence of what is happening now, and what is happening now must happen that way as the inevitable consequence of what has happened in the past. The future is not open to different possibilities among which we can choose to realize some and not others, since whatever possibilities we do choose to realize were already determined to be the real events of the future by the past causes operating on our choice. Though our choice may not in a given situation be compelled by an external or internal constraint, it is always compelled by causes beyond our control (namely, our heredity and past environment). It follows that a person cannot justifiably be blamed for his act, or be punished for it, or feel guilty about it, or be held responsible for it, since it was the only act he could have done in the circumstances.

INDETERMINISM. The second point of view, which we shall call "indeterminism," upholds man's moral responsibility by denying the principle of determinism. There are two ways in which this has been argued. The first is by asserting that man has a soul as well as a body, and that a person's act of will at the moment of choice is a function of his soul, not his body. This may be called the religious argument for indeterminism, since it is believed that God has created the soul and endowed it with the freedom to choose between good and evil. This God-given freedom means that the soul is not subject to the laws of personality development. The soul is a spiritual (nonmaterial) entity which is not discoverable by empirical observation and does not depend on the body for its existence. By means of an act of will the soul can move the body and so bring about changes in the physical world.

This point of view denies determinism because it holds that a person's heredity and environment do not completely determine his actions and choices. A person's heredity and environment may mold his general character, but within the limits of that character his will is free to choose among alternatives confronting him. And this means that at the moment of choice his will is at least partly free from the causes which have operated upon him up to that moment. The fact that man has the capacity to break into the causal chain of events and initiate changes in the physical world implies that the physical world is not a closed system. The future is open to whatever possibilities are realizable through human choices and actions.

The moral implications which the religious indeterminist draws are as follows. Since each person's choices are the direct result of the acts of his own undetermined will, and since it is a person's undetermined soul which alone has the power to make choices, it is the person himself who is morally responsible for the choices he makes. If he does an immoral act, he must accept responsibility for it (provided, of course, that he could have done otherwise and was not under external or internal constraint). He cannot excuse himself on the ground that his heredity and environment caused him to do it.

A second way of arguing for free will as opposed to determinism is not on the basis of the existence of a soul, but on the basis of our immediate consciousness of freedom which we all experience when we make a choice under the conditions we have called freedom of choice.[1] We know we are not forced by our past to choose one alternative

rather than another because careful introspection of our feelings at the moment of choice reveals no causal forces operating on us. We are free to choose because we see the alternatives open to us, and we know from past experience that we have the ability to do any of the alternatives. Freedom of the will is an undeniable fact of the moral life of man. The future has not already been determined by the operation of past causes. What the future will be depends on what happens in the present, and the present includes the choices which human beings now make. If human beings choose one way, for example, there will continue to be wars and crime and poverty in the future. If they choose another way there will eventually be no wars, crime, or poverty. The future is up to us. It all depends on how we choose from moment to moment in the present, and how we choose depends only on the efforts of our own will.

A free choice is not the choice of an undetermined soul, but the choice of our moral self. This self functions within the limits set by our personality development, but these limits allow for some freedom from past causes. Psychology may be able to explain our personality in terms of the past, but it can never explain our moral self. We can shape our moral self by our own efforts. Even though a person may have been raised under conditions which have given him, for example, an aggressive antisocial personality, this does not mean that in a particular situation of choice he must do an aggressive antisocial act. He himself has the freedom to exert his will power and self-control, so that his choice is not determined by the tendencies of his personality. Thus his moral self is the final determiner

[1] One version of this argument is given in the selection by C. A. Campbell in this chapter.

of what he does (in situations where he has freedom of choice). He is not the helpless creature of his heredity and environment, but a being with the freedom to act according to moral principles. He therefore should properly feel guilt about his own wrongdoing, and it is justifiable to blame (or praise) him, to punish (or reward) him, and to hold him responsible for his actions.

NONMECHANISTIC DETERMINISM. We now turn to a third point of view concerning the necessary conditions for moral responsibility. From this point of view, the position of mechanistic determinism and the position of indeterminism are both unacceptable, the former because it proceeds from an erroneous conception of what the principle of determinism means, the latter because it denies the principle of determinism. We call this third point of view "nonmechanistic determinism." It rejects the indeterminists' claim that we must be to some extent free from past causes if we are to be held morally responsible. It affirms that a nonmechanistic interpretation of determinism provides for all the freedom necessary for moral responsibility. Thus, although it holds that all the actions and choices of a person are totally determined by past causes in his heredity and environment, it claims that we are justified in holding the person responsible for at least some of his actions and choices. Let us see how this is argued.

According to the nonmechanistic interpretation of determinism, to say that every event has a cause is to say that it is theoretically possible to predict every event from a complete knowledge of preceding events and a complete knowledge of causal laws. The fact that there are causes by which we can explain

why something happens does not mean that these causes force (compel, necessitate) the thing to happen. It means only that the event is preceded by certain happenings in a way in which other similar events are preceded by similar happenings. Given sufficient knowledge of these preceding happenings and of the other similar events and their preceding happenings, it is possible to predict with some degree of accuracy the event in question.[2]

From this standpoint, the assertion that all human actions and choices are completely determined by past events means nothing more than that it would be possible to predict such actions and choices if we knew enough about the past. Actually we are constantly making predictions about the actions and choices of people in our daily life. Our past experience with friends and acquaintances is sufficient to give us a reasonable expectation about how they will act when we next meet them. As psychology and the social sciences advance, more and more accurate predictions about people's actions and choices will become possible. Nevertheless, we have all been in situations where people have surprised us by doing the unexpected, and in scientific predictions there is still much room for doubt. The question then is whether these failures to predict correctly and this element of doubt are not due to the fact that people's choices are at least in part uncaused, so that even if we knew everything about their personality development, we still could not predict how they were going to choose. According to the determinist, our present inability to predict stems from our ignorance of all the causes (preceding events and causal laws), not from the fact that there is an inherently unpredictable

[2] For a more detailed account of this view of determinism, see the selection by David Hume in Chapter 2.

element in human choice. A person's choice may be forever practically unpredictable in the sense that we may always lack sufficient knowledge to make a completely accurate prediction of it. To say that nevertheless the choice is totally determined by past causes is to say that theoretically it is predictable, that is, if we knew all the causes we would be able to predict it with complete accuracy.

The nonmechanistic determinist claims that despite the fact that all human choices are theoretically predictable, we are justified in holding a person responsible for some of his actions. A person can be held responsible for those of his actions which he was not forced (compelled, constrained) to do. Such actions are the ones he chooses to do in situations where he has freedom of choice, that is, where he has the ability to choose among a number of alternatives and is not under external or internal constraint. When determinism is interpreted in a nonmechanistic way, it is possible to believe that all actions are caused but not all actions are forced or constrained. The possibility of caused but unconstrained actions follows from the idea that causation means predictability, not compulsion.

Whether the nonmechanistic determinist is successful in his attempt to make moral responsibility compatible with determinism is a question the reader must ponder when he reads the selections in this chapter by David Hume, P. H. Nowell-Smith, and C. A. Campbell. Hume and Nowell-Smith both believe that people can rightly be held responsible for their actions, and both accept a nonmechanistic view of determinism. Campbell, on the contrary, argues that moral responsibility implies a "contra-causal freedom," and that we do experience such freedom

at moments when we must choose between doing what we would most like to do and what our moral duty requires. The problem of free will is also considered in "A Priori Ethics" by Immanuel Kant (Chapter 10), where the discussion of freedom is an integral part of Kant's theory of ethics.

THE PROBLEM OF FREEDOM OF THE WILL

The three positions we have just discussed are diverging points of view which philosophers have taken on the relations between causation, free will, and moral responsibility. The general problem with which all three positions have been concerned may be analyzed into several groups of questions. One group of questions centers upon causation, another upon freedom, and a third upon the conditions of praise and blame, reward and punishment, pride and guilt, and holding a person responsible. The three groups of questions may be set forth as follows:

1. Are all human actions and choices totally determined by past causes? What does determinism mean when applied to human actions and choices? What does indeterminism mean?

2. Does belief in freedom of the will contradict determinism? In what sense (if any) can a person be said to have free will, if all his actions and choices are totally determined by past causes?

3. Does morality require that we deny determinism? Is there at least one sense of "freedom of the will" (and if so, what sense) which is both consistent with determinism and sufficient for the justification of praise and blame, reward and punishment, pride and guilt, and holding a person responsible?

THE THEOLOGICAL ASPECT OF THE PROBLEM. In the history of Western philosophy the free will problem has also had a theological aspect. The theological question is whether God's omniscience is consistent with his moral goodness and justice. For if God is omniscient (all-knowing), then it would seem that God knows beforehand everything that ever happens in the world. Thus, before a person makes a choice among alternatives confronting him, God already knows which alternative he will choose. How then can the person's choice be free? Does the person really have a choice at all? When God knows beforehand that a certain person is going to choose in a certain way, the person must choose in that way and in no other way, since God's foreknowledge can never be mistaken and has no gaps in it. But if the person really had no choice, how can God be just in punishing the person for doing a bad action? Indeed, it would appear that God must be extremely unjust to give a person no choice and yet to punish him for what he could not help doing. Thus if God is omniscient it seems he cannot be just. In this chapter the theological aspect of the free will problem is considered in the selection in this chapter by St. Augustine.

DETERMINISM AND FATALISM. Much confusion about the problem of freedom of the will can be avoided if we keep in mind the difference between both mechanistic and nonmechanistic determinism on the one hand, and fatalism on the other. Fatalism is the point of view that what happens in the future does not depend on man's choice in the present. If something is fated to happen, then it will happen no matter what human beings now choose to do. The soldier on the battlefield is a fatalist when he believes that a certain bullet "has his name on it," that his death is "a matter of fate" over which he has no control. Because the fatalist is convinced that the event which is fated to happen will happen no matter what choices he makes, he develops an attitude of complete passivity and resignation toward the event. This attitude often becomes generalized into a feeling of futility and helplessness about all of life, so that he comes to regard any effort by anyone to bring about a better world as utterly hopeless, since it is out of our hands whether the future will be better or worse.

Now fatalism in this sense is radically different from nonmechanistic determinism for the following reason. The nonmechanistic determinist recognizes two kinds of future events, those which are not affected by present human choices and those which are, while a fatalist takes a fatalistic attitude toward both kinds of events. He may be fatalistic about crimes and wars as well as about earthquakes, hurricanes, and incurable diseases. If a person were fatalistic about a third world war, for example, he would be certain that it was going to happen and that there was nothing we could do about it. The nonmechanistic determinist would say that whether there will be a third world war depends entirely on the choices human beings make. That there will or that there will not be a third world war, he would say, is something which no one can be certain of, since it is too difficult to predict all the complex and multifarious human choices which would bring about the one eventuality or the other. But the person who believes that a third world war is fated to occur is absolutely certain it will, regardless of the choices people make. Thus the fatalist treats all "fated" events in the same way, disregarding the fact (which his emotions prevent him from acknowledging) that some of them are events of the kind which we know from past experience depend on human choices.

The difference between fatalism and mechanistic determinism is not as easy to recognize as the difference between fatalism and nonmechanistic determinism. (Sometimes the word "fatalism" is used to mean the very same thing as "mechanistic determinism," but, as the following discussion indicates, "fatalism" in such a sense is quite different from "fatalism" in the sense in which it is being used here.) There is a certain emotional similarity between fatalism and mechanistic determinism which should not cause us to overlook the definite conceptual difference between them. The fatalist feels resigned because the future is out of his hands. The mechanistic determinist feels resigned because the past is out of his hands. He realizes that the future will in part be determined by his own choices, but he sees himself making choices determined by the past, like a machine functioning according to the manipulation of outside forces. The future is closed (though what will happen in it is not already known with certainty) because past causes necessitate present choices and present choices necessitate future consequences. But present choices are genuinely effective in the future in the sense that what occurs in the future depends on them. If they were different, the future would be different. They never *can* be different from what they turn out to be, however, because what they turn out to be is the inevitable result of what the past has been. Now the emotional reaction to this conception of one's own choices is often similar to a fatalistic outlook on life, because one feels helpless about what will happen in the future. But the conceptual belief of fatalism is contradictory to that of mechanistic determinism at a crucial point.

The basic tenet of fatalism is that what is fated to happen is not greatly affected, or not affected at all, by human choices; and this is held to be true even of those things which past experience has shown to be greatly affected by human choices. We have seen that if a person were fatalistic about a third world war, he would be sure that it was bound to happen and that there was nothing he or anybody else could do to prevent it. A mechanistic determinist, on the other hand, would say that *if* a third world war occurs then it will be the necessary and inevitable consequence of present and past events, including the choices people made. But he does not say that a third world war is inevitable; for he knows that it will in fact occur only if human beings make certain choices, and he cannot be sure that they will make those choices. All he claims is that whatever choices are made have been necessitated by the environment and heredity of the persons making them, and these causal factors are part of world history. Thus the whole process of world history is, or is not, leading inevitably to a third world war. Whatever will happen will happen inevitably, but we do not know with certainty what will happen because we do not know with certainty how human beings will choose. The fatalist, in contrast, is absolutely certain that those things which are fated to happen will happen, and that they will happen regardless of how human beings choose.

DETERMINISM AND PREDESTINATION. Not only must both senses of determinism be clearly distinguished from fatalism, they also must be distinguished from the doctrine of predestination or foreordination. When people speak of an event as having been "predestined" or "foreordained" to happen, they imply the existence of some purposive agent behind the universe which brought the event about. It is as if the predestined event had been ordered or decreed to happen by an intelligent mind which desired it to happen. In theistic religion this intelligent mind would be God, and the event would be understood as having happened by the will of God. Belief in fatalism does not require belief in predestination, although it is possible for the two to go together. This would occur when the fated event is viewed as being willed to happen by a purposive agent.

Sometimes predestination takes the form of a belief that everything in history is the outcome of the workings of Fate or Destiny, personified as a being who has written down in one great book the complete account of history before it happens and exactly as the being has willed it to happen. The principal difference between determinism (in both senses) and predestination, then, is that determinism does not imply the existence of a purposive agent behind the world who orders things to happen in the world, while predestination does.

The reader is now invited to become acquainted with some of the ways philosophers have tried to solve the problem of freedom of the will. The reader is advised to keep in mind the differences between mechanistic determinism, nonmechanistic determinism, fatalism, and predestination. He should remember that the problem is concerned with three basic issues: (1) whether and in what sense all human actions and choices are determined, (2) whether and in what sense freedom of the will contradicts determinism, and (3) whether and in what sense morality requires freedom of the will. These issues are investigated in various ways and from various points of view in the reading selections which follow.

31. ST. AUGUSTINE
(354–430)

Free Will and God's Foreknowledge

St. Augustine (Aurelius Augustinus) was born in Tagaste, North Africa. His studies in philosophy and theology led him to accept Manichaeism, a Persian religion which at that time was a major rival of Christianity. The Manichaeans believed that there is an antagonistic dualism in the world between two principles, one of Darkness (Evil) and the other of Light (Good), and that man's body comes from the former, his soul from the latter. After teaching rhetoric in North Africa and while pursuing his studies in Milan, Augustine gave up Manichaeism and entered upon a period of skepticism. Under the influence of St. Ambrose, Bishop of Milan, Augustine was converted to Christianity. He lived for three years according to monastic rules and was finally ordained a priest. In 396 he became Bishop of Hippo, in Africa, and devoted himself to the development of Christian doctrine. His most important works are: *The Trinity; The City of God; Confessions;* and *On Free Will,* from which this reading is taken.

St. Augustine here offers his celebrated solution to the theological problem concerning freedom of the will. The problem, which is explained in the introduction to this chapter, may be briefly summarized as follows. If God has foreknowledge of everything that happens, then he knows before we make a choice how we are going to choose. Now suppose God knows beforehand that we are going to do an immoral act. It follows that we must do it, since God cannot be mistaken in his foreknowledge. This seems to imply that we could not help but do the

act, since we could not make a choice counter to God's foreknowledge. But if we could not help but do the act, we did not have a free choice to do or not to do it, and God should not punish us for doing it. Thus God's foreknowledge appears to be contradictory to his justice in punishing us for our sins.

St. Augustine uses the literary device of a dialogue to present the problem and offer us his solution. The two persons in the dialogue are Evodius and Augustine. Evodius states the problem and Augustine attempts to solve it. The reader will find no difficulty in following the argument as it is presented in this dialogue form.

The reading is from Book III, Sections ii, iii, and iv, of the *De Libero Arbitrio (On Free Will)*, as edited and translated from the Latin by Professor John H. S. Burleigh of the University of Edinburgh.

From *Augustine: Earlier Writings,* by John H. S. Burleigh,
The Westminster Press, Phila., 1953.
Used by permission of the publisher.

EVODIUS. I have a deep desire to know how it can be that God knows all things beforehand and that, nevertheless, we do not sin by necessity. Whoever says that anything can happen otherwise than as God has foreknown it is attempting to destroy the divine foreknowledge with the most insensate impiety. If God foreknew that the first man would sin—and that anyone must concede who acknowledges with me that God has foreknowledge of all future events—I do not say that God did not make him, for he made him good, nor that the sin of the creature whom he made good could be prejudicial to God. On the contrary, God showed his goodness in making man, his justice in punishing his sin, and his mercy in delivering him. I do not say, therefore, that God did not make man. But this I say. Since God foreknew that man would sin, that which God foreknew must necessarily come to pass. How then is the will free when there is apparently this unavoidable necessity? . . .

AUGUSTINE. Your trouble is this. You wonder how it can be that these two propositions are not contradictory and incompatible, namely that God has foreknowledge of all future events, and that we sin voluntarily and not by necessity. For if, you say, God foreknows that a man will sin, he must necessarily sin. But if there is necessity there is no voluntary choice in sinning, but rather fixed and unavoidable necessity. You are afraid that by that reasoning the conclusion may be reached either that God's foreknowledge of all future events must be impiously denied, or, if that cannot be denied, that sin is committed not voluntarily but by necessity. Isn't that your difficulty?

ev. Exactly that.

aug. You think, therefore, that all things of which God has foreknowledge happen by necessity and not voluntarily.

ev. Yes. Absolutely.

aug. Try an experiment, and examine yourself a little, and tell me what kind of will you are going to have tomorrow. Will you want to sin or to do right?

ev. I do not know.

aug. Do you think God also does not know?

ev. I could in no wise think that.

aug. If God knows what you are going to will tomorrow, and foresees what all men are going to will in the future, not only those who are at present alive but all who will ever be, much more will he foresee what he is going to do with the just and the impious?

ev. Certainly if I say that God has foreknowledge of my deeds, I should say with even greater confidence that he has foreknowledge of his own acts, and foresees with complete certainty what he is going to do.

aug. Don't you see that you will have to be careful lest someone say to you that, if all things of which God has foreknowledge are done by necessity and not voluntarily, his own future acts will be done not voluntarily but by necessity?

ev. When I said that all future events of which God has foreknowledge happen by necessity, I was having regard only to things which happen within his creation, and not to things which happen in God himself. Indeed, in God nothing happens. Everything is eternal.

aug. God, then, is not active within his creation?

ev. He determined once for all how the order of the universe he created was to go on, and he never changes his mind.

aug. Does he never make anyone happy?

ev. Indeed he does.

aug. He does it precisely at the time when the man in question actually becomes happy.

ev. That is so.

aug. If, then, for example, you yourself are happy one year from now, you will be made happy at that time.

ev. Exactly.

aug. God knows today what he is going to do a year hence?

EV. He eternally had that foreknowledge, but I agree that he has it now, if indeed it is to happen so.

AUG. Now tell me, are you not God's creature? And will not your becoming happy take place within your experience?

EV. Certainly I am God's creature, and if I become happy it will be within my experience.

AUG. If God, then, makes you happy, your happiness will come by necessity and not by the exercise of your will?

EV. God's will is my necessity.

AUG. Will you then be happy against your will?

EV. If I had the power to be happy, I should be so at once. For I wish to be happy but am not, because not I but God makes me happy.

AUG. The truth simply cries out against you. You could not imagine that "having in our power" means anything else than "being able to do what we will." Therefore there is nothing so much in our power as is the will itself. For as soon as we will [*volumus*] immediately will [*voluntas*] is there. We can say rightly that we do not grow old voluntarily but necessarily, or that we do not die voluntarily but from necessity, and so with other similar things. But who but a raving fool would say that it is not voluntarily that we will? Therefore though God knows how we are going to will in the future, it is not proved that we do not voluntarily will anything. When you said that you did not make yourself happy, you said it as if I had denied it. What I say is that when you become happy in the future, it will take place not against your will but in accordance with your willing. Therefore, though God has foreknowledge of your happiness in the future, and though nothing can happen otherwise than as he has foreknown it (for that would mean that there is no foreknowledge), we are not thereby compelled to think that you will not be happy voluntarily. That would be absurd and far from true. God's foreknowledge, which is even today quite certain that you are to be happy at a future date, does not rob you of your will to happiness when you actually attain happiness. Similarly if ever in the future you have a culpable will, it will be none the less your will because God had foreknowledge of it.

Observe, pray, how blind are those who say that if God has foreknowledge of what I am going to will, since nothing can happen otherwise than as he has foreknown it, therefore I must necessarily will what he has foreknown. If so, it must be admitted that I will, not voluntarily but from necessity. Strange folly! Is there, then, no difference between things that happen according to God's foreknowledge where there is no intervention of man's will at all, and things that happen because of a will of which he has foreknowledge? I omit the equally monstrous assertion of the man I mentioned a moment ago, who says I must necessarily so will. By assuming necessity he strives to do away with will altogether. If I must necessarily will, why need I speak of willing at all? But if he puts it in another way, and says that, because he must necessarily so will, his will is not in his own power, he can be countered by the answer you gave me when I asked whether you could become happy against your will. You replied that you would be happy now if the matter were in your power; for you willed to be happy but could not achieve it. And I added that the truth cries out against you; for we cannot say we do not have the power unless we do not have what we will. If we do not have the will, we may think we will but in fact we do not. If we cannot will without willing, those who will have will, and all that is in our power we have by willing. Our will would not be will unless it were in our power. Because it is in our power, it is free. We have nothing that is free which is not in our power, and if we have something it cannot be nothing. Hence it is not necessary to deny that God has foreknowledge of all things, while at the same time our wills are our own. God has foreknowledge of our will, so that of which he has foreknowledge must come to pass. In other words, we shall exercise our wills in the future because he has foreknowledge that we shall do so; and there can be no will or voluntary action unless it be in our power. Hence God has also foreknowledge of our power to will. My power is not taken from me by God's foreknowledge. Indeed, I shall be more certainly in possession of my power because he whose foreknowledge is never mistaken, foreknows that I shall have the power.

EV. Now I no longer deny that whatever God has foreknown must necessarily come to pass, nor that he has foreknowledge of our sins, but in such a way that our wills remain free and within our power.

AUG. What further difficulty do you have? Perhaps you have forgotten what we established in our first disputation, and now wish to deny that we sin voluntarily and under no compulsion from anything superior, inferior or equal to us.

EV. I do not venture to deny that at all. But I must confess I do not yet see how God's foreknowledge of our sins and our freedom of will in sinning can be other than mutually contradictory. We must confess that God is just and knows all things beforehand. But I should like to know with what justice he punishes sins which must necessarily be committed; or how they are not necessarily committed when he knows that they will be committed . . .

AUG. Why do you think our free will is opposed to God's foreknowledge? Is it because it is foreknowledge simply, or because it is God's foreknowledge?

EV. In the main because it is God's foreknowledge.

AUG. If you knew in advance that such and such a man would sin, there would be no necessity for him to sin.

EV. Indeed there would, for I should have no real foreknowledge unless I knew for certain what was going to happen.

AUG. So it is foreknowledge generally and not God's foreknowledge specially that causes the events foreknown to happen by necessity? There would be no such thing as foreknowledge unless there was certain foreknowledge.

EV. I agree. But why these questions?

AUG. Unless I am mistaken, you would not directly compel the man to sin, though you knew beforehand that he was going to sin. Nor does your prescience in itself compel him to sin even though he was certainly going to sin, as we must assume if you have real prescience. So there is no contradiction here. Simply you know beforehand what another is going to do with his own will. Similarly God compels no man to sin, though he sees beforehand those who are going to sin by their own will.

Why then should he not justly punish sins which, though he had foreknowledge of them, he did not compel the sinner to commit? Just as you apply no compulsion to past events by having them in your memory, so God by his foreknowledge does not use compulsion in the case of future events. Just as you remember your past actions, though all that you remember were not actions of your own, so God has foreknowledge of all his own actions, but is not the agent of all that he foreknows. Of evil actions he is not the agent but the just punisher. From this you may understand with what justice God punishes sins, for he has no responsibility for the future actions of men though he knows them beforehand. If he ought not to award punishment to sinners because he knew beforehand that they would sin, he ought not to reward the righteous, because he knew equally that they would be righteous. Let us confess that it belongs to his foreknowledge to allow no future event to escape his knowledge, and that it belongs to his justice to see that no sin goes unpunished by his judgment. For sin is committed voluntarily and not by any compulsion from his foreknowledge.

QUESTIONS

1. The first main argument which Augustine gives in reply to Evodius is to show that it is possible to act voluntarily even though all things are foreknown by God. What are the main points of his argument?
2. "Our will would not be will unless it were in our power. Because it is in our power, it is free." What do these two sentences mean? In your answer, give definitions of "will," "being in our power," and "free," as these terms are used by Augustine.
3. The crux of Augustine's solution to the problem lies in his attempt to justify the statement: ". . . It is not necessary to deny that God has foreknowledge of all things, while at the same time our wills are our own." How does he attempt to justify this statement? Why do you think his attempt was or was not successful?
4. How does Augustine reply to Evodius' query: "I should like to know with what justice [God] punishes sins which must necessarily be committed . . ."? Do you find his reply acceptable? Why or why not?
5. Suppose that, instead of there being an omniscient God, there were a group of psychologists in the world who could predict with a high degree of probability (though not with absolute certainty) how some people would act. Would this fact present a serious difficulty about holding those people morally responsible for their acts? Why or why not?
6. In this reading St. Augustine is concerned with the propositions: (a) human behavior is actually foreknown by an omniscient God, and (b) human behavior

is compelled or necessitated. Compare each of these propositions with: (c) human behavior is predictable, and (d) human behavior is caused. Which ones (if any) of these four propositions, in your estimation, contradict the possibility of moral responsibility? State your reasons.

32. DAVID HUME

(1711–76)

Liberty and Necessity

(A general introductory note on Hume may be found on page 116.)

In this reading Hume attempts to prove that determinism, if understood properly, does not deny any freedom which is required for religion or morality. Indeed, he concludes that determinism is itself presupposed by religion and morality. His entire argument depends on accepting the "nonmechanistic" view of determinism and rejecting the "mechanistic" view. Although Hume here gives a brief account of the "nonmechanistic" view, a more complete presentation of his theory of determinism is contained in "An Enquiry Concerning Human Understanding" in Chapter 2. The reader is advised to consult that selection for a clarification of many of the points made in the discussion of "liberty" (indeterminism) and "necessity" (determinism) in the reading which follows.

Hume distinguishes two meanings of "liberty": (1) "the liberty of spontaneity," by which he means freedom from internal and external constraints upon our will; and (2) "the liberty of indifference," which means freedom from causation or necessity, i.e., indeterminism. In his discussion of liberty Hume also points out that we have a "false sensation or experience" of freedom, which makes us mistakenly believe that we are free from necessity. Hume grants that we have freedom of the will in sense (1), but not in sense (2). He then goes on to show that morality and religion are possible even if "we can never free ourselves from the bonds of necessity." He concludes by arguing that determinism is not only consistent with but is actually required by morality and religion.

This reading is from Book II, Part III, Sections I and II of *A Treatise of Human Nature* (1738–40).

Of all the immediate effects of pain and pleasure, there is none more remarkable than the WILL; and tho', properly speaking, it be not comprehended among the passions, yet as the full understanding of its nature and properties, is necessary to the explanation of them, we shall here make it the subject of our enquiry. I desire it may be observ'd, that by the *will*, I mean nothing but *the internal impression we feel and are conscious of, when we knowingly give rise to any new motion of our body, or new perception of our mind.* This impression, like the preceding ones of pride and humility, love and hatred, 'tis impossible to define, and needless to describe any farther; for which reason we shall cut off all those definitions and distinctions, with which philosophers are wont to perplex rather than clear up this question; and entering at first upon the subject, shall examine that long disputed question concerning *liberty and necessity;* which occurs so naturally in treating of the will.

'Tis universally acknowledg'd, that the operations of external bodies are necessary, and that in the communication of their motion, in their attraction, and mutual cohesion, there are not the least traces of indifference or liberty. Every object is determin'd by an absolute fate to a certain degree and direction of its motion, and can no more depart from that precise line, in which it moves, than it can convert itself into an angel, or spirit, or any superior substance. The actions, therefore, of matter are to be regarded as instances of necessary actions; and whatever is in this respect on the same footing with matter, must be acknowledg'd to be necessary. That we may know whether this be the case with the actions of the mind, we shall begin with examining matter, and considering on what the idea of a necessity in its operations are founded, and why we conclude one body or action to be the infallible cause of another.

It has been observ'd already, that in no single instance the ultimate connexion of any objects is discoverable, either by our senses or reason, and that we can never penetrate so far into the essence and construction of bodies, as to perceive the principle, on which their mutual influence depends. 'Tis their constant union alone, with which we are acquainted; and 'tis from the constant union the necessity arises. If objects had not an uniform and regular conjunction with each other, we shou'd never arrive at any idea of cause and effect; and even after all, the necessity, which enters into that idea, is nothing but a determination of the mind to pass from one object to its usual attendant, and infer the existence of one from that of the other. Here then are two particulars, which we are to consider as essential to necessity, *viz.* the constant *union* and the *inference* of the mind; and wherever we discover these we must acknowledge a necessity. As the actions of matter have no necessity, but what is deriv'd from these circumstances, and it is not by any insight into the essence of bodies we discover their connexion, the absence of this insight, while the union and inference remain, will never, in any case, remove the necessity. 'Tis the observation of the union, which produces the inference; for which reason it might be thought sufficient, if we prove a constant union in the actions of the mind, in order to establish the inference, along with the necessity of these actions. But that I may bestow a greater force on my reasoning, I shall examine these particulars apart, and shall first prove from experience, that our actions have a constant union with our motives, tempers, and circumstances, before I consider the inferences we draw from it.

To this end a very slight and general view of the common course of human affairs will be sufficient. There is no light, in which we can take them, that does not confirm this principle. Whether we consider mankind according to the difference of sexes, ages, governments, conditions, or methods of education; the same uniformity and regular operation of natural principles are discernible. Like causes still produce like effects; in the same manner as in the mutual action of the elements and powers of nature.

There are different trees, which regularly produce fruit, whose relish is different from each other; and this regularity will be admitted as an instance of necessity and causes in external bodies. But are the products of *Guienne* and of *Champagne* more regularly different than the sentiments, actions, and passions of the two sexes, of which the one are distinguish'd by their force and maturity, the other by their delicacy and softness?

Are the changes of our body from infancy to old age more regular and certain than those of our mind and conduct? And wou'd a man be more ridiculous, who wou'd expect that an infant of four years old will raise a weight of three hundred pound, than one, who from a person of the same age, wou'd look for a philosophical reasoning, or a prudent and well-concerted action?

We must certainly allow, that the cohesion of the parts of matter arises from natural and necessary principles, whatever difficulty we may find in explaining them: And for a like reason we must allow, that human society is founded on like principles; and our reason in the latter case, is better than even that in the former; because we not only observe, that men *always* seek society, but can also explain the principles, on which this universal propensity is founded. For is it more certain, that two flat pieces of marble will unite together, than that two young savages of different sexes will copulate? Do the children arise from this copulation more uniformly, than does the parents' care for their safety and preservation? And after they have arriv'd at years of discretion by the care of their parents, are the inconveniences attending their separation more certain than their foresight of these inconveniences, and their care of avoiding them by a close union and confederacy?

The skin, pores, muscles, and nerves of a day-labourer are different from those of a man of quality: So are his sentiments, actions and manners. The different stations of life influence the whole fabric, external and internal; and these different stations arise necessarily, because uniformly, from the necessary and uniform principles of human nature. Men cannot live without society, and cannot be associated without government. Government makes a distinction of property, and establishes the different ranks of men. This produces industry, traffic, manufactures, law-suits, war, leagues, alliances, voyages, travels, cities, fleets, ports, and all those other actions and objects, which cause such a diversity, and at the same time maintain such an uniformity in human life.

Shou'd a traveller, returning from a far country, tell us, that he had seen a climate in the fiftieth degree of northern latitude, where all the fruits ripen and come to perfection in the winter, and decay in the summer, after the same manner as in *England* they are produc'd and decay in the contrary seasons, he wou'd find few so credulous as to believe him. I am apt to think a traveller wou'd meet with as little credit, who shou'd inform us of people exactly of the same character with those in *Plato's Republic* on the one hand, or those in *Hobbes's Leviathan* on the other. There is a general course of nature in human actions, as well as in the operations of the sun and the climate. There are also characters peculiar to different nations and particular persons, as well as common to mankind. The knowledge of these characters is founded on the observation of an uniformity in the actions, that flow from them; and this uniformity forms the very essence of necessity.

I can imagine only one way of eluding this argument, which is by denying that uniformity of human actions, on which it is founded. As long as actions have a constant union and connexion with the situation and temper of the agent, however we may in words refuse to acknowledge the necessity, we really allow the thing. Now some may, perhaps, find a pretext to deny this regular union and connexion. For what is more capricious than human actions? What more inconstant than the desires of man? And what creature departs more widely, not only from right reason, but from his own character and disposition? An hour, a moment is sufficient to make him change from one extreme to another, and overturn what cost the greatest pain and labour to establish. Necessity is regular and certain. Human conduct is irregular and uncertain. The one, therefore, proceeds not from the other.

To this I reply, that in judging of the actions of men we must proceed upon the same maxims, as when we reason concerning external objects. When any phenomena are constantly and invariably conjoin'd together, they acquire such a connexion in the imagination, that it passes from one to the other, without any doubt or hesitation. But below this there are many inferior degrees of evidence and probability, nor does one single contrariety of experiment entirely destroy all our reasoning. The mind ballances the contrary experiments, and deducting the inferior from the superior, proceeds with that degree of assurance or evidence, which remains. Even when these contrary experiments are entirely equal, we remove not the notion of causes and necessity; but supposing that the usual contrariety proceeds from the operation of contrary and conceal'd causes, we conclude, that the chance or indifference lies only in our judgment on account of our imperfect knowledge, not in the things themselves, which are in every case equally necessary, tho' to appearance not equally constant or certain. No union can be more constant and certain, than that of some actions with some motives and characters; and if in other cases the union is uncertain, 'tis no more than what happens in the operations of body, nor can we conclude any thing from the one irregularity, which will not follow equally from the other.

'Tis commonly allow'd that mad-men have no liberty. But were we to judge by their actions, these have less regularity and constancy than the actions of wise-men, and consequently are farther remov'd from necessity. Our way of thinking in this particular is, therefore, absolutely inconsistent; but is a natural consequence of these confus'd ideas and undefin'd terms, which we so commonly make use of in our reasonings, especially on the present subject.

We must now shew, that as the *union* betwixt motives and actions has the same constancy, as that in any natural operations, so its influence on the understanding is also the same, in *determining* us to infer the existence of one from that of another. If this shall appear, there is no known circumstance, that enters into the connexion and production of the actions of matter, that is not to be found in all the operations of the mind; and consequently we cannot, without a manifest absurdity, attribute necessity to the one, and refuse it to the other.

There is no philosopher, whose judgment is so riveted to this fantastical system of liberty, as not to acknowledge the force of *moral evidence,* and both in speculation and practice proceed upon it, as upon a reasonable foundation. Now moral evidence is nothing but a conclusion concerning the actions of men, deriv'd from the consideration of their motives, temper and situation. Thus when we see certain characters or figures describ'd upon paper, we infer that the person, who produc'd them, would affirm such facts, the death of *Caesar,* the success of *Augustus,* the cruelty of *Nero;* and remembring many other concurrent testimonies we conclude, that those facts were once really existent, and that so many men, without any interest, wou'd never conspire to deceive us; especially since they must, in the attempt, expose themselves to the derision of all their contemporaries, when these facts were asserted to be recent and universally known. The same kind of reasoning runs thro' politics, war, commerce, oeconomy, and indeed mixes itself so entirely in human life, that 'tis impossible to act or subsist a moment without having recourse to it. A prince, who imposes a tax upon his subjects, expects their compliance. A general, who conducts an army, makes account of a certain degree of courage. A merchant looks for fidelity and skill in his factor or super-cargo. A man, who gives orders for his dinner, doubts not of the obedience of his servants. In short, as nothing more nearly interests us than our own actions and those of others, the greatest part of our reasonings is employ'd in judgments concerning them. Now I assert, that whoever reasons after this manner, does *ipso facto* believe the actions of the will to arise from necessity, and that he knows not what he means, when he denies it.

All those objects, of which we call the one *cause* and the other *effect,* consider'd in themselves, are as distinct and separate from each other, as any two things in nature, nor can we ever, by the most accurate survey of them, infer the existence of the one from that of the other. 'Tis only from experience and the observation of their constant union, that we are able to form this inference; and even after all, the inference is nothing but the effects of custom on the imagination. We must not here be content with saying, that the idea of cause and effect arises from objects constantly united; but must affirm, that 'tis the very same with the idea of these objects, and that the *necessary connexion* is not discover'd by a conclusion of the understanding, but is merely a perception of the mind. Wherever, therefore, we observe the same union, and wherever the union operates in the same manner upon the belief and opinion, we have the idea of causes and necessity, tho' perhaps we may avoid those expressions. Motion in one body in all past instances, that have fallen under our observation, is follow'd upon impulse by motion in another. 'Tis impossible for the mind to penetrate farther. From this constant union it *forms* the idea of cause and effect, and by its influence *feels* the necessity. As there is the same constancy, and the same influence in what we call moral evidence, I ask no more. What remains can only be a dispute of words.

And indeed, when we consider how aptly *natural* and *moral* evidence cement together, and form only one chain of argument betwixt them, we shall make no scruple to allow, that they are of the same nature, and deriv'd from the same principles. A prisoner, who has neither money nor interest, discovers the impossibility of his escape, as well from the obstinacy of the goaler, as from the walls and bars with which he is surrounded; and in all attempts for his freedom chuses rather to work upon the stone and iron of the one, than upon the inflexible nature of the other. The same prisoner, when conducted to the scaffold, foresees his death as certainly from the constancy and fidelity of his guards as from the operation of the ax or wheel. His mind runs along a certain train of ideas: The refusal of the soldiers to consent to his escape, the action of the executioner; the separation of the head and body; bleeding, convulsive motions, and death. Here is a connected chain of natural causes and voluntary actions; but the mind feels no difference betwixt them in passing from one link to another; nor is less certain of the future event than if it were connected with the present impressions of the memory and senses by a train of causes cemented together by what we are pleas'd to call a *physical necessity*. The same experienc'd union has the same effect on the mind, whether the united objects be motives, volitions and actions; or figure and motion. We may change the names of things; but their nature and their operation on the understanding never change.

I dare be positive no one will ever endeavour to refute these reasonings otherwise than by altering my definitions, and assigning a different meaning to the terms of *cause, and effect, and necessity, and liberty, and chance*. According to my definitions, necessity makes an essential part of causation; and consequently liberty, by removing necessity, removes also causes, and is the very same thing with chance. As chance is commonly thought to imply a contradiction, and is at least directly contrary to experience, there are always the same arguments against liberty or free-will. If any one alters the definitions, I cannot pretend to argue with him, 'till I know the meaning he assigns to these terms.

I believe we may assign the three following reasons for the prevalence of the doctrine of liberty, however absurd it may be in one sense, and unintelligible in any other. First, After we have perform'd any action; tho' we confess we were influenc'd by particular views and motives; 'tis difficult for us to perswade ourselves we were govern'd by necessity, and that 'twas utterly impossible for us to have acted otherwise; the idea of necessity seeming to imply something of force, and violence, and constraint, of which we are not sensible. Few are capable of distinguishing betwixt the liberty of *spontaniety,* as it is call'd in the schools, and the liberty of *indifference;* betwixt that which is oppos'd to violence, and that which means a negation of necessity and causes. The first is even the most common sense of the word; and as 'tis only that species of liberty, which it concerns us to preserve, our thoughts have been principally turn'd towards it, and have almost universally confounded it with the other.

Secondly, there is a *false sensation or experience* even of the liberty of indifference; which is regarded as an argument for its real existence. The necessity of any action, whether of matter or of the mind, is not properly a quality in the agent, but in any thinking or intelligent being, who may consider the action, and consists in the determination of his thought to infer its existence from some preceding objects: As liberty or chance, on the other hand, is nothing but the want of that determination, and a certain looseness, which we feel in passing or not passing from the idea of one to that of the other. Now we may observe, that tho' in reflecting on human actions we seldom feel such a looseness or indifference, yet it very commonly happens, that in performing the actions themselves we are sensible of something like it: And as all related or resembling objects are readily taken for each other, this has been employ'd as a demonstrative or even an intuitive proof of human liberty. We feel that our actions are subject to our will on most occasions, and imagine we feel that the will itself is subject to nothing; because when by a denial of it we are provok'd to try, we feel that it moves easily every way, and produces an image of itself even on that side, on which it did not settle. This image or faint motion, we perswade ourselves, cou'd have been compleated into the thing itself; because, shou'd that be deny'd, we find, upon a second trial, that it can. But these efforts are all in vain; and whatever capricious and irregular actions we may perform; as the desire of showing our liberty is the sole motive of our actions; we can never free ourselves from the bonds of necessity. We may imagine we feel a liberty within ourselves; but a spectator can commonly infer our actions from our motives and character; and even where he cannot, he concludes in general, that he might, were he perfectly acquainted with every circumstance of our situation and temper, and the most secret springs of our complexion and disposition. Now this is the very essence of necessity, according to the fore-going doctrine.

A third reason why the doctrine of liberty has generally been better receiv'd in the world, than its antagonist, proceeds from *religion,* which has been very unnecessarily interested in this question. There is no method of reasoning more common, and yet none more blameable, than in philosoph-ical debates to endeavour to refute any hypothesis by a pretext of its danger-ous consequences to religion and morality. When any opinion leads us into absurdities, 'tis certainly false; but 'tis not certain an opinion is false, because 'tis of dangerous consequence. Such topics, therefore, ought entirely to be foreborn, as serving nothing to the discovery of truth, but only to make the person of an antagonist odious. This I observe in general, without pretending to draw any advantage from it. I submit myself frankly to an examination of this kind, and dare venture to affirm, that the doctrine of necessity, accord-ing to my explication of it, is not only innocent, but even advantageous to religion and morality.

I define necessity two ways, conformable to the two definitions of *cause,* of which it makes an essential part. I place it either in the constant union and conjunction of like objects, or in the inference of the mind from the one to the other. Now necessity, in both these senses, has universally, tho' tacitely, in the schools, in the pulpit, and in common life, been allow'd to belong to the will of man, and no one has ever pretended to deny, that we can draw inferences concerning human actions, and that those inferences are founded on the experienc'd union of like actions with like motives and circumstances. The only particular in which any one can differ from me, is either, that perhaps he will refuse to call this necessity. But as long as the meaning is understood, I hope the word can do no harm. Or that he will maintain there is something else in the operations of matter. Now whether it be so or not is of no consequence to religion, whatever it may be to natural philosophy. I may be mistaken in asserting, that we have no idea of any other connexion in the actions of body, and shall be glad to be farther instructed on that head: But sure I am, I ascribe nothing to the actions of the mind, but what must readily be allow'd of. Let no one, therefore, put an invidious construction on my words, by saying simply, that I assert the necessity of human actions, and place them on the same footing with the operations of senseless matter. I do not ascribe to the will that unintelligible necessity, which is suppos'd to lie in matter. But I ascribe to matter, that intelligible quality, call it necessity or not, which the most rigorous orthodoxy does or must allow to belong to the will. I change, therefore, nothing in the receiv'd systems, with regard to the will, but only with regard to material objects.

Nay I shall go farther, and assert, that this kind of necessity is so essen-tial to religion and morality, that without it there must ensue an absolute subversion of both, and that every other supposition is entirely destructive to all laws both *divine* and *human*. 'Tis indeed certain, that as all human laws are founded on rewards and punishments, 'tis suppos'd as a fundamental principle, that these motives have an influence on the mind, and both produce the good and prevent the evil actions. We may give to this influence what name we please; but as 'tis usually conjoin'd with the action, common sense requires it shou'd be esteem'd a cause, and be look'd upon as an instance of that necessity, which I wou'd establish.

This reasoning is equally solid, when apply'd to *divine* laws, so far as the deity is consider'd as a legislator, and is suppos'd to inflict punishment and bestow rewards with a design to produce obedience. But I also maintain, that even where he acts not in his magisterial capacity, but is regarded as the avenger of crimes merely on account of their odiousness and deformity, not only 'tis impossible, without the necessary connexion of cause and effect in human actions, that punishments cou'd be inflicted compatible with justice and moral equity; but also that it cou'd ever enter into the thoughts of any reasonable being to inflict them. The constant and universal object of hatred or anger is a person or creature endow'd with thought and consciousness; and when any criminal or injurious actions excite that passion, 'tis only by their relation to the person or connexion with him. But according to the doctrine of liberty or chance, this connexion is reduc'd to nothing, nor are men more accountable for those actions, which are design'd and premeditated, than for such as are the most casual and accidental. Actions are by their very nature temporary and perishing; and where they proceed not from some cause in the characters and disposition of the person, who perform'd them, they infix not themselves upon him, and can neither redound to his honour, if good, nor infamy, if evil. The action itself may be blameable; it may be contrary to all the rules of morality and religion: But the person is not responsible for it; and as it proceeded from nothing in him, that is durable or constant, and leaves nothing of that nature behind it, 'tis impossible he can, upon its account, become the object of punishment or vengeance. According to the hypothesis of liberty, therefore, a man is as pure and untainted, after having committed the most horrid crimes, as at the first moment of his birth, nor is his character any way concern'd in his actions; since they are not deriv'd from it, and the wickedness of the one can never be us'd as a proof of the depravity of the other. 'Tis only upon the principles of necessity, that a person acquires any merit or demerit from his actions, however the common opinion may incline to the contrary.

But so inconsistent are men with themselves, that tho' they often assert, that necessity utterly destroys all merit and demerit either towards mankind or superior powers, yet they continue still to reason upon these very principles of necessity in all their judgments concerning this matter. Men are not blam'd for such evil actions as they perform ignorantly and casually, whatever may be their consequences. Why? but because the causes of these actions are only momentary, and terminate in them alone. Men are less blam'd for such evil actions, as they perform hastily and unpremeditately, than for such as proceed from thought and deliberation. For what reason? but because a hasty temper, tho' a constant cause in the mind, operates only by intervals, and infects not the whole character. Again, repentance wipes off every crime, especially if attended with an evident reformation of life and manners. How is this to be accounted for? But by asserting that actions render a person criminal, merely as they are proofs of criminal passions or principles in the mind; and when by any alteration of these principles they cease to be just proofs, they likewise cease to be criminal. But according to the doctrine of *liberty* or *chance* they never were just proofs, and consequently never were criminal.

Here then I turn to my adversary, and desire him to free his own system from these odious consequences before he charge them upon others. Or if he rather chuses, that this question shou'd be decided by fair arguments before philosophers, than by declamations before the people, let him return to what I have advanc'd to prove that liberty and chance are synonimous; and concerning the nature of moral evidence and the regularity of human actions. Upon a review of these reasonings, I cannot doubt of an entire victory. . . .

QUESTIONS

1. "Necessity is regular and certain. Human conduct is irregular and uncertain." How does Hume reply to this argument for "liberty" (indeterminism)? Explain why you think his reply is satisfactory or unsatisfactory.
2. Give your reasons for agreeing (or disagreeing) with Hume's view that our inner sensation or feeling of freedom is "false." Why does he think that this feeling provides no evidence against determinism?
3. Is Hume's argument that determinism is required by religion and morality a good one? If not, where are his errors? If so, why would it ever have been thought that determinism was opposed to religion and morality?
4. Give the line of reasoning which leads Hume to say: "According to the hypothesis of liberty, therefore, a man is as pure and untainted, after having committed the most horrid crimes, as at the first moment of his birth. . . ."
5. Compare Hume's argument that a person would not be responsible for an action if it were not caused by something in his character and dispositions with the argument given by C. A. Campbell in this chapter that free will and moral responsibility have to do with actions that are *not* expressions of a person's character. Do the two philosophers mean the same thing by the word "character"? Can the two arguments be made consistent with each other? If so, show how. If not, explain why not.

33. P. H. NOWELL-SMITH
(b. 1914)

Free Will and Moral Responsibility

P. H. Nowell-Smith is Professor of Philosophy at the University of Leicester, England. He is the author of *Ethics* (1954), a volume in the Pelican Philosophy Series. The reading which follows appeared originally as an article in *Mind,* in 1948. In giving the editors of this book permission to reprint his article, Professor Nowell-Smith requested that there be published with it a short commentary on points in the article which he later came to think of as either wrongly made or not clearly made. In accordance with this request, the editors are pleased to print at the end of the article a commentary which Professor Nowell-Smith wrote in 1958 especially for this book.

The article begins with a presentation of the traditional problem of freedom of the will, and Professor Nowell-Smith states his preference for handling it without resort to any metaphysical conception (such as the appeal to a mechanistic view of the universe, or to the existence of an undetermined soul). His discussion is divided into five sections. In Sections I and II he makes a careful study of the "Libertarian's" (indeterminist's) claim that an action must be uncaused if a person is to be held morally responsible for it. He criticizes this claim by showing that the conditions under which people are ordinarily said to act "freely" and are consequently held responsible do not require that their actions be uncaused. Thus he attempts to show that moral responsibility is not incompatible with determinism. Another way of arguing the same point is to be found in Hume's "Liberty and Necessity" in this chapter. The reader will find it enlightening to compare these two arguments, and he should try to decide for himself whether either of them really is successful in establishing the point.

After arguing that the Libertarian does not provide a correct analysis of a free and morally responsible action, Professor Nowell-Smith considers what analysis would, first, *explain why* (i.e., for what purposes) we blame or punish one person for doing an action and not another for doing the same action, and second, would *justify* our doing this. In Section III of the article he considers two possible solutions to this problem, the positivist and the intuitionist, and rejects them both. A brief word about the intuitionist solution is perhaps called for here. According to the ethical intuitionist, we directly intuit moral characteristics and moral obligations. Some intuitionists believe that we intuit the quality of right or wrong in an action. Others say we intuit the relation of "fittingness" between an action and its punishment (or reward). Thus we are said to intuit that we ought to punish (i.e., that it is fitting or proper to punish) one man for an action and not another.

Having rejected the positivist and intuitionist solutions to the problem, Professor Nowell-Smith proceeds to offer his own solution in Sections IV and V. He begins with an analysis of moral judgments. Since moral judgments, according to this analysis, refer to actions which are "fit subjects for praise and blame," he is led to an account of what makes an action a fit subject for praise or blame. In Section V he attempts to show that this account provides both an *explanation* of why we punish or

blame people, and a *justification* for our doing so in certain circumstances. In the commentary on his own article, Professor Nowell-Smith makes certain qualifications of his views on punishment and the conditions of "desert" (i.e., the conditions under which a person deserves to be punished).

The reader should examine Professor Nowell-Smith's concepts of freedom, moral judgment, punishment, and desert to see, first, what they mean, and second, whether they offer a satisfactory solution to the problem of freedom of the will.

From "Free Will and Moral Responsibility,"
by P. H. Nowell-Smith, *Mind,* Vol. 57, No. 225, 1948.
Reprinted by permission of the author and the editor of *Mind.*

The traditional problem of free will has been so adequately covered in recent philosophical literature that some excuse must be offered for reopening it; and I do so because, although I believe that the traditional problem has been solved, I believe also that the solution leaves open certain further problems that are both interesting and important. It is to these problems that I propose to devote most of this paper; but, even at the risk of flogging dead horses, I feel bound to say something about the traditional problem itself.

I

The problem arises out of a *prima facie* incompatibility between the freedom of human action and the universality of causal law. It was raised in an acute form when universal determinism was believed to be a necessary presupposition of science; but it was not then new, because the incompatibility, if it exists at all, exists equally between human freedom and the foreknowledge of God. As it appears to the "plain man" the problem may be formulated as follows: "Very often I seem to myself to be acting freely, and this freedom, if it exists, implies that I could have acted otherwise than I did. If this freedom is illusory, I shall need a very convincing argument to prove that it is so, since it appears to be something of which I am immediately aware. Moreover, if there is no freedom, there is no moral responsibility; for it would not be right to praise or blame a man for something that he could not help doing. But, if a man could have acted otherwise than he did, his action must have been uncaused, and universal determinism is therefore untrue."

Broadly, there are two methods of resolving this, as any other, antinomy. We can either assume that the incompatibility is a genuine one at a certain level of thought and try to resolve it at a higher plane in which either or both the terms "freedom" and "necessity" lose their ordinary meaning or we can try to show by an analysis of these terms that no such incompatibility exists. If the latter method is successful, it will show that what is essential in our concept of freedom does not conflict with what is essential in our concept of causal necessity and that the incompatibility arises only because, at some stage in our development of one or both of these concepts, we have been tempted into making a false step. This method seems to me the better (provided always that it is successful), on the ground that it does not resort to any metaphysical conception imported *ad hoc* to solve this problem, which might be objectionable on other grounds. In the first two sections of this paper I shall give a brief outline of the analysis of the problem that I believe to be correct; and for this analysis I claim no originality. The method of presentation will, however, throw into relief the partial nature of the solution and help to indicate the further problems to be discussed in the last three sections.

Freedom, so far from being incompatible with causality, implies it. When I am conscious of being free, I am not directly conscious that my actions are uncaused, because absence of causation is not something of which one could be directly aware. That the plain man and the Libertarian philosopher are right in claiming to know directly the difference between voluntary and involuntary actions, at least in some cases, I have no doubt; but we can never have this direct knowledge that something is uncaused, since this is a general proposition and, like other general propositions, could only be established by reflection on empirical evidence. Fortunately it is not necessary here either to attempt an analysis of causality or to answer the question whether or not it is a necessary presupposition of science. It is now widely recognised that the considerations which lead scientists to suppose that strict determinism is not true are irrelevant to the problem of free will, since these considerations lend no support to the view that the phenomena with which we are concerned are not predictable; and it is to predictability, not to any special theory of the grounds of predictability, that the Libertarian objects. He claims that if our actions are predictable we are "pawns in the hands of fate" and cannot choose what we shall do. If, it is argued, someone can know what I shall do, then I have no choice but to do it.

The fallacy of this argument has often been exposed and the clearest proof that it is mistaken or at least muddled lies in showing that I could not be free to choose what I do *unless* determinism is correct. There are, indeed, grounds for supposing that strict determinism in psychology is not correct; but this, if true, constitutes not an increase but a limitation of our freedom of action. For the simplest actions could not be performed in an indeterministic universe. If I decide, say, to eat a piece of fish, I cannot do so if the fish is liable to turn into a stone or to disintegrate in mid-air or to behave in any other utterly unpredictable manner. It is precisely because physical objects have determinate causal characteristics that we are able to do what we decide to do. To this it is no answer to say that perhaps the behaviour of physical objects is determined while that of volitions is not. For we sometimes cause people to make decisions as well as to act on them. If someone shouts: "Look out! There is a bull," I shall probably run away. My action is caused by my decision to run; but my decision is itself caused by my fear, and that too is caused by what I have heard. Or, again, someone may try to influence my vote by offering me a bribe. If I accept the bribe and vote accordingly, the action is caused by the bribe, my avarice and my sense of obligation to the donor; yet this would certainly be held to be a blameworthy action, and therefore a voluntary one. A genuinely uncaused action could hardly be said to be an action *of* the agent at all; for in referring the action to an agent we are referring it to a cause.

In calling a man "honest" or "brave" we imply that he can be relied on to act honestly or bravely, and this means that we predict such actions from him. This does not mean that we can predict human actions with the same degree of assurance as that with which we predict eclipses. Psychology and the social sciences have not yet succeeded in establishing laws as reliable as those that we have established in some of the natural sciences, and maybe they never will. But any element of unreliability in our predictions of human actions decreases rather than increases the reliability of our moral judgements about them and of our consequent attributions of praise and blame. An expert chess player has less difficulty in defeating a moderate player than in defeating a novice, because the moves of the moderate player are more predictable; but they could hardly be said to be less voluntary. In calling an action "voluntary" we do not, therefore, mean that it is unpredictable; we mean that no one compelled the agent to act as he did. To say that, on the determinist view, we are "mere pawns in the hands of fate" is to confuse causality with compulsion, to confuse natural laws (descriptions) with social laws (prescriptions) and to think of fate as a malignant deity that continually thwarts our aims. What the protagonist of freedom requires, in short, is not uncaused actions, but actions that are the effects of a peculiar kind of causes. I shall be as brief as possible in saying what these causes are, since this has often been said before. But it is one thing to state the criteria by which we decide whether or not an action is voluntary and another to say why this distinction is important for ethics. The problem which the analysts have not, in my view, sufficiently considered is that of analysing the peculiar relation of "merit" or "fittingness" that is held to exist between voluntary actions and moral responsibility.

II

If someone overpowers me and compels me to fire a gun which causes a death, I should not be held guilty of murder. It would be said that my action was not voluntary; for I could not, had I so wished, have acted otherwise. On the other hand, if I kill someone because I hope to benefit under his will, my action is still caused, namely by my greed; but my action would be held to be voluntary and I should be blamed for it. The criterion here is that, while in the first case the cause is external to me, in the second it is my decision. A similar criterion would be used to distinguish a kleptomaniac from a thief. A kleptomaniac is held to be one who steals without having decided to do so, perhaps even in spite of a decision not to do so. He is not held morally responsible for his action because his action is not held to be voluntary. But in this case it is not true, as it was in the last, that his action is called involuntary because it is caused by some outside force. The cause of kleptomania is obscure; but it is not external compulsion. And, if the cause is not external, how can we say that the kleptomaniac is "compelled"? As used by psychologists, the term "compulsion" is evidently a metaphor, similar to that by which we speak of a man's doing something when "he is not himself." Evidently our moral judgements imply not merely a distinction between voluntary and compelled actions, but a further distinction among actions that are not compelled.

A third example will make it clear that some such distinction must be made. Suppose that a schoolmaster has two pupils A and B, who fail to do a simple sum correctly. A has often done sums of similar difficulty before and done them correctly, while B has always failed. The schoolmaster will, perhaps, threaten A with punishment, but he will give B extra private tuition. On the traditional view his action might be explained as follows: "A has done these sums correctly before; therefore he could have done them correctly on this occasion. His failure is due to carelessness or laziness. On the other hand, B is stupid. He has never done these sums correctly; so I suppose that he *cannot* do them. A's failure is due to a moral delinquency, B's to an intellectual defect. A therefore deserves punishment, but B does not." This is, I think, a fair summary of what the "plain man" thinks about a typical case, and the points to which I wish to draw attention are these:

(*a*) Neither failure is said to be "uncaused."

(*b*) The causes assigned are divided into two classes, moral and intellectual. (Cases of physical deficiency, *e.g.* not being strong or tall enough would go along with the intellectual class, the point being that such deficiencies are nonmoral.)

(c) Praise and blame are thought appropriate to moral but not to nonmoral defects.

(d) The criterion for deciding whether a defect is moral is "Could the agent have acted otherwise?"

I do not wish to suggest that the reasoning attributed to the plain man in this case is in any way incorrect, only that, particularly in regard to point (c) and (d) it needs explaining.

It is evident that one of the necessary conditions of moral action is that the agent "could have acted otherwise" and it is to this fact that the Libertarian is drawing attention. His case may be stated as follows: "It is a well-known maxim that 'I ought' implies 'I can.' If I cannot do a certain action, then that action cannot be my duty. On the other hand, 'I ought' as clearly implies 'I need not'; for if I cannot possibly refrain from a certain action, there can be no merit or demerit in doing it. Therefore, in every case of moral choice it is possible for the agent to do the action and also possible for him not to do it; were it not so, there would be no *choice;* for choice is between possibilities. But this implies that the action is uncaused, because a caused action cannot but occur." The fallacy in this argument lies in supposing that, when we say "A could have acted otherwise," we mean that A, being what he was and being placed in the circumstances in which he was placed, could have done something other than what he did. But in fact we never do mean this; and if we believe that voluntary action is uncaused action, that is only because we believe erroneously that uncaused action is a necessary condition of moral responsibility. The Libertarian believes that an action cannot be a moral one if the agent could not have acted otherwise, and he takes no account of possible differences in the causes that might have prevented him from acting otherwise. The Determinist, on the other hand, holds that the objective possibility of alternative actions is an illusion and that, if A in fact did X, then he could not have done any action incompatible with X. But he holds also that differences in the various causes that might have led to X may be of great importance and that it is in fact from the consideration of such differences that we discover the criterion by which we judge an action to be voluntary, and so moral.

We all blame Nero for murdering Agrippina, and the Libertarian holds that this implies that Nero could have abstained from his action. But this last phrase is ambiguous. Even if we admit that it would have been impossible for anyone to predict Nero's action with the degree of assurance with which we predict eclipses, yet an acute observer at Nero's court might have laid longish odds that Nero, being what he was and being placed in the circumstances in which he was placed, would sooner or later murder his mother. To say that Nero might have acted otherwise is to say that he could have decided to act otherwise and that he would have so decided if he had been of a different character. If Nero had been Seneca, for example, he would have preferred suicide to matricide. But what could "If Nero had been Seneca . . ." possibly mean? Unfulfilled conditionals in which both terms are names of individuals constitute, admittedly, a thorny philosophical problem; but it is clear, I think, that if "If Nero had been Seneca . . ." means anything at all, it is a quasi-general proposition which can be analysed either as "If Nero had had the character of Seneca" or "If Seneca had been emperor" or in some similar fashion. None of these analyses are incompatible with the Determinist's contention that, as things stood, Nero could not have abstained. But, adds the Determinist, the cause of his inability to abstain was not external compulsion nor some inexplicable and uncharacteristic quirk. His action was predictable because it was characteristic, and it is for the same reason that he is held to blame.

But the Libertarian's case is not yet fully answered. He might reply: "But, on this analysis, I still cannot blame Nero which in fact I do, and feel that I do justly. If the murder was caused by his character, *he* may not have been to blame. For his character may have been caused by hereditary and environmental factors over which he had no control. Can we justly blame a man if his vicious actions are due to hereditary epilepsy or to the influence of a corrupt and vicious court?" To this the answer is that we can and do. So long as we persist in supposing that, to be moral, an action must be uncaused, we can only push the moral responsibility back in time; and this, so far from solving the problem, merely shows the impossibility of any solution on these lines.

This is made abundantly clear by Aristotle's discussion of the subject, which I shall paraphrase somewhat freely in order to show that it must raise a difficulty which Aristotle does not squarely face. Aristotle says that, if a man plead that he could not help doing X because he was "the sort of man to do X," then he should be blamed for being this sort of man. His character was caused by his earlier actions, Y and Z, that made him the sort of person who would, in the given situation, inevitably do X. But suppose the criminal pleads that at the time of doing Y and Z he did not know that these were vicious actions and did not know that doing vicious actions causes a vicious character? Then, says Aristotle, all we can say in such a case is that not to know that actions create character is the mark of a singularly senseless person. But this is clearly inadequate. For the criminal might proceed: "Very well then, I was a singularly senseless person; I neither knew that Y and Z were vicious actions nor that, if I did them, I would become the sort of person to do X. And, anyhow, at the time of doing Y and Z, I was the sort of person to do Y and Z. These actions were just as much caused as was X. You say that blaming me for doing X is really blaming me for having done Y and Z. Now apply the same argument to Y and Z and see where it leads you. Furthermore my ignorance at the time of doing Y and Z which, according to you, is the real source of the trouble, was not my fault either. My father did not have me properly educated. Blame him, if you must blame some-body; but he will offer the same reply as I have done, and so *ad infinitum."* This argument carries no conviction; but it admits of no reply, and it is here that the temptation to invoke a metaphysical *deus ex machina* becomes invit-ing. If we proceed on the assumption that, to be moral, an action must be uncaused, either we shall find a genuinely uncaused action at the beginning of the chain or we shall not. If we do not, then, according to the Libertarian, there can be no moral praise and blame at all (and it was to account for these that Libertarianism was invented); and, if we do, then we must suppose that, while almost all our actions are caused, and therefore amoral, there was in the distant past some one action that was not caused and for which we can justly be praised or blamed. This bizarre theory has in fact been held; but the objections to it are clear. We praise and blame people for what they do now, not for what they might have done as babies, and any theory of moral responsibility must account for this. Secondly the same man is subjected to judgements both of praise and of blame: therefore the subject of these judge-ments cannot be one solitary act; and, thirdly, even if we were able to dis-cover this one hypothetical infantile act, would it in fact be a fit subject for either praise or blame? If it were genuinely uncaused, it could hardly be either, since it would not be an action *of* the agent.

III

So far we have discovered nothing more startling than the fact that moral actions are the effects of a peculiar kind of causes, namely the volun-tary actions of the agent. To sum up this part of the argument, I cannot do better than quote the words of Prof. Ayer: "To say that I could have acted otherwise is to say, first, that I should have acted otherwise, if I had so chosen; secondly, that my action was voluntary in the sense in which the actions say of the kleptomaniac are not; and, thirdly, that nobody compelled me to choose as I did: and these three conditions may very well be fulfilled. When they are fulfilled, I may be said to have acted freely. But this is not to say that it was a matter of chance that I acted as I did, or, in other words, that my action could not be explained. And that my actions should be capable of being explained is all that is required by the postulate of determinism." [1] With this I agree; but it leaves unsolved what is perhaps the most important part of the problem. Granted that we sometimes act "freely" in the sense defined by Ayer, in what sense is it rational or just or moral to praise or blame voluntary actions but not involuntary ones? It is surely not enough to say: "Actions of such-and-such a kind are given the name 'voluntary' and 'are praised and blamed; others are not.'" We need to explain the relation of

[1] "Freedom and Necessity," *Polemic,* No. 5, p. 43.

"fittingness" that is held to obtain between voluntary actions and moral judgement. Suppose that A and B each kill some one. We apply Ayer's tests and decide that A's was a voluntary action and B's not. We hang A, and B is immured in an asylum or regains his liberty. What needs to be explained is (*a*) Why do we do this? and (*b*) Is it morally justifiable?

Before attempting to answer these questions I shall first say something of two alternative solutions, the positivist and the intuitionist. The positivist solution might be on these lines: "Both the questions at the end of the last paragraph are pseudo-questions. We cannot explain why we do things, unless 'explaining' merely means 'discovering efficient causes.' I can discover the efficient causes of human actions, as of other phenomena, by observation; but I cannot discover final causes, because there are no such things and no good has ever come of looking for them. Look at the sterility of the natural sciences before the seventeenth century philosophers substituted explanation in terms of efficient causes for explanation in terms of final ones. Secondly, to ask whether it is moral or rational to act as we do is silly. If you like I will include such action in my definition of 'acting morally or rationally.' What is moral in a given society is what is in accordance with its customs; and to ask whether a custom is moral is to ask whether it is customary, which is ridiculous."

I shall not spend much time in discussing this solution, because the fallacy is, I believe, obvious, and the theory can be refuted without appeal to any dubious intuitions of Natural Law. It is true that in natural science the search for final causes is futile; but this is because such a search rests on the erroneous attribution of human purposes to nature. But in discussing human conduct anthropomorphic ideas are not out of place; it is their transfer to natural phenomena that is illegitimate. Though the right answer to the question "What causes an eclipse of the sun?" cannot be in the form "The sun wants to do so-and-so"; this sort of answer may very well be appropriate when the phenomenon in question is a human action. Not even the positivist denies the existence and causal efficacy of human purposes.

The intuitionist solution cannot so easily be dismissed; in fact it is never possible formally to refute someone who claims to be directly aware of something. All that we can do is to show that, in a given case, intuitionism leads to some unplausible conclusion that the intuitionist himself would be reluctant to admit. It is not my intention to show that intuitionism is in general false; indeed, the theory that our knowledge of values is grounded in intuition may very well be true. But moral judgements, as I hope to show in the next section, are not pure value judgements; they are value judgements combined with causal judgements. Whatever else we may be asserting when we call an action right or wrong, we are asserting that it was caused in a certain way; and it is difficult to see how such a causal proposition can be intuited. Furthermore, in default of widespread agreement about intuitions of this relation of fittingness, we are driven to believe that such intuitions, if they occur, are subjective. And there is no such agreement, even among

experts. If, as Kant held, the infliction of punishment on a criminal is necessarily a moral act, how is it that Westermarck can say: "The infliction of
pain is not an act that the moral consciousness regards with indifference even
in the case of a criminal." [2] Again, Ewing, after showing that the retributive
theory of punishment cannot be defended except by an appeal to intuition,
goes on to say: "Now it seems to me that, instead of being intuitively certain
that punishment should be inflicted as an end-in-itself without any consideration of consequences, the intuitive evidence is all the other way." [3] Rashdall,
again, holds that the problem must be decided "for each of us by an appeal
to his own moral consciousness" [4] and sides, rather tentatively, with the anti-
Kantians. This disagreement of experts sheds no light on the truth of the
retributive theory of punishment, but it does tend to show that the intuition
of fittingness on which that theory relies either does not in fact occur or is at
best unreliable and at worst subjective. The intuitionist who claims to be
directly aware of the relation of fittingness is, in short, telling us something
about his own mind. This may be interesting and important, but it is inconsistent with the proposition that most intuitionists would like to maintain,
that such intuitions are objectively true or false. The intuitionist theory
cannot be ruled out, but it is a safe rule not to resort to intuitions until driven
to do so, because so many alleged intuitions have, in the past, been shown to
be not merely not intuited but even false.

IV

The theory that I wish to suggest is that in every so-called moral judgement there are two distinct elements, a value judgement and a moral judgement proper. About value judgements no special theory is implied. In particular, I do not intend to prejudice any of the following issues:

(*a*) whether value judgements are or are not properly called "judgements" at all,

(*b*) whether there is or is not only one type of value (for instance,
pleasure), and

(*c*) whether or not value judgements are subjective.
It will, however, follow that, whatever values there may be, there is no such
thing as moral value, as such, but that when we attribute moral value to a
thing we are saying in a misleading way that the thing has some value or
other and is connected with a moral cause.

Whatever our reasons may be, we do in fact regard some states, objects
and events as "good" or "valuable" and others as "bad" or "disvaluable"; the
former we try to promote, the latter to prevent. Whatever may be the case

[2] *Ethical Relativity*, p. 77.
[3] *The Morality of Punishment*, p. 18.
[4] *The Theory of Good and Evil*, pp. 284 ff.

with value judgements, the strictly moral element in a moral judgement is concerned with an empirical fact and is, therefore, objective. The difference between these two types of judgement can be made clear by an example. Suppose that, for whatever reason, I regard A's life as valuable. (I may hold that all human life is valuable as such, or that A is a good man and that the lives of good men are valuable, or merely that the existence of A is propitious to some scheme in which I am interested.) A may be murdered in cold blood by B or may be run over by C in circumstances over which the latter had no control. In each of these cases I should make the same value judgement, that A's death was "bad." But, while in the first case I should make the further moral judgement that B's action was criminal, in the second I should make no additional moral judgement at all.

The theory can be divided into four parts:

(*a*) Value judgements apply only to events (including their consequences), but not to their causes.

(*b*) Events that are "good" or "bad" constitute moral actions only when they are caused by someone's voluntary decision.

(*c*) "Good" and "bad" events that are also moral actions are fit subjects for praise and blame, while other good and bad events are not.

(*d*) This "fittingness" is a causal relation, discoverable neither by a special "moral sense" nor by intuition nor by *a priori* reasoning, but by reflection on experience.

Of these propositions (*a*) and (*b*) are recommendations to employ a certain terminology in ethical matters; (*c*) is a proposition which will, I think, be generally admitted, provided the suggested terminology is accepted. But it is (*c*) that requires explanation, and the explanation is contained in (*d*). If it is true that praise and blame are means employed to bring about good events and prevent bad ones, they are appropriate not to all good and bad events, but only to those that they can in fact bring about or prevent. Since a moral action is one that can be fittingly praised or blamed, it follows that a moral action is one that can be brought about or prevented by these means. Moral actions are a subclass of good and bad events, and the traditional criterion for deciding whether or not an event belongs to this subclass was, as we saw, "Was the action voluntary, *i.e.* caused by a decision of the agent?" But the application of this criterion involves two difficulties. It is sometimes difficult to decide to what cause an action was due. Is this a case of laziness or a case of stupidity? Was the prisoner in the dock mad or was he avaricious? This is an empirical difficulty and raises no question of principle. But the other difficulty that arises in applying the criterion of voluntariness is to find a rule for deciding what classes of actions are voluntary. If the criterion I have suggested is correct, then we should find that the class of actions generally agreed to be voluntary coincides roughly with the class of actions that are caused by characteristics that can be strengthened or inhibited by praise and blame. And this is what we do in fact find; moral characteristics, as opposed to intellectual and physical ones, are just those that we believe to be alterable in this way. Now the problem of deciding whether or not a characteristic is alterable may be difficult; but the difficulty is an empirical one only, and we know at least how to set about solving it.

This theory implies a utilitarian theory of punishment. Rewards and punishments (for the sake of brevity I shall in future refer only to punishment) are distributed not because certain actions directly "merit" them, but because some useful purpose is believed to be served by inflicting them. It should be noted that the theory that punishment is purposive does not imply that its purposes must always have been those that the Utilitarians had in mind. Furthermore, the fact that some systems of punishment do not in fact produce the intended results, an argument that is often urged against the utilitarian theory, does not tend to show that no result was intended. The performance of Sellenger's Round doubtless does nothing to keep the sun on its course; but that does not prove that it is not intended to do so by the performers. Failure to produce results argues not lack of purpose but lack of skill in the practitioner.

It may be objected that this theory fails to account for the retributive element in punishment and, before elaborating it on the positive side, I shall first suggest a possible explanation both of the fact that the retributive theory is believed and of the fact that its supporters claim to intuit its truth. To do this it is necessary to distinguish between the reasons for which the theory first came to be held and the reasons for which it is held now. An adequate account of the first point would require to be based on a wider knowledge of anthropology than I possess, and I do not claim that the account here suggested is true, even in its broad outlines. Nevertheless it is, I think, plausible to suppose that retributive punishment originally had *some* purpose, even if it was quite different from the one suggested here.

The primitive morality that demands an eye for an eye is by no means incompatible with the theory that punishment is not mere retribution, but is designed to bring about some end; and such practices as the punishment of idiots, animals and even inanimate objects do not prove that their practitioners were intuitionists who claimed to be directly aware that certain actions "ought to be punished," the morality of the punishment being in no way dependent on any supposed advantage to those who inflict it. Such practices are always found in conjunction with a special theological theory as to the nature of the universe. It is held that the Gods require certain sorts of conduct on the part of human beings and that they will visit breaches of the rules with their wrath in the form of plagues, famines and other undesirable events. It is to prevent these that punishment is inflicted; and this explains why it is that what *we* call the morality of the action, which includes the condition that it be voluntary, is not held to affect the morality of punishment, a point which orthodox retributionists have some difficulty in explaining. If the volition of the agent is held to be irrelevant to the operation of

God's wrath, it will also be irrelevant to the morality of punishment, since the object of punishment is not to requite a voluntarily committed wrong but to ward off God's anger. Oedipus has committed parricide and incest. He must be punished, not because he did so, still less because he intended to do so, but because the tribe that harbours him will suffer if he is not. Punishment is expiation.

When a society holds theological beliefs other than our own we shall not be surprised to find that its moral ideas differ also. Retributive punishment does not have the object that punishment has with us, and it does not (we believe) achieve the results aimed at. But neither of these facts tends to show that it did not originally have some purpose, and it is a curious fact that the retributive practice tends to become mollified (in the form of purely ritual expiation) and finally abandoned, precisely when the crude theology on which it is based ceases to be believed. Now if retributive practices are due entirely to instinct or to an intuition of fittingness it is hard to see why this should be so. It is apparently a pure coincidence that the intuitive light grows dim precisely when a certain theological theory is abandoned. But if the purposive theory is true it is easy to see why the retributive element should tend to give way before the reformatory and deterrent elements when people abandon the belief that punishment will obviate the failure of crops but conceive (or retain) the belief that it will benefit society by inhibiting certain forms of action. When we abandon the belief that God will visit his wrath on a tribe that harbours an unwitting parricide, we no longer have any motive for punishing him. Consequently we call him innocent. A man is not punishable because he is guilty; he is guilty because he is punishable, that is to say, because some useful result is supposed to accrue from punishing him.

If this is true, we can also explain why it is that modern retributionists, who do not hold the crude theological beliefs with which I have suggested that the practice was originally linked, fall back on an intuition of fittingness. Here, as elsewhere, intuition is invoked to account for a belief that we are quite certain that we hold but for which we have forgotten the original grounds and cannot discover new ones. It often happens that a belief is retained after the theory on which it is based and which alone makes it plausible has been abandoned, and this is particularly liable to happen in ethics for the following reason. Metaphysical and scientific views are changed by the speculation of a few intellectuals, who are regarded by the many as harmless. But morals, as Hume said, excite our passions and produce and prevent action. The moral reformer, therefore, unlike the speculator, is treated as a danger to society; and for this reason morality tends to be more conservative than other branches of thought. Hence there sometimes arises a lack of logical relation between the metaphysical and scientific ideas of a society and its moral code, the latter being partly a survival from older modes of thought. When this process of survival occurs in a society not our own we call it a superstition or a taboo; when it occurs in our own we call it a Moral Law. Now the retributive theory has a logical justification if a certain theological view is accepted. That view having been abandoned, the justification no longer exists and we are forced to fall back on a direct intuition that punishment is fitting.

V

The analysis suggested at the beginning of the last section can now be applied to the examples used earlier in the paper. We saw that, apart from the empirical difficulty of deciding to what class an action belongs, there are two difficulties of principle. One is the problem of determining what classes of actions are voluntary; the other the problem of showing a connexion between being voluntary and being liable to praise or blame. It has, I think, usually been the practice to try to solve the first of these problems first; but this leaves us, as we saw, in the insuperable difficulty of libertarianism and also renders the second problem insoluble. If the theory I have suggested is correct, the second problem should come first and is simply the empirical problem of deciding what characteristics are alterable; and the solution to this problem then provides the criterion for deciding what actions are voluntary. The preliminary analysis of the case of the schoolmaster left unexplained the meaning of the vital sentence, "A could have acted otherwise, while B could not" and also the question "Why is laziness punishable and stupidity not?" It is not enough to say that A's failure was voluntary because he is known to have acted rightly before. Perhaps he was not lazy then but is now. And how do we know that his laziness now is not just as much beyond his control as was his industriousness then and as is B's stupidity now? An analysis made on these lines cannot fail to land us in the difficulty in which Aristotle left us. A will plead that his laziness was caused and therefore involuntary. On the other hand, if, instead of assuming that A ought to be punished because he is morally guilty, we suppose that he ought to be punished for some other reason, the rationale of the schoolmaster's action becomes clear. He knows from experience that, if he adds the fear of punishment to the motives actuating A, then A will tend to get these sums right in future, which is, for him, the end to be achieved. On the other hand, if B is stupid, neither threats nor promises will cause him to do better. When we say that A could have done the sum correctly, had he so chosen, we do not imply that he could, on that occasion, have so chosen. But we do imply that A is such that, under certain circumstances, he will choose to act correctly; and those circumstances can be brought about. Rewards and punishments are means of varying the causal antecedents of actions so that those we desire will occur and those we wish to prevent will not occur. Cleverness and industriousness are both valuable characteristics; the latter is called a "moral" one and the former not, because we know from experience that the former cannot be induced by means of praise and blame, while the latter can. It is surely no accident that the characteristics that we believe to be alterable in this way are precisely those that we call moral; and this also explains why, to be moral, an act must be voluntary. To say that a man could have acted otherwise is to say that he might have been the sort of person who would have acted otherwise; and to attribute his acting as he did to his moral character, as opposed to some amoral defect, is to say that his action was due to one of the characteristics that can be altered by means of rewards and punishments.

It is not necessary to undertake an elaborate analysis of the other examples used. If a man kills someone because he is physically compelled to do so, he will not be prevented from doing so again in similar circumstances by the knowledge that the action will be severely punished. But if his action is due to his own decision, this knowledge may cause him to decide otherwise in future. In the same way the basis for the distinction between the kleptomaniac and the thief is that the latter is held to have decided to steal. Here the cause in both cases lies within the agent and the distinction of internal and external causation did not help us. The fact that one commits a voluntary action and the other does not is important, but by itself it does not account for the differential treatment of the two men. Why are men who steal as a result of a decision said to be worthy of punishment, while those who steal from some other cause are not? The reason is that we believe that the fear of punishment will affect the future behaviour of the thief but not that of the kleptomaniac. If a man steals because he has decided to do so, we can prevent his doing so again by causing him to decide otherwise. If he expects to be punished, then in addition to the motive that tends to make him steal there will be a powerful motive tending to make him refrain. Now the fear of punishment has no such influence on the kleptomaniac; on the other hand, psychoanalysis, by removing the subconscious cause of his tendency to steal, may achieve the desired result. Nor is this merely an interesting but unimportant distinction between kleptomaniacs and thieves; it is the very basis for the distinction. In each case we make the same value judgement, that the abstraction of one's neighbours' goods is undesirable. If we consider the actions of the thief and the kleptomaniac simply as events, without regard to their causes, they are identical and provide no possible basis for differential treatment. Therefore the different moral judgements that we in fact make and the different treatments that we accord cannot be based on the value judgement alone. The moral judgements are concerned with the causes of the actions. But to say that avarice is a reprehensible cause and kleptomania not explains nothing. For we cannot, without appeal to dubious intuitions, assert that of two similar undesirable events one is morally reprehensible and the other not. Nor is it enough to say with the positivists that the fact that we make these distinctions is simply a brute fact about our society and requires no explanation. Some basis must be found for the distinction, and I suggest that it is to be found in the fact that, while potential thieves will be deterred by the prospect of six months' hard labour, potential kleptomaniacs will not.

Generalising from these instances, we can see that the relation that is held to exist between voluntary wrong-doing and punishability is neither an inexplicable sociological fact nor a mysterious relation of "merit" that some of us are able to intuit; it is a relation of cause and effect. If this is so, then, whatever views we may hold about the subjectivity of value judgements, moral judgements, being judgements of cause and effect, are all objective. Many moral philosophers have held subjectivist doctrines about other forms of value, such as pleasure or aesthetic taste, but have been unwilling to allow that moral judgements are subjective, and this in spite of the fact that the arguments leading to subjectivism in aesthetics appear to apply equally to morals. I think that their hesitation has been correct and has not always been due to the irrational considerations, such as the fear that subjectivity in ethics might undermine society, that have sometimes been attributed to them. If the proposed separation of the value element from the moral element in moral judgement be accepted, their unwillingness to accept a purely subjective theory of ethics will have been justified.

AUTHOR'S COMMENTARY

The main purpose of my article was to analyse the ideas of freedom and desert in terms of the empirical idea of "alterability by rewards and punishments" and thus reduce the number of intuitions required in this area. This attempt led me to conclude that "a man is not punishable because he is guilty; he is guilty because he is punishable, that is to say, because some useful purpose is supposed to accrue from punishing him." The question of freedom is too complicated for discussion in a postscript; something may be said about desert.

1. The idea that a punishment can and should "fit" a crime now seems to me to derive partly from a simple failure to distinguish punishment from damages, the purpose of civil law from the purpose of criminal law. It may be difficult to assess in monetary terms the amount of loss sustained by the plaintiff in a civil suit; but, once this is assessed, it is a simple matter to assess the damages which it is "fitting" for the court to award. For the purpose of the award is, as nearly as possible, to make good the loss. Since a *fine* of $100 awarded by a criminal court has the same effect on the pocket as an award

of $100 *damages* in a civil court, we tend to confuse the two and to suppose that the idea of "fittingness" between loss and reparation can be transferred to crime and punishment.

2. The major defect of the article lies in the failure to distinguish *cases* from *rules,* the judge's question, "Should this man in the dock, John Doe, be punished?" from the legislator's question, "Should acts of Type N be prohibited by law and, in consequence, people who do acts of Type N become liable to punishment?" When we say that John Doe deserves to be punished we certainly do not *mean* that it would be useful to punish him; nor would most of us subscribe to the *moral* view that it is just to punish him if and only if it is useful to do so. Desert is a matter of law. He deserves to be punished at all only if he has broken a law, and the severity of the punishment that he deserves is determined by what the law lays down. Considerations of utility can come in at this point only in so far as the law allows the judge a discretion to bring them in. But the legislator, I should now say, should be guided solely by considerations of utility. It is right to make a law forbidding acts of Type N only if (a) such acts are "bad" in the nonmoral sense referred to in the article and (b) the propensity to do them is one that can be weakened or eliminated by the threat of punishment.

3. In this modified theory the idea of a general fittingness between crime and punishment (as distinct from the fittingness of punishing this man in just this way) still has an important place. Deterring people from a particular type of act is never our sole aim; hence the deterrent effect of a penalty should not be the sole consideration of the legislator. While it still seems to me quite impossible to say that a certain type or degree of punishment is "fitting" to a certain type of crime, a more complex notion of fittingness is possible. Most people would agree that some types of crime are worse than others, whether or not they were prepared to analyse "worse" in terms of degree of disutility. If now we construct a scale of severity of punishment, it seems just that the punishment for a greater crime should be more severe than that for a lesser. This rule embodies a four-term relation of fittingness; it cuts across the principle of deterrence, since it may well occur that a milder penalty would deter people from the greater crime; and it can be accommodated within the framework of a utilitarian account. For a utilitarian will be more concerned to prevent greater crimes than lesser. If the penalty for a lesser crime were made equal to or greater than that for a greater crime— which it well might be if deterrence were our sole criterion—such a system, though tending to decrease the volume of the lesser crime, might increase the volume of the greater. For example, if the penalty for burglary is as great as that for murder, no doubt the number of burglaries will be reduced; but those burglars who are still not deterred will commit murder in order not to be caught. The purely deterrent rule would not then be the most "useful." As in all such matters our decision has to be made after considering the many different consequences of adopting one law rather than another. The admis-

sion of an idea of "fittingness" of this complex kind does not seem to me to entail the falsity of my thesis that desert must, *in the end,* be explained in terms of alterability by punishment; but the explanation is a good deal more complicated than I used to think.

QUESTIONS

1. Professor Nowell-Smith claims that it is fallacious for the Libertarians to argue that "if our actions are predictable we are 'pawns in the hands of fate' and cannot choose what we shall do." How does he attempt to justify this claim? Give your reasons for agreeing, or disagreeing, with him.

2. If there is not a strict determinism in psychology, Professor Nowell-Smith says, there is not an increase but a limitation of our freedom of action. What reasons does he give for saying this? Why, in your opinion, are his reasons acceptable, or unacceptable?

3. Professor Nowell-Smith argues that "freedom, so far from being incompatible with causality, implies it." In what respects is his argument similar to, and in what respects is it different from, Hume's in "Liberty and Necessity" in this chapter?

4. Professor Nowell-Smith asserts that "A could have acted otherwise" does *not* mean "A, being what he was and being placed in the circumstances in which he was placed, could have done something other than what he did." What does he assert that it *does* mean? State why you think he is, or is not, correct in his assertion about what it means. Compare your answer with the criticism of this passage by C. A. Campbell on pages 487–88. How sound are Professor Campbell's arguments?

5. ". . . 'Can we justly blame a man if his vicious actions are due to hereditary epilepsy or to the influence of a corrupt and vicious court?' To this the answer is that we can and do." How does Professor Nowell-Smith defend this answer?

6. Review Section II and the first half of the first paragraph of Section III of the reading. Then state in your own words what it means to act *freely,* according to this portion of the reading.

7. On what grounds does Professor Nowell-Smith reject the positivist explanation of why we hold one person morally responsible and not another?

8. How does Professor Nowell-Smith distinguish moral judgments from value judgments in general? How do you think he would reply to the objection that there are many actions which are "good" or "bad" and are caused by someone's voluntary decision, yet no one would think of calling them "moral" (e.g., an artist's creating a good or bad painting, a historian's writing a good or bad history book, or a chess player's making good or bad moves in a chess game)?

9. According to Professor Nowell-Smith, what is the connection between the fact that an action is voluntary and the fact that it is liable to praise or blame?

10. "A man is not punishable because he is guilty; he is guilty because he is punishable. . . ." What argument does Professor Nowell-Smith give in support of this statement?

11. In order to test your understanding of the reading, complete the following sentence as you think Professor Nowell-Smith has completed it in the reading. Then check your answer with the sentence itself. (It occurs in the first paragraph of Section V.) "Cleverness and industriousness are both valuable characteristics; the latter is called a 'moral' one and the former not, because . . ."

12. How does Professor Nowell-Smith explain why a thief is held morally responsible but not a kleptomaniac? Does his explanation make it possible for us to *justify* holding a thief but not a kleptomaniac responsible? Defend your answer.

13. In his commentary on his article, Professor Nowell-Smith says that "the major defect of the article lies in the failure to distinguish *cases* from *rules*. . . ." Explain what this distinction is, and show its bearing on the problem of justifying punishment.

34. C. A. CAMPBELL

(*b. 1897*)

Is Free Will a Pseudo-Problem?

Charles Arthur Campbell was educated at the University of Glasgow and Balliol College, Oxford. He was Professor of Logic and Rhetoric at the University of Glasgow from 1938 until his retirement in 1961. He is the author of *Scepticism and Construction* (1931) and *On Selfhood and Godhood* (1957).

In the article that follows, Professor Campbell attacks those philosophers who claim that the problem of free will is a "pseudo-problem." According to them, once the semantic confusions involved in the use of words like "free," "caused," and "responsible" are cleared up, it will be evident that there is no contradiction between determinism and moral responsibility and hence no problem about how a man can be held responsible if all his actions and decisions are caused. The only reason why anyone thinks that there is a problem is that he has mistaken ideas about what determinism means and has not analyzed with sufficient care the concepts of freedom and responsibility. Thus all that is necessary to show that there really is no such problem as freedom of the will is to correct these conceptual errors and confusions.

Professor Campbell begins by summarizing the argument of a philosopher, Moritz Schlick, who held the foregoing view. It should be noted that Schlick's position is similar to the one set forth by P. H. Nowell-Smith in the preceding selection. After presenting Schlick's argument, Professor Campbell proceeds to examine and criticize it. He concludes his article by defending the position that freedom of the will is not a pseudo-problem, but a real one. He does this by arguing that moral responsibility requires a "contra-causal" kind of freedom, that is, a kind of freedom not compatible with determinism.

From "Is 'Freewill' a Pseudo-Problem?" *Mind,* by C. A. Campbell, Vol. 60, No. 240, 1951. Reprinted by permission of the author and the editor of *Mind.*

1

. . . Chapter VII of Moritz Schlick's *Problems of Ethics* . . . the title of which is 'When is a Man Responsible?' and the first section of which bears the heading 'The Pseudo-problem of Freedom of the Will', presents in concentrated form . . . [an] argument . . . that 'Free Will', as traditionally formulated, is a pseudo-problem, begotten by mere confusion of mind. I shall first summarise, as faithfully as I can, what I take to be the distinctive points in Schlick's argument.

The traditional formulation of the problem, Schlick points out, is based on the assumption that to have 'free will' entails having a will that is, at least sometimes, exempt from causal law. It is traditionally supposed, quite rightly, that moral responsibility implies freedom in *some* sense: and it is supposed, also quite rightly, that this sense is one which is incompatible with compulsion. But because it is further supposed, quite *wrongly,* that to be subject to causal or natural law is to be subject to compulsion, the inference is drawn that the free will implied in moral responsibility is incompatible with causal continuity. The ultimate root of the error, Schlick contends, lies in a failure to distinguish between two different kinds of Law, one of which does indeed 'compel', but the other of which does *not*.[1] There are, first, *pre*scriptive laws, such as the laws imposed by civil authority, which presume contrary desires on the part of those to whom they are applied; and these may fairly be said to exercise 'compulsion'. And there are, secondly, *de*scriptive laws, such as the laws which the sciences seek to formulate; and these merely state what does as a matter of fact always happen. It is perfectly clear that the relation of the latter, the natural, causal laws, to human willing is radically different from the 'compulsive' relation of prescriptive laws to human willing, and that it is really an absurdity to talk of a species of natural law like, say, psychological laws, *compelling* us to act in this or that way. The term 'compulsion' is totally inept where, as in this case, there are no contrary desires. But the traditional discussions of Free Will, confusing descriptive with prescriptive laws, fallaciously assume 'compulsion' to be ingredient in Law as such, and it is contended accordingly that moral freedom, since it certainly implies absence of compulsion, implies also exemption from causal law.

It follows that the problem of Free Will, as traditionally stated, is a mere pseudo-problem. The statement of it in terms of exemption from causal law rests on the assumption that causal law involves 'compulsion'. And this assumption is demonstrably false. Expose the muddle from which it arises and the so-called 'problem' in its traditional form disappears.

[1] *Problems of Ethics,* Ch. VII, Section 2. (All references are to the English translation by David Rynin, published in New York in 1939 by Prentice-Hall.)

But is it quite certain that the freedom which moral responsibility implies is no more than 'the absence of compulsion'? This is the premise upon which Schlick's argument proceeds, but Schlick is himself well aware that it stands in need of confirmation from an analysis of the notion of moral responsibility. Otherwise it might be maintained that although 'the absence of compulsion' has been shown not to entail a contra-causal type of freedom, there is nevertheless some *other* condition of moral responsibility that *does* entail it. Accordingly Schlick embarks now upon a formal analysis of the nature and conditions of moral responsibility designed to show that the *only* freedom implied by moral responsibility is freedom from compulsion. It was a trifle ambitious, however, even for a master of compression like Professor Schlick, to hope to deal satisfactorily in half-a dozen very brief pages with a topic which has been so extensively debated in the literature of moral philosophy: and I cannot pretend that I find what he has to say free from obscurity. But to the best of my belief what follows does reproduce the gist of Schlick's analysis.

What precisely, Schlick asks, does the term 'moral responsibility' mean in our ordinary linguistic usage? [2] He begins his answer by insisting upon the close connexion for ordinary usage between 'moral responsibility' and *punishment* (strictly speaking, punishment and *reward:* but for convenience Schlick virtually confines the discussion to punishment, and we shall do the same). The connexion, as Schlick sees it, is this. In ordinary practice our concern with the responsibility for an act (he tells us) is with a view to determining *who is to be punished for it.* Now punishment is (I quote) 'an educative measure'. It is 'a means to the formation of motives, which are in part to prevent the wrong-doer from repeating the act (reformation), and in part to prevent others from committing a similar act (intimidation)'.[3] When we ask, then, 'Who in a given case is to be punished?'—which is the same as the question, 'Who is responsible?'—what we are really wanting to discover is some agent in the situation upon whose motives we can bring to bear the appropriate educative influences, so that in similar situations in future his strongest motive will impel him to refrain from, rather than to repeat, the act. 'The question of who is responsible' Schlick sums up, 'is . . . a matter only of knowing who is to be punished or rewarded, in order that punishment and reward function as such—be able to achieve their goal'.[4] It is not a matter, he expressly declares, of trying to ascertain what may be called the 'original instigator' of the act. That might be a great-grand-parent, from the consequence of whose behaviour vicious tendencies have been inherited by a living person. Such 'remote causes' as this are irrelevant to questions of punishment (and so to questions of moral responsibility), 'for in the first place their actual contribution cannot be determined, and in the second place they are generally out of reach'.[5]

[2] *Ibid.,* Ch. VII, Section 5.
[3] *Ibid.,* p. 152.
[4] *Ibid.,* p. 153.
[5] *Ibid.*

It is a matter for regret that Schlick has not rounded off his discussion, as one had hoped and expected he would, by formulating a precise definition of moral responsibility in terms of what he has been saying. I think, however, that the conclusion to which his argument leads could be not unfairly expressed in some such way as this: 'We say that a man is morally responsible for an act if his motives for bringing about the act are such as we can affect favourably in respect of his future behaviour by the educative influences of reward and punishment'.

Given the truth of this analysis of moral responsibility, Schlick's contention follows logically enough that the only freedom that is required for moral responsibility is freedom from compulsion. For what are the cases in which a man's motives are *not* capable of being favourably affected by reward and punishment?—the cases in which, that is, according to Schlick's analysis, we do *not* deem him morally responsible? The only such cases, it would seem, are those in which a man is subjected to some form of external constraint which prevents him from acting according to his 'natural desires'. For example, if a man is compelled by a pistol at his breast to do a certain act, or induced to do it by an externally administered narcotic, he is not 'morally responsible'; or not, at any rate, in so far as punishment would be impotent to affect his motives in respect of his future behaviour. External constraint in one form or another seems to be the sole circumstance which absolves a man from moral responsibility. Hence we may say that freedom from external constraint is the only sort of freedom which an agent must possess in order to be morally responsible. The 'contra-causal' sort of freedom which so many philosophers and others have supposed to be required is shown by a true analysis of moral responsibility to be irrelevant.

This completes the argument that 'Free Will', as traditionally formulated, is a pseudo-problem. The only freedom implied by moral responsibility is freedom from compulsion; and as we have rid ourselves of the myth that subjection to causal law is a form of compulsion, we can see that the only compulsion which absolves from moral responsibility is the external constraint which prevents us from translating our desires into action. The true meaning of the question 'Have we free will?' thus becomes simply 'Can we translate our desires into action?' And this question does not constitute a 'problem' at all, for the answer to it is not in doubt. The obvious answer is 'Sometimes we can, sometimes we can't, according to the specific circumstances of the case'.

II

Here, then, in substance is Schlick's theory. Let us now examine it.

In the first place, it is surely quite unplausible to suggest that the common assumption that moral freedom postulates some breach of causal continuity arises from a confusion of two different types of law. Schlick's distinction between descriptive and prescriptive law is, of course, sound. It was no doubt worth pointing out, too that descriptive laws cannot be said to 'compel' human behaviour in the same way as prescriptive laws do. But it seems to me evident that the usual reason why it is held that moral freedom implies some breach of causal continuity, is not a belief that causal laws 'compel' as civil laws 'compel', but simply the belief that the admission of unbroken causal continuity entails a *further* admission which is directly incompatible with moral responsibility; *viz.* the admission that ro man could have acted otherwise than he in fact did. Now it may, of course, be an error thus to assume that a man is not morally responsible for an act, a fit subject for moral praise and blame in respect of it, unless he could have acted otherwise than he did. Or, if *this* is not an error, it may still be an error to assume that a man could not have acted otherwise than he did, in the sense of the phrase that is crucial for moral responsibility, without there occurring some breach of causal continuity. Into these matters we shall have to enter very fully at a later stage. But the relevant point at the moment is that these (not *prima facie* absurd) assumptions about the conditions of moral responsibility have very commonly, indeed normally, been made, and that they are entirely adequate to explain why the problem of Free Will finds its usual formulation in terms of partial exemption from causal law. Schlick's distinction between prescriptive and descriptive laws has no bearing at all upon the truth or falsity of these assumptions. Yet if these assumptions are accepted, it is (I suggest) really inevitable that the Free Will problem should be formulated in the way to which Schlick takes exception. Recognition of the distinciton upon which Schlick and his followers lay so much stress can make not a jot of difference.

As we have seen, however, Schlick does later proceed to the much more important business of disputing these common assumptions about the conditions of moral responsibility. He offers us an analysis of moral responsibility which flatly contradicts these assumptions; an analysis according to which the only freedom demanded by morality is a freedom which is compatible with Determinism. If this analysis can be sustained, there is certainly no problem of 'Free Will' in the traditional sense.

But it seems a simple matter to show that Schlick's analysis is untenable. Let us test it by Schlick's own claim that it gives us what we mean by 'moral responsibility' in ordinary linguistic usage.

We do not ordinarily consider the lower animals to be morally responsible. But *ought* we not to do so if Schlick is right about what we mean by moral responsibility? It is quite possible, by punishing the dog who absconds with the succulent chops designed for its master's luncheon, favourably to influence its motives in respect of its future behaviour in like circumstances. If moral responsibility is to be linked with punishment as Schlick links it, and punishment conceived as a form of education, we should surely hold the dog morally responsible? The plain fact, of course, is that we don't. We don't, because we suppose that the dog 'couldn't help it': that its action (unlike what we usually believe to be true of human beings) was simply a link in a continuous chain of causes and effects. In other words, we do commonly demand the contra-causal sort of freedom as a condition of moral responsibility.

Again, we do ordinarily consider it proper, in certain circumstances, to speak of a person no longer living as morally responsible for some present situation. But *ought* we to do so if we accept Schlick's essentially 'forward-looking' interpretation of punishment and responsibility? Clearly we cannot now favourably affect the dead man's motives. No doubt they could *at one time* have been favourably affected. But that cannot be relevant to our judgment of responsibility if, as Schlick insists, the question of who is responsible 'is a matter only of knowing who is to be punished or rewarded'. Indeed he expressly tells us, as we saw earlier, that in asking this question we are not concerned with a 'great-grand-parent' who may have been the 'original instigator', because, for one reason, this 'remote cause' is 'out of reach'. We cannot bring the appropriate educative influence to bear upon it. But the plain fact, of course, is that we do frequently assign moral responsibility for present situations to persons who have long been inaccessible to any punitive action on our part. And Schlick's position is still more paradoxical in respect of our apportionment of responsibility for occurrences in the distant past. Since in these cases there is no agent whatsoever whom we can favourably influence by punishment, the question of moral responsibility here should have no meaning for us. But of course it has. Historical writings are studded with examples.

Possibly the criticism just made may seem to some to result from taking Schlick's analysis too much *au pied de la lettre*. The absurd consequences deduced, it may be said, would not follow if we interpreted Schlick as meaning that a man is morally responsible where his motive is such as can *in principle* be favourably affected by reward or punishment—whether or not we who pass the judgment are in a position to take such action. But with every desire to be fair to Schlick, I cannot see how he could accept this modification and still retain the essence of his theory. For the essence of his theory seems to be that moral responsibility has its whole meaning and importance for us in relation to our potential control of future conduct in the interests of society. (I agree that it is hard to believe that anybody *really* thinks this. But it is perhaps less hard to believe to-day than it has ever been before in the history of modern ethics.)

Again, we ordinarily consider that, in certain circumstances, the *degree* of a man's moral responsibility for an act is affected by considerations of his inherited nature, or of his environment, or of both. It is our normal habit to 'make allowances' (as we say) when we have reason to believe that a malefactor had a vicious heredity, or was nurtured in his formative years in a harmful environment. We say in such cases 'Poor chap, he is more to be pitied than blamed. We could scarcely expect him to behave like a decent citizen with *his* parentage or upbringing.' But this extremely common sort of judgment has no point at all if we mean by moral responsibility what Schlick says that we mean. On *that* meaning the degree of a man's moral responsibility must presumably be dependent upon the degree to which we can favourably affect his future motives, which is quite another matter. Now there is no reason to believe that the motives of a man with a bad heredity or a bad upbringing are either less or more subject to educative influence than those of his more fortunate fellows. Yet it is plain matter of fact that we do commonly consider the degree of a man's moral responsibility to be affected by these two factors.

A final point. The extremity of paradox in Schlick's identification of the question 'Who is morally blameworthy?' with the question 'Who is to be punished?' is apt to be partially concealed from us just because it is our normal habit to include in the meaning of 'punishment' an element of 'requital for moral transgression' which Schlick expressly denies to it. On that account we commonly think of 'punishment', in its strict sense, as implying moral blameworthiness in the person punished. But if we remember to mean by punishment what Schlick means by it, a purely 'educative measure', with no retributive ingredients, his identification of the two questions loses such plausibility as it might otherwise have. For clearly we often think it proper to 'punish' a person, in *Schlick's* sense, where we are not at all prepared to say that the person is morally blameworthy. We may even think him morally commendable. A case in point would be the unmistakably sincere but muddleheaded person who at the cost of great suffering to himself steadfastly pursues as his 'duty' a course which, in our judgment is fraught with danger to the common weal. We should most of us feel entitled, in the public interest, to bring such action to bear upon the man's motives as might induce him to refrain in future from his socially injurious behaviour: in other words, to inflict upon him what Schlick would call 'punishment'. But we should most of us feel perfectly clear that in so 'punishing' this misguided citizen we are not proclaiming his moral blameworthiness for moral wickedness.

Adopting Schlick's own criterion, then, looking simply 'to the manner in which the concept is used',[6] we seem bound to admit that constantly people do assign moral responsibility where Schlick's theory says they shouldn't, don't assign moral responsibility where Schlick's theory says they should, and assign degrees of moral responsibility where on Schlick's theory there should be no difference in degree. I think we may reasonably conclude that Schlick's account of what we mean by moral responsibility breaks down.

The rebuttal of Schlick's arguments, however, will not suffice of itself to refute the pseudo-problem theory. The indebtedness to Schlick of most

[6] *Ibid.,* Ch. VII, Section 5, p. 151.

later advocates of the theory may be conceded; but certainly it does not comprehend all of significance that they have to say on the problem. There are recent analyses of the conditions of moral responsibility containing sufficient new matter, or sufficient old matter in a more precise and telling form, to require of us now something of a fresh start. In the section which follows I propose to consider some representative samples of these analyses—all of which, of course, are designed to show that the freedom which moral responsibility implies is not in fact a contra-causal type of freedom.

But before reopening the general question of the nature and conditions of moral responsibility there is a *caveat* which it seems to me worth while to enter. The difficulties in the way of a clear answer are not slight; but they are apt to seem a good deal more formidable than they really are because of a common tendency to consider in unduly close association two distinct questions: the question 'Is a contra-causal type of freedom implied by moral responsibility?' and the question 'Does a contra-causal type of freedom anywhere exist?'. It seems to me that many philosophers (and I suspect that Moritz Schlick is among them) begin their enquiry with so firm a conviction that the contra-causal sort of freedom nowhere exists, that they find it hard to take very seriously the possibility that it is *this* sort of freedom that moral responsibility implies. For they are loth to abandon the commonsense belief that moral responsibility itself is something real. The implicit reasoning I take to be this. Moral responsibility is real. If moral responsibility is real, the freedom implied in it must be a fact. But contra-causal freedom is not a fact. Therefore contra-causal freedom is not the freedom implied in moral responsibility. I think we should be on our guard against allowing this or some similar train of reasoning (whose premises, after all, are far from indubitable) to seduce us into distorting what we actually find when we set about a direct analysis of moral responsibility and its conditions.

III

The pseudo-problem theorists usually, and naturally, develop their analysis of moral responsibility by way of contrast with a view which, while it has enjoyed a good deal of philosophic support, I can perhaps best describe as the common view. It will be well to remind ourselves, therefore, of the main features of this view.

So far as the *meaning,* as distinct from the *conditions,* of moral responsibility is concerned, the common view is very simple. If we ask ourselves whether a certain person is morally responsible for a given act (or it may be just 'in general'), what we are considering, it would be said, is whether or not that person is a fit subject upon whom to pass moral judgment; whether he can fittingly be deemed morally good or bad, morally praiseworthy or blameworthy. This does not take us any great way: but (*pace* Schlick) so far as it goes it does not seem to me seriously disputable. The really interesting and controversial question is about the *conditions* of moral responsibility, and in particular the question whether freedom of a contra-causal kind is among these conditions.

The answer of the common man to the latter question is that it most certainly *is* among the conditions. Why does he feel so sure about this? Not, I argued earlier, because the common man supposes that causal law exercises 'compulsion' in the sense that prescriptive laws do, but simply because he does not see how a person can be deemed morally praiseworthy or blameworthy in respect of an act which he could not help performing. From the stand-point of moral praise and blame, he would say—though not necessarily from other stand-points—it is a matter of indifference whether it is by reason of some external constraint or by reason of his own given nature that the man could not help doing what he did. It is quite enough to make moral praise and blame futile that in either case there were no genuine alternatives, no open possibilities, before the man when he acted. He could not have acted otherwise than he did. And the common man might not unreasonably go on to stress the fact that we all, even if we are linguistic philosophers, do in our actual practice of moral judgment appear to accept the common view. He might insist upon the point alluded to earlier in this paper, that we do all, in passing moral censure, 'make allowances' for influences in a man's hereditary nature or environmental circumstances which we regard as having made it more than ordinarily difficult for him to act otherwise than he did: the implication being that if we supposed that the man's heredity and environment made it not merely very *difficult* but actually *impossible* for him to act otherwise than he did, we could not properly assign moral blame to him at all.

Let us put the argument implicit in the common view a little more sharply. The moral 'ought' implies 'can'. If we say that A morally ought to have done X, we imply that in our opinion, he could have done X. But we assign moral blame to a man only for failing to do what we think he morally ought to have done. Hence if we morally blame A for not having done X, we imply that he could have done X even though in fact he did not. In other words, we imply that A could have acted otherwise than he did. And that means that we imply, as a necessary condition of a man's being morally blameworthy, that he enjoyed a freedom of a kind not compatible with unbroken causal continuity.

IV

Now what is it that is supposed to be wrong with this simple piece of argument?—For, of course, it must be rejected by all these philosophers who tell us that the traditional problem of Free Will is a mere pseudo-problem.

The argument looks as though it were doing little more than reading off necessary implications of the fundamental categories of our moral thinking. One's inclination is to ask 'If one is to think morally at all, how else than this *can* we think?'.

In point of fact, there is pretty general agreement among the contemporary critics as to what is wrong with the argument. Their answer in general terms is as follows. No doubt A's moral responsibility does imply that he could have acted otherwise. But this expression 'could have acted otherwise' stands in dire need of analysis. When we analyse it, we find that it is not, as is so often supposed, simple and unambiguous, and we find that in *some* at least of its possible meanings it implies *no* breach of causal continuity between character and conduct. Having got this clear, we can further discern that only in one of these *latter* meanings is there any compulsion upon our moral thinking to assert that if A is morally blameworthy for an act, A 'could have acted otherwise than he did'. It follows that, contrary to common belief, our moral thinking does *not* require us to posit a contra-causal freedom as a condition of moral responsibility.

So much of importance obviously turns upon the validity or otherwise of this line of criticism that we must examine it in some detail and with express regard to the *ipsissima verba* of the critics.

In the course of a recent article in MIND,[7] entitled 'Free Will and Moral Responsibility', Mr. Nowell Smith (having earlier affirmed his belief that 'the traditional problem has been solved') explains very concisely the nature of the confusion which, as he thinks, has led to the demand for a contra-causal freedom. He begins by frankly recognising that "It is evident that one of the necessary conditions of moral action is that the agent 'could have acted otherwise'" and he adds "it is to this fact that the Libertarian is drawing attention".[8] Then, after showing (unexceptionably, I think) how the relationship of 'ought' to 'can' warrants the proposition which he has accepted as evident, and how it induces the Libertarian to assert the existence of action that is 'uncaused', he proceeds to point out, in a crucial passage, the nature of the Libertarian's error:

> The fallacy in the argument (he contends) lies in supposing that when we say 'A could have acted otherwise' we mean that A, *being what he was and being placed in the circumstances in which he was placed,* could have done something other than what he did. But in fact we never do mean this.[9]

What then *do* we mean here by 'A could have acted otherwise'? Mr. Nowell Smith does not tell us in so many words, but the passage I have quoted leaves little doubt how he would answer. What we really mean by the expression, he implies, is not a *categorical* but a *hypothetical* proposition.

[7] January, 1948. (This article is reprinted above, beginning on p. 460.—Eds.)
[8] *Ibid.*, p. 49 (p. 465, above.—Eds.)
[9] *Ibid.* (p. 465, above.—Eds.)

We mean 'A could have acted otherwise, *if he did not happen to be what he in fact was,* or *if he were placed in circumstances other than those in which he was in fact placed'.* Now, *these* propositions, it is easy to see, are in no way incompatible with acceptance of the causal principle in its full rigour. Accordingly the claim that our fundamental moral thinking obliges us to assert a contra-causal freedom as a condition of moral responsibility is disproved.

Such is the 'analytical solution' of our problem offered (with obvious confidence) by one able philosopher of to-day, and entirely representative of the views of many other able philosophers. Yet I make bold to say that its falsity stares one in the face. It seems perfectly plain that the hypothetical propositions which Mr. Nowell Smith proposes to substitute for the categorical proposition cannot express 'what we really mean' in this context by 'A could have acted otherwise', for the simple reason that these hypothetical propositions have no bearing whatsoever upon the question of the moral responsibility of *A*. And it is *A* whose moral responsibility we are talking about—a definite person *A* with a definitive character and in a definitive set of circumstances. What conceivable significance could it have for our attitude to A's responsibility to know that someone with a *different* character (or *A* with a different character, if that collocation of words has any meaning), or A in a different set of circumstances from those in which A as we are concerned with him was in fact placed, 'could have acted otherwise'? No doubt this supposititious being *could* have acted otherwise than the definitive person A acted. But the point is that where we are reflecting, as we are supposed in this context to be reflecting, upon the question of *A*'s moral responsibility, our interest in this supposititious being is precisely *nil*.

The two hypothetical propositions suggested in Mr. Nowell Smith's account of the matter do not, however, exhaust the speculations that have been made along these lines. Another very common suggestion by the analysts is that what we really mean by 'A could have acted otherwise' is 'A could have acted otherwise *if he had willed, or chosen, otherwise'.* This was among the suggestions offered by G. E. Moore in the well-known chapter on Free Will in his *Ethics.* It is, I think, the suggestion he most strongly favoured: though it is fair to add that neither about this nor about any other of his suggestions is Moore in the least dogmatic. He does claim, for, I think, convincing reasons, that "we *very often* mean by 'could' merely 'would, *if* so-and-so had chosen' ".[10] And he concludes "I must confess that I cannot feel certain that this may not be all that we usually mean and understand by the assertion that we have Free Will".[11]

This third hypothetical proposition appears to enjoy also the support of Mr. C. L. Stevenson. Mr. Stevenson begins the chapter of *Ethics and Language* entitled 'Avoidability-Indeterminism' with the now familiar pro-

[10] *Ethics*, p. 212.
[11] *Ibid.*, p. 217.

nouncement of his School that 'controversy about freedom and determinism of the will . . . presents no permanent difficulty to ethics, being largely a product of confusions'. A major confusion (if I understand him rightly) he takes to lie in the meaning of the term 'avoidable', when we say 'A's action was avoidable'—or, I presume, 'A could have acted otherwise'. He himself offers the following definition of 'avoidable'—" 'A's action was avoidable' has the meaning of 'If A had made a certain choice, which in fact he did not make, his action would not have occurred' ".[12] This I think we may regard as in substance identical with the suggestion that what we really mean by 'A could have acted otherwise' is 'A could have acted otherwise *if* he had chosen (or willed) otherwise'. For clarity's sake we shall here keep to this earlier formulation. In either formulation the special significance of the third hypothetical proposition, as of the two hypothetical propositions already considered, is that it is compatible with strict determinism. If this be indeed all that we mean by the 'freedom' that conditions moral responsibility, then those philosophers are certainly wrong who hold that moral freedom is of the contra-causal type.

Now this third hypothetical proposition does at least possess the merit, not shared by its predecessors, of having a real relevance to the question of moral responsibility. If, *e.g.* A had promised to meet us at 2 p.m., and he chanced to break his leg at 1 p.m., we should not blame him for his failure to discharge his promise. For we should be satisfied that he *could not* have acted otherwise, even if he had so chosen; or *could not*, at any rate, in a way which would have enabled him to meet us at 2 p.m. The freedom to translate one's choice into action, which we saw earlier is for Schlick the *only* freedom required for moral responsibility, is without doubt *one* of the conditions of moral responsibility.

But it seems easy to show that this third hypothetical proposition does not exhaust what we mean, and *some*times is not even *part* of what we mean, by the expression 'could have acted otherwise' in its moral context. Thus it can hardly be even part of what we mean in the case of that class of wrong actions (and it is a large class) concerning which there is really no question whether the agent could have acted otherwise, *if* he had chosen otherwise. Take lying, for example. Only in some very abnormal situation could it occur to one to doubt whether A, whose power of speech was evinced by his telling a lie, was in a position to tell what he took to be the truth *if* he had so chosen. Of *course* he was. Yet it still makes good sense for one's moral thinking to ask whether A, when lying, 'could have acted otherwise': and we still require an affirmative answer to this question if A's moral blameworthiness is to be established. It seems apparent, therefore, that in this class of cases at any rate one does *not* mean by 'A could have acted otherwise', 'A could have acted otherwise *if* he had so chosen'.

[12] *Ethics and Language*, p. 298.

What then *does* one mean in this class of cases by 'A could have acted otherwise'? I submit that the expression is taken in its simple, categorical meaning, without any suppressed 'if' clause to qualify it. Or perhaps, in order to keep before us the important truth that it is only as expressions of *will* or *choice* that acts are of moral import, it might be better to say that a condition of A's moral responsibility is that he could have *chosen* otherwise. We saw that there is no real question whether A who told a lie could have acted otherwise *if* he had chosen otherwise. But there is a very real question, at least for any person who approaches the question of moral responsibility at a tolerably advanced level of reflexion, about whether A could have *chosen* otherwise. Such a person will doubtless be acquainted with the claims advanced in some quarters that causal law operates universally: or/and with the theories of some philosophies that the universe is throughout the expression of a single supreme principle; or/and with the doctrines of some theologians that the world is created, sustained and governed by an Omniscient and Omnipotent Being. Very understandably such world-views awaken in him doubts about the validity of his first, easy, instinctive assumption that there are genuinely open possibilities before a man at the moment of moral choice. It thus becomes for him a real question whether a man could have chosen otherwise than he actually did, and, in consequence, whether man's moral responsibility is really defensible. For how can a man be morally responsible, he asks himself, if his choices, like all other events in the universe, could not have been otherwise than they in fact were? It is precisely against the background of world-views such as these that for reflective people the problem of moral responsibility normally arises.

Furthermore, to the man who has attained this level of reflexion, it will in *no* class of cases be a sufficient condition of moral responsibility for an act that one could have acted otherwise *if* one had chosen otherwise—not even in these cases where there *was* some possibility of the operation of 'external constraint'. In these cases he will, indeed expressly recognise freedom from external constraint as a *necessary condition,* but not as a *sufficient* condition. For he will be aware that, even granted *this* freedom, it is still conceivable that the agent had no freedom to choose otherwise than he did, and he will therefore require that the latter sort of freedom be added if moral responsibility for the act is to be established.

I have been contending that, for persons at a *tolerably advanced level of reflexion,* 'A could have acted otherwise', as a condition of A's moral responsibility, means 'A could have chosen otherwise'. The qualification italicised is of some importance. The unreflective or unsophisticated person, the ordinary 'man in the street', who does not know or much care what scientists and theologians and philosophers have said about the world, sees well enough that A is morally responsible only if he could have acted otherwise, but in his intellectual innocence he will, very probably, envisage nothing capable of preventing A from having acted otherwise except some material impediment—like the broken leg in the example above. Accordingly, for the unreflective person, 'A could have acted otherwise', as a condition of moral responsibility, *is* apt to mean no more than 'A could have acted otherwise *if* he had so chosen'.

It would appear, then, that the view now favoured by many philosophers, that the freedom required for moral responsibility is merely freedom from external constraint, is a view which they share only with the less reflective type of layman. Yet it should be plain that on a matter of this sort the view of the unreflective person is of little value by comparison with the view of the reflective person. There are some contexts, no doubt, in which lack of sophistication is an asset. But this is not one of them. The question at issue here is as to the kind of impediments which might have prevented a man from acting otherwise than he in fact did: and on this question knowledge and reflexion are surely prerequisites of any answer that is worth listening to. It is simply on account of the limitations of his mental vision that the unreflective man interprets the expression 'could have acted otherwise', in its context as a condition of moral responsibility, solely in terms of external constraint. He has failed (as yet) to reach the intellectual level at which one takes into account the implications for moral choices of the world-views of science, religion, and philosophy. If on a matter of this complexity the philosopher finds that his analysis accords with the utterances of the uneducated he has, I suggest, better cause for uneasiness than for self-congratulation.

This concludes the main part of what it seems to me necessary to say in answer to the pseudo-problem theorists. My object so far has been to expose the falsity of those innovations (chiefly Positivist) in the way of argument and analysis which are supposed by many to have made it impossible any longer to formulate the problem of Free Will in the traditional manner. My contention is that, at least so far as these innovations are concerned, the simple time-honoured argument still holds from the nature of the moral ought to the conclusion that moral responsibility implies a contra-causal type of freedom.

. . .

V

[It is sometimes argued that a] contra-causal freedom, . . . such as is implied in the 'categorical' interpretation of the proposition 'A could have chosen otherwise than he did', posits a breach of causal continuity between a man's character and his conduct. Now apart from the general presumption in favour of the universality of causal law, there are special reasons for disallowing the breach that is here alleged. It is the common assumption of social intercourse that our acquaintances will act 'in character'; that their choices will exhibit the 'natural' response of their characters to the given situation. And this assumption seems to be amply substantiated, over a wide range of conduct, by the actual success which attends predictions made on this basis. Where there should be, on the contra-causal hypothesis, chaotic variability, there is found in fact a large measure of intelligible continuity. Moreover, what is the alternative to admitting that a person's choices flow from his character? Surely just that the so-called 'choice' is not *that person's* choice at all: that, relatively to the person concerned, it is a mere 'accident'. Now we cannot really believe this. But if it *were* the case, it would certainly not help to establish *moral* freedom, the freedom required for *moral* responsibility. For clearly a man cannot be morally responsible for an act which does not express his own choice but is, on the contrary, attributable simply to chance.

These are clearly considerations worthy of all respect. It is not surprising if they have played a big part in persuading people to respond sympathetically to the view that 'Free Will', in its usual contra-causal formulation, is a pseudo-problem. A full answer to them is obviously not practicable in what is little more than an appendix to the body of this paper; but I am hopeful that something can be said, even in a little space, to show that they are very far from being as conclusive against a contra-causal freedom as they are often supposed to be.

To begin with the less troublesome of the two main objections indicated—the objection that the break in causal continuity which free will involves is inconsistent with the predictability of conduct on the basis of the agent's known character. All that is necessary to meet this objection, I suggest, is the frank recognition, which is perfectly open to the Libertarian, that there is a wide area of human conduct, determinable on clear general principles, within which free will does not effectively operate. The most important of these general principles (I have no space to deal here with the others) has often enough been stated by Libertarians. Free will does not operate in these practical situations in which no conflict arises in the agent's mind between what he conceives to be his 'duty' and what he feels to be his 'strongest desire'. It does not operate here because there just is no occasion for it to operate. There is no reason whatever why the agent should here even contemplate choosing any course other than that prescribed by his strongest desire. In all such situations, therefore, he naturally wills in accordance with strongest desire. But his 'strongest desire' is simply the specific *ad hoc* expression of that system of conative and emotive dispositions which we call his 'character'. In all such situations, therefore, whatever may be the case elsewhere, his will is in effect determined by his character as so far formed. Now when we bear in mind that there are an almost immeasurably greater number of situations in a man's life that conform to *this* pattern than there are situations in which an agent is aware of a conflict between strongest desire and duty, it is apparent that a Libertarianism which accepts the limitation of free will to the *latter* type of situation is not open to the stock objection on the score of 'predictability'. For there still remains a vast area of human behaviour in which prediction on the basis of known character may be expected to succeed: an area which will accommodate without difficulty, I think, all these empirical facts about successful prediction which the critic is apt to suppose fatal to Free Will.

So far as I can see, such a delimitation of the field of effective free will denies to the Libertarian absolutely nothing which matters to him. For it is precisely that small sector of the field of choices which our principle of delimitation still leaves open to free will—the sector in which strongest desire clashes with duty—that is crucial for moral responsibility. It is, I believe, with respect to such situations, and in the last resort to such situations alone, that the agent himself recognises that moral praise and blame are appropriate. They are appropriate, according as he does or does not 'rise to duty' in the face of opposing desires; always granted, that is, that he is free to choose between these courses as genuinely open possibilities. If the reality of freedom be conceded *here,* everything is conceded that the Libertarian has any real interest in securing.

But, of course, the most vital question is, can the reality of freedom be conceded even here? In particular, can the standard objection be met which we stated, that if the person's choice does not, in these situations as elsewhere, flow from his *character,* then it is not *that person's* choice at all.

This is, perhaps, of all the objections to a contra-causal freedom, the one which is generally felt to be the most conclusive. For the assumption upon which it is based, *viz.* that no intelligible meaning can attach to the claim that an act which is not an expression of the self's *character* may nevertheless be the *self's* act, is apt to be regarded as self-evident. The Libertarian is accordingly charged with being in effect an *In*determinist, whose 'free will', in so far as it does not flow from the agent's character, can only be a matter of 'chance'. Has the Libertarian—who invariably repudiates this charge and claims to be a *Self*-determinist—any way of showing that, contrary to the assumption of his critics, we *can* meaningfully talk of an act as the self's act even though, in an important sense, it is not an expression of the self's 'character'?

I think that he has. I want to suggest that what prevents the critics from finding a meaning in this way of talking is that they are looking for it in the wrong way; or better, perhaps, with the wrong orientation. They are looking for it from the standpoint of the *external observer;* the stand-point proper to, because alone possible for, apprehension of the physical world. Now from the external stand-point we may observe processes of change. But one thing which, by common consent, *cannot* be observed from without is *creative activity.* Yet—and here lies the crux of the whole matter—it is precisely creative activity which we are trying to understand when we are trying to understand what is traditionally designated by 'free will'. For if there should be an act which is genuinely the self's act and is nevertheless not an expression of its character, such an act, in which the self 'transcends' its character as so far formed, would seem to be essentially of the nature of creative activity. It follows that to look for a meaning in 'free will' from the external stand-point is absurd. It is to look for it in a way that ensures that it will not be found. Granted that a creative activity of any kind is at least *possible* (and I know of no ground for its *a priori* rejection), there is one way, and one way only, in which we can hope to apprehend it, and that is from the *inner* stand-point of direct participation.

It seems to me therefore, that if the Libertarian's claim to find a meaning in a 'free' will which is genuinely the self's will, though not an expression of the self's character, is to be subjected to any test that is worth applying, that test must be undertaken from the inner stand-point. We ought to place ourselves imaginatively at the stand-point of the agent engaged in the typical moral situation in which free will is claimed, and ask ourselves whether from *this* stand-point the claim in question does or does not have meaning for us. That the appeal must be to introspection is no doubt unfortunate. But he would be a very doctrinaire critic of introspection who declined to make use of it when in the nature of the case no other means of apprehension is available. Everyone must make the introspective experiment for himself: but I may perhaps venture to report, though at this late stage with extreme brevity, what I at least seem to find when I make the experiment myself.

In the situation of moral conflict, then, I (as agent) have before my mind a course of action X, which I believe to be my duty; and also a course of action Y, incompatible with X, which I feel to be that which I most strongly desire. Y is, as it is sometimes expressed, 'in the line of least resistance' for me—the course which I am aware I should take if I let my purely desiring nature operate without hindrance. It is the course towards which I am aware that my *character*, as so far formed, naturally inclines me. Now, as actually engaged in this situation, I find that I cannot help believing that I *can* rise to duty and choose X; the 'rising to duty' being effected by what is commonly called 'effort of will'. And I further find, if I ask myself just what it is I am believing when I believe that I 'can' rise to duty, that I cannot help believing that it lies with me here and now, quite absolutely, which of two genuinely open possibilities I adopt; whether, that is, I make the effort of will and choose X, or, on the other hand, let my desiring nature, my character as so far formed, 'have its way', and choose Y, the course 'in the line of least resistance'. These beliefs may, of course, be illusory, but that is not at present in point. For the present argument all that matters is whether beliefs of this sort are in fact discoverable in the moral agent in the situation of 'moral temptation'. For my own part, I cannot doubt the introspective evidence that they are.

Now here is the vital point. No matter which course, X or Y, I choose in this situation, I cannot doubt, *qua* practical being engaged in it, that my choice is *not* just the expression of my formed character, and yet *is* a choice made by my *self*. For suppose I make the effort and choose X (my 'duty'). Since my very purpose in making the 'effort' is to enable me to act against the existing 'set' of desire, which is the expression of my character as so far formed, I cannot possibly regard the act itself as the expression of my *character*. On the other hand, introspection makes it equally clear that I am certain that it is *I* who choose: that the act is not an 'accident', but is genuinely *my* act. Or suppose that I choose Y (the end of 'strongest desire'). The course chosen here is, it is true, in conformity with my 'character'. But since I find myself unable to doubt that I *could* have made the effort and chosen X, I cannot possibly regard the choice of Y as *just* the expression of my character. Yet here again I find that I cannot doubt that the choice is *my* choice, a choice for which *I* am justly to be blamed.

What this amounts to is that I *can* and *do* attach meaning, *qua* moral agent, to an act which is not the self's character and yet is genuinely the self's act. And having no good reason to suppose that other persons have a fundamentally different mental constitution, it seems to me probable that anyone else who undertakes a similar experiment will be obliged to submit a similar report. I conclude, therefore, that the argument against 'free will' on the score of its 'meaninglessness' must be held to fail. 'Free Will' does have meaning; though, because it is of the nature of a creative activity, its meaning is discoverable only in an intuition of the practical consciousness of the participating agent. To the agent making a moral choice in the situation where duty clashes with desire, his 'self' is known to him as a creatively active self, a self which declines to be identified with his 'character' as so formed. Not, of course, that the self's character—let it be added to obviate misunderstanding—either is, or is supposed by the agent to be, devoid of bearing upon his choices, even in the 'sector' in which free will is held to operate. On the contrary, such a bearing is manifest in the empirically verifiable fact that we find it 'harder' (as we say) to make the effort of will required to 'rise to duty' in proportion to the extent that the 'dutiful' course conflicts with the course to which our character as so far formed inclines us. It is only in the polemics of the critics that a 'free' will is supposed to be incompatible with recognising the bearing of 'character' upon choice.

"But what" (it may be asked) "of the all-important question of the *value* of this 'subjective certainty'? Even if what you say is sound as 'phenomenology', is there any reason to suppose that the conviction on which you lay so much stress is in fact *true?*" I agree that the question is important; far more important, indeed, than is always realised, for it is not always realised that the only direct evidence there *could* be for a creative activity like 'free will' is an intuition of the practical consciousness. But this question falls outside the purview of the present paper. The aim of the paper has not been to offer a constructive defence of free will. It has been to show that the problem as traditionally posed is a real, and not a pseudo, problem. A serious threat to that thesis, it was acknowledged, arises from the apparent difficulty of attaching meaning to an act which is not the expression of the self's character and yet *is* the self's own act. The object of my brief phenomenological analysis was to provide evidence that such an act *does* have meaning for us in the one context in which there is any sense in *expecting* it to have meaning.

VI

My general conclusion is, I fear, very unexciting. It is merely that it is an error to suppose that the 'Free Will' problem, when correctly formulated, turns out not to be a 'problem' at all. Labouring to reinstate an old problem is dull work enough. But I am disposed to think that the philosophic situation to-day calls for a good deal more dull work of a similar sort.

QUESTIONS

1. Professor Campbell says that Schlick's distinction between prescriptive and descriptive laws has no bearing at all upon the truth or falsity of the common assumptions about the conditions that must exist if a man is to be held morally responsible for what he does. Explain why you agree or disagree with Campbell on this point.
2. What are Professor Campbell's arguments in support of his claim that "we do commonly demand the contra-causal sort of freedom as a condition of moral responsibility"? Assess the validity of these arguments.
3. Compare Professor Campbell's understanding of what it means to say that a person "could have done otherwise than he did" with the analysis of this phrase given by Professor Nowell-Smith in the preceding reading. Is the issue between them decidable in any way? If so, show how. If not, explain why not.
4. What answer does Professor Campbell give to the objection that "the break in causal continuity which free will involves is inconsistent with the predictability of conduct on the basis of the agent's known character"? State why you think his answer is or is not satisfactory.
5. What does Professor Campbell mean by "an act which is not the self's character and yet is genuinely the self's act"? What conclusions regarding free will does he draw from his statements about such an act? How cogent is his argument?
6. How would you go about deciding whether any problem in philosophy is a pseudo-problem? Apply your method to the problem of free will.

SUGGESTED FURTHER READING

CLASSIC WORKS

Aquinas, St. Thomas, *Summa Theologica* (1265–72), First Part of the Second Part, Questions 6–10, 12–14, 17–20. This material is contained in *The Basic Writings of St. Thomas Aquinas,* Random House, New York, Vol. 1, Chap. XI.
Aristotle, *Nicomachean Ethics,* Book III, Chaps. 1–5.

Hobbes, Thomas, *Leviathan* (1651), Chap. XXI; *Of Liberty and Necessity* (1654).
James, William, "The Dilemma of Determinism" (1884), reprinted in *Essays in Faith and Morals,* by William James.
Mill, John Stuart, *A System of Logic* (1843), Book VI, Chap. 2.
Spinoza, Benedict de, *Ethics* (1678), Parts IV and V. See also *The Philosophy of Spinoza,* Random House, New York, Chaps. XI, XIV, XV, and XIX.

INTRODUCTORY STUDIES

Ayer, A. J., "Freedom and Necessity," *Polemic,* No. 5, 1946. Reprinted in *Philosophical Essays,* by A. J. Ayer, Macmillan, London, 1954.
Brandt, R. B., *Ethical Theory,* Prentice-Hall, Englewood Cliffs, N.J., 1959, Chap. 20.
Cranston, M., *Freedom—A New Analysis,* Longmans, Green, London, 1953.
Hobart, R. E., "Free Will as Involving Determination and Inconceivable Without It," *Mind,* Vol. 43, 1934.
Hospers, John, *Human Conduct,* Harcourt, Brace, & World, New York, 1961, Chap. 10.
Moore, G. E., *Ethics,* Oxford University Press, London, 1912.
Morgenbesser, S., and J. Walsh, eds., *Free Will,* Prentice-Hall, Englewood Cliffs, N.J., 1962. (Anthology.)
Peters, R. S., *Authority, Responsibility and Education,* Allen & Unwin, London, 1959, Part II.
Raab, F. V., "Free Will and the Ambiguity of 'Could,'" *Philosophical Review,* Vol. 64, 1955.
Schlick, M., *Problems of Ethics,* trans., D. Rynin, Prentice-Hall, Englewood Cliffs, N.J., 1939, Chap. VII.
Sellars, W., and J. Hospers, eds., *Readings in Ethical Theory,* Appleton-Century-Crofts, New York, 1952, Sec. VII. (Anthology.)
Wilson, John, "Freedom and Compulsion," *Mind,* Vol. 67, 1958.
Wood, Ledger, "The Free Will Controversy," *Philosophy,* Vol. 16, 1941.

ADVANCED STUDIES

Adler, Mortimer J., *The Idea of Freedom,* Doubleday, Garden City, N.Y., 1958 and 1961. (Historical survey.)
Campbell, C. A., *Scepticism and Construction,* Allen & Unwin, London, 1931, Chaps. IV and V.
———, *On Selfhood and Godhood,* Allen & Unwin, London, 1957, Lecture IX and Appendix B.
Canfield, John, "The Compatibility of Free Will and Determinism," *Philosophical Review,* Vol. 71, 1962.
Farrer, Austin, *The Freedom of the Will,* Black, London, 1958.
Hampshire, S., W. G. Maclagen, and R. M. Hare, "The Freedom of the Will" (symposium), *Aristotelian Society Supplementary Volume 25,* Harrison & Sons, London, 1951.
Hook, Sidney, ed., *Determinism and Freedom in the Age of Modern Science,* New York University Press, New York, 1958, and Collier Books, New York, 1961. (Collection of symposium papers.)
Lehrer, Keith, "Doing the Impossible," *Australasian Journal of Philosophy,* Vol. 42, 1964.
Morris, Herbert, ed., *Freedom and Responsibility: Readings in Philosophy and Law,* Stanford University Press, Stanford, Calif., 1961. (Anthology.)

Nowell-Smith, P. H., *Ethics,* Penguin Books, Harmondsworth, Middlesex, Eng., 1954, Chaps. 19 and 20.

——, "Determinists and Libertarians," *Mind,* Vol. 63, 1954.

Ofstad, H., *An Inquiry into the Freedom of Decision,* Allen & Unwin, London, 1961.

Pears, D. F., ed., *Freedom and the Will,* Macmillan, London, 1963. (Anthology.)

Taylor, Richard, "Deliberation and Foreknowledge," *American Philosophical Quarterly,* Vol. 1, 1964.

Vivian, F., *Human Freedom and Responsibility,* Chatto & Windus, London, 1964.

Chapter 10. Moral Knowledge

WHAT IS MORALITY?

All of us possess standards of right and wrong which we acquired in childhood when our parents told us what we ought and ought not to do, when they showed their approval and disapproval, and when they rewarded and punished us. In giving us this moral guidance our parents were committing themselves, whether they were aware of it or not, to certain answers to the fundamental questions of human behavior: How should I live? What sort of person ought I to try to become? What is my duty to others and to myself? What kinds of actions are right and what kinds are wrong? Similarly, we commit ourselves to specific answers to these questions when we bring up our own children. But despite this early moral training which we all receive, we sometimes find ourselves in situations where we are not sure what we ought to do, and in our mature life we may occasionally try to find our own answers to moral questions. To reflect about such questions is to examine the principles on which our practical lives are based. The attempt to find acceptable answers to such questions is the ultimate aim of moral philosophy.

Moral questions are, of course, not the only kind of practical questions. Consider the difference between asking, "How should I live?" and asking, "What should I do in order to increase the profits of my business?" Or to take another example, consider the difference between telling a person who is learning to play baseball what the duties of a catcher are, and telling a person what his moral duty is. What is the difference? What makes a question or a statement a moral one? Perhaps the best way to answer this is by saying that moral questions are those which we answer by citing moral rules and moral standards; moral statements are those which, when challenged, we defend the same way. A *moral rule* (sometimes called a moral principle) is a rule which we believe ought to govern the conduct of human beings as human beings, in contrast to the special rules which govern the conduct of human beings as business executives, baseball players, dinner guests, or automobile drivers. The rules of successful business practice, of baseball, of etiquette, and of traffic are none of them moral rules, although they may sometimes prescribe the same actions as are prescribed by moral rules. We would not say that a baseball player was morally obligated to leave the batter's box after striking out, although we would say that he was morally obligated not to throw the game. The act of deliberately losing a baseball game is morally wrong, not because it violates any rule of the game, but because it violates the obligation of all human beings to be honest. A moral rule, then, may be defined as a rule which we expect every human being to follow, simply because he is a human being.

Similarly, a *moral standard* is a standard for judging a good way of life, rather than for judging a good way of swimming, studying, or playing chess. Such a standard determines the conditions that must be fulfilled if one is to be a good man, not the conditions for being a good swimmer, a good student, or a good chess player. As such, a moral standard is a norm which all men ought to try to live up to. *Moral ideals* are simply those concepts of moral perfection that we have when we imagine a person's character as completely fulfilling our moral standards, or a person's conduct as always being in accordance with our moral rules. In each case we are judging a person's character or conduct simply with respect to his being a human being among other human beings, and not with respect to any special role which he might have in practical life.

From these definitions we see that the moral aspect of any rule, ideal, or standard of human conduct is its claim to universal applicability, that is, its claim to apply to all human beings everywhere and at all times. For to say that a moral rule governs the conduct of human beings as human beings is to say that it is a rule which all human beings everywhere and at all times ought to follow. (This is not, however, the same as saying that all human beings everywhere and at all times actually do follow it, or even that they actually believe they ought to follow it.) Thus if we state that the rule, "In ordinary circumstances it is wrong to lie," is a moral rule, we imply that in ordinary circumstances *no* human being ought to lie. The same thing may be said of moral ideals and moral standards. If we point to the life of Abraham Lincoln or of some other historical figure as exemplifying a moral ideal, we are making the implicit value judgment that all human beings ought to try to imitate such a life. And to say, for example, that the standard for determining whether an action is morally right or wrong is whether or not it leads to the general happiness of mankind, is to say that such a standard ought to be adopted universally, and that it is the standard which does distinguish the moral rightness and wrongness of all actions of all men everywhere.

THE PROBLEM OF MORAL KNOWLEDGE

The problem of moral knowledge arises when we investigate the possibility of justifying this claim to universality. Suppose a person who asks us a moral question or who challenges our

moral judgments is not satisfied with our answer because he is unwilling to accept, as universally binding on all men, the rules, ideals, or standards to which we appeal. Or suppose that we ourselves begin to question the universal applicability of the very rules, ideals, or standards with which we have grown up and which constitute the moral code of our society. At this point we must decide whether we should continue to accept or whether we should reject those rules, ideals, and standards as genuinely moral, i.e., as applicable to all men everywhere. We are forced to examine the basis on which we have previously justified our moral judgments. And this means we must examine the grounds on which our moral knowledge rests. To do this in a clear and systematic way is to do moral philosophy.

The task of moral philosophy is to solve the problem of moral knowledge, that is, to answer the question, "How do we know what rules, ideals, and standards are applicable to all men?" This question demands that we find out, first, whether there is any basis for the justification of moral claims, and second, if there is such a basis, what it consists in. Moral philosophers have disputed about both parts of this problem. Some have denied any basis for justifying moral claims, while others have asserted that there is such a basis. But among the latter there has been fundamental disagreement about what constitutes a valid basis.

The denial of any basis for justifying moral claims is sometimes called *ethical relativism*. According to this point of view there are no rules, ideals, or standards of human conduct that can justifiably be applied to all men everywhere. Within a given society which accepts a certain set of rules, ideals, and standards, these may be applied to the individual members of the society. But there is no justification for applying them to individuals outside the society. Ethical relativism is to be contrasted with the opposite point of view known as *ethical absolutism,* according to which there are rules, ideals, and standards that are genuinely moral, i.e., applicable to all men in all societies.

ETHICAL RELATIVISM AND THE FACTS OF ETHICAL RELATIVITY

One of the arguments which ethical relativists give in support of their position is based on certain findings in history, psychology, and the social sciences. These findings may be summed up in the following three statements of fact: (1) There exists great variation in the rules, ideals, and standards accepted by different societies at different times in history. (2) Most human beings are ethnocentric, i.e., they believe the rules, ideals, and standards of their own society to be the only true ones. (3) The conscience and moral beliefs of every person come from his social environment. Let us consider these three facts briefly and see how they are claimed to provide a "scientific proof" of ethical relativism.

Through the studies of historians and anthropologists we learn that in some societies slavery has been approved of and in others it has been disapproved of, that some societies have practiced human sacrifice and others have condemned such a practice. We observe that some people have seen nothing wrong in having children work twelve hours a day in coal mines, while others have led reform movements against such "wrongs." We find that in one society public nakedness is considered a very shameful thing, while in another society it is practiced by everyone and considered perfectly proper.

We also find that in each society most people are absolutely sure that their own view of what is right and wrong represents the one true morality. The phenomenon of ethnocentrism is to be observed in the most diverse societies. People everywhere tend to think that their own way of life is superior to all others and that their own moral rules, ideals, and standards are the only acceptable ones. This trait is most pronounced in people who lead provincial lives. We may have noticed complacent, conventional people in our own communities who never have any doubts about their moral beliefs because their lives have brought them into contact only with people who agree with them.

Finally, we learn from psychology that the process by which all people acquire their moral convictions is

the process of "introjection" or incorporation into one's own mind of the precepts and moral attitudes of others, particularly of one's parents or of other persons *in loco parentis* in one's youth. As a result of this process, the attitudes of impressive persons in one's early environment (and to some extent throughout life) become a permanent part of one's own mental structure, become "second nature," as the popular expression has it. Through this process, too, moral standards and conventions become handed on from one generation to another, thus giving permanence and stability to the codes and traditions of society.[1]

Now the ethical relativists take these three facts to mean that the moral judgments of a given society are "relative"

[1] J. C. Flugel, *Man, Morals and Society,* International Universities Press, New York, 1945, p. 35. For a more detailed analysis of how we learn moral principles, see the selection by R. M. Hare in this chapter.

to the rules, ideals, and standards accepted by that society, and that those rules, ideals, and standards are themselves "relative" to that society in the sense that they can be applied only in that society. Consequently, the code of one society cannot be judged as better or worse than the code of another. There are no absolute standards of comparison since all standards are "relative" to the society in which they are "introjected" and handed on from one generation to the next. Therefore no code is universally applicable to all men. It follows that the very same kind of action which is right in one society may be wrong in another, that what are vices to us may be virtues to others, and so on. A moral judgment which we believe to be true (e.g., "genocide is wrong") is true only relatively to our own standards. The same judgment will be false relatively to other standards. A person can be said to make a mistake in his moral judgments only in the sense that they do not conform to the accepted code of his society. Thus we must say that for Nazis the judgment that all Jews ought to be exterminated was a correct moral judgment since it conformed to the code of Nazism. In our society, however, the same judgment would be false. To claim that the entire code of Nazism was mistaken, or even to claim that it was morally inferior to another code, is to set up one code as an absolute standard, and this is never justifiable. All standards and ideals come from one social environment or another. Therefore it is nothing but narrow-minded dogmatism to apply one code to all men in all societies. According to the ethical relativist, when we say that a person knows what is right and wrong all we can possibly mean is that the person knows how to apply the particular rules, ideals, and standards of his own society in making moral judgments. We cannot go farther and claim that the person is justified in accepting those rules, ideals, and standards. For ethical relativism, then, there are no grounds for a universal moral code.

ETHICAL ABSOLUTISM

The ethical absolutist, on the other hand, claims that there is one true set of moral rules, ideals, and standards which apply to all men in all societies. According to this view, people can be correct or mistaken not only in their moral judgments, but also in their rules, ideals, and standards, since one moral code may be superior to another.

It is important not to confuse ethical absolutism with ethnocentrism, dogmatism, or intolerance. The ethical absolutist theoretically need not be ethnocentric, dogmatic, or intolerant, although historically he has often been all three. The ethical absolutist may well believe, contrary to ethnocentrism, that the code of his own society is not as advanced, as enlightened, or as justified as that of some other society. Or he may have constructed in his own thought an ideal moral code which he believes is superior to any existing code, including the one in which he himself was morally educated. But he may hold his belief with some degree of doubt. He may be somewhat uncertain whether one code (either actually existing or mentally constructed) is really better than another. Indeed, to the extent that the ethical absolutist seeks reasons for accepting one code and rejecting another, and to the extent that the reasons which he finds do not yield certainty, he will be undogmatic and skeptical, holding his belief only to some degree of probability. In short, ethical absolutism without ethical dogmatism is the view *that* there are moral truths without certainty as to *what* they are. Finally the ethical absolutist may want to tolerate all sorts of moral beliefs and practices, since he may be in doubt about whether his own are really superior to those of others. He may place a high value on tolerance as a social condition necessary for carrying on the search for the most enlightened moral code. Or he may simply believe in tolerance itself as a true moral virtue and a basic principle of an ideal society. The ethical relativist, on the other hand, though often identified as the supreme advocate of tolerance, cannot in fact claim that tolerance is really a good thing since there are societies which neither practice nor preach tolerance, and in totalitarian societies tolerance is actually an evil. To be consistent the relativist must, therefore, say that tolerance is good only in a democratic type of society, but is bad in a totalitarian society.

THE FACTS OF ETHICAL RELATIVITY AS COMPATIBLE WITH BOTH RELATIVISM AND ABSOLUTISM

Is not ethical absolutism clearly false in light of the three facts which the relativist takes as a proof of the relativity of all moral judgments and of all moral codes? The answer is "No," for the following reason. The ethical absolutist can perfectly well accept all three facts without contradicting his own position. We must not confuse *the facts of ethical relativity* with *the theory of ethical relativism*. The fact that people disagree in their moral judgments and codes does not imply that they are all equally justified (or unjustified) in accepting those judgments and codes, or that there is no way to decide which of them are correct and which are mistaken. To show that what one society *believes* to be right another society *believes* to be wrong is by no means to show that what *is* right in one society

is wrong in another. The relativist's conclusion would follow only under the assumption that an action is right or wrong because it is thought to be right or wrong, and this assumption cannot be taken for granted without further proof. Similarly, the fact that each society maintains that its own moral code is the only true one does not imply that each society is justified in maintaining this. And we must remember that the absolutist himself is not necessarily ethnocentric. Finally, the fact that all moral beliefs come from the social environment has nothing to do with whether or not there are valid grounds for holding them. The grounds which justify a belief are not the same as its psychological causes or origins. We conclude, therefore, that the three facts of ethical relativity are equally compatible with ethical relativism and ethical absolutism.

The real difference between the two ethical theories concerns the possibility of finding grounds on the basis of which, not only moral judgments, but also moral rules, ideals, and standards can be justified. If moral judgments can be justified only on the grounds of rules, ideals, and standards which are themselves without any sort of justification, then ethical relativism is true. On the other hand, if we can justify the acceptance of a set of rules, ideals, and standards as universally binding on all men, then the possibility of ethical absolutism is established. But the full argument for ethical absolutism requires that we state how this can be done, that we state, in other words, how we can obtain genuine knowledge of a universally applicable moral code.

ARGUMENTS FOR AND AGAINST ETHICAL RELATIVISM AND ABSOLUTISM

Perhaps the strongest argument against ethical absolutism (and for ethical relativism) in recent moral philosophy is based on the idea that moral judgments are not really judgments at all, but are merely "emotive" utterances which express the attitudes of those who utter them. (See Ayer's "The Emotive Theory" in this chapter.) If one can show that there are no grounds on the basis of which an attitude can ultimately be justified and if, as this view maintains, moral judgments are nothing but expressions of attitudes, it follows that no moral judgment could be said to be true or false in any universal or absolute sense.

Another view that has been claimed to lend support to ethical relativism is atheistic existentialism, of which the French writer, Jean-Paul Sartre, is a leading exponent. Sartre himself argues, however, that his position does not destroy all moral judgment, but that, on the contrary, it implies that every person must take full responsibility for the decisions and choices he makes in practical life. (See *"The Ethical Outlook of Existentialism"* in this chapter.)

Any argument against ethical relativism (and for ethical absolutism) must show how it is possible to obtain genuine moral knowledge, so that we can determine in any given case whether what someone *thinks* is right or wrong is *really* right or wrong, that is, so that we can determine in any given case whether someone's moral judgment is true or false. There have been many different attempts to do this in the history of philosophy, and this chapter contains some of the most important and famous of these attempts. In each case the moral philosopher examines the grounds on which moral knowledge rests and tries to show how these grounds justify the acceptance of a certain rule of conduct, ideal of life, or standard of good behavior, or a certain set of such rules, ideals, and standards, as applicable to all men

everywhere. One philosopher finds the grounds of genuine moral knowledge in our knowledge of human nature (Aristotle); another finds such grounds in a special kind of human feeling (Hume); another in pure reason (Kant); and still another in certain consequences of human behavior (Mill). In each case there is a different conception of the ultimate basis of the justification of moral rules, ideals, and standards. It is for the reader to decide for himself which of these conceptions, if any, is correct.

In the reading by R. M. Hare we are presented with a new approach to moral philosophy. Mr. Hare studies the way people in everyday life actually use moral statements and the way they actually reason about moral questions. The logical relations among moral concepts and judgments, which are implicit in ordinary moral discourse, are then made explicit and analyzed. Whether this approach to moral philosophy leads to ethical relativism or to ethical absolutism is a matter to be determined by the reader.

THE MORAL PHILOSOPHER AND THE MORALIST

A final remark should be made about the difference between a moral philosopher and a moralist. A moralist is one who tells us what is right and wrong, what our duty is, what ideals we should strive for, what vices we should try to get rid of, and so on. That is, he is primarily concerned with uttering moral judgments and with getting people to become morally good. He may use rational arguments or he may use various other means of persuasion, such as exhortation and inspirational preaching. The moral philosopher, on the other hand, is not primarily concerned with making moral judgments but with examining their meaning and their justifiability. In other words, while the moralist *uses* moral language for moral purposes, the moral philosopher *studies* that language for intellectual purposes. The moral philosopher is trying to *discover truth* (about the meanings of moral concepts and the justification of moral judgments); the moralist is trying to *bring about a better world.* The moralist assumes, in all his activities, that certain rules, ideals, and standards are true. The moral philosopher examines these very assumptions to see whether they are justified. In the selections which follow, the authors will sometimes be found making moral judgments. They will sometimes tell us (as moralists) what they consider to be right and wrong, or what our duty is, in addition to telling us (as moral philosophers) how we can *know* these things. But the main interest in these selections is not the excellence or correctness of their moral content (according to the editors' own moral standards), but the importance of their contribution to the study of moral knowledge. It is as good moral philosophers, not as good moralists, that these particular philosophers were chosen for inclusion in this chapter.

35. ARISTOTLE

(384–322 B.C.)

Teleological Naturalism

Aristotle was a student in the Academy at Athens, where he was taught by Plato, the founder of the Academy. On the death of Plato in 347 B.C., Aristotle left the Academy and was away from Athens for about thirteen years. He spent part of this time as tutor to the young Alexander of Macedon. When Aristotle returned to Athens he founded his own college, the Lyceum, where he taught until the year before his death.

Aristotle wrote on a wide range of topics, including logic, metaphysics, physics, biology, psychology, politics, dramaturgy, and ethics. His writings have had a great influence over twenty-four centuries of Western intellectual history. The following reading is from *The Nicomachean Ethics,* named for his son, Nicomachus.

In this reading Aristotle attempts to establish our knowledge of what is morally right and wrong on the basis of our knowledge of human nature. The central idea in his ethical theory is that man is a being who seeks certain goals or ends. In order to accomplish these ends, there are certain functions which man must perform in a proper way. Aristotle thinks that if we comprehend clearly what these proper functions are, we will understand the nature of good and evil, virtue and vice. This moral philosophy is called "teleological" because its basic concept is that of *purpose.* It is called "naturalism" because it attempts to derive our moral knowledge solely from our factual knowledge of the nature of man.

This selection includes parts of Books

I, II, and X of *The Nicomachean Ethics,* as translated and edited by Professor J. A. K. Thomson. Professor

Thomson's explanatory comments are also included, printed in italics.

From *The Ethics of Aristotle,* translated by J. A. K. Thomson, Allen & Unwin, London, 1953. Reprinted by permission of the publisher.

It is thought that every activity, artistic or scientific, in fact every deliberate action or pursuit, has for its object the attainment of some good. We may therefore assent to the view which has been expressed that "the good" is "that at which all things aim." Since modes of action involving the practised hand and the instructed brain are numerous, the number of their ends is proportionately large. For instance, the end of medical science is health; of military science, victory; of economic science, wealth. All skills of that kind which come under a single "faculty"—a skill in making bridles or any other part of a horse's gear comes under the faculty or art of horsemanship, while horsemanship itself and every branch of military practice comes under the art of war, and in like manner other arts and techniques are subordinate to yet others—in all these the ends of the master arts are to be preferred to those of the subordinate skills, for it is the former that provide the motive for pursuing the latter.

Now if there is an end which as moral agents we seek for its own sake, and which is the cause of our seeking all the other ends—if we are not to go on choosing one act for the sake of another, thus landing ourselves in an infinite progression with the result that desire will be frustrated and ineffectual—it is clear that this must be the good, that is the absolutely good. May we not then argue from this that a knowledge of the good is a great advantage to us in the conduct of our lives? Are we not more likely to hit the mark if we have a target? If this be true, we must do our best to get at least a rough idea of what the good really is, and which of the sciences, pure or applied, is concerned with the business of achieving it.

Ethics is a branch of politics. That is to say, it is the duty of the statesman to create for the citizen the best possible opportunity of living the good life. It will be seen that the effect of this injunction is not to degrade morality but to moralize politics. The modern view that "you cannot make men better by act of parliament" would have been repudiated by Aristotle as certainly as by Plato and indeed by ancient philosophers in general.

Now most people would regard the good as the end pursued by that study which has most authority and control over the rest. Need I say that this is the science of politics? It is political science that prescribes what subjects are to be taught in states, which of these the different sections of the population are to learn, and up to what point. We see also that the faculties which obtain most regard come under this science: for example, the art of war, the management of property, the ability to state a case. Since, therefore, politics makes use of the other practical sciences, and lays it down besides what we must do and what we must not do, its end must include theirs. And that end, in politics as well as in ethics, can only be the good for man. For even if the good of the community coincides with that of the individual, the good of the community is clearly a greater and more perfect good both to get and to keep. This is not to deny that the good of the individual is worth while. But what is good for a nation or a city has a higher, a diviner, quality.

Such being the matters we seek to investigate, the investigation may fairly be represented as the study of politics. . . .

Let us resume our consideration of what is the end of political science. For want of a better word we call it "Happiness." People are agreed on the word but not on its meaning.

To resume. Since every activity involving some acquired skill or some moral decision aims at some good, what do we take to be the end of politics—what is the supreme good attainable in our actions? Well, so far as the name goes there is pretty general agreement. "It is happiness," say both intellectuals and the unsophisticated, meaning by "happiness" living well or faring well. But when it comes to saying in what happiness consists, opinions differ, and the account given by the generality of mankind is not at all like that given by the philosophers. The masses take it to be something plain and tangible, like pleasure or money or social standing. Some maintain that it is one of these, some that it is another, and the same man will change his opinion about it more than once. When he has caught an illness he will say that it is health, and when he is hard up he will say that it is money. Conscious that they are out of their depths in such discussions, most people are impressed by anyone who pontificates and says something that is over their heads. Now it would no doubt be a waste of time to examine all these opinions; enough if we consider those which are most in evidence or have something to be said for them. Among these we shall have to discuss the view held by some that, over and above particular goods like those I have just mentioned, there is another which is good in itself and the cause of whatever goodness there is in all these others. . . .

A man's way of life may afford a clue to his genuine views upon the nature of happiness. It is therefore worth our while to glance at the different types of life.

There is a general assumption that the manner of a man's life is a clue to what he on reflection regards as the good—in other words, happiness. Persons of low tastes (always in the majority) hold that it is pleasure. Accordingly they ask for nothing better than the sort of life which consists in having a good time. (I have in mind the three well-known types of life—that just mentioned, that of the man of affairs, that of the philosophic student.) The utter vulgarity of the herd of men comes out in their preference for the sort of existence a cow leads. Their view would hardly get a respectful hearing, were it not that those who occupy great positions sympathize with a monster of sensuality like Sardanapalus.[1] The gentleman, however, and the man of affairs identify the good with honour, which may fairly be described as the end which men pursue in political or public life. Yet honour is surely too superficial a thing to be the good we are seeking. Honour depends more on those who confer than on him who receives it, and we cannot but feel that the good is something personal and almost inseparable from its possessor. Again, why do men seek honour? Surely in order to confirm the favourable opinion they have formed of themselves. It is at all events by intelligent men who know them personally that they seek to be honoured. And for what? For their moral qualities. The inference is clear; public men prefer virtue to honour. It might therefore seem reasonable to suppose that virtue rather than honour is the end pursued in the life of the public servant. But clearly even virtue cannot be quite the end. It is possible, most people think, to possess virtue while you are asleep, to possess it without acting under its influence during any portion of one's life. Besides, the virtuous man may meet with the most atrocious luck or ill-treatment; and nobody, who was not arguing for argument's sake, would maintain that a man with an existence of that sort was "happy." The third type of life is the "contemplative," and this we shall discuss later.

As for the life of the business man, it does not give him much freedom of action. Besides, wealth obviously is not the good we seek, for the sole purpose it serves is to provide the means of getting something else. So far as that goes, the ends we have already mentioned would have a better title to be considered the good, for they are desired on their own account. But in fact even their claim must be disallowed. We may say that they have furnished the ground for many arguments, and leave the matter at that. . . .

What then is the good? If it is what all men in the last resort aim at, it must be happiness. And that for two reasons: (1) happiness is everything it needs to be, (2) it has everything it needs to have.

We return to the good which is the object of our search. What is it? The question must be asked because good seems to vary with the art or pursuit in which it appears. It is one thing in medicine and another in strategy, and so in the other branches of human skill. We must inquire, then, what is the good which is the end common to all of them. Shall we say it is that for the sake of which everything else is done? In medicine this is health, in military science victory, in architecture a building, and so on—different ends in different arts; every consciously directed activity has an end for the sake of which everything that it does is done. This end may be described as its good.

---

[1] Sardanapalus is usually identified as Assurbanipal, King of Assyria, 668–626 B.C.— Eds.

Consequently, if there be some one thing which is the end of all things consciously done, this will be the doable good; or, if there be more than one end, then it will be all of these. Thus the ground on which our argument proceeds is shifted, but the the conclusion arrived at is the same.

I must try, however, to make my meaning clearer.

In our actions we aim at more ends than one—that seems to be certain—but, since we choose some (wealth, for example, or flutes and tools or instruments generally) as means to something else, it is clear that not all of them are ends in the full sense of the word, whereas the good, that is the supreme good, is surely such an end. Assuming then that there is some one thing which alone is an end beyond which there are no further ends, we may call *that* the good of which we are in search. If there be more than one such final end, the good will be that end which has the highest degree of finality. An object pursued for its own sake possesses a higher degree of finality than one pursued with an eye to something else. A corollary to that is that a thing which is never chosen as a means to some remoter object has a higher degree of finality than things which are chosen both as ends in themselves and as means to such ends. We may conclude, then, that something which is always chosen for its own sake and never for the sake of something else is without qualification a final end.

Now happiness more than anything else appears to be just such an end, for we always choose it for its own sake and never for the sake of some other thing. It is different with honour, pleasure, intelligence and good qualities generally. We choose them indeed for their own sake in the sense that we should be glad to have them irrespective of any advantage which might accrue from them. But we also choose them for the sake of our happiness in the belief that they will be instrumental in promoting that. On the other hand nobody chooses happiness as a means of achieving them or anything else whatsoever than just happiness.

The same conclusion would seem to follow from another consideration. It is a generally accepted view that the final good is self-sufficient. By "self-sufficient" is meant not what is sufficient for oneself living the life of a solitary but includes parents, wife and children, friends and fellow-citizens in general. For man is a social animal. A self-sufficient thing, then, we take to be one which on its own footing tends to make life desirable and lacking in nothing. And we regard happiness as such a thing. Add to this that we regard it as the most desirable of all things without having it counted in with some other desirable thing. For, if such an addition were possible, clearly we should regard it as more desirable when even the smallest advantage was added to it. For the result would be an increase in the number of advantages, and the larger sum of advantages is preferable to the smaller.

Happiness then, the end to which all our conscious acts are directed, is found to be something final and self-sufficient.

But we desire a clearer definition of happiness. The way to this may be prepared by a discussion of what is meant by the "function" of a man.

But no doubt people will say, "To call happiness the highest good is a truism. We want a more distinct account of what it is." We might arrive at this if we could grasp what is meant by the "function" of a human being. If we take a flutist or a sculptor or any craftsman—in fact any class of men at all who have some special job or profession—we find that his special talent and excellence comes out in that job, and this is his function. The same thing will be true of man simply as man—that is of course if "man" does have a function. But is it likely that joiners and shoemakers have certain functions or specialized activities, while man as such has none but has been left by Nature a functionless being? Seeing that eye and hand and foot and every one of our members has some obvious function, must we not believe that in like manner a human being has a function over and above these particular functions? Then what exactly is it? The mere act of living is not peculiar to man—we find it even in the vegetable kingdom—and what we are looking for is something peculiar to him. We must therefore exclude from our definition the life that manifests itself in mere nurture and growth. A step higher should come the life that is confined to experiencing sensations. But that we see is shared by horses, cows, and the brute creation as a whole. We are left, then, with a life concerning which we can make two statements. First, it belongs to the rational part of man. Secondly, it finds expression in actions. The rational part may be either active or passive: passive in so far as it follows the dictates of reason, active in so far as it possesses and exercises the power of reasoning. A similar distinction can be drawn within the rational life; that is to say, the reasonable element in it may be active or passive. Let us take it that what we are concerned with here is the reasoning power in action, for it will be generally allowed that when we speak of "reasoning" we really mean *exercising* our reasoning faculties. (This seems the more correct use of the word.) Now let us assume for the moment the truth of the following propositions. (*a*) The function of a man is the exercise of his noncorporeal faculties or "soul" in accordance with, or at least not divorced from, a rational principle. (*b*) The function of an individual and of a *good* individual in the same class—a harp player, for example, and a good harp player, and so through the classes—is generically the same, except that we must add superiority in accomplishment to the function, the function of the harp player being merely to play on the harp, while the function of the good harp player is to play on it well. (*c*) The function of man is a certain form of life, namely an activity of the soul exercised in combination with a rational principle or reasonable ground of action. (*d*) The function of a good man is to exert such activity well. (*e*) A function is performed well when performed in accordance with the excellence proper to it. If these assumptions are granted, we conclude that the good for man is "an activity of soul in accordance with goodness" or (on the supposition that there may be more than one form of goodness) "in accordance with the best and most complete form of goodness."

Happiness is more than momentary bliss.

There is another condition of happiness; it cannot be achieved in less than a complete lifetime. One swallow does not make a summer; neither does one fine day. And one day, or indeed any brief period of felicity, does not make a man entirely and perfectly happy. . . .

Our definition of happiness compels us to consider the nature of virtue. But before we can do this we must have some conception of how the human soul is constituted. It will serve our purpose to take over (for what it is worth) the current psychology which divides the soul into "parts."

Happiness, then, being an activity of the soul in conformity with perfect goodness, it follows that we must examine the nature of goodness. When we have done this we should be in a better position to investigate the nature of happiness. There is this, too. The genuine statesman is thought of as a man who has taken peculiar pains to master this problem, desiring as he does to make his fellow-citizens good men obedient to the laws. Now, if the study of moral goodness is a part of political science, our inquiry into its nature will clearly follow the lines laid down in our preliminary observations.

Well, the goodness we have to consider is human goodness. This—I mean human goodness or (if you prefer to put it that way) human happiness—was what we set out to find. By human goodness is meant not fineness of physique but a right condition of the soul, and by happiness a condition of the soul. That being so, it is evident that the statesman ought to have some inkling of psychology, just as the doctor who is to specialize in diseases of the eye must have a general knowledge of physiology. Indeed, such a general background is even more necessary for the statesman in view of the fact that his science is of a higher order than the doctor's. Now the best kind of doctor takes a good deal of trouble to acquire a knowledge of the human body as a whole. Therefore the statesman should also be a psychologist and study the soul with an eye to his profession. Yet he will do so only as far as his own problems make it necessary; to go into greater detail on the subject would hardly be worth the labour spent on it.

Psychology has been studied elsewhere and some of the doctrines stated there may be accepted as adequate for our present purpose and used by us here. The soul is represented as consisting of two parts, a rational and an irrational. As regards the irrational part there is one subdivision of it which appears to be common to all living things, and this we may designate as having a "vegetative" nature, by which I mean that it is the cause of nutrition and growth, since one must assume the existence of some such vital force in all things that assimilate food. Now the excellence peculiar to this power is evidently common to the whole of animated nature and not confined to man. This view is supported by the admitted fact that the vegetative part of us is particularly active in sleep, when the good and the bad are hardest to distinguish. Such a phenomenon would be only natural, for sleep is a cessation of that function on the operation of which depends the goodness or badness of the soul. But enough of this, let us say no more about the nutritive part of the soul, since it forms no portion of goodness in the specifically *human* character.

But there would seem to be another constituent of the soul which, while irrational, contains an element of rationality. It may be observed in the types of men we call "continent" and "incontinent." They have a principle—a rational element in their souls—which we commend, because it encourages them to perform the best actions in the right way. But such natures appear at the same time to contain an irrational element in active opposition to the rational. In paralytic cases it often happens that when the patient wills to move his limbs to the right they swing instead to the left. Exactly the same thing may happen to the soul; the impulses of the incontinent man carry him in the opposite direction from that towards which he was aiming. The only difference is that, where the body is concerned, we see the uncontrolled limb, while the erratic impulse we do not see. Yet this should not prevent us from believing that besides the rational an irrational principle exists running opposite and counter to the other. Yet, as I said, it is not altogether irrational; at all events it submits to direction in the continent man, and may be assumed to be still more amenable to reason in the "temperate" and in the brave man, in whose moral make-up there is nothing which is at variance with reason.

We have, then, this clear result. The irrational part of the soul, like the soul itself, consists of two parts. The first of these is the vegetative, which has nothing rational about it at all. The second is that from which spring the appetites and desire in general; and this does in a way participate in reason, seeing that it is submissive and obedient to it. . . . That the irrational element in us need not be heedless of the rational is proved by the fact that we find admonition, indeed every form of censure and exhortation, not ineffective. It may be, however, that we ought to speak of the appetite part of the soul as rational, too. In that event it will rather be the rational part that is divided in two, one division rational in the proper sense of the word and in its nature, the other in the derivative sense in which we speak of a child as "listening to reason" in the person of its father.

These distinctions within the soul supply us with a classification of the virtues. Some are called "intellectual," as wisdom, intelligence, prudence. Others are "moral," as liberality and temperance. When we are speaking of a man's *character* we do not describe him as wise or intelligent but as gentle or temperate. Yet we praise a wise man, too, on the ground of his "disposition" or settled habit of acting wisely. The dispositions so praised are what we mean by "virtues."

But first we have to ask what moral virtue or goodness is. It is a con-

firmed disposition to act rightly, the disposition being itself formed by a
continuous series of right actions.

Virtue, then, is of two kinds, intellectual and moral. Of these the intellectual is in the main indebted to teaching for its production and growth, and this calls for time and experience. Moral goodness, on the other hand, is the child of habit, from which it has got its very name, ethics being derived from *ethos,* "habit," by a slight alteration in the quantity of the *e.* This is an indication that none of the moral virtues is implanted in us by Nature, since nothing that Nature creates can be taught by habit to change the direction of its development. For instance a stone, the natural tendency of which is to fall down, could never, however often you threw it up in the air, be trained to go in that direction. No more can you train fire to burn downwards. Nothing in fact, if the law of its being is to behave in one way, can be habituated to behave in another. The moral virtues, then, are produced in us neither *by* Nature nor *against* Nature. Nature, indeed, prepares in us the ground for their reception, but their complete formation is the product of habit.

Consider again these powers or faculties with which Nature endows us. We acquire the ability to use them before we do use them. The senses provide us with a good illustration of this truth. We have not acquired the sense of sight from repeated acts of seeing, or the sense of hearing from repeated acts of hearing. It is the other way round. We had these senses before we used them; we did not acquire them as a result of using them. But the moral virtues we do acquire by first exercising them. The same is true of the arts and crafts in general. The craftsman has to learn how to make things, but he learns in the process of making them. So men become builders by building, harp players by playing the harp. By a similar process we become just by performing just actions, temperate by performing temperate actions, brave by performing brave actions. Look at what happens in political societies —it confirms our view. We find legislators seeking to make good men of their fellows by making good behaviour habitual with them. That is the aim of every lawgiver, and when he is unable to carry it out effectively, he is a failure; nay, success or failure in this is what makes the difference between a good constitution and a bad.

Again, the creation and the destruction of any virtue are effected by identical causes and identical means; and this may be said, too, of every art. It is as a result of playing the harp that harpers become good or bad in their art. The same is true of builders and all other craftsmen. Men will become good builders as a result of building well, and bad builders as a result of building badly. Otherwise what would be the use of having anyone to teach a trade? Craftsmen would all be born either good or bad. Now this holds also of the virtues. It is in the course of our dealings with our fellow-men that we become just or unjust. It is our behaviour in a crisis and our habitual reactions to danger that make us brave or cowardly, as it may be. So with our desires and passions. Some men are made temperate and gentle, others profligate and passionate, the former by conducting themselves in one way, the latter by conducting themselves in another, in situations in which their feelings are involved. We may sum it all up in the generalization, "Like activities produce like dispositions." This makes it our duty to see that our activities have the right character, since the differences of quality in them are repeated in the dispositions that follow in their train. So it is a matter of real importance whether our early education confirms us in one set of habits or another. It would be nearer the truth to say that it makes a very great difference indeed, in fact all the difference in the world. . . .

After this Aristotle proceeds to lay down a proposition or generalization which is cardinal in his system of ethics. Excess or deficiency in his actions impairs the moral quality of the agent.

Let us begin with the following observation. It is in the nature of moral qualities that they can be destroyed by deficiency on the one hand and excess on the other. We can see this in the instances of bodily health and strength. Physical strength is destroyed by too much and also by too little exercise. Similarly health is ruined by eating and drinking either too much or too little, while it is produced, increased, and preserved by taking the right quantity of drink and victuals. Well, it is the same with temperance, courage, and the other virtues. The man who shuns and fears everything and can stand up to nothing becomes a coward. The man who is afraid of nothing at all, but marches up to every danger, becomes foolhardy. In the same way the man who indulges in every pleasure without refraining from a single one becomes incontinent. If, on the other hand, a man behaves like the Boor in comedy and turns his back on every pleasure, he will find his sensibilities becoming blunted. So also temperance and courage are destroyed both by excess and deficiency, and they are kept alive by observance of the mean. . . .

We have now to state the "differentia" of virtue. Virtue is a disposition; but how are we to distinguish it from other dispositions? We may say that it is such a disposition as enables the good man to perform his function well. And he performs it well when he avoids the extremes and chooses the mean in actions and feelings.

It is not, however, enough to give this account of the *genus* of virtue—that it is a disposition; we must describe its *species*. Let us begin, then, with this proposition. Excellence of whatever kind affects that of which it is the excellence in two ways. (1) It produces a good state in it. (2) It enables it to perform its function well. Take eyesight. The goodness of your eye is not only that which makes your eye good, it is also that which makes it function well. Or take the case of a horse. The goodness of a horse makes him a good horse, but it also makes him good at running, carrying a rider, and facing the enemy. Our proposition, then, seems to be true, and it enables us to say that virtue in a man will be the disposition which (*a*) makes him a good man, (*b*) enables him to perform his function well.

Every form of applied knowledge, when it performs its function well, looks to the mean and works to the standard set by that. It is because people feel this that they apply the *cliché,* "You couldn't add anything to it or take anything from it" to an artistic masterpiece, the implication being that too much and too little alike destroy perfection, while the mean preserves it. Now if this be so, and if it be true, as we say, that good craftsmen work to the standard of the mean, then, since goodness like Nature is more exact and of a higher character than any art, it follows that goodness is the quality that hits the mean. By "goodness" I mean goodness of moral character, since it is moral goodness that deals with feelings and actions, and it is in them that we find excess, deficiency, and a mean. It is possible, for example, to experience fear, boldness, desire, anger, pity, and pleasures and pains generally, too much or too little or to the right amount. If we feel them too much or too little, we are wrong. But to have these feelings at the right times on the right occasions towards the right people for the right motive and in the right way is to have them in the right measure, that is, somewhere between the extremes; and this is what characterizes goodness. The same may be said of the mean and extremes in actions. Now it is in the field of actions and feelings that goodness operates; in them we find excess, deficiency, and, between them, the mean, the first two being wrong, the mean right and praised as such. Goodness, then, is a mean condition in the sense that it aims at and hits the mean.

Consider, too, that it is possible to go wrong in more ways than one. (In Pythagorean terminology evil is a form of the Unlimited, good of the Limited.) But there is only one way of being right. That is why going wrong is easy, and going right difficult; it is easy to miss the bull's-eye and difficult to hit it. Here, then, is another explanation of why the too much and the too little are connected with evil and the mean with good. As the poet says,   Goodness is one, evil is multiform.

We are now in a position to state our definition of virtue with more precision. Observe that the kind of virtue meant here is moral, not intellectual, and that Aristotle must not be taken as saying that the kind of virtue which he regards as the highest and truest is any sort of mean.

We may now define virtue as a disposition of the soul in which, when it has to choose among actions and feelings, it observes the mean relative to us, this being determined by such a rule or principle as would take shape in the mind of a man of sense or practical wisdom. We call it a mean condition as lying between two forms of badness, one being excess and the other deficiency; and also for this reason, that, whereas badness either falls short of or exceeds the right measure in feelings and actions, virtue discovers the mean and deliberately chooses it. Thus, looked at from the point of view of its essence as embodied in its definition, virtue no doubt is a mean; judged by the standard of what is right and best, it is an extreme.

Aristotle enters a caution. Though we have said that virtue observes the mean in actions and passions, we do not say this of all acts and all feelings. Some are essentially evil and, when these are involved, our rule of applying the mean cannot be brought into operation.

But choice of a mean is not possible in every action or every feeling. The very names of some have an immediate connotation of evil. Such are malice, shamelessness, envy among feelings, and among actions adultery, theft, murder. All these and more like them have a bad name as being evil in themselves; it is not merely the excess or deficiency of them that we censure. In their case, then, it is impossible to act rightly; whatever we do is wrong. Nor do circumstances make any difference in the rightness or wrongness of them. When a man commits adultery there is no point in asking whether it is with the right woman or at the right time or in the right way, for to do anything like that is simply wrong. It would amount to claiming that there is a mean and excess and defect in unjust or cowardly or intemperate actions. If such a thing were possible, we should find ourselves with a mean quantity of excess, a mean of deficiency, an excess of excess and a deficiency of deficiency. But just as in temperance and justice there can be no mean or excess or deficiency, because the mean in a sense *is* an extreme, so there can be no mean or excess or deficiency in those vicious actions—however done, they are wrong. Putting the matter into general language, we may say that there is no mean in the extremes, and no extreme in the mean, to be observed by anybody. . . .

A recapitulation of what has been said of Happiness.

We stated that happiness is not a condition—not a state of mind or disposition of character. If it were, it might belong to a man whose whole existence was passed in sleep, while he lived the life of a vegetable, or to the victim of some appalling misfortune. So if we cannot accept this but feel that we must rather insist that happiness is some form of activity; if, moreover, activities may be classified into those which are necessary to some end desirable for the sake of something beyond themselves, and those that are desirable in and for themselves, clearly happiness must be classed among activities desirable in themselves, and not among those desirable as a means to something else. For happiness is not in need of anything—it is self-sufficient. As for activities, they are desirable in themselves when all that is asked of them is their own exercise. Actions which are in conformity with goodness evidently have this character, for the performance of morally good and beautiful actions is desirable on its own account. . . .

Aristotle gives reasons for thinking that Happiness in its highest and best manifestation is found in cultivating the "contemplative" life.

But if happiness is an activity in accordance with virtue, it is reasonable to assume that it will be in accordance with the highest virtue; and this can only be the virtue of the best part of us. Whether this be the intellect or something else—whatever it is that is held to have a natural right to govern

and guide us, and to have an insight into what is noble and divine, either
as being itself also divine or more divine than any other part of us—it is the
activity of this part in accordance with the virtue proper to it that will be
perfect happiness. Now this activity has a speculative or contemplative character. This is a conclusion which may be accepted as in harmony with the
truth. For "contemplation" is the highest form of activity, since the intellect
is the highest thing in us and the objects which come within its range are
the highest that can be known. But it is also the most continuous activity,
for we can think about intellectual problems more continuously than we can
keep up any sort of physical action. Again, we feel sure that a modicum of
pleasure must be one of the ingredients of happiness. Now it is admitted
that activity along the lines of "wisdom" is the pleasantest of all the good
activities. At all events it is thought that philosophy ("the pursuit of wisdom") has pleasures marvellous in purity and duration, and it stands to
reason that those who have knowledge pass their time more pleasantly than
those who are engaged in its pursuit. Again, self-sufficiency will be found to
belong in an exceptional degree to the exercise of the speculative intellect.
The wise man, as much as the just man and everyone else, must have the
necessaries of life. But, given an adequate supply of these, the just man also
needs people with and towards whom he can put his justice into operation;
and we can use similar language about the temperate man, the brave man,
and so on. But the wise man can do more. He can speculate all by himself,
and the wiser he is the better he can do it. Doubtless it helps to have fellow-
workers, but for all that he is the most self-sufficing of men. Finally it may
well be thought that the activity of contemplation is the only one that is
praised on its own account, because nothing comes of it beyond the act of
contemplation, whereas from practical activities we count on gaining something more or less over and above the mere action. Again, it is commonly
believed that, to have happiness, one must have leisure; we occupy ourselves
in order that we may have leisure, just as we make war for the sake of peace.
Now the practical virtues find opportunity for their exercise in politics and
in war, but these are occupations which are supposed to leave no room for
leisure. Certainly it is true of the trade of war, for no one deliberately chooses
to make war for the sake of making it or tries to bring about a war. A man
would be regarded as a bloodthirsty monster if he were to make war on a
friendly state just to produce battles and slaughter. The business of the
politician also makes leisure impossible. Besides the activity itself, politics
aims at securing positions of power and honour or the happiness of the
politician himself or his fellow-citizens—a happiness obviously distinct from
·hat which we are seeking.

   We are now in a position to suggest the truth of the following statements. (*a*) Political and military activities, while pre-eminent among good
activities in beauty and grandeur, are incompatible with leisure, and are not
chosen for their own sake but with a view to some remoter end, whereas the

activity of the intellect is felt to excel in the serious use of leisure, taking as it does the form of contemplation, and not to aim at any end beyond itself, and to own a pleasure peculiar to itself, thereby enhancing its activity. (*b*) In this activity we easily recognize self-sufficiency, the possibility of leisure and such freedom from fatigue as is humanly possible, together with all the other blessings of pure happiness. Now if these statements are received as true, it will follow that it is this intellectual activity which forms perfect happiness for a man—provided of course that it ensures a complete span of life, for nothing incomplete can be an element in happiness.

Yes, but such a life will be too high for *human* attainment. It will not be lived by us in our merely human capacity but in virtue of something divine within us, and so far as this divine particle is superior to man's composite nature, to that extent will its activity be superior to that of the other forms of excellence. If the intellect is divine compared with man, the life of the intellect must be divine compared with the life of a human creature. And we ought not to listen to those who counsel us *O man, think as man should* and *O mortal, remember your mortality*. Rather ought we, so far as in us lies, to put on immortality and to leave nothing unattempted in the effort to live in conformity with the highest thing within us. Small in bulk it may be, yet in power and preciousness it transcends all the rest. We may in fact believe that this is the true self of the individual, being the sovran and better part of him. It would be strange, then, if a man should choose to live not his own life but another's. Moreover, the rule, as I stated it a little before, will apply here—the rule that what is best and pleasantest for each creature is that which intimately belongs to it. Applying it, we shall conclude that the life of the intellect is the best and pleasantest for man, because the intellect more than anything else *is* the man. Thus it will be the happiest life as well.

The moral as distinct from the intellectual life will, though only in a secondary degree, be happy too. For the moral activities are human *par excellence*. When we display courage or justice or any other virtue it is in our dealings with our fellow men, when we are careful to observe what is due to each in all contracts and exchange of services, indeed in our actions and feelings of every kind, all of which are manifestly human experiences. Some of these, we think, are actually the products of our bodily constitution—goodness of character is felt to have in many ways an intimate connexion with the passions. Prudence, too, is bound up with moral goodness, and goodness with prudence, because the first principles from which prudence starts are given by the moral virtues, for which the right standard is set by prudence. But these virtues, thus closely linked with the passions, go to form the composite being called man. Now the virtues of our composite nature are essentially human. Therefore the life that is lived in the performance of these virtues, and the happiness that ensues from such a life, must also be purely human. But the happiness of the intellectual life is something quite distinct from this. We must leave it at that, for a detailed discussion would go beyond the scope of the question before us. It would further appear that such happiness stands in need of external accessories to but a small extent or less than the happiness founded on moral goodness. The necessaries of life are required by both, and in equal measure. Granted; in this respect the difference between them may be small. But there will be a vast difference in what they require for the exercise of their powers. Thus the liberal man will need money to practise his liberality, as will indeed the just man to meet his obligations. The brave man will need strength if he is to do something brave, and the temperate man the opportunity of being intemperate. (Otherwise how can he, or the possessor of any other virtue, prove that he possesses the virtue?) Another question is whether it is the purpose of an action or the action itself that is the most decisive factor in producing moral goodness on the assumption generally made that goodness depends on both. Well, the perfect character will obviously need both for its formation. But many extraneous things are needed for the performance of virtuous actions, and the greater and finer the actions, the more numerous will be these accessories. On the other hand the student of intellectual problems has no need of all these paraphernalia; perhaps they are rather a hindrance to his thinking. Yet after all he is a man and a member of society and, in so far as he is that, he will choose to act on moral grounds. And this means that he will have need of external goods to permit him to live on the human level.

That perfect happiness is a speculative activity will further appear from the following considerations. The gods in our conception of them enjoy the most complete blessedness and felicity. But what kind of actions can we rightly attribute to them? If we say "just actions," how absurd it will be to picture them as making contracts and restoring deposits and all that sort of thing! Shall we say "brave actions" then? Can you imagine the gods seeking glory by facing dangers and alarms? And what of liberal actions? Whom are they to be liberal to? What an odd idea that the gods actually possess coined money or something like it! Then there are temperate actions. But what could temperate actions mean in their case? What a piece of vulgarity to commend the gods for not having flagitious desires! And if we go through the whole list we shall find that all forms of virtuous activity must be paltry for the gods and unworthy of them. Nevertheless men have always thought of them as at least living beings and, if living, then doing something, for we cannot suppose that they are always asleep, like Endymion. But if from a living being there is taken away action, not to mention creation or production, what is left him but contemplation? We must conclude then that the activity of God, which is blessed above all others, must take the form of contemplation. And from this it follows that among human activities that which is most akin to God's will bring us the greatest happiness. What also goes to show the truth of this is the fact that the lower animals cannot partake of happiness, for they are utterly incapable of contemplation. The life of the gods is altogether happy, that of man is happy so far as it includes something that resembles the divine activity; but none of the other animals can be properly described as happy, because they are in no way capable of speculation or contemplation. Happiness then covers the same ground as contemplation and those who have the greatest power of contemplation are the happiest, not accidentally but as an essential element of their contemplation. For contemplation is itself beyond price. We conclude that happiness is a form of contemplation. . . .

Such then is our theory of ethics. But theory is not practice and has no effect on the practice of the average man.

Assuming then that we have adequately discussed, at least in outline, the subjects of happiness and the different forms of goodness, may we consider the task we set before us as now complete? Or would it not be better to say that in the science of conduct the end, as we have so often had occasion to say, is not to obtain a theoretical acquaintance with the different points at issue, but rather to put our theories into practice? If that be true, it is not enough to *know* about goodness; we must endeavour to possess and use it, and in some way to see to it that we become good. Now if discourses on the theory of ethics were enough in themselves to make men good,

Many and great the rewards they would win,

as Theognis has it. And they would deserve them, and all we should have to do would be to provide ourselves with such discourses. But the plain truth is that, while theories may very powerfully stimulate and encourage generous youth, and may inspire a character naturally noble and sincerely loving the beauty of goodness with a passion for virtue, they are unable to push the many in the direction of lofty principles. For it is the nature of the many to yield to the suggestions of fear rather than honour, and to abstain from evil not because of the disgrace but the penalties entailed by not abstaining. Living under the dictates of passion, they chase the pleasures fit for such natures and the means of gratifying them, and they shun the pains which are the opposite of these pleasures. But the honourable and the truly delightful—of that they have no conception, having never tasted genuine pleasure. What theory, what homily can ever reform people like that? To uproot by argument habits long embedded in the character is a difficult, perhaps an impossible, task. We may, I take it, regard ourselves as fortunate if we can get some portion of goodness by acquiring for ourselves all the recognized means of becoming good.

To become good we must have a suitable nature rightly directed by habit and education.

Now some thinkers hold that goodness comes by nature, others that we acquire it by habit, others that we are made good by teaching. The bounty of nature is clearly beyond our control; it is bestowed by some divine dispensation on those who are in the true sense of the word "fortunate." As for arguments and teaching, it is to be feared they are not efficacious in all instances. Like a piece of land, which has to be prepared for the seed that is to grow there, the mind of the pupil has to be prepared for the inculcation of good habits, if it is to like and dislike the things it ought. The man who is passion's slave will not listen to or understand the logic of anyone who tries to dissuade him from going on as he is doing. When a man is in that state, what chance have you of changing his mind by argumentation? In fact one may venture on the broad statement that passion is not amenable to reason but only to force. We must then have a character to work upon which has a natural bias towards virtue, loving the noble and hating the base.

Education in goodness is best undertaken by the state.

Yet it is far from easy to obtain a right training in goodness from youth upwards, unless one has been brought up under right laws. To live a hard and sober life is not an attractive prospect for most, especially when they are young. For this reason the nurture and the pursuits of young persons should be regulated by law, for hard conditions and sober living will cease to be painful when they have become habitual. Of course, it is not enough to receive the right nurture and supervision in youth. We must also practise what we have learnt and make a habit of it when we are grown up. So we shall need laws for the regulation of adult behaviour as well, for the whole indeed of our lives; for people are by and large readier to submit to punishment and compulsion than moved by arguments and ideals. Hence some believe that, while lawgivers are under an obligation to encourage and inspire the citizens in the pursuit of virtue for its beauty, not doubting that those who have been well brought up will respond, they are also bound to inflict chastisement and penalties on the disobedient and ill-conditioned, and to deport the hopeless cases altogether. They take the line that, while the good man no doubt, living as he does with some kind of moral standard, will listen to reason, the degraded, who are all for pleasure, must be chastised by pain like beasts of burden. This is also the reason they give for maintaining that the punishment for transgressors should take the form of those pains which come nearest to being the opposite of their darling pleasures.

Be that as it may, I repeat that, if a man is to turn out well, he must have been properly educated and trained, and must thereafter persevere in good habits of life and do no wrong either with or against his will. This result can be produced only by submitting one's life to the guidance of intelligence in some form and a right system with truth in it. Now a father has not got the power to enforce obedience to his authority, nor indeed, broadly speaking, has any individual, unless he happens to be a king or something equivalent. But law, emanating as a rule from a certain wisdom and intelligence, does have the power of compulsion. We dislike people who thwart our inclinations, even if they are entirely justified in doing so, but we do not grumble at the law when it orders what is right. Yet Sparta, with perhaps one or two other places, is the only state in which the lawgiver seems to have been at pains to regulate the nurture and day-to-day life of the community. In the majority of states the problem has not been faced, and every man does as he likes with his life in the manner of the Cyclops in Homer, "laying down the law for children and wife."

QUESTIONS

1. When Aristotle says that the good of the community is greater and more perfect than the good of the individual, does he imply that the community can justifiably sacrifice the individual's good in order to further its own good? Defend your answer by giving a general account of Aristotle's views on the relation between ethics and politics.
2. Aristotle defines the good as "an end beyond which are no further ends." Such an end is whatever a person desires for its own sake rather than for the sake of something else. It follows that whatever a person desires for its own sake is good, and there is no sense in saying that a person can desire what is in fact evil. How might Aristotle reply to this argument?
3. Explain what Aristotle means by happiness. How is it to be distinguished from pleasure?
4. Aristotle attempts to define the good for man (happiness) in terms of the peculiar function of man, which he identifies as the activity of reasoning. But there are other functions peculiar to man, such as his ability to blush or to be ashamed, and his ability to use his thumb in handling things. Clearly the fact that something is peculiar to man does not mean that it defines the good for man. For how do we know that the good for man does not lie in those functions which man has in common with animals?
   Is this a good criticism of Aristotle's position? Why or why not?
5. What is the basis for Aristotle's distinction between moral virtues and intellectual virtues? Why does he discuss intellectual virtues in a book on ethics?
6. Many people would say that the life of Jesus exemplifies moral goodness at its highest level. Yet Jesus certainly carried to great extremes his inward purity, his refusal to compromise his ideals, his honesty, and his love of humanity. Does the life of Jesus provide evidence against Aristotle's conception of virtue as a mean?
7. Try to give some examples of what Aristotle calls "contemplation." What does he think is being contemplated by a person during an act of contemplation?
8. Since our highest virtue according to Aristotle is contemplation, then a man who spends his life in contemplation leads a better life than a man who spends his life in alleviating the sufferings of others.
   State why you think this conclusion does, or does not, follow from Aristotle's point of view.
9. Aristotle's whole ethical system is based on knowledge of human nature. If we know the nature of man, he is saying, then we can derive from that knowledge the knowledge of good and evil. Do you think that knowledge of man's nature is *sufficient* for obtaining moral knowledge? Is it *necessary, but not sufficient?* Is it *neither necessary nor sufficient?* Is it *totally irrelevant* to obtaining moral knowledge? Defend your answer.

36. DAVID HUME

(1711–76)

The Moral Sense

(A general introductory note on Hume may be found on page 116.)

Hume believes that we obtain moral knowledge through what he calls "the moral sense." In order to understand what he means by this, it is necessary to begin with his discussion of human motivation. According to Hume neither our reason itself nor the knowledge which we gain by the use of our reason can directly determine our actions. Only "passion" (which includes for Hume what we now call emotions, attitudes, desires, wishes, and needs) can act as a motivating force on our behavior. Reason can tell us what the probable consequences of our actions will be, and can thus indirectly cause us to act one way rather than another, depending on whether we like or dislike the consequences of which it informs us. Reason also has the power to correct mistaken suppositions on the basis of which we act, and to tell us what means will most likely bring about an end we have already chosen. By itself, however, reason is powerless to determine the choice of an end. The conclusion which Hume draws from his study of motivation is that passion can neither be in conflict nor in harmony with reason.

Hume next proceeds to argue that, since reason cannot directly influence our actions, it cannot be a source of moral knowledge. From what source, then, do we get our moral knowledge? Hume's answer is: From the moral sense. The reader will discover for himself the full meaning of this answer when he becomes acquainted with Hume's own argument in the reading which follows.

The reading is taken from Book II, Part III, Section III, and Book III, Part I, Sections I and II of *A Treatise of Human Nature* (1738–40), and from Section IX of *An Enquiry Concerning the Principles of Morals* (1751). Hume's own section headings are used.

OF THE INFLUENCING MOTIVES OF THE WILL

Nothing is more usual in philosophy, and even in common life, than to talk of the combat of passion and reason, to give the preference to reason, and to assert that men are only so far virtuous as they conform themselves to its dictates. Every rational creature, 'tis said, is oblig'd to regulate his actions by reason; and if any other motive or principle challenge the direction of his conduct, he ought to oppose it, 'till it be entirely subdu'd, or at least brought to a conformity with that superior principle. On this method of thinking the greatest part of moral philosophy, ancient and modern, seems to be founded; nor is there an ampler field, as well for metaphysical arguments, as popular declamations, than this suppos'd pre-eminence of reason above passion. The eternity, invariableness, and divine origin of the former have been display'd to the best advantage: The blindness, unconstancy and deceitfulness of the latter have been as strongly insisted on. In order to shew the fallacy of all this philosophy, I shall endeavour to prove *first,* that reason alone can never be a motive to any action of the will; and *secondly,* that it can never oppose passion in the direction of the will.

The understanding exerts itself after two different ways, as it judges from demonstration or probability; as it regards the abstract relations of our ideas, or those relations of objects, of which experience only gives us information. I believe it scarce will be asserted, that the first species of reasoning alone is ever the cause of any action. As its proper province is the world of ideas, and as the will always places us in that of realities, demonstration and volition seem, upon that account, to be totally remov'd, from each other. Mathematics, indeed, are useful in all mechanical operations, and arithmetic in almost every art and profession: But 'tis not of themselves they have any influence. Mechanics are the art of regulating the motions of bodies *to some design'd end or purpose;* and the reason why we employ arithmetic in fixing the proportions of numbers, is only that we may discover the proportions of their influence and operation. A merchant is desirous of knowing the sum total of his accounts with any person: Why? but that he may learn what sum will have the same *effects* in paying his debt, and going to market, as all the particular articles taken together. Abstract or demonstrative reasoning, therefore, never influences any of our actions, but only as it directs our judgment concerning causes and effects; which leads us to the second operation of the understanding.

'Tis obvious, that when we have the prospect of pain or pleasure from any object, we feel a consequent emotion of aversion or propensity, and are carry'd to avoid or embrace what will give us this uneasiness or satisfaction. 'Tis also obvious, that this emotion rests not here, but making us cast our view on every side, comprehends whatever objects are connected with its original one by the relation of cause and effect. Here then reasoning takes place to discover this relation; and according as our reasoning varies, our actions receive a subsequent variation. But 'tis evident in this case, that the impulse arises not from reason, but is only directed by it. 'Tis from the prospect of pain or pleasure that the aversion or propensity arises towards any object: And these emotions extend themselves to the causes and effects of that object, as they are pointed out to us by reason and experience. It can never in the least concern us to know, that such objects are causes, and such others effects, if both the causes and effects be indifferent to us. Where the objects themselves do not affect us, their connexion can never give them any influence; and 'tis plain, that as reason is nothing but the discovery of this connexion, it cannot be by its means that the objects are able to affect us.

Since reason alone can never produce any action, or give rise to volition, I infer, that the same faculty is as incapable of preventing volition, or of disputing the preference with any passion or emotion. This consequence is necessary. 'Tis impossible reason cou'd have the latter effect of preventing volition, but by giving an impulse in a contrary direction to our passion; and that impulse, had it operated alone, wou'd have been able to produce volition. Nothing can oppose or retard the impulse of passion, but a contrary impulse; and if this contrary impulse ever arises from reason, that latter faculty must have an original influence on the will, and must be able to cause, as well as hinder any act of volition. But if reason has no original influence, 'tis impossible it can withstand any principle, which has such an efficacy, or ever keep the mind in suspense a moment. Thus it appears, that the principle, which opposes our passion, cannot be the same with reason, and is only call'd so in an improper sense. We speak not strictly and philosophically when we talk of the combat of passion and of reason. Reason is, and ought only to be the slave of the passions, and can never pretend to any other office than to serve and obey them. As this opinion may appear somewhat extraordinary, it may not be improper to confirm it by some other considerations.

A passion is an original existence, or, if you will, modification of existence, and contains not any representative quality, which renders it a copy of any other existence or modification. When I am angry, I am actually possest with the passion, and in that emotion have no more a reference to any other object, than when I am thirsty, or sick, or more than five foot high. 'Tis impossible, therefore, that this passion can be oppos'd by, or be contradictory to truth and reason; since this contradiction consists in the disagreement of ideas, consider'd as copies, with those objects, which they represent.

What may at first occur on this head, is, that as nothing can be contrary to truth or reason, except what has a reference to it, and as the judgments of our understanding only have this reference, it must follow, that passions can be contrary to reason only so far as they are *accompany'd* with some judgment or opinion. According to this principle, which is so obvious and natural, 'tis only in two senses, that any affection can be call'd unreasonable. First, When a passion, such as hope or fear, grief or joy, despair or security, is founded on the supposition of the existence of objects, which really do not exist. Secondly, When in exerting any passion in action, we chuse means insufficient for the design'd end, and deceive ourselves in our judgment of causes and effects. Where a passion is neither founded on false suppositions, nor chuses means insufficient for the end, the understanding can neither justify nor condemn it. 'Tis not contrary to reason to prefer the destruction of the whole world to the scratching of my finger. 'Tis not contrary to reason for me to chuse my total ruin, to prevent the least uneasiness of an *Indian* or person wholly unknown to me. 'Tis as little contrary to reason to prefer even my own acknowledg'd lesser good to my greater, and have a more ardent affection for the former than the latter. A trivial good may, from certain circumstances, produce a desire superior to what arises from the greatest and most valuable enjoyment; nor is there any thing more extraordinary in this, than in mechanics to see one pound weight raise up a hundred by the advantage of its situation. In short, a passion must be accompany'd with some false judgment, in order to its being unreasonable; and even then 'tis not the passion, properly speaking, which is unreasonable, but the judgment.

The consequences are evident. Since a passion can never, in any sense, be call'd unreasonable, but when founded on a false supposition, or when it chuses means insufficient for the design'd end, 'tis impossible, that reason and passion can ever oppose each other, or dispute for the government of the will and actions. The moment we perceive the falshood of any supposition, or the insufficiency of any means, our passions yield to our reason without any opposition. I may desire any fruit as of an excellent relish; but whenever you convince me of my mistake, my longing ceases. I may will the performance of certain actions as means of obtaining any desir'd good; but as my willing of these actions is only secondary, and founded on the supposition, that they are causes of the propos'd effect; as soon as I discover the falshood of that supposition, they must become indifferent to me.

'Tis natural for one, that does not examine objects with a strict philosophic eye, to imagine, that those actions of the mind are entirely the same, which produce not a different sensation, and are not immediately distinguishable to the feeling and perception. Reason, for instance, exerts itself without producing any sensible emotion; and except in the more sublime disquisitions of philosophy, or in the frivolous subtilties of the schools, scarce ever conveys any pleasure or uneasiness. Hence it proceeds, that every action of the mind, which operates with the same calmness and tranquillity, is confounded with reason by all those, who judge of things from the first view and appearance. Now 'tis certain, there are certain calm desires and tendencies, which, tho' they be real passions, produce little emotion in the mind, and are more known by their effects than by the immediate feeling or sensation. These desires are of two kinds; either certain instincts originally implanted in our natures, such as benevolence and resentment, the love of life, and kindness to children; or the general appetite to good, and aversion to evil, consider'd merely as such. When any of these passions are calm, and cause no disorder in the soul, they are very readily taken for the determinations of reason, and are suppos'd to proceed from the same faculty, with that, which judges of truth and falshood. Their nature and principles have been suppos'd the same, because their sensations are not evidently different.

Beside these calm passions, which often determine the will, there are certain violent emotions of the same kind, which have likewise a great influence on that faculty. When I receive any injury from another, I often feel a violent passion of resentment, which makes me desire his evil and punishment, independent of all considerations of pleasure and advantage to myself. When I am immediately threaten'd with any grievous ill, my fears, apprehensions, and aversions rise to a great height, and produce a sensible emotion.

The common error of metaphysicians has lain in ascribing the direction of the will entirely to one of these principles, and supposing the other to have no influence. Men often act knowingly against their interest: For which reason the view of the greatest possible good does not always influence them. Men often counter-act a violent passion in prosecution of their interests and designs: 'Tis not therefore the present uneasiness alone, which determines them. In general we may observe, that both these principles operate on the will; and where they are contrary, that either of them prevails, according to the *general* character or *present* disposition of the person. What we call strength of mind, implies the prevalence of the calm passions above the violent; tho' we may easily observe, there is no man so constantly possess'd of this virtue, as never on any occasion to yield to the sollicitations of passion and desire. From these variations of temper proceeds the great difficulty of deciding concerning the actions and resolutions of men, where there is any contrariety of motives and passions.

. . .

MORAL DISTINCTIONS NOT DERIV'D FROM REASON

. . .

It has been observ'd, that nothing is ever present to the mind but its perceptions; and that all the actions of seeing, hearing, judging, loving, hating, and thinking, fall under this denomination. The mind can never exert itself in any action, which we may not comprehend under the term of *perception;* and consequently that term is no less applicable to those judgments, by which we distinguish moral good and evil, than to every other operation of the mind. To approve of one character, to condemn another, are only so many different perceptions.

Now as perceptions resolve themselves into two kinds, viz. *impressions* and *ideas,* this distinction gives rise to a question, with which we shall open up our present enquiry concerning morals, *Whether 'tis by means of our* ideas *or* impressions *we distinguish betwixt vice and virtue, and pronounce an action blameable or praise-worthy?* This will immediately cut off all loose discourses and declamations, and reduce us to something precise and exact on the present subject.

Those who affirm that virtue is nothing but a conformity to reason, that there are eternal fitnesses and unfitnesses of things, which are the same to every rational being that considers them; that the immutable measures of right and wrong impose an obligation, not only on human creatures, but also on the Deity himself: All these systems concur in the opinion, that morality, like truth, is discern'd merely by ideas, and by their juxta-position and comparison. In order, therefore, to judge of these systems, we need only consider, whether it be possible, from reason alone, to distinguish betwixt moral good and evil, or whether there must concur some other principles to enable us to make that distinction.

If morality had naturally no influence on human passions and actions, 'twere in vain to take such pains to inculcate it; and nothing wou'd be more fruitless than that multitude of rules and precepts, with which all moralists abound. Philosophy is commonly divided into *speculative* and *practical;* and as morality is always comprehended under the latter division, 'tis supposed to influence our passions and actions, and to go beyond the calm and indolent judgments of the understanding. And this is confirm'd by common experience, which informs us, that men are often govern'd by their duties, and are deter'd from some actions by the opinion of injustice, and impell'd to others by that of obligation.

Since morals, therefore, have an influence on the actions and affections, it follows, that they cannot be deriv'd from reason; and that because reason alone, as we have already prov'd, can never have any such influence. Morals excite passions, and produce or prevent actions. Reason of itself is utterly impotent in this particular. The rules of morality, therefore, are not conclusions of our reason.

No one, I believe, will deny the justness of this inference; nor is there any other means of evading it, than by denying that principle, on which it is founded. As long as it is allow'd, that reason has no influence on our passions and actions, 'tis in vain to pretend, that morality is discover'd only by a deduction of reason. An active principle can never be founded on an inactive; and if reason be inactive in itself, it must remain so in all its shapes and appearances, whether it exerts itself in natural or moral subjects, whether it considers the powers of external bodies, or the actions of rational beings.

. . .

Reason is the discovery of truth or falshood. Truth or falshood consists in an agreement or disagreement either to the *real* relations of ideas, or to *real* existence and matter of fact. Whatever, therefore, is not susceptible of this agreement or disagreement, is incapable of being true or false, and can never be an object of our reason. Now 'tis evident our passions, volitions, and actions, are not susceptible of any such agreement or disagreement; being original facts and realities, compleat in themselves, and implying no reference to other passions, volitions, and actions. 'Tis impossible, therefore, they can be pronounced either true or false, and be either contrary or conformable to reason.

This argument is of double advantage to our present purpose. For it proves *directly,* that actions do not derive their merit from a conformity to reason, nor their blame from a contrariety to it; and it proves the same truth more *indirectly,* by shewing us, that as reason can never immediately prevent or produce any action by contradicting or approving of it, it cannot be the source of moral good and evil, which are found to have that influence. Actions may be laudable or blameable; but they cannot be reasonable or unreasonable: Laudable or blameable, therefore, are not the same with reasonable or unreasonable. The merit and demerit of actions frequently contradict, and sometimes controul our natural propensities. But reason has no such influence. Moral distinctions, therefore, are not the offspring of reason. Reason is wholly inactive, and can never be the source of so active a principle as conscience, or a sense of morals.

. . .

But to make these general reflexions more clear and convincing, we may illustrate them by some particular instances, wherein this character of moral good or evil is the most universally acknowledged. Of all crimes that human creatures are capable of committing, the most horrid and unnatural is ingratitude, especially when it is committed against parents, and appears in the more flagrant instances of wounds and death. This is acknowledg'd by all mankind, philosophers as well as the people; the question only arises among philosophers, whether the guilt or moral deformity of this action be discover'd by demonstrative reasoning, or be felt by an internal sense, and by means of some sentiment, which the reflecting on such an action naturally occasions. This question will soon be decided against the former opinion, if we can shew the same relations in other objects, without the notion of any guilt or iniquity attending them. Reason or science is nothing but the comparing of ideas, and the discovery of their relations; and if the same relations have different characters, it must evidently follow, that those characters are not discover'd merely by reason. To put the affair, therefore, to this trial, let us chuse any inanimate object, such as an oak or elm; and let us suppose, that by the dropping of its seed, it produces a sapling below it, which springing up by degrees, at last overtops and destroys the parent tree: I ask, if in this instance there be wanting any relation, which is discoverable in parricide or ingratitude? Is not the one tree the cause of the other's existence; and the latter the cause of the destruction of the former, in the same manner as when a child murders his parent? 'Tis not sufficient to reply, that a choice or will is wanting. For in the case of parricide, a will does not give rise to any *different* relations, but is only the cause from which the action is deriv'd; and consequently produces the *same* relations, that in the oak or elm arise from some other principles. 'Tis a will or choice, that determines a man to kill his parent; and they are the laws of matter and motion, that determine a sapling to destroy the oak, from which it sprung. Here then the same relations have different causes; but still the relations are the same: And as their discovery is not in both cases attended with a notion of immorality, it follows, that that notion does not arise from such a discovery.

But to chuse an instance, still more resembling; I would fain ask any one, why incest in the human species is criminal, and why the very same action, and the same relations in animals have not the smallest moral turpitude and deformity? If it be answer'd, that this action is innocent in animals, because they have not reason sufficient to discover its turpitude; but that man, being endow'd with that faculty, which *ought* to restrain him to his duty, the same action instantly becomes criminal to him; should this be said, I would reply, that this is evidently arguing in a circle. For before reason can perceive this turpitude, the turpitude must exist; and consequently is independent of the decisions of our reason, and is their object more properly than their effect. According to this system, then, every animal, that has sense, and appetite, and will; that is, every animal must be susceptible of all the same virtues and vices, for which we ascribe praise and blame to human creatures. All the difference is, that our superior reason may serve to discover the vice or virtue, and by that means may augment the blame or praise: But still this discovery supposes a separate being in these moral distinctions, and a being, which depends only on the will and appetite, and which, both in thought and reality, may be distinguish'd from the reason. Animals are susceptible of the same relations, with respect to each other, as the human species, and therefore wou'd also be susceptible of the same morality, if the essence of morality consisted in these relations. Their want of a sufficient degree of reason may hinder them from perceiving the duties and obligations of morality, but can never hinder these duties from existing; since they must antecedently exist, in order to their being perceiv'd. Reason must find them, and can never produce them. This argument deserves to be weigh'd, as being, in my opinion, entirely decisive.

Nor does this reasoning only prove, that morality consists not in any relations, that are the objects of science; but if examin'd, will prove with equal certainty, that it consists not in any *matter of fact,* which can be discover'd by the understanding. This is the *second* part of our argument; and if it can be made evident, we may conclude, that morality is not an object of reason. But can there be any difficulty in proving, that vice and virtue are not matters of fact, whose existence we can infer by reason? Take any action allow'd to be vicious: Wilful murder, for instance. Examine it in all lights, and see if you can find that matter of fact, or real existence, which you call *vice.* In which-ever way you take it, you find only certain passions, motives, volitions and thoughts. There is no other matter of fact in the case. The vice entirely escapes you, as long as you consider the object. You never can find it, till you turn your reflexion into your own breast, and find a sentiment of disapprobation, which arises in you, towards this action. Here is a matter of fact; but 'tis the object of feeling, not of reason. It lies in yourself, not in the object. So that when you pronounce any action or character to be vicious, you mean nothing, but that from the constitution of your nature you have a feeling or sentiment of blame from the contemplation of it. Vice and virtue, therefore, may be compar'd to sounds, colours, heat and cold, which, according to modern philosophy, are not qualities in objects, but perceptions in the mind: And this discovery in morals, like that other in physics, is to be regarded as a considerable advancement of the speculative sciences; tho', like that too, it has little or no influence on practice. Nothing can be more real, or concern us more, than our own sentiments of pleasure and uneasiness; and if these be favourable to virtue, and unfavourable to vice, no more can be requisite to the regulation of our conduct and behaviour.

I cannot forbear adding to these reasonings an observation, which may, perhaps, be found of some importance. In every system of morality, which I have hitherto met with, I have always remark'd, that the author proceeds for some time in the ordinary way of reasoning, and establishes the being of a God, or makes observations concerning human affairs; when of a sudden I am surpriz'd to find, that instead of the usual copulations of propositions, *is,* and *is not,* I meet with no proposition that is not connected with an *ought,* or an *ought not.* This change is imperceptible; but is, however, of the last consequence. For as this *ought,* or *ought not,* expresses some new relation or affirmation, 'tis necessary that it shou'd be observ'd and explain'd; and at the same time that a reason should be given, for what seems altogether inconceivable, how this new relation can be a deduction from others, which are entirely different from it. But as authors do not commonly use this precaution, I shall presume to recommend it to the readers; and am persuaded, that this small attention wou'd subvert all the vulgar systems of morality, and let us see, that the distinction of vice and virtue is not founded merely on the relations of objects, nor is perceiv'd by reason.

MORAL DISTINCTIONS DERIV'D FROM A MORAL SENSE

Thus the course of the argument leads us to conclude, that since vice and virtue are not discoverable merely by reason, or the comparison of ideas, it must be by means of some impression or sentiment they occasion, that we are able to mark the difference betwixt them. Our decisions concerning moral rectitude and depravity are evidently perceptions; and as all perceptions are either impressions or ideas, the exclusion of the one is a convincing argument for the other. Morality, therefore, is more properly felt than judg'd of; tho' this feeling or sentiment is commonly so soft and gentle, that we are apt to confound it with an idea, according to our common custom of taking all things for the same, which have any near resemblance to each other.

The next question is, Of what nature are these impressions, and after what manner do they operate upon us? Here we cannot remain long in suspense, but must pronounce the impression arising from virtue, to be agreeable, and that proceeding from vice to be uneasy. Every moment's experience must convince us of this. There is no spectacle so fair and beautiful as a noble and generous action; nor any which gives us more abhorrence than one that is cruel and treacherous. No enjoyment equals the satisfaction we receive from the company of those we love and esteem; as the greatest of all punishments is to be oblig'd to pass our lives with those we hate or contemn. A very play or romance may afford us instances of this pleasure, which virtue conveys to us; and pain, which arises from vice.

Now since the distinguishing impressions, by which moral good or evil is known, are nothing but *particular* pains or pleasures; it follows, that in all enquiries concerning these moral distinctions, it will be sufficient to shew the principles, which make us feel a satisfaction or uneasiness from the survey of any character, in order to satisfy us why the character is laudable or blameable. An action, or sentiment, or character is virtuous or vicious; why? because its view causes a pleasure or uneasiness of a particular kind. In giving a reason, therefore, for the pleasure or uneasiness, we sufficiently explain the vice or virtue. To have the sense of virtue, is nothing but to *feel* a satisfaction of a particular kind from the contemplation of a character. The very *feeling* constitutes our praise or admiration. We go no farther; nor do we enquire into the cause of the satisfaction. We do not infer a character to be virtuous, because it pleases: But in feeling that it pleases after such a particular manner, we in effect feel that it is virtuous. The case is the same as in our judgments concerning all kinds of beauty, and tastes, and sensations. Our approbation is imply'd in the immediate pleasure they convey to us.

I have objected to the system, which establishes eternal rational measures of right and wrong, that 'tis impossible to shew, in the actions of reasonable creatures, any relations, which are not found in external objects; and therefore, if morality always attended these relations, 'twere possible for inanimate matter to become virtuous or vicious. Now it may, in like manner, be objected to the present system, that if virtue and vice be determin'd by pleasure and pain, these qualities must, in every case, arise from the sensations; and consequently any object, whether animate or inanimate, rational or irrational, might become morally good or evil, provided it can excite a satisfaction or uneasiness. But tho' this objection seems to be the very same, it has by no means the same force, in the one case as in the other. For, *first,* 'tis evident, that under the term *pleasure,* we comprehend sensations, which are very different from each other, and which have only such a distant resemblance, as is requisite to make them be express'd by the same abstract term. A good composition of music and a bottle of good wine equally produce pleasure; and what is more, their goodness is determin'd merely by the pleasure. But shall we say upon that account, that the wine is harmonious, or the music of a good flavour? In like manner an inanimate object, and the character or sentiments of any person may, both of them, give satisfaction; but as the satisfaction is different, this keeps our sentiments concerning them from being confounded, and makes us ascribe virtue to the one, and not to the other. Nor is every sentiment of pleasure or pain, which arises from characters and actions, of that *peculiar* kind, which makes us praise or condemn. The good qualities of an enemy are hurtful to us; but may still command our esteem and respect. 'Tis only when a character is considered in general, without reference to our particular interest, that it causes such a feeling or sentiment, as denominates it morally good or evil. 'Tis true, those sentiments, from interest and morals, are apt to be confounded, and naturally run into one another. It seldom happens, that we do not think an enemy vicious, and can distinguish betwixt his opposition to our interest and real villainy or baseness. But this hinders not, but that the sentiments are, in themselves, distinct; and a man of temper and judgment may preserve himself from these illusions. In like manner, tho' 'tis certain a musical voice is nothing but one that naturally gives a *particular* kind of pleasure; yet 'tis difficult for a man to be sensible, that the voice of an enemy is agreeable, or to allow it to be musical. But a person of a fine ear, who has the command of himself, can separate these feelings, and give praise to what deserves it.

. . .

CONCLUSION

It is sufficient for our present purpose, if it be allowed, what surely, without the greatest absurdity, cannot be disputed, that there is some benevolence, however small, infused into our bosom; some spark of friendship for humankind; some particle of the dove kneaded into our frame, along with the elements of the wolf and serpent. Let these generous sentiments be supposed ever so weak, let them be insufficient to move even a hand or finger of our body, they must still direct the determinations of our mind and, where everything else is equal, produce a cool preference of what is useful and serviceable to mankind above what is pernicious and dangerous. A *moral distinction,* therefore, immediately arises; a general sentiment of blame and approbation; a tendency, however faint, to the objects of the one, and a proportionable aversion to those of the other. Nor will those reasoners who so earnestly maintain the predominant selfishness of humankind be anywise scandalized at hearing of the weak sentiments of virtue implanted in our nature. On the contrary, they are found as ready to maintain the one tenet as the other; and their spirit of satire (for such it appears, rather than of corruption) naturally gives rise to both opinions which have, indeed, a great and almost an indissoluble connection together.

Avarice, ambition, vanity, and all passions vulgarly, though improperly, comprised under the denomination of *self-love* are here excluded from our theory concerning the origin of morals, not because they are too weak, but because they have not a proper direction for that purpose. The notion of morals implies some sentiment common to all mankind, which recommends the same object to general approbation and makes every man, or most men, agree in the same opinion or decision concerning it. It also implies some sentiment so universal and comprehensive as to extend to all mankind, and render the actions and conduct, even of the persons the most remote, an object of applause or censure, according as they agree or disagree with that rule of right which is established. These two requisite circumstances belong alone to the sentiment of humanity here insisted on. The other passions produce, in every breast, many strong sentiments of desire and aversion, affection and hatred, but these neither are felt so much in common nor are so comprehensive as to be the foundation of any general system and established theory of blame or approbation.

When a man denominates another his *enemy,* his *rival,* his *antagonist,* his *adversary,* he is understood to speak the language of self-love and to express sentiments peculiar to himself and arising from his particular circumstances and situation. But when he bestows on any man the epithets of *vicious* or *odious* or *depraved,* he then speaks another language and expresses sentiments in which he expects all his audience are to concur with him. He must here, therefore, depart from his private and particular situation and must choose a point of view common to him with others, he must move some universal principle of the human frame and touch a string to which all mankind have an accord and symphony. If he means, therefore, to express that this man possesses qualities whose tendency is pernicious to society, he has chosen this common point of view and has touched the principle of humanity in which every man, in some degree, concurs. While the human heart is compounded of the same elements as at present, it will never be wholly indifferent to public good, nor entirely unaffected with the tendency of characters and manners. And though this affection of humanity may not generally be esteemed so strong as vanity or ambition, yet being common to all men, it can alone be the foundation of morals or of any general system of blame or praise. One man's ambition is not another's ambition, nor will the same event or object satisfy both; but the humanity of one man is the humanity of everyone and the same object touches this passion in all human creatures.

But the sentiments which arise from humanity are not only the same in all human creatures and produce the same approbation or censure, but they also comprehend all human creatures; nor is there anyone whose conduct or character is not, by their means, an object, to everyone, of censure or approbation. On the contrary, those other passions, commonly denominated selfish, both produce different sentiments in each individual, according to his particular situation and also contemplate the greater part of mankind with the utmost indifference and unconcern. Whoever has a high regard and esteem for me, flatters my vanity; whoever expresses contempt, mortifies and displeases me. But as my name is known but to a small part of mankind, there are few who come within the sphere of this passion, or excite, on its account, either my affection or disgust. But if you represent a tyrannical, insolent, or barbarous behavior, in any country or in any age of the world, I soon carry my eye to the pernicious tendency of such a conduct and feel the sentiment of repugnance and displeasure toward it. No character can be so remote as to be, in this light, wholly indifferent to me. What is beneficial to society or to the person himself must still be preferred. And every quality or action of every human being must by this means be ranked under some class or denomination expressive of general censure or applause.

What more, therefore, can we ask to distinguish the sentiments dependent on humanity from those connected with any other passion, or to satisfy us why the former are the origin of morals, not the latter? Whatever conduct gains my approbation, by touching my humanity, procures also the applause of all mankind by affecting the same principle in them; but what serves my avarice or ambition pleases these passions in me alone and affects not the avarice and ambition of the rest of mankind. There is no circumstance of conduct in any man, provided it have a beneficial tendency, that is not agreeable to my humanity, however remote the person; but every man, so far removed as neither to cross nor serve my avarice and ambition, is regarded as wholly indifferent by those passions. The distinction, therefore, between these species of sentiment being so great and evident, language must soon be molded upon it and must invent a peculiar set of terms in order to express those universal sentiments of censure or approbation which arise from humanity, or from views of general usefulness and its contrary. *Virtue* and *vice* become then known: morals are recognized; certain general ideas are framed of human conduct and behavior; such measures are expected from men in such situations. This action is determined to be conformable to our abstract rule; that other, contrary. And by such universal principles are the particular sentiments of self-love frequently controlled and limited.

QUESTIONS

1. How does Hume attempt to show that "reason alone can never produce any action, or give rise to volition . . ."?
2. What is Hume's argument that from reason alone we cannot derive the distinction between good and evil? Explain in your own words the point of his arguments concerning ingratitude and incest.
3. Why, according to Hume, are vice and virtue not objective matters of fact?
4. "The *ought* cannot be derived solely from the *is*." In the light of Hume's moral philosophy, state what you would take this sentence to mean, and then explain why Hume would or would not accept it.
5. Does Hume, like Aristotle, attempt to base our knowledge of right and

wrong on our knowledge of man's nature? If so, how do the two philosophers differ in their ways of arguing? If not, on what does Hume attempt to base our knowledge of right and wrong? (Aristotle's views are to be found in the preceding selection of this chapter.)

6. From Hume's point of view, why is not a good composition of music or a bottle of good wine *morally* good? Can Hume's method for distinguishing moral goodness from other kinds of goodness be used to distinguish correctly between moral goodness and prudence (knowing how to achieve one's own ends)? Explain and defend your answer.

7. Hume's moral philosophy has been attacked on the following grounds:

"According to Hume's position, what makes murder wrong is the fact that people disapprove of murder. This implies that if people came to approve of murder, it would no longer be wrong but would thereby become right. But such a consequence outrages the moral feelings of all decent people, and therefore Hume's theory must be false."

What do you think of this argument?

8. Would it be possible for a person who accepted Hume's theory to be an ethical absolutist, or must he be an ethical relativist? (For the meaning of "ethical absolutist" and "ethical relativist," see the introduction to this chapter.)

9. What line of reasoning leads Hume to make the shocking statement: "It is not contrary to reason to prefer the destruction of the whole world to the scratching of my finger"?

10. Professor C. D. Broad has said:

. . . The logical consequence of Hume's theory is . . . that . . disputes on moral questions . . . *could* be settled, and that the way to settle them is to collect statistics of how people in fact do feel. And to me this kind of answer seems utterly irrelevant to this kind of question. If I am right in this, Hume's theory must be false.[1]

Is this a good argument against Hume?

[1] C. D. Broad, *Five Types of Ethical Theory,* Routledge and Kegan Paul, London, 1930, p. 115.

37. IMMANUEL KANT

(1724–1804)

A Priori Ethics

(A general introductory note on Kant may be found on page 130.)

This reading consists of the major portion of Kant's *Fundamental Principles of the Metaphysic of Morals.* In this book Kant is trying to make explicit the moral concepts which are implicit in the ethical outlook of ordinary peo-

ple in everyday life. The entire book is basically a study, in Kant's words, of "the common idea of duty and of moral laws." Kant is not trying to impose on us his own moral opinions, nor is he making a special theory of his own about moral knowledge which he wishes others to adopt. Instead of trying to get us to think about moral matters in a way different from the way we have always thought about them, his object is to make clear to us the logical foundations underlying the way in which we actually do think about moral matters in our practical life. He is trying to answer the question: What is it that, upon careful reflection, all of us really believe to be the essence of our moral duty?

Kant's fundamental thesis is that moral knowledge is a priori, that is, it is knowledge which rests solely on grounds of pure reason. He attempts to prove this by a detailed analysis of the meaning of moral duty. He begins by considering what it means for a person to have moral worth. A person has moral worth, according to Kant, when he has a good will, and a good will is the disposition to do our duty just because it is our duty. In other words, a person has a good will when his actions are motivated, not by his desires or "inclinations," but only by his duty. The intentions of the person, not the consequences of his actions, are the only thing relevant to his moral worth.

To act from duty, however, requires that we know what our duty is, and Kant claims that the nature of our duty can be derived from pure reason alone. The key to his argument lies in his conception of moral law; for duty is simply obedience to the moral law, and, therefore, if we understand what the moral law is, we know what our duty is. Kant believes that if a law is to be a moral law, it must be both universal and necessary. It must apply without exception not only to all men but to all rational beings, so that if there should exist somewhere in the universe beings who have nothing in common with men but the capacity to reason, the same moral law which commands men will also command them, and their moral duty will be identical with that of men. Now, according to Kant, the only kind of law which would have these characteristics would be a law *which commands nothing but obedience to law as such.* Our moral duty, therefore, is to act in accordance with the conception of law itself, in short, to act lawfully. And this means to act in accordance with a universal rule or principle which applies impartially to all rational beings in the universe. Thus each person is to act in the way that he would be willing as a rational being to have everyone else act. As Kant puts it: Each person is to act so that he can will that the maxim of his action become a universal law. It follows that what is right or wrong for one person is right or wrong for everyone—indeed, for all rational beings—in all places and at all times. The moral law, then, being a universal concept which applies to the world but is independent of all contingencies in the world, can only rest on grounds of pure reason.

What it means to try to put this ethical theory into practice the reader will discover for himself when he becomes acquainted with Kant's full argument. It should be remarked that Kant gives a number of examples to illustrate his meaning, and the careful reader will raise the question whether Kant's examples are always consistent with his theory.

The general result for moral knowledge implied by Kant's theory is a total separation, an impassable gulf, between science and ethics, between our knowledge of what is and our knowledge of what ought to be, between the realm of facts and the realm of values. Kant was emphatic in asserting that empirical knowledge of the natural world is completely irrelevant to our knowledge of what is right and wrong. In his own words, his central purpose was "to con-

struct a pure moral philosophy, perfectly cleared of everything which is
only empirical, and which belongs to
anthropology." (Kant's use of "anthropology," the science of man, covers
what would now be called psychology
and the social sciences.) This is what
Kant meant by a "metaphysic of mor-

als": an account of moral principles
which shows them to be derivable from
pure reason alone.

This selection is taken from T. K.
Abbott's translation of the *Fundamental Principles of the Metaphysic of Morals*. All headings not bracketed are
Kant's own.

From Kant: *Fundamental Principles of the Metaphysic of Morals,*
translated by Thomas K. Abbott with an introduction by Marvin
Fox (The Library of Liberal Arts No. 16, N. Y., 1949). Reprinted
by permission of the Liberal Arts Press Division of
The Bobbs-Merrill Company, Inc.

PREFACE

. . .

As my concern here is with moral philosophy, I limit the question suggested to this: whether it is not of the utmost necessity to construct a pure
moral philosophy, perfectly cleared of everything which is only empirical,
and which belongs to anthropology? For that such a philosophy must be
possible is evident from the common idea of duty and of the moral laws.
Everyone must admit that if a law is to have moral force, that is, to be the
basis of an obligation, it must carry with it absolute necessity; that, for
example, the precept, "Thou shalt not lie," is not valid for men alone, as if
other rational beings had no need to observe it; and so with all the other
moral laws properly so called; that, therefore, the basis of obligation must
not be sought in the nature of man, or in the circumstances in the world in
which he is placed, but *a priori* simply in the conceptions of pure reason;
and although any other precept which is founded on principles of mere
experience may be in certain respects universal, yet in as far as it rests even
in the least degree on an empirical basis, perhaps only as to a motive, such
a precept, while it may be a practical rule, can never be called a moral law.

Thus not only are moral laws with their principles essentially distinguished from every other kind of practical knowledge in which there is
anything empirical, but all moral philosophy rests wholly on its pure part.
When applied to man, it does not borrow the least thing from the knowledge of man himself (anthropology), but gives laws *a priori* to him as a
rational being. No doubt these laws require a judgment sharpened by experience, in order, on the one hand, to distinguish in what cases they are
applicable, and, on the other, to procure for them access to the will of the
man, and effectual influence on conduct; since man is acted on by so many

inclinations that, though capable of the idea of a practical pure reason, he is not so easily able to make it effective *in concreto* in his life.

A metaphysic of morals is therefore indispensably necessary, not merely for speculative reasons, in order to investigate the sources of the practical principles which are to be found *a priori* in our reason, but also because morals themselves are liable to all sorts of corruption as long as we are without that clue and supreme canon by which to estimate them correctly. For in order that an action should be morally good, it is not enough that it *conform* to the moral law, but it must also be done *for the sake of the law,* otherwise that conformity is only very contingent and uncertain; since a principle which is not moral, although it may now and then produce actions conformable to the law, will also often produce actions which contradict it. Now it is only in a pure philosophy that we can look for the moral law in its purity and genuineness (and, in a practical matter, this is of the utmost consequence): we must, therefore, begin with pure philosophy (metaphysic), and without it there cannot be any moral philosophy at all. That which mingles these pure principles with the empirical does not deserve the name of philosophy (for what distinguishes philosophy from common rational knowledge is that it treats in separate sciences what the latter only comprehends confusedly); much less does it deserve that of moral philosophy, since by this confusion it even spoils the purity of morals themselves and counteracts its own end.

. . .

First Section

TRANSITION FROM THE COMMON RATIONAL KNOWLEDGE OF MORALITY TO THE PHILOSOPHICAL

[The Good Will]

Nothing can possibly be conceived in the world, or even out of it, which can be called good without qualification, except a *good will*. Intelligence, wit, judgment, and the other *talents* of the mind, however they may be named, or courage, resolution, perseverance, as qualities of temperament, are undoubtedly good and desirable in many respects; but these gifts of nature may also become extremely bad and mischievous if the will which is to make use of them, and which, therefore, constitutes what is called *character,* is not good. It is the same with the *gifts of fortune.* Power, riches, honor, even health, and the general well-being and contentment with one's condition which is called *happiness,* inspire pride, and often presumption, if there is not a good will to correct the influence of these on the mind, and with this also to rectify the whole principle of acting, and adapt it to its end. The sight of a being who is not adorned with a single feature of a pure and good will, enjoying unbroken prosperity, can never give pleasure to an impartial rational spectator. Thus a good will appears to constitute the indispensable condition even of being worthy of happiness.

There are even some qualities which are of service to this good will itself, and may facilitate its action, yet which have no intrinsic unconditional value, but always presuppose a good will, and this qualifies the esteem that we justly have for them, and does not permit us to regard them as absolutely good. Moderation in the affections and passions, self-control, and calm deliberation are not only good in many respects, but even seem to constitute part of the intrinsic worth of the person; but they are far from deserving to be called good without qualification, although they have been so unconditionally praised by the ancients. For without the principles of a good will, they may become extremely bad; and the coolness of a villain not only makes him far more dangerous, but also directly makes him more abominable in our eyes than he would have been without it.

A good will is good not because of what is performs or effects, not by its aptness for the attainment of some proposed end, but simply by virtue of the volition—that is, it is good in itself, and considered by itself is to be esteemed much higher than all that can be brought about by it in favor of any inclination, nay, even of the sum-total of all inclinations. Even if it should happen that, owing to special disfavor of fortune, or the niggardly provision of a step-motherly nature, this will should wholly lack power to accomplish its purpose, if with its greatest efforts it should yet achieve nothing, and there should remain only the good will (not, to be sure, a mere wish, but the summoning of all means in our power), then, like a jewel, it would still shine by its own light, as a thing which has its whole value in itself. Its usefulness or fruitlessness can neither add to nor take away anything from this value. It would be, as it were, only the setting to enable us to handle it the more conveniently in common commerce, or to attract to it the attention of those who are not yet connoisseurs, but not to recommend it to true connoisseurs, or to determine its value.

[Why Reason Was Made to Guide the Will]

There is, however, something so strange in this idea of the absolute value of the mere will, in which no account is taken of its utility, that notwithstanding the thorough assent of even common reason to the idea, yet a suspicion must arise that it may perhaps really be the product of mere high-flown fancy, and that we may have misunderstood the purpose of nature in assigning reason as the governor of our will. Therefore we will examine this idea from this point of view.

In the physical constitution of an organized being, that is, a being adapted suitably to the purposes of life, we assume it as a fundamental principle that no organ for any purpose will be found but what is also the fittest and best adapted for that purpose. Now in a being which has reason and a will, if the proper object of nature were its *conservation,* its *welfare,* in a word, its *happiness,* then nature would have hit upon a very bad arrangement in selecting the reason of the creature to carry out this purpose. For all the actions which the creature has to perform with a view to this purpose, and the whole rule of its conduct, would be far more surely prescribed to it by instinct, and that end would have been attained thereby much more certainly than it ever can be by reason. Should reason have been communicated to this favored creature over and above, it must only have served it to contemplate the happy constitution of its nature, to admire it, to congratulate itself thereon, and to feel thankful for it to the beneficent cause, but not that it should subject its desires to that weak and delusive guidance, and meddle bunglingly with the purpose of nature. In a word, nature would have taken care that reason should not break forth into *practical exercise,* nor have the presumption, with its weak insight, to think out for itself the plan of happiness and of the means of attaining it. Nature would not only have taken on herself the choice of the ends but also of the means, and with wise foresight would have entrusted both to instinct.

And, in fact, we find that the more a cultivated reason applies itself with deliberate purpose to the enjoyment of life and happiness, so much the more does the man fail of true satisfaction. And from this circumstance there arises in many, if they are candid enough to confess it, a certain degree of *misology,* that is, hatred of reason, especially in the case of those who are most experienced in the use of it, because after calculating all the advantages they derive—I do not say from the invention of all the arts of common luxury, but even from the sciences (which seem to them to be after all only a luxury of the understanding)—they find that they have, in fact, only brought more trouble on their shoulders rather than gained in happiness; and they end by envying rather than despising the more common stamp of men who keep closer to the guidance of mere instinct, and do not allow their reason much influence on their conduct. And this we must admit, that the judgment of those who would very much lower the lofty eulogies of the advantages which reason gives us in regard to the happiness and satisfaction of life, or who would even reduce them below zero, is by no means morose or ungrateful to the goodness with which the world is governed, but that there lies at the root of these judgments the idea that our existence has a different and far nobler end, for which, and not for happiness, reason is properly intended, and which must, therefore, be regarded as the supreme condition to which the private ends of man must, for the most part, be postponed.

For as reason is not competent to guide the will with certainty in regard to its objects and the satisfaction of all our wants (which it to some extent even multiplies), this being an end to which an implanted instinct would have led with much greater certainty; and since, nevertheless, reason is imparted to us as a practical faculty, that is, as one which is to have influence on the *will*, therefore, admitting that nature generally in the distribution of her capacities has adapted the means to the end, its true destination must be to produce a *will*, not merely good as a *means* to something else, but *good in itself*, for which reason was absolutely necessary. This will then, though not indeed the sole and complete good, must be the supreme good and the condition of every other, even of the desire of happiness. Under these circumstances, there is nothing inconsistent with the wisdom of nature in the fact that the cultivation of the reason, which is requisite for the first and unconditional purpose, does in many ways interfere, at least in this life, with the attainment of the second, which is always conditional—namely, happiness. Nay, it may even reduce it to nothing, without nature thereby failing of her purpose. For reason recognizes the establishment of a good will as its highest practical destination, and in attaining this purpose is capable only of a satisfaction of its own proper kind, namely, that from the attainment of an end, which end again is determined by reason only, notwithstanding that this may involve many a disappointment to the ends of inclination.

[*The First Proposition of Morality*]

We have then to develop the notion of a will which deserves to be highly esteemed for itself, and is good without a view to anything further, a notion which exists already in the sound natural understanding, requiring rather to be cleared up than to be taught, and which in estimating the value of our actions always takes the first place and constitutes the condition of all the rest. In order to do this, we will take the notion of duty, which includes that of a good will, although implying certain subjective restrictions and hindrances. These, however, far from concealing it or rendering it unrecognizable, rather bring it out by contrast and make it shine forth so much the brighter.

I omit here all actions which are already recognized as inconsistent with duty, although they may be useful for this or that purpose, for with these the question whether they are done *from duty* cannot arise at all, since they even conflict with it. I also set aside those actions which really conform to duty, but to which men have *no* direct *inclination*, performing them because they are impelled thereto by some other inclination. For in this case we can readily distinguish whether the action which agrees with duty is done *from duty* or from a selfish view. It is much harder to make this distinction when the action accords with duty, and the subject has besides a *direct* inclination to it. For example, it is always a matter of duty that a dealer should not overcharge an inexperienced purchaser; and wherever there is much commerce the prudent tradesman does not overcharge, but keeps a fixed price for everyone, so that a child buys of him as well as any other. Men are thus *honestly* served; but this is not enough to make us believe that the tradesman has so acted from duty and from principles of honesty; his own advantage required it; it is out of the question in this case to suppose that he might besides have a direct inclination in favor of the buyers, so that, as it were, from love he should give no advantage to one over another. Accordingly the action was done neither from duty nor from direct inclination, but merely with a selfish view.

On the other hand, it is a duty to maintain one's life; and, in addition, everyone has also a direct inclination to do so. But on this account the often anxious care which most men take for it has no intrinsic worth, and their maxim has no moral import. They preserve their life *as duty requires,* no doubt, but not *because duty requires.* On the other hand, if adversity and hopeless sorrow have completely taken away the relish for life, if the unfortunate one, strong in mind, indignant at his fate rather than desponding or dejected, wishes for death, and yet preserves his life without loving it—not from inclination or fear, but from duty—then his maxim has a moral worth.

To be beneficent when we can is a duty; and besides this, there are many minds so sympathetically constituted that, without any other motive of vanity or self-interest, they find a pleasure in spreading joy around them, and can take delight in the satisfaction of others so far as it is their own work. But I maintain that in such a case an action of this kind, however proper, however amiable it may be, has nevertheless no true moral worth, but is on a level with other inclinations, for example, the inclination to honor, which, if it is happily directed to that which is in fact of public utility and accordant with duty, and consequently honorable, deserves praise and encouragement, but not esteem. For the maxim lacks the moral import, namely, that such actions be done *from duty,* not from inclination. Put the case that the mind of that philanthropist was clouded by sorrow of his own, extinguishing all sympathy with the lot of others, and that while he still has the power to benefit others in distress, he is not touched by their trouble because he is absorbed with his own; and now suppose that he tears himself out of this dead insensibility and performs the action without any inclination to it, but simply from duty, then first has his action its genuine moral worth. Further still, if nature has put little sympathy in the heart of this or that man, if he, supposed to be an upright man, is by temperament cold and indifferent to the sufferings of others, perhaps because in respect of his own he is provided with the special gift of patience and fortitude, and supposes, or even requires, that others should have the same—and such a man would certainly not be the meanest product of nature—but if nature had not specially framed him for a philanthropist, would he not still find in himself a source from whence to give himself a far higher worth than that of a good-natured temperament could be? Unquestionably. It is just in this that the moral worth of the character is brought out which is incomparably the highest of all, namely, that he is beneficent, not from inclination, but from duty.

To secure one's own happiness is a duty, at least indirectly; for discontent with one's condition, under a pressure of many anxieties and amidst unsatisfied wants, might easily become a great *temptation to transgression of duty*. But here again, without looking to duty, all men have already the strongest and most intimate inclination to happiness, because it is just in this idea that all inclinations are combined in one total. But the precept of happiness is often of such a sort that it greatly interferes with some inclinations, and yet a man cannot form any definite and certain conception of the sum of satisfaction of all of them which is called happiness. It is not then to be wondered at that a single inclination, definite both as to what it promises and as to the time within which it can be gratified, is often able to overcome such a fluctuating idea, and that a gouty patient, for instance, can choose to enjoy what he likes, and to suffer what he may, since, according to his calculation, on this occasion at least, he has [only] not sacrificed the enjoyment of the present moment to a possibly mistaken expectation of a happiness which is supposed to be found in health. But even in this case, if the general desire for happiness did not influence his will, and supposing that in his particular case health was not a necessary element in this calculation, there yet remains in this, as in all other cases, this law—namely, that he should promote his happiness not from inclination but from duty, and by this would his conduct first acquire true moral worth.

It is in this manner, undoubtedly, that we are to understand those passages of Scripture also in which we are commanded to love our neighbor, even our enemy. For love, as an affection, cannot be commanded, but beneficence for duty's sake may, even though we are not impelled to it by any inclination—nay, are even repelled by a natural and unconquerable aversion. This is *practical* love, and not *pathological*—a love which is seated in the will, and not in the propensions of sense—in principles of action and not of tender sympathy; and it is this love alone which can be commanded.

[*The Second Proposition of Morality*]

The second [1] proposition is: That an action done from duty derives its moral worth, *not from the purpose* which is to be attained by it, but from the maxim by which it is determined, and therefore does not depend on the realization of the object of the action, but merely on the *principle of volition* by which the action has taken place, without regard to any object of desire. It is clear from what precedes that the purposes which we may have in view in our actions, or their effects regarded as ends and springs of the will, cannot give to actions any unconditional or moral worth. In what, then, can their worth lie if it is not to consist in the will and in reference to its expected effect? It cannot lie anywhere but in the *principle of the will* without regard to the ends which can be attained by the action. For the will stands between its *a priori* principle, which is formal, and its *a posteriori* spring, which is

---

[1] The first proposition was that to have moral worth an action must be done from duty.

material, as between two roads, and as it must be determined by something, it follows that it must be determined by the formal principle of volition when an action is done from duty, in which case every material principle has been withdrawn from it.

[*The Third Proposition of Morality*]

The third proposition, which is a consequence of the two preceding, I would express thus: *Duty is the necessity of acting from respect for the law.* I may have *inclination* for an object as the effect of my proposed action, but I cannot have *respect* for it just for this reason that it is an effect and not an energy of will. Similarly, I cannot have respect for inclination, whether my own or another's; I can at most, if my own, approve it; if another's, sometimes even love it, that is, look on it as favorable to my own interest. It is only what is connected with my will as a principle, by no means as an effect—what does not subserve my inclination, but overpowers it, or at least in case of choice excludes it from its calculation—in other words, simply the law of itself, which can be an object of respect, and hence a command. Now an action done from duty must wholly exclude the influence of inclination, and with it every object of the will, so that nothing remains which can determine the will except objectively the *law,* and subjectively *pure respect* for this practical law, and consequently the maxim [2] that I should follow this law even to the thwarting of all my inclinations.

Thus the moral worth of an action does not lie in the effect expected from it, nor in any principle of action which requires to borrow its motive from this expected effect. For all these effects—agreeableness of one's condition, and even the promotion of the happiness of others—could have been also brought about by other causes, so that for this there would have been no need of the will of a rational being; whereas it is in this alone that the supreme and unconditional good can be found. The pre-eminent good which we call moral can therefore consist in nothing else than *the conception of law* in itself, *which certainly is only possible in a rational being,* in so far as this conception, and not the expected effect, determines the will. This is a good which is already present in the person who acts accordingly, and we have not to wait for it to appear first in the result.

[*The Supreme Principle of Morality:*
The Categorical Imperative]

But what sort of law can that be the conception of which must determine the will, even without paying any regard to the effect expected from it, in order that this will may be called good absolutely and without qualifica-

---

[2] A *maxim* is the subjective principle of volition. The objective principle (*i.e.*, that which would also serve subjectively as a practical principle to all rational beings if reason had full power over the faculty of desire) is the practical *law.*

tion? As I have deprived the will of every impulse which could arise to it from obedience to any law, there remains nothing but the universal conformity of its actions to law in general, which alone is to serve the will as a principle, that is, I am never to act otherwise than so *that I could also will that my maxim should become a universal law*. Here, now, it is the simple conformity to law in general, without assuming any particular law applicable to certain actions, that serves the will as its principle, and must so serve it if duty is not to be a vain delusion and a chimerical notion. The common reason of men in its practical judgments perfectly coincides with this, and always has in view the principle here suggested. Let the question be, for example: May I when in distress make a promise with the intention not to keep it? I readily distinguish here between the two significations which the question may have: whether it is prudent or whether it is right to make a false promise? The former may undoubtedly often be the case. I see clearly indeed that it is not enough to extricate myself from a present difficulty by means of this subterfuge, but it must be well considered whether there may not hereafter spring from this lie much greater inconvenience than that from which I now free myself, and as, with all my supposed *cunning*, the consequences cannot be so easily foreseen but that credit once lost may be much more injurious to me than any mischief which I seek to avoid at present, it should be considered whether it would not be more *prudent* to act herein according to a universal maxim, and to make it a habit to promise nothing except with the intention of keeping it. But it is soon clear to me that such a maxim will still only be based on the fear of consequences. Now it is a wholly different thing to be truthful from duty, and to be so from apprehension of injurious consequences. In the first case, the very notion of the action already implies a law for me; in the second case, I must first look about elsewhere to see what results may be combined with it which would affect myself. For to deviate from the principle of duty is beyond all doubt wicked; but to be unfaithful to my maxim of prudence may often be very advantageous to me, although to abide by it is certainly safer. The shortest way, however, and an unerring one, to discover the answer to this question whether a lying promise is consistent with duty, is to ask myself, Should I be content that my maxim (to extricate myself from difficulty by a false promise) should hold good as a universal law, for myself as well as for others; and should I be able to say to myself, "Every one may make a deceitful promise when he finds himself in a difficulty from which he cannot otherwise extricate himself"? Then I presently become aware that, while I can will the lie, I can by no means will that lying should be a universal law. For with such a law there would be no promises at all, since it would be in vain to allege my intention in regard to my future actions to those who would not believe this allegation, or if they over-hastily did so, would pay me back in my own coin. Hence my maxim, as soon as it should be made a universal law, would necessarily destroy itself.

I do not, therefore, need any far-reaching penetration to discern what

I have to do in order that my will may be morally good. Inexperienced in the course of the world, incapable of being prepared for all its contingencies, I only ask myself: Canst thou also will that thy maxim should be a universal law? If not, then it must be rejected, and that not because of a disadvantage accruing from it to myself or even to others, but because it cannot enter as a principle into a possible universal legislation, and reason extorts from me immediate respect for such legislation. I do not indeed as yet *discern* on what this respect is based (this the philosopher may inquire), but at least I understand this—that it is an estimation of the worth which far outweighs all worth of what is recommended by inclination, and that the necessity of acting from *pure* respect for the practical law is what constitutes duty, to which every other motive must give place because it is the condition of a will being good *in itself,* and the worth of such a will is above everything.

Thus, then, without quitting the moral knowledge of common human reason, we have arrived at its principle. And although, no doubt, common men do not conceive it in such an abstract and universal form, yet they always have it really before their eyes and use it as the standard of their decision.

·   ·   ·

Second Section

TRANSITION FROM POPULAR MORAL PHILOSOPHY TO THE METAPHYSIC OF MORALS

[*The Impossibility of an Empirical Moral Philosophy*]

If we have hitherto drawn our notion of duty from the common use of our practical reason, it is by no means to be inferred that we have treated it as an empirical notion. On the contrary, if we attend to the experience of men's conduct, we meet frequent and, as we ourselves allow, just complaints that one cannot find a single certain example of the disposition to act from pure duty. Although many things are done in *conformity* with what *duty* prescribes, it is nevertheless always doubtful whether they are done strictly *from duty,* so as to have a moral worth. Hence there have at all times been philosophers who have altogether denied that this disposition actually exists at all in human actions, and have ascribed everything to a more or less refined self-love. Not that they have on that account questioned the soundness of the conception of morality; on the contrary, they spoke with sincere regret of the frailty and corruption of human nature, which, though noble enough to take as its rule an idea so worthy of respect, is yet too weak to follow it and employs reason, which ought to give it the law only for the purpose of providing for the interest of the inclinations, whether singly or at the best in the greatest possible harmony with one another.

In fact, it is absolutely impossible to make out by experience with complete certainty a single case in which the maxim of an action, however right in itself, rested simply on moral grounds and on the conception of duty. Sometimes it happens that with the sharpest self-examination we can find nothing beside the moral principle of duty which could have been powerful enough to move us to this or that action and to so great a sacrifice; yet we cannot from this infer with certainty that it was not really some secret impulse of self-love, under the false appearance of duty, that was the actual determining cause of the will. We like then to flatter ourselves by falsely taking credit for a more noble motive; whereas in fact we can never, even by the strictest examination, get completely behind the secret springs of action since, when the question is of moral worth, it is not with the actions which we see that we are concerned, but with those inward principles of them which we do not see.

Moreover, we cannot better serve the wishes of those who ridicule all morality as a mere chimera of human imagination overstepping itself from vanity, than by conceding to them that notions of duty must be drawn only from experience (as from indolence, people are ready to think is also the case with all other notions); for this is to prepare for them a certain triumph. I am willing to admit out of love of humanity that even most of our actions are correct, but if we look closer at them we everywhere come upon the dear self which is always prominent, and it is this they have in view, and not the strict command of duty, which would often require self-denial. Without being an enemy of virtue, a cool observer, one that does not mistake the wish for good, however lively, for its reality, may sometimes doubt whether true virtue is actually found anywhere in the world, and this especially as years increase and the judgment is partly made wiser by experience, and partly also more acute in observation. This being so, nothing can secure us from falling away altogether from our ideas of duty, or maintain in the soul a well-grounded respect for its law, but the clear conviction that although there should never have been actions which really sprang from such pure sources, yet whether this or that takes place is not at all the question; but that reason of itself, independent on all experience, ordains what ought to take place, that accordingly actions of which perhaps the world has hitherto never given an example, the feasibility even of which might be very much doubted by one who founds everything on experience, are nevertheless inflexibly commanded by reason; that, for example, even though there might never yet have been a sincere friend, yet not a whit the less is pure sincerity in friendship required of every man, because, prior to all experience, this duty is involved as duty in the idea of a reason determining the will by *a priori* principles.

When we add further that, unless we deny that the notion of morality has any truth or reference to any possible object, we must admit that its law must be valid, not merely for men, but for all *rational creatures generally,* not merely under certain contingent conditions or with exceptions, but *with absolute necessity,* then it is clear that no experience could enable us to infer even the possibility of such apodictic laws. For with what right could we bring into unbounded respect as a universal precept for every rational nature that which perhaps holds only under the contingent conditions of humanity? Or how could laws of the determination of *our* will be regarded as laws of the determination of the will of rational beings generally, and for us only as such, if they were merely empirical and did not take their origin wholly *a priori* from pure but practical reason?

Nor could anything be more fatal to morality than that we should wish to derive it from examples. For every example of it that is set before me must be first itself tested by principles of morality, whether it is worthy to serve as an original example, that is, as a pattern, but by no means can it authoritatively furnish the conception of morality. Even the Holy One of the Gospels must first be compared with our ideal of moral perfection before we can recognize Him as such; and so He says of Himself, "Why call ye Me [whom you see] good; none is good [the model of good] but God only [whom ye do not see]?" But whence have we the conception of God as the supreme good? Simply from the *idea* of moral perfection, which reason frames *a priori* and connects inseparably with the notion of a free will. Imitation finds no place at all in morality, and examples serve only for encouragement, that is, they put beyond doubt the feasibility of what the law commands, they make visible that which the practical rule expresses more generally, but they can never authorize us to set aside the true original which lies in reason, and to guide ourselves by examples.

·   ·   ·

From what has been said, it is clear that all moral conceptions have their seat and origin completely *a priori* in the reason, and that, moreover, in the commonest reason just as truly as in that which is in the highest degree speculative; that they cannot be obtained by abstraction from any empirical, and therefore merely contingent, knowledge; that it is just this purity of their origin that makes them worthy to serve as our supreme practical principle, and that just in proportion as we add anything empirical, we detract from their genuine influence and from the absolute value of actions; that it is not only of the greatest necessity, in a purely speculative point of view, but is also of the greatest practical importance, to derive these notions and laws from pure reason, to present them pure and unmixed, and even to determine the compass of this practical or pure rational knowledge, that is, to determine the whole faculty of pure practical reason; and, in doing so, we must not make its principles dependent on the particular nature of human reason, though in speculative philosophy this may be permitted, or may even at times be necessary; but since moral laws ought to hold good for every rational creature, we must derive them from the general concept of a rational being. In this way, although for its *application* to man morality has need of anthropology, yet, in the first instance, we must treat it independently as pure philosophy, that is, as metaphysic, complete in itself (a thing which in such distinct branches of science is easily done); knowing well that, unless we are in possession of this, it would not only be vain to determine the moral element of duty in right actions for purposes of speculative criticism, but it would be impossible to base morals on their genuine principles, even for common practical purposes, especially of moral instruction, so as to produce pure moral dispositions, and to engraft them on men's minds to the promotion of the greatest possible good in the world.

But in order that in this study we may not merely advance by the natural steps from the common moral judgment (in this case very worthy of respect) to the philosophical, as has been already done, but also from a popular philosophy, which goes no further than it can reach by groping with the help of examples, to metaphysics (which does not allow itself to be checked by anything empirical and, as it must measure the whole extent of this kind of rational knowledge, goes as far as ideal conceptions, where even examples fail us), we must follow and clearly describe the practical faculty of reason, from the general rules of its determination to the point where the notion of duty springs from it.

[*Imperatives: Hypothetical and Categorical*]

Everything in nature works according to laws. Rational beings alone have the faculty of acting according *to the conception* of laws—that is, according to principles, that is, have a *will*. Since the deduction of actions from principles requires *reason,* the will is nothing but practical reason. If reason infallibly determines the will, then the actions of such a being which are recognized as objectively necessary are subjectively necessary also, that is, the will is a faculty to choose *that only* which reason independent on inclination recognizes as practically necessary, that is, as good. But if reason of itself does not sufficiently determine the will, if the latter is subject also to subjective conditions (particular impulses) which do not always coincide with the objective conditions, in a word, if the will does not *in itself* completely accord with reason (which is actually the case with men), then the actions which objectively are recognized as necessary are subjectively contingent, and the determination of such a will according to objective laws is *obligation,* that is to say, the relation of the objective laws to a will that is not thoroughly good is conceived as the determination of the will of a rational being by principles of reason, but which the will from its nature does not of necessity follow.

The conception of an objective principle, in so far as it is obligatory for a will, is called a command (of reason), and the formula of the command is called an Imperative.

All imperatives are expressed by the word *ought* [or *shall*], and thereby indicate the relation of an objective law of reason to a will which from its subjective constitution is not necessarily determined by it (an obligation). They say that something would be good to do or to forebear, but they say it to a will which does not always do a thing because it is conceived to be good to do it. That is practically *good,* however, which determines the will by means of the conceptions of reason, and consequently not from subjective causes, but objectively, that is, on principles which are valid for every rational being as such. It is distinguished from the *pleasant* as that which influences the will only by means of sensation from merely subjective causes, valid only for the sense of this or that one, and not as a principle of reason which holds for every one.

A perfectly good will would therefore be equally subject to objective laws (viz., laws of good), but could not be conceived as *obliged* thereby to act lawfully, because of itself from its subjective constitution it can only be determined by the conception of good. Therefore no imperatives hold for the Divine will, or in general for a *holy* will; *ought* is here out of place because the volition is already of itself necessarily in unison with the law. Therefore imperatives are only formulae to express the relation of objective laws of all volition to the subjective imperfection of the will of this or that rational being, for example, the human will.

Now all *imperatives* command either *hypothetically* or *categorically.* The former represent the practical necessity of a possible action as means to something else that is willed (or at least which one might possibly will). The categorical imperative would be that which represented an action as necessary of itself without reference to another end, that is, as objectively necessary.

Since every practical law represents a possible action as good, and on this account, for a subject who is practically determinable by reason as necessary, all imperatives are formulae determining an action which is necessary according to the principle of a will good in some respects. If now the action is good only as a means *to something else,* then the imperative is *hypothetical;* if it is conceived as good *in itself* and consequently as being necessarily the principle of a will which of itself conforms to reason, then it is *categorical.*

Thus the imperative declares what action possible by me would be good, and presents the practical rule in relation to a will which does not forthwith perform an action simply because it is good, whether because the subject does not always know that it is good, or because, even if it know this, yet its maxims might be opposed to the objective principles of practical reason.

Accordingly the hypothetical imperative only says that the action is good for some purpose, *possible* or *actual.* In the first case it is a *problemat-*

ical, in the second an *assertorial* practical principle. The categorical imperative which declares an action to be objectively necessary in itself without reference to any purpose, that is, without any other end, is valid as an *apodictic* (practical) principle.

Whatever is possible only by the power of some rational being may also be conceived as a possible purpose of some will; and therefore the principles of action as regards the means necessary to attain some possible purpose are in fact infinitely numerous. All sciences have a practical part consisting of problems expressing that some end is possible for us, and of imperatives directing how it may be attained. These may, therefore, be called in general imperatives of *skill.* Here there is no question whether the end is rational and good, but only what one must do in order to attain it. The precepts for the physician to make his patient thoroughly healthy, and for a poisoner to ensure certain death, are of equal value in this respect, that each serves to effect its purpose perfectly. Since in early youth it cannot be known what ends are likely to occur to us in the course of life, parents seek to have their children taught a *great many things,* and provide for their *skill* in the use of means for all sorts of arbitrary ends, of none of which can they determine whether it may not perhaps hereafter be an object to their pupil, but which it is at all events *possible* that he might aim at; and this anxiety is so great that they commonly neglect to form and correct their judgment on the value of the things which may be chosen as ends.

There is *one* end, however, which may be assumed to be actually such to all rational beings (so far as imperatives apply to them, viz., as dependent beings), and, therefore, one purpose which they not merely *may* have, but which we may with certainty assume that they all actually *have* by a natural necessity, and this is *happiness.* The hypothetical imperative which expresses the practical necessity of an action as means to the advancement of happiness is *assertorial.* We are not to present it as necessary for an uncertain and merely possible purpose, but for a purpose which we may presuppose with certainty and *a priori* in every man, because it belongs to his being. Now skill in the choice of means to his own greatest well-being may be called *prudence,* in the narrowest sense. And thus the imperative which refers to the choice of means to one's own happiness, that is, the precept of prudence, is still always *hypothetical;* the action is not commanded absolutely, but only as means to another purpose.

Finally, there is an imperative which commands a certain conduct immediately, without having as its condition any other purpose to be attained by it. This imperative is *categorical.* It concerns not the matter of the action, or its intended result, but its form and the principle of which it is itself a result; and what is essentially good in it consists in the mental disposition, let the consequence be what it may. This imperative may be called that of *morality.*

There is a marked distinction also between the volitions on these three sorts of principles in the *dissimilarity* of the obligation of the will. In order to mark this difference more clearly, I think they would be most suitably named in their order if we said they are either *rules* of skill, or *counsels* of prudence, or *commands* (*laws*) of morality. For it is *law* only that involves the conception of an *unconditional* and objective necessity, which is consequently universally valid; and commands are laws which must be obeyed, that is, must be followed, even in opposition to inclination. *Counsels,* indeed, involve necessity, but one which can only hold under a contingent subjective condition, viz., they depend on whether this or that man reckons this or that as part of his happiness; the categorical imperative, on the contrary, is not limited by any condition, and as being absolutely, although practically, necessary may be quite properly called a command. We might also call the first kind of imperatives *technical* (belonging to art), the second *pragmatic* (belonging to welfare), the third *moral* (belonging to free conduct generally, that is, to morals).

[*The Rational Ground of Hypothetical Imperatives*]

Now arises the question, how are all these imperatives possible? This question does not seek to know how we can conceive the accomplishment of the action which the imperative ordains, but merely how we can conceive the obligation of the will which the imperative expresses. No special explanation is needed to show how an imperative of skill is possible. Whoever wills the end wills also (so far as reason decides his conduct) the means in his power which are indispensably necessary thereto. This proposition is, as regards the volition, analytical; for in willing an object as my effect there is already thought the causality of myself as an acting cause, that is to say, the use of the means; and the imperative educes from the conception of volition of an end the conception of actions necessary to this end. Synthetical propositions must no doubt be employed in defining the means to a proposed end; but they do not concern the principle, the act of the will, but the object and its realization. For example, that in order to bisect a line on an unerring principle I must draw from its extremities two intersecting arcs; this no doubt is taught by mathematics only in synthetical propositions; but if I know that it is only by this process that the intended operation can be performed, then to say that if I fully will the operation, I also will the action required for it, is an analytical proposition; for it is one and the same thing to conceive something as an effect which I can produce in a certain way, and to conceive myself as acting in this way.

If it were only equally easy to give a definite conception of happiness, the imperatives of prudence would correspond exactly with those of skill, and would likewise be analytical. For in this case as in that, it could be said whoever wills the end wills also (according to the dictate of reason necessarily) the indispensable means thereto which are in his power. But, unfortunately, the notion of happiness is so indefinite that although every man wishes to attain it, yet he never can say definitely and consistently what it is that he really wishes and wills. The reason of this is that all the elements which belong to the notion of happiness are altogether empirical, that is, they must be borrowed from experience, and nevertheless the idea of happiness requires an absolute whole, a maximum of welfare in my present and all future circumstances. Now it is impossible that the most clear-sighted and at the same time most powerful being (supposed finite) should frame to himself a definite conception of what he really wills in this. Does he will riches, how much anxiety, envy, and snares might he not thereby draw upon his shoulders? Does he will knowledge and discernment, perhaps it might prove to be only an eye so much the sharper to show him so much the more fearfully the evils that are now concealed from him and that cannot be avoided, or to impose more wants on his desires, which already give him concern enough. Would he have long life? Who guarantees to him that it would not be a long misery? Would he at least have health? How often has uneasiness of the body restrained from excesses into which perfect health would have allowed one to fall, and so on. In short, he is unable, on any principle, to determine with certainty what would make him truly happy; because to do so he would need to be omniscient. We cannot therefore act on any definite principles to secure happiness, but only on empirical counsels, for example, of regimen, frugality, courtesy, reserve, etc., which experience teaches do, on the average, most promote well-being. Hence it follows that the imperatives of prudence do not, strictly speaking, command at all, that is, they cannot present actions objectively as practically *necessary;* that they are rather to be regarded as counsels (*consilia*) than precepts (*praecepta*) of reason, that the problem to determine certainly and universally what action would promote the happiness of a rational being is completely insoluble, and consequently no imperative respecting it is possible which should, in the strict sense, command to do what makes happy; because happiness is not an ideal of reason but of imagination, resting solely on empirical grounds, and it is vain to expect that these should define an action by which one could attain the totality of a series of consequences which is really endless. This imperative of prudence would, however, be an analytical proposition if we assume that the means to happiness could be certainly assigned; for it is distinguished from the imperative of skill only by this that in the latter the end is merely *possible,* in the former it is *given;* as, however, both only ordain the means to that which we suppose to be willed as an end, it follows that the imperative which ordains the willing of the means to him who wills the end is in both cases analytical. Thus there is no difficulty in regard to the possibility of an imperative of this kind either.

[*The Rational Ground of the Categorical Imperative*]

On the other hand, the question, how the imperative of *morality* is possible, is undoubtedly one, the only one, demanding a solution, as this is not at all hypothetical, and the objective necessity which it presents cannot rest on any hypothesis, as is the case with the hypothetical imperatives. Only here we must never leave out of consideration that we *cannot* make out *by any example,* in other words, empirically, whether there is such an imperative at all; but it is rather to be feared that all those which seem to be categorical may yet be at bottom hypothetical. For instance, when the precept is: Thou shalt not promise deceitfully; and it is assumed that the necessity of this is not a mere counsel to avoid some other evil, so that it should mean: Thou shalt not make a lying promise, lest if it become known thou shouldst destroy thy credit, but that an action of this kind must be regarded as evil in itself, so that the imperative of the prohibition is categorical; then we cannot show with certainty in any example that the will was determined merely by the law, without any other spring of action, although it may appear to be so. For it is always possible that fear of disgrace, perhaps also obscure dread of other dangers, may have a secret influence on the will. Who can prove by experience the non-existence of a cause when all that experience tells us is that we do not perceive it? But in such a case the so-called moral imperative, which as such appears to be categorical and unconditional, would in reality be only a pragmatic precept, drawing our attention to our own interests, and merely teaching us to take these into consideration.

We shall therefore have to investigate *a priori* the possibility of a categorical imperative, as we have not in this case the advantage of its reality being given in experience, so that [the elucidation of] its possibility should be requisite only for its explanation, not for its establishment. In the meantime it may be discerned beforehand that the categorical imperative alone has the purport of a practical law; all the rest may indeed be called *principles* of the will but not laws, since whatever is only necessary for the attainment of some arbitrary purpose may be considered as in itself contingent, and we can at any time be free from the precept if we give up the purpose; on the contrary, the unconditional command leaves the will no liberty to choose the opposite, consequently it alone carries with it that necessity which we require in a law.

Secondly, in the case of this categorical imperative or law of morality, the difficulty (of discerning its possibility) is a very profound one. It is an *a priori* synthetical practical proposition;[3] and as there is so much difficulty

---

[3] I connect the act with the will without presupposing any condition resulting from any inclination, but *a priori,* and therefore necessarily (though only objectively, that is, assuming the idea of a reason possessing full power over all subjective motives). This is accordingly a practical proposition which does not deduce the willing of an action by mere analysis from another already presupposed (for we have not such a perfect

in discerning the possibility of speculative propositions of this kind, it may readily be supposed that the difficulty will be no less with the practical.

[*First Formulation of the Categorical Imperative: Universal Law*]

In this problem we will first inquire whether the mere conception of a categorical imperative may not perhaps supply us also with the formula of it, containing the proposition which alone can be a categorical imperative; for even if we know the tenor of such an absolute command, yet how it is possible will require further special and laborious study, which we postpone to the last section.

When I conceive a hypothetical imperative, in general I do not know beforehand what it will contain until I am given the condition. But when I conceive a categorical imperative, I know at once what it contains. For as the imperative contains besides the law only the necessity that the maxims [4] shall conform to this law, while the law contains no conditions restricting it, there remains nothing but the general statement that the maxim of the action should conform to a universal law, and it is this conformity alone that the imperative properly represents as necessary.

There is therefore but one categorical imperative, namely, this: *Act only on that maxim whereby thou canst at the same time will that it should become a universal law.*

Now if all imperatives of duty can be deduced from this one imperative as from their principle, then, although it should remain undecided whether what is called duty is not merely a vain notion, yet at least we shall be able to show what we understand by it and what this notion means.

Since the universality of the law according to which effects are produced constitutes what is properly called *nature* in the most general sense (as to form)—that is, the existence of things so far as it is determined by general laws—the imperative of duty may be expressed thus: *Act as if the maxim of thy action were to become by thy will a universal law of nature.*

[*Four Illustrations*]

We will now enumerate a few duties, adopting the usual division of them into duties to ourselves and to others, and into perfect and imperfect duties.

---

will), but connects it immediately with the conception of the will of a rational being, as something not contained in it.

[4] A maxim is a subjective principle of action, and must be distinguished from the *objective principle,* namely, practical law. The former contains the practical rule set by reason according to the conditions of the subject (often its ignorance or its inclinations), so that it is the principle on which the subject *acts;* but the law is the objective

1. A man reduced to despair by a series of misfortunes feels wearied of life, but is still so far in possession of his reason that he can ask himself whether it would not be contrary to his duty to himself to take his own life. Now he inquires whether the maxim of his action could become a universal law of nature. His maxim is: From self-love I adopt it as a principle to shorten my life when its longer duration is likely to bring more evil than satisfaction. It is asked then simply whether this principle founded on self-love can become a universal law of nature. Now we see at once that a system of nature of which it should be a law to destroy life by means of the very feeling whose special nature it is to impel to the improvement of life would contradict itself, and therefore could not exist as a system of nature; hence that maxim cannot possibly exist as a universal law of nature, and consequently would be wholly inconsistent with the supreme principle of all duty.

2. Another finds himself forced by necessity to borrow money. He knows that he will not be able to repay it, but sees also that nothing will be lent to him unless he promises stoutly to repay it in a definite time. He desires to make this promise, but he has still so much conscience as to ask himself: Is it not unlawful and inconsistent with duty to get out of a difficulty in this way? Suppose, however, that he resolves to do so, then the maxim of his action would be expressed thus: When I think myself in want of money, I will borrow money and promise to repay it, although I know that I never can do so. Now this principle of self-love or of one's own advantage may perhaps be consistent with my whole future welfare; but the question now is, Is it right? I change then the suggestion of self-love into a universal law, and state the question thus: How would it be if my maxim were a universal law? Then I see at once that it could never hold as a universal law of nature, but would necessarily contradict itself. For supposing it to be a universal law that everyone when he thinks himself in a difficulty should be able to promise whatever he pleases, with the purpose of not keeping his promise, the promise itself would become impossible, as well as the end that one might have in view in it, since no one would consider that anything was promised to him, but would ridicule all such statements as vain pretenses.

3. A third finds in himself a talent which with the help of some culture might make him a useful man in many respects. But he finds himself in comfortable circumstances and prefers to indulge in pleasure rather than to take pains in enlarging and improving his happy natural capacities. He asks, however, whether his maxim of neglect of his natural gifts, besides agreeing with his inclination to indulgence, agrees also with what is called duty. He sees then that a system of nature could indeed subsist with such a universal law, although men (like the South Sea islanders) should let their talents rest and resolve to devote their lives merely to idleness, amusement, and propagation of their species—in a word, to enjoyment; but he cannot possibly *will*

principle valid for every rational being, and is the principle on which it *ought to act*— that is—an imperative.

that this should be a universal law of nature, or be implanted in us as such by a natural instinct. For, as a rational being, he necessarily wills that his faculties be developed, since they serve him, and have been given him, for all sorts of possible purposes.

4. A fourth, who is in prosperity, while he sees that others have to contend with great wretchedness and that he could help them, thinks: What concern is it of mine? Let everyone be as happy as Heaven pleases, or as he can make himself; I will take nothing from him nor even envy him, only I do not wish to contribute anything to his welfare or to his assistance in distress! Now no doubt, if such a mode of thinking were a universal law, the human race might very well subsist, and doubtless even better than in a state in which everyone talks of sympathy and good-will, or even takes care occasionally to put it into practice, but, on the other side, also cheats when he can, betrays the rights of men, or otherwise violates them. But although it is possible that a universal law of nature might exist in accordance with that maxim, it is impossible to *will* that such a principle should have the universal validity of a law of nature. For a will which resolved this would contradict itself, inasmuch as many cases might occur in which one would have need of the love and sympathy of others, and in which, by such a law of nature, sprung from his own will, he would deprive himself of all hope of the aid he desires.

These are a few of the many actual duties, or at least what we regard as such, which obviously fall into two classes on the one principle that we have laid down. We must be *able to will* that a maxim of our action should be a universal law. This is the canon of the moral appreciation of the action generally. Some actions are of such a character that their maxim cannot without contradiction be even *conceived* as a universal law of nature, far from it being possible that we should *will* that it *should* be so. In others, this intrinsic impossibility is not found, but still it is impossible to *will* that their maxim should be raised to the universality of a law of nature, since such a will would contradict itself. It is easily seen that the former violate strict or rigorous (inflexible) duty; the latter only laxer (meritorious) duty. Thus it has been completely shown by these examples how all duties depend as regards the nature of the obligation (not the object of the action) on the same principle.

[Transgressions of the Moral Law]

If now we attend to ourselves on occasion of any transgression of duty, we shall find that we in fact do not will that our maxim should be a universal law, for that is impossible for us; on the contrary, we will that the opposite should remain a universal law, only we assume the liberty of making an *exception* in our own favor or (just for this time only) in favor of our inclination. Consequently, if we considered all cases from one and the same point of view, namely, that of reason, we should find a contradiction in our own will, namely, that a certain principle should be objectively necessary as a universal law, and yet subjectively should not be universal, but admit of exceptions. As, however, we at one moment regard our action from the point of view of a will wholly conformed to reason, and then again look at the same action from the point of view of a will affected by inclination, there is not really any contradiction, but an antagonism of inclination to the precept of reason, whereby the universality of the principle is changed into a mere generality, so that the practical principle of reason shall meet the maxim half way. Now, although this cannot be justified in our own impartial judgment, yet it proves that we do really recognize the validity of the categorical imperative and (with all respect for it) only allow ourselves a few exceptions which we think unimportant and forced from us.

[*The Need for an A Priori Proof of the Categorical Imperative*]

We have thus established at least this much—that if duty is a conception which is to have any import and real legislative authority for our actions, it can only be expressed in categorical, and not at all in hypothetical imperatives. We have also, which is of great importance, exhibited clearly and definitely for every practical application the content of the categorical imperative, which must contain the principle of all duty if there is such a thing at all. We have not yet, however, advanced so far as to prove *a priori* that there actually is such an imperative, that there is a practical law which commands absolutely of itself and without any other impulse, and that the following of this law is duty.

With the view of attaining to this it is of extreme importance to remember that we must not allow ourselves to think of deducing the reality of this principle from the *particular attributes of human nature*. For duty is to be a practical, unconditional necessity of action; it must therefore hold for all rational beings (to whom an imperative can apply at all), and *for this reason only* be also a law for all human wills. On the contrary, whatever is deduced from the particular natural characteristics of humanity, from certain feelings and propensions, nay, even, if possible, from any particular tendency proper to human reason, and which need not necessarily hold for the will of every rational being—this may indeed supply us with a maxim but not with a law; with a subjective principle on which we may have a propension and inclination to act, but not with an objective principle on which we should be *enjoined* to act, even though all our propensions, inclinations, and natural dispositions were opposed to it. In fact, the sublimity and intrinsic dignity of the command in duty are so much the more evident, the less the subjective impulses favor it and the more they oppose it, without being able in the slightest degree to weaken the obligation of the law or to diminish its validity.

Here then we see philosophy brought to a critical position, since it has to be firmly fixed, notwithstanding that it has nothing to support it in heaven or earth. Here it must show its purity as absolute director of its own laws, not the herald of those which are whispered to it by an implanted sense or who knows what tutelary nature. Although these may be better than nothing, yet they can never afford principles dictated by reason, which must have their source wholly *a priori* and thence their commanding authority, expecting everything from the supremacy of the law and the due respect for it, nothing from inclination, or else condemning the man to self-contempt and inward abhorrence.

Thus every empirical element is not only quite incapable of being an aid to the principle of morality, but is even highly prejudicial to the purity of morals; for the proper and inestimable worth of an absolutely good will consists just in this that the principle of action is free from all influence of contingent grounds, which alone experience can furnish. We cannot too much or too often repeat our warning against this lax and even mean habit of thought which seeks for its principle among empirical motives and laws; for human reason in its weariness is glad to rest on this pillow, and in a dream of sweet illusions (in which, instead of Juno, it embraces a cloud) it substitutes for morality a bastard patched up from limbs of various derivation, which looks like anything one chooses to see in it; only not like virtue to one who has once beheld her in her true form.[5]

The question then is this: Is it a necessary law *for all rational beings* that they should always judge of their actions by maxims of which they can themselves will that they should serve as universal laws? If it is so, then it must be connected (altogether *a priori*) with the very conception of the will of a rational being generally. But in order to discover this connection we must, however reluctantly, take a step into metaphysic, although into a domain of it which is distinct from speculative philosophy—namely, the metaphysic of morals. In a practical philosophy, where it is not the reasons of what *happens* that we have to ascertain, but the laws of what *ought to happen,* even although it never does, that is, objective practical laws, there it is not necessary to inquire into the reasons why anything pleases or displeases, how the pleasure of mere sensation differs from taste, and whether the latter is distinct from a general satisfaction of reason; on what the feeling of pleasure or pain rests, and how from it desires and inclinations arise, and from these again maxims by the cooperation of reason; for all this belongs to an empirical psychology, which would constitute the second part of physics, if we regard physics as the *philosophy* of nature, so far as it is based on *empirical laws*. But here we are concerned with objective practical laws, and consequently with the relation of the will to itself so far as it is determined

[5] To behold virtue in her proper form is nothing else but to contemplate morality stripped of all admixture of sensible things and of every spurious ornament of reward or self-love. How much she then eclipses everything else that appears charming to the affections, every one may readily perceive with the least exertion of his reason, if it be not wholly spoiled for abstraction.

by reason alone, in which case whatever has reference to anything empirical is necessarily excluded; since if *reason of itself alone* determines the conduct (and it is the possibility of this that we are now investigating), it must necessarily do so *a priori*.

[Second Formulation of the Categorical Imperative: Humanity as an End in Itself]

The will is conceived as a faculty of determining oneself to action *in accordance with the conception of certain laws*. And such a faculty can be found only in rational beings. Now that which serves the will as the objective ground of its self-determination is the *end*, and if this is assigned by reason alone, it must hold for all rational beings. On the other hand, that which merely contains the ground of possibility of the action of which the effect is the end, this is called the *means*. The subjective ground of the desire is the *spring*, the objective ground of the volition is the *motive;* hence the distinction between subjective ends which rest on springs, and objective ends which depend on motives valid for every rational being. Practical principles are *formal* when they abstract from all subjective ends; they are *material* when they assume these, and therefore particular, springs of action. The ends which a rational being proposes to himself at pleasure as *effects* of his actions (material ends) are all only relative, for it is only their relation to the particular desires of the subject that gives them their worth, which therefore cannot furnish principles universal and necessary for all rational beings and for every volition, that is to say, practical laws. Hence all these relative ends can give rise only to hypothetical imperatives.

Supposing, however, that there were something *whose existence* has *in itself* an absolute worth, something which, being *an end in itself,* could be a source of definite laws, then in this and this alone would lie the source of a possible categorical imperative, that is, a practical law.

Now I say: man and generally any rational being *exists* as an end in himself, *not merely as a means* to be arbitrarily used by this or that will, but in all his actions, whether they concern himself or other rational beings, must be always regarded at the same time as an end. All objects of the inclinations have only a conditional worth; for if the inclinations and the wants founded on them did not exist, then their object would be without value. But the inclinations themselves, being sources of want, are so far from having an absolute worth for which they should be desired that, on the contrary, it must be the universal wish of every rational being to be wholly free from them. Thus the worth of any object which is *to be acquired* by our action is always conditional. Beings whose existence depends not on our will but on nature's, have nevertheless, if they are nonrational beings, only a relative value as means, and are therefore called *things;* rational beings, on the contrary, are called *persons,* because their very nature points them out as ends in themselves, that is, as something which must not be used merely as means, and so far therefore restricts freedom of action (and is an object of respect). These, therefore, are not merely subjective ends whose existence has a worth *for us* as an effect of our action, but *objective ends,* that is, things whose existence is an end in itself—an end, moreover, for which no other can be substituted, which they should subserve *merely* as means, for otherwise nothing whatever would possess *absolute worth;* but if all worth were conditioned and therefore contingent, then there would be no supreme practical principle of reason whatever.

If then there is a supreme practical principle or, in respect of the human will, a categorical imperative, it must be one which, being drawn from the conception of that which is necessarily an end for everyone because it is *an end in itself,* constitutes an *objective* principle of will, and can therefore serve as a universal practical law. The foundation of this principle is: *rational nature exists as an end in itself.* Man necessarily conceives his own existence as being so; so far then this is a *subjective* principle of human actions. But every other rational being regards its existence similarly, just on the same rational principle that holds for me [6] so that it is at the same time an objective principle from which as a supreme practical law all laws of the will must be capable of being deduced. Accordingly the practical imperative will be as follows: *So act as to treat humanity, whether in thine own person or in that of any other, in every case as an end withal, never as means only.* We will now inquire whether this can be practically carried out.

[*Four Illustrations*]

To abide by the previous examples:

First, under the head of necessary duty to oneself: He who contemplates suicide should ask himself whether his action can be consistent with the idea of humanity *as an end in itself.* If he destroys himself in order to escape from painful circumstances, he uses a person merely as *a mean* to maintain a tolerable condition up to the end of life. But a man is not a thing, that is to say, something which can be used merely as means, but must in all his actions be always considered as an end in himself. I cannot, therefore, dispose in any way of a man in my own person so as to mutilate him, to damage or kill him. (It belongs to ethics proper to define this principle more precisely, so as to avoid all misunderstanding, for example, as to the amputation of the limbs in order to preserve myself; as to exposing my life to danger with a view to preserve it, etc. This question is therefore omitted here.)

Secondly, as regards necessary duties, or those of strict obligation, towards others; He who is thinking of making a lying promise to others will see at once that he would be using another man *merely as a mean,* without

[6] This proposition is here stated as a postulate. The ground of it will be found in the concluding section.

the latter containing at the same time the end in himself. For he whom I propose by such a promise to use for my own purposes cannot possibly assent to my mode of acting towards him, and therefore cannot himself contain the end of this action. This violation of the principle of humanity in other men is more obvious if we take in examples of attacks on the freedom and property of others. For then it is clear that he who transgresses the rights of men intends to use the person of others merely as means, without considering that as rational beings they ought always to be esteemed also as ends, that is, as beings who must be capable of containing in themselves the end of the very same action.[7]

Thirdly, as regards contingent (meritorious) duties to oneself; It is not enough that the action does not violate humanity in our own person as an end in itself, it must also *harmonize with* it. Now there are in humanity capacities of greater perfection which belong to the end that nature has in view in regard to humanity in ourselves as the subject; to neglect these might perhaps be consistent with the *maintenance* of humanity as an end in itself, but not with the *advancement* of this end.

Fourthly, as regards meritorious duties towards others: The natural end which all men have is their own happiness. Now humanity might indeed subsist although no one should contribute anything to the happiness of others, provided he did not intentionally withdraw anything from it; but after all, this would only harmonize negatively, not positively, with *humanity as an end in itself,* if everyone does not also endeavor, as far as in him lies, to forward the ends of others. For the ends of any subject which is an end in himself ought as far as possible to be *my* ends also, if that conception is to have its *full* effect with me.

[*Third Formulation of the Categorical Imperative: The Autonomy of the Will as Universal Legislator*]

This principle that humanity and generally every rational nature is *an end in itself* (which is the supreme limiting condition of every man's freedom of action), is not borrowed from experience, *first,* because it is universal, applying as it does to all rational beings whatever, and experience is not capable of determining anything about them; *secondly,* because it does not present humanity as an end to men (subjectively), that is, as an object which men do of themselves actually adopt as an end; but as an

---

[7] Let it not be thought that the common: *quod tibi non vis fieri, etc.* [that which you do not want to be done to you, do not do to others] could serve here as the rule or principle. For it is only a deduction from the former, though with several limitations; it cannot be a universal law, for it does not contain the principle of duties to oneself, nor of the duties of benevolence to others (for many a one would gladly consent that others should not benefit him, provided only that he might be excused from showing benevolence to them), nor finally that of duties of strict obligation to one another, for on this principle the criminal might argue against the judge who punishes him, and so on.

objective end which must as a law constitute the supreme limiting condition of all our subjective ends, let them be what we will; it must therefore spring from pure reason. In fact the objective principle of all practical legislation lies (according to the first principle) in *the rule* and its form of universality which makes it capable of being a law (say, for example, a law of nature); but the *subjective* principle is in the *end;* now by the second principle, the subject of all ends is each rational being inasmuch as it is an end in itself. Hence follows the third practical principle of the will, which is the ultimate condition of its harmony with the universal practical reason, viz., the idea of *the will of every rational being as a universally legislative will.*

On this principle all maxims are rejected which are inconsistent with the will being itself universal legislator. Thus the will is not subject to the law, but so subject that it must be regarded *as itself giving the law,* and on this ground only subject to the law (of which it can regard itself as the author).

In the previous imperatives, namely, that based on the conception of the conformity of actions to general laws, as in a *physical system of nature,* and that based on the universal *prerogative* of rational beings as *ends* in themselves—these imperatives just because they were conceived as categorical excluded from any share in their authority all admixture of any interest as a spring of action; they were, however, only *assumed* to be categorical, because such an assumption was necessary to explain the conception of duty. But we could not prove independently that there are practical propositions which command categorically, nor can it be proved in this section; one thing, however, could be done, namely, to indicate in the imperative itself, by some determinate expression, that in the case of volition from duty all interest is renounced, which is the specific criterion of categorical as distinguished from hypothetical imperatives. This is done in the present (third) formula of the principle, namely, in the idea of the will of every rational being as a *universally legislating will.*

For although a will *which is subject to laws* may be attached to this law by means of an interest, yet a will which is itself a supreme lawgiver, so far as it is such, cannot possibly depend on any interest, since a will so dependent would itself still need another law restricting the interest of its self-love by the condition that it should be valid as universal law.

Thus the *principle* that every human will is *a will which in all its maxims gives universal laws,*[8] provided it be otherwise justified, would be very *well adapted* to be the categorical imperative, in this respect, namely, that just because of the idea of universal legislation it is *not based on any interest,* and therefore it alone among all possible imperatives can be *unconditional.* Or still better, converting the proposition, if there is a categorical

---

[8] I may be excused from adducing examples to elucidate this principle, as those which have already been used to elucidate the categorical imperative and its formula would all serve for the like purpose here.

imperative (that is, a law for the will of every rational being), it can only command that everything be done from maxims of one's will regarded as a will which could at the same time will that it should itself give universal laws, for in that case only the practical principle and the imperative which it obeys are unconditional, since they cannot be based on any interest.

Looking back now on all previous attempts to discover the principle of morality, we need not wonder why they all failed. It was seen that man was bound to laws by duty, but it was not observed that the laws to which he is subject are *only those of his own giving,* though at the same time they are *universal,* and that he is only bound to act in conformity with his own will—a will, however, which is designed by nature to give universal laws. For when one has conceived man only as subject to a law (no matter what), then this law required some interest, either by way of attraction or constraint, since it did not originate as a law from *his own* will, but this will was according to a law obliged by *something else* to act in a certain manner. Now by this necessary consequence all the labor spent in finding a supreme principle of *duty* was irrevocably lost. For men never elicited duty, but only a necessity of acting from a certain interest. Whether this interest was private or otherwise, in any case the imperative must be conditional, and could not by any means be capable of being a moral command. I will therefore call this the principle of *Autonomy* of the will, in contrast with every other which I accordingly reckon as *Heteronomy.*

[The Kingdom of Ends]

The conception of every rational being as one which must consider itself as giving in all the maxims of its will universal laws, so as to judge itself and its actions from this point of view—this conception leads to another which depends on it and is very fruitful, namely, that of a *kingdom of ends.*

By a "kingdom" I understand the union of different rational beings in a system by common laws. Now since it is by laws that ends are determined as regards their universal validity, hence, if we abstract from the personal differences of rational beings, and likewise from all the content of their private ends, we shall be able to conceive all ends combined in a systematic whole (including both rational beings as ends in themselves, and also the special ends which each may propose to himself), that is to say, we can conceive a kingdom of ends, which on the preceding principles is possible.

For all rational beings come under the *law* that each of them must treat itself and all others *never merely as means,* but in every case *at the same time as ends in themselves.* Hence results a systematic union of rational beings by common objective laws, that is, a kingdom which may be called a kingdom of ends, since what these laws have in view is just the relation of these beings to one another as ends and means. It is certainly only an ideal.

A rational being belongs as a *member* to the kingdom of ends when, although giving universal laws in it, he is also himself subject to these laws. He belongs to it *as sovereign* when, while giving laws, he is not subject to the will of any other.

A rational being must always regard himself as giving laws either as member or as sovereign in a kingdom of ends which is rendered possible by the freedom of will. He cannot, however, maintain the latter position merely by the maxims of his will, but only in case he is a completely independent being without wants and with unrestricted power adequate to his will.

Morality consists then in the reference of all action to the legislation which alone can render a kingdom of ends possible. This legislation must be capable of existing in every rational being, and of emanating from his will, so that the principle of this will is never to act on any maxim which could not without contradiction be also a universal law, and accordingly always so to act *that the will could at the same time regard itself as giving in its maxims universal laws.* If now the maxims of rational beings are not by their own nature coincident with this objective principle, then the necessity of acting on it is called practical necessitation that is, *duty.* Duty does not apply to the sovereign in the kingdom of ends, but it does to every member of it and to all in the same degree.

The practical necessity of acting on this principle, that is, duty, does not rest at all on feelings, impulses, or inclinations, but solely on the relation of rational beings to one another, a relation in which the will of a rational being must always be regarded as *legislative,* since otherwise it could not be conceived as *an end in itself.* Reason then refers every maxim of the will, regarding it as legislating universally, to every other will and also to every action towards oneself; and this not on account of any other practical motive or any future advantage, but from the idea of the *dignity* of a rational being, obeying no law but that which he himself also gives.

In the kingdom of ends everything has either *value* or *dignity.* Whatever has a value can be replaced by something else which is *equivalent;* whatever, on the other hand, is above all value, and therefore admits of no equivalent, has a dignity.

Whatever has reference to the general inclinations and wants of mankind has a *market value;* whatever, without presupposing a want, corresponds to a certain taste, that is, to a satisfaction in the mere purposeless play of our faculties, has a *fancy value;* but that which constitutes the condition under which alone anything can be an end in itself, this has not merely a relative worth, that is, value, but an intrinsic worth, that is, *dignity.*

Now morality is the condition under which alone a rational being can be an end in himself, since by this alone it is possible that he should be a legislating member in the kingdom of ends. Thus morality, and humanity as capable of it, is that which alone has dignity. Skill and diligence in labor have a market value; wit, lively imagination, and humor have fancy value; on the other hand, fidelity to promises, benevolence from principle (not from instinct), have an intrinsic worth. Neither nature nor art contains anything which in default of these it could put in their place, for their worth consists not in the effects which spring from them, not in the use and advantage which they secure, but in the disposition of mind, that is, the maxims of the will which are ready to manifest themselves in such actions, even though they should not have the desired effect. These actions also need no recommendation from any subjective taste or sentiment, that they may be looked on with immediate favor and satisfaction: they need no immediate propension or feeling for them; they exhibit the will that performs them as an object of an immediate respect, and nothing but reason is required to *impose* them on the will; not to *flatter* it into them, which, in the case of duties, would be a contradiction. This estimation therefore shows that the worth of such a disposition is dignity, and places it infinitely above all value, with which it cannot for a moment be brought into comparison or competition without as it were violating its sanctity.

What then is it which justifies virtue or the morally good disposition, in making such lofty claims? It is nothing less than the privilege it secures to the rational being of participating in the giving of universal laws, by which it qualifies him to be a member of a possible kingdom of ends, a privilege to which he was already destined by his own nature as being an end in himself, and on that account legislating in the kingdom of ends; free as regards all laws of physical nature, and obeying those only which he himself gives, and by which his maxims can belong to a system of universal law, to which at the same time he submits himself. For nothing has any worth except what the law assigns it. Now the legislation itself which assigns the worth of everything must for that very reason possess dignity, that is, an unconditional incomparable worth; and the word *respect* alone supplies a becoming expression for the esteem which a rational being must have for it. *Autonomy* then is the basis of the dignity of human and of every rational nature.

. . .

The Autonomy of the Will as the Supreme Principle of Morality

Autonomy of the will is that property of it by which it is a law to itself (independently on any property of the objects of volition). The principle of autonomy then is: Always so to choose that the same volition shall comprehend the maxims of our choice as a universal law. We cannot prove that this practical rule is an imperative, that is, that the will of every rational being is necessarily bound to it as a condition, by a mere analysis of the conceptions which occur in it, since it is a synthetical proposition; we must advance beyond the cognition of the objects to a critical examination of the subject, that is, of the pure practical reason, for this synthetic proposition which commands apodictically must be capable of being cognized wholly *a priori*. This matter, however, does not belong to the present section. But that the principle of autonomy in question is the sole principle of morals can be readily shown by mere analysis of the conceptions of morality. For by this analysis we find that its principle must be a categorical imperative, and that what this commands is neither more nor less than this very autonomy.

Heteronomy of the Will as the Source of All Spurious Principles of Morality

If the will seeks the law which is to determine it *anywhere else* than in the fitness of its maxims to be universal laws of its own dictation, consequently if it goes out of itself and seeks this law in the character of any of its objects, there always results *heteronomy*. The will in that case does not give itself the law, but it is given by the object through its relation to the will. This relation, whether it rests on inclination or on conceptions of reason, only admits of hypothetical imperatives: I ought to do something *because I wish for something else*. On the contrary, the moral, and therefore categorical, imperative says: I ought to do so and so, even though I should not wish for anything else. For example, the former says: I ought not to lie if I would retain my reputation; the latter says: I ought not to lie although it should not bring me the least discredit. The latter therefore must so far abstract from all objects that they shall have no *influence* on the will, in order that practical reason (will) may not be restricted to administering an interest not belonging to it, but may simply show its own commanding authority as the supreme legislation. Thus, for example, I ought to endeavor to promote the happiness of others, not as if its realization involved any concern of mine (whether by immediate inclination or by any satisfaction indirectly gained through reason), but simply because a maxim which excludes it cannot be comprehended as a universal law in one and the same volition.

. . .

Third Section

TRANSITION FROM THE METAPHYSIC OF MORALS TO THE CRITIQUE OF PURE PRACTICAL REASON

The Concept of Freedom Is the Key that Explains the Autonomy of the Will

The *will* is a kind of causality belonging to living beings in so far as they are rational, and *freedom* would be this property of such causality that it can be efficient, independently on foreign causes *determining* it; just as *physical necessity* is the property that the causality of all irrational beings has of being determined to activity by the influence of foreign causes.

The preceding definition of freedom is *negative,* and therefore unfruitful for the discovery of its essence; but it leads to a *positive* conception which is so much the more full and fruitful. Since the conception of causality involves that of laws, according to which, by something that we call cause, something else, namely, the effect, must be produced [laid down]; hence, although freedom is not a property of the will depending on physical laws, yet it is not for that reason lawless; on the contrary, it must be a causality acting according to immutable laws, but of a peculiar kind; otherwise a free will would be an absurdity. Physical necessity is a heteronomy of the efficient causes, for every effect is possible only according to this law—that something else determines the efficient cause to exert its causality. What else then can freedom of the will be but autonomy, that is, the property of the will to be a law to itself? But the proposition: The will is in every action a law to itself, only expresses the principle to act on no other maxim than that which can also have as an object itself as a universal law. Now this is precisely the formula of the categorical imperative and is the principle of morality, so that a free will and a will subject to moral laws are one and the same.

On the hypothesis, then, of freedom of the will, morality together with its principle follows from it by mere analysis of the conception. However, the latter is a synthetic proposition; viz., an absolutely good will is that whose maxim can always include itself regarded as a universal law; for this property of its maxim can never be discovered by analyzing the conception of an absolutely good will. Now such synthetic propositions are only possible in this way—that the two cognitions are connected together by their union with a third in which they are both to be found. The *positive* concept of freedom furnishes this third cognition, which cannot, as with physical causes, be the nature of the sensible world (in the concept of which we find conjoined the concept of something in relation as cause to *something else* as effect). We cannot now at once show what this third is to which freedom points us, and of which we have an idea *a priori,* nor can we make intelligible how the concept of freedom is shown to be legitimate from principles of pure practical reason, and with it the possibility of a categorical imperative; but some further preparation is required.

FREEDOM

Must Be Presupposed as a Property of the Will of All Rational Beings

It is not enough to predicate freedom of our own will, from whatever reason, if we have not sufficient grounds for predicating the same of all rational beings. For as morality serves as a law for us only because we are *rational beings,* it must also hold for all rational beings; and as it must be deduced simply from the property of freedom, it must be shown that freedom also is a property of all rational beings. It is not enough, then, to prove it from certain supposed experiences of human nature (which indeed is quite impossible, and it can only be shown *a priori*), but we must show that it belongs to the activity of all rational beings endowed with a will. Now I say every being that cannot act except *under the idea of freedom* is just for that reason in a practical point of view really free, that is to say, all laws which are inseparably connected with freedom have the same force for him as if his will had been shown to be free in itself by a proof theoretically conclusive.[9] Now I affirm that we must attribute to every rational being which has a will that it has also the idea of freedom and acts entirely under this idea. For in such a being we conceive a reason that is practical, that is, has causality in reference to its objects. Now we cannot possibly conceive a reason consciously receiving a bias from any other quarter with respect to its judgments, for then the subject would ascribe the determination of its judgment not to its own reason, but to an impulse. It must regard itself as the author of its principles independent on foreign influences. Consequently, as practical reason or as the will of a rational being it must regard itself as free, that is to say, the will of such a being cannot be a will of its own except under the idea of freedom. This idea must therefore in a practical point of view be ascribed to every rational being.

Of the Interest Attaching to the Ideas of Morality

We have finally reduced the definite conception of morality to the idea of freedom. This latter, however, we could not prove to be actually a property of ourselves or of human nature; only we saw that it must be presupposed if we would conceive a being as rational and conscious of its causality in respect of its actions, that is, as endowed with a will; and so we find that on just the same grounds we must ascribe to every being endowed with reason and will this attribute of determining itself to action under the idea of its freedom.

Now it resulted also from the presupposition of this idea that we became aware of a law that the subjective principles of action, that is, maxims, must also be so assumed that they can also hold as objective, that is, universal principles, and so serve as universal laws of our own dictation. But why, then, should I subject myself to this principle and that simply as a rational being, thus also subjecting to it all other beings endowed with reason? I will

[9] I adopt this method of assuming freedom merely *as an idea* which rational beings suppose in their actions, in order to avoid the necessity of proving it in its theoretical aspect also. The former is sufficient for my purpose; for even though the speculative proof should not be made out, yet a being that cannot act except with the idea of freedom is bound by the same laws that would oblige a being who was actually free. Thus we can escape here from the onus which presses on the theory.

allow that no interest *urges* me to this, for that would not give a categorical imperative, but I must *take* an interest in it and discern how this comes to pass; for this "I ought" is properly an "I would," valid for every rational being, provided only that reason determined his actions without any hindrance. But for beings that are in addition affected as we are by springs of a different kind, namely, sensibility, and in whose case that is not always done which reason alone would do, for these that necessity is expressed only as an "ought," and the subjective necessity is different from the objective.

It seems, then, as if the moral law, that is, the principle of autonomy of the will, were properly speaking only presupposed in the idea of freedom, and as if we could not prove its reality and objective necessity independently. In that case we should still have gained something considerable by at least determining the true principle more exactly than had previously been done; but as regards its validity and the practical necessity of subjecting oneself to it, we should not have advanced a step. For if we were asked why the universal validity of our maxim as a law must be the condition restricting our actions, and on what we ground the worth which we assign to this manner of acting—a worth so great that there cannot be any higher interest—and if we were asked further how it happens that it is by this alone a man believes he feels his own personal worth, in comparison with which that of an agreeable or disagreeable condition is to be regarded as nothing, to these questions we could give no satisfactory answer.

We find indeed sometimes that we can take an interest in a personal quality which does not involve any interest of external condition, provided this quality makes us capable of participating in the condition in case reason were to effect the allotment; that is to say, the mere being worthy of happiness can interest of itself even without the motive of participating in this happiness. This judgment, however, is in fact only the effect of the importance of the moral law which we before presupposed (when by the idea of freedom we detach ourselves from every empirical interest); but that we ought to detach ourselves from these interests, that is, to consider ourselves as free in action and yet as subject to certain laws, so as to find a worth simply in our own person which can compensate us for the loss of everything that gives worth to our condition; this we are not yet able to discern in this way, nor do we see how it is possible so to act—in other words, *whence the moral law derives its obligation.*

It must be freely admitted that there is a sort of circle here from which it seems impossible to escape. In the order of efficient causes we assume ourselves free, in order that in the order of ends we may conceive ourselves as subject to moral laws; and we afterwards conceive ourselves as subject to these laws because we have attributed to ourselves freedom of will; for freedom and self-legislation of will are both autonomy, and therefore are reciprocal conceptions, and for this very reason one must not be used to explain the other or give the reason of it, but at most only for logical purposes to reduce apparently different notions of the same object to one single concept (as we reduce different fractions of the same value to the lowest terms).

[*The Two Points of View*]

One resource remains to us, namely, to inquire whether we do not occupy different points of view when by means of freedom we think ourselves as causes efficient *a priori,* and when we form our conception of ourselves from our actions as effects which we see before our eyes.

It is a remark which needs no subtle reflection to make, but which we may assume that even the commonest understanding can make, although it be after its fashion by an obscure discernment of judgment which it calls feeling, that all the "ideas" that come to us involuntarily (as those of the senses) do not enable us to know objects otherwise than as they affect us; so that what they may be in themselves remains unknown to us, and consequently that as regards "ideas" of this kind even with the closest attention and clearness that the understanding can apply to them, we can by them only attain to the knowledge of *appearances,* never to that of *things in themselves.* As soon as this distinction has once been made (perhaps merely in consequence of the difference observed between the ideas given us from without, and in which we are passive, and those that we produce simply from ourselves, and in which we show our own activity), then it follows of itself that we must admit and assume behind the appearance something else that is not an appearance, namely, the things in themselves; although we must admit that, as they can never be known to us except as they affect us, we can come no nearer to them, nor can we ever know what they are in themselves. This must furnish a distinction, however crude, between a *world of sense* and the *world of understanding,* of which the former may be different according to the difference of the sensuous impressions in various observers, while the second which is its basis always remains the same. Even as to himself, a man cannot pretend to know what he is in himself from the knowledge he has by internal sensation. For as he does not as it were create himself, and does not come by the conception of himself *a priori* but empirically, it naturally follows that he can obtain his knowledge even of himself only by the inner sense, and consequently only through the appearances of his nature and the way in which his consciousness is affected. At the same time, beyond these characteristics of his own subject, made up of mere appearances, he must necessarily suppose something else as their basis, namely, his *ego,* whatever its characteristics in itself may be. Thus in respect to mere perception and receptivity of sensations he must reckon himself as belonging to the *world of sense;* but in respect of whatever there may be of pure activity in him (that which reaches consciousness immediately and not through affecting the senses), he must reckon himself as belonging to the *intellectual world,* of which, however, he has no further knowledge. To such a conclusion the reflecting man must come with respect to all the things which can be presented to him; it is probably to be met with even in persons of the commonest understanding, who, as is well known, are very much inclined to suppose behind the objects of the senses something else invisible and acting of itself. They spoil it, however, by presently sensualizing this invisible again; that is to say, wanting to make it an object of intuition, so that they do not become a whit the wiser.

Now man really finds in himself a faculty by which he distinguishes himself from everything else, even from himself as affected by objects, and that is *reason.* This being pure spontaneity is even elevated above the *understanding.* For although the latter is a spontaneity and does not, like sense, merely contain intuitions that arise when we are affected by things (and are therefore passive), yet it cannot produce from its activity any other conceptions than those which merely serve *to bring the intuitions of sense under rules,* and thereby to unite them in one consciousness, and without this use of the sensibility it could not think at all; whereas, on the contrary, reason shows so pure a spontaneity in the case of what I call "ideas" [Ideal Conceptions] that it thereby far transcends everything that the sensibility can give it, and exhibits its most important function in distinguishing the world of sense from that of understanding, and thereby prescribing the limits of the understanding itself.

For this reason a rational being must regard himself *qua* intelligence (not from the side of his lower faculties) as belonging not to the world of sense, but to that of understanding; hence he has two points of view from which he can regard himself, and recognize laws of the exercise of his faculties, and consequently of all his actions; *first,* so far as he belongs to the world of sense, he finds himself subject to laws of nature (heteronomy); *secondly,* as belonging to the intelligible world, under laws which, being independent on nature, have their foundation not in experience but in reason alone.

As a reasonable being, and consequently belonging to the intelligible world, man can never conceive the causality of his own will otherwise than on condition of the idea of freedom, for independence on the determining causes of the sensible world (an independence which reason must always ascribe to itself) is freedom. Now the idea of freedom is inseparably connected with the conception of *autonomy,* and this again with the universal principle of morality which is ideally the foundation of all actions of *rational* beings, just as the law of nature is of all phenomena.

Now the suspicion is removed which we raised above, that there was a latent circle involved in our reasoning from freedom to autonomy, and from this to the moral law, viz., that we laid down the idea of freedom because of the moral law only that we might afterwards in turn infer the latter from freedom, and that consequently we could assign no reason at all for this law, but could only [present] it as a *petitio principii* which well-disposed minds would gladly concede to us, but which we could never put forward as a provable proposition. For now we see that when we conceive ourselves as free we transfer ourselves into the world of understanding as members of it, and recognize the autonomy of the will with its consequence, morality; whereas, if we conceive ourselves as under obligation, we consider ourselves as belonging to the world of sense, and at the same time to the world of understanding.

How Is a Categorical Imperative Possible?

Every rational being reckons himself *qua* intelligence as belonging to the world of understanding, and it is simply as an efficient cause belonging to that world that he calls his causality a *will*. On the other side, he is also conscious of himself as a part of the world of sense in which his actions, which are mere appearances [phenomena] of that causality, are displayed; we cannot, however, discern how they are possible from this causality which we do not know; but instead of that, these actions as belonging to the sensible world must be viewed as determined by other phenomena, namely, desires and inclinations. If therefore I were only a member of the world of understanding, then all my actions would perfectly conform to the principle of autonomy of the pure will; if I were only a part of the world of sense, they would necessarily be assumed to conform wholly to the natural law of desires and inclinations, in other words, to the heteronomy of nature. (The former would rest on morality as the supreme principle, the latter on happiness.) Since, however, *the world of understanding contains the foundation of the world of sense, and consequently of its laws also,* and accordingly gives the law to my will (which belongs wholly to the world of understanding) directly, and must be conceived as doing so, it follows that, although on the one side I must regard myself as a being belonging to the world of sense, yet, on the other side, I must recognize myself, as an intelligence, as subject to the law of the world of understanding, that is, to reason, which contains this law in the idea of freedom, and therefore as subject to the autonomy of the will; consequently I must regard the laws of the world of understanding as imperatives for me, and the actions which conform to them as duties.

And thus what makes categorical imperatives possible is this—that the idea of freedom makes me a member of an intelligible world, in consequence of which, if I were nothing else, all my actions *would* always conform to the autonomy of the will; but as I at the same time intuit myself as a member of the world of sense, they *ought* so to conform, and this *categorical* "ought" implies a synthetic *a priori* proposition, inasmuch as besides my will as affected by sensible desires there is added further the idea of the same will, but as belonging to the world of the understanding, pure and practical of itself, which contains the supreme condition according to reason of the former will;

precisely as to the intuitions of sense there are added concepts of the understanding which of themselves signify nothing but regular form in general, and in this way synthetic *a priori* propositions become possible, on which all knowledge of physical nature rests.

The practical use of common human reason confirms this reasoning. There is no one, not even the most consummate villain, provided only that he is otherwise accustomed to the use of reason, who, when we set before him examples of honesty of purpose, of steadfastness in following good maxims, of sympathy and general benevolence (even combined with great sacrifices of advantages and comfort), does not wish that he might also possess these qualities. Only on account of his inclinations and impulses he cannot attain this in himself, but at the same time he wishes to be free from such inclinations which are burdensome to himself. He proves by this that he transfers himself in thought with a will free from the impulses of the sensibility into an order of things wholly different from that of his desires in the field of the sensibility; since he cannot expect to obtain by that wish any gratification of his desires, nor any position which would satisfy any of his actual or supposable inclinations (for this would destroy the preeminence of the very idea which wrests that wish from him) he can only expect a greater intrinsic worth of his own person. This better person, however, he imagines himself to be when he transfers himself to the point of view of a member of the world of the understanding, to which he is involuntarily forced by the idea of freedom, that is, of independence on *determining* causes of the world of sense; and from this point of view he is conscious of a good will, which by his own confession constitutes the law for the bad will that he possesses as a member of the world of sense—a law whose authority he recognizes while transgressing it. What he morally "ought" is then what he necessarily "would" as a member of the world of the understanding, and is conceived by him as an "ought" only inasmuch as he likewise considers himself as a member of the world of sense.

On the Extreme Limits of All Practical Philosophy

. . .

The claims to freedom of will made even by common reason are founded on the consciousness and the admitted supposition that reason is independent on merely subjectively determined causes which together constitute what belongs to sensation only, and which consequently come under the general designation of sensibility. Man considering himself in this way as an intelligence places himself thereby in a different order of things and in a relation to determining grounds of a wholly different kind when on the one hand he thinks of himself as an intelligence endowed with a will, and consequently with causality, and when on the other he perceives himself as a phenomenon in the world of sense (as he really is also), and affirms that his causality is subject to external determination according to laws of nature. Now he soon becomes aware that both can hold good, nay, must hold good at the same time. For there is not the smallest contradiction in saying that a *thing in appearance* (belonging to the world of sense) is subject to certain laws on which the very same *as a thing* or being *in itself* is independent; and that he must conceive and think of himself in this two-fold way, rests as to the first on the consciousness of himself as an object affected through the senses, and as to the second on the consciousness of himself as an intelligence, that is, as independent on sensible impressions in the employment of his reason (in other words as belonging to the world of understanding).

Hence it comes to pass that man claims the possession of a will which takes no account of anything that comes under the head of desires and inclinations, and on the contrary conceives actions as possible to him, nay, even as necessary, which can only be done by disregarding all desires and sensible inclinations. The causality of such actions lies in him as an intelligence and in the laws of effects and actions [which depend] on the principles of an intelligible world, of which indeed he knows nothing more than that in it pure reason alone independent on sensibility gives the law; moreover, since it is only in that world, as an intelligence, that he is his proper self (being as man only the appearance of himself), those laws apply to him directly and categorically, so that the incitements of inclinations and appetites (in other words, the whole nature of the world of sense) cannot impair the laws of his volition as an intelligence. Nay, he does not even hold himself responsible for the former or ascribe them to his proper self, that is, his will; he only ascribes to his will any indulgence which he might yield them if he allowed them to influence his maxims to the prejudice of the rational laws of the will.

When practical reason *thinks* itself into a world of understanding, it does not thereby transcend its own limits, as it would if it tried to enter it by *intuition* or *sensation*. The former is only a negative thought in respect of the world of sense, which does not give any laws to reason in determining the will, and is positive only in this single point that this freedom as a negative characteristic is at the same time conjoined with a (positive) faculty and even with a causality of reason, which we designate a will, namely, a faculty of so acting that the principle of the actions shall conform to the essential character of a rational motive, that is, the condition that the maxim have universal validity as a law. But were it to borrow an *object of will,* that is, a motive, from the world of understanding, then it would overstep its bounds and pretend to be acquainted with something of which it knows nothing. The conception of a world of the understanding is then only a *point of view* which reason finds itself compelled to take outside the appearances in order to *conceive itself as practical,* which would not be possible if the influences of the sensibility had a determining power on man, but which is necessary unless he is to be denied the consciousness of himself as an intelligence, and consequently as a rational cause, energizing by reason, that is, operating freely. This thought certainly involves the idea of an order and a system of laws different from that of the mechanism of nature which belongs to the sensible world; and it makes the conception of an intelligible world necessary (that is to say, the whole system of rational beings as things in themselves). But it does not in the least authorize us to think of it further than as to its *formal* condition only, that is, the universality of the maxims of the will as laws, and consequently the autonomy of the latter, which alone is consistent with its freedom; whereas, on the contrary, all laws that refer to a definite object give heteronomy, which only belongs to laws of nature, and can only apply to the sensible world.

But reason would overstep all its bounds if it undertook to *explain how* pure reason can be practical, which would be exactly the same problem as to explain *how freedom is possible.*

For we can explain nothing but that which we can reduce to laws the object of which can be given in some possible experience. But freedom is a mere *idea* [ideal conception], the objective reality of which can in no wise be shown according to laws of nature, and consequently not in any possible experience; and for this reason it can never be comprehended or understood because we cannot support it by any sort of example or analogy. It holds good only as a necessary hypothesis of reason in a being that believes itself conscious of a will, that is, of a faculty distinct from mere desire (namely, a faculty of determining itself to action as an intelligence, in other words, by laws of reason independently on natural instincts). Now where determination according to laws of nature ceases, there all *explanation* ceases also, and nothing remains but *defense,* that is, the removal of the objections of those who pretend to have seen deeper into the nature of things, and thereupon boldly declare freedom impossible. We can only point out to them that the supposed contradiction that they have discovered in it arises only from this, that in order to be able to apply the law of nature to human actions, they must necessarily consider man as an appearance; then when we demand of them that they should also think of him *qua* intelligence as a thing in itself, they still persist in considering him in this respect also as an appearance. In this view it would no doubt be a contradiction to suppose the causality of the same subject (that is, his will) to be withdrawn from all the natural laws of the sensible world. But this contradiction disappears if they would only bethink themselves and admit, as is reasonable, that behind the appearances there must also lie at their root (although hidden) the things in themselves, and that we cannot expect the laws of these to be the same as those that govern their appearances.

. . .

The question, then, How a categorical imperative is possible, can be answered to this extent that we can assign the only hypothesis on which it is possible, namely, the idea of freedom; and we can also discern the necessity of this hypothesis, and this is sufficient for the *practical exercise* of reason, that is, for the conviction of the *validity of this imperative,* and hence of the moral law; but how this hypothesis itself is possible can never be discerned by any human reason. On the hypothesis, however, that the will of an intelligence is free, its *autonomy,* as the essential formal condition of its determination, is a necessary consequence. . . .

QUESTIONS

1. What reasons does Kant give for saying that for an action to be morally good, it must not only conform to the moral law but also must be done for the sake of the law?
2. What does Kant mean by saying that only a good will can be called good without qualification? What arguments does he give in support of this view? How valid do you think his arguments are?
3. What would you say is the difference between our desires and our will, in Kant's sense of "will"? What does he mean by saying, ". . . the will is nothing but practical reason"?
4. Kant distinguishes: (a) actions inconsistent with duty, (b) actions consistent with duty, but not done from duty, and (c) actions consistent with duty and done from duty. Give an example of each and explain why Kant considers this distinction important for morals.
5. When Kant says that the actions of people who take delight in helping others have "no true moral worth," does he mean that our moral duty is to help others, not out of love for them, but only with a kind of cold determination and grim disposition to be morally upright? Defend your answer by specific references to the text of the reading.
6. According to Kant, is our own personal happiness always opposed to our moral duty? Why or why not?
7. What are Kant's three propositions of morality? He claims that the third proposition is a consequence of the first two. Give a careful appraisal of the justifiability of that claim.
8. Not conformity to any particular law, but "simple conformity to law in general" defines our moral duty. What does Kant mean by "simple conformity to law in general"? To clarify your answer give some examples, but do not give the same examples that Kant does.
9. Kant says that although common men do not conceive the moral law (Act only so that you can will that your maxim become a universal law.) in such an abstract and universal form, "yet they always have it really before their eyes and use it as the standard of their decision." Does Kant give any argument in defense of this assertion? If so, what is it, and is it in your opinion sound? If not, what argument do you think could be made for it, or against it?
10. Suppose someone objected to Kant's theory, saying that it was too idealistic, that is, it would be impossible to put into practice. What would Kant be likely to say in reply?
11. According to Kant, why must the moral law be valid "not merely for men, but for all *rational creatures generally,* not merely under certain contingent conditions or with exceptions, but *with absolute necessity"*?
12. Explain clearly the difference between a hypothetical and a categorical imperative. Show how this distinction is used by Kant in describing three kinds of imperatives: imperatives of skill, of prudence, and of morality. Give examples.

13. The categorical imperative is "an *a priori* synthetical practical proposition." State what this means in your own words. (You may refer to Kant's "Analytic and Synthetic" in Chapter 2 for an explanation of the terms "a priori" and "synthetical.")

14. Analyze the four examples Kant gives of "duties to ourselves and to others" and "perfect and imperfect duties," in order to determine whether any of these examples fail to exemplify what they are supposed to exemplify.

15. Summarize the steps in Kant's line of reasoning to show that the "practical imperative" ("So act to treat humanity, whether in thine own person or in that of any other, in every case as an end withal, never as means only.") means essentially the same thing as the "categorical imperative" ("So act that the maxim of thine action can become a universal law.").

16. Explain what Kant means by a "kingdom of ends." How is this concept connected with the concept of the moral law?

17. What does Kant mean by the "autonomy of the will"? If you have read selections from Chapter 9, "Freedom of the Will," state why you think that Kant has succeeded, or has not succeeded, in providing either a partial or a whole solution to the problem of freedom of the will.

18. Study Kant's entire theory to see whether there are any traces of empirical arguments (arguments based on what we learn from experience) in it. Point out any places where Kant has failed to remain within the boundaries of a priori reasoning.

19. Is the following statement a fair criticism? Defend your answer.
"Kant's theory rests upon a fundamental logical error. He tries to deduce from the general concept of moral duty what our duty is, and this is the same mistake as trying to deduce from an analysis of the meaning of the word 'vote' how a person ought to vote."

20. Construct a reply which Kant might make to the statement that his whole theory is merely an elaborate psychological "rationalization" of his Pietistic upbringing. (Kant's parents were members of a Protestant sect known as Pietism, whose moral code tended to condemn personal pleasures.) Is such a statement at all relevant to the truth of what Kant has to say about morality? Why or why not?

21. Suppose it were claimed that Kant's entire moral philosophy is simply an argument to the effect that we should all obey the Golden Rule: Do unto others as you would have them do unto you. Is it true that the Golden Rule follows from Kant's conception of moral duty? If it does, is this *all* Kant's theory amounts to? In answering these questions, consult Kant's footnote on page 564.

22. In the introduction to this selection, it was said that the general result of Kant's theory is that there is a total separation, an impassable gulf, between science and ethics, between our knowledge of what is and our knowledge of what ought to be, between the realm of facts and the realm of values. Outline the main reasons for which you now think this is, or is not, so.

38. JOHN STUART MILL

(1806–73)

Utilitarianism

John Stuart Mill was the son of a famous British economist and social philosopher, James Mill. Through his philosophical writings, the son established a greater name than his father's. In 1843 he published *A System of Logic, Ratiocinative and Inductive,* a major work in its field. His other important works include the *Essay on Liberty* (1859); *An Examination of Sir William Hamilton's Philosophy* (1865); and his chief study in moral philosophy, *Utilitarianism* (1863). Mill had a strong social conscience and became a leader of liberalism and social reform in Victorian England, putting into practice many of the principles he had set forth in his moral philosophy.

In the first part of this reading, Mill is trying to clarify the meaning of the utilitarian standard of morality. In particular he is defending it against certain distortions of meaning which it suffered at the hands of both its opponents and its popularizers. In the second part, Mill attempts to show that utilitarianism is a true ethical system. Here he is directly concerned with the central problem of moral philosophy: the justification of a moral standard. Mill not only tries to justify utilitarianism, he also discusses the difficulties involved in any attempt to "prove" an ethical system. In this discussion he critically examines the ultimate grounds of moral knowledge.

This selection comes from Chapters II and IV of *Utilitarianism.* Mill's own chapter titles are used.

From Mill: *Utilitarianism* (The Library of Liberal Arts No. 1, N. Y., 1957). Reprinted by permission of the Liberal Arts Press Division of The Bobbs-Merrill Company, Inc.

WHAT UTILITARIANISM IS

A passing remark is all that needs be given to the ignorant blunder of supposing that those who stand up for utility as the test of right and wrong use the term in that restricted and merely colloquial sense in which utility is opposed to pleasure. An apology is due to the philosophical opponents of utilitarianism for even the momentary appearance of confounding them with anyone capable of so absurd a misconception; which is the more extraordinary, inasmuch as the contrary accusation, of referring everything to pleasure, and that, too, in its grossest form, is another of the common charges against utilitarianism: and, as has been pointedly remarked by an able writer, the same sort of persons, and often the very same persons, denounce the theory "as impracticably dry when the word 'utility' precedes the word 'pleasure,' and as too practically voluptuous when the word 'pleasure' precedes the word 'utility.'" Those who know anything about the matter are aware that every writer, from Epicurus to Bentham, who maintained the theory of utility meant by it, not something to be contradistinguished from pleasure, but pleasure itself, together with exemption from pain; and instead of opposing the useful to the agreeable or the ornamental, have always declared that the useful means these, among other things. Yet the common herd, including the herd of writers, not only in newspapers and periodicals, but in books of weight and pretension, are perpetually falling into this shallow mistake. Having caught up the word "utilitarian," while knowing nothing whatever about it but its sound, they habitually express by it the rejection or the neglect of pleasure in some of its forms: of beauty, of ornament, or of amusement. Nor is the term thus ignorantly misapplied solely in disparagement, but occasionally in compliment, as though it implied superiority to frivolity and the mere pleasures of the moment. And this perverted use is the only one in which the word is popularly known, and the one from which the new generation are acquiring their sole notion of its meaning. Those who introduced the word, but who had for many years discontinued it as a distinctive appellation, may well feel themselves called upon to resume it if by doing so they can hope to contribute anything toward rescuing it from this utter degradation.

The creed which accepts as the foundation of morals "utility" or the "greatest happiness principle" holds that actions are right in proportion as they tend to promote happiness; wrong as they tend to produce the reverse of happiness. By happiness is intended pleasure and the absence of pain; by unhappiness, pain and the privation of pleasure. To give a clear view of the moral standard set up by the theory, much more requires to be said; in particular, what things it includes in the ideas of pain and pleasure, and to what extent this is left an open question. But these supplementary explanations do not affect the theory of life on which this theory of morality is grounded—namely, that pleasure and freedom from pain are the only things desirable as ends; and that all desirable things (which are as numerous in the utilitarian as in any other scheme) are desirable either for pleasure inherent in themselves or as means to the promotion of pleasure and the prevention of pain.

Now such a theory of life excites in many minds, and among them in some of the most estimable in feeling and purpose, inveterate dislike. To suppose that life has (as they express it) no higher end than pleasure—no better and nobler object of desire and pursuit—they designate as utterly mean and groveling, as a doctrine worthy only of swine, to whom the followers of

Epicurus were, at a very early period, contemptuously likened; and modern holders of the doctrine are occasionally made the subject of equally polite comparisons by its German, French, and English assailants.

When thus attacked, the Epicureans have always answered that it is not they, but their accusers, who represent human nature in a degrading light, since the accusation supposes human beings to be capable of no pleasures except those of which swine are capable. If this supposition were true, the charge could not be gainsaid, but would then be no longer an imputation; for if the sources of pleasure were precisely the same to human beings and to swine, the rule of life which is good enough for the one would be good enough for the other. The comparison of the Epicurean life to that of beasts is felt as degrading, precisely because a beast's pleasures do not satisfy a human being's conceptions of happiness. Human beings have faculties more elevated than the animal appetites and, when once made conscious of them, do not regard anything as happiness which does not include their gratification. I do not, indeed, consider the Epicureans to have been by any means faultless in drawing out their scheme of consequences from the utilitarian principle. To do this in any sufficient manner, many Stoic, as well as Christian, elements require to be included. But there is no known Epicurean theory of life which does not assign to the pleasures of the intellect, of the feelings and imagination, and of the moral sentiments a much higher value as pleasures than to those of mere sensation. It must be admitted, however, that utilitarian writers in general have placed the superiority of mental over bodily pleasures chiefly in the greater permanency, safety, uncostliness, etc., of the former—that is, in their circumstantial advantages rather than in their intrinsic nature. And on all these points utilitarians have fully proved their case; but they might have taken the other and, as it may be called, higher ground with entire consistency. It is quite compatible with the principle of utility to recognize the fact that some kinds of pleasure are more desirable and more valuable than others. It would be absurd that, while in estimating all other things quality is considered as well as quantity, the estimation of pleasure should be supposed to depend on quantity alone.

If I am asked what I mean by difference of quality in pleasures, or what makes one pleasure more valuable than another, merely as a pleasure, except its being greater in amount, there is but one possible answer. Of two pleasures, if there be one to which all or almost all who have experience of both give a decided preference, irrespective of any feeling of moral obligation to prefer it, that is the more desirable pleasure. If one of the two is, by those who are competently acquainted with both, placed so far above the other that they prefer it, even though knowing it to be attended with a greater amount of discontent, and would not resign it for any quantity of the other pleasure which their nature is capable of, we are justified in ascribing to the preferred enjoyment a superiority in quality so far outweighing quantity as to render it, in comparison, of small account.

Now it is an unquestionable fact that those who are equally acquainted with and equally capable of appreciating and enjoying both do give a most marked preference to the manner of existence which employs their higher faculties. Few human creatures would consent to be changed into any of the lower animals for a promise of the fullest allowance of a beast's pleasures; no intelligent human being would consent to be a fool, no instructed person would be an ignoramus, no person of feeling and conscience would be selfish and base, even though they should be persuaded that the fool, the dunce, or the rascal is better satisfied with his lot than they are with theirs. They would not resign what they possess more than he for the most complete satisfaction of all the desires which they have in common with him. If they ever fancy they would, it is only in cases of unhappiness so extreme that to escape from it they would exchange their lot for almost any other, however undesirable in their own eyes. A being of higher faculties requires more to make him happy, is capable probably of more acute suffering, and certainly accessible to it at more points, than one of an inferior type; but in spite of these liabilities, he can never really wish to sink into what he feels to be a lower grade of existence. We may give what explanation we please of this unwillingness; we may attribute it to pride, a name which is given indiscriminately to some of the most and to some of the least estimable feelings of which mankind are capable; we may refer it to the love of liberty and personal independence, an appeal to which was with the Stoics one of the most effective means for the inculcation of it; to the love of power or to the love of excitement, both of which do really enter into and contribute to it; but its most appropriate appellation is a sense of dignity, which all human beings possess in one form or other, and in some, though by no means in exact, proportion to their higher faculties, and which is so essential a part of the happiness of those in whom it is strong that nothing which conflicts with it could be otherwise than momentarily an object of desire to them. Whoever supposes that this preference takes place at a sacrifice of happiness —that the superior being, in anything like equal circumstances, is not happier than the inferior—confounds the two very different ideas of happiness and content. It is indisputable that the being whose capacities of enjoyment are low has the greatest chance of having them fully satisfied; and a highly endowed being will always feel that any happiness which he can look for, as the world is constituted, is imperfect. But he can learn to bear its imperfections, if they are at all bearable; and they will not make him envy the being who is indeed unconscious of the imperfections, but only because he feels not at all the good which those imperfections qualify. It is better to be a human being dissatisfied than a pig satisfied; better to be Socrates dissatisfied than a fool satisfied. And if the fool, or the pig, are of a different opinion, it is because they only know their own side of the question. The other party to the comparison knows both sides.

It may be objected that many who are capable of the higher pleasures occasionally, under the influence of temptation, postpone them to the lower.

But this is quite compatible with a full appreciation of the intrinsic superiority of the higher. Men often, from infirmity of character, make their election for the nearer good, though they know it to be the less valuable; and this no less when the choice is between two bodily pleasures than when it is between bodily and mental. They pursue sensual indulgences to the injury of health, though perfectly aware that health is the greater good. It may be further objected that many who begin with youthful enthusiasm for everything noble, as they advance in years, sink into indolence and selfishness. But I do not believe that those who undergo this very common change voluntarily choose the lower description of pleasures in preference to the higher. I believe that, before they devote themselves exclusively to the one, they have already become incapable of the other. Capacity for the nobler feelings is in most natures a very tender plant, easily killed, not only by hostile influences, but by mere want of sustenance; and in the majority of young persons it speedily dies away if the occupations to which their position in life has devoted them, and the society into which it has thrown them, are not favorable to keeping that higher capacity in exercise. Men lose their high aspirations as they lose their intellectual tastes, because they have not time or opportunity for indulging them; and they addict themselves to inferior pleasures, not because they deliberately prefer them, but because they are either the only ones to which they have access or the only ones which they are any longer capable of enjoying. It may be questioned whether anyone who has remained equally susceptible to both classes of pleasures ever knowingly and calmly preferred the lower, though many, in all ages, have broken down in an ineffectual attempt to combine both.

From this verdict of the only competent judges, I apprehend there can be no appeal. On a question which is the best worth having of two pleasures, or which of two modes of existence is the most grateful to the feelings, apart from its moral attributes and from its consequences, the judgment of those who are qualified by knowledge of both, or, if they differ, that of the majority among them, must be admitted as final. And there needs be the less hesitation to accept this judgment respecting the quality of pleasures, since there is no other tribunal to be referred to even on the question of quantity. What means are there of determining which is the acutest of two pains, or the intensest of two pleasurable sensations, except the general suffrage of those who are familiar with both? Neither pains nor pleasures are homogeneous, and pain is always heterogeneous with pleasure. What is there to decide whether a particular pleasure is worth purchasing at the cost of a particular pain, except the feelings and judgment of the experienced? When, therefore, those feelings and judgment declare the pleasures derived from the higher faculties to be preferable *in kind,* apart from the question of intensity, to those of which the animal nature, disjoined from the higher faculties, is susceptible, they are entitled on this subject to the same regard.

I have dwelt on this point as being a necessary part of a perfectly just conception of utility or happiness considered as the directive rule of human conduct. But it is by no means an indispensable condition to the acceptance of the utilitarian standard; for that standard is not the agent's own greatest happiness, but the greatest amount of happiness altogether; and if it may possibly be doubted whether a noble character is always the happier for its nobleness, there can be no doubt that it makes other people happier, and that the world in general is immensely a gainer by it. Utilitarianism, therefore, could only attain its end by the general cultivation of nobleness of character, even if each individual were only benefited by the nobleness of others, and his own, so far as happiness is concerned, were a sheer deduction from the benefit. But the bare enunciation of such an absurdity as this last renders refutation superfluous.

According to the greatest happiness principle, as above explained, the ultimate end, with reference to and for the sake of which all other things are desirable—whether we are considering our own good or that of other people—is an existence exempt as far as possible from pain, and as rich as possible in enjoyments, both in point of quantity and quality; the test of quality and the rule for measuring it against quantity being the preference felt by those who, in their opportunities of experience, to which must be added their habits of self-consciousness and self-observation, are best furnished with the means of comparison. This, being according to the utilitarian opinion the end of human action, is necessarily also the standard of morality, which may accordingly be defined "the rules and precepts for human conduct," by the observance of which an existence such as has been described might be, to the greatest extent possible, secured to all mankind; and not to them only, but, so far as the nature of things admits, to the whole sentient creation.

. . .

The utilitarian morality does recognize in human beings the power of sacrificing their own greatest good for the good of others. It only refuses to admit that the sacrifice is itself a good. A sacrifice which does not increase or tend to increase the sum total of happiness, it considers as wasted. The only self-renunciation which it applauds is devotion to the happiness, or to some of the means of happiness, of others, either of mankind collectively or of individuals within the limits imposed by the collective interests of mankind.

I must again repeat what the assailants of utilitarianism seldom have the justice to acknowledge, that the happiness which forms the utilitarian standard of what is right in conduct is not the agent's own happiness but that of all concerned. As between his own happiness and that of others, utilitarianism requires him to be as strictly impartial as a disinterested and benevolent spectator. In the golden rule of Jesus of Nazareth, we read the complete spirit of the ethics of utility. "To do as you would be done by," and "to love your neighbor as yourself," constitute the ideal perfection of utilitarian morality. As the means of making the nearest approach to this ideal, utility would enjoin, first, that laws and social arrangements should place the happiness or (as, speaking practically, it may be called) the interest of every individual as nearly as possible in harmony with the interest of the whole; and, secondly, that education and opinion, which have so vast a power over human character, should so use that power as to establish in the mind of every individual an indissoluble association between his own happiness and the good of the whole, especially between his own happiness and the practice of such modes of conduct, negative and positive, as regard for the universal happiness prescribes; so that not only he may be unable to conceive the possibility of happiness to himself, consistently with conduct opposed to the general good, but also that a direct impulse to promote the general good may be in every individual one of the habitual motives of action, and the sentiments connected therewith may fill a large and prominent place in every human being's sentient existence. If the impugners of the utilitarian morality represented it to their own minds in this its true character, I know not what recommendation possessed by any other morality they could possibly affirm to be wanting to it; what more beautiful or more exalted developments of human nature any other ethical system can be supposed to foster, or what springs of action, not accessible to the utilitarian, such systems rely on for giving effect to their mandates.

The objectors to utilitarianism cannot always be charged with representing it in a discreditable light. On the contrary, those among them who entertain anything like a just idea of its disinterested character sometimes find fault with its standard as being too high for humanity. They say it is exacting too much to require that people shall always act from the inducement of promoting the general interests of society. But this is to mistake the very meaning of a standard of morals and confound the rule of action with the motive of it. It is the business of ethics to tell us what are our duties, or by what test we may know them; but no system of ethics requires that the sole motive of all we do shall be a feeling of duty; on the contrary, ninety-nine hundredths of all our actions are done from other motives, and rightly so done if the rule of duty does not condemn them. It is the more unjust to utilitarianism that this particular misapprehension should be made a ground of objection to it, inasmuch as utilitarian moralists have gone beyond almost all others in affirming that the motive has nothing to do with the morality of the action, though much with the worth of the agent. He who saves a fellow creature from drowning does what is morally right, whether his motive be duty or the hope of being paid for his trouble; he who betrays the friend that trusts him is guilty of a crime, even if his object be to serve another friend to whom he is under greater obligations.[1] But to speak only

[1] An opponent, whose intellectual and moral fairness it is a pleasure to acknowledge (the Rev. J. Llewellyn Davies), has objected to this passage, saying, "Surely the right-

of actions done from the motive of duty, and in direct obedience to principle: it is a misapprehension of the utilitarian mode of thought to conceive it as implying that people should fix their minds upon so wide a generality as the world, or society at large. The great majority of good actions are intended not for the benefit of the world, but for that of individuals, of which the good of the world is made up; and the thoughts of the most virtuous man need not on these occasions travel beyond the particular persons concerned, except so far as is necessary to assure himself that in benefiting them he is not violating the rights, that is, the legitimate and authorized expectations, of anyone else. The multiplication of happiness is, according to the utilitarian ethics, the object of virtue: the occasions on which any person (except one in a thousand) has it in his power to do this on an extended scale—in other words, to be a public benefactor—are but exceptional; and on these occasions alone is he called on to consider public utility; in every other case, private utility, the interest or happiness of some few persons, is all he has to attend to. Those alone the influence of whose actions extends to society in general need concern themselves habitually about so large an object. In the case of abstinences indeed—of things which people forbear to do from moral considerations, though the consequences in the particular case might be beneficial—it would be unworthy of an intelligent agent not to be consciously aware that the action is of a class which, if practiced generally, would be generally injurious, and that this is the ground of the obligation to abstain from it. The amount of regard for the public interest implied in this recognition is no greater than is demanded by every system of morals, for they all enjoin to abstain from whatever is manifestly pernicious to society.

. . .

ness or wrongness of saving a man from drowning does depend very much upon the motive with which it is done. Suppose that a tyrant, when his enemy jumped into the sea to escape from him, saved him from drowning simply in order that he might inflict upon him more exquisite tortures, would it tend to clearness to speak of that rescue as 'a morally right action'? Or suppose again, according to one of the stock illustrations of ethical inquiries, that a man betrayed a trust received from a friend, because the discharge of it would fatally injure that friend himself or someone belonging to him, would utilitarianism compel one to call the betrayal 'a crime' as much as if it had been done from the meanest motive?"

I submit that he who saves another from drowning in order to kill him by torture afterwards does not differ only in motive from him who does the same thing from duty or benevolence; the act itself is different. The rescue of the man is, in the case supposed, only the necessary first step of an act far more atrocious than leaving him to drown would have been. Had Mr. Davies said, "The rightness or wrongness of saving a man from drowning does depend very much" not upon the motive, but "upon the *intention*," no utilitarian would have differed from him. Mr. Davies, by an oversight too common not to be quite venial, has in this case confounded the very different ideas of Motive and Intention. There is no point which utilitarian thinkers (and Bentham preeminently) have taken more pains to illustrate than this. The morality of the action depends entirely upon the intention—that is, upon what the agent *wills to do*. But the motive, that is, the feeling which makes him will so to do, if it makes no difference in the act, makes none in the morality: though it makes a great difference in our moral estimation of the agent, especially if it indicates a good or a bad habitual *disposition*—a bent of character from which useful, or from which hurtful actions are likely to arise.

It may not be superfluous to notice a few more of the common misapprehensions of utilitarian ethics, even those which are so obvious and gross that it might appear impossible for any person of candor and intelligence to fall into them; since persons, even of considerable mental endowment, often give themselves so little trouble to understand the bearings of any opinion against which they entertain a prejudice, and men are in general so little conscious of this voluntary ignorance as a defect that the vulgarest misunderstandings of ethical doctrines are continually met with in the deliberate writings of persons of the greatest pretensions both to high principle and to philosophy. We not uncommonly hear the doctrine of utility inveighed against as a *godless* doctrine. If it be necessary to say anything at all against so mere an assumption, we may say that the question depends upon what idea we have formed of the moral character of the Deity. If it be a true belief that God desires, above all things, the happiness of his creatures, and that this was his purpose in their creation, utility is not only not a godless doctrine, but more profoundly religious than any other. If it be meant that utilitarianism does not recognize the revealed will of God as the supreme law of morals, I answer that a utilitarian who believes in the perfect goodness and wisdom of *God* necessarily believes that whatever God has thought fit to reveal on the subject of morals must fulfill the requirements of utility in a supreme degree. But others besides utilitarians have been of the opinion that the Christian revelation was intended, and is fitted, to inform the hearts and minds of mankind with a spirit which should enable them to find for themselves what is right, and incline them to do it when found, rather than to tell them, except in a very general way, what it is; and that we need a doctrine of ethics, carefully followed out, to *interpret* to us the will of God. Whether this opinion is correct or not, it is superfluous here to discuss; since whatever aid religion, either natural or revealed, can afford to ethical investigation is as open to the utilitarian moralist as to any other. He can use it as the testimony of God to the usefulness or hurtfulness of any given course of action by as good a right as others can use it for the indication of a transcendental law having no connection with usefulness or with happiness.

Again, utility is often summarily stigmatized as an immoral doctrine by giving it the name of "expediency," and taking advantage of the popular use of that term to contrast it with principle. But the expedient, in the sense in which it is opposed to the right, generally means that which is expedient for the particular interest of the agent himself; as when a minister sacrifices the interests of his country to keep himself in place. When it means anything better than this, it means that which is expedient for some immediate object, some temporary purpose, but which violates a rule whose observance is expedient in a much higher degree. The expedient, in this sense, instead of being the same thing with the useful, is a branch of the hurtful. Thus it would often be expedient, for the purpose of getting over some momentary embarrassment, or attaining some object immediately useful to ourselves or others, to tell a lie. But inasmuch as the cultivation in ourselves of a sensitive feeling on the subject of veracity is one of the most useful, and the enfeeblement of that feeling one of the most hurtful, things to which our conduct can be instrumental; and inasmuch as any, even unintentional, deviation from truth does that much toward weakening the trustworthiness of human assertion, which is not only the principal support of all present social well-being, but the insufficiency of which does more than any one thing that can be named to keep back civilization, virtue, everything on which human happiness on the largest scale depends—we feel that the violation, for a present advantage, of a rule of such transcendent expediency is not expedient, and that he who, for the sake of convenience to himself or to some other individual, does what depends on him to deprive mankind of the good, and inflict upon them the evil, involved in the greater or less reliance which they can place in each other's word, acts the part of one of their worst enemies. Yet that even this rule, sacred as it is, admits of possible exceptions is acknowledged by all moralists; the chief of which is when the withholding of some fact (as of information from a malefactor, or of bad news from a person dangerously ill) would save an individual (especially an individual other than oneself) from great and unmerited evil, and when the withholding can only be effected by denial. But in order that the exception may not extend itself beyond the need, and may have the least possible effect in weakening reliance on veracity, it ought to be recognized and, if possible, its limits defined; and, if the principle of utility is good for anything, it must be good for weighing these conflicting utilities against one another and marking out the region within which one or the other preponderates.

. . .

OF WHAT SORT OF PROOF THE PRINCIPLE OF UTILITY IS SUSCEPTIBLE

. . . Questions of ultimate ends do not admit of proof, in the ordinary acceptation of the term. To be incapable of proof by reasoning is common to all first principles, to the first premises of our knowledge, as well as to those of our conduct. But the former, being matters of fact, may be the subject of a direct appeal to the faculties which judge of fact—namely, our senses and our internal consciousness. Can an appeal be made to the same faculties on questions of practical ends? Or by what other faculty is cognizance taken of them?

Questions about ends are, in other words, questions what things are desirable. The utilitarian doctrine is that happiness is desirable, and the only thing desirable, as an end; all other things being only desirable as means to that end. What ought to be required of this doctrine, what conditions is it requisite that the doctrine should fulfill—to make good its claim to be believed?

The only proof capable of being given that an object is visible is that people actually see it. The only proof that a sound is audible is that people hear it; and so of the other sources of our experience. In like manner, I apprehend, the sole evidence it is possible to produce that anything is desirable is that people do actually desire it. If the end which the utilitarian doctrine proposes to itself were not, in theory and in practice, acknowledged to be an end, nothing could ever convince any person that it was so. No reason can be given why the general happiness is desirable, except that each person, so far as he believes it to be attainable, desires his own happiness. This, however, being a fact, we have not only all the proof which the case admits of, but all which it is possible to require, that happiness is a good, that each person's happiness is a good to that person, and the general happiness, therefore, a good to the aggregate of all persons. Happiness has made out its title as *one* of the ends of conduct and, consequently, one of the criteria of morality.

But it has not, by this alone, proved itself to be the sole criterion. To do that, it would seem, by the same rule, necessary to show, not only that people desire happiness, but that they never desire anything else. Now it is palpable that they do desire things which, in common language, are decidedly distinguished from happiness. They desire, for example, virtue and the absence of vice no less really than pleasure and the absence of pain. The desire of virtue is not as universal, but it is as authentic a fact as the desire of happiness. And hence the opponents of the utilitarian standard deem that they have a right to infer that there are other ends of human action besides happiness, and that happiness is not the standard of approbation and disapprobation.

But does the utilitarian doctrine deny that people desire virtue, or maintain that virtue is not a thing to be desired? The very reverse. It maintains not only that virtue is to be desired, but that it is to be desired disinterestedly, for itself. Whatever may be the opinion of utilitarian moralists as to the original conditions by which virtue is made virtue, however they may believe (as they do) that actions and dispositions are only virtuous because they promote another end than virtue, yet this being granted, and it having been decided, from considerations of this description, what *is* virtuous, they not only place virtue at the very head of the things which are good as means to the ultimate end, but they also recognize as a psychological fact the possibility of its being, to the individual, a good in itself, without looking to any end beyond it; and hold that the mind is not in a right state, not in a state conformable to utility, not in the state most conducive to the general happiness, unless it does love virtue in this manner—as a thing desirable in itself, even although, in the individual instance, it should not produce those other desirable consequences which it tends to produce, and on account of which it is held to be virtue. This opinion is not, in the smallest degree, a departure from the happiness principle. The ingredients of happiness are very various, and each of them is desirable in itself, and not merely when considered as swelling an aggregate. The principle of utility does not mean that any given pleasure, as music, for instance, or any given exemption from pain, as for example health, is to be looked upon as means to a collective something termed happiness, and to be desired on that account. They are desired and desirable in and for themselves; besides being means, they are a part of the end. Virtue, according to the utilitarian doctrine, is not naturally and originally part of the end, but it is capable of becoming so; and in those who live it disinterestedly it has become so, and is desired and cherished, not as a means to happiness, but as a part of their happiness.

To illustrate this further, we may remember that virtue is not the only thing originally a means, and which if it were not a means to anything else would be and remain indifferent, but which by association with what it is a means to comes to be desired for itself, and that too with the utmost intensity. What, for example, shall we say of the love of money? There is nothing originally more desirable about money than about any heap of glittering pebbles. Its worth is solely that of the things which it will buy; the desires for other things than itself, which it is a means of gratifying. Yet the love of money is not only one of the strongest moving forces of human life, but money is, in many cases, desired in and for itself; the desire to possess it is often stronger than the desire to use it, and goes on increasing when all the desires which point to ends beyond it, to be compassed by it, are falling off. It may, then, be said truly that money is desired not for the sake of an end, but as part of the end. From being a means to happiness, it has come to be itself a principal ingredient of the individual's conception of happiness. The same may be said of the majority of the great objects of human life: power, for example, or fame, except that to each of these there is a certain amount of immediate pleasure annexed, which has at least the semblance of being naturally inherent in them—a thing which cannot be said of money. Still, however, the strongest natural attraction, both of power and of fame, is the immense aid they give to the attainment of our other wishes; and it is the strong association thus generated between them and all our objects of desire which gives to the direct desire of them the intensity it often assumes, so as in some characters to surpass in strength all other desires. In these cases the means have become a part of the end, and a more important part of it than any of the things which they are means to. What was once desired as an instrument for the attainment of happiness has come to be desired for its own sake. In being desired for its own sake it is, however, desired as *part* of happiness. The person is made, or thinks he would be made, happy by its mere possession; and is made unhappy by failure to obtain it. The desire of it is not a different thing from the desire of happiness any more than the love of music or the desire of health. They are included in happiness. They are some of the elements of which the desire of happiness is made up. Happiness is not an abstract idea but a concrete whole; and these are some of its parts. And the utilitarian standard sanctions and approves their being so. Life would be a poor thing, very ill provided with sources of happiness, if there were not this provision of nature by which things originally indifferent, but conducive to, or otherwise associated with, the satisfaction of our primitive desires, become in themselves sources of pleasure more valuable than the primitive pleasures, both in permanency, in the space of human existence that they are capable of covering, and even in intensity.

Virtue, according to the utilitarian conception, is a good of this description. There was no original desire of it, or motive to it, save its conduciveness to pleasure, and especially to protection from pain. But through the association thus formed it may be felt a good in itself, and desired as such with as great intensity as any other good; and with this difference between it and the love of money, of power, or of fame—that all of these may, and often do, render the individual noxious to the other members of the society to which he belongs, whereas there is nothing which makes him so much a blessing to them as the cultivation of the disinterested love of virtue. And consequently, the utilitarian standard, while it tolerates and approves those other acquired desires, up to the point beyond which they would be more injurious to the general happiness than promotive of it, enjoins and requires the cultivation of the love of virtue up to the greatest strength possible, as being above all things important to the general happiness.

It results from the preceding considerations that there is in reality nothing desired except happiness. Whatever is desired otherwise than as a means to some end beyond itself, and ultimately to happiness, is desired as itself a part of happiness, and is not desired for itself until it has become so. Those who desire virtue for its own sake desire it either because the consciousness of it is a pleasure, or because the consciousness of being without it is a pain, or for both reasons united; as in truth the pleasure and pain seldom exist separately, but almost always together—the same person feeling pleasure in the degree of virtue attained, and pain in not having attained more. If one of these gave him no pleasure, and the other no pain, he would not love or desire virtue, or would desire it only for the other benefits which it might produce to himself or to persons whom he cared for.

We have now, then, an answer to the question, of what sort of proof the principle of utility is susceptible. If the opinion which I have now stated is psychologically true—if human nature is so constituted as to desire nothing which is not either a part of happiness or a means of happiness—we can have no other proof, and we require no other, that these are the only things desirable. If so, happiness is the sole end of human action, and the promotion of it the test by which to judge of all human conduct; from whence it necessarily follows that it must be the criterion of morality, since a part is included in the whole.

And now to decide whether this is really so, whether mankind do desire nothing for itself but that which is a pleasure to them, or of which the absence is a pain, we have evidently arrived at a question of fact and experience, dependent, like all similar questions, upon evidence. It can only be determined by practiced self-consciousness and self-observation, assisted by observation of others. I believe that these sources of evidence, impartially consulted, will declare that desiring a thing and finding it pleasant, aversion to it and thinking of it as painful, are phenomena entirely inseparable or, rather, two parts of the same phenomenon—in strictness of language, two different modes of naming the same psychological fact; that to think of an object as desirable (unless for the sake of its consequences) and to think of it as pleasant are one and the same thing; and that to desire anything except in proportion as the idea of it is pleasant is a physical and metaphysical impossibility.

So obvious does this appear to me that I expect it will hardly be disputed; and the objection made will be, not that desire can possibly be directed to anything ultimately except pleasure and exemption from pain, but that the will is a different thing from desire; that a person of confirmed virtue or any other person whose purposes are fixed carries out his purposes without any thought of the pleasure he has in contemplating them or expects to derive from their fulfillment, and persists in acting on them, even though these pleasures are much diminished by changes in his character or decay of his passive sensibilities, or are outweighed by the pains which the pursuit of the purposes may bring upon him. All this I fully admit and have stated it elsewhere as positively and emphatically as anyone. Will, the active phenomenon, is a different thing from desire, the state of passive sensibility, and, though originally an offshoot from it, may in time take root and detach itself from the parent stock, so much so that in the case of a habitual purpose, instead of willing the thing because we desire it, we often desire it only because we will it. This, however, is but an instance of that familiar fact, the power of habit, and is nowise confined to the case of virtuous actions. Many indifferent things which men originally did from a motive of some sort they continue to do from habit. Sometimes this is done unconsciously, the consciousness coming only after the action; at other times with conscious volition, but volition which has become habitual and is put in operation by the force of habit, in opposition perhaps to the deliberate preference, as often happens with those who have contracted habits of vicious or hurtful indulgence. Third and last comes the case in which the habitual act of will in the individual instance is not in contradiction to the general intention prevailing at other times, but in fulfillment of it, as in the case of the person of confirmed virtue and of all who pursue deliberately and consistently any determinate end. The distinction between will and desire thus understood is an authentic and highly important psychological fact; but the fact consists solely in this—that will, like all other parts of our constitution, is amenable to habit, and that we may will from habit what we no longer desire for itself, or desire only because we will it. It is not the less true that will, in the beginning, is entirely produced by desire, including in that term the repelling influence of pain as well as the attractive one of pleasure. Let us take into consideration no longer the person who has a confirmed will to do right, but him in whom that virtuous will is still feeble, conquerable by temptation, and not to be fully relied on; by what means can it be strengthened? How can the will to be virtuous, where it does not exist in sufficient force, be implanted or awakened? Only by making the person *desire* virtue— by making him think of it in a pleasurable light, or of its absence in a painful one. It is by associating the doing right with pleasure, or the wrong with pain, or by eliciting and impressing and bringing home to the person's experience the pleasure naturally involved in the one or the pain in the other, that it is possible to call forth that will to be virtuous which, when confirmed, acts without any thought of either pleasure or pain. Will is the child of desire, and passes out of the dominion of its parent only to come under that of habit. That which is the result of habit affords no presumption of being intrinsically good; and there would be no reason for wishing that the purpose of virtue should become independent of pleasure and pain were it not that the influence of the pleasurable and painful associations which prompt to virtue is not sufficiently to be depended on for unerring constancy of action until it has acquired the support of habit. Both in feeling and in conduct, habit is the only thing which imparts certainty; and it is because of the importance to others of being able to rely absolutely on one's feelings and conduct, and to oneself of being able to rely on one's own, that the will to do right ought to be cultivated into this habitual independence. In other words, this state of the will is a means to good, not intrinsically a good; and does not contradict the doctrine that nothing is a good to human beings but in so far as it is either itself pleasurable or a means of attaining pleasure or averting pain.

But if this doctrine be true, the principle of utility is proved. Whether it is so or not must now be left to the consideration of the thoughtful reader.

QUESTIONS

1. "An act is right if it is useful." "An act is right if it brings pleasure." Mill says that the principle of utilitarianism is not identical with either of these statements, but in a sense combines them both. Explain in what sense it is a combination of both statements.
2. Mill distinguishes quality of pleasure from quantity of pleasure. What does he mean by this difference? Elucidate your answer by means of examples. Suppose an action brought about a great quantity of low quality pleasure, and another action brought about a small quantity of high quality pleasure. How would Mill decide which action was the better?
3. "Human beings have faculties more elevated than the animal appetites. . . ." What standard is Mill using here to determine the degree of "elevation" of our faculties? Is this standard derivable from the "greatest happiness principle"? Why or why not?
4. What would Mill be likely to reply to the following objection?
   "You say: 'Better to be a human being dissatisfied than a pig satisfied.' But by your own test of competent acquaintance with both experiences as the

method for deciding which is the better, you have no grounds for making that statement, for you have never been a pig."

5. Does Mill ever provide a satisfactory answer to the fundamental question: Why should I seek the greatest happiness for all if my doing so interferes with my own happiness? Defend your answer.

6. ". . . The motive has nothing to do with the morality of the action, though much with the worth of the agent." From the point of view of utilitarianism, what is meant by "the morality of the action" as distinct from "the worth of the agent"? Is there any connection between the two? Explain by means of examples.

7. State why you think Mill does, or does not, adequately reply to the objection that "utilitarianism does not recognize the revealed will of God as the supreme law of morals. . . ."

8. After reading the selection by Kant in this chapter, analyze the different grounds on which Mill and Kant, respectively, would base the moral judgment, "It is wrong to lie." Would there ever be an action which Kant would approve of and Mill disapprove of, or an action which Kant would disapprove of and Mill approve of? If so, give examples and explain why they would disagree in each case. If not, explain in detail why not.

9. It is now widely accepted among philosophers that there is a glaring error in the following argument. Where is it?

"The only proof capable of being given that an object is visible is that people actually see it. The only proof that a sound is audible is that people hear it; and so of the other sources of our experience. In like manner, I apprehend, the sole evidence it is possible to produce that anything is desirable is that people do actually desire it."

10. What differences and what similarities do you find between Mill's conception of happiness and Aristotle's? (See "Teleological Naturalism" in this chapter.)

11. From the point of view of Kant's ethical theory (see his "A Priori Ethics" in this chapter) the promotion of happiness has nothing to do with deciding what is morally right and wrong. For Mill, on the other hand, the promotion of happiness is itself the "criterion of morality." Is there any possible way to determine which of these views is justified? If so, briefly outline the way. If not, show clearly why not.

39. A. J. AYER

(b. 1910)

The Emotive Theory

(A general introductory note on A. J. Ayer may be found on page 185.)

In this reading Professor Ayer is concerned with the question whether moral statements are empirically verifiable. The reader is advised to consult the selection by Professor Ayer in Chapter 3, in order to understand the general position from which he approaches the problem of moral knowledge.

Professor Ayer begins by rejecting two types of moral philosophy: naturalism and non-naturalism (or intuitionism). Naturalism is the view that moral statements are empirically verifiable, that is, moral knowledge is simply knowledge of a certain set of empirical facts. The moral philosophies of Aristotle, of Hume, and of Mill may all be considered different forms of naturalism. Non-naturalism, on the other hand, is the view that moral statements are not empirically verifiable, but are nevertheless genuinely true or false. The theory of Kant may be considered a version of this point of view. It should be noted that Professor Ayer calls non-naturalism the "absolutist view," but this term is not used in the same way as the term "ethical absolutism" is used in the introduction to this chapter.

After giving his arguments against both naturalism and non-naturalism, Professor Ayer sets forth his own position, which has come to be known as "the emotive theory." According to this theory, moral statements do not express propositions, which can be true or false. They express emotions or attitudes, which can be neither true nor false. Since truth and falsity do not apply to moral statements, there is consequently no such thing as moral knowledge. The general principle of "radical empiricism," which Professor Ayer is trying to defend throughout his book, Language, Truth and Logic, is thus preserved: All statements which are "synthetic," i.e., which express propositions conveying information about the world, are empirically verifiable. All other statements are either (1) "analytic," i.e., they express propositions which are true or false a priori and do not describe anything in the world, or (2) "emotive," i.e., utterances which express no propositions at all and therefore cannot be true or false. Moral statements, Ayer claims, belong in the latter category.

This selection is taken from Chapter VI of Language, Truth and Logic.

From Language, Truth and Logic, by Alfred Jules Ayer, reprinted through permission by the author and by Dover Publications, Inc., New York 10, N. Y. ($1.25, paperbound).

The ordinary system of ethics, as elaborated in the works of ethical philosophers, is very far from being a homogeneous whole. Not only is it apt to contain pieces of metaphysics, and analyses of nonethical concepts: its actual ethical contents are themselves of very different kinds. We may divide them, indeed, into four main classes. There are, first of all, propositions which express definitions of ethical terms, or judgements about the legitimacy or possibility of certain definitions. Secondly, there are propositions describing the phenomena of moral experience, and their causes. Thirdly, there are exhortations to moral virtue. And, lastly, there are actual ethical judgements. It is unfortunately the case that the distinction between these four classes, plain as it is, is commonly ignored by ethical philosophers; with the result that it is often very difficult to tell from their works what it is that they are seeking to discover or prove.

In fact, it is easy to see that only the first of our four classes, namely that which comprises the propositions relating to the definitions of ethical terms, can be said to constitute ethical philosophy. The propositions which describe the phenomena of moral experience, and their causes, must be assigned to the science of psychology, or sociology. The exhortations to moral virtue are not propositions at all, but ejaculations or commands which are designed to provoke the reader to action of a certain sort. Accordingly, they do not belong to any branch of philosophy or science. As for the expressions of ethical judgements, we have not yet determined how they should be classified. But inasmuch as they are certainly neither definitions nor comments upon definitions, nor quotations, we may say decisively that they do not belong to ethical philosophy. A strictly philosophical treatise on ethics should therefore make no ethical pronouncements. But it should, by giving an analysis of ethical terms, show what is the category to which all such pronouncements belong. And this is what we are now about to do.

A question which is often discussed by ethical philosophers is whether it is possible to find definitions which would reduce all ethical terms to one or two fundamental terms. But this question, though it undeniably belongs to ethical philosophy, is not relevant to our present enquiry. We are not now concerned to discover which term, within the sphere of ethical terms, is to be taken as fundamental; whether, for example, "good" can be defined in terms of "right" or "right" in terms of "good," or both in terms of "value." What we are interested in is the possibility of reducing the whole sphere of ethical terms to nonethical terms. We are enquiring whether statements of ethical value can be translated into statements of empirical fact.

That they can be so translated is the contention of those ethical philosophers who are commonly called subjectivists, and of those who are known as utilitarians. For the utilitarian defines the rightness of actions, and the goodness of ends, in terms of the pleasure, or happiness, or satisfaction, to which they give rise; the subjectivist, in terms of the feelings of approval which a certain person, or group of people, has towards them. Each of these types of definition makes moral judgements into a subclass of psychological or sociological judgements; and for this reason they are very attractive to us. For, if either was correct, it would follow that ethical assertions were not generically different from the factual assertions which are ordinarily contrasted with them; and the account which we have already given of empirical hypotheses would apply to them also.

Nevertheless we shall not adopt either a subjectivist or a utilitarian analysis of ethical terms. We reject the subjectivist view that to call an action right, or a thing good, is to say that it is generally approved of, because it is not self-contradictory to assert that some actions which are generally approved of are not right, or that some things which are generally approved of are not good. And we reject the alternative subjectivist view that a man who asserts that a certain action is right, or that a certain thing is good, is saying that he himself approves of it, on the ground that a man who confessed that he sometimes approved of what was bad or wrong would not be contradicting himself. And a similar argument is fatal to utilitarianism. We cannot agree that to call an action right is to say that of all the actions possible in the circumstances it would cause, or be likely to cause, the greatest happiness, or the greatest balance of pleasure over pain, or the greatest balance of satisfied over unsatisfied desire, because we find that it is not self-contradictory to say that it is sometimes wrong to perform the action which would actually or probably cause the greatest happiness, or the greatest balance of pleasure over pain, or of satisfied over unsatisfied desire. And since it is not self-contradictory to say that some pleasant things are not good, or that some bad things are desired, it cannot be the case that the sentence "*x* is good" is equivalent to "*x* is pleasant," or to "*x* is desired." And to every other variant of utilitarianism with which I am acquainted the same objection can be made. And therefore we should, I think, conclude that the validity of ethical judgements it not determined by the felicific tendencies of actions, any more than by the nature of people's feelings; but that it must be regarded as "absolute" or "intrinsic," and not empirically calculable.

If we say this, we are not, of course, denying that it is possible to invent a language in which all ethical symbols are definable in nonethical terms, or even that it is desirable to invent such a language and adopt it in place of our own; what we are denying is that the suggested reduction of ethical to nonethical statements is consistent with the conventions of our actual language. That is, we reject utilitarianism and subjectivism, not as proposals to replace our existing ethical notions by new ones, but as analyses of our existing ethical notions. Our contention is simply that, in our language, sentences which contain normative ethical symbols are not equivalent to sentences which express psychological propositions, or indeed empirical propositions of any kind.

It is advisable here to make it plain that it is only normative ethical symbols, and not descriptive ethical symbols, that are held by us to be indefinable in factual terms. There is a danger of confusing these two types of symbols, because they are commonly constituted by signs of the same sensible form. Thus a complex sign of the form "*x* is wrong" may constitute a sentence which expresses a moral judgement concerning a certain type of conduct, or it may constitute a sentence which states that a certain type of conduct is repugnant to the moral sense of a particular society. In the latter case, the symbol "wrong" is a descriptive ethical symbol, and the sentence in which it occurs expresses an ordinary sociological proposition; in the former case, the symbol "wrong" is a normative ethical symbol, and the sentence in which it occurs does not, we maintain, express an empirical proposition at all. It is only with normative ethics that we are at present concerned; so that whenever ethical symbols are used in the course of this argument without qualification, they are always to be interpreted as symbols of the normative type.

In admitting that normative ethical concepts are irreducible to empirical concepts, we seem to be leaving the way clear for the "absolutist" view of ethics—that is, the view that statements of value are not controlled by observation, as ordinary empirical propositions are, but only by a mysterious "intellectual intuition." A feature of this theory, which is seldom recognized by its advocates, is that it makes statements of value unverifiable. For it is notorious that what seems intuitively certain to one person may seem doubtful, or even false, to another. So that unless it is possible to provide some criterion by which one may decide between conflicting intuitions, a mere appeal to intuition is worthless as a test of a proposition's validity. But in the case of moral judgements, no such criterion can be given. Some moralists claim to settle the matter by saying that they "know" that their own moral judgements are correct. But such an assertion is of purely psychological interest, and has not the slightest tendency to prove the validity of any moral judgement. For dissentient moralists may equally well "know" that their ethical views are correct. And, as far as subjective certainty goes, there will be nothing to choose between them. When such differences of opinion arise in connection with an ordinary empirical proposition, one may attempt to resolve them by referring to, or actually carrying out, some relevant empirical test. But with regard to ethical statements, there is, on the "absolutist" or "intuitionist" theory, no relevant empirical test. We are therefore justified in saying that on this theory ethical statements are held to be unverifiable. They are, of course, also held to be genuine synthetic propositions.

Considering the use which we have made of the principle that a synthetic proposition is significant only if it is empirically verifiable, it is clear that the acceptance of an "absolutist" theory of ethics would undermine the whole of our main argument. And as we have already rejected the "naturalistic" theories which are commonly supposed to provide the only alternative to "absolutism" in ethics, we seem to have reached a difficult position. We shall meet the difficulty by showing that the correct treatment of ethical statements is afforded by a third theory, which is wholly compatible with our radical empiricism.

We begin by admitting that the fundamental ethical concepts are unanalysable, inasmuch as there is no criterion by which one can test the validity of the judgements in which they occur. So far we are in agreement with the absolutists. But, unlike the absolutists, we are able to give an explanation of this fact about ethical concepts. We say that the reason why they are unanalysable is that they are mere pseudo-concepts. The presence of an ethical symbol in a proposition adds nothing to its factual content. Thus if I say to someone, "You acted wrongly in stealing that money," I am not stating anything more than if I had simply said, "You stole that money."

In adding that this action is wrong I am not making any further statement about it. I am simply evincing my moral disapproval of it. It is as if I had said, "You stole that money," in a peculiar tone of horror, or written it with the addition of some special exclamation marks. The tone, or the exclamation marks, adds nothing to the literal meaning of the sentence. It merely serves to show that the expression of it is attended by certain feelings in the speaker.

If now I generalise my previous statement and say, "Stealing money is wrong," I produce a sentence which has no factual meaning—that is, expresses no proposition which can be either true or false. It is as if I had written "Stealing money!!" where the shape and thickness of the exclamation marks show, by a suitable convention, that a special sort of moral disapproval is the feeling which is being expressed. It is clear that there is nothing said here which can be true or false. Another man may disagree with me about the wrongness of stealing, in the sense that he may not have the same feelings about stealing as I have, and he may quarrel with me on account of my moral sentiments. But he cannot, strictly speaking, contradict me. For in saying that a certain type of action is right or wrong, I am not making any factual statement, not even a statement about my own state of mind. I am merely expressing certain moral sentiments. And the man who is ostensibly contradicting me is merely expressing his moral sentiments. So that there is plainly no sense in asking which of us is in the right. For neither of us is asserting a genuine proposition.

What we have just been saying about the symbol "wrong" applies to all normative ethical symbols. Sometimes they occur in sentences which record ordinary empirical facts besides expressing ethical feeling about those facts: sometimes they occur in sentences which simply express ethical feeling about a certain type of action, or situation, without making any statement of fact. But in every case in which one would commonly be said to be making an ethical judgment, the function of the relevant ethical word is purely "emotive." It is used to express feeling about certain objects, but not to make any assertion about them.

It is worth mentioning that ethical terms do not serve only to express feeling. They are calculated also to arouse feeling, and so to stimulate action. Indeed some of them are used in such a way as to give the sentences in which they occur the effect of commands. Thus the sentence "It is your duty to tell the truth" may be regarded both as the expression of a certain sort of ethical feeling about truthfulness and as the expression of the command "Tell the truth." The sentence "You ought to tell the truth" also involves the command "Tell the truth," but here the tone of the command is less emphatic. In the sentence "It is good to tell the truth" the command has become little more than a suggestion. And thus the "meaning" of the word "good," in its ethical usage, is differentiated from that of the word "duty" or the word "ought." In fact we may define the meaning of the various ethical words in terms both of the different feelings they are ordinarily taken to express, and also the different responses which they are calculated to provoke.

We can now see why it is impossible to find a criterion for determining the validity of ethical judgements. It is not because they have an "absolute" validity which is mysteriously independent of ordinary sense-experience, but because they have no objective validity whatsoever. If a sentence makes no statement at all, there is obviously no sense in asking whether what it says is true or false. And we have seen that sentences which simply express moral judgements do not say anything. They are pure expressions of feeling and as such do not come under the category of truth and falsehood. They are unverifiable for the same reason as a cry of pain or a word of command is unverifiable—because they do not express genuine propositions.

Thus, although our theory of ethics might fairly be said to be radically subjectivist, it differs in a very important respect from the orthodox subjectivist theory. For the orthodox subjectivist does not deny, as we do, that the sentences of a moralizer express genuine propositions. All he denies is that they express propositions of a unique nonempirical character. His own view is that they express propositions about the speaker's feelings. If this were so, ethical judgements clearly would be capable of being true or false. They would be true if the speaker had the relevant feelings, and false if he had not. And this is a matter which is, in principle, empirically verifiable. Furthermore they could be significantly contradicted. For if I say, "Tolerance is a virtue," and someone answers, "You don't approve of it," he would, on the ordinary subjectivist theory, be contradicting me. On our theory, he would not be contradicting me, because, in saying that tolerance was a virtue, I should not be making any statement about my own feelings or about anything else. I should simply be evincing my feelings, which is not at all the same thing as saying that I have them.

The distinction between the expression of feeling and the assertion of feeling is complicated by the fact that the assertion that one has a certain feeling often accompanies the expression of that feeling, and is then, indeed, a factor in the expression of that feeling. Thus I may simultaneously express boredom and say that I am bored, and in that case my utterance of the words, "I am bored," is one of the circumstances which make it true to say that I am expressing or evincing boredom. But I can express boredom without actually saying that I am bored. I can express it by my tone and gestures, while making a statement about something wholly unconnected with it, or by an ejaculation, or without uttering any words at all. So that even if the assertion that one has a certain feeling always involves the expression of that feeling, the expression of a feeling assuredly does not always involve the assertion that one has it. And this is the important point to grasp in considering the distinction between our theory and the ordinary subjectivist theory. For whereas the subjectivist holds that ethical statements actually assert the existence of certain feelings, we hold that ethical statements are expressions and excitants of feeling which do not necessarily involve any assertions.

We have already remarked that the main objection to the ordinary subjectivist theory is that the validity of ethical judgements is not determined by the nature of their author's feelings. And this is an objection which our theory escapes. For it does not imply that the existence of any feelings is a necessary and sufficient condition of the validity of an ethical judgement. It implies, on the contrary, that ethical judgements have no validity.

There is, however, a celebrated argument against subjectivist theories which our theory does not escape. It has been pointed out by Moore that if ethical statements were simply statements about the speaker's feelings, it would be impossible to argue about questions of value. To take a typical example: if a man said that thrift was a virtue, and another replied that it was a vice, they would not, on this theory, be disputing with one another. One would be saying that he approved of thrift, and the other that *he* didn't; and there is no reason why both these statements should not be true. Now Moore held it to be obvious that we do dispute about questions of value, and accordingly concluded that the particular form of subjectivism which he was discussing was false.

It is plain that the conclusion that it is impossible to dispute about questions of value follows from our theory also. For as we hold that such sentences as "Thrift is a virtue" and "Thrift is a vice" do not express propositions at all, we clearly cannot hold that they express incompatible propositions. We must therefore admit that if Moore's argument really refutes the ordinary subjectivist theory, it also refutes ours. But, in fact, we deny that it does refute even the ordinary subjectivist theory. For we hold that one really never does dispute about questions of value.

This may seem, at first sight, to be a very paradoxical assertion. For we certainly do engage in disputes which are ordinarily regarded as disputes about questions of value. But, in all such cases, we find, if we consider the matter closely, that the dispute is not really about a question of value, but about a question of fact. When someone disagrees with us about the moral value of a certain action or type of action, we do admittedly resort to argument in order to win him over to our way of thinking. But we do not attempt to show by our arguments that he has the "wrong" ethical feeling towards a situation whose nature he has correctly apprehended. What we attempt to show is that he is mistaken about the facts of the case. We argue that he has misconceived the agent's motive: or that he has misjudged the effects of the action, or its probable effects in view of the agent's knowledge; or that he has failed to take into account the special circumstances in which the agent was placed. Or else we employ more general arguments about the effects which actions of a certain type tend to produce, or the qualities which are usually manifested in their performance. We do this in the hope that we have only to get our opponent to agree with us about the nature of the empirical facts for him to adopt the same moral attitude towards them as we do. And as the people with whom we argue have generally received the same moral education as ourselves, and live in the same social order, our expectation is usually justified. But if our opponent happens to have undergone a different process of moral "conditioning" from ourselves, so that, even when he acknowledges all the facts, he still disagrees with us about the moral value of the actions under discussion, then we abandon the attempt to convince him by argument. We say that it is impossible to argue with him because he has a distorted or undeveloped moral sense; which signifies merely that he employs a different set of values from our own. We feel that our own system of values is superior, and therefore speak in such derogatory terms of his. But we cannot bring forward any arguments to show that our system is superior. For our judgement that it is so is itself a judgement of value, and accordingly outside the scope of argument. It is because argument fails us when we come to deal with pure questions of value, as distinct from questions of fact, that we finally resort to mere abuse.

In short, we find that argument is possible on moral questions only if some system of values is presupposed. If our opponent concurs with us in expressing moral disapproval of all actions of a given type *t*, then we may get him to condemn a particular action A, by bringing forward arguments to show that A is of type *t*. For the question whether A does or does not belong to that type is a plain question of fact. Given that a man has certain moral principles, we argue that he must, in order to be consistent, react morally to certain things in a certain way. What we do not and cannot argue about is the validity of these moral principles. We merely praise or condemn them in the light of our own feelings.

QUESTIONS

1. According to Professor Ayer, both subjectivists and utilitarians translate moral statements into statements of empirical fact. How does he attempt to show this? Taking Hume as an example of a subjectivist and Mill as an example of a utilitarian, show that Professor Ayer's argument does, or does not, hold for the views of these two philosophers. (For Hume's and Mill's views, see their selections in this chapter.)
2. On what grounds does Professor Ayer reject the subjectivist and utilitarian analyses of ethical terms? Appraise the validity of his argument.
3. On what basis does Professor Ayer claim that a person who says, "You acted wrongly in stealing that money," is not stating anything more than if he had said, "You stole that money"? Many people have been shocked by this claim and have called it outrageously immoral. Others have said it is obviously untrue. Do you think it is immoral? Do you think it is obviously untrue? Defend your answers.
4. Sometimes the emotive theory of ethics is called "the imperative theory" because the sentence "It is your duty to tell the truth" is said to be the expression of the command "Tell the truth." The imperative theory has been attacked on the grounds that it cannot account for the fact that, while the

command "Tell the truth" has a moral statement corresponding to it, the commands "Shut the door," "Smoke Camels," "Throw a pass on the next play" do not. Thus, the argument runs, the imperative theory cannot explain the difference between moral and nonmoral commands. Could Professor Ayer satisfactorily answer this objection? If so, how?

5. A criticism which many have raised against the emotive theory is that when one person says, "Euthanasia is wrong," and another says, "Euthanasia is not wrong," they are contradicting one another. That is, if what one is saying is true, what the other is saying must be false. But according to Professor Ayer's theory, there is no contradiction in such a situation. Give your reasons for deciding that Professor Ayer does, or does not, successfully reply to this criticism.

6. Explain by means of examples the difference between the expression of a feeling and the assertion of a feeling. Of what importance is this distinction in understanding the emotive theory of ethics?

7. A philosopher has attacked Ayer's position by saying that if it were true, then a murderer could remove the wrongness of his deed by crying, "Hurrah for murder!"

Is this a good criticism?

8. Compare carefully Ayer's view of moral statements with Hume's theory of the moral sense. How do the two views differ? (Compare Question 7 above with Question 7 on Hume, page 537.)

9. Are all disputes about values really disputes about facts, as Ayer claims? When we say that a person has a "distorted or undeveloped moral sense," is it true that we mean "merely that he employs a different set of values from our own"?

10. Why does Ayer's theory imply ethical relativism? (For the meaning of "ethical relativism," see the introduction to this chapter.)

40. JEAN-PAUL SARTRE

(b. 1905)

The Ethical Outlook of Existentialism

Jean-Paul Sartre, who now resides in Paris, has been Professor of Philosophy at the Lycée of Le Havre, the Lycée of Laon, and the Lycée Condorcet in Neuilly, France. During the Second World War he served in the French army until he was taken prisoner in 1940. In the spring of 1941 he escaped, and during the German occupation of France he was active in the Resistance Movement. After the liberation in 1944 he devoted himself entirely to writing—fiction, drama, literary criticism, and philosophical essays. His novels include *Nausea* (1938) and *Roads to Freedom* (1945–49). *The Flies* (1943) and *No Exit* (1944) are two of his best known plays. Among his philosophical works are *Being and Nothingness* (1943) and *Existentialism*

(1946), from which the following selection is taken.

Sartre begins by explaining what is meant when existentialists say that "existence comes before essence." There is no fixed human nature or essence of man to which individuals must conform. Instead, each individual "will be what he makes of himself." Since there is no God who can tell him to be one kind of person rather than another, he must take the responsibility of deciding for himself what kind of person to be. Now, Sartre's argument continues, to become a certain kind of person is to realize a certain type of humanity; therefore, when one chooses to create oneself, one chooses for all humanity. In Sartre's words: "I am creating a certain image of man of my own choosing. In choosing myself, I choose man."

What is to guide an individual in making such a choice? Sartre does not appeal to universal rules of conduct because he thinks that these are too abstract to be of much help in the concrete circumstances of choice. Nor does he believe that we can be guided by specific moral standards, since these would have to come from outside human choice and in denying the existence of God he thinks he has taken away the only possible source of such standards. Instead, each person must make a free commitment to standards he has chosen for himself when (1) he fully senses his own responsibility as a maker of an image of humanity, and (2) he is aware of the basic facts about the human condition which all men share with him. Sartre then attempts to show why this view of ethical choice does not entail the breakdown of all moral judgment.

From *Existentialism,* by Jean-Paul Sartre, translated by Bernard Frechtman, Philosophical Library, New York, 1947. Reprinted by permission of the publisher.

. . . There are two kinds of existentialist; first, those who are Christian, among whom I would include Jaspers and Gabriel Marcel, both Catholic; and on the other hand the atheistic existentialists, among whom I class Heidegger, and then the French existentialists and myself. What they have in common is that they think that existence precedes essence, or, if you prefer, that subjectivity must be the starting point.

Just what does that mean? Let us consider some object that is manufactured, for example, a book or a paper-cutter: here is an object which has been made by an artisan whose inspiration came from a concept. He referred to the concept of what a paper-cutter is and likewise to a known method of production, which is part of the concept, something which is, by and large, a routine. Thus, the paper-cutter is at once an object produced in a certain way and, on the other hand, one having a specific use; and one can not postulate a man who produces a paper-cutter but does not know what it is used for. Therefore, let us say that, for the paper-cutter, essence—that is, the ensemble of both the production routines and the properties which enable it to be both produced and defined—precedes existence. Thus, the presence of the paper-cutter or book in front of me is determined. Therefore, we have here a technical view of the world whereby it can be said that production precedes existence.

When we conceive God as the Creator, He is generally thought of as a superior sort of artisan. Whatever doctrine we may be considering, whether one like that of Descartes or that of Leibnitz, we always grant that will more or less follows understanding or, at the very least, accompanies it, and that when God creates He knows exactly what He is creating. Thus, the concept of man in the mind of God is comparable to the concept of paper-cutter in the mind of the manufacturer, and, following certain techniques and a conception, God produces man, just as the artisan, following a definition and a technique, makes a paper-cutter. Thus, the individual man is the realisation of a certain concept in the divine intelligence.

In the eighteenth century, the atheism of the *philosophes* discarded the idea of God, but not so much for the notion that essence precedes existence. To a certain extent, this idea is found everywhere; we find it in Diderot, in Voltaire, and even in Kant. Man has a human nature; this human nature, which is the concept of the human, is found in all men, which means that each man is a particular example of a universal concept, man. In Kant, the result of this universality is that the wild-man, the natural man, as well as the bourgeois, are circumscribed by the same definition and have the same basic qualities. Thus, here too the essence of man precedes the historical existence that we find in nature.

Atheistic existentialism, which I represent, is more coherent. It states that if God does not exist, there is at least one being in whom existence precedes essence, a being who exists before he can be defined by any concept, and that this being is man, or, as Heidegger says, human reality. What is meant here by saying that existence precedes essence? It means that, first of all, man exists, turns up, appears on the scene, and, only afterwards, defines himself. If man, as the existentialist conceives him, is indefinable, it is because at first he is nothing. Only afterward will he be something, and he himself will have made what he will be. Thus, there is no human nature, since there is no God to conceive it. Not only is man what he conceives himself to be, but he is also only what he wills himself to be after this thrust toward existence.

Man is nothing else but what he makes of himself. Such is the first principle of existentialism. It is also what is called subjectivity, the name we are labeled with when charges are brought against us. But what do we mean by this, if not that man has a greater dignity than a stone or table? For we mean that man first exists, that is, that man first of all is the being who hurls himself toward a future and who is conscious of imagining himself as being in the future. Man is at the start a plan which is aware of itself, rather than a patch of moss, a piece of garbage, or a cauliflower; nothing exists prior to this plan; there is nothing in heaven; man will be what he will have planned to be. Not what he will want to be. Because by the word "will" we generally mean a conscious decision, which is subsequent to what we have already made of ourselves. I may want to belong to a political party, write a book, get married; but all that is only a manifestation of an earlier, more spontaneous choice that is called "will." But if existence really does precede essence, man is responsible for what he is. Thus, existentialism's first move is to make every man aware of what he is and to make the full responsibility of his existence rest on him. And when we say that a man is responsible for himself, we do not only mean that he is responsible for his own individuality, but that he is responsible for all men.

The word subjectivism has two meanings, and our opponents play on the two. Subjectivism means, on the one hand, that an individual chooses and makes himself; and, on the other, that it is impossible for man to transcend human subjectivity. The second of these is the essential meaning of existentialism. When we say that man chooses his own self, we mean that every one of us does likewise; but we also mean by that that in making this choice he also chooses all men. In fact, in creating the man that we want to be, there is not a single one of our acts which does not at the same time create an image of man as we think he ought to be. To choose to be this or that is to affirm at the same time the value of what we choose, because we can never choose evil. We always choose the good, and nothing can be good for us without being good for all.

If, on the other hand, existence precedes essence, and if we grant that we exist and fashion our image at one and the same time, the image is valid for everybody and for our whole age. Thus, our responsibility is much greater than we might have supposed, because it involves all mankind. If I am a workingman and choose to join a Christian trade-union rather than be a communist, and if by being a member I want to show that the best thing for man is resignation, that the kingdom of man is not of this world, I am not only involving my own case—I want to be resigned for everyone. As a result, my action has involved all humanity. To take a more individual matter, if I want to marry, to have children; even if this marriage depends solely on my own circumstances or passion or wish, I am involving all humanity in monogamy and not merely myself. Therefore, I am responsible for myself and for everyone else. I am creating a certain image of man of my own choosing. In choosing myself, I choose man.

This helps us understand what the actual content is of such rather grandiloquent words as anguish, forlornness, despair. As you will see, it's all quite simple.

First, what is meant by anguish? The existentialists say at once that man is anguish. What that means is this: the man who involves himself and who realizes that he is not only the person he chooses to be, but also a law-maker who is, at the same time, choosing all mankind as well as himself, can not help escape the feeling of his total and deep responsibility. Of course, there are many people who are not anxious; but we claim that they are hiding their anxiety, that they are fleeing from it. Certainly, many people believe that when they do something, they themselves are the only ones involved, and when someone says to them, "What if everyone acted that way?" they shrug their shoulders and answer, "Everyone doesn't act that way." But really, one should always ask himself, "What would happen if everybody looked at things that way?" There is no escaping this disturbing thought except by a kind of double-dealing. A man who lies and makes excuses for himself by saying "not everybody does that," is someone with an uneasy conscience, because the act of lying implies that a universal value is conferred upon the lie.

Anguish is evident even when it conceals itself. This is the anguish that Kierkegaard called the anguish of Abraham. You know the story: an angel has ordered Abraham to sacrifice his son; if it really were an angel who has come and said, "You are Abraham, you shall sacrifice your son," everything would be all right. But everyone might first wonder, "Is it really an angel, and am I really Abraham? What proof do I have?"

There was a madwoman who had hallucinations; someone used to speak to her on the telephone and give her orders. Her doctor asked her, "Who is it who talks to you?" She answered, "He says it's God." What proof did she really have that it was God? If an angel comes to me, what proof is there that it's an angel? And if I hear voices, what proof is there that they come from heaven and not from hell, or from the subconscious, or a pathological condition? What proves that they are addressed to me? What proof is there that I have been appointed to impose my choice and my conception of man on humanity? I'll never find any proof or sign to convince me of that. If a voice addresses me, it is always for me to decide that this is the angel's voice; if I consider that such an act is a good one, it is I who will choose to say that it is good rather than bad.

Now, I'm not being singled out as an Abraham, and yet at every moment I'm obliged to perform exemplary acts. For every man, everything happens as if all mankind had its eyes fixed on him and were guiding itself by what he does. And every man ought to say to himself, "Am I really the kind of man who has the right to act in such a way that humanity might guide itself by my actions?" And if he does not say that to himself, he is masking his anguish.

There is no question here of the kind of anguish which would lead to quietism, to inaction. It is a matter of a simple sort of anguish that anybody who has had responsibilities is familiar with. For example, when a military officer takes the responsibility for an attack and sends a certain number of men to death, he chooses to do so, and in the main he alone makes the choice. Doubtless, orders come from above, but they are too broad; he interprets them, and on this interpretation depend the lives of ten or fourteen or twenty men. In making a decision he can not help having a certain anguish. All leaders know this anguish. That doesn't keep them from acting; on the contrary, it is the very condition of their action. For it implies that they envisage a number of possibilities, and when they choose one, they realize that it has value only because it is chosen. We shall see that this kind of anguish, which is the kind that existentialism describes, is explained, in addition, by a direct responsibility to the other men whom it involves. It is not a curtain separating us from action, but is part of action itself.

When we speak of forlornness, a term Heidegger was fond of, we mean only that God does not exist and that we have to face all the consequences of this. The existentialist is strongly opposed to a certain kind of secular ethics which would like to abolish God with the least possible expense. About 1880, some French teachers tried to set up a secular ethics which went something like this: God is a useless and costly hypothesis; we are discarding it; but, meanwhile, in order for there to be an ethics, a society, a civilization, it is essential that certain values be taken seriously and that they be considered as having an *a priori* existence. It must be obligatory, *a priori,* to be honest, not to lie, not to beat your wife, to have children, etc., etc. So we're going to try a little device which will make it possible to show that values exist all the same, inscribed in a heaven of ideas, though otherwise God does not exist. In other words—and this, I believe, is the tendency of everything called reformism in France—nothing will be changed if God does not exist. We shall find ourselves with the same norms of honesty, progress, and humanism, and we shall have made of God an outdated hypothesis which will peacefully die off by itself.

The existentialist, on the contrary, thinks it very distressing that God does not exist, because all possibility of finding values in a heaven of ideas disappears along with Him; there can no longer be an *a priori* Good, since there is no infinite and perfect consciousness to think it. Nowhere is it written that the Good exists, that we must be honest, that we must not lie; because the fact is we are on a plane where there are only men. Dostoievsky said, "If God didn't exist, everything would be possible." That is the very starting point of existentialism. Indeed, everything is permissible if God does not exist, and as a result man is forlorn, because neither within him nor without does he find anything to cling to. He can't start making excuses for himself.

If existence really does precede essence, there is no explaining things away by reference to a fixed and given human nature. In other words, there is no determinism, man is free, man is freedom. On the other hand, if God does not exist, we find no values or commands to turn to which legitimize our conduct. So, in the bright realm of values, we have no excuse behind us, nor justification before us. We are alone, with no excuses.

That is the idea I shall try to convey when I say that man is condemned to be free. Condemned, because he did not create himself, yet, in other respects is free; because, once thrown into the world, he is responsible for everything he does. The existentialist does not believe in the power of passion. He will never agree that a sweeping passion is a ravaging torrent which fatally leads a man to certain acts and is therefore an excuse. He thinks that man is responsible for his passion.

The existentialist does not think that man is going to help himself by finding in the world some omen by which to orient himself. Because he thinks that man will interpret the omen to suit himself. Therefore, he thinks that man, with no support and no aid, is condemned every moment to invent man. Ponge, in a very fine article, has said, "Man is the future of man." That's exactly it. But if it is taken to mean that this future is recorded in heaven, that God sees it, then it is false, because it would really no longer be a future. If it is taken to mean that, whatever a man may be, there is a future to be forged, a virgin future before him, then this remark is sound. But then we are forlorn.

To give you an example which will enable you to understand forlornness better, I shall cite the case of one of my students who came to see me under the following circumstances: his father was on bad terms with his mother, and, moreover, was inclined to be a collaborationist; his older brother had been killed in the German offensive of 1940, and the young man, with somewhat immature but generous feelings, wanted to avenge him. His mother lived alone with him, very much upset by the half-treason of her husband and the death of her older son; the boy was her only consolation.

The boy was faced with the choice of leaving for England and joining the Free French Forces—that is, leaving his mother behind—or remaining with his mother and helping her to carry on. He was fully aware that the woman lived only for him and that his going-off—and perhaps his death— would plunge her into despair. He was also aware that every act that he did for his mother's sake was a sure thing, in the sense that it was helping her to carry on, whereas every effort he made toward going off and fighting was an uncertain move which might run aground and prove completely useless; for example, on his way to England he might, while passing through Spain, be detained indefinitely in a Spanish camp; he might reach England or Algiers and be stuck in an office at a desk job. As a result, he was faced with two very different kinds of action: one, concrete, immediate, but concerning only one individual; the other concerned an incomparably vaster group, a national collectivity, but for that very reason was dubious, and might be interrupted en route. And, at the same time, he was wavering between two kinds of ethics. On the one hand, an ethics of sympathy, of personal devotion; on the other, a broader ethics, but one whose efficacy was more dubious. He had to choose between the two.

Who could help him choose? Christian doctrine? No. Christian doctrine says, "Be charitable, love your neighbor, take the more rugged path, etc., etc." But which is the more rugged path? Whom should he love as a brother? The fighting man or his mother? Which does the greater good, the vague act of fighting in a group, or the concrete one of helping a particular human being to go on living? Who can decide *a priori?* Nobody. No book of ethics can tell him. The Kantian ethics says, "Never treat any person as a means, but as an end." Very well, if I stay with my mother, I'll treat her as an end and not as a means; but by virtue of this very fact, I'm running the risk of treating the people around me who are fighting, as means; and, conversely, if I go to join those who are fighting, I'll be treating them as an end, and, by doing that, I run the risk of treating my mother as a means.

If values are vague, and if they are always too broad for the concrete and specific case that we are considering, the only thing left for us is to trust our instincts. That's what this young man tried to do; and when I saw him, he said, "In the end, feeling is what counts. I ought to choose whichever pushes me in one direction. If I feel that I love my mother enough to sacrifice everything else for her—my desire for vengeance, for action, for adventure— then I'll stay with her. If, on the contrary, I feel that my love for my mother isn't enough, I'll leave."

But how is the value of a feeling determined? What gives his feeling for his mother value? Precisely the fact that he remained with her. I may say that I like so-and-so well enough to sacrifice a certain amount of money for him, but I may say so only if I've done it. I may say "I love my mother well enough to remain with her" if I have remained with her. The only way to determine the value of this affection is, precisely, to perform an act which confirms and defines it. But, since I require this affection to justify my act, I find myself caught in a vicious circle.

On the other hand, Gide has well said that a mock feeling and a true feeling are almost indistinguishable; to decide that I love my mother and will remain with her, or to remain with her by putting on an act, amount somewhat to the same thing. In other words, the feeling is formed by the acts one performs; so, I can not refer to it in order to act upon it. Which means that I can neither seek within myself the true condition which will impel me to act, nor apply to a system of ethics for concepts which will permit me to act. You will say, "At least, he did go to a teacher for advice." But if you seek advice from a priest, for example, you have chosen this priest; you already knew, more or less, just about what advice he was going to give you. In other words, choosing your adviser is involving yourself. The proof of this is that if you are a Christian, you will say, "Consult a priest." But some priests are collaborating, some are just marking time, some are resisting. Which to choose? If the young man chooses a priest who is resisting or collaborating, he has already decided on the kind of advice he's going to get. Therefore, in coming to see me he knew the answer I was going to give him, and I had only one answer to give: "You're free, choose, that is, invent." No general ethics can show you what is to be done; there are no omens in the world. The Catholics will reply, "But there are." Granted—but, in any case, I myself choose the meaning they have.

When I was a prisoner, I knew a rather remarkable young man who was a Jesuit. He had entered the Jesuit order in the following way: he had had a number of very bad breaks; in childhood, his father died, leaving him in poverty, and he was a scholarship student at a religious institution where he was constantly made to feel that he was being kept out of charity; then, he failed to get any of the honors and distinctions that children like; later on, at about eighteen, he bungled a love affair; finally, at twenty-two, he failed in military training, a childish enough matter, but it was the last straw.

This young fellow might well have felt that he had botched everything. It was a sign of something, but of what? He might have taken refuge in bitterness or despair. But he very wisely looked upon all this as a sign that he was not made for secular triumphs, and that only the triumphs of religion, holiness, and faith were open to him. He saw the hand of God in all this, and so he entered the order. Who can help seeing that he alone decided what the sign meant?

Some other interpretation might have been drawn from this series of setbacks; for example, that he might have done better to turn carpenter or revolutionist. Therefore, he is fully responsible for the interpretation. Forlornness implies that we ourselves choose our being. Forlornness and anguish go together.

As for despair, the term has a very simple meaning. It means that we shall confine ourselves to reckoning only with what depends upon our will, or on the ensemble of probabilities which make our action possible. When we want something, we always have to reckon with probabilities. I may be counting on the arrival of a friend. The friend is coming by rail or street-car; this supposes that the train will arrive on schedule, or that the street-car will not jump the track. I am left in the realm of possibility; but possibilities are to be reckoned with only to the point where my action comports with the ensemble of these possibilities, and no further. The moment the possibilities I am considering are not rigorously involved by my action, I ought to disengage myself from them, because no God, no scheme, can adapt the world and its possibilities to my will. When Descartes said, "Conquer yourself rather than the world," he meant essentially the same thing.

. . .

Subjectivity of the individual is indeed our point of departure, and this for strictly philosophic reasons. Not because we are bourgeois, but because we want a doctrine based on truth and not a lot of fine theories, full of hope but with no real basis. There can be no other truth to take off from than this: *I think; therefore, I exist.* There we have the absolute truth of consciousness becoming aware of itself. Every theory which takes man out of the moment in which he becomes aware of himself is, at its very beginning, a theory which confounds truth, for outside the Cartesian *cogito,* all views are only probable, and a doctrine of probability which is not bound to a truth dissolves into thin air. In order to describe the probable, you must have a firm hold on the true. Therefore, before there can be any truth whatsoever, there must be an absolute truth; and this one is simple and easily arrived at; it's on everyone's doorstep; it's a matter of grasping it directly.

Secondly, this theory is the only one which gives man dignity, the only one which does not reduce him to an object. The effect of all materialism is to treat all men, including the one philosophizing, as objects, that is, as an ensemble of determined reactions in no way distinguished from the ensemble of qualities and phenomena which constitute a table or a chair or a stone. We definitely wish to establish the human realm as an ensemble of values distinct from the material realm. But the subjectivity that we have thus arrived at, and which we have claimed to be truth, is not a strictly individual subjectivity, for we have demonstrated that one discovers in the *cogito* not only himself, but others as well.

The philosophies of Descartes and Kant to the contrary, through the *I think* we reach our own self in the presence of others, and the others are just as real to us as our own self. Thus, the man who becomes aware of himself through the *cogito* also perceives all others, and he perceives them as the condition of his own existence. He realizes that he can not be anything (in the sense that we say that someone is witty or nasty or jealous) unless others recognize it as such. In order to get any truth about myself, I must have contact with another person. The other is indispensable to my own existence, as well as to my knowledge about myself. This being so, in discovering my inner being I discover the other person at the same time, like a freedom placed in front of me which thinks and wills only for or against me. Hence, let us at once announce the discovery of a world which we shall call intersubjectivity; this is the world in which man decides what he is and what others are.

Besides, if it is impossible to find in every man some universal essence which would be human nature, yet there does exist a universal human condition. It's not by chance that today's thinkers speak more readily of man's condition than of his nature. By condition they mean, more or less definitely, the *a priori* limits which outline man's fundamental situation in the universe. Historical situations vary; a man may be born a slave in a pagan society or a feudal lord or a proletarian. What does not vary is the necessity for him to exist in the world, to be at work there, to be there in the midst of other people, and to be mortal there. The limits are neither subjective or objective, or, rather, they have an objective and a subjective side. Objective because they are to be found everywhere and are recognizable everywhere; subjective because they are *lived* and are nothing if man does not live them, that is, freely determine his existence with reference to them. And though the configurations may differ, at least none of them are completely strange to me, because they all appear as attempts either to pass beyond these limits or recede from them or deny them or adapt to them. Consequently, every configuration, however individual it may be, has a universal value.

Every configuration, even the Chinese, the Indian, or the Negro, can be understood by a Westerner. "Can be understood" means that by virtue of a situation that he can imagine, a European of 1945 can, in like manner, push himself to his limits and reconstitute within himself the configuration of the Chinese, the Indian, or the African. Every configuration has universality in the sense that every configuration can be understood by every man. This does not at all mean that this configuration defines man forever, but that it can be met with again. There is always a way to understand the idiot, the child, the savage, the foreigner, provided one has the necessary information.

In this sense we may say that there is a universality of man; but it is not given, it is perpetually being made. I build the universal in choosing myself; I build it in understanding the configuration of every other man, whatever age he might have lived in. This absoluteness of choice does not do away with the relativeness of each epoch. At heart, what existentialism shows is the connection between the absolute character of free involvement, by virtue of which every man realizes himself in realizing a type of mankind, an involvement always comprehensible in any age whatsoever and by any person whosoever, and the relativeness of the cultural ensemble which may result from such a choice; it must be stressed that the relativity of Cartesianism and the absolute character of Cartesian involvement go together. In this sense, you may, if you like, say that each of us performs an absolute act in breathing, eating, sleeping, or behaving in any way whatever. There is no difference between being free, like a configuration, like an existence which chooses its essence, and being absolute. There is no difference between being an absolute temporarily localised, that is, localised in history, and being universally comprehensible.

This does not entirely settle the objection to subjectivism. In fact, the objection still takes several forms. First, there is the following: we are told, "So you're able to do anything, no matter what!" This is expressed in various ways. First we are accused of anarchy; then they say, "You're unable to pass judgment on others, because there's no reason to prefer one configuration to another"; finally they tell us, "Everything is arbitrary in this choosing of yours. You take something from one pocket and pretend you're putting it into the other."

These three objections aren't very serious. Take the first objection. "You're able to do anything, no matter what" is not to the point. In one sense choice is possible, but what is not possible is not to choose. I can always choose, but I ought to know that if I do not choose, I am still choosing. Though this may seem purely formal, it is highly important for keeping fantasy and caprice within bounds. If it is true that in facing a situation, for example, one in which, as a person capable of having sexual relations, of having children, I am obliged to choose an attitude, and if I in any way assume responsibility for a choice which, in involving myself, also involves all mankind, this has nothing to do with caprice, even if no *a priori* value determines my choice.

If anybody thinks that he recognizes here Gide's theory of the arbitrary act, he fails to see the enormous difference between this doctrine and Gide's. Gide does not know what a situation is. He acts out of pure caprice. For us, on the contrary, man is in an organized situation in which he himself is involved. Through his choice, he involves all mankind, and he can not avoid making a choice: either he will remain chaste, or he will marry without having children, or he will marry and have children; anyhow, whatever he may do, it is impossible for him not to take full responsibility for the way he handles this problem. Doubtless, he chooses without refering to pre-established values, but it is unfair to accuse him of caprice. Instead, let us say that moral choice is to be compared to the making of a work of art. And before going any further, let it be said at once that we are not dealing here with an aesthetic ethics, because our opponents are so dishonest that they even accuse us of that. The example I've chosen is a comparison only.

Having said that, may I ask whether anyone has ever accused an artist who has painted a picture of not having drawn his inspiration from rules set up *a priori?* Has anyone ever asked, "What painting ought he to make?" It is clearly understood that there is no definite painting to be made, that the artist is engaged in the making of his painting, and that the painting to be made is precisely the painting he will have made. It is clearly understood that there are no *a priori* aesthetic values, but that there are values which appear subsequently in the coherence of the painting, in the correspondence between what the artist intended and the result. Nobody can tell what the painting of tomorrow will be like. Painting can be judged only after it has once been made. What connection does that have with ethics? We are in the same creative situation. We never say that a work of art is arbitrary. When we speak of a canvas of Picasso, we never say that it is arbitrary; we understand quite well that he was making himself what he is at the very time he was painting, that the ensemble of his work is embodied in his life.

The same holds on the ethical plane. What art and ethics have in common is that we have creation and invention in both cases. We can not decide *a priori* what there is to be done. I think that I pointed that out quite sufficiently when I mentioned the case of the student who came to see me, and who might have applied to all the ethical systems, Kantian or other-wise, without getting any sort of guidance. He was obliged to devise his law himself. Never let it be said by us that this man—who, taking affection, individual action, and kind-heartedness toward a specific person as his ethical first principle, chooses to remain with his mother, or who, preferring to make a sacrifice, chooses to go to England—has made an arbitrary choice. Man makes himself. He isn't ready made at the start. In choosing his ethics, he makes himself, and force of circumstances is such that he can not abstain from choosing one. We define man only in relationship to involvement. It is therefore absurd to charge us with arbitrariness of choice.

In the second place, it is said that we are unable to pass judgment on others. In a way this is true, and in another way, false. It is true in this sense, that, whenever a man sanely and sincerely involves himself and chooses his configuration, it is impossible for him to prefer another configuration, regardless of what his own may be in other respects. It is true in this sense, that we do not believe in progress. Progress is betterment. Man is always the same. The situation confronting him varies. Choice always remains a choice in a situation. The problem has not changed since the time one could choose between those for and those against slavery, for example, at the time of the Civil War, and the present time, when one can side with the [M.R.P., or Mouvement Républicain Populaire] or with the Communists.

But, nevertheless, one can still pass judgment, for, as I have said, one makes a choice in relationship to others. First, one can judge (and this is perhaps not a judgment of value, but a logical judgment) that certain choices are based on error and others on truth. If we have defined man's situation as a free choice, with no excuses and no recourse, every man who takes refuge behind the excuse of his passions, every man who sets up a determinism, is a dishonest man.

The objection may be raised, "But why mayn't he choose himself dishonestly?" I reply that I am not obliged to pass moral judgment on him, but that I do define his dishonesty as an error. One can not help considering the truth of the matter. Dishonesty is obviously a falsehood because it belies the complete freedom of involvement. On the same grounds, I maintain that there is also dishonesty if I choose to state that certain values exist prior to me; it is self-contradictory for me to want them and at the same time state that they are imposed on me. Suppose someone says to me, "What if I want to be dishonest?" I'll answer, "There's no reason for you not to be, but I'm saying that that's what you are, and that the strictly coherent attitude is that of honesty."

Besides, I can bring moral judgment to bear. When I declare that freedom in every concrete circumstance can have no other aim than to want itself, if man has once become aware that in his forlornness he imposes values, he can no longer want but one thing, and that is freedom, as the basis of all values. That doesn't mean that he wants it in the abstract. It means simply that the ultimate meaning of the acts of honest men is the quest for freedom as such. A man who belongs to a communist or revolutionary union wants concrete goals; these goals imply an abstract desire for freedom; but this freedom is wanted in something concrete. We want freedom for freedom's sake and in every particular circumstance. And in wanting freedom we discover that it depends entirely on the freedom of others, and that the freedom of others depends on ours. Of course, freedom as the definition of man does not depend on others, but as soon as there is involvement, I am obliged to want others to have freedom at the same time that I want my own freedom. I can take freedom as my goal only if I take that of others as a goal as well. Consequently, when, in all honesty, I've recognized that man is a being in whom existence precedes essence, that he is a free being who, in various circumstances, can want only his freedom, I have at the same time recognized that I can want only the freedom of others.

Therefore, in the name of this will for freedom, which freedom itself implies, I may pass judgment on those who seek to hide from themselves the complete arbitrariness and the complete freedom of their existence. Those who hide their complete freedom from themselves out of a spirit of seriousness or by means of deterministic excuses, I shall call cowards; those who try to show that their existence was necessary, when it is the very contingency of man's appearance on earth, I shall call stinkers. But cowards or stinkers can be judged only from a strictly unbiased point of view.

Therefore though the content of ethics is variable, a certain form of it is universal. Kant says that freedom desires both itself and the freedom of others. Granted. But he believes that the formal and the universal are enough to constitute an ethics. We, on the other hand, think that principles which are too abstract run aground in trying to decide action. Once again, take the case of the student. In the name of what, in the name of what great moral maxim do you think he could have decided, in perfect peace of mind, to abandon his mother or to stay with her? There is no way of judging. The content is always concrete and thereby unforeseeable; there is always the element of invention. The one thing that counts is knowing whether the inventing that has been done, has been done in the name of freedom. . . .

QUESTIONS

1. "There is no human nature, since there is no God to conceive it." What does Sartre mean by this? What bearing does it have on ethics, in his view? Must an atheist deny a human nature? Why or why not?
2. According to atheistic existentialism, there are three fundamental aspects or characteristics of human life: anguish, forlornness, and despair. What meaning does Sartre give to each of these terms? Discuss the objection that this is an overly pessimistic view of life.
3. With regard to the choice by which an individual determines what kind of person he will be, are there reasons for choosing one way and not another, according to Sartre? If so, what would constitute such reasons? If not, is the choice completely arbitrary?
4. On what grounds is a person responsible for his choices, according to Sartre?
5. Compare Sartre's theory of ethical choice with Kant's conception of the moral law. (See the reading by Kant in this chapter.) What do the two views have in common? How do they differ?

6. Critically analyze the argument by which Sartre supports the claim: "No general ethics can show you what is to be done."

7. What does Sartre mean by asserting that moral choice is comparable to the making of a work of art, and on what grounds does he justify this assertion? Is his argument acceptable?

41. R. M. HARE

(b. 1919)

Moral Reasoning

Richard Mervyn Hare is a Fellow of Balliol College, Oxford. He is the author of *The Language of Morals* (1952) and *Freedom and Reason* (1963).

In this reading, which is taken from *The Language of Morals,* Mr. Hare approaches the problems of moral philosophy by way of the study of moral language. In order to answer the question, "What are the grounds on which moral knowledge rests?" he examines the way in which people in everyday life use words and sentences when they arrive at moral decisions, justify moral judgments, and learn moral principles. Mr. Hare is concerned with the psychology of moral reasoning only as it enlightens us about the logic of moral reasoning. That is to say, his basic purpose is not to describe the actual process by which people are morally educated and by which they morally educate others, but to clarify the logical nature of the grounds on which our claim to moral knowledge rests. In this way he attempts to work out a solution to the problem of moral knowledge which is based on the meanings of moral words and the relations between moral statements as they arise out of the practical situations of everyday life.

The reading is from Chapter 4 of *The Language of Morals.*

From *The Language of Morals,* by R. M. Hare, The Clarendon Press, Oxford, 1952. Reprinted by permission of the publisher.

Without principles, most kinds of teaching are impossible, for what is taught is in most cases a principle. In particular, when we learn *to do* something, what we learn is always a principle. Even to learn or be taught a fact (like the names of the five rivers of the Punjab) is to learn how to answer a question; it is to learn the principle "When asked 'What are the names of the five rivers of the Punjab?' answer 'The Jhelum, the Chenab, etc.'" By this I do not of course mean that to learn to do anything is to learn to recite by rote some universal imperative sentence. This would involve us in a vicious regress; for learning to recite is a kind of learning, and must have its principles; but in that case we should have to learn to recite the principles of reciting. The point is rather this, that to learn to do anything is never to learn to do an individual act; it is always to learn to do acts of a certain kind in a certain kind of situation; and this is to learn a principle. Thus, in learning to drive, I learn, not to change gear *now*, but to change gear when my engine makes a certain kind of noise. If this were not so, instruction would be of no use at all; for if all an instructor could do were to tell us to change gear *now*, he would have to sit beside us for the rest of our lives in order to tell us just when, on each occasion, to change gear.

Thus without principles we could not learn anything whatever from our elders. This would mean that every generation would have to start from scratch and teach itself. But even if each generation were able to teach itself, it could not do so without principles; for self-teaching, like all other teaching, is the teaching of principles. This may be seen by [an] artificial example. Let us suppose that [a man] made all his choices on some principle, but always forgot, as soon as he had made the choice, what the principle had been. He would have, accordingly, each time he made a decision, to go over all the effects of the alternative actions. This would be so time-consuming that he would not have the leisure to make many decisions in the course of his life. He would spend his whole time deciding matters like whether to step off with the right or the left foot, and would never reach what we should call the more important decisions. But if he could remember the principles on which he acted, he would be in a much better position; he could *learn* how to act in certain kinds of circumstance; he could learn to single out quickly the relevant aspects of a situation, including the effects of the various possible actions, and so choose quickly, and in many cases habitually. Thus his powers of considered decision would be set free for more momentous decisions. When the cabinet-maker has learnt how to make a dovetail without thinking much about it, he will have time to think about such things as the proportions and aesthetic appearance of the finished product. And it is the same with our conduct in the moral sphere; when the performance of the lesser duties has become a matter of habit, we have time to think about the greater.

There is a limit in practice to the amount that can be taught to someone by someone else. Beyond this point, self-teaching is necessary. The limit is set by the variety of conditions which may be met with in doing whatever is being taught; and this variety is greater in some cases than in others. A sergeant can teach a recruit almost all there is to be known about fixing bayonets on parade, because one occasion of fixing bayonets on parade is much like another; but a driving instructor cannot do more than begin to teach his pupil the art of driving, because the conditions to be met with in driving are so various. In most cases, teaching cannot consist in getting the learner to perform faultlessly a fixed drill. One of the things that has to be included in any but the most elementary kinds of instruction is the opportunity for the learner to make decisions for himself, and in so doing to examine, and even modify to suit particular types of case, the principles which are being taught. The principles that are taught us initially are of a provisional kind. Our training, after the initial stages, consists in taking these principles, and making them less provisional; we do this by using them continually in our own decisions, and sometimes making exceptions to them; some of the exceptions are made because our instructor points out to us that certain cases are instances of classes of exceptions to the principle; and some of the exceptions we decide on for ourselves. . . .

We may illustrate this process of modifying principles from the example already used, that of learning to drive. I am told, for instance, always to draw into the side of the road when I stop the car; but later I am told that this does not apply when I stop before turning into a sideroad to the off-side—for then I must stop near the middle of the road until it is possible for me to turn. Still later I learn that in this manoeuvre it is not necessary to stop at all if it is an uncontrolled junction and I can see that there is no traffic which I should obstruct by turning. When I have picked up all these modifications to the rule, and the similar modifications to all the other rules, and practice them habitually as so modified, then I am said to be a good driver, because my car is always in the right place on the road, travelling at the right speed, and so on. The good driver is, among other things, one whose actions are so exactly governed by principles which have become a habit with him, that he normally does not have to *think* just what to do. But road conditions are exceedingly various, and therefore it is unwise to let all one's driving become a matter of habit. One can never be certain that one's principles of driving are perfect—indeed, one can be very sure that they are not; and therefore the good driver not only drives well from habit, but constantly attends to his driving habits, to see whether they might not be improved; he never stops learning.

It is hardly necessary to point out that principles of driving, like other principles, are normally not inculcated by their verbal repetition, but by example, demonstration, and other practical means. We learn to drive, not by precept, but by being shown how to do particular bits of driving; the precepts are usually only explanatory or mnemonic of what we are being shown. Thereafter, we try to do the particular manoeuvres ourselves, and are criticized for failures, commended when we do them well, and so gradually get the hang of the various principles of good driving. For although our instruction is far from being purely verbal, nevertheless what we are being taught are principles. The fact that the derivation of particular acts (or commands to do them) from principles is normally done nonverbally does not show that it is not a logical process, any more than the inference:

The clock has just struck seven times
The clock strikes seven times at seven o'clock only
∴. It is just after seven o'clock

is shown to be nonlogical because it is never made explicitly in words.

Drivers often know just what to do in a certain situation without being able to enunciate in words the principle on which they act. This is a very common state of affairs with all kinds of principles. Trappers know just where to set their traps, but often cannot explain just why they have put a trap in a particular place. We all know how to use words to convey our meaning; but if a logician presses us for the exact definition of a word we have used, or the exact rules for its use, we are often at a loss. This does not mean that the setting of traps or the use of words or the driving of cars does not proceed according to principles. One may know how, without being able to say how—though if a skill is to be taught, it is easier if we *can* say how.

We must not think that, if we can decide between one course and another without further thought (it seems self-evident to us, which we should do), this necessarily implies that we have some mysterious intuitive faculty which tells us what to do. A driver does not know when to change gear by intuition; he knows it because he has learnt and not forgotten; what he knows is a principle, though he cannot formulate the principle in words. The same is true of moral decisions which are sometimes called "intuitive." We have moral "intuitions" because we have learnt how to behave, and have different ones according to how we have learnt to behave.

It would be a mistake to say that all that had to be done to a man to make him into a good driver was to tell him, or otherwise inculcate into him, a lot of general principles. This would be to leave out the factor of decision. Very soon after he begins to learn, he will be faced with situations to deal with which the provisional principles so far taught him require modification; and he will then have to decide what to do. He will very soon discover which decisions were right and which wrong, partly because his instructor tells him, and partly because having seen the effects of the decisions he determines in future not to bring about such effects. On no account must we commit the mistake of supposing that decisions and principles occupy two separate spheres and do not meet at any point. All decisions except those, if any, that are completely arbitrary are to some extent decisions of principle. We are always setting precedents for ourselves. It is not a case of the principle settling everything down to a certain point, and decision dealing with everything below that point. Rather, decision and principles interact throughout the whole field. Suppose that we have a principle to act in a certain way in certain circumstances. Suppose then that we find ourselves in circumstances which fall under the principle, but which have certain other peculiar features, not met before, which make us ask "Is the principle really intended to cover cases like this, or is it incompletely specified—is there here a case belonging to a class which should be treated as exceptional?" Our answer to this question will be a decision, but a decision of principle, as is shown by the use of the value-word "should." If we decide that this should be an exception, we thereby modify the principle by laying down an exception to it.

Suppose, for example, that in learning to drive I have been taught always to signal before I slow down or stop, but have not yet been taught what to do when stopping in an emergency; if a child leaps in front of my car, I do not signal, but keep both hands on the steering-wheel; and thereafter I accept the former principle with this exception, that in cases of emergency it is better to steer than to signal. I have, even on the spur of the moment, made a decision of principle. To understand what happens in cases like this is to understand a great deal about the making of value-judgements.

I do not wish to seem to be pressing too far my comparison, in respect of the way in which they are learnt, between principles of driving and principles of conduct. It is necessary also to bear in mind some distinctions. In the first place, the expression "good driver" is itself ambiguous in that it is not immediately clear what standard is being applied. It might be simply a standard of expertness; we might call a person a good driver if he were able to do just what he wanted with his car; we might say "Although a very good driver, he is most inconsiderate to other road users." On the other hand, we sometimes expect a good driver to have moral qualities as well; we do not, according to this criterion, call a man a good driver if he drives expertly, but without the slightest heed for the convenience or safety of other people. The line between these two standards of good driving is not easy to draw in practice. There is also a third standard, according to which a driver is said to be good if he conforms to the accepted principles of good driving as laid down, for example, in the *Highway Code*. Since the *Highway Code* is compiled with a definite purpose in view, this standard coincides to a great extent with the second.

Secondly, there are two ways of looking at driving instruction:

(1) We establish at the beginning certain ends, for example the avoidance of collisions, and instruction consists in teaching what practices are conducive to those ends. According to this way of looking at them, the principles of good driving are hypothetical imperatives.

(2) We teach at first simple rules of thumb, and the learner only gradually comes to see what the ends are, at which the instruction is aimed.

It must not be thought that either (1) or (2) by itself gives a complete account of our procedure. Which method we adopt depends to a great extent on the maturity and intelligence of the learner. In teaching African soldiers to drive, we might incline more to the second method; if I had to teach my two-year-old son to drive, I should have to adopt the same methods as I now adopt for teaching him to refrain from interfering with the controls when I am driving myself. With a highly intelligent learner, on the other hand, we may adopt a method which has more of (1) in it than of (2).

It must not be thought, however, that method (2) is ever entirely without a place even in the case of the most rational of learners. It may be that the desirability of avoiding collisions is at once understood and accepted even by comparatively stupid learners; but there are a great many more ends than this which a good driver has to aim at. He has to avoid causing many kinds of avoidable inconvenience both to himself and to others; he has to learn not to do things which result in damage to his vehicle, and so on. It is of no use to establish at the beginning a general end, "the avoidance of avoidable inconvenience"; for "inconvenience" is a value-word, and until he has had experience of driving, the learner will not know what sorts of situation are to count as avoidable inconvenience. The general end or principle is vacuous until by our detailed instruction we have given it content. Therefore it is always necessary to start, to some extent, by teaching our learner *what* to do, and leaving it for him to find out later *why*. We may therefore say that although moral principles, which are normally taught us when we are immature, are taught largely by method (2), and principles of driving preponderantly by method (1), there is not an absolute division between the two sorts of principle in this respect. What I have just said about first learning *what* to do, and about the initial vacuity of the general end, is borrowed from Aristotle. The one fundamental distinction between principles of driving and principles of conduct is that the latter are, in Aristotle's term, "architectonic" of the former; for the ends of good driving (safety, the avoidance of inconvenience to others, the preservation of property, and so on) are justified ultimately, if justification is sought, by appeal to moral considerations.

It would be folly, however, to say that there is only one way of learning a skill or any other body of principles, or of justifying a particular decision made in the practice of it. There are many ways, and I have tried to make the above account sufficiently general to cover all of them. It is sometimes said by writers on morals that we have to justify an act by reference to its effects, and that we tell which effects are to be sought, which avoided, by reference to some principle. Such a theory is that of the utilitarians, who bid us look at the effects, and examine these in the light of the principle of utility, to see which effects would maximize pleasure. Sometimes, on the other hand, it is said that an act is justified directly by reference to the principles which it observes, and these principles in their turn by reference to the effects of always observing them. Sometimes it is said that we should observe principles and ignore the effects—though for the reasons given above "effects" cannot be here intended in the sense in which I have been using it. What is wrong with these theories is not what they say, but their assumption that they are telling us the only way to justify actions, or decide what actions to do. We do, indeed, justify and decide on actions in all these ways; for example, sometimes, if asked why we did A, we say, "Because it was a case falling under principle P," and if asked to justify P in turn, we go into the effects of observing it and of not observing it. But sometimes, when asked the same question "Why did you do A?" we say "Because if I hadn't, E would have happened," and if asked what was wrong about E happening, we appeal to some principle.

The truth is that, if asked to justify as completely as possible any decision, we have to bring in both effects—to give content to the decision—and principles, and the effects in general of observing those principles, and so on, until we have satisfied our inquirer. Thus a complete justification of a decision would consist of a complete account of its effects, together with a complete account of the principles which it observed, and the effects of observing those principles—for, of course, it is the effects (what obeying them in fact consists in) which give content to the principles too. Thus, if pressed to justify a decision completely, we have to give a complete specification of the way of life of which it is a part. This complete specification it is impossible in practice to give; the nearest attempts are those given by the great religions, especially those which can point to historical persons who carried out the way of life in practice. Suppose, however, that we can give it. If the inquirer still goes on asking "But why *should* I live like that?" then there is no further answer to give him, because we have already, *ex hypothesi,* said everything that could be included in this further answer. We can only ask him to make up his own mind which way he ought to live; for in the end everything rests upon such a decision of principle. He has to decide whether to accept that way of life or not; if he accepts it, then we can proceed to justify the decisions that are based upon it; if he does not accept it, then let him accept some other, and try to live by it. The sting is in the last clause. To describe such ultimate decisions as arbitrary, because *ex hypothesi* everything which could be used to justify them has already been included in the decision, would be like saying that a complete description of the universe was utterly unfounded, because no further fact could be called upon in corroboration of it. This is not how we used the words "arbitrary" and "unfounded." Far from being arbitrary, such a decision would be the most well-founded of decisions, because it would be based upon a consideration of everything upon which it could possibly be founded.

It will be noticed how, in talking of decisions of principle, I have inevitably started talking value-language. Thus we decide that the principle *should* be modified, or that it is *better* to steer than to signal. . . . To make a value-judgement is to make a decision of principle. To ask whether I ought to do A in these circumstances is (to borrow Kantian language with a small though important modification) to ask whether or not I will that doing A in such circumstances should become a universal law. . . . The same question could be put in other words by asking "What attitude shall I adopt and recommend towards doing A in such circumstances?"; for "attitude," if it means anything, means a principle of action.

As Kant points out in the important passage on the Autonomy of the Will, we have to make our own decisions of principle. Other people cannot make them for us unless we have first decided to take their advice or obey their orders. There is an interesting analogy here with the position of the scientist, who also has to rely on his own observations. It might be said that there is a difference here between decisions and observations, to the detriment of the former, in that an observation, once made, is public property, whereas decisions have to be made by the agent himself on each occasion. But the difference is only apparent. A scientist would not have become a scientist unless he had convinced himself that the observations of other scientists were in general reliable. He did this by making some observations of his own. When we learnt elementary chemistry at school, we had some theoretical periods and some practical. In the theoretical periods we studied books; in the practical periods we made experiments, and found, if we were lucky, that the results tallied with what the books said. This showed us that what the books said was not all nonsense; so that even if, by reason of disturbing factors ignored by us, our experiments came out wrong, we were inclined to trust the books and acknowledge that we had made a mistake. We were confirmed in this assumption by the fact that we often discovered later what the mistake had been. If our observations, however carefully we did them, were always at variance with the textbooks, we should not be tempted to make science our profession. Thus the confidence of the scientist in other people's observations is ultimately based, among other things, on his own observations and his own judgements about what is reliable. He has in the end to rely on himself.

The case of the moral agent is not dissimilar. When in our early days we are given our elementary moral instruction, there are some things that we are told, and some things that we do. If, when we did as we were told, the total effects of our so doing, when they happened, were always such as we would not have chosen, had we known, then we should seek better advice, or, if prevented from so doing, either work out our own salvation or become moral defectives. If we are in general given what we subsequently come to see to have been good advice, we decide in general to follow the advice and adopt the principles of those who have given us this good advice in the past. This is what happens to any child who is well brought up. Just as the scientist does not try to rewrite all that is in the textbooks, but takes that for granted and sticks to his own particular researches, so this fortunate child will take over bodily the principles of his elders and adapt them in detail, by his own decisions, to suit his own circumstances from time to time. This is how in a well-ordered society morality remains stable, and at the same time gets adapted to changing circumstances.

There are, however, many ways in which this happy state of affairs can deteriorate. Let us consider a process that seems to occur quite often in history; it occurred in Greece during the fifth and fourth centuries, and it has occurred in our own time. Suppose that the people of a certain generation —I will call it the first generation—have got very settled principles, inherited from their fathers. Suppose that they have become so settled as to be second nature, so that generally speaking people act on the principles without thinking, and their power of making considered decisions of principle becomes atrophied. They act always by the book, and come to no harm, because the state of the world in their time remains much the same as that for which the principles were thought out. But their sons, the second generation, as they grow up, find that conditions have changed (e.g. through a protracted war or an industrial revolution), and that the principles in which they have been brought up are no longer adequate. Since, in their education, much stress has been laid on observing principles, and very little on making the decisions on which these principles are ultimately based, their morality has no roots, and becomes completely unstable. Books on "The Whole Duty of Man" are no longer written or read. Often, when they do what it says in such books, they subsequently find cause to regret their decisions; and there are too many cases of this kind for any confidence in the old principles, as a body, to remain. No doubt there are among these old principles certain very general ones, which will remain acceptable unless human nature and the state of the world undergo a most fundamental change; but the second generation, not having been brought up to make decisions of principle, but to do what it says in the book, will not, most of them, be able to make those crucial decisions which would determine which principles to keep, which to modify, and which to abandon. Some people will have been so steeped in the old principles that they just follow them come what may; and these will on the whole be more fortunate than the others, for it is better to have some principles, even if they sometimes lead to decisions which we regret, than to be morally adrift. The bulk of the second generation, and still more perhaps of the third, will not know which of the principles to keep and which to reject; and so they will come more and more to live from day to day—not a bad thing, because it trains their powers of decision, but it is an unpleasant and dangerous state to be in. A few among them, the rebels, will shout from the housetops that some or all of the old moral principles are worthless; some of these rebels will advocate new principles of their own; some will have nothing to offer. Though they increase the confusion, these rebels perform the useful function of making people decide between their rival principles; and if they not only advocate new principles, but sincerely try to live by them, they are conducting a moral experiment which may be of the utmost value to man (in which case they go down in history as great moral teachers), or may, on the other hand, prove disastrous both to them and to their disciples.

It may take several generations for this disease to play itself out. Morality regains its vigour when ordinary people have learnt afresh to decide for themselves what principles to live by, and more especially what principles to teach their children. Since the world, though subject to vast material changes, changes only very slowly in matters that are fundamental from the moral point of view, the principles which win the acceptance of the mass of people are not likely to differ enormously from those which their fathers came to distrust. The moral principles of Aristotle resemble those of Aeschylus more than they differ from them, and we ourselves shall perhaps come back to something recognizably like the morality of our grandfathers. But there will be some changes; some of the principles advocated by the rebels will have been adopted. That is how morality progresses—or retrogresses. The process is reflected by very subtle changes in the uses of value-words; the impossibility of translating Aristotle's catalogue of virtues into modern English may serve as an example, and the disappearance without trace of the word "righteous" may serve as another.

The question "How shall I bring up my children?" which we have mentioned, is one to the logic of which, since ancient times, few philosophers have given much attention. A child's moral upbringing has an effect upon him which will remain largely untouched by anything that happens to him thereafter. If he has had a stable upbringing, whether on good principles or on bad ones, it will be extremely difficult for him to abandon those principles in later life—difficult but not impossible. They will have for him the force of an objective moral law; and his behaviour will seem to give much evidence in support of intuitionist ethical theories, provided that it is not compared with the behaviour of those who stick just as firmly to quite different principles. But nevertheless, unless our education has been so thorough as to transform us into automata, we can come to doubt or even reject these principles; that is what makes human beings, whose moral systems change, different from ants, whose moral system does not. Therefore, even if for me the question "What shall I do in such and such a situation?" is almost invariably answered without ambiguity by the moral intuition which my upbringing has given me, I may, if I ask myself "How shall I bring up my children?" pause before giving an answer. It is here that the most fundamental moral decisions of all arise; and it is here, if only moral philosophers would pay attention to them, that the most characteristic uses of moral words are to be found. Shall I bring up my children *exactly* as I was brought up, so that they have the same intuitions about morals as I have? Or have circumstances altered, so that the moral character of the father will not provide a suitable equipment for the children? Perhaps I shall try to bring them up like their father, and shall fail; perhaps their new environment will be too strong for me, and they will come to repudiate my principles. Or I may have become so bewildered by the strange new world that, although I still act from force of habit on the principles that I have learnt, I simply do not know what principles to impart to my children, if, indeed, one in my condition can impart any settled principles at all. On all these questions, I have to make up my mind; only the most hide-bound father will try to bring up his children, without thinking, in exactly the way that he himself was brought up; and even he will usually fail disastrously.

Many of the dark places of ethics become clearer when we consider this dilemma in which parents are liable to find themselves. We have already noticed that, although principles have in the end to rest upon decisions of principle, decisions as such cannot be taught; only principles can be taught. It is the powerlessness of the parent to make for his son those many decisions of principle which the son during his future career will make, that gives moral language its characteristic shape. The only instrument which the parent possesses is moral education—the teaching of principles by example and precept, backed up by chastisement and other more up-to-date psychological methods. Shall he use these means, and to what extent? Certain generations of parents have had no doubts about this question. They have used them to the full; and the result has been to turn their children into good intuitionists, able to cling to the rails, but bad at steering round corners. At other times parents—and who shall blame them?—suffer from lack of confidence; they are not sure enough what they themselves think, to be ready to impart to their children a stable way of life. The children of such a generation are likely to grow up opportunists, well able to make individual decisions, but without the settled body of principles which is the most priceless heritage that any generation can leave to its successors. For, though principles are in the end built upon decisions of principle, the building is the work of many generations, and the man who has to start from the beginning is to be pitied; he will not be likely, unless he is a genius, to achieve many conclusions of importance, any more than the average boy, turned loose without instruction upon a desert island, or even in a laboratory, would be likely to make any of the major scientific discoveries.

The dilemma between these two extreme courses in education is plainly a false one. Why it is a false one is apparent, if we recall what was said earlier about the dynamic relation between decisions and principles. It is very like learning to drive. It would be foolish, in teaching someone to drive, to try to inculcate into him such fixed and comprehensive principles that he would never have to make an independent decision. It would be equally foolish to go to the other extreme and leave it to him to find his own way of driving. What we do, if we are sensible, is to give him a solid basis of principles, but at the same time ample opportunity of making the decisions upon which these principles are based, and by which they are modified, improved, adapted to change circumstances, or even abandoned if they become entirely unsuited to a new environment. To teach only the principles, without giving the opportunity of subjecting them to the learner's own decisions of principle, is like teaching science exclusively from the textbooks without entering the laboratory. On the other hand, to abandon one's child or one's driving-pupil to his own self-expression is like putting a boy into a laboratory and saying "Get on with it." The boy may enjoy himself or kill himself, but will probably not learn much science.

The moral words, of which we may take "ought" as an example, reflect in their logical behaviour this double nature of moral instruction—as well they may, for it is in moral instruction that they are most typically used. The sentences in which they appear are normally the expression of decisions of principle—and it is easy to let the decisions get separated, in our discussion of the subject, from the principles. This is the source of the controversy between the "objectivists," as intuitionists sometimes call themselves, and the "subjectivists," as they often call their opponents. The former lay stress on the fixed principles that are handed down by the father, the latter on the new decisions which have to be made by the son. The objectivist says "Of course you know what you ought to do; look at what your conscience tells you, and if in doubt go by the consciences of the vast majority of men." He is able to say this, because our consciences are the product of the principles which our early training has indelibly planted in us, and in one society these principles do not differ much from one person to another. The subjectivist, on the other hand, says "But surely, when it comes to the point—when I have listened to what other people say, and given due weight to my own intuitions, the legacy of my upbringing—I have in the end to decide for myself what I ought to do. To deny this is to be a conventionalist; for both common moral notions and my own intuitions are the legacy of tradition, and—apart from the fact that there are so many different traditions in the world— traditions cannot be started without someone doing what I now feel called upon to do, decide. If I refuse to make my own decisions, I am, in merely copying my fathers, showing myself a lesser man than they; for whereas they must have initiated, I shall be merely accepting." This plea of the subjectivist is quite justified. It is the plea of the adolescent who wants to be adult. To become morally adult is to reconcile these two apparently conflicting positions by learning to make decisions of principle; it is to learn to use "ought"-sentences in the realization that they can only be verified by reference to a standard or set of principles which we have by our own decision accepted and made our own. This is what our present generation is so painfully trying to do.

QUESTIONS

1. ". . . Without principles we could not learn anything whatever from our elders." Why not, according to Mr. Hare? In your answer make clear what is meant by a "principle."

2. Mr. Hare claims that when we say we have "moral intuitions," all we really mean is that we have learned how we ought to act in a given situation without having to think about it. Is this a good reason for rejecting the ethical intuitionist's view of moral knowledge? Why or why not?

3. Mr. Hare asserts that to give a complete justification of any decision we can only specify the total way of life of which it is a part, and then let the person make up his own mind what way of life he wants to live. Does this imply that morality is merely a matter of personal taste, concerning which we cannot argue? Defend your answer.

4. Why does Mr. Hare think that an ultimate decision to adopt one way of life rather than another is not "arbitrary"? State your reasons for agreeing, or disagreeing, with him.

5. Defend or attack the claim that Mr. Hare has discovered a consistent way to combine the utilitarian outlook in ethics with the Kantian outlook. (For these outlooks, see the readings by Mill and Kant in this chapter.)

6. Why are the learning of principles and the making of decisions *both* important in moral education, according to Mr. Hare?

7. ". . . The world, though subject to vast material changes, changes only very slowly in matters that are fundamental from the moral point of view. . . ." Give your reasons for accepting, or for doubting, this statement.

8. Why does Mr. Hare think that the study of the way children are brought up is important for understanding the nature of moral reasoning?

9. At the end of the reading, Mr. Hare offers an explanation of the subjectivist-objectivist dispute in moral philosophy. How plausible is his explanation, in your opinion? What would a subjectivist such as Hume be likely to say about this explanation? What would an objectivist such as Kant be likely to say about it? (See the selections by Hume and Kant in this chapter.)

10. After reading the account of moral statements given by Professor A. J. Ayer in this chapter, what criticisms do you think he might raise against Mr. Hare's view of the justification of moral decisions and the learning of moral principles? How might Mr. Hare reply to these criticisms?

11. Referring to the meanings of "ethical relativism" and "ethical absolutism" explained in the introduction to this chapter, would you say that Mr. Hare's views lead to ethical relativism, to ethical absolutism, or to neither? Why?

SUGGESTED FURTHER READING

ANTHOLOGIES

Abelson, Raziel, ed., *Ethics and Metaethics: Readings in Ethical Philosophy,* St Martin's, New York, 1963.

Brandt, Richard B., ed., *Value and Obligation: Systematic Readings in Ethics,* Harcourt, Brace & World, New York, 1961.

Dewey, R., F. W. Gramlich, and D. Loftsgordon, eds., *Problems of Ethics: A Book of Readings,* Macmillan, New York, 1961.

Johnson, Oliver A., ed., *Ethics: Selections from Classical and Contemporary Writers,* Holt, Rinehart & Winston, New York, 1961.

Jones, W. T., F. Sontag, M. D. Beckner, and R. J. Fogelin, eds., *Approaches to Ethics: Representative Selections from Classical Times to the Present,* McGraw-Hill, New York, 1962.

Melden, Abraham I., ed., *Ethical Theories: A Book of Readings,* Prentice-Hall, Englewood Cliffs, N. J., 1950. Second Edition, 1955.

Mothersill, Mary, ed., *Ethics,* Macmillan, New York, 1965.

Oldenquist, Andrew, ed., *Readings in Moral Philosophy,* Houghton Mifflin, Boston, Mass., 1965.

Ramsey, Paul, ed., *Nine Modern Moralists,* Prentice-Hall, Englewood Cliffs, N. J., 1962.

Sellars, W., and J. Hospers, eds., *Readings in Ethical Theory,* Appleton-Century-Crofts, New York, 1952.

Taylor, Paul W., ed., *The Moral Judgment: Readings in Contemporary Meta-Ethics,* Prentice-Hall, Englewood Cliffs, New York, 1963.

CLASSIC WORKS

Bentham, Jeremy, *An Introduction to the Principles of Morals and Legislation* (1789).

Bradley, F. H., *Ethical Studies* (1876).

Butler, Joseph, *Sermons Upon Human Nature* (1726).

Green, T. H., *Prolegomena to Ethics* (1883).

Moore, G. E., *Principia Ethica* (1903).

Plato, *Republic; Protagoras; Gorgias; Philebus.*

Price, Richard, *A Review of the Principal Questions of Morals* (1760).

Sidgwick, Henry, *The Methods of Ethics* (1874).

Smith, Adam, *The Theory of Moral Sentiments* (1759).

Spinoza, Benedict de, *Ethics* (1678).

INTRODUCTORY STUDIES

Baier, K., *The Moral Point of View,* Cornell University Press, Ithaca, N.Y., 1958.

Broad, C. D., *Five Types of Ethical Theory,* Routledge and Kegan Paul, London, 1930.

Dewey, John, *Reconstruction in Philosophy,* Holt, New York, 1920, Chap. VII.

———, *The Quest for Certainty,* Allen & Unwin, London, 1930, Chap. X.

Ewing, A. C., *Ethics,* English Universities Press, London, 1953.

Frankena, W. K., *Ethics,* Prentice-Hall, Englewood Cliffs, N. J., 1963.

Gauthier, D. P., *Practical Reasoning,* Oxford University Press, London, 1963.

Gotshalk, D. W., *Patterns of Good and Evil,* University of Illinois Press, Urbana, Ill., 1963.

Hospers, John, *Human Conduct,* Harcourt, Brace & World, New York, 1961.

Mayo, B., *Ethics and the Moral Life,* Macmillan, London, 1958.

Parker, Dewitt H., *The Philosophy of Value,* University of Michigan Press, Ann Arbor, 1957.

Pepper, S. C., *Ethics,* Appleton-Century-Crofts, New York, 1960.

Perry, Ralph Barton, *General Theory of Value,* Longmans, Green, New York, 1926.

———, *Realms of Value,* Harvard University Press, Cambridge, Mass., 1954.

Schlick, Moritz, *Problems of Ethics,* tr. by David Rynin, Prentice-Hall, Englewood Cliffs, N. J., 1939.

Sesonske, A., *Value and Obligation,* University of California Press, Berkeley, Calif., 1957, and Oxford University Press, New York, 1964.

Shirk, Evelyn, *The Ethical Dimension,* Appleton-Century-Crofts, New York, 1965.

Stace, W. T., *The Concept of Morals,* Macmillan, New York, 1937.

Toulmin, Stephen E., *An Examination of the Place of Reason in Ethics,* Cambridge University Press, London, 1950.

Von Wright, G. H., *The Varieties of Goodness,* Humanities Press, New York, 1963.

ADVANCED STUDIES

Aiken, H. D., *Reason and Conduct,* Alfred A. Knopf, New York, 1962.

Blanshard, Brand, *Reason and Goodness,* Allen & Unwin, London, 1961.

Brandt, R. B., *Ethical Theory,* Prentice-Hall, Englewood Cliffs, N. J., 1959.

Costaneda, H. N., and G. Nakhnikian, eds., *Morality and the Language of Conduct,* Wayne State University Press, Detroit, 1963. (Collection of Essays.)

Dewey, John, *Theory of Valuation,* Vol. 2, No. 4, *International Encyclopedia of Unified Science,* University of Chicago Press, Chicago, 1939.

Edel, Abraham, *Ethical Judgment,* Free Press, Glencoe, Ill., 1955.

Edwards, Paul, *The Logic of Moral Discourse,* Free Press, Glencoe, Ill., 1955.

Ewing, A. C., *The Definition of Good,* Macmillan, New York, 1947.

Graham, A. C., *The Problem of Value,* Hutchinson University Library, London, 1961.

Hare, R. M., *Freedom and Reason,* Oxford University Press, London, 1963.

Hartmann, Nicolai, *Ethics,* tr. by Stanton Coit, Macmillan, New York, 1932, 3 vols.

Ladd, John, *The Structure of a Moral Code,* Harvard University Press, Cambridge, Mass., 1957, Parts I and II.

Lewis, C. I., *An Analysis of Knowledge and Valuation,* Open Court Publishing Co., La Salle, Ill., 1946.

Melden, A. I., ed., *Essays in Moral Philosophy,* University of Washington Press, Seattle, 1958. (Collection of Essays.)

Nowell-Smith, P. H., *Ethics,* Penguin Books, Harmondsworth, Middlesex, Eng., 1954.

Raphael, D. D., *Moral Judgement,* Allen & Unwin, London, 1955.

Rice, Philip Blair, *On the Knowledge of Good and Evil,* Random House, New York, 1955.

Ross, W. D., *The Right and the Good,* Oxford University Press, London, 1930.

————, *Foundations of Ethics,* Oxford University Press, London, 1939.

Singer, M. G., *Generalization in Ethics,* Alfred A. Knopf, New York, 1961.

Stevenson, Charles L., *Ethics and Language,* Yale University Press, New Haven, Conn., 1944.

————, *Facts and Values,* Yale University Press, New Haven, Conn., 1963.

Taylor, P. W., *Normative Discourse,* Prentice-Hall, Englewood Cliffs, N. J., 1961.

Zink, S., *The Concepts of Ethics,* St Martin's, New York, 1962.

PERIODICALS

Many excellent articles on the problem of moral knowledge are to be found in recent and current issues of the following periodicals:

American Philosophical Quarterly; Analysis; Aristotelian Society Supplementary Volumes; Ethics; Inquiry; Journal of Philosophy; Mind; Philosophical Quarterly; Philosophical Review; Philosophy; Philosophy and Phenomenological Research; and *Proceedings of the Aristotelian Society.*

Chapter 11. Problems of Aesthetics

Aesthetics, or the philosophy of art, is the study of problems regarding the appreciation and evaluation of works of fine art. These problems may conveniently be divided into three groups as follows: (1) the concept of art, (2) beauty and the aesthetic experience, and (3) the nature and justification of aesthetic criticism and appraisal. This chapter contains one essay on each of these three topics, and a fourth essay in which certain questions are raised about the proper aims and methods of the whole discipline of aesthetics. We shall now examine in more detail the three basic groups of problems that have been the central concern of philosophers of art.

THE WORK OF ART

The word "art" is perhaps most commonly used to refer to painting and sculpture, but in aesthetics we use the word to refer to all works created in the various media of what are called "the fine arts": painting, sculpture, music, literature, drama, architecture, and the dance. Philosophers of art have carried on lengthy disputes about what, if anything, should be added to or subtracted from this list. Some have argued that certain "mixed" arts (e.g., opera—a combination of music, drama, and the dance—and the film—a combination of photography, drama, and music), as distinct from the "pure" arts listed, should be included among the fine arts. Whether photography is to be considered one of the "pure" arts is also questionable. In trying to decide such questions, philosophers have proposed various definitions of "fine art," trying to state exactly what property or set of properties a man-made object must have in order correctly to be called a work of fine art. Let us briefly consider some of these definitions.

Sometimes it is said that a work of art is any product of artistic creation, and the unique purpose of artistic creation is the making of something that will be enjoyed by people quite regardless of any practical use to which it can be put. The essence of fine art is found by contrasting it with practical or technical art, which is the making of tools, machines, and other artifacts to be used as instruments to accomplish some practical end. Thus a fire extinguisher is a work of practical art. It is made to serve a useful function. A painting, on the other hand, is not meant to be used as a means to some end. It is an end in itself. The reader may already be objecting: But exactly what does it mean to speak of an end in itself? Can the distinction between contemplation and use be clearly made? And what about objects like an ancient Greek vase or a Chippendale chair, that were made to be both useful and enjoyable to look at? Are they not also works of fine art? These are all legitimate questions to be raised concerning this way of defining art.

A second kind of definition is not in terms of the purpose for which a work of art is made, but in terms of certain properties that are supposed to characterize the work itself. One such definition is that of the aesthetician, Clive Bell: Art is significant form. Any man-made object which has form that is emotionally significant to a contemplator of it is a work of art. This definition has evoked many criticisms, mainly about the meaning—or lack of meaning—of the terms "significance" and "form." But Clive Bell did claim to have discovered what he called "the essential quality in a work of art, the quality that distinguishes works of art from all other classes of objects."

Another definition has been set forth and defended by the so-called "expression" theory of art: A work of art is

PROBLEMS OF AESTHETICS 637

the expression of emotion. This definition is quite similar to that which is proposed by the great Russian writer, Leo Tolstoy, in his book *What Is Art?* His definition might be summed up in the statement: Art is the communication of feelings. The selections from Tolstoy's book given in this chapter begin with his rejection of another definition of art: that a work of art is simply anything which people find to be beautiful.

This definition of art in terms of beauty raises the question: What is beauty? Tolstoy has some things to say about this, but a more thorough discussion of this question will be found in "The Nature of Beauty," by George Santayana. The theory of beauty brings us to the second main area of aesthetic problems, but before turning to it, we should mention the fact that in recent writings in aesthetics the whole endeavor to define art has been brought into question. Can art be defined at all? Is there such a thing as the essence of art, that is, a property or set of properties that are common to all works of fine art and that are not found in anything else? Or is the attempt to arrive at a true definition of art basically confused? Is the philosopher who offers a definition of art doing anything more than stipulating his own definition, merely telling us how he has decided to use the word "art"? And if this is all he is doing, of what use to us is his theory of art? These critical challenges to all traditional definitions of art are brought out by Professor William Kennick in "Does Traditional Aesthetics Rest On A Mistake?"

BEAUTY AND AESTHETIC EXPERIENCE

The second group of questions of central importance in aesthetics is con-cerned with the concepts of beauty and aesthetic appreciation or contemplation. We apply the word "beautiful" not only to works of art, but to things we see and hear even when they are not the product of human acts, such as a sunset or the song of a bird. Thus, though works of art may be beautiful, not all beautiful things are works of art. And many philosophers have argued that not all works of art—not even all good ones—are beautiful. The first claim would require us to separate the concept of beauty from that of a work of art. The second would require us to separate the concept of beauty from standards of artistic excellence and judgments of aesthetic merit. Putting aside the second claim until the next section, let us look at the first claim more closely.

Since beauty is to be found outside man-made objects, a work of art cannot be identified with whatever is beautiful. This contradicts the definition of art that a work of art is anything which people find to be beautiful. However, a slight revision in the definition would get around this difficulty. We need only say that a work of art is any man-made object or product of human skill that is found to be beautiful. With regard to this revised definition we must immediately inquire: Found *by whom* to be beautiful? And found to be beautiful *under what conditions?* The first question arises because what one person finds beautiful another person might not. Where there are cultural differences, variation in the experience of beauty is often extreme. The relativity of taste has been cited by some philosophers as a reason why we should consider beauty to be subjective rather than objective. Beauty is said to be in the beholder, not in the object beheld. Thus to say that an object is beautiful is not to make an assertion about some property of the object itself, but is simply to assert that someone enjoys looking at it. According to this theory, the same work may be both beautiful and not beautiful at the same time, since one person may be responding to it positively and another responding to it negatively. Whether something is beautiful, then, depends on who is contemplating it and whether he finds satisfaction in contemplating it.

It has been argued, however, that genuine beauty is to be discovered in an object only when a person experiences it in a certain way, or under certain conditions. Not every response to an object is to be classed as an *aesthetic* experience, and it is only if an object pleases a person when he views it aesthetically, or when he takes an aesthetic attitude toward it, that we are entitled to call the object beautiful. This position is developed by the American philosopher, George Santayana. Exactly what an aesthetic experience is remains a matter of dispute in contemporary aesthetics. It has even been questioned whether there is such a thing at all. But all philosophers are now agreed on the point that if aesthetic contemplation does occur, it can only occur under special conditions, and that it is the task of any philosopher who believes that it occurs to specify just what those conditions are.

Even if the reality of aesthetic experience were established, there would still be two basic issues to be resolved by the aesthetician: (1) Would the relativity of taste be shown to be false? If all nonaesthetic considerations were excluded as irrelevant to the appreciation of a work and only aesthetic factors were allowed to influence one's response to it, would all men find the same works to be beautiful? Would all

variation in taste be eliminated if everyone who viewed a work did so in a purely aesthetic way? (2) Is aesthetic experience cognitive, that is, is it a way of knowing some truth about a work of art? In particular, would it be right to claim that in an aesthetic experience a person apprehends objective beauty?

These issues are taken up in "The Nature of Beauty," by George Santayana, and "What Is Art?" by Leo Tolstoy.

INTERPRETATION
AND EVALUATION

In the preceding section we put aside for later consideration the question: Can a work of art be a good work and yet not be beautiful? Most philosophers of art have separated the two questions: What do we mean by saying that an object is beautiful? and What makes a good work of art good? Aesthetic enjoyment and the experience of beauty are one thing; critical interpretation and evaluation are another. Perhaps a person who can determine when a work of art is good has a more developed, cultivated, or enlightened taste than a person who cannot. He may be said to be able to appreciate art better than one who lacks critical judgment. But he need not always find beautiful those works that he judges to be good. The ugliness of a work, when viewed aesthetically, may even be an appropriate aspect of it and add to its overall worth. Paintings that depict the horrors of war or of social injustice, for example, may lose some of their force if they contain nothing that appears ugly or repulsive to us.

Leaving the problem of the relation between beauty and artistic excellence, let us examine the sorts of questions that aesthetics tries to answer regarding artistic excellence itself. We are here concerned with what is ordinarily called art criticism. The word "criticism" covers two activities: "interpretation" and "evaluation." The main difference between these activities is that the first is aimed at coming fully to understand a work, without making any value judgment about whether the work is good, bad, or indifferent, while the second is the attempt to determine the aesthetic merits and deficiencies of the work so that a value judgment of its overall worth can be made. Books and articles written by art historians and critics (including music, literary, and drama critics) usually contain both sorts of statements, an interpretation and an appraisal of the work. Both activities of the critical intelligence are the philosopher's concern.

With regard to the interpretation of a work of art, the philosopher investigates the critic's activity by inquiring into the meaning and truth of his statements about the work. If the critic uses terms like "style," "form," "content," and "structure," the aesthetician carefully analyzes how he uses them. The aesthetician also examines the logical cogency of the critic's arguments supporting his interpretation of the work. This in turn requires a philosophical investigation of what it means to say that some interpretations are correct, true, or adequate, while others are incorrect, false, or inadequate. Criteria for determining the correctness or incorrectness of an interpretation must be made explicit. Finally, a defense must be given for using these criteria. Thus aesthetics ultimately concerns itself with the justification of the criteria of truth and falsity in the critical understanding and analysis of a work of art.

With regard to the evaluation or appraisal of a work of art, aesthetics has similar tasks to perform. It must examine the meaning of value terms like "excellent," "superb," "a masterpiece," "great," "mediocre," "worthless," which critics use. The philosopher must make explicit (if the critic has not done so) the aesthetic standards that are being applied to the work in evaluating it. For only when the standards are known can the critic's judgments be clearly understood and either defended as sound, cogent, justified, or attacked as unsound, weak, unjustified. Finally, the rules of reasoning used in aesthetic argument must be investigated. When critics support their evaluations by giving reasons, the philosopher tries to make clear the logical structure of their arguments. He analyzes what it means to say that some reasons given in support of a judgment are good (that is, they bind all people who wish to think rationally and soundly about the merits of works of art) while other reasons are bad or poor. This in turn involves the study of criteria of validity and rationality in critical evaluation, and the justification of such criteria in terms of the whole enterprise of aesthetic criticism of works of art.

This chapter includes one philosophical investigation by an aesthetician of the activity of critical evaluation: "The Use of 'Good' in Aesthetic Judgments," by Helen Knight. Mrs. Knight studies the meaning of the word "good" as it is applied to works of art. What she has to say about this word could also be said about other evaluative terms, such as "superb," "outstanding," "profound," "shallow," or "a failure." Some of Mrs. Knight's questions are also discussed by Professor Kennick, who makes suggestions about right and wrong ways of justifying the use of standards of evaluation. Mrs. Knight calls these standards "criteria" for applying such words as "good" to a work.

Both of these philosophers raise important issues that are still being discussed in aesthetics today.

PHILOSOPHY OF ART AND CRITICISM OF ART

It should now be clear that aesthetics, or the philosophy of art, is quite different from art criticism. While the subject matter dealt with by the critic is the particular work of art he is interpreting or evaluating, the subject matter of the philosopher of art is the critic's activity itself. The critic makes assertions about a work of art; the aesthetician makes assertions about the meaning and truth of the critic's assertions. The aesthetician tries to clarify the concept of a work of art (as distinct from analyzing and judging particular works), and also tries to place the entire activity of criticism within the wider field of aesthetic experience. Thus philosophy remains true to its traditional goal of understanding the interrelatedness of all aspects of human life. By taking an overall view of the logic of criticism, by analyzing man's experience of beauty, and by making clear the nature of art, the philosopher enables us to see the aesthetic life of man as a whole. Since the creation and appreciation of the arts is a basic aspect of every culture, and since the experience of beauty is universal in human consciousness, aesthetics adds an essential element to our understanding of what it means to be human.

42. GEORGE SANTAYANA

(1863–1952)

The Nature of Beauty

The American philosopher, George Santayana, was born in Madrid, Spain. He was educated in America and taught philosophy at Harvard University for a number of years. He returned to Europe in 1912 and lived in Italy until his death in 1952. His major philosophical works are *The Sense of Beauty* (1896), *The Life of Reason* (1905–06), and *The Realms of Being* (four volumes, 1927–40).

In the reading that follows, Santayana attempts to give a definition of "beauty" or "the beautiful" by specifying the conditions that an object must fulfill to be correctly judged as beautiful. He first distinguishes aesthetic judgments, of which judgments of beauty are one type, from moral judgments. Both of these are value judgments, so Santayana's search for the definition of beauty involves him in a general discussion of different kinds of values. Moreover, since the direct perception or appreciation of beauty in an object is an experience that gives us pleasure, Santayana finds he must separate aesthetic pleasure from other types of pleasure in order to arrive at what is distinctive in the experience of beauty. He finds that the distinguishing mark of aesthetic pleasure is neither its "disinterestedness" nor its "universality," but rather its "objectification." What Santayana means by these three characteristics is clarified by the examples he gives in the reading. Thus, by a process of logical discrimination in successive steps, Santayana finally reaches his definition of beauty as "pleasure objectified."

The reading is taken from *The Sense of Beauty: Being the Outlines of Aesthetic Theory,* Part 1: "The Nature of Beauty." The section headings are Santayana's.

Reprinted with the permission of Charles Scribner's Sons
from *The Sense of Beauty,* pp. 13, 19–24, 28–31, 32–41,
by George Santayana (1896).

THE PHILOSOPHY OF BEAUTY IS A THEORY OF VALUES

It would be easy to find a definition of beauty that should give in a few words a telling paraphrase of the word. We know on excellent authority that beauty is truth, that it is the expression of the ideal, the symbol of divine perfection, and the sensible manifestation of the good. A litany of these titles of honour might easily be compiled, and repeated in praise of our divinity. Such phrases stimulate thought and give us a momentary pleasure, but they hardly bring any permanent enlightenment. A definition that should really define must be nothing less than the exposition of the origin, place, and elements of beauty as an object of human experience. We must learn from it, as far as possible, why, when, and how beauty appears, what conditions an object must fulfill to be beautiful, what elements of our nature make us sensible of beauty, and what the relation is between the constitution of the object and the excitement of our susceptibility. Nothing less will really define beauty or make us understand what aesthetic appreciation is. The definition of beauty in this sense will be the task of this whole book, a task that can be only very imperfectly accomplished within its limits.

· · ·

CONTRAST BETWEEN MORAL AND AESTHETIC VALUES

The relation between aesthetic and moral judgments, between the spheres of the beautiful and the good, is close, but the distinction between them is important. One factor of this distinction is that while aesthetic judgments are mainly positive, that is, perceptions of good, moral judgments are mainly and fundamentally negative, or perceptions of evil. Another factor of the distinction is that whereas, in the perception of beauty, our judgment is necessarily intrinsic and based on the character of the immediate experience, and never consciously on the idea of an eventual utility in the object, judgments about moral worth, on the contrary, are always based, when they are positive, upon the consciousness of benefits probably involved. Both these distinctions need some elucidation.

Hedonistic ethics have always had to struggle against the moral sense of mankind. Earnest minds, that feel the weight and dignity of life, rebel against the assertion that the aim of right conduct is enjoyment. Pleasure usually appears to them as a temptation, and they sometimes go so far as to make avoidance of it a virtue. The truth is that morality is not mainly concerned with the attainment of pleasure; it is rather concerned, in all its deeper and more authoritative maxims, with the prevention of suffering. There is something artificial in the deliberate pursuit of pleasure; there is something absurd in the obligation to enjoy oneself. We feel no duty in that direction; we take to enjoyment naturally enough after the work of life is done, and the freedom and spontaneity of our pleasures is what is most essential to them.

The sad business of life is rather to escape certain dreadful evils to which our nature exposes us,—death, hunger, disease, weariness, isolation, and contempt. By the awful authority of these things, which stand like spectres behind every moral injunction, conscience in reality speaks, and a mind which they have duly impressed cannot but feel, by contrast, the hopeless triviality of the search for pleasure. It cannot but feel that a life abandoned to amusement and to changing impulses must run unawares into fatal dangers. The moment, however, that society emerges from the early pressure of the environment and is tolerably secure against primary evils, morality grows lax. The forms that life will farther assume are not to be imposed by moral authority, but are determined by the genius of the race, the opportunities of the moment, and the tastes and resources of individual minds. The reign of duty gives place to the reign of freedom, and the law and the covenant to the dispensation of grace.

The appreciation of beauty and its embodiment in the arts are activities which belong to our holiday life, when we are redeemed for the moment from the shadow of evil and the slavery to fear, and are following the bent of our nature where it chooses to lead us. The values, then, with which we here deal are positive; they were negative in the sphere of morality. The ugly is hardly an exception, because it is not the cause of any real pain. In itself it is rather a source of amusement. If its suggestions are vitally repulsive, its presence becomes a real evil towards which we assume a practical and moral attitude. And, correspondingly, the pleasant is never, as we have seen, the object of a truly moral injunction.

WORK AND PLAY

We have here, then, an important element of the distinction between aesthetic and moral values. It is the same that has been pointed to in the famous contrast between work and play. These terms may be used in different senses and their importance in moral classification differs with the meaning attached to them. We may call everything play which is useless activity, exercise that springs from the physiological impulse to discharge the energy which the exigencies of life have not called out. Work will then be all action that is necessary or useful for life. Evidently if work and play are thus objectively distinguished as useful and useless action, work is a eulogistic term and play a disparaging one. It would be better for us that all our energy should be turned to account, that none of it should be wasted in aimless motion. Play, in this sense, is a sign of imperfect adaptation. It is proper to childhood, when the body and mind are not yet fit to cope with the environment, but it is unseemly in manhood and pitiable in old age, because it marks an atrophy of human nature, and a failure to take hold of the opportunities of life.

Play is thus essentially frivolous. Some persons, understanding the term in this sense, have felt an aversion, which every liberal mind will share, to classing social pleasures, art, and religion under the head of play, and by that epithet condemning them, as a certain school seems to do, to gradual extinction as the race approaches maturity. But if all the useless ornaments of our life are to be cut off in the process of adaptation, evolution would impoverish instead of enriching our nature. Perhaps that is the tendency of evolution, and our barbarous ancestors amid their toils and wars, with their flaming passions and mythologies, lived better lives than are reserved to our well-adapted descendants.

We may be allowed to hope, however, that some imagination may survive parasitically even in the most serviceable brain. Whatever course history may take,—and we are not here concerned with prophecy,—the question of what is desirable is not affected. To condemn spontaneous and delightful occupations because they are useless for self-preservation shows an uncritical prizing of life irrespective of its content. For such a system the worthiest function of the universe should be to establish perpetual motion. Uselessness is a fatal accusation to bring against any act which is done for its presumed utility, but those which are done for their own sake are their own justification.

At the same time there is an undeniable propriety in calling all the liberal and imaginative activities of man play, because they are spontaneous, and not carried on under pressure of external necessity or danger. Their utility for self-preservation may be very indirect and accidental, but they are not worthless for that reason. On the contrary, we may measure the degree of happiness and civilization which any race has attained by the proportion of its energy which is devoted to free and generous pursuits, to the adornment of life and the culture of the imagination. For it is in the spontaneous play of his faculties that man finds himself and his happiness. Slavery is the most degrading condition of which he is capable, and he is as often a slave to the niggardness of the earth and the inclemency of heaven, as to a master or an institution. He is a slave when all his energy is spent in avoiding suffering and death, when all his action is imposed from without, and no breath or strength is left him for free enjoyment.

Work and play here take on a different meaning, and become equivalent to servitude and freedom. The change consists in the subjective point of view from which the distinction is now made. We no longer mean by work all that is done usefully, but only what is done unwillingly and by the spur of necessity. By play we are designating, no longer what is done fruitlessly, but whatever is done spontaneously and for its own sake, whether it have or not an ulterior utility. Play, in this sense, may be our most useful occupation. So far would a gradual adaptation to the environment be from making this play obsolete, that it would tend to abolish work, and to make play universal. For with the elimination of all the conflicts and errors of instinct, the race would do spontaneously whatever conduced to its welfare and we should live safely and prosperously without external stimulus or restraint.

ALL VALUES ARE IN ONE SENSE AESTHETIC

In this second and subjective sense, then, work is the disparaging term and play the eulogistic one. All who feel the dignity and importance of the things of the imagination, need not hesitate to adopt the classification which designates them as play. We point out thereby, not that they have no value, but that their value is intrinsic, that in them is one of the sources of all worth. Evidently all values must be ultimately intrinsic. The useful is good because of the excellence of its consequences; but these must somewhere cease to be merely useful in their turn, or only excellent as means; somewhere we must reach the good that is good in itself and for its own sake, else the whole process is futile, and the utility of our first object illusory. We here reach the second factor in our distinction, between aesthetic and moral values, which regards their immediacy.

. . .

AESTHETIC AND PHYSICAL PLEASURE

We have now separated with some care . . . moral judgments from the sphere of our subject, and found that we are to deal only with perceptions of value, and with these only when they are positive and immediate. But even with these distinctions the most remarkable characteristic of the sense of beauty remains undefined. All pleasures are intrinsic and positive values, but all pleasures are not perceptions of beauty. Pleasure is indeed the essence of that perception, but there is evidently in this particular pleasure a complication which is not present in others and which is the basis of the distinction made by consciousness and language between it and the rest. It will be instructive to notice the degrees of this difference.

The bodily pleasures are those least resembling perceptions of beauty. By bodily pleasures we mean, of course, more than pleasures with a bodily seat; for that class would include them all, as well as all forms and elements of consciousness. Aesthetic pleasures have physical conditions, they depend on the activity of the eye and the ear, of the memory and the other ideational functions of the brain. But we do not connect those pleasures with their seats except in physiological studies; the ideas with which aesthetic pleasures are associated are not the ideas of their bodily causes. The pleasures we call physical, and regard as low, on the contrary, are those which call our attention to some part of our own body, and which make no object so conspicuous to us as the organ in which they arise.

There is here, then, a very marked distinction between physical and aesthetic pleasure; the organs of the latter must be transparent, they must not intercept our attention, but carry it directly to some external object. The greater dignity and range of aesthetic pleasure is thus made very intelligible. The soul is glad, as it were, to forget its connexion with the body and to fancy that it can travel over the world with the liberty with which it changes the objects of its thought. The mind passes from China to Peru without any conscious change in the local tensions of the body. This illusion of disembodiment is very exhilarating, while immersion in the flesh and confinement to some organ gives a tone of grossness and selfishness to our consciousness. The generally meaner associations of physical pleasures also help to explain their comparative crudity.

THE DIFFERENTIA OF AESTHETIC PLEASURE NOT ITS DISINTERESTEDNESS

The distinction between pleasure and the sense of beauty has sometimes been said to consist in the unselfishness of aesthetic satisfaction. In other pleasures, it is said, we gratify our senses and passions; in the contemplation of beauty we are raised above ourselves, the passions are silenced and we are happy in the recognition of a good that we do not seek to possess. The painter does not look at a spring of water with the eyes of a thirsty man, nor at a beautiful woman with those of a satyr. The difference lies, it is urged, in the impersonality of the enjoyment. But this distinction is one of intensity and delicacy, not of nature, and it seems satisfactory only to the least aesthetic minds.

In the second place, the supposed disinterestedness of aesthetic delights is not very fundamental. Appreciation of a picture is not identical with the desire to buy it, but it is, or ought to be, closely related and preliminary to that desire. The beauties of nature and of the plastic arts are not consumed by being enjoyed; they retain all the efficacy to impress a second beholder. But this circumstance is accidental, and those aesthetic objects which depend upon change and are exhausted in time, as are all performances, are things the enjoyment of which is an object of rivalry and is coveted as much as any other pleasure. And even plastic beauties can often not be enjoyed except by a few, on account of the necessity of travel or other difficulties of access, and then this aesthetic enjoyment is as selfishly pursued as the rest.

The truth which the theory is trying to state seems rather to be that when we seek aesthetic pleasures we have no further pleasure in mind; that we do not mix up the satisfactions of vanity and proprietorship with the delight of contemplation. This is true, but it is true at bottom of all pursuits and enjoyments. Every real pleasure is in one sense disinterested. It is not sought with ulterior motives, and what fills the mind is no calculation, but the image of an object or event, suffused with emotion.

. . .

THE DIFFERENTIA OF AESTHETIC PLEASURE NOT ITS UNIVERSALITY

The supposed disinterestedness of our love of beauty passes into another characteristic of it often regarded as essential,—its universality. The pleasures of the senses have, it is said, no dogmatism in them; that anything gives me pleasure involves no assertion about its capacity to give pleasure to another. But when I judge a thing to be beautiful, my judgment means that the thing is beautiful in itself, or (what is the same thing more critically expressed) that it should seem so to everybody. The claim to universality is, according to this doctrine, the essence of the aesthetic; what makes the perception of beauty a judgment rather than a sensation. All aesthetic precepts would be impossible, and all criticism arbitrary and subjective, unless we admit a paradoxical universality in our judgment, the philosophical implications of which we may then go on to develop. But we are fortunately not required to enter the labyrinth into which this method leads; there is a much simpler and clearer way of studying such questions, which is to challenge and analyze the assertion before us and seek its basis in human nature. Before this is done, we should run the risk of expanding a natural misconception or inaccuracy of thought into an inveterate and pernicious prejudice by making it the centre of an elaborate construction.

That the claim of universality is such a natural inaccuracy will not be hard to show. There is notoriously no great agreement upon aesthetic matters; and such agreement as there is, is based upon similarity of origin, nature, and circumstance among men, a similarity which, where it exists, tends to bring about identity in all judgments and feelings. It is unmeaning to say that what is beautiful to one man *ought* to be beautiful to another. If their senses are the same, their associations and dispositions similar, then the same thing will certainly be beautiful to both. If their natures are different, the form which to one will be entrancing will be to another even invisible, because his classifications and discriminations in perception will be different, and he may see a hideous detached fragment or a shapeless aggregate of things, in what to another is a perfect whole—so entirely are the unities of objects unities of function and use. It is absurd to say that what is invisible to a given being *ought* to seem beautiful to him. Evidently this obligation of recognizing the same qualities is conditioned by the possession of the same faculties. But no two men have exactly the same faculties, nor can things have for any two exactly the same values.

What is loosely expressed by saying that any one ought to see this or that beauty is that he would see it if his disposition, training, or attention were what our ideal demands for him; and our ideal of what any one should be has complex but discoverable sources. We take, for instance, a certain pleasure in having our own judgments supported by those of others; we are intolerant, if not of the existence of a nature different from our own, at least of its expression in words and judgments. We are confirmed or made happy in our doubtful opinions by seeing them accepted universally. We are unable to find the basis of our taste in our own experience and therefore refuse to look for it there. If we were sure of our ground, we should be willing to acquiesce in the naturally different feelings and ways of others, as a man who is conscious of speaking his language with the accent of the capital confesses its arbitrariness with gayety, and is pleased and interested in the variations of it he observes in provincials; but the provincial is always zealous to show that he has reason and ancient authority to justify his oddities. So people who have no sensations, and do not know why they judge, are always trying to show that they judge by universal reason.

Thus the frailty and superficiality of our own judgments cannot brook contradiction. We abhor another man's doubt when we cannot tell him why we ourselves believe. Our ideal of other men tends therefore to include the agreement of their judgments with our own; and although we might acknowledge the fatuity of this demand in regard to natures very different from the human, we may be unreasonable enough to require that all races should admire the same style of architecture, and all ages the same poets.

The great actual unity of human taste within the range of conventional history helps the pretension. But in principle it is untenable. Nothing has less to do with the real merit of a work of imagination than the capacity of all men to appreciate it; the true test is the degree and kind of satisfaction it can give to him who appreciates it most. The symphony would lose nothing if half mankind had always been deaf, as nine-tenths of them actually are to the intricacies of its harmonies; but it would have lost much if no Beethoven had existed. And more: incapacity to appreciate certain types of beauty may be the condition *sine qua non* for the appreciation of another kind; the greatest capacity both for enjoyment and creation is highly specialized and exclusive, and hence the greatest ages of art have often been strangely intolerant.

The invectives of one school against another, perverse as they are philosophically, are artistically often signs of health, because they indicate a vital appreciation of certain kinds of beauty, a love of them that has grown into a jealous passion. The architects that have pieced out the imperfections of ancient buildings with their own thoughts, like Charles V. when he raised his massive palace beside the Alhambra, may be condemned from a certain point of view. They marred much by their interference; but they showed a splendid confidence in their own intuitions, a proud assertion of their own taste, which is the greatest evidence of aesthetic sincerity. On the contrary, our own gropings, eclecticism, and archaeology are the symptoms of impotence. If we were less learned and less just, we might be more efficient. If our appreciation were less general, it might be more real, and if we trained our imagination into exclusiveness, it might attain to character.

THE DIFFERENTIA OF AESTHETIC PLEASURE: ITS OBJECTIFICATION

There is, however, something more in the claim to universality in aesthetic judgments than the desire to generalize our own opinions. There is the expression of a curious but well-known psychological phenomenon, viz., the transformation of an element of sensation into the quality of a thing. If we say that other men should see the beauties we see, it is because we think those beauties *are in the object,* like its colour, proportion, or size. Our judgment appears to us merely the perception and discovery of an external existence, of the real excellence that is without. But this notion is radically absurd and contradictory. Beauty, as we have seen, is a value; it cannot be conceived as an independent existence which affects our senses and which we consequently perceive. It exists in perception, and cannot exist otherwise. A beauty not perceived is a pleasure not felt, and a contradiction. But modern philosophy has taught us to say the same thing of every element of the perceived world; all are sensations; and their grouping into objects imagined to be permanent and external is the work of certain habits of our intelligence. We should be incapable of surveying or retaining the diffused experiences of life, unless we organized and classified them, and out of the chaos of impressions framed the world of conventional and recognizable objects.

How this is done is explained by the current theories of perception. External objects usually affect various senses at once, the impressions of which are thereby associated. Repeated experiences of one object are also associated on account of their similarity; hence a double tendency to merge and unify into a single percept, to which a name is attached, the group of those memories and reactions which in fact had one external thing for their cause. But this percept, once formed, is clearly different from those particular experiences out of which it grew. It is permanent, they are variable. They are but partial views and glimpses of it. The constituted notion therefore comes to be the reality, and the materials of it merely the appearance. The distinction between substance and quality, reality and appearance, matter and mind, has no other origin.

The objects thus conceived and distinguished from our ideas of them, are at first compacted of all the impressions, feelings, and memories, which offer themselves for association and fall within the vortex of the amalgamating imagination. Every sensation we get from a thing is originally treated as one of its qualities. Experiment, however, and the practical need of a simpler conception of the structure of objects lead us gradually to reduce the qualities of the object to a minimum, and to regard most perceptions as an effect of those few qualities upon us. These few primary qualities, like extension which we persist in treating as independently real and as the quality of a substance, are those which suffice to explain the order of our experiences. All the rest, like colour, are relegated to the subjective sphere, as merely effects upon our minds, and apparent or secondary qualities of the object.

But this distinction has only a practical justification. Convenience and economy of thought alone determine what combination of our sensations we shall continue to objectify and treat as the cause of the rest. The right and tendency to be objective is equal in all, since they are all prior to the artifice of thought by which we separate the concept from its materials, the thing from our experiences.

The qualities which we now conceive to belong to real objects are for the most part images of sight and touch. One of the first classes of effects to be treated as secondary were naturally pleasures and pains, since it could commonly conduce very little to intelligent and successful action to conceive our pleasures and pains as resident in objects. But emotions are essentially capable of objectification, as well as impressions of sense; and one may well believe that a primitive and inexperienced consciousness would rather people the world with ghosts of its own terrors and passions than with projections of those luminous and mathematical concepts which as yet it could hardly have formed.

This animistic and mythological habit of thought still holds its own at the confines of knowledge, where mechanical explanations are not found. In ourselves, where nearness makes observation difficult, in the intricate chaos of animal and human life, we still appeal to the efficacy of will and ideas, as also in the remote night of cosmic and religious problems. But in all the intermediate realm of vulgar day, where mechanical science has made progress, the inclusion of emotional or passionate elements in the concept of the reality would be now an extravagance. Here our idea of things is composed exclusively of perceptual elements, of the ideas of form and of motion.

The beauty of objects, however, forms an exception to this rule. Beauty is an emotional element, a pleasure of ours, which nevertheless we regard as a quality of things. But we are now prepared to understand the nature of this exception. It is the survival of a tendency originally universal to make every effect of a thing upon us a constituent of its conceived nature. The scientific idea of a thing is a great abstraction from the mass of perceptions and reactions which that thing produces; the aesthetic idea is less abstract, since it retains the emotional reaction, the pleasure of the perception, as an integral part of the conceived thing.

Nor is it hard to find the ground of this survival in the sense of beauty of an objectification of feeling elsewhere extinct. Most of the pleasures which objects cause are easily distinguished and separated from the perception of the object: the object has to be applied to a particular organ, like the palate, or swallowed like wine, or used and operated upon in some way before the pleasure arises. The cohesion is therefore slight between the pleasure and the other associated elements of sense; the pleasure is separated in time from the perception, or it is localized in a different organ, and consequently is at once recognized as an effect and not as a quality of the object. But when the process of perception itself is pleasant, as it may easily be, when the intellectual operation, by which the elements of sense are associated and projected, and the concept of the form and substance of the thing produced, is naturally delightful, then we have a pleasure intimately bound up in the thing, inseparable from its character and constitution, the seat of which in us is the same as the seat of the perception. We naturally fail, under these circumstances, to separate the pleasure from the other objectified feelings. It becomes, like them, a quality of the object, which we distinguish from pleasures not so incorporated in the perception of things, by giving it the name of beauty.

THE DEFINITION OF BEAUTY

We have now reached our definition of beauty, which, in the terms of our successive analysis and narrowing of the conception, is value positive, intrinsic, and objectified. Or, in less technical language, Beauty is pleasure regarded as the quality of a thing.

This definition is intended to sum up a variety of distinctions and identifications which should perhaps be here more explicitly set down. Beauty is a value, that is, it is not a perception of a matter of fact or of a relation: it is an emotion, an affection of our volitional and appreciative nature. An object cannot be beautiful if it can give pleasure to nobody: a beauty to which all men were forever indifferent is a contradiction in terms.

In the second place, this value is positive, it is the sense of the presence of something good, or (in the case of ugliness) of its absence. It is never the perception of a positive evil, it is never a negative value. That we are endowed with the sense of beauty is a pure gain which brings no evil with it. When the ugly ceases to be amusing or merely uninteresting and becomes disgusting, it becomes indeed a positive evil: but a moral and practical, not an aesthetic one. In aesthetics that saying is true—often so disingenuous in ethics—that evil is nothing but the absence of good: for even the tedium and vulgarity of an existence without beauty is not itself ugly so much as lamentable and degrading. The absence of aesthetic goods is a moral evil: the aesthetic evil is merely relative, and means less of aesthetic good than was expected at the place and time. No form in itself gives pain, although some forms give pain by causing a shock of surprise even when they are really beautiful: as if a mother found a fine bull pup in her child's cradle, when her pain would not be aesthetic in its nature.

Further, this pleasure must not be in the consequence of the utility of the object or event, but in its immediate perception; in other words, beauty is an ultimate good, something that gives satisfaction to a natural function, to some fundamental need or capacity of our minds. Beauty is therefore a positive value that is intrinsic; it is a pleasure. These two circumstances sufficiently separate the sphere of aesthetics from that of ethics. Moral values are generally negative, and always remote. Morality has to do with the avoidance of evil and the pursuit of good: aesthetics only with enjoyment.

Finally, the pleasures of sense are distinguished from the perception of beauty, as sensation in general is distinguished from perception; by the objectification of the elements and their appearance as qualities rather of things than of consciousness. The passage from sensation to perception is gradual, and the path may be sometimes retraced: so it is with beauty and the pleasures of sensation. There is no sharp line between them, but it depends upon the degree of objectivity my feeling has attained at the moment whether I say "It pleases me," or "It is beautiful." If I am selfconscious and critical, I shall probably use one phrase; if I am impulsive and susceptible, the other. The more remote, interwoven, and inextricable the pleasure is, the more objective it will appear; and the union of two pleasures often makes one beauty. In Shakespeare's LIVth sonnet are these words:

> O how much more doth beauty beauteous seem
> By that sweet ornament which truth doth give!
> The rose looks fair, but fairer we it deem
> For that sweet odour which doth in it live.
> The canker-blooms have full as deep a dye
> As the perfumèd tincture of the roses,
> Hang on such thorns, and play as wantonly
> When summer's breath their maskèd buds discloses.
> But, for their beauty only is their show,
> They live unwooed and unrespected fade;
> Die to themselves. Sweet roses do not so:
> Of their sweet deaths are sweetest odours made.

One added ornament, we see, turns the deep dye, which was but show and mere sensation before, into an element of beauty and reality; and as truth is here the co-operation of perceptions, so beauty is the co-operation of pleasures. If colour, form, and motion are hardly beautiful without the sweetness of the odour, how much more necessary would they be for the sweetness itself to become a beauty! If we had the perfume in a flask, no one would think of calling it beautiful: it would give us too detached and controllable a sensation. There would be no object in which it could be easily incorporated. But let it float from the garden, and it will add another sensuous charm to objects simultaneously recognized, and help to make them beautiful. Thus beauty is constituted by the objectification of pleasure. It is pleasure objectified.

QUESTIONS

1. How does Santayana distinguish between moral and aesthetic judgments? State why you would accept or reject his way of distinguishing between them.
2. "The appreciation of the arts is useless."
   "The appreciation of the arts is one of the most useful things in human life."
   How might each of these statements be defended? What play on the words "useless" and "useful" is involved? How would Santayana regard the truth or falsity of each statement?
3. "It is unmeaning to say that what is beautiful to one man *ought* to be beautiful to another." Why, according to Santayana? Does Santayana's reasoning commit him to a position of aesthetic relativism (the view that no judgments of beauty are true or universally valid)? Defend your answer.
4. "By defining beauty as a kind of pleasure, Santayana takes the position of a subjectivist about beauty. That is, a statement that an object is beautiful, according to him, is equivalent to a statement about someone's emotional reactions to the object." Show why this is an accurate account of Santayana's theory, or if it is not, show in what way it distorts his theory.
5. How does Santayana differentiate beauty from bodily pleasures and the pleasures of the senses? Assess the validity of his arguments.
6. "Beauty . . . is a value." What does Santayana mean by this? In your opinion, is this statement empirically verifiable? Why or why not?
7. Do you think the word "beauty" can be defined at all? In answering this question, consider what difficulties are involved in determining whether any proposed definition is true or false.

43. LEO TOLSTOY

(1828–1910)

What Is Art?

The Russian writer, Leo Tolstoy (Lev Nikolayevich Tolstoi) was born of a noble family and, as a young man, served in the Russian army. He became interested in social reform and strove to help the serfs, but his main energies turned to writing, and in the period between 1865 and 1877 he produced what are considered to be two of the greatest novels ever written: *War and Peace* (1865–69) and *Anna Karenina* (1875–77). In 1876 he experienced a sudden deepening of his belief in Christianity as a religion of universal brotherly love. This religious experience changed his whole life, and he became an advocate of nonviolence, compassion, and forgiveness in all relations among men. It was in this period that he wrote a series of philosophical essays, including *What Is Art?* from which this reading is taken.

The first definition of art examined by Tolstoy may be stated thus: Art is the manifestation of beauty in any man-made object. This definition leads to an analysis of the concept of beauty, which Tolstoy finds to be both subjective and relative. For something is considered beautiful when it pleases people who have a certain aesthetic taste, and the same object may not be considered beautiful by other people who have a different taste. The definition of art in terms of beauty, then, does not give Tolstoy what he wants, which is a definition of "true art" that can be used as a basis for deciding, as he puts it, "what is and what is not good art by judging whether a work conforms or does not conform to this definition."

Tolstoy then turns to three new definitions of art, all of which he rejects on the ground that they consider only "the pleasure art may give, and not the purpose it may serve in the life of man and of humanity." The definition which he finally accepts may be summed up in the statement: Art is the communication of feeling, necessary for civilized life and the moral progress of humanity. After explaining what is meant by the communication of feeling, Tolstoy then considers the purpose of art. He arrives at his conclusions about the purpose of art by examining the relation between art and religion.

Having determined what the true purpose of art is, he proceeds to set forth what he regards as valid criteria for distinguishing good art from bad art. He lists three standards for judging good art which do not take into account the feelings that are the subject matter of art, and one standard which does take such feelings into account. This last standard is defined as the degree to which a work fulfills the true purpose of art.

The reading includes parts of Chapters 2, 4, 5, 6, 15, and 16 of *What Is Art?*

From Leo Tolstoy: *What Is Art?* translated by Aylmer Maude, 1898, Oxford University Press, Inc., London and New York. Reprinted by permission of the publisher.

'What is art? What a question! Art is architecture, sculpture, painting, music, and poetry in all its forms,' usually replies the ordinary man, the art amateur or even the artist himself, imagining the matter about which he is talking to be perfectly clear and uniformly understood by everybody. But in architecture, one inquires further, are there not simple buildings which are not objects of art, and buildings with artistic pretensions which are unsuccessful and ugly and therefore not to be considered works of art? Wherein lies the characteristic sign of a work of art?

It is the same in sculpture, in music, and in poetry. Art in all its forms is bounded on one side by the practically useful, and on the other by unsuccessful attempts at art. How is art to be marked off from each of these? The ordinary educated man of our circle, and even the artist who has not occupied himself specially with aesthetics, will not hesitate at this question either. He thinks the solution was found long ago and is well known to everyone.

'Art is activity that produces beauty,' says such a man.

If art consists in that,—then is a ballet or an operetta art? you inquire.

'Yes,' says the ordinary man, though with some hesitation, 'a good ballet or a graceful operetta is also art, in so far as it manifests beauty.'

But without even asking the ordinary man what differentiates the 'good' ballet and the 'graceful' operetta from their opposites (a question he would have much difficulty in answering), if you ask him whether the activity of costumers and hairdressers, who ornament the figures and faces of the women for the ballet and the operetta, is art; or the activity of Worth, the dressmaker; of scent-makers and men-cooks, then he will in most cases deny that their activity belongs to the domain of art. But in this the ordinary man makes a mistake just because he is an ordinary man and not a specialist, and because he has not occupied himself with aesthetic questions.

. . .

The ordinary man . . . is firmly convinced that all questions of art may be simply and clearly solved by acknowledging beauty to be the content of art. To him it seems clear and comprehensible that art consists in manifesting beauty, and that a reference to beauty will serve to explain all questions about art.

But what is this beauty which forms the content of art? How is it defined? What is it?

. . .

All the aesthetic definitions of beauty lead to two fundamental conceptions. The first is that beauty is something having an independent existence (existing in itself), that it is one of the manifestations of the absolutely Perfect, of the Idea, of the Spirit, of Will, or of God; the other is that beauty is a kind of pleasure received by us not having personal advantage for its object.

. . .

On the one hand beauty is viewed as something mystical and very elevated, but unfortunately at the same time very indefinite, and consequently embracing philosophy, religion, and life itself (as in the theories of Schelling and Hegel and their German and French followers); or on the other hand (as necessarily follows from the definition of Kant and his adherents), beauty is simply a certain kind of disinterested pleasure received by us. And this conception of beauty, although it seems very clear, is unfortunately again inexact; for it widens out on the other side, that is, it includes the pleasure derived from drink, from food, from touching a delicate skin, and so forth.

. . .

In its subjective aspect, we call beauty that which supplies us with a particular kind of pleasure.

In its objective aspect, we call beauty something absolutely perfect, and we acknowledge it to be so only because we receive from the manifestation of this absolute perfection a certain kind of pleasure: so that this objective definition is nothing but the subjective conception differently expressed. In reality both conceptions of beauty amount to one and the same thing, namely, the reception by us of a certain kind of pleasure; that is to say, we call 'beauty' that which pleases us without evoking in us desire.

. . .

There is no objective definition of beauty. The existing definitions (both the metaphysical and the experimental) amount only to one and the same subjective definition, which is (strange as it seems to say so), that art is that which makes beauty manifest, and beauty is that which pleases (without exciting desire). Many aestheticians have felt the insufficiency and instability of such a definition, and in order to give it a firm basis have asked themselves why a thing pleases. And they have converted the discussion on beauty into a question of taste, as did Hutcheson, Voltaire, Diderot, and others. But all attempts to define what taste is must lead to nothing, as the reader may see both from the history of aesthetics and experimentally. There is and can be no explanation of why one thing pleases one man and displeases another, or *vice versa;* so that the whole existing science of aesthetics fails to do what we might expect from it as a mental activity calling itself a science, namely, it does not define the qualities and laws of art, or of the beautiful (if that be the content of art), or the nature of taste (if taste decides the question of art and its merit), and then on the basis of such definitions acknowledge as art those productions which correspond to these laws and reject those which do not come under them. But this science of aesthetics consists in first acknowledging a certain set of productions to be art (because they please us), and then framing such a theory of art as all these productions which please a certain circle of people can be fitted into. There exists an art-canon according to which certain productions favoured by our circle are acknowledged as being art,—the works of Phidias, Sophocles, Homer, Titian, Raphael, Bach, Beethoven, Dante, Shakespeare, Goethe, and others,—and the aesthetic laws must be such as to embrace all these productions. In aesthetic literature you will constantly meet with opinions on the merit and importance of art, founded not on any certain laws by which this or that is held to be good or bad, but merely on consideration as to whether this art tallies with the art-canon we have drawn up.

. . .

All the existing aesthetic standards are built on this plan. Instead of giving a definition of true art and then deciding what is and what is not good art by judging whether a work conforms or does not conform to this definition, a certain class of works which for some reason pleases a certain circle of people is accepted as being art, and a definition of art is then devised to cover all these productions. . . .

So that the theory of art founded on beauty, expounded by aesthetics and in dim outline professed by the public, is nothing but the setting up as good of that which has pleased and pleases us, that is, pleases a certain class of people.

In order to define any human activity, it is necessary to understand its sense and importance; and in order to do this it is primarily necessary to examine that activity in itself, in its dependence on its causes and in connexion with its effects, and not merely in relation to the pleasure we can get from it.

If we say that the aim of any activity is merely our pleasure and define it solely by that pleasure, our definition will evidently be a false one. But this is precisely what has occurred in the efforts to define art. Now if we consider the food question it will not occur to any one to affirm that the importance of food consists in the pleasure we receive when eating it. Everybody understands that the satisfaction of our taste cannot serve as a basis for our definition of the merits of food, and that we have therefore no right to presuppose that dinners with cayenne pepper, Limburg cheese, alcohol, and so on, to which we are accustomed and which please us, form the very best human food,

In the same way beauty, or that which pleases us, can in no sense serve as a basis for the definition of art; nor can a series of objects which afford us pleasure serve as the model of what art should be.

To see the aim and purpose of art in the pleasure we get from it, is like assuming (as is done by people of the lowest moral development, for instance by savages) that the purpose and aim of food is the pleasure derived when consuming it.

Just as people who conceive the aim and purpose of food to be pleasure cannot recognize the real meaning of eating, so people who consider the aim of art to be pleasure cannot realize its true meaning and purpose, because they attribute to an activity the meaning of which lies in its connexion with the other phenomena of life, the false and exceptional aim of pleasure. People come to understand that the meaning of eating lies in the nourishment of the body, only when they cease to consider that the object of that activity is pleasure. And it is the same with regard to art. People will come to understand the meaning of art only when they cease to consider that the aim of that activity is beauty, that is to say, pleasure. The acknowledgment of beauty (that is, of a certain kind of pleasure received from art) as being the aim of art, not only fails to assist us in finding a definition of what art is, but on the contrary by transferring the question into a region quite foreign to art (into metaphysical, psychological, physiological, and even historical, discussions as to why such a production pleases one person and such another displeases or pleases some one else), it renders such definition impossible. And since discussions as to why one man likes pears and another prefers meat do not help towards finding a definition of what is essential in nourishment, so the solution of questions of taste in art (to which the discussions on art involuntarily come) not only does not help to make clear in what this particular human activity which we call art really consists, but renders such elucidation quite impossible until we rid ourselves of a conception which justifies every kind of art at the cost of confusing the whole matter.

. . .

What is art if we put aside the conception of beauty, which confuses the whole matter? The latest and most comprehensible definitions of art, apart from the conception of beauty, are the following:—(1) *a,* Art is an activity arising even in the animal kingdom, and springing from sexual desire and the propensity to play (Schiller, Darwin, Spencer), and *b,* accompanied by a pleasurable excitement of the nervous system (Grant Allen). This is the physiological-evolutionary definition. (2) Art is the external manifestation, by means of lines, colours, movements, sounds, or words, of emotions felt by man (Véron). This is the experimental definition. According to the very latest definition (Sully), (3) Art is 'the production of some permanent object or passing action which is fitted not only to supply an active enjoyment to the producer, but to convey a pleasurable impression to a number of spectators or listeners, quite apart from any personal advantage to be derived from it.'

Notwithstanding the superiority of these definitions to the metaphysical definitions which depended on the conception of beauty, they are yet far from exact. The first, the physiological-evolutionary definition (1) *a,* is inexact, because instead of speaking about the artistic activity itself, which is the real matter in hand, it treats of the derivation of art. The modification of it, *b,* based on the physiological effects on the human organism, is inexact because within the limits of such definition many other human activities can be included, as has occurred in the neo-aesthetic theories which reckon as art the preparation of handsome clothes, pleasant scents, and even of victuals.

The experimental definition, (2), which makes art consist in the expression of emotions, is inexact because a man may express his emotions by means of lines, colours, sounds, or words and yet may not act on others by such expression—and then the manifestation of his emotions is not art.

The third definition (that of Sully) is inexact because in the production of objects or actions affording pleasure to the producer and a pleasant emotion to the spectators or hearers apart from personal advantage, may be included the showing of conjuring tricks or gymnastic exercises, and other activities which are not art. And further, many things the production of which does not afford pleasure to the producer and the sensation received from which is unpleasant, such as gloomy, heart-rending scenes in a poetic description or a play, may nevertheless be undoubted works of art.

The inaccuracy of all these definitions arises from the fact that in them all (as also in the metaphysical definitions) the object considered is the pleasure art may give, and not the purpose it may serve in the life of man and of humanity.

In order to define art correctly it is necessary first of all to cease to consider it as a means to pleasure, and to consider it as one of the conditions of human life. Viewing it in this way we cannot fail to observe that art is one of the means of intercourse between man and man.

Every work of art causes the receiver to enter into a certain kind of relationship both with him who produced or is producing the art, and with all those who, simultaneously, previously, or subsequently, receive the same artistic impression.

Speech transmitting the thoughts and experiences of men serves as a means of union among them, and art serves a similar purpose. The peculiarity of this latter means of intercourse, distinguishing it from intercourse by means of words, consists in this, that whereas by words a man transmits his thoughts to another, by art he transmits his feelings.

The activity of art is based on the fact that a man receiving through his sense of hearing or sight another man's expression of feeling, is capable of experiencing the emotion which moved the man who expressed it. To take the simplest example: one man laughs, and another who hears becomes merry, or a man weeps, and another who hears feels sorrow. A man is excited or irritated, and another man seeing him is brought to a similar state of mind. By his movements or by the sounds of his voice a man expresses courage and determination or sadness and calmness, and this state of mind passes on to others. A man suffers, manifesting his sufferings by groans and spasms, and this suffering transmits itself to other people; a man expresses his feelings of admiration, devotion, fear, respect, or love, to certain objects, persons, or phenomena, and others are infected by the same feelings of admiration, devotion, fear, respect, or love, to the same objects, persons, or phenomena.

And it is on this capacity of man to receive another man's expression of feeling and to experience those feelings himself, that the activity of art is based.

If a man infects another or others directly, immediately, by his appearance or by the sounds he gives vent to at the very time he experiences the feeling; if he causes another man to yawn when he himself cannot help yawning, or to laugh or cry when he himself is obliged to laugh or cry, or to suffer when he himself is suffering—that does not amount to art.

Art begins when one person with the object of joining another or others to himself in one and the same feeling, expresses that feeling by certain external indications. To take the simplest example: a boy having experienced, let us say, fear on encountering a wolf, relates that encounter, and in order to evoke in others the feeling he has experienced, describes himself, his condition before the encounter, the surroundings, the wood, his own lightheartedness, and then the wolf's appearance, its movements, the distance between himself and the wolf, and so forth. All this, if only the boy when telling the story again experiences the feelings he had lived through, and infects the hearers and compels them to feel what he had experienced—is art. Even if the boy had not seen a wolf but had frequently been afraid of one, and if wishing to evoke in others the fear he had felt, he invented an encounter with a wolf and recounted it so as to make his hearers share the feelings he experienced when he feared the wolf, that also would be art. And just in the same way it is art if a man, having experienced either the fear of suffering or the attraction of enjoyment (whether in reality or in imagination), expresses these feelings on canvas or in marble so that others are infected by them. And it is also art if a man feels, or imagines to himself, feelings of delight, gladness, sorrow, despair, courage, or despondency, and the transition from one to another of these feelings, and expresses them by sounds so that the hearers are infected by them and experience them as they were experienced by the composer.

The feelings with which the artist infects others may be most various—very strong or very weak, very important or very insignificant, very bad or very good: feelings of love of one's country, self-devotion and submission to fate or to God expressed in a drama, raptures of lovers described in a novel, feelings of voluptuousness expressed in a picture, courage expressed in a triumphal march, merriment evoked by a dance, humour evoked by a funny story, the feeling of quietness transmitted by an evening landscape or by a lullaby, or the feeling of admiration evoked by a beautiful arabesque—it is all art.

If only the spectators or auditors are infected by the feelings which the author has felt, it is art.

To evoke in oneself a feeling one has once experienced and having evoked it in oneself then by means of movements, lines, colours, sounds, or forms expressed in words, so to transmit that feeling that others experience the same feeling—this is the activity of art.

Art is a human activity consisting in this, that one man consciously by means of certain external signs, hands on to others feelings he has lived through, and that others are infected by these feelings and also experience them.

Art is not, as the metaphysicians say, the manifestation of some mysterious Idea of beauty or God; it is not, as the aesthetic physiologists say, a game in which man lets off his excess of stored-up energy; it is not the expression of man's emotions by external signs; it is not the production of pleasing objects; and, above all, it is not pleasure; but it is a means of union among men joining them together in the same feelings, and indispensable for the life and progress towards well-being of individuals and of humanity.

As every man, thanks to man's capacity to express thoughts by words, may know all that has been done for him in the realms of thought by all humanity before his day, and can in the present, thanks to this capacity to understand the thoughts of others, become a sharer in their activity and also himself hand on to his contemporaries and descendants the thoughts he has assimilated from others as well as those that have arisen in himself; so, thanks to man's capacity to be infected with the feelings of others by means of art, all that is being lived through by his contemporaries is accessible to him, as well as the feelings experienced by men thousands of years ago, and he has also the possibility of transmitting his own feelings to others.

If people lacked the capacity to receive the thoughts conceived by men who preceded them and to pass on to others their own thoughts, men would be like wild beasts, or like Kasper Hauser.[1]

And if men lacked this other capacity of being infected by art, people might be almost more savage still, and above all more separated from, and more hostile to, one another.

And therefore the activity of art is a most important one, as important as the activity of speech itself and as generally diffused.

As speech does not act on us only in sermons, orations, or books, but in all those remarks by which we interchange thoughts and experiences with one another, so also art in the wide sense of the word permeates our whole life, but it is only to some of its manifestations that we apply the term in the limited sense of the word.

We are accustomed to understand art to be only what we hear and see in theatres, concerts, and exhibitions; together with buildings, statues, poems, and novels. . . . But all this is but the smallest part of the art by which we communicate with one another in life. All human life is filled with works of art of every kind—from cradle-song, jest, mimicry, the ornamentation of houses, dress, and utensils, to church services, buildings, monuments, and triumphal processions. It is all artistic activity. So that by art, in the limited sense of the word, we do not mean all human activity transmitting feelings but only that part which we for some reason select from it and to which we attach special importance.

This special importance has always been given by men to that part of this activity which transmits feelings flowing from their religious perception, and this small part they have specifically called art, attaching to it the full meaning of the word.

.   .   .

The estimation of the value of art (or rather, of the feelings it transmits) depends on men's perception of the meaning of life; depends on what they

---

[1] 'The foundling of Nuremberg,' found in the marketplace of that town on 23rd May 1828, apparently some sixteen years old. He spoke little and was almost totally ignorant even of common objects. He subsequently explained that he had been brought up in confinement underground and visited by only one man, whom he saw but seldom.

hold to be the good and the evil of life. And what is good and what is evil is defined by what are termed religions.

Humanity unceasingly moves forward from a lower, more partial and obscure, understanding of life to one more general and more lucid. And in this as in every movement there are leaders—those who have understood the meaning of life more clearly than others—and of these advanced men there is always one who has in his words and by his life expressed this meaning more clearly, lucidly, and strongly, than others. This man's expression of the meaning of life, together with those superstitions, traditions, and ceremonies, which usually form round the memory of such a man, is what is called a religion. Religions are the exponents of the highest comprehension of life accessible to the best and foremost men at a given time in a given society—a comprehension towards which all the rest of that society must inevitably and irresistibly advance. And therefore religions alone have always served, and still serve, as bases for the valuation of human sentiments. If feelings bring men nearer the ideal their religion indicates, if they are in harmony with it and do not contradict it, they are good; if they estrange men from it and oppose it they are bad.

If the religion places the meaning of life in worshipping one God and fulfilling what is regarded as His will, as was the case among the Jews, then the feelings flowing from love of that God and of His law, when successfully transmitted through the art of poetry, by the prophets, by the psalms, or by the epic of the book of Genesis, are good, high art. All opposing that, as for instance the transmission of feelings of devotion to strange gods, or of feelings incompatible with the law of God, would be considered bad art. Or if, as was the case among the Greeks, the religion places the meaning of life in earthly happiness, in beauty and in strength, then art successfully transmitting the joy and energy of life would be considered good art, but art transmitting feelings of effeminacy or despondency would be bad art. If the meaning of life is seen in the well-being of one's nation, or in honouring one's ancestors and continuing the mode of life led by them, as was the case among the Romans and the Chinese respectively, then art transmitting feelings of joy at the sacrifice of one's personal well-being for the common weal, or at the exaltation of one's ancestors and the maintenance of their traditions, would be considered good art; but art expressing feelings contrary to these would be regarded as bad. If the meaning of life is seen in freeing oneself from the yoke of animalism, as is the case among the Buddhists, then art successfully transmitting feelings that elevate the soul and humble the flesh will be good art, and all that transmits feelings strengthening the bodily passions will be bad art.

In every age and in every human society there exists a religious sense of what is good and what is bad common to that whole society, and it is this religious conception that decides the value of the feelings transmitted by art.

· · ·

Art in our society has become so perverted that not only has bad art come to be considered good, but even the very perception of what art really is has been lost. In order to be able to speak about the art of our society it is, therefore, first of all necessary to distinguish art from counterfeit art.

There is one indubitable sign distinguishing real art from its counterfeit—namely, the infectiousness of art. If a man without exercising effort and without altering his standpoint, on reading, hearing, or seeing another man's work experiences a mental condition which unites him with that man and with others who are also affected by that work, then the object evoking that condition is a work of art. And however poetic, realistic, striking, or interesting, a work may be, it is not a work of art if it does not evoke that feeling (quite distinct from all other feelings) of joy and of spiritual union with another (the author) and with others (those who are also infected by it).

It is true that this indication is an *internal* one and that there are people who, having forgotten what the action of real art is, expect something else from art (in our society the great majority are in this state), and that therefore such people may mistake for this aesthetic feeling the feeling of diversion and a certain excitement which they receive from counterfeits of art. But though it is impossible to undeceive these people just as it may be impossible to convince a man suffering from colour-blindness that green is not red, yet for all that, this indication remains perfectly definite to those whose feeling for art is neither perverted nor atrophied, and it clearly distinguishes the feeling produced by art from all other feelings.

The chief peculiarity of this feeling is that the recipient of a truly artistic impression is so united to the artist that he feels as if the work were his own and not some one else's—as if what it expresses were just what he had long been wishing to express. A real work of art destroys in the consciousness of the recipient the separation between himself and the artist, and not that alone, but also between himself and all whose minds receive this work of art. In this freeing of our personality from its separation and isolation, in this uniting of it with others, lies the chief characteristic and the great attractive force of art.

If a man is infected by the author's condition of soul, if he feels this emotion and this union with others, then the object which has effected this is art; but if there be no such infection, if there be not this union with the author and with others who are moved by the same work—then it is not art. And not only is infection a sure sign of art, but the degree of infectiousness is also the sole measure of excellence in art.

The stronger the infection the better is the art, as art, speaking of it now apart from its subject-matter—that is, not considering the value of the feelings it transmits.

And the degree of the infectiousness of art depends on three conditions:—

(1) On the greater or lesser individuality of the feeling transmitted; (2) on the greater or lesser clearness with which the feeling is transmitted; (3) on the sincerity of the artist, that is, on the greater or lesser force with which the artist himself feels the emotion he transmits.

The more individual the feeling transmitted the more strongly does it act on the recipient; the more individual the state of soul into which he is transferred the more pleasure does the recipient obtain and therefore the more readily and strongly does he join in it.

Clearness of expression assists infection because the recipient who mingles in consciousness with the author is the better satisfied the more clearly that feeling is transmitted which, as it seems to him, he has long known and felt and for which he has only now found expression.

But most of all is the degree of infectiousness of art increased by the degree of sincerity in the artist. As soon as the spectator, hearer, or reader, feels that the artist is infected by his own production and writes, sings, or plays, for himself, and not merely to act on others, this mental condition of the artist infects the recipient; and, on the contrary, as soon as the spectator, reader, or hearer, feels that the author is not writing, singing, or playing, for his own satisfaction—does not himself feel what he wishes to express, but is doing it for him, the recipient—resistance immediately springs up, and the most individual and the newest feelings and the cleverest technique not only fail to produce any infection but actually repel.

I have mentioned three conditions of contagion in art, but they may all be summed up into one, the last, sincerity; that is, that the artist should be impelled by an inner need to express his feeling. That condition includes the first; for if the artist is sincere he will express the feeling as he experienced it. And as each man is different from every one else, his feeling will be individual for every one else; and the more individual it is—the more the artist has drawn it from the depths of his nature—the more sympathetic and sincere will it be. And this same sincerity will impel the artist to find clear expression for the feeling which he wishes to transmit.

Therefore this third condition—sincerity—is the most important of the three. It is always complied with in peasant art, and this explains why such art always acts so powerfully; but it is a condition almost entirely absent from our upper-class art, which is continually produced by artists actuated by personal aims of covetousness or vanity.

Such are the three conditions which divide art from its counterfeits, and which also decide the quality of every work of art considered apart from its subject-matter.

The absence of any one of these conditions excludes a work from the category of art and relegates it to that of art's counterfeits. If the work does not transmit the artist's peculiarity of feeling and is therefore not individual, if it is unintelligibly expressed, or if it has not proceeded from the author's inner need for expression—it is not a work of art. If all these conditions are present even in the smallest degree, then the work even if a weak one is yet a work of art.

The presence in various degrees of these three conditions: individuality, clearness, and sincerity, decides the merit of a work of art as art, apart from subject-matter. All works of art take order of merit according to the degree in which they fulfill the first, the second, and the third, of these conditions. In one the individuality of the feeling transmitted may predominate; in another, clearness of expression; in a third, sincerity; while a fourth may have sincerity and individuality but be deficient in clearness; a fifth, individuality and clearness, but less sincerity; and so forth, in all possible degrees and combinations.

Thus is art divided from what is not art, and thus is the quality of art, as art, decided, independently of its subject-matter, that is to say, apart from whether the feelings it transmits are good or bad.

But how are we to define good and bad art with reference to its content or subject-matter?

. . .

Art like speech is a means of communication and therefore of progress, that is, of the movement of humanity forward towards perfection. Speech renders accessible to men of the latest generations all the knowledge discovered by the experience and reflection both of preceding generations and of the best and foremost men of their own times; art renders accessible to men of the latest generations all the feelings experienced by their predecessors and also those felt by their best and foremost contemporaries. And as the evolution of knowledge proceeds by truer and more necessary knowledge dislodging and replacing what was mistaken and unnecessary, so the evolution of feeling proceeds by means of art—feelings less kind and less necessary for the well-being of mankind being replaced by others kinder and more needful for that end. That is the purpose of art. And speaking now of the feelings which are its subject-matter, the more art fulfils that purpose the better the art, and the less it fulfils it the worse the art.

The appraisement of feelings (that is, the recognition of one or other set of feelings as more or less good, more or less necessary for the well-being of mankind) is effected by the religious perception of the age.

In every period of history and in every human society there exists an understanding of the meaning of life, which represents the highest level to which men of that society have attained—an understanding indicating the highest good at which that society aims. This understanding is the religious perception of the given time and society. And this religious perception is always clearly expressed by a few advanced men and more or less vividly perceived by members of the society generally. Such a religious perception and its corresponding expression always exists in every society. If it appears to us that there is no religious perception in our society, this is not because there really is none, but only because we do not wish to see it. And we often wish not to see it because it exposes the fact that our life is inconsistent with that religious perception.

Religious perception in a society is like the direction of a flowing river. If the river flows at all it must have a direction. If a society lives, there must be a religious perception indicating the direction in which, more or less consciously, all its members tend.

And so there always has been, and is, a religious perception in every society. And it is by the standard of this religious perception that the feelings transmitted by art have always been appraised. It has always been only on the basis of this religious perception of their age, that men have chosen from amid the endlessly varied spheres of art that art which transmitted feelings making religious perception operative in actual life. And such art has always been highly valued and encouraged, while art transmitting feelings already outlived, flowing from the antiquated religious perceptions of a former age, has always been condemned and despised. All the rest of art transmitting those most diverse feelings by means of which people commune with one another was not condemned and was tolerated if only it did not transmit feelings contrary to religious perception. Thus for instance among the Greeks, art transmitting feelings of beauty, strength, and courage (Hesiod, Homer, Phidias) was chosen, approved, and encouraged, while art transmitting feelings of rude sensuality, despondency, and effeminacy, was condemned and despised. Among the Jews, art transmitting feelings of devotion and submission to the God of the Hebrews and to His will (the epic of Genesis, the prophets, the Psalms) was chosen and encouraged, while art transmitting feelings of idolatry (the Golden Calf) was condemned and despised. All the rest of art—stories, songs, dances, ornamentation of houses, of utensils, and of clothes—which was not contrary to religious perception, was neither distinguished nor discussed. Thus as regards its subject-matter has art always and everywhere been appraised and thus it should be appraised, for this attitude towards art proceeds from the fundamental characteristics of human nature, and those characteristics do not change.

I know that according to an opinion current in our times religion is a superstition humanity has outgrown, and it is therefore assumed that no such thing exists as a religious perception common to us all by which art in our time can be appraised. I know that this is the opinion current in the pseudo-cultured circles of today. People who do not acknowledge Christianity in its true meaning because it undermines their social privileges, and who therefore invent all kinds of philosophic and aesthetic theories to hide from themselves the meaninglessness and wrongfulness of their lives, cannot think otherwise. These people intentionally, or sometimes unintentionally, confuse the notion of a religious cult with the notion of religious perception, and think that by denying the cult they get rid of the perception.

. . .

The religious perception of our time in its widest and most practical application is the consciousness that our well-being, both material and spiritual, individual and collective, temporal and eternal, lies in the growth of brotherhood among men—in their loving harmony with one another. This perception is not only expressed by Christ and all the best men of past ages, it is not only repeated in most varied forms and from most diverse sides by the best men of our times, but it already serves as a clue to all the complex labour of humanity, consisting as this labour does on the one hand in the destruction of physical and moral obstacles to the union of men, and on the other hand in establishing the principles common to all men which can and should unite them in one universal brotherhood. And it is on the basis of this perception that we should appraise all the phenomena of our life and among the rest our art also: choosing from all its realms and highly prizing and encouraging whatever transmits feelings flowing from this religious perception, rejecting whatever is contrary to it, and not attributing to the rest of art an importance that does not properly belong to it.

QUESTIONS

1. What objections does Tolstoy raise against defining art as a manifestation of beauty? Outline his arguments and then give your own appraisal of their validity.
2. What similarities and what differences can you find between Tolstoy's conception of beauty and the definition of beauty presented by George Santayana in the preceding reading? Analyze your own notion of beauty by showing how the word "beautiful" is used in everyday life. How does your analysis differ from the views of Tolstoy and Santayana?
3. Examine carefully the definition of art proposed by Tolstoy, considering the following questions: Is the definition too broad, that is, is there anything which would satisfy the conditions set forth in the definition but would not properly be called art? Is the definition too narrow, that is, is there anything that would properly be called a work of art but which would not satisfy the definitional conditions? What elements in the definition are unclear or vaguely expressed? Can they be clarified without changing the basic idea of art embodied in the definition? If so, show how. If not, explain why not.
4. ". . . Art in the wide sense of the word permeates our whole life, but it is only to some of its manifestations that we apply the term in the limited sense of the word." Distinguish carefully between what is meant by the wide sense of the word "art" and the limited sense. Does this distinction help to clarify Tolstoy's original definition of art? Why or why not?
5. What is religion, according to Tolstoy, and how is it related to art? Would it be impossible for an atheist to be an artist, if Tolstoy's views are accepted? If an atheist could be an artist, could he ever be a good artist (that is, create good works of art)? Defend your answers.
6. Critically analyze the way Tolstoy distinguishes art from counterfeit art. Can counterfeit art be differentiated from bad (but real) art, in Tolstoy's theory? If so, show how. If not, explain why not.
7. What are the standards for evaluating good art, according to Tolstoy? Assess

the strengths and weaknesses of the arguments he uses to validate or justify these standards.

8. How would Tolstoy be able to separate art from political propaganda? From religious sermonizing? From moral exhortation?

9. Some aestheticians have argued that Tolstoy's theory of art destroys the integrity and autonomy of the artist, since it implies that every artist has the duty to serve moral, political, or religious ends set up by the society in which he lives. Must this conclusion be drawn from the theory? Why or why not?

44. HELEN KNIGHT

(b. 1899)

The Use of "Good" in Aesthetic Judgments

Helen Knight received her B.A. and Ph.D. degrees from Bedford College, University of London. She was a research student at Newnham College, Cambridge, from 1921 to 1925, a Research Fellow from 1932 to 1935, and continued research until 1941. After a period of school teaching in England, she became a tutor in English Literature at Trinity College, Melbourne University, Australia, where she has been since 1949. She is the author of a number of philosophical articles.

Mrs. Knight begins by stating that her problem is to explain the relation between goodness and its criteria, in judgments of works of art. The problem may be reworded as: the relation between the meaning or use of "good" in aesthetic judgments and the criteria of goodness that are referred to when someone tries to justify such judgments. Let us suppose a person says that a certain painting is a good painting. We can then ask for his reasons for judging it to be good. There are three ways in which such a demand

is ordinarily made: Why is it a good painting? What is good about it? What makes it a good painting? However we word our question, it must be answered by showing that the painting satisfies certain criteria of goodness in a painting. In other words, the person who attempts to justify his value judgment "This is a good painting" must refer to some aesthetic *standards* by which he is judging this painting and must show that the painting has "good-making characteristics," that is, it fulfills the conditions for a good painting set by the judge's standards. It is always possible, of course, to challenge the standards used, but this is a further question which Mrs. Knight puts off for discussion until the last part of her article.

Mrs. Knight distinguishes a specific sense of "good" and a general sense. The specific sense limits the application of the word to a certain class of objects. To say that something is a good painting, for example, is to judge it *as a painting,* that is, as a member of the class of paintings. Similarly, to say that someone is a good tennis player is to evaluate him within the class of tennis players. He is being compared with other tennis players, not with baseball players, artists, or scientists (unless they are also tennis players, in which case he is being compared with them *as* tennis players, not *as* baseball players, artists, or scientists). The general sense of "good" occurs when we judge an experience or an activity as a good thing. Thus to say "Listening to music is good" is like saying "It is a good thing to listen to music." There is no specific or limited class of "things" with which listening to music is being compared.

The importance of this distinction between the specific and general uses of "good" is this. In the case of the general use, there is some plausibility in claiming that a naturalistic analysis of "good" provides a fairly accurate account of its meaning, but the same cannot be said in the case of the specific use of "good." A naturalistic analysis of "good" (or any other value word) is an analysis according to which any statement in which the word "good" occurs as a predicate (that is, any value judgment) is equivalent in meaning to a factual or empirical statement. By what is perhaps the most common naturalistic analysis, "This is good" means the same as "I (the speaker) like this" or "I (the speaker) desire this." So if we say "Listening to music is good," using "good" in the general sense, it is at least not obviously false to claim that what we are saying amounts to "I like listening to music." But, according to Mrs. Knight, it does not at all follow from this that "I like this painting" is anywhere near what we mean when we say "This is a good painting." Indeed, what is missing from "I like this painting" which is present in "This is

a good painting" is the implicit reference to criteria of goodness in painting, that is, to aesthetic standards of appraisal or evaluation. Thus if a person seriously judges a painting to be a good one, the questions "Why is it good?" and "What makes it good?" are not correctly answered by saying "The reason why it is good is that I like it" or "The fact that I like it makes it good." Such answers would appear to be completely out of order or inappropriate if two people were seriously considering the aesthetic merits of a painting which they were both viewing with careful attention. This is the reasoning behind Mrs. Knight's statement that "my *liking* a picture is never a criterion of its goodness."

In any instance of the specific use of "good," then, we may always look for the criteria or standards being referred to in judging something to be good. But, Mrs. Knight then goes on to argue, we cannot say that the full meaning of "good" in the specific sense is exhausted by citing the "criterion-characteristics" (good-making characteristics) of the object being judged. For we normally say: "X is a good painting *because* it has such-and-such characteristics," and this is clearly saying more than the empty statement: "X has such-and-such characteristics because it has those characteristics." The word "good," Mrs. Knight concludes, has a greater generality (even in its specific sense) than do empirical words referring to good-making properties. And that is why it is perfectly correct to use the same word "good" about an object even when we apply different criteria to it and hence refer to different characteristics of the object as good-making ones. Whatever criteria we use, we judge the object to be good when it fulfills the conditions set by our criteria. If the criteria differ, then what makes the object good will be different. But "good" still means that the object satisfies the criteria.

At the end of the first part of her article, Mrs. Knight mentions three possible analyses of the meaning of "good." One is that the word names a simple property, goodness itself, which is a "non-naturalistic" property because it cannot be identified with any set of empirical properties. According to this analysis, to say "This is a good painting" is to say "This painting has the objective property of goodness in it." Mrs. Knight rejects this analysis because it does not account for the relation between calling an object good and showing that it satisfies criteria of goodness. The second analysis is a naturalistic one which, contrary to the first analysis, identifies the meaning of "good" with a set of empirical properties. For the reasons given in the preceding paragraph, this analysis is also

rejected. This leaves a third analysis, according to which "good" is not the name of any property, naturalistic or non-naturalistic, but instead is an evaluative word applied to an object when we find that it has good-making properties, that is, those empirical properties in virtue of which the object fulfils the conditions set by the criteria or standards of evaluation by reference to which we are judging it.

In the second part of her article, Mrs. Knight considers cases of people disagreeing in their aesthetic judgments, and examines the possible sources of such disagreements. In the light of her previous study of the meaning of "good," she attempts to bring out the sorts of arguments by which such disagreements may be rationally resolved.

The title of this reading is the title of the original article, which is here reprinted in its entirety.

From "The Use of 'Good' in Aesthetic Judgments," by Helen Knight, *Proceedings of the Aristotelian Society,* Vol. 36, 1935–36. Reprinted by permission of the author and The Aristotelian Society.

I

I intend to speak about "good" in such judgments as "Most of Cézanne's pictures are good," "*Howard's End* is a good novel," "This is a good film." But the main points apply to "beautiful" as much as to "good." It is largely a matter of choosing different illustrations for the same general point, and I have chosen "good" in preference to "beautiful" as I want to speak about works of art, and in particular, about pictures. On the whole we commend the works of man for their goodness, and the works of nature for their beauty.

I am raising a philosophic question. When we get into philosophic difficulty about the use of "good" we are puzzled by the difference between goodness and its criteria, the reasons for goodness—the difference, for example, between "this is good" and "this object balances that," "this line

repeats that," "the placing of this figure brings out the psychological significance of the event." We become interested in what differentiates the use of
"good" from the use of expressions for its criteria, we become interested in
its generality.

This is the problem, and I shall try to show that we can only get light
on it by considering the goodness-criteria relation. But this involves a significant denial. Many people have tried to solve their difficulty by giving
a naturalistic analysis of "good" or "beautiful." It is suggested for example
that when anyone says that a work of art is good he means that he likes it,
or that it satisfies a desire, or that it gives him a feeling of "objectified self-
affirmation." But analysis throws no light at all on the goodness-criteria relation, and I shall try to show that no analysis will give us what we want.
We shall also see that all naturalistic analyses misrepresent the situation in
one way or other.

I will introduce my view by asking you to consider two different uses
of "good," one of which is also a group of uses. There is the use exemplified
by "good tennis player," "good knitter," "good Pekingese," "good piece of
steak" etc. We use "good" in these cases for what is good of its kind. The
goodness of these things depends on their satisfying the criteria of goodness
for things of their kind. So this use embraces a group of *specific* uses. On
the other hand we have the *general* use exemplified in "aesthetic experience
is good," "philosophic discussion is good." We can bring out the contrast by
comparing "philosophic discussion is good" with "that was a good philosophic discussion," we should use quite different arguments to establish
each of these statements.

These uses are different—but in what respect? Certainly not because
"good" occupies different positions in the sentence. It makes no difference
to our meaning whether we say "that tennis player is good" or "that's a good
tennis player." Whereas we do get the difference when we say "that discussion was good" (as ordinarily used) and "discussion is good" (but we might
use "that discussion was good" to exemplify the general use). The difference
does not lie in the position of "good," nor in another, and far more important fact. For in *each* case we show the meaning of "good" by considering
its criteria—and not by giving an analysis. There is, however, this difference.
Whenever we get a specific "good" we can always use a certain type of expression—"is a good *picture*," "is a good *knitter*," "is a good *Pekingese*"
etc.; and the words "picture," "knitter" and "Pekingese" contribute to the
meaning of the sentence. But if we try to put the general "good" in this
form we can only get "is a good *thing*"; and "is a good thing" means
exactly the same as "is good." But I want in particular to notice another
(though related) difference. It is highly plausible to suppose that my desire
for aesthetic experience or philosophic discussion is a criterion for their goodness in the general sense; and indeed, that my desire for *x* is a criterion for
the goodness of *x* in this sense, whatever *x* may be. But it is not plausible to

suppose that any of my mental states is a criterion for the goodness of Helen Wills' tennis. The contrast I am pointing to is this:—On the one hand we get my desire as a criterion for the goodness of everything that is good in the general sense. On the other hand we get a number of completely different sets of criteria—criteria for tennis, for knitting, for Pekingese dogs, for pieces of steak, and so on. And this is a point I want to emphasize when I class the "good" of aesthetic judgments among the specific uses.

When we say "Cézanne's *Green Jar* is good," we are not using "good" in the general, but in one of the specific senses. It belongs to the group exemplified by "good tennis playing" and "good Pekingese." I shall try to show that this is the natural view to take. And I shall try to say as much as I can about what it involves. The main thing to consider is the goodness-criteria relation. This is the central fact, and explains the generality of "good." On the other hand we must also consider the criteria specific to aesthetic goodness. I propose to discuss the goodness-criteria relation in a relatively simple case, and conclude this discussion with some general observations about the use of "good." But all this is extremely difficult, and I know that the discussion is most inadequate. I then hope to show that aesthetic goodness involves this relation. But why, it may be asked, has the point been overlooked? This is not surprising. The aesthetic situation is very complicated, and its complications have obscured the main structure of aesthetic reasoning. But if we see the structure in a simple case we may recognise it in a more complicated one. And accordingly I lay great stress on the analogy.

Suppose I am looking at a game of tennis and say "that's a good player." If someone asks me "why?" or "what do you mean?" I answer by pointing out features of his playing. I say, for example, that his strokes are swift, that his placing is accurate, and point to the speed of his footwork. In making these remarks I am showing that he satisfies the criteria. I am indicating features of his playing that are criteria for its goodness. And this is what my questioner expected. It is the only answer that any of us expects in our ordinary conversations. We give our meaning by pointing out criterion-characters.

But suppose that my questioner wants a philosophic discussion, and says that this answer neglects the generality of "good." It is clear that "he's a good player" is not equivalent to any one of the reasons suggested above, nor to a group of such reasons. The mere fact of their being *reasons* shows that they are not equivalent, as no proposition is a reason for itself. But it is also obvious that "he's a good player" says in a sense far less than "his aim is accurate," and "she's a good knitter" says far less than "her knitting is even." But though "he's a good player" says less than *one* reason, yet in a sense it stretches over all.

It is at this point that analysis crops up. Suppose we persist in asking "But what do we mean when we say his playing is good? what are we saying?" We no longer expect the normal answer. We want someone to say: "I mean by 'his playing is good' that it is so-and-so," where "so-and-so" is a set of words that provides an analysis. But such an answer, if it could be found, would not really satisfy us. For we want to understand the generality of "good," and the key to this lies in the goodness-criteria relation. Thus at this point the question: what do we mean? is misleading. For neither an enumeration of criteria nor an analysis will give us what we want.

But let us consider what analysis might be suggested. We shall find the case of knitting quite instructive, for here I can see no candidate at all. It is plain that there just are different criteria, evenness, speed, capacity to do intricate patterns etc. In the case of tennis, someone might suggest "has winning ability." It would then be natural to retort: "and what about style?" This is of course a criterion of goodness, though a steady and reliable player would be good without it. In winning ability and style we have simply found two criteria of a very general type. A player is good *because* of his style and *because* he is able to win. Let us suppose we are looking at two stylish players, neither of whom is able to win. One of them, we can see, is unlikely to improve, in spite of his style he is bad. But the other is promising, "Look at his style," we say, "he is good even though he can't win." These cases show us something about the goodness-criteria relation. Style is a criterion, but a player may be good without it; and a knitter may be good without speed. On the other hand a player may have style and not be good, a knitter may be quick and not be good. And consider this: One player is good because of his smashing service and speed of returns, another because of his careful and unexpected placing of the ball, another because of his smashing service and spectacular backhand strokes, another because he never misses a ball. These variations are typical. We sometimes get one set of criteria, sometimes another; and the sets overlap, providing a number of different combinations. It is through considering such examples, and the more of them the better, that we get to know what the goodness-criteria relation is like. It is not however just a matter of collecting facts, but of seeing how elastic the relation is.

I shall now attempt to sum up some general points that I think have emerged about the use of "good," and these contain as much as I can say about its generality. We have seen that the meaning of "good" is determined by its criteria. And this is to say: that the truth and falsity of "he is a good so-and-so" depends on whether he possesses criterion-characters or not; and that the natural answer to the question, "what do you mean?" lies in pointing out these characters. But, on the other hand, "he is a good so-and-so" is not equivalent to any proposition which asserts the possession of a criterion-character, nor to a group of such propositions. This lack of equivalence is marked by the use of "because" which introduces the criterion propositions. A clear way of stating the difference would be to give a great many cases in which goodness and criterion propositions are differently used.

For example: "he is good, but his placing is not accurate"; "he is not good, but has a smashing service"; "he is good, his service is smashing and his returns are speedy"; "he is good, he is steady and reliable, his service is not smashing and his returns are not speedy."

On different occasions, as we have seen, we judge by different criteria— "he is good because his service is smashing and his returns are speedy"; "he is good because he is steady and reliable." This is certainly not ambiguity. There are not several meanings of "good" as there are two meanings of "plain" or two meanings of "see" when we distinguish "seeing a physical object" from "seeing a sense-datum." The situation, as I have tried to show, is totally different. But none the less I should like to speak about variations in the meaning of "good," to say that its meaning varies when we use different criteria. Some of the differences, I suggest, are striking enough to merit this description. I shall raise the point later on in connection with aesthetic judgments.

Let us now see how the meaning of "good" in aesthetic judgments is determined by its criteria. It will be useful to look at a word like "piquant." Suppose I say that a certain woman is beautiful, and someone replies "Not beautiful, but piquant." I am quite likely to accept this correction, why? Because I see that her features are piquant as distinct from beautiful. And we might point out the marks of piquancy. We might say that her nose is retroussé, her chin pointed, her expression vivacious. But in any case we can see that her piquancy depends on her features or expression. And in distinguishing piquancy from beauty we imply that beauty depends on other features (though there may be overlapping).

This example is useful because "piquant" is the same kind of word as "good." But the range of its criteria is narrower, and this makes its dependence on them easier to see. "Good" is exactly the same kind of word as "piquant" and "beautiful," but its use is far wider. It is used with *this* set of criteria and with *that;* and so on through an extremely wide range of overlapping sets. On any *one* occasion it is used with one set only, but on this occasion with this set, on that occasion with that, and so on. This in a way drains it of meaning, it is empty as compared with "piquant." So we see the relation between "piquant" and its criteria more readily, but with a little more attention we can see it just as clearly in the case of "good."

Suppose I say that Cézanne's *Green Jar* is a good picture and someone asks me "why?" or "what do you mean?" I should answer by describing it. I should point out a number of facts about its organization, for example: that apple is placed so that it exactly balances the main mass on the right; the lines of table-cloth, knife and shadows repeat each other; the diagonal of the knife counteracts the diagonals of the shadows. All these objects, I might continue, are exceedingly solid and the shadows exceedingly deep— each thing "is infallibly in its place." I might point out a number of important problems that Cézanne has solved, for example, that he combines a geometrical scheme with the variety we get in natural appearances. And finally I might allude to the profundity and gravity of the picture. In this description I have pointed out criterion-characters, the *Green Jar* is good because it possesses them.

This is the type of reasoning that runs through critical writings. I shall give a few illustrations. Consider Reynolds' discussion of the principal lights in a picture.[1] He praises the *Bacchus and Ariadne* of Titian. The figure of Ariadne dressed in blue and the sea behind her form a cold contrast to the mellow colours of the principal group. But by giving Ariadne a red scarf and one of the Bacchante some blue drapery Titian prevents a division of the picture into separate sections. On the other hand Le Brun in *The Tent of Darius* mismanages the light. The picture has a heavy air because the principal light falls on Statira who is dressed in pale blue. Reynolds then gives the *Landscape in Moonlight* by Rubens as an example of modifying natural appearance for the sake of harmony. On the one hand Rubens introduces more colour contrast, and on the other hand modifies the natural brightness of the moon. The natural brightness could only be preserved by making everything else very dark. Rembrandt in his *Man in Armour* preserves the natural brightness of the armour, and as a result the picture is too black. We get a similar type of criterion when Berenson praises Giotto for presenting just those lines, those lights and shadows which convey solidity,[2] and when Fry points out how Cézanne emphasizes just those aspects of colour which convey plastic form.[3] We get quite another type when Reynolds condemns Bernini's *David* for the meanness of its expression,[4] and Delacroix points out that Millet's peasants are a little too ambitious—this, he explains, is because Millet only reads the Bible.[5]

We find in these cases the same kind of reasoning as in discussions about tennis—he is good because his returns are speedy, it is good because the red scarf and blue drapery preserve the balance. And the question "what do you mean by saying it's good?" provokes the same kind of answer, "I mean that the lines balance each other, that it combines geometric structure with variety, that it is profound."

Let us now consider some cases in which I change my judgment. I decide that a picture is bad. Then someone points out its construction, and I see the picture in a new way. The figures had seemed a mere haphazard collection. I now see a diagonal movement in which the figures participate, and as I follow this movement the space recedes, giving a strong impression of depth. And I reverse my judgment. What determines the change? My perception of how the picture is constructed, my recognition of a criterion-

[1] Discourses, Seeley & Co., Lond., 1905, pp. 245–252.
[2] The Italian Painters of the Renaissance. The Clarendon Press, Oxford, 1930, pp. 70–71.
[3] Cézanne. Hogarth Press, London, 1927, pp. 39–40.
[4] Discourses, p. 71.
[5] Journal Librairie Plon. Paris, 1893. Vol. 2, p. 61.

character. Or take these cases. I believe that the *Death of Chatterton* and the *Last Goodbye* are good, the one because of its dramatic presentation, the other because of its pathos. But someone convinces me that the one is theatrical and the other sentimental. And I now decide that these pictures are bad.

It is worth while to notice that my *liking* a picture is never a criterion of its goodness. We never say "this picture is good because I like it." I fully admit that we value aesthetic experience because it includes enjoyment. It is obvious that liking is important, but we must not mistake its role. It is not a criterion. Nor is it true, as we may be inclined to think, that we always like what we judge to be good, and dislike what we judge to be bad. It is common to find indifference combined with approval—"I can't see anything in so-and-so, but I believe it's good." And we also find liking combined with disapproval. I may have a taste for the sentimental, and like *East Lynne*, even if I know that *East Lynne* is sentimental and that sentimentality is bad. Or I may like a novel because it deals with a problem that interests me, and because I agree with its views. But I may believe that its treatment of the problem is unsuited to the novel form. And in both these cases I condemn the novels for the very characters I like.

I have tried to show that the goodness of pictures depends on their possession of criterion-characters. We give reasons for goodness by pointing them out. The judgment "this is good" or "this is bad" depends on their presence or absence. And this means that we understand the "good" of aesthetic judgments by understanding the goodness-criteria relation. Its meaning is determined by criterion-characters, but the proposition "this is good" is not equivalent to any criterion proposition. And there are rules which determine the truth of the former in relation to the truth of the latter.

And now a few last words about analysis. It is irrelevant to our problem because it tells us nothing about the goodness-criteria relation. I believe we become increasingly convinced of this the more we consider this relation, and that desire for analysis dwindles away. We have indeed found a third alternative, previously overlooked. Our puzzle started when we became convinced that "good" does not name an indefinable quality, and we tried to remove the puzzle by defining "good" in naturalistic terms. We now see that "good" may be indefinable and yet not stand for an indefinable quality, and that it has significance even though in one sense it stands for nothing.

We also see how naturalistic analyses distort the situation. Most of them select a state of mind such as our liking which is not even a criterion of goodness. In looking for such an analysis we tend to look for a mental state which constantly accompanies the judgment that a work of art is good or beautiful. We are struck by some one or other experience such as liking, satisfaction of desire, increased vitality, and analyse aesthetic judgments in terms of this experience. But let us suppose that we *do* find a mental state that constantly accompanies the judgment that a work of art is good or beautiful. What then? It will only provide us with a psychological generalisation: whenever anyone judges a work of art to be good he always likes it or it always satisfies a desire, or it always increases his vitality. It does not solve any philosophic problem about the use of "good."

II

There are many points to notice about the criteria of aesthetic merit, and many problems to consider. I am passing over many of these, but certainly not because I think them of little importance. I shall first give examples to show the diversity of aesthetic criteria, and then consider variations in the use of "good" to which this diversity leads. If we look at certain cases of disagreement from this point of view we shall be inclined to interpret them as linguistic differences.

One picture is good for one sort of thing, and another for something quite different. We may praise a water colour for its translucency and an oil for the thickness and richness of its impasto. We praise the brightness and clarity of an Impressionist painting, but do not condemn a Rembrandt for lacking these qualities. It is clear that we look for something different in each case. We praise a Botticelli for the poetry of its theme and a Degas for its realism. And how do we praise a realistic picture? We say that the artist has caught the exact pose, the kind of thing one might see at any moment. And the very banality of that pose (in the case of Degas) is a merit. But we do not condemn Botticelli because we fail to meet his goddesses and nymphs as we walk through the street. On the contrary we praise him for imagination of the ideal. And we praise him for his flowing rhythm, but do not condemn Byzantine art for being rigid, nor Cézanne for being ponderous. Suppose we are considering the work of a colourist, a member let us say, of the Venetian school. We praise it for subtle nuances of colour and for atmospheric unity, the kind that obscures the contour of things. We praise it for richness of paint, for richness and vitality of effect. And if it fails in these respects we condemn it. But of course we do not condemn a fresco painting of the fifteenth century because it has none of these qualities. In this kind of painting we look for something quite different, for perfection in each part, for unity achieved by the balance of independent wholes, for simplicity in colour and thinness of paint, for its simple and dignified effect.

These examples show that there are a great many alternative standards. To a large extent these are set by the artist or school. An artist tries to produce a certain effect, and his purpose is shaped by a number of factors:— the use of a certain medium (oil, tempera etc.), interest in a certain kind of appearance (sunlight, depth etc.), in a certain kind of form (classical, baroque etc.), in a certain kind of subject (the poetic, the commonplace etc.).

All these factors provide criteria and each provides a large number of alternative criteria. I do not say that the artist's aim is our only critical measure, but it is extremely important and mainly responsible for the diversity of standards.

It is natural to suggest that we can classify criteria, or at least a great many of them, under the headings of form and representation. This classification is convenient and enlightening. But it may suggest misleading ideas. We may think, for example, that we class all formal criteria together because of a common property to which "formal" refers. But the class of formal properties is heterogeneous. We praise a picture because the parts balance each other, because the colours are orchestrated, because the figures are solid, because the colours are brilliant. These are all formal criteria, but we do not class them together because of a common property. Classification is important, but it does not reduce the diversity of criteria.

I now want to discuss this diversity from the linguistic point of view. We have seen that different pictures are good for different reasons. Accordingly when we say "this picture is good" we are often judging by different criteria. We can translate this into a statement about language: when we say "this picture is good" we are often using "good" with different meanings. Only we must remember that "good" is not ambiguous, and that the variations of meaning are distinctive.

These variations occur very frequently. We have already seen one reason for this, namely that pictures are good by different criteria. But there is another reason, that some people *habitually* judge by certain criteria and not by others. It is a commonplace that some people always praise a picture for its form and others for its subject. Each set habitually selects criteria from another group, and, as we shall see, there are other cases. It may be a matter of ignorance. Without historical and technical training we do not know what artists are aiming at, and accordingly are ignorant of a great many criteria. But there is a far more curious reason. We *refuse* to use criteria of which we are well aware. And this is by no means uncommon. Suppose I say to someone that *After Office Hours* is a good film and he denies it. I then point out its competent acting, its slickness and smartness. He does not deny that it has these qualities, but answers "that's not goodness." But there are many different criteria of goodness in films and these are among them. His answer amounts to saying "I don't want to accept these criteria of goodness—I don't want to use 'good' in this way." We also get more serious cases of this refusal. Thus Delacroix complains of the "modern schools" who look on colour as an inferior and "earthy" aspect of painting, and exhort artists to reject the technique of the colourist. Again what does this come to? "We don't want to accept these criteria of goodness." Even Reynolds maintains that the highest art requires simplicity, in fact monotony of colour, and must renounce the harmony of subtle nuances. This partly explains his depreciation of Tintoretto, Veronese and Rubens. And what does his criticism come to? "I have *decided* to degrade these criteria, and in consequence these artists only paint 'ornamental' pictures."

The point then is this. Either through ignorance or prejudice many people habitually use "good" with certain meanings and not with others. And when we look at the matter in this light we see that a great deal of aesthetic disagreement is linguistic. It is disagreement in the use of "good." Suppose that two people are looking at a picture by Picasso, the kind in which we get abstract treatment of actual objects. One of them says "this is good" and the other "this is bad." The first is judging by its form, and the other points scornfully to the representation (or lack of it). The appropriate comment is, I suggest, "They are using 'good' with different meanings." And this also applies to the dispute about *After Office Hours*. But we need not only consider such complete disagreement. Delacroix, for example, places Rubens much higher than Reynolds places him, and this is partly because Delacroix is willing, in fact anxious, to accept colour criteria at their full value.

It is important to notice that when people disagree in this way they may completely agree about the nature of what they are discussing. The filmgoers may agree that *After Office Hours* is competent in acting, smart and slick. Reynolds fully agrees with Delacroix that Rubens excels in colour technique. This agreement is significant, and fits in very happily with the linguistic explanation. Suppose, on the other hand, that Reynolds was disputing Rubens' excellence as a colourist. This would be a dispute of quite another kind. It would be a factual dispute about Rubens' technique.

There are two more points I must raise before concluding. I shall treat them both in a very sketchy manner, but cannot leave the subject without indicating the lines along which my answer to them would run.

The first is concerned with comparative judgments, "this picture is better than that." Such judgments are most profitable when we compare pictures that resemble each other pretty closely, two water colours, two Impressionist paintings, two Baroque paintings etc. In such cases we judge both pictures by the same criteria.

But what about the comparison of pictures which are good for different reasons? I believe that in some cases this would be nonsensical. It is nonsense to ask whether Raphael or Rembrandt is the better artist, whether rugged scenery is better than soft, or Gothic architecture than Norman. In these cases we can only state a preference for one or the other. But we *do* make comparative judgments where the criteria are different. Raphael's *School of Athens* is better than a water colour by Crome or a cartoon by Max Beerbohm. But Crome and Beerbohm were aiming at completely different ends from Raphael, and their pictures may be perfect of their kind. The explanation of these comparative judgments is, I believe, that some criteria are higher than others. I mean by this simply that when pictures excel by some criteria we say they are better than if they excel by others. The criteria by which Raphael excels, such as space, composition, organization of groups, expressiveness, dignity, are among the very highest.

The second question is closely connected, and has probably been provoked by many of my statements. What is the guarantee of a criterion? What determines the truth of "so-and-so is a criterion for goodness in pictures"? The guarantee, I would answer, lies in its being used as a criterion. Organization of groups, space composition, profundity etc., are criteria of goodness because they are used as such. But we must face a difficulty. Who is it that uses them? It is true that some are in general use. A large number of people would praise a picture for its profundity. There is also the important fact that we often use criteria without being able to name or distinguish them. But we must acknowledge that some are only used by critics, and not even by all of them. We must admit that criteria are not firmly fixed, like the points (at any one time) of a Pekingese. But it completely misrepresents the situation to say they are not fixed at all.

Perhaps I should also point out that the fixing of criteria is one thing, and their use another. When we make aesthetic judgments we are using criteria, and not talking about the circumstances in which they are fixed. They are fixed by certain people who no doubt have their reasons for preferring some to others. But we do not refer to these facts in our aesthetic judgments.

I have been constantly harping in this paper on the judicial office of aesthetic judgments, and feel that I must supply an antidote, for I have no desire to exalt this office. I believe, it is true, that the judgments we make in pointing out criteria are the most profitable judgments to make. But we need not make them with judicial intent. It is far better to say "Cézanne was interested in that and that, we can find so-and-so in his pictures." The great thing is to discover what a work of art is like.

QUESTIONS

1. At the beginning of her essay, Mrs. Knight claims that the main points of her analysis of the meaning of "good" also apply to the meaning of "beautiful." In the light of the discussions of beauty by George Santayana and Leo Tolstoy in the earlier readings of this chapter, consider the justifiability of this claim.

2. What objections does Mrs. Knight raise against naturalistic analyses of "good"? Would her objections hold against the so-called "ideal observer theory" of aesthetics, according to which "This is a good painting" means the same as "An ideal aesthetic observer (one who is a competent judge of painting) approves of this painting"? Why or why not?

3. After distinguishing the general use of "good" from its specific uses, Mrs. Knight says: "I class the 'good' of aesthetic judgments among the specific uses." Explain the difference between the general and the specific uses of "good," and then give an argument either in defense of, or in opposition to, Mrs. Knight's statement.

4. While maintaining that the meaning of "good" varies when different criteria of goodness are used, Mrs. Knight also maintains that a judgment that something is a good so-and-so ". . . is not equivalent to any proposition which asserts the possession of a criterion-character, nor to a group of such propositions." Show why these two positions maintained by Mrs. Knight are, or are not, consistent with each other.

5. Explain in detail the difference between liking a painting and judging it to be good, according to Mrs. Knight's theory. Assess the soundness of her argument that we do not always like what we judge to be good or dislike what we judge to be bad. Give examples.

6. If one accepted Mrs. Knight's views on the meaning of "good" in aesthetic judgments, would one have to reject Tolstoy's theory of good art, set forth in the preceding reading? If so, show why. If not, explain why the two theories are mutually consistent.

7. What are the main sources of the diversity of standards for judging paintings, according to Mrs. Knight? Discuss the question whether there can be any method of validating or justifying some standards rather than others, in the light of these sources of diversity.

8. Mrs. Knight says: "It is nonsense to ask whether Raphael or Rembrandt is the better artist, whether rugged scenery is better than soft, or Gothic architecture than Norman." What is the meaning of the word "nonsense" in this statement? Give your reasons for considering the statement true or false. Must Mrs. Knight be classed as an aesthetic relativist for having made the statement? In your answer, make clear what you mean by "aesthetic relativism."

9. ". . . A great deal of aesthetic disagreement is linguistic." What is the reasoning behind this sentence, and why would you accept it or reject it? Suppose the sentence had read, "*All* aesthetic disagreement . . ." instead of "A great deal. . . ." Would you then disagree with it? Why or why not?

10. "What is the guarantee of a criterion? . . . The guarantee, I would answer, lies in its being used as a criterion." Suppose Mrs. Knight were asked: Used by whom? What would her reply be? Show how you would decide whether her answer was satisfactory.

45. WILLIAM E. KENNICK

(b. 1923)

Does Traditional Aesthetics Rest on a Mistake?

William Elmer Kennick received his Ph.D. degree from Cornell University. He has taught philosophy and served as Chairman of the Philosophy Department at Oberlin College. Since 1956 he has been on the faculty of Amherst College, where he is now Professor of Philosophy. He is the author of a number of philosophical articles and the editor of *Art and Philosophy: Readings in Aesthetics* (1964).

Professor Kennick makes clear at the

very beginning of this reading that his answer to the question stated in the title is "Yes." There are not just one, but two mistakes made by traditional aesthetics, according to Professor Kennick. The first mistake is to propound definitions that are supposed to tell us what is the essence of beauty or what is the true nature of art. The second mistake is to use such definitions as the basis for setting up universal criteria or standards for judging all works of art. Good examples of what Professor Kennick means by traditional aesthetics are Santayana's "The Nature of Beauty" and Tolstoy's "What Is Art?" in this chapter.

Professor Kennick begins by considering the nature of definitions. (His discussion may be usefully supplemented by reference to Professor Max Black's account of definition in "The Definition of Scientific Method," in Chapter 4.) Traditional theories of art and beauty have offered definitions of the words "art" and "beauty" which were attempts to specify the essential properties common to every work of art or every beautiful thing. These properties were also meant to differentiate art and beauty from everything else in the world. They were proposed as a true and complete list of the "defining characteristics" of art and beauty. Professor Kennick critically analyzes this view of a definition and tries to show why it is mistaken. However, he does not rest his case on this negative point. He takes a fresh look at aesthetic theories and points out that they have an importance and a validity when taken as recommendations or instructions for viewing art in new ways.

Concerning the second mistake, Professor Kennick examines a typical theory of the traditional sort which attempts to establish standards of good art or criteria of aesthetic merit on the basis of a theory of the essential nature of art. He then presents his own view of the function of aesthetic standards or criteria in the making of critical judgments. He concludes with a study of how such standards might be justified.

The reading consists of Professor Kennick's entire article, originally published in 1958.

From "Does Traditional Aesthetics Rest on a Mistake?" by William E. Kennick, *Mind,* Vol. 67, No. 267, 1958. Reprinted by permission of the author and the editor of *Mind.*

Does traditional aesthetics rest on a mistake? It rests, I think, on at least two of them, and the purpose of this paper is to explore the claim that it does.

By 'traditional aesthetics' I mean that familiar philosophical discipline which concerns itself with trying to answer such questions as the following: What is Art? What is Beauty? What is the Aesthetic Experience? What is the Creative Act? What are the criteria of Aesthetic Judgement and Taste? What is the function of Criticism? To be sure, there are others, like: Are the aesthetic object and the work of art the same? or, Does art have any cognitive content?—but these questions are commonly taken to be subordinate to those of the first group, which might be called the 'basic questions' of traditional aesthetics.

1. *The Basic Questions as Requests for Definitions.* If someone asks me 'What is helium?' I can reply: 'It's a gas' or 'It's a chemical element' or 'It's a gaseous element, inert and colourless, whose atomic number is 2 and whose atomic weight is 4.003'. A number of replies will do, depending upon whom I am talking to, the aim of his question, and so on. It is a pretty straightforward business; we get answers to such questions every day from dictionaries, encyclopedias, and technical manuals.

Now someone asks me 'What is Space?' or 'What is Man?' or 'What is Religion?' or 'What is Art?' His question is of the same form as the question 'What is helium?' but how vastly different! There is something very puzzling about these questions; they cannot be answered readily by appealing to dictionaries, encyclopedias, or technical manuals. They are philosophical questions, we say, giving our puzzlement a name, although we should not think of calling 'What is helium?' a philosophical question. Yet we expect something of the same sort of answer to both of them. There's the rub.

We say that questions like 'What is Space?' or 'What is Art?' are requests for information about the nature or essence of Space or of Art. We could say that 'What is helium?' is a request for information about the nature or essence of helium, but we rarely, if ever, do; although we do use questions like 'What is helium?' as analogues of questions like 'What is Space?' to show the sort of reply we are looking for. What we want, we say, is a definition of Space or of Art, for as Plato and Aristotle taught us long ago, "definition is the formula of the essence". So, just as the traditional metaphysicians have long sought for the nature or essence of Space and of Time, of Reality and of Change, the traditional aesthetician has sought for the essence of Art and of Beauty, of the Aesthetic Experience and the Creative Act. Most of the basic questions of traditional aesthetics are requests for definitions; hence the familiar formulae that constitute the results of traditional aesthetic inquiry: 'Art is Expression' (Croce), 'Art is Significant Form' (Clive Bell), 'Beauty is Pleasure Objectified' (Santayana), and so on. Given these definitions we are supposed to know what Art is or what Beauty is, just as we are supposed to know what helium is if someone tells us that it is a chemical element, gaseous, inert, and colourless, with an atomic number of 2 and an atomic weight of 4.003. F. J. E. Woodbridge once remarked that metaphysics searches for the nature of reality and finds it by definition. We might say that traditional aesthetics searches for the nature of Art or Beauty and finds it by definition.

But why should it be so difficult to discern the essence of Art or Beauty? Why should it take so much argument to establish or defend such formulae as 'Art is Expression'? And once we have arrived at such formulae or have been given them in answer to our question, why should they be so dissatisfying?

To come closer to an answer to these questions, we must look at what it is the aesthetician expects of a definition of Art or Beauty. De Witt Parker has stated with unusual clarity the "assumption" of the aesthetician in asking and answering such questions as 'What is Art?'; at the beginning of his essay on "The Nature of Art" (note the title) he says:

> The assumption underlying every philosophy of art is the existence of some *common nature* present in all the arts, despite their differences in form and content; something the *same* in painting and sculpture; in poetry and drama; in music and architecture. Every single work of art, it is admitted, has a unique flavour, a *je ne sais quoi* which makes it incomparable with every other work; nevertheless, there is some mark or set of marks which, if it applies to any work of art, applies to *all* works of art, *and to nothing else*— a common denominator, so to say, which constitutes the definition of art, and serves to separate . . . the field of art from other fields of human culture.[1]

What we are after, it should be clear, is what the traditional logic texts call a 'definition *per genus et differentiam*' of Art and Beauty.

2. The Assumption Questioned; the First Mistake. The assumption that, despite their differences, all works of art must possess some common nature, some distinctive set of characteristics, which serves to separate Art from everything else, a set of necessary and sufficient conditions for their being works of art at all, is both natural and disquieting, and constitutes what I consider to be the first mistake on which traditional aesthetics rests. It is natural, because, after all, we do use the word 'art' to refer to a large number of very different things—pictures and poems and musical compositions and sculptures and vases and a host of other things; and yet the word is one word. Surely, we are inclined to say, there must be something common to them all or we should not call them all by the same name. *Unum nomen; unum nominatum.*

Yet the assumption is disquieting when we come to search for the common nature which we suppose all works of art to possess. It is so elusive. We ought to be able to read a poem by Donne or by Keats, a novel by George Eliot or Joseph Conrad, or a play by Sophocles or Shakespeare, to listen to Mozart and Stravinsky, and to look at the pictures of Giotto and Cezanne and the Chinese masters and *see* what Art is. But when we look we do not see what Art is. So we are inclined to suppose that its essence must be something hidden, something that only an aesthetician can see, like the sounds that only a dog can hear, or else, as Parker, for example, supposes, that it must be something very complex, involving many characteristics (*op. cit.* p. 93). This explains why an adequate definition of Art is so hard to arrive at, why it is so much harder to answer questions like 'What

---

[1] De Witt H. Parker, "The Nature of Art," *Revue Internationale de Philosophie,* July 1939, p. 684; reprinted in E. Vivas and M. Krieger, eds., *The Problems of Aesthetics* (New York, 1953), p. 90. Italics mine.

is Art?' than it is to answer questions like 'What is helium?' Perhaps this also explains why there is a Philosophy of Art when there is no Philosophy of Helium?

But this explanation will not do. It will not do, that is, to suppose simply that the essence or nature of Art is elusive, very hard to detect, or very complex. It suggests that what we are faced with is a problem of scrutinizing, that what we have to do is to look long and hard at works of art, examine them carefully and diligently and, *voila!* we shall *see*. But no amount of looking and scrutinizing gives us what we want. All we see is this poem and that play, this picture and that statue, or some feature of them that catches our attention; and if we find some resemblances between poems or plays or pictures, or even between poems *and* pictures, pictures *and* musical compositions, these resemblances quickly disappear when we turn to other poems and plays and pictures. That is why in aesthetics it is best not to look at too many works of art and why, incidentally, aesthetics is best taught without concrete examples; a few will do. We can readily believe that we have seen the essence of Art when we have selected our examples properly; but when we range farther afield we lose it.

Despite the temptation to think that if we look long enough and hard enough at works of art we shall find the common denominator in question, after all the fruitless scrutinizing that has already been done, it is still more tempting to think that we are looking for something that is not there, like looking for the equator or the line on the spectrum that separates orange from red. No wonder that in aesthetics we soon begin to feel the frustration of St. Augustine when he asked himself 'What is Time?': "If I am not asked, I know; if I am asked, I know not". Something must be wrong.

What is wrong, as I see it, has nothing to do with the nature or essence of Art at all; that is, there is neither anything mysterious nor anything complicated about works of art which makes the task of answering the question 'What is Art?' so difficult. Like St. Augustine with Time, we do know quite well what Art is; it is only when someone asks us that we do not know. The trouble lies not in the works of art themselves but in the concept of Art. The word 'art', unlike the word 'helium', has a complicated variety of uses, what is nowadays called a complex 'logic'. It is not a word coined in the laboratory or the studio to name something that has hitherto escaped our attention; nor is it a relatively simple term of common parlance like 'star' or 'tree' which names something with which we are all quite familiar. As Professor Kristeller has shown us,[2] it is a word with a long, involved, and interesting history; a complicated concept indeed, but not for the reasons which the aestheticians suppose. Any good dictionary will indicate some of its many meanings, some of the variety of uses which the word 'art' has; but no dictionary will give us the kind of formula which the aestheticians seek.

[2] P. O. Kristeller, "The Modern System of the Arts: A Study in the History of Aesthetics", *Journal of the History of Ideas,* xii (1951), 496–527; xiii (1952), 17–46.

That is why we suppose that the nature of Art is a philosophical problem and why there is a Philosophy of Art but no Philosophy of Helium. It is the complicated concepts like those of Space, Time, Reality, Change, Art, Knowledge, and so on that baffle us. Dictionaries and their definitions are of use in making short shrift of questions of the form 'What is X?' only in relatively simple and comparatively trivial cases; in the hard and more interesting cases they are frustrating and disappointing.

Doubtless there is an answer to this, and it might run somewhat as follows: "We know that the word 'Art' has a variety of uses in English. Most commonly it is used to refer to pictures alone; when we visit an art museum or consult an art critic, we expect to see pictures or to hear pictures talked about. We say that painting, painting pictures, *not* painting houses or fences, is *an* art, that cooking and sewing and basket-weaving, book-binding and selling are *arts,* but only some pictures do we call *works* of art, and rarely do we refer to dishes or garments or baskets as works of art, except honorifically. We speak of the liberal arts and the industrial arts and of the art of war. But all of this is beside the point. As aestheticians we are interested only in what are sometimes called the 'fine arts', or what Colling-wood calls 'art proper'—works of art. Surely all of these have something in common, else how should we be able to separate those paintings and draw-ings and poems and plays, musical compositions and buildings which are works of art from those which are not?"

To answer the last question first and make a long story short: we are able to separate those objects which are works of art from those which are not, because we know English; that is, we know how correctly to use the word 'art' and to apply the phrase 'work of art'. To borrow a statement from Dr. Waismann and change it to meet my own needs, "If anyone is able to use the word 'art' or the phrase 'work of art' correctly, in all sorts of contexts and on the right sort of occasions, he knows 'what art is', and no formula in the world can make him wiser".[3] "Art proper" is simply what is properly called 'art'. The 'correctly' and 'properly' here have nothing to do with any 'common nature' or 'common denominator' of all works of art; they have merely to do with the rules that govern the actual and commonly accepted usage of the word 'art'.

Imagine a very large warehouse filled with all sorts of things—pictures of every description, musical scores for symphonies and dances and hymns, machines, tools, boats, houses, churches and temples, statues, vases, books of poetry and of prose, furniture and clothing, newspapers, postage stamps, flowers, trees, stones, musical instruments. Now we instruct someone to enter the warehouse and bring out all of the works of art it contains. He will be able to do this with reasonable success, despite the fact that, as even the aestheticians must admit, he possesses no satisfactory definition of Art

[3] See F. Waismann, "Analytic-Synthetic II", *Analysis,* 11 (1950), p. 27.

in terms of some common denominator, because no such definition has yet been found. Now imagine the same person sent into the warehouse to bring out all objects with Significant Form, or all objects of Expression. He would rightly be baffled; he knows a work of art when he sees one, but he has little or no idea what to look for when he is told to bring an object that possesses Significant Form.

To be sure, there are many occasions on which we are not sure whether something is a work of art or not; that is, we are not sure whether to call a given drawing or musical composition a work of art or not. Are "Nearer My God to Thee" and the political cartoons of Mr. Low works of art? But this merely reflects the systematic vagueness of the concepts in question, or what Dr. Waismann on another occasion has called their 'open texture'; a vagueness, note, which the definitions of the aestheticians do nothing at all to remove. On such occasions we can, of course, tighten the texture, remove some of the vagueness, by making a decision, drawing a line; and perhaps curators and purchasing committees of art museums are sometimes forced for obvious practical reasons to do this. But in doing so, they and we are not discovering anything about Art.

We do know what art is when no one asks us what it is; that is, we know quite well how to use the word 'art' and the phrase 'work of art' correctly. And when someone asks us what art is, we do *not* know; that is, we are at a loss to produce any simple formula, or any complex one, which will neatly exhibit the logic of this word and this phrase. It is the compulsion to reduce the complexity of aesthetic concepts to simplicity, neatness, and order that moves the aesthetician to make his first mistake, to ask 'What is Art?' and to expect to find an answer like the answer that can be given to 'What is helium?'

What I have said about Art in this section applies, *mutatis mutandis,* to Beauty, the Aesthetic Experience, the Creative Act, and all of the other entities with which traditional aesthetics concerns itself.

Where there is no mystery, there is no need for removing a mystery and certainly none for inventing one.

3. *Common Denominators and Similarities.* Is the search for common characteristics among works of art, then, a fool's errand? That depends upon what we expect to find. If we expect to find some common denominator in Parker's sense, we are bound to be disappointed. We shall get ourselves enmeshed in unnecessary difficulties, and the definitions which we hope will free us from the net will be specious at best. If we say 'Art is Significant Form' we may feel momentarily enlightened; but when we come to reflect upon what we mean by 'significant form' we shall find ourselves entangled again. For the notion of Significant Form is clearly more obscure than is that of Art or Beauty, as the example of the warehouse above amply illustrates; the same holds for Expression, Intuition, Representation, and the other favoured candidates of the aestheticians. Nor will it do to say, as Pro-

fessor Munro does,[4] that "art is skill in providing stimuli to satisfactory aesthetic experience". This has merely a scientific *sound,* and this sound is about as close as the effort to make aesthetics scientific comes to science. The notion of aesthetic experience is fraught with the same difficulties as the notion of art. To put it dogmatically, there is no such thing as *the* Aesthetic Experience; different sorts of experiences are properly referred to as aesthetic. Do not say they must all be contemplative. Does that really help at all?

There is, however, a fruitful and enlightening search for similarities and resemblances in art which the search for the common denominator sometimes furthers, the search for what, to torture a phrase of Wittgenstein's, we can call 'family resemblances'. When we squint we can sometimes see features of an object which otherwise we should miss. So in aesthetics, when we narrow our view, when in the search for the common denominator we carefully select our examples and restrict our sight, we may not see what we are looking for, but we may see something of more interest and importance. The simplifying formulae of the aestheticians are not to be scrapped merely because they fail to do what they are designed to do. What fails to do one thing may do another. The mistake of the aestheticians can be turned to advantage. The suspicion that aesthetics is not nonsense is often justified. For the idea that there is a unity among the arts, properly employed, can lead to the uncovering of similarities which, when noticed, enrich our commerce with art. Croce's supposed discovery that Art is Expression calls our attention to, among other things, an interesting feature of some, if not all, works of art, namely, their indifference to the distinction between the real and the unreal.

Or, to take examples from critics, when F. R. Leavis says of Crabbe, "His art is that of the short-story writer",[5] and when Professor Stechow compares the fourth movement of Schumann's "Rhenish" Symphony with certain features of the Cologne Cathedral,[6] we have something of interest and importance. Our attention is refocused on certain works, and we see them in a new light. One of the offices of creative criticism, as of creative aesthetics, is the finding and pointing out of precisely such similarities.

4. *Aesthetic Theories Reconsidered.* Philosophical mistakes are rarely downright howlers; they have a point. What I have said is, I think, correct, but it neglects an important facet of the quest for essences, a by-product of that search, so to speak, which we should not ignore. An aesthetic theory, by which I mean a systematic answer to such questions as 'What is Art?' 'What is Beauty?' and the like, frequently does something quite other than

---

[4] Thomas Munro, *The Arts and Their Interrelations* (New York, 1949), p. 108.

[5] F. R. Leavis, *Revaluation: Tradition and Development in English Poetry* (London, 1936), p. 125.

[6] Wolfgang Stechow, "Problems of Structure in Some Relations Between the Visual Arts and Music", *The Journal of Aesthetics and Art Criticism,* xi (1953), 325.

what it sets out to do. The assumption underlying traditional aesthetics, as Parker states it in the passage quoted above, is wrong, and I hope I have shown why it is wrong. It does not follow from this, however, that aesthetic theories are wholly without point, that they are merely mistaken, that formulae like 'Art is Significant Form' are worthless, useless, or meaningless. They do serve a purpose, but their purpose is not that which Parker assigns them. Considered in context, in the historical or personal context, for example, they are frequently seen to have a point which has nothing to do with the philosophical excuses that are made for them.

Take Bell's famous dictum that 'Art is Significant Form'. It does not help us to understand what art is at all, and to that extent it is a failure; its shortcomings in this direction have been exposed on numerous occasions. It is easy to beat Bell down; he is so vulnerable. But when we stop to consider that he was an Englishman and when he wrote his book on art (1913) and what the taste of the English was like then and of his association with Roger Fry, the statement that 'Art is Significant Form' loses some of its mystifying sound. It has a *point*. Not the point that Bell thinks it has, for Bell was also looking for the common denominator; another point. We might put it this way. The taste of Edwardian Englishmen in art was restricted to what we pejoratively call the 'academic'. Subject-matter was of prime importance to them—portraits of eminent persons, landscapes with or without cows, genre scenes, pictures of fox hunts, and the rest. Bell had seen the paintings of Cezanne, Matisse, and Picasso, and he was quick to see that subject-matter was not of prime importance in them, that the value of the paintings did not rest on realism or sentimental associations. It rested on what? Well, 'significant form'; lines and colours and patterns and harmonies that stir apart from associations evoked by subject-matter. He found also that he could look at other paintings, older paintings, paintings by the Venetian and Dutch masters, for example, and at vases and carpets and sculptures in the same way he looked at Cezanne. He found such looking rewarding, exciting. But when he turned to the pictures of the academicians, the thrill disappeared; they could not be looked at profitably in this way. What was more natural, then, than that he should announce his discovery by saying 'Art *is* Significant Form'? He *had* discovered something for himself. Not the essence of Art, as the philosophers would have it, although he thought that this is what he found, but *a new way of looking at pictures.* He wanted to share his discovery with others and to reform English taste. *Here* is the point of his dictum; 'Art is Significant Form' is a slogan, the epitome of a platform of aesthetic reform. It has work to do. Not the work which the philosophers assign it, but a work of teaching people a new way of looking at pictures.

When we blow the dust of philosophic cant away from aesthetic theories and look at them in this way, they take on an importance which otherwise they seem to lack. Read Aristotle's *Poetics,* not as a philosophical exercise in definition, but as instruction in one way to read tragic poetry, and it takes on a new life. Many of the other dicta of the aestheticians can also be examined in this light. We know that as definitions they will not do; but as instruments of instruction or reform they will do. Perhaps that is why they have had more real weight with practising critics than they have had with philosophers. The critics have caught the point, where the philosophers, misguided from the start by a foolish preoccupation with definition, have missed it.

5. *Aesthetics and Criticism; the Second Mistake.* One of the prime reasons for the aesthetician's search for definitions of Art, Beauty, and the rest, is his supposition that unless we know what Art or Beauty is, we cannot say what good art or beautiful art is. Put it in the form of an assumption: Criticism presupposes Aesthetic Theory. This assumption contains the second mistake on which traditional aesthetics rests, namely, the view that responsible criticism is impossible without standards or criteria universally applicable to all works of art. The second mistake is in this way closely related to the first.

To see more clearly how this assumption operates, we can turn to a recent book by Mr. Harold Osborne,[7] *Aesthetics and Criticism.* Osborne believes that "a theory of the nature of artistic excellence is implicit in every critical assertion which is other than autobiographical record", and he thinks that "until the theory has been made explicit the criticism is without meaning" (p. 3). By a 'theory of the nature of artistic excellence' Osborne means a theory of the nature of Beauty (p. 3).

Osborne examines several theories of the nature of Beauty and finds them all wanting. His moves against them are instructive. Take, for example, his move against a version of the Realistic Theory in Chapter V, that theory holding that artistic excellence consists in 'truth to life'—or so Osborne states it. He correctly notes that practising critics have rarely insisted that verisimilitude is a necessary condition of artistic excellence, and we should all agree that it is not. "But", says Osborne, "if correspondence with real or possible actuality is not a necessary condition of artistic excellence, then most certainly it is not and cannot be of itself an *artistic* virtue, or an aesthetic merit, in those works of literature where it happens to occur" (p. 93). This is a curious argument. It seems to contain a glaring non-sequitur. But what leads Osborne from his protasis to his conclusion is the assumption that the only acceptable reason offerable for a critical judgement of a work of art is one framed in terms of a characteristic which all works of art, *qua* works of art, must possess. Since we admit that not all works of art must possess truth to life or verisimilitude, we cannot use their adventitious possession of this property as a reason for praising, judging, or commending them as works of art.

Now surely this is mistaken. We can agree that correspondence with real or possible actuality, whatever that may mean, is not a *necessary* condition

---

[7] Routledge and Kegan Paul Ltd., London, 1955.

of artistic excellence; that is, it is *not* necessary that it appear among the reasons offerable for the judgement that a given work of art is good or beautiful. But it does not follow that therefore it does not and cannot appear as *a* reason for such a judgement. We can and do praise works of art, *as* works of art, whatever the force of that is, for a variety of reasons, and not always the same variety. Osborne's reply here is that in doing so we are being 'illogical and inconsistent'. Attacking the users of the Hedonistic Criterion, he says, "In so far as he [the critic] also uses other criteria [than the hedonistic one] for grading and assessing works of art, he is being illogical and incon- sistent with himself whenever he does introduce the hedonistic—or emotional —assumption" (p. 139). But why? There is nothing whatever illogical or inconsistent about praising, grading, or judging a work of art for more than one reason, unless we assume with Osborne that one and only one reason is offerable on pain of inconsistency, which is clearly not the case in art or anywhere else.

Osborne, true to the assumptions of traditional aesthetics, is looking for that condition which is both necessary and sufficient for artistic excellence or merit. His own candidate for that condition is what he calls "configura- tional coherence". But if anything pointed were needed to convince us of the emptiness of the search, it is the unintelligibility of Osborne's account of "beauty as configuration". If what I have said above about the concepts of Art and Beauty is true, we should not be surprised by this. For 'art' and 'beauty' do not name one and only one substance and attribute respectively; no wonder we cannot find the one thing they name or render intelligible the felt discovery that they do name one thing. We can *make* each of them name one thing if we wish. But why should be bother? We get along very well with them as they are.

6. *Ethics and Criticism; the Second Mistake Again.* 'But surely', someone will say, 'this cannot be the whole story. We can and do say that this work of art, this picture, for example, is better than that, or that this is a good one and that one is not. Do we not presuppose certain standards or criteria when we make such judgements? And isn't this really all that Osborne and other aestheticians have in mind when they insist that criticism presupposes aes- thetic theory? They are looking for the standards of critical judgement and taste in the nature of art, just as many moralists have looked for the standards of right conduct in the nature of man. They may be looking in the wrong place, but clearly they are right in assuming that there must be something to find.'

My reply is this: they are not looking in the wrong place so much as they are looking for the wrong thing. The bases of responsible criticism are indeed to be found *in* the work of art and nowhere else, but this in no way implies that critical judgements presuppose any canons, rules, standards, or criteria applicable to all works of art.

When we say that a certain knife is a good knife, we have in mind certain features of the knife, or of knives in general, which we believe will substantiate or support this claim: the sharpness of the blade, the sturdiness of the handle, the durability of the metal, the way it fits the hand, and so on. There are a number of such considerations, all of which refer to characteristics of the knife and not to our feelings about or attitudes towards it, which may be said to constitute the criteria of a good knife. Special criteria may be adduced for fishing knives as opposed to butcher knives, and so on, but this does not affect the issue in question. Note first that there is no definite or exhaustively specifiable list of criteria in common and universal employment; it does not make sense to ask how many there are or whether we have considered them all. But there are generally accepted criteria with which we are all familiar which we use to support our judgements, though in cases of special instruments or implements, like ophthalmoscopes, only specialists are acquainted with the criteria. Secondly, note how the criteria are related to the purposes or functions of knives, to the uses to which we put them, the demands we make upon them. 'Knife', we might say, is a function-word, a word that names something which is usually defined by its function or functions. The criteria, we can say loosely, are derivable from the definition. This second consideration has led some aestheticians to look for the standards of taste and criticism in the function of art.

Now take apples. They have, of course, no function. We use them, we do things with them—eat them, use them for decoration, feed them to pigs, press cider from them, and so on—but none of these things can be said to constitute the function of an apple. Depending, however, on how we use them or what we use them for, we can frame lists of criteria similar to the lists for knives. The best apples for decoration are not always the best for eating, nor are the best for making pies always the best for making cider. Now take mathematicians. A mathematician, unless he is assigned a particular work to do, again has no function. There are certain things a mathematician does, however, and in terms of these we can again frame criteria for judging, praising, grading, and commending mathematicians. Finally, take men in general. We often praise a man, *as* a man, as opposed to as a plumber or a mathematician, and we call this sort of praise moral praise. Here again, we have criteria for assessing the moral worth of men, although, theological considerations aside, we do not frame them in terms of man's function, purpose, or task, even if some moralists, like Aristotle, have tried to frame them in terms of man's end. But we make demands on men, moral demands on all men, and our criteria reflect these demands.

Let us turn now to art. The question we have to raise is this: Are critical judgements of pictures and poems logically symmetrical to the sorts of judgements we have been considering? I think they are not, or not entirely. Not because they are somehow more subjective or unreliable than other value judgements (this issue is as false as an issue can be!), but because the pattern of justification and support which is appropriate to them is of a different sort.

Any critical judgement, to be justified, must be supported by reasons; this goes without saying, for this is what 'justification' means. But must the reasons offerable and acceptable in cases of critical appraisal be of the same order or type as those offerable and acceptable in cases of instruments, implements, useful objects, professional services, jobs, offices, or moral conduct? In particular, must there be any general rules, standards, criteria, canons, or laws applicable to all works of art by which alone such critical appraisals can be supported? I think not.

In the first place, we should note that only a man corrupted by aesthetics would think of judging a work of art *as* a work of art in general, as opposed to as this poem, that picture, or this symphony. There is some truth in the contention that the notions of Art and Work of Art are special aestheticians' concepts. This follows quite naturally from the absence of any distinguishing feature or features common to all works of art as such, and from the absence of any single demand or set of demands which we make on all works of art as such. Despite the occasional claim that it has, Art has no function or purpose, in the sense in which knives and ophthalmoscopes have functions, and this is an insight to be gained from the 'art for art's sake' position. This does not mean that we cannot use individual works of art for special purposes; we can and do. We can use novels and poems and symphonies to put us to sleep or wake us up; we can use pictures to cover spots on the wall, vases to hold flowers, and sculptures for paper weights or door stops. This is what lends point to the distinction between judging something *as* a work of art and judging it *as* a sedative, stimulant, or paper weight; but we cannot conclude from this that Art has some special function or purpose in addition to the purposes to which it can be put.

Similarly there is no one thing which we *do* with all works of art: some we hang, some we play, some we perform, some we read; some we look at, some we listen to, some we analyse, some we contemplate, and so on. There is no special aesthetic use of works of art, even though it may make sense, and even be true, to say that a person who uses a statue as a door stop is not using it as a work of art; he is not doing one of the things we normally do with works of art; he is not treating it properly, we might say. But the proper treatment of works of art varies from time to time and from place to place. It was quite proper for a cave man to hurl his spear at the drawing of a bison, just as it was quite proper for the Egyptians to seal up paintings and sculptures in a tomb. Such treatment does not render the object thus treated not a work of art. The attempt to define Art in terms of what we do with certain objects is as doomed as any other. From this and the first consideration it follows that there is no way by which we can derive the criteria of taste and criticism from the function of art or from its use.

The remaining parallel is with moral appraisal, and this is the most interesting of them all. It has been, and perhaps still is, a common view among philosophers that Beauty and Goodness are two species of the same genus, namely, Value, and that therefore there are at least two classes of value judgements, namely, moral judgements and aesthetic judgements. For this reason there is a tendency further to suppose that there is a logical symmetry between the two. But the supposition of symmetry is a mistake, and I am led to suspect that it does little but harm to suppose that Beauty and Goodness are two species of the same genus at all. There are clearly certain similarities between the two, that is, between the logic of statements of the form 'This is good' and the logic of statements of the form 'This is beautiful' —they are used in many of the same ways—but this must not blind us to the differences. Criticism suffers from a very natural comparison with ethics.

Moral appraisal is like the other forms of appraisal, in this respect; it expresses a desire for uniformity. It is when we are interested in uniformity of size, milk producing capacity, conduct, and so on, that standards or criteria become so important. We maintain standards in products and in workmanship; we enforce them, hold ourselves up to them, teach them to our children, insist on them, and so on, all for the sake of a certain uniformity. In morals we *are* interested in uniformity, at least in what we expect men not to do; that is one reason why rules and laws are necessary and why they play such an important rôle in moral appraisal. But in art, unless, like Plato, we wish to be legislators and to require something of art, demand that it perform a specified educational and social service, we are not as a rule interested in uniformity. Some critics and aestheticians are, of course, interested in uniformity—uniformity in the works of art themselves or uniformity in our approach to them. For them it is quite natural to demand criteria. For them it is also quite natural to formulate theories of Art and Beauty. Remember what we said about aesthetic theories above: the definitions in which they issue are often slogans of reform. As such they are also often devices for the encouragement of uniformity. But this merely betrays the persuasive character of many aesthetic theories, and the peculiar legislative posture of some critics and aestheticians is no warrant for the assumption that the criteria in question are necessary for responsible criticism. Nor should it blind us to the fact that we do quite well without them. Criticism has in no way been hampered by the absence of generally applicable canons and norms, and where such norms have been proposed they have either, like the notorious Unities in the case of tragedy, been shown to be absurd, or else, like the requirements of balance, harmony, and unity in variety, they have been so general, equivocal, and empty as to be useless in critical practice. Ordinarily we feel no constraint in praising one novel for its verisimilitude, another for its humour, and still another for its plot or characterization. We remark on the richness of Van Gogh's impasto, but we do not find it a fault in a Chinese scroll painting that it is flat and smooth. Botticelli's lyric grace is his glory, but Giotto and Chardin are not to be condemned because their poetry is of another order. The merits of Keats and Shelley are not those of Donne and Herbert. And why should Shakespeare and Aeschylus be measured by the same rod? Different works of art are, or may be, praiseworthy or blame-worthy for different reasons, and not always the same reasons. A quality that is praiseworthy in one painting may be blameworthy in another; realism is not always a virtue, but this does not mean that it is not sometimes a virtue.[8]

Mr. Hampshire has put the reason why the criteria sought by the aesthe-ticians are so 'elusive' and why the parallel with ethics is a mistake in this way: "A work of art", he says, "is gratuitous. It is not *essentially* the answer to a question or the solution of a presented problem" (*op. cit.* p. 162). There is no one problem being solved or question answered by all poems, all pic-tures, all symphonies, let alone all works of art. If we set a number of people to doing the same thing, we can rate them on how well they do it. We have, or can frame, a criterion. But not all artists are doing the same thing—solving the same problem, answering the same question, playing the same game, running the same race. Some of them may be, we do group artists together by 'schools', and in other ways, to indicate precisely this kind of similarity; but only in so far as they are does it make sense to compare and appraise them on the same points. It is no criticism of Dickens that he did not write like Henry James. Writing a novel or a lyric poem may, in some interesting respects, be like playing a game or solving a problem, we in fact speak of artists as solving problems. But it is also different; so that if we wish to retain the analogy we must call attention to the differences by saying that not all poets or novelists are playing the *same* game, solving the *same* problems. There is indeed a certain gratuitousness in art which destroys the parallelism or symmetry between moral and aesthetic appraisal.

But there is also a gratuitousness in aesthetic criticism. Moral appraisal, like legal judgement, is a practical necessity; aesthetic appraisal is not. That is why the claim that in art it is all a matter of taste is tolerable, even if it is false, when this sounds so shocking in morals. We can live side by side in peace and amity with those whose tastes differ quite radically from our own; similar differences in moral standards are more serious. And yet, of course, aesthetic criticism is not merely a matter of taste, if by taste we mean un-reasoned preferences. Taste does play an important part in the differences among critical appraisals, but we are clearly not satisfied when, in answer to our question 'Why is it good?' or 'What's good about it?', we are told 'It's good because I like it'. Mrs. Knight correctly notes that "my *liking* a picture is never a criterion of its goodness" (*op. cit.* p. 154). That is, my liking a picture is no reason for its *being* good, though it may be a reason for my *saying* that it is good.

But if it is not all a matter of liking and disliking, why is it that a certain feature is a virtue in a given work of art? If someone tells me that a certain work of art is good for such and such reasons, how can I tell whether the

[8] I owe much in this section to Helen Knight's "The Use of 'Good' in Aesthetic Judgments", *Aesthetics and Language*, William Elton edn. (Oxford, 1954), pp. 147 ff., and to Stuart Hampshire's "Logic and Appreciation", *ibid.*, pp. 161 ff.

reasons he offers are good reasons or not, or even if they are relevant? These questions are not easily answered, for in practice we adduce many considerations for saying that a work of art is good or that a certain feature of it is a virtue. I will make no attempt to canvass these considerations but will close with some observations on a logical feature of the problem.

We are confronted, I think, with a problem that is really two problems: there is the problem of saying why a given work of art is good or bad, and there is the problem of saying why our reasons are good or bad, or even relevant. We may praise a picture, say, for its subtle balance, colour contrast, and draughtsmanship; this is saying why the picture is good. We may now go on to raise the more 'philosophical' question of what makes balance, or this sort of colour contrast, or this kind of draughtsmanship an artistic virtue. The first sort of question, the question of why the work of art is good or bad, is decided by appeal to the 'good-making characteristics' or 'criterion-characters' of the work of art in question, that is, by an appeal to certain objectively discriminable characteristics of the work under discussion. These characteristics are many and various; there is a large variety of reasons offerable for a work of art's being a good or bad work of art. The second sort of question, the question of the worth or relevance of the reasons offered in answer to the first question, is settled by appeal either to custom or to decision. In this respect aesthetic criticism is very like moral appraisal. We either simply praise what is customarily praised and condemn what is customarily condemned or we *decide* what the criteria shall be. This does not mean that the criteria, that is, the reasons offerable for a work of art's being good or bad, are arbitrary. There may be plenty of reasons why one feature is a 'criterion-character' and another is not. Part of the reason may be psychological, part sociological, part metaphysical, or even religious and ethical. Only an aesthete ignores, or tries to ignore, the many relations of a poem or picture to life and concentrates on what are called the purely 'formal' values of the work at hand; but in doing so he *determines* what he will accept as a reason for a work of art's being good or bad. That a work of art assists the cause of the proletariat in the class struggle *is* a reason for its being a good work of art to a convinced Marxist, but it is not a reason, let alone a good reason, to the bourgeois aesthete. That a picture contains nude figures is a reason, to the puritan and the prude, for condemning it, though no enlightened man can be brought to accept it. Thus morals and politics and religion do enter into our critical judgements, even when we claim that they should not.

I noted above that there is no one use which we make of all works of art, nor is there any one demand or set of demands which we make on them. This is, I think, important, and serves to explain, at least in part, the actual relativity of aesthetic criteria. What one age looks for in painting or in literature, another age may neglect. What one group demands, another forbids. We are not always consistent in even our own demands on art, and I can see no reason why we should be. We can be interested in works of art for many reasons, and some of these reasons may be more decisive at one time or in one set of circumstances than they are at another time or in another set of circumstances. This affects the very logic of critical appraisal by determining the relevance and merit of the reasons we offer for our judgements. We are well aware of the fact that the estimate of a given poet or painter changes from period to period. El Greco's or Shakespeare's reputation has not always been what it is, and no one should be surprised if it should change in the future. But if we examine the reasons that have been offered for the different estimates, we find that they too are different. Different reasons are persuasive at different times and in different contexts. The same explanation is operative: the needs and interests that art gratifies are different from time to time and, to a lesser extent perhaps, from person to person. But as the needs and interests vary, so also will the criteria and the weight we place on them. This is a vicious relativism only to those who are morally disposed to insist on the uniformity of taste.

Summary: I have tried to show (1) that the search for essences in aesthetics is a mistake, arising from the failure to appreciate the complex but not mysterious logic of such words and phrases as 'art', 'beauty', 'the aesthetic experience', and so on. But (2) although the characteristics common to all works of art are the object of a fool's errand, the search for similarities in sometimes very different works of art can be profitably pursued, and this search is occasionally stimulated by the formulae of the aestheticians. (3) Although the definitions of the aestheticians are useless for the role usually assigned to them, we must not ignore the live purpose they frequently serve as slogans in the effort to change taste and as instruments for opening up new avenues of appreciation. (4) If the search for the common denominator of all works of art is abandoned, abandoned with it must be the attempt to derive the criteria of critical appreciation and appraisal from the nature of art. (5) Traditional aesthetics mistakenly supposes that responsible criticism is impossible without a set of rules, canons, or standards applicable to all works of art. This supposition arises from an uncritical assimilation of the pattern of critical appraisal to that of appraisal in other areas, particularly morals, and from a failure to appreciate the gratuitousness of art and the manner in which reasons are operative in the justification of critical judgements.

QUESTIONS

1. What is wrong about searching for the common nature of all works of art, according to Professor Kennick? Suppose someone said: "The fact that this is a very difficult thing to discover doesn't mean it isn't there." What would Professor Kennick reply? Give your reasons for accepting or rejecting his reply.
2. "We are able to separate those objects which are works of art from those which are not, because we know English. . . ." What is the reasoning behind this statement?
3. Professor Kennick argues that aesthetic theories frequently do something

other than what their originators had in mind in propounding them. Analyze and assess the validity of Professor Kennick's argument and apply it to the aesthetic theories of George Santayana and Leo Tolstoy, presented in this chapter.

4. The second mistake of traditional aesthetics, according to Professor Kennick, is "the view that responsible criticism is impossible without standards or criteria universally applicable to all works of art." Explain clearly what is meant by the words quoted, and give Professor Kennick's reasons for claiming that this view is a mistake. Then set forth your own position regarding the quote.

5. What points does Professor Kennick bring out by comparing judgments of good knives and good apples with aesthetic judgments of good works of art? What similarities and what differences does he find?

6. ". . . Only a man corrupted by aesthetics would think of judging a work of art *as* a work of art in general. . . ." Give a reasoned argument in support of, or in opposition to, this statement.

7. Professor Kennick denies that there is one specific *aesthetic* use of works of art. How does he try to show this? Suppose someone were to argue that, although there may be no one proper aesthetic way of treating works of art, at least there are *improper* ways of treating them, for example, using them as means to practical ends. How might Professor Kennick reply to this? Would his reply be satisfactory, in your opinion? Defend your answer.

8. In a footnote Professor Kennick acknowledges an indebtedness to Helen Knight's article, "The Use of 'Good' in Aesthetic Judgments," for some of his thoughts on the function and justification of aesthetic criteria. After reading Mrs. Knight's article, make a careful comparison of her views on aesthetic criteria with those of Professor Kennick. In your comparison consider the following questions: Are they agreed on all points? Do they try to answer the same questions? Are their arguments equally sound?

9. At the end of his article Professor Kennick distinguishes two problems: why a given work of art is good or bad, and why our reasons for judging the work are good reasons or bad reasons, or even relevant ones. Explain the distinction between these two problems in terms of the different ways they must be solved. Does the solution to one depend on the solution to the other? If so, show how. If not, explain why not.

10. "Morals and politics and religion do enter into our critical judgments, even when we claim that they should not." Does this imply that Professor Kennick's theory of aesthetic judgment is in basic agreement with that of Tolstoy, presented in the reading, "What Is Art?" Why or why not?

SUGGESTED FURTHER READING

ANTHOLOGIES

Aschenbrenner, K., and A. Isenberg, eds., *Aesthetic Theories: Studies in the Philosophy of Art,* Prentice-Hall, Englewood Cliffs, N. J., 1965.

Elton, William, ed., *Aesthetics and Language,* Blackwell, Oxford, 1954.

Kennick, William E., ed., *Art and Philosophy: Readings in Aesthetics,* St Martin's, New York, 1964.

Levich, Marvin, ed., *Aesthetics and the Philosophy of Criticism,* Random House, New York, 1963.

Margolis, Joseph, ed., *Philosophy Looks at the Arts: Contemporary Readings in Aesthetics,* Scribner's, New York, 1962.

Philipson, Morris, ed., *Aesthetics Today,* Meridian Books, New York, 1961.
Rader, Melvin, ed., *A Modern Book of Esthetics,* Third Edition, Holt, Rinehart & Winston, New York, 1962.
Vivas, Eliseo, and Murray Krieger, eds., *The Problems of Aesthetics,* Holt, Rinehart & Winston, New York, 1953.
Weitz, Morris, ed., *Problems in Aesthetics,* Macmillan, New York, 1959.

CLASSIC WORKS

Aquinas, St. Thomas, *Summa Theologica* (1265–72).
Aristotle, *Poetics.*
Bacon, Francis, *Of Beauty* (1597).
Burke, Edmund, *A Philosophical Enquiry into the Origin of Our Ideas of the Sublime and Beautiful* (1756).
Hegel, G. W. F., *Lectures on Esthetics* (1835).
Home, Henry (Lord Kames), *Elements of Criticism* (1761).
Hutcheson, Francis, *An Inquiry into the Original of our Ideas of Beauty and Virtue* (1725).
Kant, Immanuel, *Critique of Judgment* (1790).
Leonardo da Vinci, *Treatise on Painting; Notebooks* (c. 1485).
Lessing, G. E., *Laocoön* (1766).
Longinus, *On the Sublime* (Third Century A.D.).
Nietzsche, F., *The Birth of Tragedy* (1872).
Plato, *Ion; Symposium; Republic.*
Ruskin, John, *Lectures on Art* (1893).
Schelling, F. W. J., *Philosophy of Art* (1803).
Schiller, F., *Letters on the Esthetic Education of Humanity* (1795).
Schopenhauer, A., *The World as Will and Idea* (1818).

INTRODUCTORY STUDIES

Aldrich, Virgil C., *Philosophy of Art,* Prentice-Hall, Englewood Cliffs, N. J., 1963.
Bell, Clive, *Art,* Chatto & Windus, London, 1914.
Carritt, E. F., *An Introduction to Aesthetics,* Hutchinson's University Library, London, 1949.
Collingwood, R. G., *The Principles of Art,* Oxford University Press, London, 1938.
Croce, Benedetto, *Aesthetic as Science of Expression and General Linguistic,* trans. by Douglas Ainslie, Second Edition, Macmillan, New York, 1922.
Dewey, John, *Art as Experience,* Minton, Balch, New York, 1934, and Capricorn Books, New York, 1958.
Ducasse, Curt John, *The Philosophy of Art,* Dial, New York, 1929.
———, *Art, the Critics and You,* Liberal Arts, New York, 1944.
Forster, E. M., "The *Raison d'Etre* of Criticism in the Arts"; "Art for Art's Sake"; in *Two Cheers for Democracy,* Harcourt, Brace & World, New York, 1938.
Gilbert, K. E., and H. Kuhn, *A History of Esthetics,* Second Edition, Indiana University Press, Bloomington, Ind., 1953.
Gotshalk, D. W., "A Next Step for Aesthetics," *Journal of Aesthetics and Art Criticism,* Vol. 18, 1959.
———, *Art and the Social Order,* Revised Edition, Dover Publications, New York, 1962.
Hospers, John, "The Collingwood-Croce Theory of Art," *Philosophy,* Vol. 31, 1956.

Munro, Thomas, *The Arts and their Interrelations,* Liberal Arts, New York, 1949.

———, *Toward Science in Aesthetics,* Liberal Arts, New York, 1958.

Osborne, Harold, *Aesthetics and Criticism,* Routledge & Kegan Paul, London, 1955.

Parker, D. H., *The Principles of Aesthetics,* Silver, Burdett, New York, 1920.

———, *The Analysis of Art,* Yale University Press, New Haven, Conn., 1926.

Prall, D. W., *Aesthetic Analysis,* Crowell, New York, 1936.

Read, Sir Herbert, *Icon and Idea: The Function of Art in the Development of Human Consciousness,* Harvard University Press, Cambridge, Mass., 1955.

———, *The Forms of Things Unknown: Essays Toward an Aesthetic Philosophy,* Horizon, New York, 1960.

Reid, L. A., *A Study in Aesthetics,* Macmillan, New York, 1931.

Tsugawa, Albert, "The Objectivity of Aesthetic Judgments," *Philosophical Review,* Vol. 70, 1961.

Ziff, Paul, "The Task of Defining a Work of Art," *Philosophical Review,* Vol. 62, 1953.

ADVANCED STUDIES

Beardsley, Monroe, *Aesthetics: Problems in the Philosophy of Criticism,* Harcourt, Brace & World, New York, 1958.

Cannavo, S., and L. Hyman, "Literary Uniqueness and Critical Communication," *British Journal of Aesthetics,* Vol. 5, 1965.

Dickie, George, "The Myth of the Aesthetic Attitude," *American Philosophical Quarterly,* Vol. 1, 1964.

Greene, T. M., *The Arts and the Art of Criticism,* Princeton University Press, Princeton, N. J., 1940.

Harré, R., "Quasi-Aesthetic Appraisals," *Philosophy,* Vol. 33, 1958.

Harrison, B., "Some Uses of 'Good' in Criticism," *Mind,* Vol. 69, 1960.

Hoffman, Robert, "Aesthetic Argument—Interpretative and Evaluative," *Philosophical Quarterly,* Vol. 11, 1961.

Hospers, John, *Meaning and Truth in the Arts,* University of North Carolina Press, Chapel Hill, N. C., 1946.

Hungerland, Isabel C., *Poetic Discourse,* University of California Publications in Philosophy, Berkeley and Los Angeles, Calif., 1958.

———, "The Logic of Aesthetic Concepts," *Proceedings and Addresses of the American Philosophical Association (1962–63),* Antioch, Yellow Springs, Ohio, 1963.

Langer, Susanne K., *Feeling and Form,* Routledge & Kegan Paul, London, 1953.

Lewis, C. I., *An Analysis of Knowledge and Valuation,* Open Court, La Salle, Ill., 1946.

Margolis, Joseph, "Mr. Weitz and the Definition of Art," *Philosophical Studies,* Vol. 9, 1958.

———, "Proposals on the Logic of Aesthetic Judgments," *Philosophical Quarterly,* Vol. 9, 1959.

Pepper, Stephen C., *Aesthetic Quality,* Scribner's, New York, 1937.

———, *Principles of Art Appreciation,* Harcourt, Brace & World, New York, 1949.

———, *The Basis of Criticism in the Arts,* Harvard University Press, Cambridge, Mass., 1949.

———, *The Work of Art,* Indiana University Press, Bloomington, Ind., 1955.

Pratt, Caroll C., *The Meaning of Music: A Study in Psychological Aesthetics,* McGraw-Hill, New York, 1931.

Schapiro, Meyer, *Vincent Van Gogh,* Abrams, New York, 1950.

———, *Paul Cezanne,* Abrams, New York, 1952.

———, "The Nature of Abstract Art," *Marxist Quarterly,* January–March, 1937.

Schwyzer, H. R. G., "Sibley's Aesthetic Concepts," *Philosophical Review,* Vol. 72, 1963.

Sibley, Frank, "Aesthetic Concepts," *Philosophical Review,* Vol. 68, 1959.

———, "Aesthetic and Nonaesthetic," *Philosophical Review,* Vol. 74, 1965.

Sparshott, F. E., *The Structure of Aesthetics,* Routledge & Kegan Paul, London, 1963.

Stevenson, Charles L., "On 'What Is a Poem?'" *Philosophical Review,* Vol. 66, 1957.

———, "Interpretation and Evaluation in Aesthetics," in *Philosophical Analysis,* ed., Max Black, Prentice-Hall, Englewood Cliffs, N. J., 1950.

Stolnitz, Jerome, "On Objective Relativism in Aesthetics," *Journal of Philosophy,* Vol. 57, 1960.

Ushenko, Andrew P., *Dynamics of Art,* Indiana University Press, Bloomington, Ind., 1953.

Weitz, Morris, *The Philosophy of the Arts,* Harvard University Press, Cambridge, Mass., 1950.

———, "The Role of Theory in Aesthetics," *Journal of Aesthetics and Art Criticism,* Vol. 15, 1956.

PERIODICALS

There are two scholarly journals exclusively devoted to aesthetics and the philosophy of art:

The British Journal of Aesthetics
The Journal of Aesthetics and Art Criticism.

Other articles in this field may be found in recent and current issues of the periodicals listed at the end of Chapter 10.